Early Childhood Education

Third Canadian Edition

Introduction to

Early Childhood *Education*

Third Canadian Edition

Eva Essa
University of Nevada (Reno)

Rosemary Young
Brock University

THOMSON

NELSON

Australia   Canada   Mexico   Singapore   Spain   United Kingdom   United States

THOMSON

✳ ™

NELSON

Introduction to Early Childhood Education, Third Canadian Edition

Eva Essa and Rosemary Young

Editorial Director and Publisher:
Evelyn Veitch

Executive Editor:
Joanna Cotton

Marketing Manager:
Chantal Lanning

Developmental Editor:
Joanne Sutherland

Production Editor:
Natalia Denesiuk

Senior Production Coordinator:
Hedy Sellers

Copy Editor and Proofreader:
Rodney Rawlings

Creative Director:
Angela Cluer

Interior and Cover Design:
Suzanne Peden

Cover Image:
Richard Price/Getty Images

Compositor:
Carol Magee

Printer:
Transcontinental

National Library of Canada Cataloguing in Publication Data

Essa, Eva
    Introduction to early childhood education / Eva Essa, Rosemary Young. — 3rd Canadian ed.

First ed. written by Rosemary Young. Includes bibliographical references and index.
ISBN 0-17-616909-1

    1. Early childhood education.
2. Early childhood education—Canada. I. Young, Rosemary Elaine. II. Title.

LB1139.3.C3Y685 2002   372.21
C2002-902219-3

This book is affectionately dedicated to Catharine Young, my mother,
and to Margaret Shattuck, my mother-in-law.
Without their assistance and support, there might not be a book.

Brief Contents

Preface xxii

Part 1: What?

Chapter 1: The Scope of Early Childhood Education   2
Chapter 2: The History of Early Childhood Education   38
Chapter 3: Early Childhood Education Program Models   68
Chapter 4: Early Childhood Education in Canada   106

Part 2: Who?

Chapter 5: Children and Their Families   150
Chapter 6: The Early Childhood Educator   191

Part 3: How? The Basics

Chapter 7: Play and Developmentally Appropriate Practice   220
Chapter 8: Guidance: Routines, Group Activities, and Behaviours   275

Part 4: How? Curriculum

Chapter 9: Curriculum   320
Chapter 10: Development Through the Curriculum   353

Part 5: Why?

Chapter 11: Quality in Early Childhood Programs   402
Chapter 12: The Future of Early Childhood Education   430

Glossary of Key Terms 447

References 461

Name Index 505

Subject Index 510

Contents

List of Exhibits   xix

List of Boxes   xxi

Preface   xxii

Part 1: What?

Chapter 1: The Scope of Early Childhood Education   2

The Growth of Early Childhood Education   4
  Changes in Family Life   4
  Benefits of Early Childhood Education   8
  Child Advocacy   8
When Is Early Childhood?   9
What Is Included in Early Childhood Education?   9
  Purpose of Programs   10
  Program Settings   12
  Ages of Children   16
  Sources of Support for Programs   20
Defining Quality in Early Childhood Programs   25
  Group Size   25
  Teacher Qualifications   26
  Teacher-Child Ratio   27
  Mixed-Age Grouping   28
  Developmental Appropriateness of the Program   29
  Teacher-Child Interaction   31
  Teacher Consistency   32
  Respect and Concern for Teachers   33
  Physical Environment   33
  Family Involvement   34
  Quality as a Combination of Factors   34

Key Terms   34

Key Points   35

Key Questions   36

Chapter 2: The History of Early Childhood Education   38

A Look Back—Children Through Time   39

Views of Children   41

Influential People in the History of Early Childhood Education   43

    Martin Luther (1483–1546)   43

    John Amos Comenius (1592–1670)   43

    John Locke (1632–1704)   44

    Jean-Jacques Rousseau (1712–1778)   44

    Johann Pestalozzi (1746–1827)   45

    Robert Owen (1771–1858)   45

    Friedrich Froebel (1782–1852)   46

    John Dewey (1859–1952)   47

    Margaret McMillan (1860–1931)   48

    Maria Montessori (1870–1952)   49

    Loris Malaguzzi (1920–1994)   50

    More Influential People   51

Influential Theorists of Child Development   51

    Sigmund Freud (1856–1939)   52

    Jean Piaget (1896–1980)   54

    J. B. Watson (1878–1958)   56

    B. F. Skinner (1904–1990)   58

    Arnold Gessell (1880–1961)   60

    Erik Erikson (1902–1994)   61

    Lev Vygotsky (1896–1934)   61

Influential Events in Early Childhood Education   62

    Sputnik and Educational Upheaval   63

    Research and the Rediscovery of the Early Childhood Years   64

Key Terms   65

Key Points   66

Key Questions   67

Chapter 3: Early Childhood Education Program Models   68

Application of Theories in Early Childhood Education   69

    Montessori Programs   70

    Open Education   74

    Project Head Start   77

    Cognitively Oriented Curriculum (COC)   80

    The Bereiter-Engelmann Model (DISTAR)   84

    The Reggio Emilia Model   87

Research and Evaluation of Program Models   93

    Comparisons of Program Models   95

    Evaluations of Individual Models   97

Additional Research on Early Childhood Education   101

Key Terms   103

Key Points   104

Key Questions   105

Chapter 4: Early Childhood Education in Canada   106

The Roots of ECE and Regulation of the Field   107
   British Columbia   107
   Alberta   109
   Saskatchewan   111
   Manitoba   113
   Ontario   115
   Quebec   120
   New Brunswick   123
   Prince Edward Island   124
   Nova Scotia   126
   Newfoundland and Labrador   128
   Yukon Territory   131
   Northwest Territories   134
   Nunavut   136
Current Practices and Future Directions in ECE in Canada   136
   Teacher-Child Ratios, Group Size, and Centre Size in Canada   137
   Regulation of Teacher Training and Program Availability   142
   Scope of Licensed Child Care in Canada and Parental Needs   145

Key Terms   147

Key Points   147

Key Questions   148

Part 2: Who?

Chapter 5: Children and Their Families   150

Children   151
   Recognizing Similarities   151
   Age-Related Similarities Among Children   152
   Need for Self-Esteem   158
   Need for Play   160
   Respecting Differences   161
   Inclusion   162
Families   164
   Families—A Theoretical Perspective   165
   The Changing Canadian Family   166
   Family Forms   166

Family Variations   168
Families in Poverty   170
The Needs of Families   171
Parenthood   172
Empowerment, Partnerships, and Advocacy   172
Coordinating Needs and Programs   173
Communicating with Families   174
Individual Communication Methods   175
Informal Contact with Families   175
Formal Contact with Families   176
When Problems Arise Between Parents and Teachers   179
Group Communication Methods   180
Physical Environment   180
Written Communiqués   180
Bulletin Boards   181
Meetings and Other Group Functions   182
Family Involvement   183
Families as Resources   184
Family Members in the Classroom   184
Family Members as Decision Makers   185
Adult Education and Lifelong Learning   185

Key Terms   187

Key Points   188

Key Questions   189

Chapter 6: The Early Childhood Educator   191

The Early Childhood Educator   192
Qualities of the Early Childhood Educator   192
Professionalism   194
    Core Knowledge Base of the Early Childhood Education Profession   196
    Standards of Practice—Rights, Roles, and Responsibilities   198
    Ethics   200
    Training and Regulation in Early Childhood Education   201
Careers in Early Childhood Education   202
Teachers' Developmental Stages   202
Staffing in Early Childhood Programs—Relationships and Team Building   205
    Director and/or Supervisor   207
    Resource Teacher   207
    Home Visitors   208
    Teaching Staff   208
    The Senior Teacher   208
    The Assistant Teacher   209
    Team Teaching   209
    Volunteers   210

Support Staff   210
Board of Directors   211
Community Professionals   211
Teacher Evaluation   213
Professional Organizations   214
Canada   214
United States   215
Benefits of Student Memberships   216

Key Terms   217

Key Points   217

Key Questions   218

Part 3: How? The Basics

Chapter 7: Play and Developmentally Appropriate Practice   220

The Relationship Between Play, Guidance, and Emotional Development   220
Your Role as Nurturer   221
Emotional Development   221
Play   223
Theories of Play   223
Freud's Theory of Play   225
Piaget's Theory of Play   225
Vygotsky's Theory of Play   226
What Is Play?   227
Definitions of Play   228
Play as Creativity   228
Overview of Play: Play from Infancy Through to the Early School Years   229
Play in Infancy   229
Play in the Preschool and Early School Years   230
Pretend Play   230
Research and Value of Play   234
A Note on Superheroes   235
Cooperative Games   236
Guidance   237
Appropriate Practices in Early Childhood Education   237
Developmentally Appropriate Programs   239
Age-Appropriate Programs   240
Individually Appropriate Inclusive Programs   241
Developmentally Appropriate Environment   245
Impact of the Environment on Children   248
Impact of the Environment on Teachers   249
Developmentally Appropriate Equipment   250
Criteria for Selecting Equipment   250

Computers   250
Developmentally Appropriate Materials   252
  Criteria for Selecting Materials   252
  Teacher-Made Materials and Resources   255
  A Note About Learning Centres   256
Developmentally Appropriate Schedules   257
Components of the Developmentally Appropriate Program   260
  Activity Time   261
  Large-Group or Circle Activities   262
  Small-Group Activities   263
  Outdoor Activities   263
  Routines   265
  Cleanup   265
  Meals and Snacks   266
  Nap or Rest   267
  Transitions   267
Guidelines for Program Planning   267
  Alternating Active and Quiet Times   267
  Balancing Child-Initiated and Teacher-Initiated Activities   268
  Activity Level of the Children   268
  Developmental Level of the Children   269
  Group Size   269
  Family Groupings   270
  Arrival of Children   270
  Seasonal Considerations   270
  "Wasted Time"   270

Key Terms   272

Key Points   272

Key Questions   273

Chapter 8: Guidance: Routines, Group Activities, and Behaviours   275

Guidance and Discipline   276
What Behaviours Do We Expect of Young Children?   277
Factors in Selecting Guidance Techniques   278
Arrival at School   280
  Morning Health Check   281
  The New Child at School   281
Meals and Eating Behaviour   282
  Providing Nutritious Meals That Children Will Eat   282
  Encouraging Healthy Eating Habits   284
  Problem Eating Behaviours   284

Toileting   285
   Toilet Accidents   285
   Bathroom Facilities   287
   Toothbrushing   287
Sleep and Rest Times   288
   Children Who Don't Need to Sleep   288
   Nap Guidelines   288
   Problem Sleepers   289
Factors That Affect Group Behaviour   290
   The Physical Environment   290
   Developmentally Appropriate Expectations   290
   Conveying Expectations   291
   Rules   292
Group Guidance and the Program   292
   Activity Time   293
   Meals   294
   Group Times   295
Transitions   297
The Unusual Situation   299
   Planned Unusual Situations   299
   Unplanned Unusual Events   300
   What Is the Difference Between Normal and Problem Behaviour?   301
   Factors That Affect Children's Behaviour   304
   Clear-Cut Guidelines   304
   Health and Related Problems   305
   Individual Temperament   306
   The Child's Family   307
   Some Guidance Techniques   309
   Thorough and Creative Planning   309
   Prevention   310
   Redirection   310
   Positive Reinforcement   310
   Attention   311
   Modelling   313
   Shaping   313
   Cuing   313
   Ignoring   313
   Time-Out   314
   Discussion   315

Key Terms   *315*

Key Points   *316*

Key Questions   *317*

Part 4: How? Curriculum

Chapter 9: Curriculum   320

What Is Curriculum?   320
Elements of the Curriculum   321
  Program Philosophy and Curriculum   322
  Standards, Learning Outcomes, and Curriculum   322
  Observation and Curriculum   322
  Assessment, Evaluation, and Curriculum   323
  Children's Development and Curriculum   323
Curriculum Content   323
  Children as the Focus of the Curriculum   324
  The Family as the Focus of the Curriculum   324
  The Community as the Focus of the Curriculum   325
Planning the Curriculum   327
  Themes and Projects   328
  Activities   330
  Environment   330
  Team Planning   331
Accountability   333
  Standards and Learning Outcomes   334
  Observation and Documentation   337
  Confidentiality and Objectivity   337
  Documentation   338
  Parental Involvement   338
  Types of Observations   338
  Characteristics of Good Observations   339
  Interpreting Observations   340
  Some Observational Techniques   341
Assessment   341
  Instruments   341
  Concerns About Using Assessment Instruments   345
Evaluation   347
  Selecting and Using Assessment and Evaluation Methods   348
  Information About Children   348
  Information for Program Planning   348
  Information for Parent Feedback   349

Key Terms   350

Key Points   351

Key Questions   352

Chapter 10: Development Through the Curriculum   353

Creative Development   354

What Is Creativity?   356

Esthetic Appreciation   357

Environments That Encourage Creativity   358

Attitudes That Encourage Creativity   361

Factors That Decrease Creativity   363

Physical Development   364

What Is Physical Development?   365

Environments That Encourage Physical Development   366

Attitudes That Encourage Physical Fitness, Health, and Well Being   366

Cognitive Development   371

What Is Cognition?   372

Environments and Attitudes That Encourage Cognitive Development   373

Language Development   374

What Is Language?   377

What Is Communication?   377

What Is Multilingualism?   378

Environments and Attitudes That Encourage Language Development   379

Social Development   387

What Is Social Development?   387

Environments and Attitudes That Encourage Social Development   387

Inclusion and Diversity   389

Moral Development   396

Development of Prosocial Behaviours   398

Key Terms   398

Key Points   399

Key Questions   399

Part 5: Why?

Chapter 11: Quality in Early Childhood Programs   402

Program Quality   402

Cost, Quality, and Child Outcomes Study   408

Child Care and Child Development: The NICHD Study of Early Child Care   410

You Bet I Care! Series of Studies   411

A Canada-wide Study on: Wages, Working Conditions, and Practices in Child Care Centres   412

Caring and Learning Environments: Quality in Child Care Centres Across Canada   417

Caring and Learning Environments: Quality in Regulated Family Child Care Across Canada   422

Policies and Practices in Canadian Family Child Care Agencies   425

What Have We Learned About the Quality of Child Care?   426

Key Terms   428

Key Points   428

Key Questions   429

Chapter 12: The Future of Early Childhood Education   430

Some Current Issues and Dilemmas   430
   A Historical Perspective   431
   Teacher Shortage/Turnover   432
   Teacher Turnover and Low Pay   433
   Low Wages and Affordable Child Care   435
   Burnout Syndrome   437
   Men in Early Childhood Education   438
   Changes in Professional Education for an Early Childhood Workforce   439
   Empowerment and Activism   440
The Future of Early Childhood Education   442

Key Terms   445

Key Points   446

Key Questions   446

Glossary of Key Terms   447

References   461

Name Index   505

Subject Index   510

List of Exhibits

Exhibit 1-1   Number of Canadian Children 0–9 Years of Age: Caregiving Needs and Arrangements   6

Exhibit 1-2   Some Dimensions of ECE Programs   10

Exhibit 1-3   Canadian Child Care Arrangements: Percentage of Total Number of Children in Each Caregiving Setting by Age   13

Exhibit 1-4   Percentage of Canadian Children in Different Types of Care, 1994–1995   14

Exhibit 1-5   Recommendations for Teacher-Child Ratios Within Different Group Sizes   28

Exhibit 2-1   People in the Field of Early Childhood Education   42

Exhibit 2-2   Erikson's and Freud's Developmental Sequences   53

Exhibit 2-3   The Ego Mediates   54

Exhibit 2-4   Piaget's Periods of Cognitive Development   57

Exhibit 2-5   Skinner's View of Reinforcement and Punishment   59

Exhibit 4-1   Legislation of Child Care, Coverage of Ratios, and Group Size in the Current Regulations   138

Exhibit 4-2   Teacher-Child Ratios and Group Size for Centre-Based Care— Breakdown by Province for Infants   138

Exhibit 4-3   Teacher-Child Ratios and Group Size for Centre-Based Care— Breakdown by Province for Toddlers   139

Exhibit 4-4   Teacher-Child Ratios and Group Size for Centre-Based Care— Breakdown by Province for Children 3 to 5 Years   140

Exhibit 4-5   Teacher-Child Ratios and Group Size for Centre-Based Care— Breakdown by Province for Children 5 Years and Older   141

Exhibit 4-6   Summary of Space Requirements in Child Care Settings in Canada   142

Exhibit 4-7   Legislation of Teacher Qualifications and Availability of Teacher Training   143

Exhibit 4-8   Summary of Teacher Education Programs in Canada   144

Exhibit 4-9   Scope of Child Care in Canada and Needs of Parents   146

Exhibit 6-1   Staffing Patterns   206

Exhibit 7-1   Positive Emotional Development   224

Exhibit 7-2   Parten's Categories of Social Play   231

Exhibit 7-3   Smilansky's Categories of Cognitive Play   232

Exhibit 7-4   Play Rating Sheet Using Rubin's Combination of Smilansky's and Parten's Categories   232

Exhibit 7-5   Guidelines for Organizing Classroom Space   246

Exhibit 7-6   Basic Equipment and Materials for a Preschool Classroom   253

Exhibit 9-1   The Self-Concept Curriculum Model   326

Exhibit 9-2   Observations   340

Exhibit 10-1   Guidelines for Supporting Physical Development   368

Exhibit 10-2   Guidelines for Supporting Cognitive Development   375

Exhibit 10-3   Guidelines for Supporting Language and Literacy Development   385

Exhibit 10-4   Guidelines for Supporting Social Development I   390

Exhibit 10-5   Guidelines for Supporting Social Development II   393

Exhibit 10-6   Guidelines for Supporting Social Development III   397

Exhibit 11-1   Variables an Early Childhood Educator Can Influence   405

Exhibit 11-2   Example of the Rating System and Items Used in ECERS and ITERS   407

Exhibit 11-3   Educational Levels in the *You Bet I Care!* Study   414

Exhibit 11-4   Characteristics of Canadian Teachers Responding to QCCCC Study Questionnaire   418

Exhibit 11-5   Characteristics of Canadian Teachers Observed in QCCCC Study   418

Exhibit 11-6   Characteristics of Centre Directors Responding to QCCCC Study Questionnaire   418

Exhibit 11-7   ECERS and ITERS Scores for Centres in QCCCC Study   420

Exhibit 11-8   Range of FDCRS Scores for QFCCC Study   424

List of Boxes

A Canadian Professional Speaks Out

Integration of Children with Hearing Loss   17
Froebel Education in Canada   46
The Birth of the Reggio Emilia Approach   88
Child Care Issues for First Nations   133
Custody Disputes and Pick-up Authorization   168
Inviting Success in Early Childhood Education   203
Team Building and Collaboration   212
Anti-Bias Education: A Personal and Professional Challenge for Early Childhood Educators   241
The Needs of the ADHD Child   303
Inclusion in Early Childhood Education   335
Tailoring Curriculums to Ability and Interest   355
Creativity in Art: An Expression of the Inner Self   359
Early Language Acquisition   376
Havenwood Place: An Integrated Services Approach to School Readiness   410
Certification within Regulation   436

Partnerships

Parental Values for Cognitive Development   30
When Parents Ask for Advice about Choosing a School   94
Helpful Strategies for Parent-Teacher Conferences   177
Reflections of Family Culture and Values   243
Developmentally Appropriate Programs in Transition   271
Working Together with Parents to Solve Behaviour Problems   279
Sharing Evaluations with Parents   349
Parental Involvement in the Curriculum   360

A Closer Look

Mapmaking   31
Assimilation and Accommodation at the Zoo   55
The Concept of Inclusion: Children with Diverse Needs   161
Parents' Role in the Early Childhood Environment   186
David and Rita   259
Shirley's "Accidents"   286
The Plight of Drug-Exposed Children   308
Environments that Support Curriculum   331
St. Peter's and Jack Sprat   444

Preface

*T*his is the third Canadian edition of *An Introduction to Early Childhood Education.* My gratitude and respect go to Eva Essa for writing the first and second U.S. editions of *Introduction to Early Childhood Education.*

This is an exciting time to be in the field of early childhood education in Canada. You will find many challenges await you, and your responses to these challenges can heighten interest in young children. Current research has reaffirmed the fact that "early experiences can fundamentally alter the brain structure and ultimately behaviour" (McCain & Mustard, 1999, p. 28). Although that finding was quite evident in the 1960s (e.g., Hunt, 1961), it seemed to be forgotten for a period of time. The public eye is focused again on the early years, and this bodes well for those entering the profession. What you and I do as early childhood professionals can help to keep the early years in the forefront of the public eye.

The need for a Canadian text in the field was evident when the first edition was being prepared in 1992/1993. At that time, there was a dearth of published Canadian material on early childhood education. Then, most Canadian students in introductory courses—including my students—were using American texts. At best, those texts had an add-on chapter or two on Canadian issues. Consequently, college and university instructors in this country had to assemble supplementary Canadian materials for their early childhood education courses. Considerable progress has been made in a decade. There are more Canadian texts, and more importantly, there is a growing body of research on early childhood education in Canada.

Early childhood education in Canada has its own proud history that dates back to the 19th century, its own professional organizations, and its own legislation and practices. Early childhood educators in Canada also have their own challenges that range from planning outdoor play during a lengthy winter, to offering educational programs for early childhood professionals in our northern reaches, and persuading our politicians to make high-quality early childhood programs accessible and affordable for all Canadians. I believe that in this book we have captured the uniqueness of early childhood education in Canada.

The philosophy underlying this third Canadian edition is still that early childhood educators are entrusted with the responsibility of designing a program that fosters development and provides the nurture and care that all young children need. This is an introductory text that aims to provide an overview of the field, its historical and theoretical origins, and the day-to-day work of professionals working in early childhood programs. The text can be used in full courses in two-year community college programs, three- and four-year university programs, and in-service courses for elementary school teachers who want to transfer into the early childhood division.

Terminology

The choice of terminology has been difficult at times because it is not consistent across all provinces and territories. For example, the definitions of **infant** and **toddler** vary from one Canadian jurisdiction to another. Similarly, a **teacher** in one jurisdiction would be a **caregiver** in another and a **child care worker** in yet another. I have chosen to use the terms **early childhood teacher** and **early childhood educator** synonymously in this text. *Caring for a Living* (Canadian Child Day Care Federation [CCDCF], 1992), a Canadian study of individuals working in child care settings, found that there was a high level of training among these individuals, even in those Canadian jurisdictions where it was not required. Similarly, individuals working in elementary schools also have considerable training. Consequently, we use the term "teacher" as freely as the term "caregiver" for all of those who work with young children. In some contexts, the term "teacher" has a more positive connotation among the public and it truly reflects the high degree of professionalism found in Canadian teachers in early childhood programs.

Highlights of the Third Canadian Edition

● Organization of the Text

The third Canadian edition of *Introduction to Early Childhood Education* provides thorough coverage of the field. We hope the tone of the book is positive, inviting, and inclusive. The updating of references is extensive, and the text includes current research in the field. The book is organized into five sections.

Part 1, **What?**, provides an overview of the field, its history, current models, and early childhood education in Canada.

Chapter 1, **The Scope of Early Childhood Education**, delves into what is included in this field. It examines changes in Canadian society that have shaped the scope of the field, the variety of programs that exist for young children, and some factors that influence the quality of these programs.

In Chapter 2, **The History of Early Childhood Education**, we examine the historical and theoretical foundations of the field by considering the works and ideas of important educators and theorists who have shaped the field of early childhood education as we know it today.

The links between theory and practice become clearer in Chapter 3, **Early Childhood Education Program Models.** Five program models are examined in detail, and more eclectic models are discussed. The latest research on the effectiveness of these models is also considered so that students can better evaluate the short- and long-term effectiveness of these models.

In Chapter 4, **Early Childhood Education in Canada**, we consider the history and scope of early childhood education in *each province and territory*, as well as current regulations governing these programs. We then look at the strengths and weaknesses of the field from a national perspective, and consider its future.

Part 2, **Who?**, looks at the different people in early childhood education—the children, their families, and their educators.

Chapter 5, **Children and Their Families** looks at the characteristics of young children—the things they have in common and the things that make each child unique. Then we look at parents and other family members with whom early childhood teachers share the responsibility for raising young children.

Chapter 6, **The Early Childhood Educator**, examines the different roles of those who work in early childhood programs. We consider early childhood education as a Canadian profession, our national organizations, and some issues faced by teachers in the field today.

Part 3, **How? The Basics**, focuses on the basic hows of early childhood education. We will examine the following fundamental components of high-quality early childhood education programs.

In Chapter 7, **Play and Developmentally Appropriate Practice**, we examine some of the basic constructs in early childhood education programs, including the role of play and its importance, the implementation of **developmentally appropriate practices**, and the importance of a curriculum that does not encourage bias or stereotypes. Some basic components of that curriculum and planning guidelines are then addressed.

In Chapter 8, **Guidance: Routines, Group Activities, and Behaviours,** we examine a number of important aspects of the early childhood program. Guidance suggestions for routines, transitions, and group activities are provided to help the teacher work effectively with the class as a whole. We also discuss the principles and strategies that teachers use to help children meet appropriate expectations.

In Part 4, **How? Curriculum**, we explore the basic hows of early childhood education in high-quality programs. Some basic components of the environment and curriculum, such as materials and planning and implementation guidelines, are addressed.

In Chapter 9, **Curriculum**, we discuss curriculum in terms of process and content. Then we address the issue of accountability, examining observation, assessment, standards, learning outcomes, and evaluation.

Chapter 10, **Development Through the Curriculum**, focuses on creative, physical, cognitive, language, and social development, and we talk about how the curriculum can foster development in these spheres.

In Part 5, **Why?**, we consider Canadian research on issues related to program quality, and speculate about the future.

In Chapter 11, **Quality in Early Childhood Programs**, we discuss current research on the quality of early childhood education programs across the country. The different variables that contribute to high-quality programs are discussed with special reference to recent Canadian studies.

In Chapter 12 of this final section, **The Future of Early Childhood Education,** we consider where the profession will go now that we are at the dawn of the 21st century. What issues and challenges do we face and what new ones will arise? What problems must the profession confront? What does the future hold for early childhood education in Canada? How can we ensure the availability of affordable, high-quality child care for very young Canadians?

Student-Friendly Features

While writing this edition, I have tried to keep the learning needs of adult students in mind.

The text features a number of unique learning aids:

- **A Canadian Professional Speaks Out** boxes are written by a person (or persons) with a vested interest in early childhood education on a topic pertinent to the chapter. Through these boxes, students are introduced to issues of concern to professionals on both coasts, in urban and rural settings, and in the far north.

- **Partnerships** boxes highlight topics and issues that directly affect relationships between the partners in early childhood education: families, children, teachers, and community. They offer ideas to enhance working together.

- **A Closer Look** boxes investigate in greater depth a topic or idea mentioned in the chapter. They offer further resources, suggestions, and practical tips.

- **Exhibits**, such as charts, tables, and figures, help organize and simplify information. The exhibits visually integrate the information and present it in a concise, at-your-fingertips, ready-to-use format.

- **Key Terms** are bolded and listed at the end of each chapter for quick reference. These terms are then defined in the Glossary of Key Terms at the back of the book.

- **Key Points**, another end-of-chapter feature, capture the underlying messages as opposed to simply reiterating facts from the chapter.

● New to This Edition

- Each chapter now ends with a series of **Key Questions** designed to encourage critical thinking and discussion of the issues raised within the chapter.

- **Reflective Exercises** are included throughout each chapter. These are designed to help the reader grapple with issues that arise from the text. The Reflective Exercises might also be used for class discussions.

- **Web icons** are included throughout the book and cue students to access the Nelson ECE Resource Centre Web site <ece.nelson.com>.

Supplemental Materials

- An **Instructor's Guide** is available for the third Canadian edition of *Introduction to Early Childhood Education*. The guide contains chapter summaries, key terms, suggestions for course planning, class discussion topics, and student assignments and activities. Key articles and related films and videos are listed as potential resources for each chapter. The Instructor's guide also contains test questions. Multiple-choice, fill-in-the-blank, and short essay questions are provided for each of the text chapters.

The **Nelson ECE Resource Centre Web site** <ece.nelson.com> contains many additional resources, including free downloadable activities and links to dozens of ECE-related Web sites.

From a Grateful Author

This book would not have been completed if others had not been generous with their knowledge and their time. To all of them, I owe a great deal of thanks. While I cannot thank everyone who has helped, several individuals deserve special recognition. Over the years, Don Rutledge, Ian Begg, and Glenn MacDonald have influenced my thinking about many issues. John Novak has been an outstanding colleague and friend who has humoured me through the process. Mary Louise Vanderlee, Coral Mitchell, and Alice Schutz also have helped in many ways. Dean Michael Manley-Casimir has supported my writing efforts. Lynn Duhaime and Cynthia Peterson have had to bear with me throughout the process, and they have worked on references and printed and copied multiple drafts of the manuscript for me. Suguna Loganathan and Dyah Kartiningdyah have helped in countless ways and, along with Lynn and Cynthia, have provided comic relief on a regular basis.

The late Polly Richardson, a former coordinator of the Early Childhood Education program at Mohawk College and former president of the Association for Early Childhood Education–Ontario, taught me much about working with young children and about the profession when I was a student, a teacher in the "lab school," and an instructor in the program. Polly came to Ontario from Winnipeg, helped establish Hamilton's war-time day nurseries, and was active in both the NEAO's training programs for early childhood educators in Ontario and the founding of ECE programs in Ontario's community colleges. She remains a source of inspiration.

The students I have taught at Brock University and, some years ago, at Mohawk College have helped me formulate ideas about the field and taught me a great deal about teaching. They also emphasized their need to know the Canadian story of early childhoood education. The many children I have worked with, both as a teacher and as a psychologist, at the Mohawk College Laboratory Preschool, the Laneway School, and the Toronto and Peel Boards of Education have challenged my thinking and broadened my understanding. Thanks are also due to the many teachers who have welcomed me into their classrooms.

Many talented Canadian professionals with an interest in early childhood education have enriched the book with their contributions to the **A Canadian Professional Speaks Out** boxes. The children and teachers at Power Glen Cooperative Nursery School, Hillfield-Strathallan College, and Wheatley School of Montessori Education have allowed me to take photos in their classes. Friends and colleagues also have been generous with photographs.

It has been a great pleasure to work with the many people at Nelson who have been involved in the production of this book. Joanna Cotton, Executive Editor, deserves special mention for her guidance. Joanne Sutherland has been involved in many aspects of the book. Natalia Denesiuk, the Production Editor, has been a great help in the latter stages of the book. Rodney Rawlings, a thoughtful freelance editor, knows the manuscript almost as well as I do.

My family has helped in less obvious, but equally important, ways. They have seen me in front of a computer for many months, and they have pitched in with each successive deadline. Don Shattuck, my husband, has solved multiple problems and has spent many hours in father–son activities while I was writing. Daniel, our son, was just over two years of age when the first edition was being written; back then, he would say "What? Aren't you finished yet?" Now at 12 years of age, he asks when the next edition is due. My mother, Catharine Young, has endured the many hours when I was unavailable with grace.

Finally, I must thank Canadian reviewers for their comments and criticisms of the proposal for this edition of the text. I have tried to incorporate their suggestions into the text and have appreciated their feedback on its organization and content. All of the following reviewers have helped to produce a textbook for Canadian students learning about early childhood education in their country: Terri Cody, Lethbridge Community College; Kathleen Fischer, Niagara College; Donna Mese, Cambrian College; Pamela Taylor, Grant MacEwan College; and Mary Louise Vanderlee, Brock University.

Part 1

What?

Each section of this book focuses on a different aspect of early childhood education (ECE), beginning with defining just what this field is. Part 1 addresses the what of early childhood education in the following ways:

- In Chapter 1, **The Scope of Early Childhood Education**, we will delve into the question of what is involved in this field. We will examine the many variations that exist today in programs for young children. As part of this examination, we will look at the need for such programs, particularly the social factors that have shaped the scope of the field. We will also begin to explore issues related to the quality of early childhood programs.

- In Chapter 2, **The History of Early Childhood Education**, we will examine some of the historical and theoretical foundations of the field by considering the works and ideas of important predecessors of early childhood education today.

- In Chapter 3, **Early Childhood Education Program Models**, we will consider the linkage between theory and practice as we review several model programs based on specific theories.

- In Chapter 4, Early **Childhood Education in Canada**, we consider the history and scope of early childhood education in the provinces and territories, as well as legislation and teacher training.

Chapter 1

The Scope of Early Childhood Education

*E*arly childhood education (ECE)—this is the field you are exploring through this text and the course in which you are enrolled. What is early childhood education? Is it the same in all the provinces and in the territories, or does it vary like other aspects of Canadian education? And just when is early childhood, or does that also vary from one location to the next? What place does early childhood education have in Canadian society? What are its roots? What is its future?

As you begin learning about this field of study, the answers to some of these questions will gain greater significance and become more focused. But first, let's clarify terminology: we will use the Canadian term **early childhood educator**. However, other terms, particularly **teacher**, **caregiver**, and **child care worker**, will also be used interchangeably. The broad scope of the early childhood educator's role leads to this multiplicity of terms—early childhood educators serve as both caregivers and teachers for the young children in their programs.

This chapter presents an overview of the field of early childhood education, while later chapters introduce new topics and issues. The following outline provides you with a synopsis of the chapter:

1. A number of social factors have contributed to the expansion of early childhood programs and brought early childhood education into the public consciousness. We will examine three factors:

   - Changes in family life such as an increased number of two-earner families and single parents

   - Growing evidence of the benefits of early education for children from poverty, children who are physically or mentally challenged, and other children at risk

   - Child advocacy, which has helped bring the needs of young children and their families to public and legislative prominence

2. There is considerable diversity in the types of early childhood programs both within and between the provinces and territories. We will look at the following ways in which programs may differ:

   - Purposes of programs

   - Program settings

   - Ages of the children

   - Sources of funding support

3. A most important factor in describing early childhood programs is quality. We can only begin our discussion of quality in early childhood education programs in this chapter, but will return to it in later chapters. In this chapter, we should at least examine the following elements that contribute to the quality of early childhood programs:

   - Teacher-child ratio

   - Group size

   - Mixed-age grouping

   - Developmental appropriateness of the program

   - Quality of child-adult interaction

   - Staff qualifications

   - Staff consistency

   - Respect and concern for the staff

   - Ongoing professional development

   - Quality of the physical environment

   - Family involvement

   - Quality as a combination of factors

The Growth of Early Childhood Education

Although the importance and value of education in the early years of life have been acknowledged for more than 2000 years (Carter, 1987), relatively recent factors have brought early childhood education to the forefront of public awareness. Fundamental changes in the economy, family life, public awareness, and public support have had a profound effect on early childhood education. You have undoubtedly seen recent newspaper headlines and national magazine covers that have directed a spotlight on child care. Much of their focus has been on changes in family life that have brought about the need for child care outside the home. These changes result from an interplay of many complex factors including the rising cost of living, a rising number of dual-income families, an increase in single-parent families, an increased number of teenage parents, greater family mobility, and a decrease in the impact of the extended family.

But the needs of working families are not the only reason that early childhood has been in the public focus. Over the past quarter-century, the success of some publicly funded early childhood programs in Canada and the United States has shown us that high-quality early educational intervention can combat poverty and dysfunction. There has also been increased attention to the needs of special populations of young children and how to bring them into the mainstream of society; for instance, children who are physically challenged, mentally challenged, abused, or culturally different have benefited from such programs.

Finally, many professionals are outspoken and eloquent advocates for the rights of children. They continue to lobby for governmental changes that will improve the lives of young children.

Changes in Family Life

"Typical" family life has changed considerably since the end of World War II. Demographic information indicates that increasing numbers of women are entering the workforce (e.g., Statistics Canada, 1985, 1996, 1998b, 1998c, 1998f, 1999b, 1999d; Women's Bureau, 1990). No longer do most mothers stay at home to rear their young children. In some families, both parents work because of the desire for personal and professional development rather than for economic reasons. In other cases, economic need forces families to rely on two salaries because one simply does not provide for all of their financial needs. And in some families, both parents work both for personal and economic reasons.

Two-Income Families.   Whereas in 1951, only 11 percent of Canadian married women worked, that figure had risen to 44 percent in 1975, 56 percent in 1987, 60 percent in 1989, and almost 70 percent in 1993 (Doxey, 1990, 1996, 1998; Women's Bureau, 1970a; Women's Bureau, 1970b; Women's Bureau, 1990; Statistics Canada, 1993). Unfortunately, in the 1950s and 1960s, government studies of women in the workforce had an unusual definition of working mothers: in addition to having children under 14, they had to have been married at some

---

Reflective Exercise 1-1

Did you spend any time in child care arrangements because your mother was working? In your class, how many students were in child care and how many were home with non-working mothers? What are your memories of your early childhood years? Can you apply your experiences to today's young children?

---

time (e.g., Women's Bureau, 1970a). Of course, that definition of a working mother eliminated single parents from consideration, and it now makes comparisons of recent studies of working mothers that include all mothers regardless of marital status somewhat difficult. Nevertheless, it is clear that there has been a steady increase in the number of married and unmarried women in the workplace since 1975.

A look at Exhibit 1-1 will give you some idea of the number of Canadian children 9 years and younger, the percentage of children who do not require supplemental care, and the arrangements of those who need it (Pence et al., 1992).

There is some regional variation in these figures that is related, at least in part, to employment opportunities. Nevertheless, women in all areas of the country are far less likely to be home rearing their children in the new millennium than they were in previous decades. About 75 percent of Canadian women were employed by the mid-1990s (Statistics Canada, 1996). Between the 1950s and 1990s, dual-income families were less frequent when there were children under 6 years of age in the home. In 1981, for example, only 38 percent of Canadian families with children under 6 years had both parents working; by 1996, that figure had risen to 56 percent (Statistics Canada, 1996, 1998h). The pattern is similar for single-parent families. Almost 40 percent of single parents with children between birth and 5 years work (Statistics Canada, 1996; 1998, June 9). Although it is still true that both parents are more likely to work if their children are 6 years or older, in recent years there has been a dramatic shift in the number of mothers returning to work after their infants are born. By the mid-1990s, about 90 percent of Canadian mothers returned to work within the year of the birth (Statistics Canada, 1999, Sept. 1).

The changes in the number of women in the workforce has led to a much greater need for child care. The recent trend for most new mothers to return to work within a year of giving birth also has escalated the need for infant and toddler programs.

Single-Parent Families. Another family change that has increased the demand for child care is the rise in the number of single parents. While the majority of single-parent families are created through divorce, there also is a growing number of never-married parents, some still finishing their high school

EXHIBIT 1-1   *Number of Canadian Children 0–9 Years of Age:*
Caregiving Needs and Arrangements

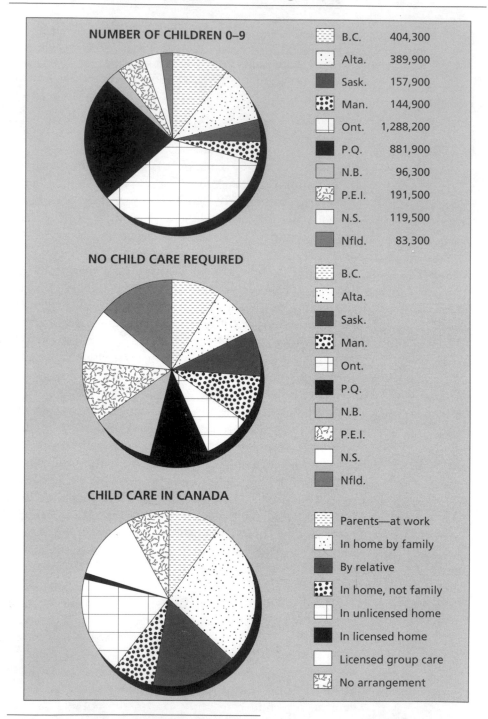

SOURCE: A. Pence et al. (1992). "An overview of NCCS data for British Columbia." In A. Pence
(Ed.), *Canadian child care in context: Perspectives from the provinces and territories* (pp. 67, 83).
Ottawa, ON: Statistics Canada and Health and Welfare Canada.

education, and some older who choose to remain single. Prior to changes in Canada's divorce laws in 1968, divorces were rare—only 1.6 married women per 1000 divorced in 1961 (Ram, 1990). That figure jumped to 6.1 in 1971, to 11.3 in 1981, and to 12.4 in 1986 (Ram, 1990). The divorce rate slowly levelled off after the flurry of activity that followed the 1968 Divorce Act. By 1991, it had dropped back to 2.7 per 1000 people and remained about the same, at 2.6 per 1000 in 1995 (Dumas, 1997; Statistics Canada, 1993a).

The marriage rate in Canada also has steadily declined, and the number of common-law relationships has steadily increased (Statistics Canada, 1997, Oct. 14). Additionally, the number of never-married individuals reported in Canadian census data has continued to increase (Statistics Canada, 1997, Oct. 14). The data from the 1996 Canadian census show that the number of single-parent families increased 19 percent between the 1991 and 1996 censuses; the data from the May 2001 census will not be available for several years, but this trend is likely to continue. Almost one of every five children in Canada lived in a single-parent family in 1996 whereas it was 1 of every 6 children in 1991. The percentage of single-parent families varies somewhat by province and territory, from a low of just under 13 percent in Alberta to highs of 15.9, 16.5, and 17.1 percent in Quebec, the Yukon, and the Northwest Territories respectively (Statistics Canada, 1997, Oct. 14).

The divorced single parent with custody of the children, most frequently the mother, typically experiences a significant decrease in income and standard of living. In addition, the single parent usually has to work (or work longer hours) to support the family. Of course, to work outside the home, the single, divorced parent, male or female, needs to find appropriate child care. Single parents who have never married face similar challenges when it comes to child care. A number of them, however—teenage mothers who have chosen to keep a child, for example—do not have the skills required to enter the workforce. Between 1991 and 1995, the incomes of both male and female single parents declined by 8 percent, twice as much as it did in two-parent families (Statistics Canada, 1998, May 12). Male single parents had the largest decrease in income, dropping by 10 percent, perhaps because of difficulties finding appropriate child care (Statistics Canada, 1998, May 12). Statistics Canada has an excellent Web site filled with information about the demographics of the Canadian family. Try visiting it as a class to find out more about the changing Canadian family.

Increasing Family Mobility. A third change in family life is the increasing mobility of many of today's families. Work demands cause some families to move away from relatives who might otherwise provide support. Family mobility, involving only the small nuclear family, has contributed to the declining influence of the extended family, that network of relatives such as grandparents, uncles, and aunts, or adult brothers and sisters beyond the immediate family.

Traditionally, the most prevalent form of child care was having a relative look after the children. One reason is that many parents seem more comfortable leaving a young child with a relative than with a stranger. In addition, relatives may charge little or no money for taking care of the child, making this a financially attractive alternative. While relatives are still a frequently used source of care, the **Canadian National Child Care Study (CNCCS)** (Pence, Read, Lero, Goelman, & Brockman, 1992) found that non-relatives now are more likely to care for Canadian children than relatives. Quite often, female relatives, who traditionally would have been home, are working. A similar pattern has been noted in the United States: from 1960 to 1980, the rate of preschool child care provided by a relative dropped from two-thirds to less than one-half of the total number of children in care (Wash & Brand, 1990).

Changes such as increasing numbers of dual-income families and single-parent families, and a decline in the impact of the extended family, have dramatically raised the demand for child care and brought early childhood education to the forefront of public attention. "Child care is now as essential to family life as the automobile or the refrigerator" (Scarr, Phillips, & McCartney, 1990, p. 26). Statistics Canada has a daily journal, called *The Daily*, and will report the results of the 2001 census as they become available. Visit the site on a regular basis to find out what demographic changes there are in the new census data.

● Benefits of Early Childhood Education

The need of working parents for child care makes early childhood education a topic of national prominence, but this is not the only reason for its increasing importance. A great deal of research, which we will discuss later in this chapter, has shown that high-quality child care programs have positive effects on the development of young children. On a parallel though separate track, there has been extensive discussion and research about the benefits of early education for special populations of children and families. Thus, children from poverty backgrounds, children with disabilities, and children at risk for other reasons have been enrolled in publicly funded programs. Since the mid-1960s, financial support has increased as a result of mounting evidence that high-quality early childhood programs can and do make a long-term difference that carries into adulthood. Researchers have concluded that good early childhood programs not only improve the lives of the children and families involved, but also result in substantial economic benefits for society. Although early intervention programs are expensive, their cost is more than recovered in subsequent years through greater schooling success, decreased need for special education, lowered delinquency and arrest rates, and decreased welfare dependence (Berrueta-Clement, Schweinhart, Barnett, Epstein, & Weikart, 1984; Wright, 1983).

● Child Advocacy

A third factor that has brought early childhood education into the public consciousness is the urgency with which many professionals view the plight of increasing numbers of children and families. Of particular concern are the many families that face extreme poverty, lacking the most basic necessities.

In Canada, on average, one in five children lives in circumstances that fall below the poverty line; in some regions of the country, for example the Atlantic, that figure is higher, while it is lower in other areas (Campaign 2000, 1998; Chisholm, 1997). Despite the fact that the United Nations has ranked Canada as number one in terms of quality of life for several recent years, Chisholm (1997) notes that Canada has the second-highest child poverty rate among industrialized nations. Yet the social problems reach beyond the needs of the poor, to working parents with moderate incomes who are beset by the scarcity of affordable, high-quality care. A report from the **National Day Care Study (NDCS)**, *Status of Day Care in Canada 1990* (National Child Care Information Centre, 1991), suggested that available licensed child care settings may serve less than 8 percent of children under 3 years who need child care and only 27 percent of Canadian children between 3 and 5 years who need child care. Organizations such as the Childcare Advocacy Association of Canada and the Canadian Child Care Federation, as well as many provincial organizations, actively advocate for young children in Canada and for high-quality early childhood programs.

The needs of children and families have become political concerns. They have come to the attention of both political leaders and the public at large through the astute efforts of those dedicated to advocating the rights of children, including early childhood professionals. But there is a continuing need to promote a common concern for the welfare of all children.

When Is Early Childhood?

If you were to ask several individuals to define the term "early childhood," it is likely that you would receive a different answer from each person. In fact, even early childhood educators have difficulty with using terms consistently. Some of this uncertainty stems from the fact that the definition of early childhood has widened over the past thirty years as has the range of early childhood programs (Doxey, 1990). In this text, the term **early childhood** refers to the period from birth to age 8, and most current works would agree with this definition.

What Is Included in Early Childhood Education?

We have looked at some of the historical roots of early childhood education and reasons for the rapid growth of the field. But **early childhood education** is a broad term and includes a variety of approaches and programs. Nursery schools and child care centres (formerly referred to as day care centres), parent cooperative preschools and infant stimulation programs, and junior kindergartens and kindergartens are but a few of the early childhood programs that exist in Canada. Toy-lending libraries, home-based child care, and employer-sponsored child care centres also fall within the definition of early childhood education programs. The Assiniboia Downs Race Track Child Care Centre in Winnipeg and the Edmonton Hospital Workers' Day Care are early childhood programs offered by the workplace. Other programs include the Pairiviq Child Care Centre in Iqaluit, Northwest Territories, an Inuit child care centre, and Gizhaadaawgamik, a day care centre for Indian children in Toronto, which derives its name from the Ojibwa word that means "a place to care for children." Some early childhood programs, such as drop-in centres, do not have explicit educational goals, while other programs such as babysitting cooperatives and drop-off child centres do not have formal programs. All of these programs, however, aim to provide an experience for young children that they would not ordinarily receive from their parents at home.

Clearly, early childhood education refers to a wide variety of programs. The programs may vary on a number of dimensions, and just some of them are shown in Exhibit 1-2.

EXHIBIT 1-2   *Some Dimensions of ECE Programs*

Settings	Ages of Children	Sources of Funding	Purposes
Family child care homes—licensed and not licensed Centre-based programs	Infants < 18 months Toddlers 18–35 months Preschoolers 3–5 years Kindergarten children –5 years Primary-level children 6–8 years	For-profit Nonprofit Employer-supported University-and college-affiliated Publicly supported	Care Enrichment Compensation

Other variations will become evident in later chapters. We will now examine some of the classifications into which programs can be grouped.

● Purpose of Programs

Child care programs are designed with many purposes in mind and differ from one another on a number of dimensions. We have already touched on some basic differences in programs that stem from their underlying thrust. Some programs serve special populations such as shift workers or parents with unusual working hours. Other programs are available for emergency care, and still others are for stay-at-home parents. The vast majority of programs, however, are designed to meet the needs of working parents. In the section below, we will consider some of the goals common to child care programs.

Care of Children.   Of course, a major purpose of many child care programs is to care for children while their parents work. The rapid rise in recent years in the numbers of children in full-day care, either in child care centres or in family child care homes, has parallelled the increasing prevalence of working mothers. Parents look for programs that will provide a safe and nurturing environment for their children during their working hours.

Enrichment.   Enrichment is a second aim of many child care programs, and this aim is especially prevalent particularly in part-time preschools such as cooperatives. These programs usually include specific activities to enhance socialization, cognitive skills, or overall development of young children. The underlying notion is that children will benefit from experiences that they may not receive at home, for instance, participating in group activities, playing with a group of agemates, or learning specific concepts from specially trained teachers.

Hurrying or Hothousing.   One phenomenon that has been growing recently is that of the "hurried child" or "hothousing," apt terms that have become popular. Hothousing is aimed at accelerating some aspect of young children's development; it is of considerable concern to many early childhood professionals (e.g., Elkind, 1981, 1987b; Gallagher & Coche, 1987; Hills, 1987; Sigel, 1987). It differs from enrichment by the nature of its activities and by its lack of developmental appropriateness. A University of Michigan study reported in *Time* magazine in 1998 (Labi, 1998) reported that leisure time for children between 3 and 9 years of age had decreased from 40 percent in 1981 to only 25 percent in 1997. Clearly, child burnout is becoming an issue. Moreover, the issue of child burnout is not confined to the United States, as the "Better Babies" installment of the CBC program *The Nature of Things* shows. Academically oriented programs for very young children are generally designed to meet the expectations of "upwardly mobile 'yuppy' [sic] parents, who want designer diapers and designer degrees in Greek, Suzuki, and computer programming for their infants" (Clarke-Stewart, 1988b, p. 147).

Reflective Exercise 1-2

Discuss the controversial topic of hothousing young children. Consider the differences between a program in which young children are encouraged to learn actively through exploration and play in a stimulating environment and one where they are involved in structured activities like reading, swimming, ballet, and music lessons.

The Canadian Toy Testing Council evaluates toys and software every year and gives awards for the best ones. In fact, they look at how appropriate the toy is for age recommended as well as at the play value of the toy. Visit their Web site and see if you can find toys that would contribute to hothousing and ones that are more age-appropriate.

Compensation.   A third major purpose of child care programs, found most frequently in publicly funded programs, is compensation. Compensatory programs aim to make up for some lack in children's backgrounds. The basic philosophy of compensatory programs, such as Mary Wright's (1983) University of Western Ontario Preschool, is to provide experiences that will help children enter the mainstream of society more successfully. Such experiences sometimes include a range of services, encompassing early childhood education, nutrition, and parent education.

Cultural Preservation.   An additional purpose of programs such as the Gizhaadaawgamik Centre mentioned above is the preservation and transmission of cultural traditions and languages. Similarly, some but by no means all church-based schools aim to provide educational programs in a religious context.

These categories, although descriptive of some underlying differences among programs, are not mutually exclusive. Few child care centres are concerned with only the physical well-being and care of children. Most also provide enriching experiences that further children's development. At the same time, preschool programs have to be concerned with appropriate nurture and safety while the children are in their care. Similarly, compensatory programs are also concerned with enriching experiences and caring for children, whereas child care or preschool programs may serve to compensate for something lacking in the backgrounds of some of the children.

● Program Settings

Programs for young children can be divided into home-based and centre-based settings. In 1992, the **Canadian National Child Care Study (CNCCS)** (Pence et al., 1992) provided a detailed examination of the types of caregiving arrangements Canadian parents reported using for children between 0 and 9 years of age. The results, shown in Exhibit 1-3, clearly show that home-based care is more frequent than centre-based care. However, parents favour different types of care for children of different ages, with centre-based care being most frequent for preschoolers. Exhibit 1-4 displays the updated information for 1994 to 1995 from the National Longitudinal Survey of Children and Youth (NLSCY) (1996), but a more detailed breakdown by age and type of care is not available for that time period.

Centre-Based Programs.   Centre-based programs include full-day **child care centres** and **nursery schools** or preschools, and more children enrolled in them than in home-based programs. Typically, child care centres are located in either a separate building of their own or any of a variety of buildings that have extra space

EXHIBIT 1-3 *Canadian Child Care Arrangements: Percentage of Total Number of Children in Each Caregiving Setting by Age*

Type of Care	Children's Ages			
	0–17 Months	18–35 Months	3–5 Years	6–9 Years
Parents—at work	10.0%	11.2%	10.7%	9.3%
Parents—at home	20.0%	15.6%	17.5%	24.6%
Sibling(s)	...	...	...	6.9%
Self	—	—	...	5.3%
Relatives in child's home	10.4%	7.5%	7.5%	5.9%
Relatives *not* in child's home	14.3%	11.8%	8.3%	6.5%
Non-relative in child's home	9.3%	10.5%	8.0%	6.0%
Non-relative *not* in child's home—licensed	...	2.7%*	1.7%*	0.8%*
Non-relative *not* in child's home—unlicensed	26.3%	25.1%	18.7%	12.7%
Preschool	—	—	2.8%	...
Kindergarten	—	—	6.0%	...
Child care centre	5.4%	12.5%	13.9%	1.6%
Before/after school program	—	—	1.1%*	4.7%
No arrangement	...	...	2.4%	15.6%
Total Number of Children	**223,300**	**269,600**	**570,200**	**862,600**

Legend:
...   Too small a sample
—   Nil
*   Estimate

SOURCE: Pence et al., 1992, p. 83.

available and a need for child care or the desire to offer it. Schools, churches, colleges and universities, hospitals, YWCA and YMCA buildings, and office towers are among the many locations with child care centres. Nursery schools and preschools are less likely than centres to be in a building on their own. Nursery schools or preschools usually are part-day programs with *primarily* an educational orientation that serve children from 2 to 5 years of age. Colleges and universities often have nursery schools attached to them that are used as demonstration centres for teacher education courses, and as laboratories for research on child development and education.

EXHIBIT 1-4 *Percentage of Canadian Children in Different Types of Care, 1994–1995*

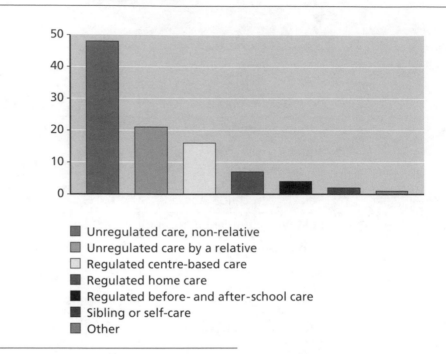

■ Unregulated care, non-relative
■ Unregulated care by a relative
□ Regulated centre-based care
■ Regulated home care
■ Regulated before- and after-school care
■ Sibling or self-care
■ Other

NOTE: Percentages from National Longitudinal Survey of Children and Youth (1996).

Parent cooperative nursery schools, which emerged in Toronto in the 1930s, and in Victoria, Saskatoon, Montreal, and Vancouver in the 1940s (Stevenson, 1990), are another type of nursery school created and controlled by parents. The parents employ the teachers, and historically, parents have had to assist in the program.

Child care centres, in contrast to nursery schools, offer full-day programs for infants and children of working parents, so the custodial aspect of child care must be included as *one* of their purposes. However, child care centres and nursery schools are by no means mutually exclusive. The better nursery schools emphasize education and care as do the better child care centres. Moreover, child care centres often have half-day options, and nursery schools sometimes have before- and after-school options. Nevertheless, the child care centre typically is open for a minimum of ten hours a day. Consequently, child care programs must provide meals and opportunities for naps or quiet times, and deal with the realities of diaper changes, toilet training, and toothbrushes and combs. Historically, many child care centres only provided custodial care, but there has been a gradual shift in focus and it probably would be difficult to find a Canadian child care centre in the 1990s that did not, at least, express an interest in the education of the children. Frequently, the interest is not just expressed, but clearly evident in practice, so that child care centres offer a comprehensive program that aims to encourage development in all areas.

In Canada, centre-based programs have increased more than any other type of child care. While in 1971, only 17,000 Canadian children were cared for in centre-based settings, close to 300,000 Canadian children were in licensed child care settings in 1990 (National Child Care Information Centre, 1991). By 1994–1995, that figure had stabilized at 235,500 (NLSCY, 1996).

Home-Based Settings. In Canada (NLSCY, 1996), as in the United States (Hofferth & Phillips, 1987), when all ages of children are considered, the largest number are cared for in homes. Some children are cared for in their own homes, while others are in family child care homes. A family child care home is someone else's home where a caregiver provides child care. As we will see below, these homes may or may not be licensed, and the quality of care ranges from excellent to atrocious. Licensed family care has increased slowly but steadily in Canada. Between 1971 to 1990, for example, the number of children cared for in licensed family child care homes increased from 600 to 38,000 (National Child Care Information Centre, 1991). By 1995, only 168,000 of the 1,500,000 children between birth and 11 years studied in the NLSCY were in licensed homes, while 1,047,000 of them were in unlicensed settings. Canadian infants and toddlers in particular are cared for in family child care homes (Pence et al., 1992). In some cases, this is because parents of very young children prefer a more intimate, home-

like setting. Parents with several children often prefer this setting, as it means that they do not have to drop off three children, for example, at three different locations on their way to work. Still other parents choose this arrangement for very young children as they do not want them exposed to the plethora of illnesses one may encounter in a large centre. But for many parents, the main reason they choose family child care is that it is readily available and often considerably cheaper than centre-based care. In Saskatchewan and Newfoundland centre-based care for infants is still not permitted, so family child care may be the only alternative in those areas.

Most provinces require licensing or registration of family child care homes that receive government funding, but the vast majority of homes are unlicensed (Halpern, 1987; Pence, 1992). Certainly, the vast majority of Canadian children in family child care are in unlicensed facilities (cf. Exhibit 1-1 and Exhibit 1-3). While licensing does not ensure quality, it does provide some safeguards. For example, the building must be safe and pass fire regulations, and there are limits on the number and ages of children who can be in the home at any time. Moreover, licensed homes are inspected on a regular basis. Later, in our discussion of the scope of child care in each province, you will note that the number of licensed spaces for infants and toddlers, in particular, across the country is consistently low in both family- and centre-based child care programs. While it may be like trying to determine if the chicken or egg comes first, it is possible that parents would choose licensed centre-based care for the very young more frequently if more spaces were available.

Exhibit 1-3 also shows that many Canadian children under 5 years are cared for in their own homes, by a relative or non-relative, but this arrangement is less frequent for school-aged children. A small number of these homes may be family child care homes where the caregiver looks after her own children and several others. Frequently, however, parents arrange to have a **nanny** come into the home on a daily or a live-in basis. Nannies have become an attractive child care option for families where both parents work and/or have schedules that do not conform to centre-based programs. Some nannies have training in child care, and they may attend to other household tasks such as cooking and light cleaning. In 1993, Canada's immigration polices required that nannies from abroad have Grade 12 education and six months of on-the-job training to enter the country. In fact, there are also a number of illegal immigrants, in both Canada and the United States, who seek employment as nannies (and both Presidents Bush and Clinton became painfully aware of this, during their pre-inaugural searches for Attorneys General in 1993 and 2000. At least three successive female candidates for that powerful, top-lawmaker position have had to withdraw their nominations as they had employed illegal immigrants and avoided paying federal taxes!).

Reflective Exercise 1-3

Family life has changed considerably over the past two decades—while you and many of your classmates were in your formative years. Families in which both parents work are much more common, as are single-parent families and teenage parents. In addition, the extended family is less of a force and family mobility has increased. Have these changes affected the people in your group? How will they affect today's young children?

● Ages of Children

The classification of early childhood spans from birth to age 8, which includes infants, toddlers, and children in kindergarten and the primary grades. Needless to say, working parents need care for children of varying ages.

Infants and Toddlers.   One of the most dramatic increases in recent years has been in infant and toddler programs. But what is an infant and what is a toddler? The answer is not as clear as it might be. In eight of the thirteen provinces and territories, **infants** are defined as being *between 0 and 18 months old,* so we will use the majority's definition. Canadians seem to have more difficulty with the term **toddler**, so we will use the most common definition: toddlers range *from 19 to 35 months old.*

Not all infant/toddler programs fall under the heading of child care, however. A number of compensatory programs, such as **infant stimulation programs** for infants at risk for developmental delays, enroll children and parents from infancy. Programs for infants and toddlers with special needs, such as a visual or hearing impairment, also start early parent-child education programs as soon as possible. In the A Canadian Professional Speaks Out box here, Dr. Janet Olds describes a research program for children with hearing impairments that was offered through the Children's Hospital of Eastern Ontario. Other programs with a compensatory focus involve infants and toddlers and their families in programs as a way of intervening in the poverty cycle.

A Canadian Professional Speaks Out

INTEGRATION OF CHILDREN WITH HEARING LOSS

Dr. J. M. Olds, Children's Hospital of Eastern Ontario

Hearing loss may place a child at risk for delays in the development of communication which, in turn, may have a impact on learning, as well as on social and emotional development. For example, it has been documented for almost a century that literacy skills in many children with hearing loss is below their hearing peers. However, we do know that the earlier a hearing impairment is identified, the greater opportunity children will have to develop their language and other abilities.

The goals of early intervention programs for children with hearing loss range from integration with hearing peers to education fostering a Deaf culture identity. However, there is little information about how successful each of these approaches are in meeting their goals. This information is important for parents, so that they can make informed decisions for their children It is also important for professionals to know if the interventions work, what facets of the program contribute to success, and what areas need to be improved. In general, research which would provide this information is still in its infancy.

One approach for children with hearing impairments is auditory-verbal therapy. This approach has been developed with the goal of optimizing a child's residual hearing to develop listening skills and the ability to communicate orally. The principles of auditory-verbal therapy include early identification of a hearing loss with prompt medical and audiological management, integrating listening in all areas of communication, and incorporating parents as partners and primary language models. Auditory-verbal therapists work closely with parents, and then later, with teachers and other professionals involved with each child. However, like most intervention programs, until very recently there has been little research investigating the effectiveness of auditory-verbal therapy.

(cont'd)

INTEGRATION OF CHILDREN WITH HEARING LOSS *cont'd*

Our research team was particularly interested in how children do after participating in auditory-verbal therapy. Our team consists of researchers at the Children's Hospital of Eastern Ontario in Ottawa and at the University of Ottawa, who work with children with hearing loss as audiologists, psychologists or educators or who have done so in the past. In our research, we gathered information from young people who, as preschoolers, were diagnosed with a hearing impairment and who had participated in auditory-verbal therapy. We were interested in whether the goals of auditory-verbal therapy were met, particularly whether children developed good communication abilities, achieved academically and functioned effectively in their homes and communities. We were particularly interested in their experience with integration, and what factors facilitated or posed barriers to integration into their schools and communities.

We collected information in a variety of ways. In our first phase, we asked these young people and their parents to complete very long questionnaires about their lives, as well as their past experiences in their schools and community. We also asked the young people to complete a series of standardized tests, so we could measure how well they were doing compared to other young people their age who could hear normally. In addition, we asked these young people, their parents, and teachers of children with hearing impairments to participate in focus groups to discuss what factors enhanced or limited integration.

Our results were very encouraging. As a group, young people with hearing loss were functioning within the average range on measures of oral communication, academic skill and self-perception compared to age peers with normal hearing. This was in contrast to the finding of a century ago which suggested limited achievement associated with hearing loss. In addition, about half the participants reported that they were still in school (42%); of those who had graduated from high school, many had continued with postsecondary studies (72%) and/or were now working. In addition, most reported that they had been integrated into a regular classroom for all (65%) or much (17%) of their school years, or secondarily had attended special education classes for hearing children with disabilities.

Young people, parents, and teachers provided us with further information about their experience with integration from their discussions in focus groups. A number of factors were mentioned as either very important in facilitating integration or in the opposite form, were major barriers to integration. At home, families that facilitated integration were those who were encouraging of their child, not only by participating in auditory-verbal therapy, but in developing social relationships and independence, as well as developing supportive networks for themselves. In the community, involvement in extracurricular activities, developing a close circle of friends and having the support of family and other people with hearing loss were some of the factors which were identified as important to facilitating integration. These factors, as well as others, were seen as assisting the student with hearing loss to become a well-adjusted member of their family and community. Other factors associated with school were identified as important in children's development. In particular, a team approach, which included school staff and parents working together to meet the needs of students with hearing loss, was identified as an important facilitator of integration. The importance of professionals specialized in hearing impairment was identified as important, whether for teaching communication, academic or social skills directly, or in providing strategies and support to classroom teachers. This was also seen as important in helping classroom teachers understand the unique needs of students with hearing impairments and to implementing specialized strategies in the classroom to meet these needs. The team approach was also considered to be important in encouraging social opportunities and social development.

Our results suggest that partnerships between parents, school staff and other professionals can work to help children with hearing loss develop into young people who are a part of their schools and communities. We feel this information is important to parents as their make choices on behalf of their children, as well as to teachers and others who work with them. In the future, we hope to follow children's development so we can continue to collect information from children as they and to continue to learn from them about what works well for them.

Preschoolers.   The largest segment of children in licensed Canadian early childhood programs are between 3 and 5 years of age (Pence et al., 1992). About 22.5 percent of the parents in the CNCCS indicated they used nursery schools, child care centres, and kindergartens for their 3-to-5-year-old children. Another 20.3 percent of children in this age group were in family child care homes, while 15.5 percent were cared for in their own homes by a relative or non-relative. The 1991 NDCS suggested that the available licensed child care spaces would serve only 27.7 percent of Canadian working women, and about 24 percent of the CNCCS sample reported using these facilities. Again, these numbers suggest that there are simply not enough licensed spaces to meet parental needs.

There are many different types of preschool programs, some more developmentally appropriate than others. A number of different models will be discussed in later chapters.

Kindergarten and Primary Children.   Most definitions of early childhood include children up to age 8. Thus, directions for curriculum, teaching strategies, and the environment in kindergartens and primary classrooms derive (or should derive) from what is known about the development and mode of learning of young, school-aged children.

Developmentally appropriate practice for this age group, just as for earlier ages, involves an integrated approach. An integrated curriculum acknowledges the importance of all aspects of human development—social, emotional, physical, cognitive, language, and creative—rather than focus primarily on the cognitive. It also involves learning experiences that promote all aspects of development and does not segment the day into separate times, such as for math, reading, physical education, or social studies. Through the use of learning centres (to be discussed in Chapter 8) and themes (Chapter 9), such subjects are fully integrated and considered an inseparable part of each other (Bredekamp, 1987).

Before- and After-School Care. Young school-aged children whose parents work full-time also require care when they are not in school. This is often provided through before- and after-school programs and full-day holiday and summer care (Musson, 1994). Such programs generally focus on recreation and care, rather than education, and particularly on self-directed and self-initiated activities, since the children spend the bulk of their day in school (Alexander, 1986; Musson, 1994).

The 1991 NDCS indicated that school-aged child care is growing faster than any other kind of program in Canada. However, the NDCS also indicated that there were only spaces for 5.56 percent of the children of all Canadian working women. Similarly, the NLSCY (1996) found only 4 percent of Canadian children in regulated before- and after-school programs, and the NDCS found just under 5 percent of school-aged children in these programs. The parents of 15.6 percent (134,900) Canadian 6-to-9-year-olds in the CNCCS had made no child care arrangements (Pence et al., 1992). In another 5.3 percent or 45,800 cases, the parents said the children looked after themselves. While the NLSCY (1996) did not provide such a fine-grained breakdown by age, it also identified a group of 37,500 children with no care arrangements. These children without formal before- and after-school programs are often labelled "latchkey" or "self-care" children. They arrive at school with the latchkey around their necks and return to an empty home after school. Concerns about the safety, vulnerability, and lack of judgment of young school-aged children have prompted an increase in before- and after-school programs. Relatively little research, however, has been carried out to measure the long-term effects of various arrangements for the school-aged children of working parents (Powell, 1987a).

● Sources of Support for Programs

One way of grouping early childhood programs is by auspice or the base of their support, especially financial. Many early childhood programs are privately owned, for-profit businesses, whereas others are not-for-profit enterprises operated through public funds or sponsored by an agency or church. A growing number of early childhood programs are also supported by employers.

For-Profit Programs. In Canada, around 30 to 40 percent of all licensed child care centres are operated for profit (Doherty, Lero, Goelman, Tougas, & La Grange, 2000; Friendly, 1994; National Child Care Information Centre, 1991; Prentice, 2000). The number of Canadian profit-making centres has dropped sharply since

1968 when 75 percent of all the licensed Canadian child care spaces were in for-profit centres. However, there is considerable regional disparity in these figures. Presumably, government incentives for nonprofit centres have played a significant role in this decline. In Saskatchewan, for example, only nonprofit centres were eligible for government funds until 1990, and there were no profit-making centres in the province then. However, one might expect to see a change in the distribution of centres there, now that funding is available. Other provinces, Manitoba and Ontario, for example, give nonprofit centres subsidies that allow them to increase teacher salaries. Current figures (Doherty et al., 1999; Friendly, 1994) suggest that Saskatchewan, Quebec, Ontario, and Manitoba have the highest percentage of nonprofit centres.

The Canadian figures stand in sharp contrast to those for the United States, where at least 50 percent of all child care programs are operated for profit, either as a single, independently owned business or as part of a regional or national chain (Gestwicki, 1997; Wash & Brand, 1990). This is a rapidly rising figure in the United States, and it is expected to continue to increase. For many years, most child care in most American communities was provided by local owners who operated one or two centres. Over the past two decades, however, child care chains, which have experienced tremendous growth—increasing by as much as a thousandfold—have moved into virtually every metropolitan area (Neugebauer, 1988). There is some concern that they may want to move into the Canadian market in the future. Child care chains are big business! Some even sell stock that is traded on the New York Stock Exchange, deal in mergers and takeovers, and utilize sophisticated marketing strategies. Kindercare in the United States, for example, has about 1200 centres and capacity for 180,000 children, and La Petite Academy has 792 centres with space for 100,000 children (Exchange Top 100, 1994; Gestwicki, 1997). These are not small operations run by a family!

In both Canada and the United States, a series of concerns about the quality of for-profit child care have emerged (e.g., Baynham, Russell, & Ross, 1988; Kagan & Newton, 1989; Doherty-Derkowski, 1995; Doherty et al., 1999; McIntosh & Rauhala, 1989; Miesels & Sternberg, 1989; Neugebauer, 1991; National Child Care Staffing Study, 1989; Prentice, 2000; Vandell & Su, 1999; West, 1988). A poorer quality of care, lower salaries and poorer benefits, less educated teaching staff, more frequent teacher turnover, and more frequent licensing violations in for-profit centres have been documented in both Canada and the United States. Without question, some of these difficulties stem from these centres' need to make a profit. In Canada, the National Council of Welfare (1988, p. 27) has clearly outlined the source of the difficulties:

> *Profits are made by keeping costs down—paying low salaries to caregivers, raising child-staff ratios or compromising health, safety or nutritional standards—all of which hurt children.*

This is not to say that every for-profit centre does this, and that every nonprofit centre does not. In the United States, Neugebauer (1991) found that there was a wide range of quality in for-profit centres as in other types of centres. Kagan and

Newton (1989) reported similar findings about overall quality, but noted that non-profit centres had more favourable teacher-child ratios, more services, better management, and more child-centred environments. The controversy continues, and, more and more in Canada, there is a tendency for provincial and territorial governments to provide subsidies only to nonprofit centres.

Nonprofit Programs.   In for-profit early childhood programs, what is left over after expenses are paid is profit that goes back to the owner or stockholders. In nonprofit programs, such monies generally are *incorporated back into the program* or are *returned to the sponsoring agency*. Undoubtedly, in some cases, there is not a major difference between returning the money to the nonprofit sponsoring agent versus the owner of a profit-making centre; however, if the profits are returned to the program, this is likely to have a positive effect on all aspects of the program.

Nonprofit centres gain their status through incorporation or sponsorship from an entity that is itself not operated for profit. Groups such as parent-run organizations, social service agencies, churches, YMCAs, YWCAs, municipalities, hospitals, colleges, and universities, are the most common sponsors of nonprofit early childhood programs. However, you probably can find nonprofit schools where the operators are paid very large salaries and little profit returns to the program. In fact, as one of the reviewers of this text suggested, students may want to discuss this issue as it relates to your community.

Nonetheless, nonprofit child care centres in Canada generally have been founded by groups sincerely interested in providing affordable, high-quality child care. In the 1970s and 1980s, when the need for child care for working parents became a more pressing social concern, many groups such as churches and the YMCA and YWCA responded to that need by opening their facilities during the week or offering them to nonprofit groups. Often, YMCA, YWCA, and church buildings included nursery, preschool, or recreational rooms that were used primarily on weekends. Some church programs are affiliated with and incorporate the religion of their churches, but many are secular. Not all church-based programs are nonprofit, however. Sometimes an enterprising member of a congregation arranges to rent the facilities for a for-profit centre.

A unique form of nonprofit early childhood program is the parent-cooperative. Parent-cooperatives, usually part-day preschool programs, are based on a staffing structure that includes a paid professional head teacher and a rotating staff of parents. As part of enrolling their children in the program, parents are required to assist a specified number of days in the classroom. This arrangement serves both a staffing and a parent education function. With increasing numbers of parents entering the workforce full-time, however, fewer parents have the time to participate in cooperative programs. Nonetheless, they continue to be popular with families with a stay-at-home parent, and with those who work part-time. Cooperative groups are also finding ways of offering full-day child care programs, and having working parents involved in fundraising and maintenance activities.

Publicly Supported Programs.   Another significant supporter of early childhood programs is the public sector, whether it be the federal, provincial, or territorial governments or the municipalities. Although there was some activity in the field of early childhood during the war years, the **Canada Assistance Plan (CAP)**, enacted in 1966, was the first piece of federal legislation that had a significant impact on child care arrangements in the provinces and territories (Clifford, 1992; Townson, 1985). The long-term aim of the CAP was to alleviate the effects of poverty and it included provisions regarding social assistance or "welfare" as well as child care services, rehabilitation and homemaker services, and counselling for those who qualify for social assistance. CAP permitted the federal government to share 50 percent of the costs of child care with the provinces and territories, but *only for those persons in need.* There still is considerable variation between the provincial and territorial definitions of "in need."

The federal government also provides some support for child care on Indian reserve lands through Indian and Northern Affairs Canada (Child Care Resource Unit, 1990). Some provinces and territories (e.g., Ontario and the Yukon) also fund Indian and Inuit programs, while others do not (e.g., Manitoba and Newfoundland).

Similarly, it is worth noting that the provinces and territories and many municipalities in Canada make significant financial contributions to early childhood programs. In fact, some provinces provide more support for early childhood programs than CAP requires, and many municipalities provide early childhood programs for their residents. Some ministries of education are involved also in providing child care to school-aged children when they are not in school.

Employer-Supported Programs. One of the fastest-growing groups with a stake in early childhood programs are employers. Many companies maintain that their interest in the needs and concerns of parent-employees has resulted in a more productive and stable workforce. For the working parents of young children, work and family are not separable and, in fact, often overlap. Child care, in particular, is not just a family issue but also a concern to employers. Employees with young children, compared to other workers, are more often late for work, leave work early, miss work altogether, and deal with personal issues while at work. When employers support child care in some way, they often report that the result is lower absenteeism, greater stability and loyalty, better morale, decreased stress, and less distraction among their employees (Fernandez, 1986; Mayfield, 1990; Milkovich & Gomez, 1976; Rothman Beach Associates, 1985). However, research has not yet fully documented these claims.

There are many ways in which employers can support their workers' child care needs. Some large companies have created child care centres in or near the place of work. For example, Statistics Canada in Ottawa, the National Film Board in St. Laurent, and Nanisivik Mines in the Northwest Territories have established workplace child care centres. In some instances, employers also make arrangements with community child care centres, such as offering vouchers or direct subsidies. Such an arrangement can ensure that employees are given priority when child care openings are available. Another way in which employers help their workers is by banding together with several other employers to support a child care centre that meets the joint needs of their employees. The Edmonton Hospital Workers Day Care, for example, is run by a consortium of employers. As part of a strike settlement, several Edmonton hospitals banded together to form a nonprofit child care facility that includes family-based child care for shift workers and young infants as well as a child care centre for older children and day workers. Larger corporations also are expressing a greater interest in employee child care—and elder care. In July 1992, 12 large American companies, including giant corporations such as IBM, AT&T, Xerox, and Kodak, announced they were committing millions of dollars to build and expand facilities for the care of their employees' children and elderly relatives (U.S. firms join forces to build day-care centres, 1992).

Not all employers, however, operate on such a large scale. Some employers provide referral services to help match the employee's need with available resources in the community. Other companies have helped develop and train a community network of family child care homes to meet their workers' needs. A growing trend among employers is to provide more responsive scheduling options, for instance, job sharing or flextime. Child care is increasingly becoming a benefits option as companies allow their employees to select from a menu rather than provide a common benefits package for all. Some companies, recognizing the significant problem posed by children who are ill, have begun to explore sick-child care options (Friedman, 1989; NAEYC Information Service, 1990).

University- and College-Affiliated Programs.   A sizable group of early childhood programs are linked to higher education. The institution in which you are enrolled may, in fact, have such a program. Some are specifically laboratory or training programs that support student practice-teaching experiences and provide subjects for research; others serve primarily as campus child care centres for the young children of students, staff, and faculty. Many combine these two functions, offering child care to the campus community while utilizing the children and families for practicum and research purposes.

Some programs are operated as a joint campus venture, others are affiliated with a specific department or unit, and others only rent space from the university or college. Campus programs that are laboratory schools are generally high-quality, incorporating what has been learned about young children and early childhood programs through research, theory, and professional practice. However, not all campus programs are high-quality. In some cases, universities and colleges simply rent space to child care programs so that there will be some child care on campus.

Public School Involvement.   A relatively recent development in early childhood program sponsorship is the involvement of public schools. A few provinces have provided services to young children below kindergarten age for a number of years, and more public schools are considering extending their programs to preschoolers. Some provinces have appropriated monies for prekindergarten programs and others have placed early childhood programs high on their agendas.

In addition, public schools have, for many years, provided early childhood centres as part of high school or vocational training programs. Recent additions of secondary courses on the family are accelerating this trend.

Although many early childhood educators feel that public school involvement is a natural and inevitable step, some persistent issues surround this move. One of the most serious concerns is that prekindergarten programs in public schools will focus on school readiness rather than developmental appropriateness, simply offering a downward extension of the kindergarten and first-grade curriculum and methods (Elkind, 1988a, 1988b; Morado, 1986).

A recent U.S. study of public school prekindergartens provides support that such fears may, in many instances, be legitimate. "We saw some wonderful programs, full of child-centred and interesting activities. Others were rigid and boring. Still others sounded good on paper, but observations revealed that classroom practice in no way resembled written philosophy" (Mitchell & Modigliani, 1989, p. 57). The authors of this report go on to say, however, that their finding of a mix of good and inappropriate practice in public school programs was not so different from what they saw in community-based early childhood programs.

Public-school sponsorship of early childhood programs is, of course, subject to the same limited supply of money that constrains other publicly supported programs. Typically, therefore, existing programs serve a limited group of children, and they are most likely to be available in large urban centres.

Defining Quality in Early Childhood Programs

Up to this point, we have discussed early childhood programs in fairly concrete, descriptive terms, looking at characteristics by which programs can be grouped. Programs can and should also be examined in terms of how they best meet the needs and consider the well-being of children. Such considerations are related to quality.

Current research is, in fact, focusing on identifying factors that create good early childhood programming for young children. The old questions about whether child care is good or bad for children or what type of care is best are now obsolete; today's research questions seek to find out how to make child care better for young children (Doherty-Derkowski, 1995; Phillips, 1987). Current research is attempting to determine which variables make a program a "good program." The emerging picture tells us that quality in child care is not dependent on single, separable factors but is a result of the presence and interaction among a variety of complex elements (Clarke-Stewart, 1987a; Doherty-Derkowski, 1995).

● Group Size

In the late 1970s, the large-scale U.S. National Day Care Study (Ruopp, Travers, Glantz, & Coelen, 1979) published its findings, and despite its age, Canadians have found the report to be of continuing relevance to our early childhood programs.

The study also has influenced the direction of subsequent studies on issues related to quality. The study showed that group size was one of two consistently important variables that define quality of care for young children. In smaller groups, children were more cooperative, innovative, and verbal; they showed less hostility and conflict than children in larger groups; and they made greater gains over time on cognitive and language tests. The association between test gains and group size was particularly marked in centres serving low-income children. Children in smaller groups were also less likely to be uninvolved in activities, and to be observed wandering aimlessly. Furthermore, teachers in smaller groups spent more time interacting with children and less time in detached observation. Another study found more elaborate play, including more pretend play, among children in smaller rather than larger groups (Bruner, 1980). One recent study summarized that with a moderate number of children in a group, children seem to demonstrate greater social competence (Clarke-Stewart, 1987b). When teachers are in charge of large groups of children, on the other hand, they tend to be less responsive to the children, and they provide less social stimulation (Howes, 1983). As group size increases beyond 18 children, teachers spend more time in management activities and show a marked increase in the time they spend passively observing activities and interactions (Ruopp et al., 1979).

Ideal group size cannot really be defined because other variables, including the parameters of the physical environment, need to be considered. As Exhibit 1-5 indicates, the recommended group size varies with the age of the children and the setting.

● Teacher Qualifications

Research has given us some indication about teachers who are most likely to provide a high-quality early childhood program. We have just discussed how the National Day Care Study (Ruopp et al., 1979) found group size to be one of two important quality variables. The other significant variable that emerged from this study was the importance of a staff with *specific training in early childhood education and development.* Of course, it should please you as a student studying this very field to know that the knowledge and skills you acquire in your courses and placements really do lead to better teaching. Many additional studies have both replicated and refined these findings (e.g., Arnett, 1987; Berk, 1985; Doherty-Derkowski, 1995; Friesen, 1992; Howes, 1983; Pollilo, 2000; Snider & Fu, 1990; Vout-Sszick, 2001; Whitebook et al., 1990). So what do teachers with specific training in early childhood education and development do differently? They engage in more interactions with the children, and, in turn, the children with trained teachers show greater social and cognitive abilities compared to children whose teachers lacked such training. These findings, particularly in relation to children's more advanced cognitive and language ability, have been supported in other research (Clarke-Stewart, 1987a; Clarke-Stewart & Gruber, 1984; Howes, 1983). In addition, teachers with early childhood training were rated as more positive and less punitive, employing a less authoritarian style of interaction with the children (Arnett, 1987).

Early childhood education students who study at the college level sometimes wonder if they have missed something by not going to university. Several studies also provide additional information on this question. Teachers with postsecondary education, including both college and university degrees in areas other than ECE or child development, are comparable to those with only a high school diploma when tested about developmentally appropriate practice (Pollilo, 2000; Snider & Fu, 1990; Vout-Szick, 2001).

● Teacher-Child Ratio

It has generally been assumed that when caregivers are responsible for large numbers of children, the quality of care is affected adversely. A number of studies have addressed this assumption and found that the ratio significantly affects children's behaviour and teacher-child interactions (Phillips & Howes, 1987). Ratio is a concept that people sometimes have difficulty defining by the terms "high" and "low" so we will talk about a **good ratio** where teachers have fewer children and a **poor ratio** where teachers have too many children.

Researchers have found that when the ratio is poor, there is less verbal interaction among adults and children than when the **teacher-child ratio** is higher. Conversations are brief and routine and contain more prohibitions (Smith & Connolly, 1981). A significant factor in providing quality care has to do with giving children individualized attention, confirming their unique identity and worth as individuals. When an adult is responsible for a large number of children, that adult is less able to provide such attention and more concerned instead with controlling and managing the group. Teachers also spend more time in activity centres with children when the teacher-child ratio is good (Ruopp et al., 1979). Moreover, children are more likely to show interest in activities and to persist at an activity when the teacher-child ratio is good (Ruopp et al., 1979).

What is an appropriate teacher-child ratio? There is no definitive answer, although there are some suggested guidelines. Exhibit 1-5 shows guidelines for teacher-child ratios and **group size** for centre-based programs that were developed by experts from across Canada (Canadian Child Day Care Federation, 1991).

In a study that looked at the quality of caregiving and the presence of developmentally appropriate activities, Howes and her colleagues (Howes, Phillips, & Whitebook, 1992) came to similar conclusions about ideal teacher-child ratios. They found, for example, that almost all infants received quality care and appropriate activities when there was a 1:3 ratio. When the ratio jumped to 1:4, only about half of the infants received quality care and engaged in age-appropriate activities. A similar pattern was found for toddlers: a ratio of 1:4 was associated with high-quality care, but a jump to a 1:6 ratio meant almost half of the toddlers had poor caregiving and inappropriate activities. The change from a 1:8 to a 1:9 ratio led to a parallel decrement in quality for 3-to-5-year-old children.

Keep in mind, however, that teacher-child ratio is one variable that interacts with other factors, such as group size and teacher qualifications. "We should avoid blanket statements about high teacher-child ratios being good and low ratios being bad until we check out the *limits* beyond which a low ratio is bad and the *outcome* for which a high ratio is good" (Clarke-Stewart, 1987a, p. 114; italics in original).

EXHIBIT 1-5   *Recommendations for Teacher-Child Ratios Within Different Group Sizes*

Group Size[1]	Ages						
	0–12 Months	12–24 Months	2 Years	3 Years	4–5 Years	5–6 Years	6–9 Years
6	1:3[2]	1:3					
8		1:4	1:4				
10			1:5	1:5			
12				1:6			
14				1:7			
16					1:8	1:8	
18					1:9	1:9	
20							1:10
22							1:11
24							1:12

1. In mixed-age groupings, the teacher-child ratio and group size should be based on the age of the majority of children in the group. However, if there are infants, ratios and group sizes for infants should be maintained at all times.

2. The ratios assume that the teachers are full-time in the program. If they have other duties such as administration or parent interviewing, an additional teacher should be present to maintain the ratios.

SOURCE: Canadian Child Day Care Federation, 1991, p. 9.

● Mixed-Age Grouping

Only in relatively recent times has our society stratified children into narrow groups defined by age, particularly in the educational context. "Although humans are not usually born in litters, we seem to insist that they be educated in them" (Katz, Evangelou, & Hartman, 1990, p. viii). Many theorists and researchers have expressed concern about the increasing separation of people into age-segregated groups in education, housing, recreation, work, and other aspects of life (Bronfenbrenner, 1971). It is more natural, they say, that people of all ages interact and share various aspects of their lives. Throughout history, socialization was facilitated because people of all ages learned from and helped each other.

Early childhood education programs are also often segregated into narrow, homogeneous age groups, with the 3-year-olds in one class, 4-year-olds across the

hall in another, and the mature 5-year-olds in their own environment. But many educators suggest that heterogeneous or **mixed-age grouping** will benefit both younger and older children. Positive social behaviours such as sharing, turn taking, and helpfulness are encouraged in mixed-age groups (McClellan, 1991, 1993). Similarly, older children have more opportunities to practise leadership skills, and young children become involved in more complex forms of pretend play (e.g., Goldman, 1981; Howes & Farver, 1987; Rothstein-Fisch & Howes, 1988). Children also appear to reap cognitive benefits from mixed-age grouping (Katz et al., 1990). In addition, children in some mixed-age settings stay with the same teacher for several years and this stability can be reassuring. Recently, a few public schools have been organizing mixed-age classes at the primary level, and teachers in those classes talk enthusiastically about the experience. However, other teachers, accustomed to single age classes, cringe at the suggestion that mixed-age classes may become more common.

As we have already mentioned, quality in early childhood programs depends on many factors. There are certainly many outstanding, high-quality programs in which children are grouped by narrow age criteria; other equally good programs utilize a mixed-age model. Nonetheless, research suggests that children receive some unique benefits from being placed in groups that contain a wider age-range of children. For this reason, mixed-age grouping is included as a criterion of quality.

● Developmental Appropriateness of the Program

Child development theory and research have given us a good understanding of what young children are like and under what conditions they thrive and learn best. From such information, we are able to plan environments, develop activities, and set expectations that match children's needs and characteristics. Throughout this book—particularly in Chapters 6 and 7, which consider how to structure an appropriate environment, Chapter 8, in which we consider guidance principles, Chapters 9 and 10, in which we examine how various components of the curriculum reinforce development, and Chapter 11, which emphasizes quality—we will focus on developmentally appropriate practice (Bredekamp, 1997; Bredekamp & Rosegrant, 1992; Bredekamp & Copple, 1997; Gestwicki, 1999).

In recent years, there has been increasing concern that public education is not adequately preparing children for the challenges of the future. This concern, expressed by those in the **back-to-basics movement**, has led to a push to return to "the basics" in education. Some have interpreted this to include young children, with the idea that an earlier introduction to academics will result in better prepared and educated children.

But, as we will consider in various contexts in this book, early childhood professionals and researchers have expressed grave apprehensions about this trend to "hothousing," which pushes preschoolers into inappropriate tasks for which they are not developmentally ready (Gallagher & Coche, 1987). Young children can learn a lot of material in a mechanistic, rote manner, but if these experiences are meaningless, such information has little relevance (Sigel, 1987). Thus, for an early childhood program to meet quality criteria, it must respect the emerging abilities of young children without imposing inappropriate expectations.

Partnerships

PARENTAL VALUES FOR COGNITIVE DEVELOPMENT

As with all areas of the early childhood curriculum, it is very important to share with parents a clear statement of the school's philosophy about how to support and further children's cognitive development. Parents should be aware, for instance, that the program is built on the conviction that children learn best through concrete, hands-on activity; that children are able to select meaningful activities on their own; and that play and learning go together. Conversely, such a philosophy means that the program does not engage in abstract and developmentally inappropriate teaching practices that require the child to sit quietly and inactively.

Today's parents are bombarded by pressures to succeed, which includes having successful children as well. Thus, many well-intentioned parents feel a need to see evidence that their children are indeed learning in their early childhood program. For instance, parents may say to you, "But Marcia does nothing but play all day; when will she learn something?" or "Ron starts kindergarten next year; shouldn't he be learning to read?" or " I want Singh to learn to sit quietly and work on his numbers" or "I'm thinking of enrolling Betsy in the school where my neighbour's son goes; he comes home with dittoes every day and Betsy only brings home paintings." How do you respond in a way that respects the parents' concerns but maintains the integrity of your program?

Conveying to parents your philosophy of how children best learn involves frequent explanation and supportive information. First, it requires that you, as the teacher, be secure in your understanding of how young children learn and acquire concepts so you can answer parents' questions and concerns. It is also important to make information from experts, which supports your approach, available to parents.

This might be done through a parental library, which includes such books as *Playtime Learning Games for Young Children*, by Alice Honig. In addition, you can distribute reprints of well-written articles to each family, prominently post short quotes on the parent bulletin board, invite an appropriate speaker to a parent meeting, or plan parent discussions groups with a knowledgeable facilitator. Let parents know about *Developmentally Appropriate Practice in Early Childhood Programs Serving Children from Birth Through Age 8* (Bredekamp & Copple, 1997), that supports your approach. In other words, let them know that your work with the children is founded on and backed by research and theory.

One teacher dealt creatively with the questions posed by some parents concerning what exactly it was their children were learning. She videotaped the children one day during a half-hour of self-selected activities. Then, during a parent meeting, she followed the showing of the videotape by discussing how the children engaged in problem solving and concept formation through their activities. The parents were amazed at how much learning was going on!

Although it is important to convey your approach and philosophy to parents, it is also vital to recognize that parents are the most important elements in their children's lives. When parents share anecdotes and experiences with you, convey the value you place on the importance of their role as their child's primary teacher and mentor. Recognize the parents' expertise and invite them to share it with all of the children. Also inform parents of special community events or exhibits that they might want to attend or visit with their children.

● Teacher-Child Interaction

Although many factors contribute to the quality of an early childhood program, perhaps the most important factor on which quality depends is the interaction between the teachers and the children. In a good program, teachers are involved with children, they are nurturing and responsive, there is ample verbal exchange, and interactions aim to teach, not just to control (Clarke-Stewart, 1987a). A wonderful physical facility, an exemplary teacher-child ratio, and a favourable group size would all be negated by uncaring and unresponsive teacher-child interaction. It is, after all, the teachers who determine the tone and the character—in effect, the quality—of a program. The mapmaking activity in A Closer Look, for example, was dependent on positive and frequent interactions between the children and their teachers.

A Closer Look

MAPMAKING

The children were on a walk around the block. Teachers Ardith and Marilyn encouraged them to pay close attention to everything they saw on the way, including buildings, trees, stop signs, the parking lot next to the dentist's office, and other features. "Remember, when we get back we're going to make a map of our block. So we have to pay really close attention to everything we see, " Marilyn told them. The children discussed and described all sorts of features that, on previous walks, had gone unnoticed. Lynette, for instance, found a doghouse in a yard behind the brown house. Chad noticed a bed of tulips and daffodils along the side of the blue house.

When the children got back to their classroom, Ardith put out a large sheet of butcher paper as a starting point for the map. The children decided to start their map at the school. "Our school is on the corner, so we should put it right here," said James, pointing to the lower left-hand corner of the paper.

"Let's build the school," suggested Miriam, and got some blocks from the block area. She and James built the school with several unit blocks and enclosed it with a "fence" of connected, longer blocks.

"I want to put in the doghouse," said Lynette.

"Where is the brown house?" asked Ardith.

"Let's put it here," said Lynette, pointing next to the school.

"Is the brown house next to our school?" asked Ardith.

"No, it's on this side of the block," said Gene, pointing along the other side of the map.

Because the brown house was not on the map yet, Lynette decided to draw a picture of the doghouse. She got a piece of paper and crayons from the art shelf.

"Maybe we should think about what we saw in the order that we saw it on our walk," suggested Ardith. "What was the first thing we saw when we got past the playground fence?" The children discussed the various buildings and houses, and soon they began putting up more block structures as they recalled the spatial relationships of the various features.

Lynette finished her drawing of the doghouse and cut it out with the scissors. It was placed behind the brown house when that was put on the map. Chad wanted to paint the blocks for the blue house so it would be the right colour.

"I don't think we ought to paint our blocks, Chad. What else could you use to make the blue house?" Ardith asked.

After a moment's thought, Chad said he would find the materials for the house in the woodworking area. He found a piece of scrap lumber that was just the right size and painted it blue. Later, Chad and Melissa drew flowers on the butcher paper along the house's side. Stop signs, trees, cars, the snail that the children had seen along the side of the road, and the sign outside the dentist's office were all added to the map.

The teachers left the map out for several days. Children continued to add items to it, particularly things they noticed on following days on their way to and from school.

● Teacher Consistency

A serious concern among professionals and parents alike is the high rate of teacher turnover in early childhood programs. The low wages of professionals in the field, documented by a current Canadian study, *Caring for a Living* (Canadian Child Day Care Federation & Canadian Day Care Advocacy Association, 1992), have been identified as a significant factor in this turnover. Nevertheless, many young children spend the bulk of their waking hours in child care, with adults other than their parents, and consistency in caregivers is important. One important task of the early years is forming a secure attachment relationship to adults. Although primary attachment is with parents, research has shown that young children certainly do become attached to their teachers. But when children lose a teacher with whom they have formed such an attachment, the loss can be profound (Phillips & Howes, 1987).

One study found that there is less teacher-child interaction in centres with a high teacher turnover rate (Phillips, Scarr, & McCartney, 1987). This is not surprising when interaction is dependent in part on establishing a relationship, something that takes time to develop. In general, research supports the finding that children seem to be better adjusted, less dependent, less anxious, and more sociable in programs with a low staff turnover rate (Clarke-Stewart, 1987a).

● Respect and Concern for Teachers

As we have discussed, a nurturing, well-trained, and consistent staff is important to a quality program, but a reciprocal concern for the well-being of the teaching staff also is needed. Working with young children is a demanding, challenging job. Thus, it is in the best interests of the children, the families, and the employer if staff members receive appropriate pay and benefits, and work in a satisfying environment. In such a setting, the needs of the staff are seriously considered, an atmosphere of camaraderie is fostered, autonomy is encouraged in planning an appropriate program for the children, and the physical environment includes space for adults (Jorde-Bloom, 1988a). Chapter 5 will discuss some of the parameters and some of the issues associated with providing such an environment for the staff.

● Physical Environment

Even though we will discuss this topic in greater detail in later chapters, it is necessary to note here that the physical facility is another important factor contributing to program quality. According to research, children demonstrate higher

cognitive skill levels and greater social competence in schools that are safe and orderly, contain a wide variety of stimulating equipment and materials, and are organized into learning centres on the basis of similar materials and activities when compared with children in programs that lack these features (Clarke-Stewart, 1987b).

A child-oriented environment conveys to children that this place is meant for them. There are interesting and worthwhile things to do in a child-oriented environment because it was designed with the characteristics, ages, and abilities of the children in mind. A child-centred environment also requires fewer restrictions and prohibitions because it was fashioned specifically for children. This contributes toward a positive and pleasant atmosphere. In short, a good environment conveys to children that this is a good place to be, that people here care about them, that they are able to satisfy their desire to learn and their innate curiosity, and that it is safe to try without fear of failure.

● Family Involvement

With increasing numbers of children spending many hours per day in child care, parents and teachers are more than ever partners in many aspects of child rearing and socialization. Studies have shown that the children benefit when parents and the early childhood staff share a common commitment to the best interests of the children, communicate openly, and have mutual respect. On the other hand, if there is a lack of communication so that parents do not know what happened at school and teachers are not informed of significant events in the child's home life, there is lack of continuity for the child. In Chapter 5 we will explore this home-school link in much greater detail.

● Quality as a Combination of Factors

For the purposes of discussion, we have isolated a number of components that contribute to quality early childhood programming, including teacher-child ratio, group size, teacher qualifications, mixed-age grouping, developmental appropriateness of the program, teacher-child interaction, staff consistency, concern for staff, the physical environment, and family involvement. It is important to keep in mind, however, that quality can best be understood and studied as a combination of components (Phillips, 1987). As you further your understanding and knowledge of the field of early childhood education, remember that quality is not defined by a single factor but depends on the complex interaction of a variety of elements in which you, as an early childhood professional, play a key role.

At this point, you have a broad overview of early childhood education and the factors that define quality programs. In the next chapter, we will examine the field's historical roots. Where did our ideas about the field come from and where were the methods developed?

Key Terms

back-to-basics movement
Canada Assistance Plan (CAP)
Canadian National Child Care Study
    (CNCCS)
caregiver
child care centres
child care worker

early childhood
early childhood education
early childhood educator
good ratio
group size
infant stimulation programs
infants

mixed-age grouping
nanny
National Day Care Study (NDCS)
nursery schools
parent cooperative

poor ratio
teacher
teacher-child ratio
toddler

Ch I

Key Points

1. Increasing numbers of women are entering the workforce. More than 50 percent of mothers of preschoolers now work and require child care for their youngsters.

2. There are significantly more single parents today than ever before, mostly because of the increase in the divorce rate. These parents need care for their children while they work.

3. Families today move more than families did in the past. Migration within the country and immigration to Canada from other countries means that many Canadian children are far away from relatives who might have been available to provide child care while the parents work.

4. Research has shown that good early childhood education programs have a lasting effect on children from disadvantaged backgrounds.

5. Investment in such programs has substantial social and financial benefits for society.

6. Some professionals participate in child advocacy, bringing to public and legislative attention the needs of children and families in poverty as well as the needs for affordable child care for families with moderate incomes.

7. Early childhood programs can be defined by their purpose. The main purpose of many programs is child care; the goal of others is enrichment. A third category includes programs whose main aim is compensation for some lack in the children's backgrounds.

8. Programs are either home-based, such as family child care homes, or centre-based, located in a school facility and usually serving larger groups of children.

9. Programs are specially designed for children of varying ages, such as infants and toddlers, preschoolers, and school-aged children.

10. Centre-based infant/toddler programs are one of the fastest-growing types of programs today.

11. Centres that serve school-aged children before and after school are an alternative to leaving these children, termed latchkey children, alone at home. They are increasing at a faster rate than any other child care programs in Canada.

12. The majority of early childhood programs are operated on a nonprofit basis. However, limited government funding for child care may mean that some of the U.S. child care chains will continue to expand across the border, particularly in metropolitan areas where there often is a shortage of spaces.

13. A number of nonprofit organizations and agencies can sponsor early childhood programs.

14. Another type of early childhood program is sponsored or supported by an employer for the children of employees. Child care as a work benefit is thought to increase worker productivity and loyalty.

15. Early childhood programs affiliated with institutions of higher learning provide training for students and child care for student, parents, faculty, and staff.

16. The Canada Assistance Plan requires the federal government to share child care funding with the provinces on a 50-50 basis. Increases in federal funding seem unlikely at this time, but the more affluent provinces and municipalities are likely to increase their contributions to child care.

17. School boards across the country are beginning to offer programs for preschoolers, and to provide child care services. This trend seems likely to continue.

18. Research has shown that a moderate group size results in children who are more socially and intellectually competent than those who spend their day in large groups.

19. When an adult is in charge of too many children, the behaviour of both the children and the adult is adversely affected by this poor teacher-child ratio.

20. Grouping children of varying ages together has benefits for both younger and older children in many developmental areas.

21. High-quality programs have developmentally appropriate expectations and activities and do not push children into inappropriate, accelerated activities.

22. Frequent and responsive interaction between adults and children is a necessity in high-quality programs.

23. Research shows that teachers with specific early childhood training are important in a high-quality program.

24. Staff consistency is important, because high staff turnover has a negative impact on young children.

25. A good staff, which provides an appropriate program for young children, has to be respected and nurtured.

26. A child-oriented environment and family involvement also contribute to the quality of a program.

Key Questions

1. Interview several parents whose preschool-aged children are enrolled in an early childhood program. Why are their children in such a program? How did the parents select the program? What program criteria were important to them?

2. If you have a local compensatory education program, arrange to visit it. What benefits do you see for the children? Talk to a teacher member and find out what services are provided for the children and their families.

3. If you were given "three wishes" to bring about changes for young children and their families, what would these be? Share your choices with others in your class. From a combined list, develop several child and family issues that you think child advocates might address.

4. Visit an early childhood program in your community and share your experience with other members of your class who have visited different programs. Classify the programs according to their characteristics, for instance, purpose, setting, ages of children served, and source of support. Does your community have a variety? Which types of programs predominate? What family needs do these programs meet?

5. If you were asked by the parent of a young child, "How do I find a good child care program?" what would your answer be? How can you help a parent recognize quality indicators?

6. Projections for the future, as we have discussed, indicate an increased need for good early childhood programs. What changes do you think are needed to bring about improvements for children and for early childhood professionals?

7. In some communities, you can probably find nonprofit schools where the operators are paid very large salaries and little profit returns to the program. Is this an issue in your community?

Chapter 2

The History of Early Childhood Education

*H*ow we approach the education and care of young children in the new millennium depends, to a great extent, on the work of many people over many centuries. Current ideas about children and how they should be treated can be traced back through centuries. Plato, for example, thought that adults should observe children's play and organize village playgroups, and Quintillian, a Roman, thought that play would foster intellectual development in the young child (Caplan & Caplan, 1974).

Learning about the historical roots of early childhood education is important for several reasons. First, it valuable to know that our current practices are based on a blend of ideas and traditions that have evolved over centuries. At times, ideas become unfashionable, but they often reemerge in a slightly altered way. Understanding these cycles of change will make it easier for you to accept and explain the ongoing changes in early childhood education that you will experience as a professional, a parent, and/or an interested observer. Second, if you are a professional in the field, you will find that your knowledge of the history of early childhood education can be a source of support, pride, and inspiration. Many of the early educators and thinkers in the field were driven to improve the quality of young children's lives, and they persisted in their efforts, even when they paid a personal toll. Finally, knowing the theories that explain *why* you do things in a certain way can be empowering. If you are questioned about your practices, you can confidently explain the theoretical underpinnings and developmental appropriateness of what you do.

Some of our current educational practices can be traced back to Greek and Roman times, but, in the interests of brevity, we can just touch on those early times. We will also examine several aspects of the history of early childhood education:

1. We will explore the writings and work of many individuals through history who have contributed to our contemporary ideas about young children and early childhood education.

2. We will also look at the theories that have influenced the field. Particularly in this century, a number of individuals have formulated theories that help us understand the nature of young children and how best to meet their needs.

- Some theorists—in the **nature** camp—believe that children's development follows an inborn plan.

- Others—in the **nurture** camp—contend that children's development is affected primarily by external factors.

- Still others—the interactionists—think that children's development is determined by an **interaction** of inborn and external factors.

A Look Back—Children Through Time

Interest in the care and education of young children goes back thousands of years. Our Western tradition is traced to ancient Greece, where the writings of philosophers such as Plato and Aristotle reflected a keen sensitivity to the needs of children and the importance of appropriate education in shaping their character (deMause, 1974; Greenleaf, 1978). These educated Greeks saw human development as a transformation from the imperfect state of childhood to the ideal of adulthood, and the Greek tradition included education for girls as well as for boys (Sameroff, 1983). Unfortunately, however, this sensitivity to the needs of young children was not shared by all, and infanticide was also common in this era (deMause, 1974). Infanticide was more likely to occur with females, and estimates suggest that the male-to-female ratio was 4:1 (deMause, 1974). Harsh discipline, beatings, and extreme isolation produced by locking children in closets and drawers persisted for centuries, even though laws against infanticide emerged as early as the 4th century A.D. (deMause, 1974). Children of the wealthy were rarely cared for by their own parents, but rather by hired wet nurses and teachers. Children of the poor were less fortunate, and were sent to be apprentices, servants, and slaves at an early age.

By the Middle Ages, even the concept of childhood seemed to have been lost. Children became little more than property and were put to work, for instance, in the fields or tending animals, just as soon as they were big enough. "The typical man or woman emerged straight out of his babyhood into a sort of junior adult status" (Braun & Edwards, 1972, p. 6). Schools and formal education as a way of passing on cultural traditions had virtually disappeared in Europe except in a few places, notably Islamic Spain, where learning was highly valued.

The Renaissance led to slight improvements in the child's lot in life, but the period from 0 to 7 years was still viewed as an unfortunate waiting period for entry into the adult world. Education became more common, but it generally was limited to the sons of the wealthy. The children of the poor went to work, not school. The 17th century saw little improvement: the Puritans' children in the Old and New World were born "ignorant and sinful" (Borstellman, 1983, p. 15). Puritan parents, as well as the Quakers, often resorted to restraint, harsh discipline, and "the rod" to ensure their children became holy. The Enlightenment was to bring welcome changes. John Locke, the child of strict Puritans, and Rousseau, a

product of Geneva's strict Calvinism, became children of the Enlightenment, and emphasized the importance of the early years. Since their time, there have been slow but steady improvements in views about the young child and early childhood education.

Significant changes in attitudes about children began to take shape in the 19th century, and kindergarten programs became part of the educational system in some locations by the middle of the century. In fact, the first *public* kindergarten in North America was established in Toronto in 1873 by Dr. J. L. Hughes (Young, 1981). Hester Howe, a school principal, became concerned that the school children had to bring their preschool-aged siblings to school with them as their mothers were working. Hughes suggested opening a crèche for these preschool children, and in 1892, the crèche, which is now Victoria Day Care Services in Toronto, was opened. Other significant events in early childhood education in Canada soon followed, especially in the more populated provinces.

The 20th century, while a relatively short period in time, represents a very active time for the field of education. For one thing, education for all children came to be increasingly accepted, and this reinforced the idea that childhood was a separate period in life. Education in North America, in the eyes of such progressive educators as John Dewey, was a training ground for democracy, a way of equalizing social inequities by imbuing children from a young age with democratic ideals. Philosophers and scientists, who proclaimed the early years as especially relevant, also contributed to the field. Among these, Sigmund Freud focused unprecedented attention on earliest experiences as the foundation of personality.

The 20th century also has seen the development of scientific methods of observation that led to the **child study movement**, out of which grew many university preschool laboratory programs designed to facilitate the careful study of young children. For example, the University of Toronto's Institute for Child Study was opened in 1926, and the St. George's Nursery School was an integral part of the Institute (Young, 1981).

Still another contribution to today's field is the notion of early childhood education as a means to social reform. Important programs were developed throughout this century with the idea of rescuing the poor from poverty. A common purpose motivated those who helped move young children out of factories into schools at the turn of the century, and those who developed Canadian and American compensatory programs in the 1960s. The 1960s compensatory programs, often known as Head Start programs, were designed to give young children from poverty backgrounds an "edge" or "head start" the summer before they entered school, as the research showed they typically were less successful in school than their more affluent peers.

Finally, another change that has profoundly affected early childhood education today is the steadily increasing need for child care, which we will discuss below.

Although recent changes in the economy and family life have brought the proliferation of child care programs available today, such programs are not new. During World War II, many women were required to work and needed arrangements for care of their young children (Braun & Edwards, 1972; Carter, 1987; Greenberg, 1987; Siegel & White, 1982; Stapleford, 1976; Weber, 1984). Child care centres were established in Canada and the United States for mothers employed in the defence industries during that time, but most were closed after the war. Nursery schools seem to have been concentrated in affluent, urban areas in the 1950s. However, the compensatory education movement of the 1960s coupled with the steadily increasing number of women in the workforce since that time has led to the exponential growth of the field during the past thirty years.

Views of Children

Traditionally, the way people view young children has been determined by the intellectual, social, and economic context of each period. Because children are vulnerable and dependent, their image and treatment tends to be shaped by the needs of the times. When needs have changed, influential thinkers and writers like Locke and Rousseau have shaken the very foundation of thoughts about children.

Today, at least in the developed world, we view children much more benignly than in the past, although many would maintain we still do not place a high enough value on the care of the very young. Nevertheless, we at least acknowledge that the childhood years are unique and important, we provide children with special environments, and we promote education as a social and personal necessity. Today's view of children is based to a greater extent on theory and research rather than on the religious or political ideas that, in part, dictated the image of children in the past. However, children in underdeveloped countries are not so fortunate, and child labour is not a thing of the past. Well-organized protests in India in 1993, for example, highlighted the plight of child carpet makers who "are not fed properly, seldom paid, and often beaten if they make mistakes while weaving" (Kids freed from carpet factories join protest against child labor, 1993, p. C10). Similar problems are common in many areas of Africa, Central America, and Asia. Closer to home, over one million children of migrant farm workers are thought to be working illegally in the United States (Morrison, 2001). Some children are still waiting to benefit from the more benign view of childhood that has evolved over the centuries.

Let us now turn to some of the important figures in our historical account of early childhood education and see how their ideas have shaped our thinking. After that, we will then review the work of influential theorists whose conceptualizations have further refined our ideas of young children.

EXHIBIT 2-1   *People in the Field of Early Childhood Education*

(Clockwise from top) Jean-Jacques Rousseau, Johann Pestalozzi, Friedrich Froebel, Maria Montessori, Lev Vygotsky, Erik Erikson, Jean Piaget, and B. F. Skinner

Influential People in the History of Early Childhood Education

Many individuals have contributed to our current view of young children and their care and education. We will touch on the works of only a few of them in this text. Some developed their ideas because of their direct work with children, often the poor and underprivileged; others' theories emerged out of political and philosophical concerns about the problems of society and how reforms could be brought about.

The Renaissance and Reformation periods led to profound changes in thinking about education and young children. Philosophers, writers, and church leaders of this time generated many new ideas that have influenced thinking in the field of early childhood education.

● Martin Luther (1483–1546)

The name Luther usually is associated with the Protestant Reformation, but he also wrote extensively about education. During Luther's time, education had been restricted to the sons of the wealthy who were tutored in the Latin language. Luther believed that education should be accessible to all, and to further that aim he recommended that teaching should be done in one's native language. He thought that the way to salvation was through reading the Bible, and he translated it into German so that it would be readily available for German families. You can learn more about Luther's influence by visiting various Web sites.

● John Amos Comenius (1592–1670)

Comenius, like Luther, was involved with the church. He was a bishop in Moravia, later Czechoslovakia, and an advocate of universal education. Perhaps more than any of his predecessors, Comenius understood and stressed the importance of the early years. In *The Great Didactic* (1967), he wrote:

> It is the nature of everything that comes into being, that while tender it is easily bent and formed, but that, when it has grown hard, it is not easy to alter. …
> A young plant can be planted, transplanted, pruned, and bent this way or that. When it has become a tree, these processes are impossible. (P. 58)

Comenius also emphasized the value of active learning, hands-on experiences, and the involvement of parents in their children's education, especially before they were 6 years of age. His 1658 publication *Orbis Pictus* ("The World of Pictures") is viewed as the first picture book for children, and it reflects his commitment to providing tangible learning materials that are appealing to the senses. Comenius, like Montessori and Piaget centuries later, also maintained that a child's development followed an internal timetable, and that teachers needed to work with that natural order. In that sense, he was perhaps the first critic of "hothousing": to him education could succeed only "if the mind be duly prepared to receive it [and] if the pupil be not overburdened by too many subjects" (Comenius, 1967, p. 127). Comenius was honoured in a 1997 *Life* magazine article titled "The Invention of Childhood" that you can access on the Web.

● John Locke (1632–1704)

John Locke was an English physician and philosopher who spent time in exile in Holland because of his opposition to the throne. Locke proposed that children were born *tabula rasa* (literally, "blank slate"), and that experience would determine what the infant became. Locke maintained that education should be pleasant for the young child rather than devoted to rote drills and learning. He also encouraged parents to abandon harsh discipline procedures as well as restrictive practices such as swaddling babies in fabric and constraining their physical activity.

● Jean-Jacques Rousseau (1712–1778)

Rousseau was not an early childhood educator, but his ideas have certainly influenced the field. As a philosopher writing in the context of the corrupt French society of his time, Rousseau developed the idea that society actually hindered human beings from developing according to their nature. Society, with its hierarchy of the few who were rich and powerful, only imposed misery on the masses, a state that is not natural. Rousseau, in fact, considered anything natural and primitive to be good. Thus, he argued, if children could develop without the artificial trappings of civilization, they would be able to achieve their true potential of being moral and good.

According to Rousseau, young children are innately pure and noble, but they need to be protected from the evil influences of society. In a protected rural environment, they learn from what is concrete and natural, through trial and error and experimentation. Rousseau recognized that children's mode of thinking and learning is different from that of adults and considered *good education to be based on the stage of development of the child, not on adult-imposed criteria.* A child-centred, uncorrupted education will, eventually, result in adults who are moral and interested in the common good of society.

Rousseau never worked with children—in fact, he actually abandoned all of his own children to foundling homes—but he wrote extensively about his philosophy in his novels and essays. Today we agree with Rousseau that children have a unique nature that needs to be nurtured and protected in an appropriate environment. Although his highly idealistic view of childhood and human nature was never fully adopted by his followers, Rousseau nonetheless had a great influence on later early childhood educators, as we shall soon see (Braun & Edwards, 1972; Carter, 1987; Grimsley, 1976; Weber, 1984).

● Johann Pestalozzi (1746–1827)

Pestalozzi, a native of Switzerland, was deeply influenced by Rousseau's educational ideas. He felt that all people, even the poorest, had the right to an education as a way of helping them develop their moral and intellectual potential. He believed in education according to nature and considered that learning for young children is intricately tied to concrete experiences and observation. Unlike Rousseau, however, he stressed the important role of the mother in children's earliest years.

Also unlike Rousseau, Pestalozzi actually worked with children, developing educational methods that are still used today. For instance, he stressed the importance of recognizing individual differences among children and the relevance of children's self-activity rather than rote as the basis of learning. One of the schools he established became world-famous, drawing visitors and students from all over Europe. He is considered to be the first to actually teach young children of pre-school age, marking the beginning of the kindergarten movement (Braun & Edwards, 1972; Ulich, 1967; Weber, 1984).

● Robert Owen (1771–1858)

Robert Owen, a disciple of Pestalozzi, was a British industrialist, philosopher, philanthropist, and social reformer (Pence, 1990; Weber, 1971). When he began to manage a textile mill in New Lanark, Scotland, he became concerned about the plight of young children who typically began to work in the mill at 6 years. Owen disliked the image of dark, satanic mills, which Dickens so aptly painted, and wanted life in New Lanark to be better both for children and their parents. Owen quickly changed the minimum age for employment to 10 years, improved housing, opened a low-cost company store, and set up schools for children and their parents.

In 1816, Owen's infant school was opened for the young children in New Lanark who attended once they could walk. Owen had visited Pestalozzi, and had read his works as well as Rousseau's, but he adopted Locke's view of the child as a *tabula rasa*. Singing, dancing, outdoor experiences, and play were major components of his program; Owen wanted learning to stem from the child's natural curiosity rather than rigid lessons. Corporal punishment was not permitted and there was no fixed schedule. Rousseau's emphasis on learning from nature was evident in Owen's program, which highlighted learning from gardens, animals, woods, and orchards.

News of Owen's school spread throughout Great Britain and to North America, and similar infant schools were founded in both locations. However, they did not survive for long, and the infant schools that survived in Britain soon adopted a rigid, custodial approach to their task. Nevertheless, Owen's school provided us with a model for the education of young children, and Owen's enlightened attitude toward preserving childhood as a distinct period and eliminating child labour eventually took hold in Britain. The breadth of Owen's writings becomes apparent when you research using the Internet.

● Friedrich Froebel (1782–1852)

Friedrich Froebel, a German, was one of the visitors at Pestalozzi's school, observing it with some mixed feelings. He greatly admired Pestalozzi's skills but was concerned over his inability to articulate his methods. Froebel, however, was better able to put into words his educational principles. Like his predecessors Rousseau and Pestalozzi, Froebel believed in the interrelatedness of nature and the child's developing mind. He also advocated that education should harmonize with the child's inner development, recognizing that children are in different stages at various ages. He saw childhood as a separate stage that was not just a transition to adulthood but a stage with great intrinsic value in its own right.

Froebel also stressed the important role of play in young children's development—play was a pure and natural mode of learning through which children achieve harmony (Braun & Edwards, 1972; Carter, 1987; Ulich, 1947; Ulich, 1967; Weber, 1984). Froebel developed a carefully programmed curriculum and specific materials that are described by Barbara Corbett in the A Canadian Professional Speaks Out box.

A Canadian Professional Speaks Out

FROEBEL EDUCATION IN CANADA

Barbara E. Corbett, The Froebel Education Centre, Mississauga, Ontario

As a Canadian I am grateful that our ancestors had the foresight to incorporate Froebel's kindergarten in our public education system. Planted into our thinking by that act were Froebel's theories and practices of education through child development. Friedrich Froebel (1782–1852) was the German educator who invented the kindergarten for children from ages 3 to 7—the time when the educational foundation for learning is formed. His first kindergarten was in Bad Blankenberg, Germany, in 1837. Toronto has the distinction of having the first public kindergarten in Canada (1883) and Ontario, in 1887, was the first government system to give grants to Froebel's kindergarten as part of the public school system.

The word kindergarten reveals Froebel's thought. The children are individual plants tended and cultivated by a kindergartner (gardener) in the social setting, the garden of children. Froebel's kindergarten provides for a five-year bridge from the home where cultivation for the 3-year-old is individual, to the school, from Grade 3 on, where the groupings are larger and socially more complex. His kindergarten combines the intimate family grouping—where the ratio can be one to eight for the youngest children, increasing to one to twelve for 6- or 7-

year-olds—with the more relaxed plays of children whereby the seeds of all future learning are planted. The Froebel Gifts, which are toys consisting of solid geometrical shapes, tablets, lines, and points, allow the child to objectively build her inner world as well as to imitate the outer environment in which she lives and moves every day. These planned plays are pleasant as well as informative and creative for the child who is in the process of becoming.

In becoming, children are educated to be thinkers. It is not enough to know the known. In Froebel's view the child must also be encouraged to think creatively as he learns the known. Thus, on becoming an adult, he will be able to use the known in new, creative ways. Children so educated will become the leadership that will take us into the 21st century.

Since we opened our Froebel Kindergarten in 1970, and seven years later expanded to include the school grades to eight, we have seen this leadership emerging. It is evident in our graduates who have gone on to high school and university as well as in children who presently attend our Froebel Education Centre in Mississauga, Ontario. It is the rare child who ever says, "What shall I do now?" Most of our children have so many ideas that it takes all the teachers' skills to guide each one through the process of self-education. For the child, that process requires concentrated effort, and for the kindergartner it is the process of helping a child become the best of who she is. Isn't that what education is—leading the child out of himself into all his relationships with his fellow human beings and the natural world?

Froebel's view of children differed from Locke's *tabula rasa* notion. While Locke emphasized the importance of *nurture* or the environment, Froebel leaned toward the *nature* or maturational side of this centuries-old controversy. Like plants, children arrived in the world with some predetermined traits that the teacher in the garden for children should help to unfold. However, just as a seed of corn could not grow into a rose even with the best gardener, so the teacher could not fundamentally alter the child's inborn characteristics.

● John Dewey (1859–1952)

John Dewey, the father of **progressive education**, led the American attack on traditional forms of public schooling. In the late 1800s, schools in the United States were very teacher-centred and subject-centred, and the curriculum, rather than the individual child's needs, determined what happened on any day. Harsh punishment and rote learning were the norm, and students were passive receptacles to be filled with knowledge by the teacher.

Dewey studied under G. Stanley Hall, who had introduced child study and, ultimately, developmental psychology to North America (Cairns, 1983). Clearly,

---

Reflective Exercise 2-1

Do you know of any schools in your community where harsh punishment and rote learning are still the norm? Are there still schools in your community where students are viewed as passive receptacles that the teacher will fill with knowledge? Could Dewey persuade them to view things differently?

---

public education was not geared toward the child in Dewey's and Hall's time, and they both warned parents and teachers about the negative consequences of traditional instruction (Borstellman, 1983; Dewey, 1897, 1900, 1902). Dewey advocated that educators use the child's interests and that education should emphasize active learning through real experiences; activity would lead to knowledge. He ran a model early childhood program at the University of Chicago, and demonstrated a **child-centred approach**, rather than a subject-centred approach in his work.

The principles of progressive education influenced a number of developments in early childhood education. For example, the Open Education model in Britain and some areas of Canada, which we will discuss in the next chapter, grew out of Dewey's work (e.g., Weber, 1971). The nursery school movement with its emphasis on play and parent education also can be traced to Dewey (Fein & Clarke-Stewart, 1973). Dewey's work also had an impact on the popularity of the programs of other educators, including Froebel and Maria Montessori (Hunt, 1968).

● Margaret McMillan (1860–1931)

Margaret McMillan and her sister Rachel were born in the United States, but moved to Britain when they were children. Margaret became a social activist, and in the late 19th century, as a member of a school board, she became an outspoken advocate for poor children in the schools. Many children had significant medical and social problems that festered in urban slums, and although 80 percent of newborns were healthy at birth, only 20 percent of them were still healthy when they entered school at age 5. Margaret, with Rachel's assistance, set up an medical clinic in Deptford, a London slum, in 1902, and it soon expanded to include an "open air" camp. In 1911, the McMillans opened their play-oriented, open-air nursery school. In addition to teaching self-care and hygiene, the McMillans experimented with open-air sheds. The shed was a shelter in a garden playground, and the children could wander freely from the indoors to the outdoors. Creativity was highly valued, and clay, drawing, block play, and movement were an integral part of these play-based programs.

Rachel died in 1917, but Margaret worked in nursery education until her death in 1931. Chiefly because of Margaret's ongoing advocacy, the British government

agreed to fund nursery schools for 3-to-5-year-olds in 1918, but the war and the economic devastation it brought slowed their spread until the 1930s. Margaret's work also influenced developments in North America, and most of the nursery schools founded in the 1920s and 1930s were modelled after the open-air nurseries. Of course, the term "nursery school" also comes from the McMillans, and their program remains one of the first models for compensatory education programs (Gardner, 1949; McMillan, 1919, 1930; Weber, 1971).

Maria Montessori (1870–1952)

A true feminist of her time, Maria Montessori was the first woman to become a medical doctor in Italy. Her psychiatric interest led her to work with children with cognitive disabilities, who, in her era, were placed in psychiatric institutions. Montessori thought their problems were often educational more than medical, and she proved her point when a number of these institutionalized children easily passed regular school exams after she had worked with them. In 1907, the city of Rome asked Montessori to take charge of a children's day nursery that was attached to a housing tenement for the poor. The housing authorities wanted someone who would keep the children off the stairs and prevent them from dirtying the newly painted walls. But Montessori found in this *casa dei bambini* (children's house) the opportunity to explore her teaching methods with normal children.

Montessori's methods were based on the principle that young children learn in a way that is fundamentally different from how adults learn. She was particularly impressed with the great capacity of children to learn so much during the first few years of life. She called this capacity the **absorbent mind**, analogous to a sponge soaking up liquid. She felt that all children have a fundamental, inborn intellectual structure that unfolds gradually as they develop, although individual differences are due to different environmental experiences.

If children's absorbent minds are exposed to appropriate learning experiences in the developmental stages, their minds will grow. This is especially true during **sensitive periods**, times when children are most receptive to absorbing specific learning. For instance, during one sensitive period, children are especially receptive to developing sensory perception; during another, they are concerned with a sense of order in their environment; in yet another, their energies focus on coordination and control of movement.

Montessori developed a curriculum that takes advantage of these sensitive periods by making appropriate experiences available to children at times when they are most ready to learn from them. She used the term **prepared environment** to describe this match of the right materials to children's stages of development. Her school included many learning activities that she herself developed to help children acquire skills. Some of these related to sensory discrimination, matching and sorting by size, shape, sound, colour, smell, or any other dimension; others helped children learn practical skills such as polishing shoes or setting a table. More advanced materials were aimed at teaching reading, writing, and math skills through hands-on manipulation.

Reflective Exercise 2-2

Montessori's ideas were almost revolutionary during her time. For example, not having the teacher lecture to children seated in neat rows was considered outrageous by her critics. Which ideas of Montessori's do you think were novel for early childhood education? What materials are still relevant in our times? Which practices do you find outdated?

Much of Montessori's philosophy and approach, particularly her **self-correcting materials** and strong sense of **respect for children**, have had an enduring impact on early childhood education. Whether by design in contemporary Montessori schools or by common acceptance in other programs, Montessori's influence is still strongly felt today (Braun & Edwards, 1972; Carter, 1987; Chattin-McNichols, 1992; Elkind, 1983; Gettman, 1987; Simons & Simons, 1986).

● Loris Malaguzzi (1920–1994)

Loris Malaguzzi, born in Correggio, Italy, was the driving force behind the establishment of the schools in the Italian town of Reggio Emilia. While teaching, Malaguzzi specialized in psychology at the Center for National Research in Rome. He became an advocate for the innovative Reggio schools, recognizing their uniqueness and potential. In the past decade, the schools' philosophy and methods have gained considerable attention and support worldwide.

Malaguzzi devised a complete system of education with a basis in the principles of Dewey, Piaget, and Vygotsky in which the school's first priority is in presenting and upholding its **image of the child** as an active and vital participant in constructing his/her own knowledge. The municipality of Reggio Emilia took a systems approach to education with relationships, interactions, and collaboration being at the centre. Children, parents, and teachers were equal partners in learning. Visual arts and an esthetically pleasing environment provided the framework for learning through a teacher called an **atelierista** and a workshop called an **atelier**. An **emergent curriculum**, which evolves through continuous dialogue and documentation, frames learning as children devise and engage in **projects**.

Shortly before his death in 1994, as worldwide attention to Reggio grew, Malaguzzi was very concerned with protecting the purpose of the schools. Two organizations were formed. These are called Reggio Children and Friends of Reggio Children. These, together with the

Courtesy of George Brown College.

International Reggio Exchange, are affiliated with the Merrill-Palmer Institute at Wayne State University in Detroit, Michigan. The Reggio program is outlined in Chapter 5.

The people of Reggio Emilia, Italy, wanted their schools to be different. They had a "universal aspiration … that their children first of all had to be taken seriously and believed in" (Malaguzzi, 1993, p. 51). They felt that all members of the community should gain great joy from learning and sharing. The first school was established in 1963 on the basis of schools started by the people in the 1940s.

● More Influential People

The "baby" doctors have written extensively on child development and child care, particularly for parents. Dr. Benjamin Spock was the forerunner of this when he wrote *The Common Sense Book of Baby and Child Care* in 1946. Generations have been raised on Dr. Spock. Since then, Dr. Burton White, Dr. Berry Brazelton, Frank and Theresa Caplan and Penelope Leach have published excellent child development books for parents.

Stanley Greenspan and Nancy Thorndike Greenspan published *First Feelings: Milestones in the Emotional Development of Your Baby and Child* in 1985. In 1988, David Elkind wrote *The Hurried Child: Growing Up Too Fast, Too Soon*, sounding the early warning that childhood was again in danger of disappearing. He recognized that views of children had begun again to mirror views from former eras, including the view of children as mini-adults, as we dressed, employed, punished, and pushed our children to accelerate at extreme paces. These authors have since published many books and articles on child care and have proven to be excellent resources.

Reflective Exercise 2-3

Interview your own parents about child-rearing practices when you were young. Ask what child care manual was popular and what they remember about it. As a class, compare the perspectives of the different parents.

Influential Theorists of Child Development

Although many of the predecessors of early childhood education developed a theoretical or philosophical viewpoint about how children develop, it was not until our century that such ideas were founded on a more systematic base through observations and research. A **human development theory** is a way of describing what happens as individuals move from infancy through adulthood, identifying significant events commonly experienced by all people, and explaining why changes occur as they do. It is useful to have a grasp of different theories as you develop your own professional identity and beliefs. This not only gives you a way of assessing your personal values but offers some alternative views about how children develop and should be treated (Thomas, 1990a). We will now do an overview of just a few of the most influential developmental theorists whose ideas have contributed, directly or indirectly, to the field of early childhood education today. Separate texts and courses on development consider these theorists and others in considerably more detail, and they are invaluable for those planning a career in early childhood education.

Some child development theorists maintain that behaviour, knowledge, and skills are innate or genetic, that they unfold in predictable stages, in sequence, at predictable ages in all people and, hence, the environment has little impact on development. Other theorists like the behaviourists maintain that the environment is the most important factor in development and that most behaviour, knowledge, and skills are learned and therefore can be taught, observed, influenced, or changed gradually and continuously. You will have many debates in your career about concepts such as nature versus nurture, heredity versus environment, and maturation versus experience. Are learning and behaviour shaped by inborn characteristics and a biological clock, by outside forces, or by an interaction between an individual's inborn disposition and the environment? Below we highlight five theories on how children develop—constructivist, psychosocial, behavioural, sociohistoric, and motivational theories.

Sigmund Freud (1856–1939)

Freud, the founder of **psychoanalytic theory**, proposed a way of viewing development that radically challenged many of the previously held ideas about childhood. Even though many of Freud's students and followers altered a number of his ideas, his influence on early childhood education has nonetheless been significant. Freud was the first to emphasize the importance of the early years as a foundation for later development. His work with adults who suffered psychological problems led him to the conclusion that the roots of their ills lay in their early experiences of childhood. Today, we acknowledge the significance of the early years, although we recognize their value not just in personality formation but in all areas of development.

Freud described stages of development, summarized in Exhibit 2-2, centred on the part of the body from which the child derives most pleasure at that time. Freud's notion of stages is still considered valid by many.

According to Freud, all behaviour is motivated by the **pleasure principle**, a desire to maximize what is pleasant. Three facets of personality are involved in this search for pleasure.

1. The first is the **id**, which is dominant during the earliest years and seeks immediate pleasure in any way possible through the satisfaction of needs.

EXHIBIT 2-2 *Erikson's and Freud's Developmental Sequences*

Erikson's Psychosocial Stages	Freud's Psychosexual Stages	Developmental Task	Positive Influences
Trust vs. Mistrust (0–18 months)	Oral stage (0–18 months)	Developing trust in the world (negative outcome is suspicion)	Warm and caring caregivers, especially the primary ones
Autonomy vs. Shame and Doubt (18 months–3 years)	Anal stage (18 months–3 or 4 years)	Developing a positive sense of autonomy (negative outcome is shame, doubt, and low self-confidence)	Allowing the child to be independent and to explore
Initiative vs. Guilt (3–5 years)	Phallic stage (3 or 4 years–6 years)	Developing a positive view of one's own actions and wishes (negative outcome is guilt over own actions)	Allowing the child to form own ideas, plans, and desires; supportive parents and caregivers
Industry vs. Inferiority (6 years–puberty)	Latency stage (6 years–puberty)	Developing confidence in one's own accomplishments (negative outcome is sense of inadequacy)	Parents, teachers, and caregivers who support child's efforts and do not constantly compare child to others
Identity vs. Identity Diffusion (adolescent years)	Genital stage (puberty on)	Developing a sense of identity (negative outcome is role confusion and aimlessness)	
Intimacy vs. Isolation (early adulthood)		Development of close, rewarding relationships (negative outcome is flight from close ones)	
Generativity vs. Stagnation (middle age)		Developing responsibilities to help others, including children (negative outcome is being self-absorbed)	
Integrity vs. Despair (old age)		Developing a sense of satisfaction with one's life (negative outcome is a sense of bitterness and failure)	

2. The ego, the rational part of the personality, operates on the **reality principle**, and helps the id find appropriate ways to achieve pleasure.

3. The **superego**, or conscience, develops during the preschool years, and is based on the moral norms of society that are passed on by parents and other adults.

Freud maintained that the ego mediates between the id and the superego in the manner described in Exhibit 2-3.

EXHIBIT 2-3   *The Ego Mediates*

Three-year-old Cassie sees her classmate Tito riding the new tricycle that the school had just purchased.

"I *want* that trike and I *want* it now! It's bright red. It's shiny. It's faster than any other trike in the world! I *want* it!" clamours Cassie's id.

"But," whispers her superego, "you can't just grab that tricycle. Remember the rule. Tito has it so it is his until he is finished playing with it."

Having to deal with the conflicting id and superego, the ego tries to mediate: "Look, if you just grab that tricycle, you will get in trouble. Why not go to Tito and ask him if you can ride it when he is done?"

Thus, Cassie compromises. She can't have the tricycle immediately, but she will get it through conventional channels and will not suffer the consequences of breaking the school's rules.

Freud's influence on thinking about children was marked during the first half of the 20th century. He also influenced the thinking of many neo-Freudians who continue to shape our views of the young child (Douvan, 1990; Weber, 1984; Zimiles, 1982).

Jean Piaget (1896–1980)

One of the most influential forces in early childhood education today is Jean Piaget. Piaget's **cognitive development theory** presents a complex picture of how children's intelligence and thinking abilities emerge. Piaget did not suggest specific educational applications of his work, but educators have transformed his theory into actual models more than any other.

Piaget, a biologist by training, thought cognitive development was similar to how all organisms function physiologically, adapting to and organizing the environment around them. A common example illustrates our own biological adaptation to the physical environment: if the temperature becomes too warm or too cold, we sweat or shiver to adapt. In a way similar to this physiological adaptation, we also adapt mentally to changes in the environment. At the same time we adapt, we mentally organize what we perceive in our environment so that it makes sense to us.

In a cognitive sense, *adaptation* is involved any time new information or a new experience occurs. The person must adapt to incorporate any new information or experience into the psychological structure. When something new presents itself, however, the existing mental structure is "upset" or put into **disequilibrium** because this new information or experience does not exactly fit into the old structures. To return to balance or **equilibrium**, **adaptation** takes place through the complementary processes of **assimilation** and **accommodation**. Assimilation occurs when the person tries to make the new information or experience fit into an existing concept or schema. Accommodation takes place when the schema is modified or a new concept is formed to incorporate the new information or experience. The A Closer Look box illustrates how these two types of adaptation operate in a group of preschoolers on a field trip to the zoo.

A Closer Look

ASSIMILATION AND ACCOMMODATION AT THE ZOO

Many of the children have often visited this zoo, and they are familiar with the animals. Raymond, for example, has always enjoyed the cats and can identify the lions, tigers, leopards, lynxes, and ocelots. Before Raymond visited this time, the zoo acquired a pair of panthers, animals Raymond had not seen before. "Look!" he exclaims, "there are two black leopards!" Raymond fit the new animals into an existing mental structure that told him that the new cats were leopards of a different colour. After all, his pet cat Fluffy is multicoloured and his other cat Eclipse is black, indicating that cats of all sorts come in different colours. Raymond is using assimilation, making the new information fit into what he already knows.

For Monique, who has recently moved to the area, this is the first time she has ever visited a zoo. There are many novel experiences for her, because before her visit she had only seen some wild animals in books and on television. Seeing the llamas, Monique considers what these animals might be. They somewhat resemble horses, but she immediately dismisses this category because she knows that horses have smooth hair and shorter necks. She has seen pictures of camels, but the animals she sees now do not have humps on their backs. She finally decides that these must be animals she does not know; after all, she has seen many other new animals today. Monique goes to one of the teachers who tells her about llamas, thus helping her in the process of accommodation, creating a new concept into which this new information can be fitted.

Organization is a process that is complementary to adaptation. While adaptation allows for new information and experiences to be incorporated into existing mental structures, organization defines how such information and experiences are related to each other. Consider a pedal. By itself it is a small, flat, rectangular item made of red plastic. However, in proper context, fitted on a tricycle, the pedal takes on an entirely different meaning as it allows the child to turn the wheels that, in turn, make the tricycle move. Organization allows us to expand the visual cues about the pedal to include information about its function as part of a whole.

Piaget called the cognitive structures into which we adapt and organize our environment **schemata** ("schema" is the singular form). Schemata are concepts or mental representations of experiences that we constantly create, refine, and reorganize. One popular analogy of schemata is an index card file. Babies are born with only a few "index cards," but, with experience, they create new cards and "dividers" as their store of information becomes more complex.

As a **stage theorist**, Piaget conceived of qualitatively different characteristics and accomplishments in cognitive ability during the four stages of development known as the **sensorimotor period**, the **preoperational period**, the **concrete operations period**, and the **formal operations period**. (See Exhibit 2-4.) Each stage is built on and incorporates the accomplishments of the previous one. **Maturation**, which interacts with experiences to determine the course of development, sets limits on when children are capable of achieving specific cognitive abilities. (You might note that Piaget acknowledges the importance of experience as well as maturational factors, in contrast to other theorists who discount the role of experience.)

Thus, the infant, dependent on movement and the senses, learns through those avenues. By age 2, however, a distinctly new ability emerges, **mental representation** of objects. This opens up a world of new possibilities, but this age group is still limited by the observable characteristics of objects. Reasoning is not yet logical, although by about 7 years children begin to apply **logical thinking** to concrete problems. Finally, by adolescence, the young person may be able to apply logic and **abstract thinking** to a wide range of problems.

Early childhood teachers are concerned primarily with children in the preoperational period, but they need to be aware of developments in preceding and subsequent periods. An understanding of the characteristics, abilities, and limits of young children is vital to appropriate teaching (Ginsburg & Opper, 1969; Lavatelli, 1970; Piaget, 1983; Saunders & Bingham-Newman, 1984; Thomas, 1990a, 1990b; Tribe, 1982; Wadsworth, 1984).

J. B. Watson (1878–1958)

Many of the theorists and educators we have considered to this point believed that there is an inborn plan according to which children develop. Rousseau, Pestalozzi, Froebel, and Montessori all felt that, given an appropriate environment and understanding adults, children would develop according to nature's plan into healthy, responsible, intelligent adults. Freud and Piaget likewise believed that development is predetermined and will follow the same stages in each person. John Locke, on the other hand, strongly disagreed with the maturational or growing plants view of development. In this sense, Locke could be seen as the forerunner of **behaviourism**. As has been mentioned above, Locke maintained that children were born *tabula rasa*, and that their experiences would determine their develop-

EXHIBIT 2-4 *Piaget's Periods of Cognitive Development*

Stage 1: Sensorimotor Period (0–2 years)

The first period is characterized by motor behaviour through which schemata are formed. The child does not yet represent events mentally but relies on coordination of senses and movement, on **object permanence** development, on learning to differentiate means from ends, and on beginning to understand the relationship of objects in space in order to learn about the environment.

Stage 2: Preoperational Period (2–7 years)

Language and other forms of representation develop during this period, although thinking is not yet logical. Children's internal mental representations, which allow them to think of objects even if these are not physically present, is the major accomplishment of this period. Children have an egocentric view of the world, in terms of their own perspective. Early classification, seriation, and role playing begin.

Stage 3: Concrete Operations Period (7–11 years)

The child has internalized some physical tasks or operations and no longer depends only on what is visible, but can apply logic to solving problems. The child now is able to reverse operations (for instance, $5 - 3 = 2$ is the same as $3 + 2 = 5$). The child can also practise conservation—recognize that an object does not change in amount even if its physical appearance changes (stretching a ball of clay into a snake).

Stage 4: Formal Operations Period (11–15 years)

The final period, rare even in adults, is characterized by sophisticated, abstract thinking and logical reasoning abilities applied to physical as well as social and moral problems.

ment. The behaviourists of the twentieth century would agree with Locke; they maintain that children are shaped by external, environmental forces rather than internal ones.

The father of behaviourism was John Broadus Watson, an American psychologist, who "shook the house of psychology to its foundations" (Kessen, 1965, p. 228) between 1913 and 1920 with his behavioural theory (Watson, 1925a, 1925b, 1928). At that time, psychology emphasized the contents of the mind, and the introspective method was considered the appropriate way to study the mind. Watson maintained that results based on the introspective method were unreliable, especially in the study of young children and animals. He argued that the observation of behaviour was the correct way to gather information; the effect of his theory was that psychology changed from a discipline that studied the mind

using introspective methods to one that studied observable behaviours and responses.

Watson used the techniques of **classical conditioning** to study fear in young children; today, however, many of his studies would be seen as unethical (Kaplan, 1991). Classical conditioning is a learning technique in which a stimulus that usually evokes a reflex (e.g., fear) is paired with one that does not usually evoke the reflex (e.g., a rat), until the latter eventually evokes the reflex by itself. For example, in his now infamous studies of Albert, a 9-month-old baby in hospital, he and a colleague (Watson & Rayner, 1920) conditioned Albert to fear rats by showing him a rat and following that with a loud noise. Albert eventually began to fear all furry objects. (Watson did not decondition him even though he knew a month in advance that Albert would be leaving hospital.) The success that Watson and his followers had in changing children's behaviour in such studies led them to argue that development was environmentally determined, and parents had an important role to play. Watson (1925a) also argued that a child's environment would determine that child's behaviour:

> Give me a dozen healthy infants, well-formed, and my own specified world to bring them up in and I'll guarantee to take any one of them at random and train him [sic] to become any type of specialist I might select—doctor, lawyer, merchant, chief, and yes, even beggarman and thief, regardless of his talents, penchants, abilities, vocations and race of his ancestors. (P. 104)

● B. F. Skinner (1904–1990)

Certainly, Watson's view of development emphasizes the importance of early experience and education, and some of his followers have applied behaviourist principles to parenting and teaching. B. F. Skinner, the most famous of Watson's followers, both popularized and extended behaviourism so that it was the dominant force in psychology until at least the 1980s. Skinner's writings and those of his many followers have had a widespread influence on all aspects of education, including the early childhood years. The application of his theoretical and experimental work can be seen in **behaviour modification**, which operates on the underlying principle that behaviour can be changed or modified by manipulating the environment, which includes both physical and social components.

Skinner emphasized that almost all behaviours are learned through experience, and can be increased or decreased in frequency as a function of what follows them. In other words, if something pleasant or enjoyable consistently happens after the child engages in a specific behaviour (the teacher smiles when Jeremy helps to put away the blocks), he is likely to repeat that behaviour. Conversely, if something unpleasant or painful follows a behaviour (Larissa burns her finger when she touches the stove), she is likely not to repeat it. Deliberately attempting to increase or decrease behaviour by controlling consequences is called **operant conditioning**.

Skinner used the term **reinforcement** to describe the *immediate consequence of behaviour* that is likely to strengthen it. Reinforcement can be either positive or negative: positive reinforcement entails providing something rewarding for the behaviour, while negative reinforcement entails the removal of something unpleasant or aversive. Whether consciously using the behavioural approach or not, early childhood educators frequently use **positive reinforcement** because of its powerful effect on children's behaviour. For example, teachers of young children are most likely to use **social reinforcers**—for instance, a smile, a hug, attention, or involvement—when they see a child engaging in a behaviour they consider desirable. Teachers may also provide **negative reinforcement**; for example, if Don Lon is hitting Rana, and the teacher intervenes at Rana's request, Rana would be reinforced for the behaviour assuming Don Lon stopped hitting once the teacher intervened. Reinforcement of both types is a very effective way of controlling behaviour.

Punishment, an unpleasant or aversive consequence that *immediately* follows a behaviour is likely to weaken that behaviour. According to Skinner (and almost all early childhood professionals), *punishment is not a very effective way of controlling behaviour*. Like reinforcement, punishment can be either *positive* or *negative*. As with reinforcement, positive punishment entails adding an unpleasant stimulus, while negative punishment entails the removal of a pleasant one. Assuming that Don Lon in the above example likes to be with other children, the teacher would be using negative punishment if she removed him from the group for hitting. Alternatively, if Rana had hit him back, she would have been giving positive punishment for his behaviour (and then the teacher would have a greater challenge). Exhibit 2-5 summarizes Skinner's view of positive and negative reinforcement and punishment. (If you think of the mathematical signs that go with these terms, + and −, it may be easier to remember the difference between positive and negative.)

EXHIBIT 2-5　*Skinner's View of Reinforcement and Punishment*

	POSITIVE (+ for adding)	NEGATIVE (– for removing)
REINFORCEMENT— strengthens frequency of the behaviour	Add something pleasant (e.g., candy, smile, praise, etc.)	Remove something unpleasant (e.g., hitting child, pinching object, etc.)
PUNISHMENT— reduces frequency of the behaviour	Add something unpleasant (e.g., hitting, etc.)	Remove something pleasant (e.g., candy, friends, praise, etc.)

In addition, other techniques, such as systematic attention to behaviour and its consequences, can be used to encourage new behaviours or eliminate undesirable ones. However, we will leave discussion of these techniques until we consider children's behaviour. Teachers in many programs frequently use a number of behavioural techniques, even if they do not strictly adhere to behavioural theory (Braun & Edwards, 1972; Bushell, 1982; Peters, Neisworth, & Yawkey, 1985; Neisworth & Buggey, 1993; Sameroff, 1983; Skinner, 1969; Skinner, 1974; Weber, 1984).

● Arnold Gessell (1880–1961)

Gessell, like John Dewey, was a student of G. Stanley Hall, and he has had a major influence on both early childhood education and developmental psychology in the 20th century (Cairns, 1983). Gessell initially worked in the field of education, and then returned to school in the middle of his career to pursue a degree in medicine at Yale. In 1911, after completing his M.D., he founded the Gessell Institute, a child study establishment that still exists at Yale, where he worked until his death. Unlike Dewey, Gessell (and Montessori) accepted Hall's view that development is predetermined and that intelligence is fixed (Hunt, 1968). However, by Gessell's time that notion had been altered somewhat, and Gessell used the term *maturation* to describe how children unfold in predetermined patterns.

Gessell studied the regularities in children's development for over 40 years, often with the assistance of his colleagues, Francis Ilg and Louise Bates Ames. They observed large numbers of children and studied their motor and language development, adaptive behaviours, and personal-social skills. They recorded their observations of each child, and averaged them for each age group so that they could present an overview of the typical child at different age levels. In 1928, he published *Infancy and Human Growth*, a report on growth in infants, and by the time of his death he had studied children through to 10 years of age. The overviews of infants and children at different ages outlined in Chapter 5 follow Gessell's approach, and are referred to as **norms**. Gessell found the norms to be so orderly that, in the same year Watson wrote his polemic on early stimulation, he wrote about "the inevitableness and surety of maturation" (1928, p. 378).

The growth of the nursery school movement in the 1920s was partly the result of Gessell's emphasis on the importance of the early years as "biologically the most important period in the development of the individual" (1923, p. 3). Moreover, Gessell's child study institute, and the University of Iowa's Child Welfare Research Station and their laboratory schools, became models for other institutes that were established in Canada and the United States in the 1920s and 1930s. As noted above, the Institute for Child Study, founded in 1925, was the first Canadian centre, but child study was soon a focus in a number of centres across the country—in Montreal, Saskatoon, and Winnipeg, for example (Northway, 1973). Advanced degrees in the study of early childhood became available at these institutes, and many of the professionals who have shaped the field in both Canada and the United States were trained in these facilities (Northway, 1973).

Other lasting contributions of Gessell include the perhaps archaic but persistent notion of **school readiness**. With his belief that maturation is predictable and orderly, Gessell discouraged parents and teachers from interfering with a child's development in most areas. According to him, only social development was subject to environmental influences, and as a consequence, most early childhood programs from the 1920s until the 1960s emphasized social growth and did not tamper with or try to stimulate growth in the other spheres of development. If a child did not seem ready for a program—kindergarten, for example—the child was kept home for an additional year of unfolding, rather than given stimulation to encourage development in the areas where there was a lag.

● Erik Erikson (1902–1994)

One of Freud's followers, Erik Erikson, modified and refined Freud's stages of development with psychosocial theory in a way that is much more acceptable to us today. Like Freud, Erikson sees each stage defined by conflict, but he sees such conflict as healthy, resulting in opportunities for personal growth. Each stage and its attendant conflict are seen as not just centred on the person alone but concerned with relationships to others. Although Freud's five stages ended with adolescence, Erikson's theory includes eight stages that span infancy through adulthood. Erikson believes these stages, which are summarized in Exhibit 2-1, occur in all human beings in the described sequence at the time in life when their emergence is most critical.

The first four are particularly important to early childhood education because they describe significant tasks that occur in the young child's life. Erikson describes four later stages that are also summarized in Exhibit 2-2. These additional stages build on the foundations of the ones we have described. Stages occur at critical times in development, but never completely disappear. Thus, trust is still important beyond infancy; children continue to struggle with the balance between autonomy and dependency; and initiative and industry are relevant even beyond the early years, though in a more mature form. Erikson emphasizes the importance of play in meeting the tasks of autonomy and initiative during the preschool years. Erikson's stages highlight some of the important issues for young children and the balance we must provide to help them achieve healthy development (Erikson, 1963; Maier, 1965; Maier, 1990; Tribe, 1982; Weber, 1984).

● Lev Vygotsky (1896–1934)

Vygotsky, born in Orsha, Russia, died early in life, yet his disagreements with Piaget over the relationships both between thought and language and between thought and social development continue to captivate readers. An intense yet very social person with the capacity to inspire others, Vygotsky was deeply interested in a variety of fields and topics ranging from literature to art and psychology. He believed that social and historic forces shape intellectual ability such that we are the product of our times. He saw language as the primary tool for conveying society's values.

By the time Vygotsky was 15, he was organizing intellectually oriented seminars for his peers; this ability to structure the environment so others could learn contributed to the formulation of his ideas about the **zone of proximal development (ZPD)**—the range of activities the child (or adult) cannot perform independently, but can perform with assistance. A related concept is that of **scaffolding**. A child's

ZPD may mean that the child finds a task too difficult to complete alone, but can accomplish it with the "scaffolding," i.e., assistance, you provide. The teacher who says "See what happens if you turn the piece around" to a child struggling to fit a puzzle piece is providing scaffolding within the child's ZPD.

Vygotsky is unique among the theorists we have discussed in his emphasis on the importance of the social environment to human development. In the past two decades, his ideas have gained renewed prominence, and acted as a springboard for cross-cultural studies of child development and child-rearing practices. Vygotsky proposed that social interaction, especially dialogue, between children and adults is the mechanism through which specific cultural values, customs, and beliefs are transmitted from generation to generation.

Vygotsky was particularly intrigued by the question of how young children develop complex thinking. He concluded that the same mechanism through which culture is transmitted—social interaction—is the way in which increasingly more complex thinking develops, as part of learning about culture. Children gain knowledge and skills through shared experiences between themselves and adults or older peers. Furthermore, the dialogues that accompany these experiences gradually become part of children's thinking. Thus, Vygotsky conceived of cognitive development as dependent on, not independent of, **social mediation**. This view contrasts with Piaget's, which conceives of the child as gradually becoming more social and less self-focused. In Vygotsky's view, the child is socially dependent at the beginning of his cognitive life, and becomes increasingly independent in his thinking through many experiences in which adults or older peers help.

Vygotsky's ideas have acquired new relevance in early childhood education. The focus on finding the appropriate ZPD for each child has validated the long-held concern with individualization in early childhood programs. Vygotsky's theory also suggests that, in addition to providing a stimulating environment in which young children are active explorers and participants, early educators need to promote discovery by modelling, explaining, and providing suggestions to suit each child's zone of proximal development (Gallimore & Tharp, 1990; Morrison, 2001; Seifert, 1993).

Influential Events in Early Childhood Education

With the exception of the flurry of activity during World War II, there was little change in early childhood education from the 1920s until the 1960s. Dewey and Hall's emphasis on child-centred programs became popular, and criticisms of the teacher-centred approach of Froebel led to the demise of his model in North America. Similarly, Montessori programs, which were popular in the United States between 1910 and 1918, were attacked by William Heard Kilpatrick in his 1914 work *The Montessori System Examined*. Kilpatrick was a lecturer at Teachers College in New York where he was known as "the million-dollar professor" (Hunt, 1968, p. 108). Kilpatrick was an ardent follower of Dewey, and was "compelled to say that in the content of her doctrine, she belongs to the mid-nineteenth century, some fifty years behind the present development of educational theory" (Kilpatrick, 1914, pp. 62–63). Kilpatrick's work was circulated widely to both students and educators, and led to the demise of Montessori programs until the 1960s.

Gessell's emphasis on maturation seemed to govern thinking about education in the early years until the 1960s: there was little to do with young children other than wait for them to unfold, except in the area of social development. Thus, most early childhood programs, which were patronized by middle-class families, emphasized social growth, and avoided interfering with cognitive development. Allowing the child to flourish in a supportive environment was sufficient. While day care centres were available, they had a welfare orientation (except during the war) and were a service to those families who needed daytime care for their children (Young, 1981).

During the late 1940s and throughout the 1950s, there was strong pressure on families to have the mother stay at home with children, at least until they were 3 years of age. Studies of infants and young children who were reared in orphanages where there was little human contact and virtually no stimulation had repeatedly found significant delays in the development of these unfortunate youngsters (e.g., Skeels, 1966; Spitz, 1945). Moreover, these problems persisted through adolescence when personality problems also were apparent (e.g., Goldfarb, 1943). These studies culminated in John Bowlby's now-classic 1951 monograph, *Maternal Care and Mental Health*. Bowlby, after reviewing the orphanage studies, concluded that the best environment for a child, at least until age 3, was at home with his or her mother or permanent mother substitute. While this guiding principle was accepted in the 1950s, partly because it was consistent with the social and political climate of the times, it was quickly debunked in the 1960s (Caldwell, 1968, 1971, 1973a, 1973b). At that time, many researchers (e.g., Casler, 1961; Yarrow, 1961) realized that the *sensory deprivation experienced by institutionalized infants and children bore no resemblance to short-term intermittent separations from a mother*.

● Sputnik and Educational Upheaval

In 1957, the Russians launched the first space missile, Sputnik. The success of the Soviet space program and, conversely, the failure of the Americans to be the first in space also launched an attack on the school system in the United States that soon filtered up to Canada. Outmoded teaching techniques, dull curricula, and too little emphasis on the sciences were seen as part of the reason the Americans lagged behind the Russians. The U.S. civil rights movement in the United States spawned further examinations of the school system. The schools were seen to be failing the middle classes and not producing the desired rocket scientists; poor children did worse in school than their middle-class counterparts; and black children in the U.S. South were the poorest in terms of their educational accomplishments (e.g., Coleman, 1966; Riessman, 1962). While the school system could be held accountable for the performance of children of poor families, marked differences between poor children and their more advantaged peers were found at the time of school entry. These latter differences pointed to the importance of experience in the preschool years.

Reflective Exercise 2-4

The terrorist attacks in the United States on September 11, 2001, will undoubtedly be described as an influential event in books written centuries from now. How do you think the events of that day will influence children in this century? Have you seen any changes in approaches to children since that bleak day?

● Research and the Rediscovery of the Early Childhood Years

A number of important advances in psychological knowledge, which were critical for our understanding of the early childhood years, also occurred shortly after Sputnik was launched. Interestingly, these new psychological understandings were remarkably in tune with the political and educational pressures of the time. Perhaps the most important psychological advance was the replacement of the maturational view of development with the interactional view, which said that development is determined by both environmental and genetic factors. J. McVicker Hunt, in his 1961 book *Intelligence and Experience*, systematically presented evidence from studies showing the relationship between experience and development in humans and animals. (Much of the research Hunt discussed had been completed at Canadian universities, especially at McGill where Donald Hebb and his students studied the effects of early experience on the neural development and behaviour of animals.) Hunt concluded: "The assumption that intelligence is fixed and that its development is predetermined by the genes [was] no longer tenable" (p. 342).

The early childhood years were identified as the period when intelligence was most susceptible to the effects of experience. Benjamin Bloom reviewed a number of longitudinal studies of intelligence in his 1964 text *Stability and Change in Human Characteristics*, and concluded: "marked changes in the environment in the early years can produce greater changes in intelligence than will equally marked changes in the environment at later periods of development" (pp. 88–89). The work of Bloom and Hunt work clearly had different implications for early childhood educators than Gessell's maturational theory.

Another advance in psychological knowledge of children was North America's belated discovery of Piaget's extensive investigations into the origins of intelligence in the young child. Dr. Daniel Berlyne from the University of Toronto, an eminent psychologist with a behaviourist background, can be credited with leading North America to discover Piaget (e.g., Rowland & McGuire, 1968). Piaget's work had been ignored in North America for two reasons: (1) his clinical method was unorthodox in the heyday of behaviourism and (2) "the lack of adequate translations into English of his elegant but difficult French" (Rowland & McGuire, 1968, p. 145) meant that his works were not available to the English-speaking world. Berlyne was among the first to recognize the severity of this problem and act upon it.

Courtesy of Eglinton Public School.

In 1950, Berlyne, in collaboration with M. Piercy, translated Piaget's *Psychology of Intelligence* into English. In that book, Piaget had outlined his theory of mental development. Berlyne spent time with Piaget in Geneva and continued to disseminate Piaget's thinking to North America and to integrate it into his own work. The post-Sputnik discovery of Piaget forced psychologists such as Burton White (1968) and educators to realize that "if we pay little attention to the events occurring in the first years of life, much of the story may be over by the time we begin to 'educate' the child, even if we start as early as age 3, let alone age 6" (White, 1968, p. 145).

A third factor that influenced North Americans' view of the young child in the 1960s was, in Ira Gordon's (1967) somewhat satirical words, the "rediscovery in sociology that language learning begins in the home" (p. 12). The theoretical work of Basil Bernstein in England indicated that social class had a profound effect on the type of language a child developed and ultimately on the cognitive style the child adopted. Bernstein's work emphasized the significance of language learning in the early years and spawned considerable North American research in this area (e.g., Hess & Shipman, 1965a, 1965b, 1968).

The rediscovery of infancy and early childhood created a new series of challenges, at least for politicians, educators, psychologists, and sociologists, if not for society at large. Gordon (1968) summarized the challenge:

> *Our old norms are shaken. ... Our present theory of the child as competent, as active, as individual ... requires that we intervene, that we do something during this period. ... We cannot sit idly by and let [the child] flower, because he [she] will not. We have to find and define the optimum environment and then we have to convince our public that it needs to provide it. (P. 20)*

Now that you have some appreciation of the historical roots of early childhood education, we will examine some current program models that have been used in the past century. Several of the program models described in Chapter 3 were developed in response to the challenges Gordon summarized above, while others, such as Montessori's model and Open Education, were rediscovered and refined in response to these same challenges.

Key Terms

absorbent mind	adaptation
abstract thinking	assimilation
accommodation	atelier

atelierista	object permanence
autonomy vs. shame and doubt	operant conditioning
behaviour modification	organization
behaviourism	pleasure principle
casa dei bambini	positive reinforcement
child study movement	preoperational period
child-centred approach	prepared environment
classical conditioning	progressive education
cognitive development theory	projects
concrete operations period	psychoanalytic theory
disequilibrium	punishment
ego	reality principle
emergent curriculum	reinforcement
equilibrium	respect for children
formal operations period	scaffolding
human development theory	schemata
id	school readiness
image of the child	self-correcting materials
initiative vs. guilt	sensitive periods
interaction	sensorimotor period
logical thinking	social mediation
maturation	social reinforcers
mental representation	stage theorist
nature	superego
negative reinforcement	trust vs. mistrust
norms	zone of proximal development (ZPD)
nurture	

Key Points

A Look Back—Children Through Time

1. The concept of childhood and treatment of children through history has always been tied to economic, religious, and social factors.

2. During the 20th century, the view of early childhood as an important part of human development was particularly promoted.

Influential People in the History of Early Childhood Education

3. Rousseau advanced the notions that children are innately noble and good, that their way of learning is different from that of adults, and that they should be removed from the corrupting influences of society.

4. Pestalozzi believed that young children learned actively, from concrete experiences, a philosophy he implemented in the schools he established.

5. Froebel, who is credited with originating the kindergarten, put great emphasis on the importance of play.

6. Montessori, working with slum children in Rome, developed a successful method of early education that is still widely followed today.

Influential Theorists of Child Development

7. Freud's psychoanalytic theory ascribes great importance to the early years. Freud proposed a structure of personality in which conscious and unconscious elements operate to balance the child's continual goal of maximizing pleasure.

8. Erikson's psychosocial theory, which spans childhood and adulthood, focuses on specific social tasks that need to emerge for healthy development in each of the eight stages.

9. Piaget's cognitive development theory, one of the most influential on early childhood education, describes how children's thinking is unique in each of four stages.

10. Skinner, one of the important proponents of behavioural theory, emphasized that almost all behaviour is learned and can be increased by positive and decreased by negative consequences.

11. A number of human development theories have been applied to early childhood education through specific models.

12. Although today there is great variation across Montessori programs, the traditional Montessori environment and materials include unique features; the role of the teacher and the children's activities differ from those in other types of early childhood programs.

Key Questions

1. Historical events have a great impact on our view of children and how we treat them. What social and political events have taken place during your life that have had an impact on young children and their education? Also ask this question of a relative or friend who was born in an earlier era.

2. What was your earliest school experience? How does it compare to the type of program you see for young children today?

3. Observe an early childhood program. What evidence do you see of the influence of one or more theorists, for instance Piaget, Erikson, or the behaviourists? Ask one of the teachers if he or she draws on any particular human development theories and compare them to your observation.

4. Observe a Montessori school in your community. How does it differ from other early childhood programs you have seen? How is it similar? What elements of Maria Montessori's original program do you see?

Chapter 3

Early Childhood Education Program Models

*H*ow we approach the education and care of young children depends, to a great extent, on what we believe children are like. Programs for preschoolers are often structured around some underlying assumptions about the nature of children. For instance, a belief that children learn actively by exploring their environment would result in a different type of early education program than one based on the idea that children learn passively by being taught specific information and skills. Similarly, a belief that children are basically unruly and need strict control would result in a different approach than the notion that children generally strive toward social acceptance.

A number of early childhood education program models founded on particular theoretical perspectives have emerged over the years. These *program models* describe typical goals, materials, roles, and sometimes even schedules; frequently, they also specify a particular theoretical stance (e.g., behaviourist, maturationist, etc.). We will consider some of these models in this chapter when exploring the following questions:

1. What theories of development have been applied to the development of early childhood education programs and what are some of the models that have evolved? We will examine six of these models.

   - Montessori programs
   - Open education
   - Project Head Start
   - Cognitively Oriented Curriculum (COC)
   - The Bereiter-Engelmann model (DISTAR)
   - The Reggio Emilia model

   These models differ in a number of ways, including their view of development. As you study the models, try to determine if they have a *nature*, *nurture*, or *interactionist orientation*, and see which theories of development you would associate with them.

2. What does the research tell us about the effectiveness of these models? We will examine the available research on these models, and the research on programs that follow an **eclectic approach.** These eclectic programs have selected ideas and practices from different models, and blended them into a composite program.

Application of Theories in Early Childhood Education

Theories of human development are important to early childhood education when they influence program practices and methods. This has happened over the years as a number of early childhood education program models, founded on a particular theoretical view, were developed. Such models represent a coherent approach to working with young children, and they may specify a philosophical and theoretical base, goals, instructional practices, methods, and materials. In some cases, models also are quite specific about the role of teachers, children, and parents in the program, while others are less rigid.

There was a great proliferation of early childhood models in the 1960s and 1970s when educators and researchers were encouraged (and funded) to develop alternative approaches for Head Start programs. Most of these models were designed to examine different ways of helping children, at risk for later academic failure, to improve school performance. But the research on these models has implications for all children (Evans, 1982).

Roopnarine and Johnson (1993) described 14 **early childhood education models,** including home-based and centre-based ones. The centre-based models could each be placed in one of three categories: (1) Montessori models, (2) behaviourist models, and (3) interactionist models. We should not, however, assume that all early childhood programs conform to one of these carefully prescribed views. Quite frequently, programs are very eclectic in their approach. In fact, if you asked a number of teachers in early childhood programs to describe their program's philosophical foundations, you would likely find that many adhere only to a vaguely recognized theory.

Nevertheless, it is beneficial to examine how some specific models have taken the views of a particular theorist (or theorists) and transformed these into program application. We will examine only six models here, although many alternative approaches exist. These six were selected to illustrate how particular views of child development can be implemented in practice. Included will be a brief overview of Montessori programs as they exist today. We will also consider the *open education* approach, which is derived from the works of Dewey and Freud among others and was developed first in the British infant schools. The U.S. Project Head Start has been influential and has led to the development of several alternative models, so it merits discussion. A description of the Cognitively Oriented Curriculum (COC) is also included. The COC, based, in part, on Piaget's principles and developed as a variant of Project Head Start, has been the focus of research; a number of eclectic models draw on components of the COC. We will also consider the Bereiter-Engelmann model, a behaviourist one developed as well in the 1960s. Finally, we will look at the Reggio Emilia model we outlined in Chapter 2 when discussing the work of Loris Malaguzzi, the driving force behind the schools in the Italian town.

For each model, we will describe the environment, the children and teachers, the role of parents, the schedule or lack thereof, and the materials and curriculum. Then, we will discuss the available research on these models and several eclectic ones.

● Montessori Programs

Maria Montessori's ideas and methods found a receptive audience in the 1910s in the United States, where Montessori programs briefly flourished (Hunt, 1968). Then, in the 1960s, when early childhood programs were multiplying rapidly, Montessori was "rediscovered" and programs based on her model proliferated (Chattin-McNichols, 1992; Hunt, 1968; Spitz, 1986). Many of the programs established in the 1960s still exist in the 1990s, and, in some communities, many additional ones have also been established.

Montessori might best be considered as an eclectic, rather than a human development theorist per se. Her model was based on some carefully considered ideas about how young children learn and a clearly articulated philosophy of education. Montessori maintained that children were inherently good and insisted that *respect for the child* was the cornerstone of successful educational programs. Her ongoing belief in the goodness of the child can be traced to Rousseau, but her emphasis on the vital importance of early experience—and her attempts to teach those who had been labelled "idiots"—place her clearly in the Lockian tradition. The heavy emphasis on **sensory education** in Montessori's program stems from her fascination with Jean-Marc-Gaspard Itard's work with a **feral child**, the so-called "wild boy of Aveyron." (*Feral children* are ones who, lost or abandoned by their parents, were thought to have been reared by animals in the wild.) She also studied the work of Edouard Séguin, a disciple of Itard. She visited his programs for "idiots" in London and Paris, and, feeling the need for a period of quiet meditation, translated over 1000 pages of Itard's and Séguin's works into Italian so she could "weigh

the sense of each word, and … read the *spirit* of the author" (Montessori, 1965, p. 41). Some of her materials were adapted from Séguin, but she developed many on her own. Her philosophy of education was unique.

Montessori, like Piaget, maintained that children's thinking was different from adults', and she saw the years from 0 to 6 as critical for development. During those years, children had an **absorbent mind**, that allowed them to learn without direct instruction. Between 3 and 6 years, children were in a **sensitive period**, one in which they were especially receptive to learning certain things, language skills for example. Montessori maintained that children learn best in a **prepared environment**. The teacher's role is to prepare the environment by selecting and arranging materials that will interest children. Then, the process of **self-education** or **auto-education** will occur; that is, the child will educate herself or himself by activity in the prepared environment.

Today, a wide range of Montessori programs can be found. Some adhere quite rigidly to the original techniques, whereas others follow an approach that has been adapted to better fit the current social context (Chattin-McNichols, 1992). There are some excellent Web sites on Montessori if you wish to learn more. It is interesting to note that although Montessori devised her program to meet the needs of impoverished children and help them learn important life skills, Montessori programs today are, for the most part, attended by children from more affluent homes. *let the children learn their own*

The Environment.   If you visit a traditional Montessori classroom, you will soon observe some of the prominent features of such a program, some similar to other types of early childhood settings, some unique to Montessori. You will quickly notice the sense of order inherent in the room. In addition, you may find the noise level in the class to be quite low, relative to programs like the Cognitively Oriented Curriculum described below.

You will not see a teacher's desk at the front of the classroom and rows of desks for the children. While this is not surprising in the new millennium, it was highly unusual (and threatening for some) when Montessori originated her program at the turn of the century. Child-sized equipment and movable furniture was even more unusual in her time, but Montessori saw it as a sign of respect for the child. Child-sized, movable furniture, rather than fixed rows of desks, are now in every early childhood program, and this is part of Montessori's legacy. The materials are clearly organized on shelves that are easily accessible to the children. There are distinct areas, each containing materials unique to promoting the tasks to be mastered in that area. The environment is also set up to be esthetically pleasing, with plants, flowers, and attractive furnishings and materials. The logic, order, and beauty are all integral to the Montessori philosophy.

The Children.   You will also note children of different ages, mostly from affluent homes, are involved in individual activities, as Montessori believed in multi-age groupings in classrooms. Generally, Montessori programs are designed to include children who span at least a three-year age spread. Typically, children from 2 $\frac{1}{2}$ or 3 to 5 years of age are found in one classroom, while the 6-to-9-year-old children would be in another class. The individualized nature of the Montessori program will also be apparent to you on your visit. Children initiate activities and are free to engage in whatever projects they choose, defining a work space for their selected activity on a mat on the floor or a tabletop. Children are self-directed, and the younger ones usually work independently, although, at times, you will see them working in pairs or small groups. Younger children may be learning how to participate in specific activities by observing and imitating their older classmates.

The Teachers.   There appears to be little adult control in a Montessori class. The teacher's involvement is unobtrusive and quiet. In fact, Montessori saw the teacher as a **director** of activities, and in many programs the teachers are known by that term. You are unlikely to see a Montessori teacher leading a large group activity or lesson. However, you probably would see the teacher both observing children carefully and demonstrating the use of materials to children who have not used them before. The teacher does not reinforce or praise children for their work, since the activities are intended to be self-rewarding and intrinsically motivating so the children do not have to be persuaded or cajoled to use them.

In Canada, some Montessori teachers take a postsecondary school program while others learn about the methods and curriculum through an intensive course of study after they have completed a first degree. Post-diploma courses are also available at some college settings. Typically, the teacher education programs are supervised by either the American Montessori Society (AMS) or the Association for Montessori Internationale (AMI).

The Parents.   Parents are rarely involved in Montessori programs as classroom helpers. While they may visit in some classes, generally they are asked to sit and be unobtrusive observers. In responding to criticisms about the lack of parent involvement in Montessori programs, Chattin-McNichols (1992) comments:

> *Some parents can't seem to resist walking around, following their child, or even* interrupting other children *to ask them about their work, praise them, or pat their heads. Needless to say, this is not welcomed by Montessori teachers. (P. 20; emphasis added)*

The Schedule.   Most Montessori programs allow periods of time for indoor and outdoor activities, and for snacks. However, the focus is on the individual versus the group, and group "lessons" would not occur every day. Rather, in this child-centred program, children determine when they will use the different materials, and they may have five-to-ten-minute group times one or two times during a week.

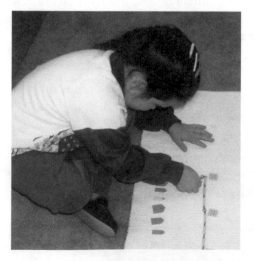

The Materials.   As you look more closely at the materials, you will see that they have some special characteristics. Montessori materials are **didactic**, each designed to teach a specific lesson. In addition, they are **self-correcting** so the child gets immediate feedback from the material after correctly (or incorrectly) completing a task. Materials are graduated from the simple to the more complex; therefore, children are challenged by progressively more difficult concepts. The materials are carefully and attractively constructed, usually made of natural materials such as varnished wood.

The Curriculum.   Different materials fit into each of the three distinct areas of the curriculum. When children first

enter a Montessori program, they are introduced to the **daily living** component, in which practical activities are emphasized. Such activities focus on self-help and environmental care skills such as buttoning, brushing hair, watering plants, washing windows, and sweeping.

The second set of activities and materials are **sensorial**, helping children develop, organize, broaden, and refine sensory perceptions of sight, sound, touch, smell, and taste. To foster visual discrimination, for instance, children use the **Pink Tower**, ten cubes increasing in regular increments of one centimetre, stacked from largest to smallest. A more complex visual discrimination task is involved with the set of **Colour Tablets**, which require the child to arrange hues of one colour from the darkest to the lightest; an even more advanced task might require the child to find the second-darkest hue of each of the seven graded colours when all of the tablets are placed out at random. Other children might be using materials that are designed to encourage auditory discrimination. The **Sound Boxes**, for example, consist of two sets of cylindrical boxes that are filled with materials like salt and rice, and children match the boxes on the basis of the sounds they make. Similarly, the **Tonal Bells**, two sets of bells that vary only in colour, are matched by sound. In addition to being self-correcting, **isolation of a single quality** also is a characteristic of the sensorial materials; they vary in tone, or colour, or size, for example, but not on all three dimensions, and this allows the child to use the materials with minimal adult assistance.

The third aspect of the program involves **conceptual** or **academic materials**. The practical and sensorial skills learned in the first two areas have laid the groundwork on which writing, reading, and mathematics are built. Conceptual learning activities are concrete and multisensory, and actively involve the child. Thus, children use their fingers to trace letters cut out of sandpaper or to trace letters in cornmeal, or use the **Movable Alphabet** to manipulate letters to form words. Many of the math materials are based on a decimal system; for instance, the **Golden Beads** come singly or in units of 10, 100, and 1000. Other activities promote cultural understanding, including maps and animal and plant pictures to identify and classify.

You may notice that some traditional early childhood activities are absent in the Montessori school. Montessori maintained that children under 6 were not able to handle fantasy, so you are not likely to find a dramatic play area in most traditional programs. Research suggests that Montessori teachers vary considerably in their tolerance (or intolerance) of disruptions caused by children using materials for fantasy play (Chattin-McNichols, 1992). Some stop it immediately, while others allow it to continue, especially if the materials are being used constructively.

Montessori's emphasis on reality also means that many programs will not have a creative art corner, or other activities that invite children to freely use their imagination. If you look carefully, you also might be puzzled by the fact that children do not combine materials in their play; that is because there usually is a restriction on how children may use materials. As David Elkind (1983) points out, once children have mastered the use of a particular material in the established manner, they should be free to act on the material and use it freely, in a more experimental way. However, the Montessori method typically allows materials to be used only in the prescribed procedure. For example, a child would not be permitted to use the Pink Tower and Colour Tablets together to build a castle or yard.

You may also note less emphasis on encouraging language learning. The emphasis is placed on showing children how to do things, rather than telling them, and then letting them complete tasks on their own. However, in Montessori programs for culturally deprived and language-delayed children, it is likely that you would notice a much greater emphasis on language. Critics would also suggest that you would not see enough activities that foster social development in a Montessori program, but if you carefully observe children in the program over several days, you will observe opportunities for cooperation, collaboration, and playful social interaction in most programs.

● Open Education

Many American textbooks on education and curriculum (e.g., Lay-Dopyera & Dopyera, 1987; Lawton, 1988; Schwarz & Robison, 1982) discuss the **Bank Street Model**, developed at the Bank Street College of Education in New York, but fail to acknowledge that its roots and earlier history can be traced to Britain where **open education** was developed in the **British Infant School** (Goffin, 1994; Weber, 1971). In fact, as a number of American authors note (e.g., Feeney, Christensen, & Moravcik, 1991; Gordon & Browne, 1993; Evans, 1975; Morrison, 1984; Weber, 1971), North Americans showed little interest in open education until the 1960s. Then, school reformers in Canada and the United States flocked to Britain to study the infant schools.

Lillian Weber (1971) visited British nursery and infant schools in the mid-1960s. Her book, *The English Infant School and Informal Education*, provides an excellent description of open education, its philosophical roots, and its refinement during the 20th century.

Susan and Nathan Isaacs, a husband–wife team who taught at Cambridge and the University of London, formulated the rationale for the open model. They drew heavily upon the works of Dewey, Piaget, and Freud, and upon Susan's own observations and studies at her famous nursery school, the **Malting House School** in Cambridge. Susan's work at the Malting House became known to and emulated by a whole generation of teachers who studied under her at the University of London, and this helped to ensure the success of the open model. To fully appreciate the richness of her program (and to find an abundance of program ideas), consult Isaacs' (1937) vivid description of her school in *Intellectual Growth in Young Children*.

Of course, the roots of the open model predate the Isaacs by at least a century. They can be traced to Owen's 1816 infant school in New Lanark, as well as to the

McMillans' 1911 open-air nursery. Nevertheless, the Isaacs formally defined the open model, and successfully fostered its application on a national level, something that has not happened in any other country.

The open model was applied in both the nursery schools for 3-to-5-year-olds and the infant schools for 5-to-8-year-olds. Nursery schools as well as infant schools were funded through the Department of Education and Science as early as 1918, a fact that may be surprising to some Canadians, especially residents of Prince Edward Island, who have just seen publicly funded kindergartens established in the 1990s. Unlike Canada, there is a remarkable continuity between the methods used in the British nursery and infant schools. While many of our early childhood programs in Canada would compare favourably with those Weber visited in Britain, we are far less likely to have comparable programs for our children between 5 and 8 years of age. Consequently, in reviewing the features of open education, for comparison you might try to keep in mind a typical primary-level class in your community.

Open programs are **child-centred**, and the different subjects are integrated into **activities** and children learn through **discovery**. For example, children in an open program might visit a firehall. Upon return to the classroom, some might become firefighters in the dramatic play area, while others draw firetrucks, and still others dictate or write stories and poems about the experience. The next day, some might make a papier maché model of the firehall and the firetrucks, while others go to the library and find additional resources on firefighting. Three weeks later, one or two children might still be pursuing the firehall theme, but others would have moved on to new topics.

Children's ability to learn through play and to choose experiences that interest them underlie learning in the open model. The school, in turn, must foster and maintain this boundless curiosity by providing a rich environment that allows the children to learn; the child determines how that learning will occur.

The Environment.   If you were to visit an open classroom, you would quickly observe many features that are shared by quality early childhood programs, but it is likely that a number of practices would vary greatly from those of the primary-level classrooms in your community. Perhaps the most striking feature would be the gradual admission time; some children enroll in September, others in January, and others in April. This eases the difficulties that are so often associated with school entry. In fact, you may also see children who will enroll in the program only after several months of visiting with a parent: this gradual introduction to the school setting is encouraged. You also may wonder at the fact that in the open nursery schools, children arrive over a lengthy period of time, and leave at quite different times.

As in the Montessori program, multi-age or family groupings are a standard feature of the open model; the 5-to-8-year-old children are grouped in the infant school and the 3-to-5-year-old children are in the nursery. You also might be puzzled by the **integrated day**: there are no lessons at prescribed times, but there are many **activity centres**. In addition, some of the children might not be in the classroom, but out of the room, working on several different projects. For example, three of them might be in the garden, with a senior citizen from the community, tending their tomatoes and measuring their growth, while others are in the library. In addition, you see several children playing at the water table and the carpentry bench in the corridor. You also see some large blocks and easels there. Open schools use space beyond the classroom, and there is freedom of movement in and out of the class for older children that is rare on this side of the Atlantic. The emphasis on the outdoors as a learning resource also is a striking feature that can be traced back to the McMillan sisters. Quite frequently, North American children at the primary level see the outdoors only at recess—even in warm weather, it is an undervalued resource in Canada—but that is not the case in the open class. You are almost overwhelmed by the number of available materials, many of them homemade. Teachers see this profusion of materials as necessary for sustaining the child's curiosity.

The Children.   The children in open programs come from widely differing backgrounds just as children in our neighbourhood-based elementary schools do. If you visit an open class, you would not find the children in rows and the teacher at a desk. However, you will find more collaborative activity and probably a higher noise level than you would in a Montessori program. You would undoubtedly notice that children are free to use materials in the way they want, and that they enjoy their freedom of movement. Children initiate projects, and the teacher serves as a resource person. Older and younger children may be playing together, and a variety of things are happening at the same time.

The Teachers.   The teachers in open schools see themselves as being there to support the child's interests. Teachers in the open class have to keep careful records on each child, as they have to know what each child understands and how he or she arrived at that understanding. Consequently, the teacher's notes do not include just final accomplishments—being able to count to 5, for example—they also include information on the activities the child engaged in that led to this accomplishment.

In the infant schools, in particular, teachers traditionally have not shared their North American colleagues' concerns about covering certain topics before the children go on to the next grade. Children in Britain have been moved from one to another group on the basis of age, not achievement. Two factors seem to account for this difference: (1) until the 1990s, the curriculum was determined at a local level (unlike in Canada, where the curriculum has been set down by the provinces since schools began) and (2) children in open classes do not receive regular report cards, which are more common in this country.

The Parents.   Parents are frequent visitors and volunteers in the open classroom, as are other members of the community. During her year-and-a-half of visits, Weber notes that she never found a school that did not have some parents present. The gradual arrival and admission procedures described above facilitate the development of positive relationships between teachers and parents.

Britain's history also helped to forge the warm bond that exists between parents and teachers in the open schools. During World War II, many children in England had to be evacuated from their homes because of the frequent bombings. While the conditions were not as extreme as those in the orphanages we discussed in Chapter 2, the great void in the lives of the evacuated children who were separated from their homes and neighbourhoods was evident. Teachers were frequently the people who had to care for the children if they were evacuated from their homes. In so doing, their understanding of the importance of the home to the child grew so that they were more likely to encourage a close relationship with the home. North Americans do not have that history, and too often, teachers, especially at the primary level, are reluctant to foster that closeness.

The Schedule. While there usually is a meeting time when all children in the school gather together several days a week, you will not find a set schedule in an open school. The entire group of children is never the focus of a set lesson; teachers work with small groups and there are many different activities in progress at one time—and often, they are occurring in several different locations. However, there typically are set times for movement and physical education, and lunch.

The Materials. As noted above, materials are abundant in the open class. Sand, water, and clay are in every class, as are materials for movement in the nursery classes and physical education in the infant classes. A wide range of painting supplies is available, in both the classes and the corridors, and workbenches and stoves are plentiful. Dramatic play areas and musical instruments are found in every class. Blocks, "beautiful junk" for assembling things, and manipulative toys like puzzles and Lego also are in every class. Many of the materials are homemade or donated, and you seldom see materials prepared for use on just one occasion.

The Curriculum. Britain has not had a history of a government-prescribed curriculum, nor the fixed standards for each grade that characterize North American programs. In an excellent Canadian guidebook about how to introduce the open model in Canadian classrooms, *Change: One Step at a Time*, Lois Napier-Anderson (1981) warned Canadians that the provincially dictated curricula made open education more difficult to implement here. Weber issued similar cautions to her American audience, and noted that Dewey's progressivism never became a reality in the United States because of a standardized curriculum.

● Project Head Start

In 1964, with the Economic Opportunity Act, the United States government launched the largest, most significant early childhood education project the world has seen. Project Head Start was a response to both the civil rights movement and the post-Sputnik educational crisis facing the United States. The project aimed to break the poverty cycle by providing children and their families with the educational, medical, dental, nutritional, psychological, and social services they required to escape from poverty. Rather than a model per se, Head Start might be better viewed as the grandparent of a number of model early childhood programs. In fact, three of the remaining four models we will discuss in this chapter originated in response to the availability of funds to develop variants of the program and to evaluate their effectiveness. The Internet contains many interesting Web sites on the Head Start program.

Canadians and Head Start. Head Start is relevant to Canadians in the field of early childhood education for several reasons. First, the scope of the project and the emphasis it placed on the importance of the early years had an impact that was felt far beyond the U.S. boundaries. Second, much of the significant research on the effectiveness of early childhood programs has been completed because Head Start emphasized an evaluation component, and researchers acknowledged the importance of this activity. Finally, many Canadians were seeing generic Head Start programs in their own communities, including at least one in Nova Scotia that predated the United States project.

Canadians also were hearing legislators talk about making funds available for Head Start projects in the 1960s (a time when funds were available). For example, in 1965, inspired by Head Start, Ontario's Minister of Education, William G. Davis, spoke in the legislature of his concerns about early childhood education (Ontario, 1965, pp. 3582–3583).

Not surprisingly, generic Head Start programs soon became available in larger urban centres in Ontario. Some were junior kindergartens, funded by school boards and the province (e.g., Toronto and Hamilton). Canadian university students, administrators, and alumni also founded a number of programs in the 1960s, the decade of social concern. The University of Western Ontario's Community Action Project (CAP), for instance, was initiated by students who found funding from the university, and governments at several levels as well as donations from local corporations. The Varsity Downtown Education Project (VDEP) in Toronto was somewhat larger in scope, and included two different centres. VDEP was funded for several years by contributions from a charitable foundation (Atkinson Foundation) and from the University of Toronto's Students' Administrative Council, Board of Governors, and alumni. VDEP then turned into a full-time alternative school, primarily for "graduates" of the summer program, that relied at first on self-raised funds and later on funds from the Toronto Board of Education.

The East Coast also saw a flurry of activity, as did the Far North. Nova Scotia perhaps saw the greatest increase in Canadian "Head Start" projects in the 1960s, as the provincial government made funds available for disadvantaged communities (Irwin & Canning, 1992). Some programs also received federal and provincial funding, while others searched for local funds. A number the programs were interracial and aimed to improve relations between whites, blacks, and Natives in communities such as Halifax, Truro, and Hants County. In fact, one program, the Brunswick-Cornwallis Pre-school Program, predated Project Head Start by two years. Alexa McDonough, in Nova Scotia, supervised nine such programs with a staff of 30. In Newfoundland, the St. John's Club of the Canadian Federation of University Women initiated an 11-week pilot program that drew on the university and community volunteers for staff and evaluations (Glassman, 1992). The program was extended and eventually received federal funding as a demonstration project. It continues today as a parent cooperative. The Skookum Jim Society in Whitehorse, Yukon, also started a generic Head Start program in 1968 with funding from the Department of Indian Affairs and a lot of volunteer efforts (Johnson & Joe, 1992).

When the federal government made Local Initiatives Program and Opportunities for Youth funding available in the early 1970s, the number of generic Head Start programs in certain areas of the country multiplied rapidly. Many of those programs continue to serve young children in the 1990s.

The Environment.   There is no one Head Start program, but many variants that are developed at the local level to be consistent with broad national goals. Children are to experience a learning environment that fosters development in all areas, and parents are to be involved in the program. Some programs are full-day ones, while others are half-day. Typically, medical, dental, and nutritional services are made available for children in the program. Children receive at least one hot meal a day, and regular medical and dental examinations are provided, and immunizations are kept up to date. The early identification of developmental delays and learning problems is encouraged, and referrals to psychologists for complete assessments are made if a problem is suspected. An individual who helps families obtain needed social services is also part of the program.

The Children.   Family income is the main criterion for admission to a Head Start program. At least 90 percent of the children in a program must come from families that meet the federal government's defined poverty level. In addition, federal guidelines require that a minimum of 10 percent of the children in the program must have disabilities.

The Parents.   Parenting education and parent involvement are also integral elements of Head Start. Teachers in Head Start, like teachers in open models, recognize that parents are the dominant influence in a young child's life. If the child's life is to improve, so must that of the parent. Many parents have found employment through the program because it gives them priority for any available nonprofessional Head Start jobs. Consequently, parents usually work as the bus driver, cook, and teacher assistants. Parents also are involved with the advisory council for the programs.

The Teachers.   Minimum standards for U.S. early childhood teachers are determined at the state level. Some states require little or no training for those working in early childhood programs, including Head Start, but others have stringent criteria.

The **Child Development Associate (CDA)** program, a **competency-based program,** was developed in the United States during the 1970s to facilitate **in-service** training of early childhood professionals. Approximately 80 percent of the recipients of a CDA have come from Head Start programs. The program has been a model for Canadian jurisdictions, which are in the process of introducing teacher-training requirements for early childhood educators. A program such as the CDA tries to credit an untrained teacher with extensive experience for the knowledge and skills obtained on the job, and then requires the person to fill in the missing knowledge and skill gaps.

The CDA has been described as an alternative avenue toward professionalism for people who traditionally have been excluded from higher education, specifically those from low-income backgrounds (Peters, 1988). The CDA model may also be relevant in those areas of Canada where travel to postsecondary institutions is a problem. In the Yukon, the Northwest Territories, Newfoundland, and Northern British Columbia, for example, attending a training program in early childhood education program located far from one's home can be a major hardship. Similarly, moving to a major urban centre from a reserve in order to study can be very difficult proposition, and many students fail to complete the programs as the cultural adjustment process coupled with the demanding program can be simply too great.

The Schedule.   Just as there is no standard Head Start environment, scheduling varies from one program to another. A Montessori Head Start program would follow the Montessori scheduling pattern, while a Head Start program following the Cognitively Oriented Curriculum would have a schedule similar to that program's.

The Materials and Curriculum.   There are not any standard materials in Head Start programs, nor is there a national curriculum. Some Head Start programs follow a Montessori approach, while in others the open model, as exemplified by the Bank Street College of Education (Gilkeson & Bowman, 1976), can be found.

● Cognitively Oriented Curriculum (COC)

A number of programs based on the theoretical precepts of Jean Piaget have evolved over the past several decades. One of these, the Cognitively Oriented Curriculum (Weikart & Schweinhart, 1993), was developed by the High/Scope Foundation of Ypsilanti, Michigan, under the leadership of David Weikart. This approach was initially designed in the early 1960s as a program for children from impoverished backgrounds, but it has since been adopted more widely, partly through the publication of its carefully outlined curriculum manual, *Young Children in Action* (Hohmann, Banet, & Weikart, 1995). Mary Wright (1983) adopted this model in her University of Western Ontario (UWO) preschool, and it has also been adopted by many preschools and some primary programs in

Canada. Prior to the many amalgamations of school boards in Ontario in the late 1990s, the Niagara South Board of Education, for example, had programs for 4-year-olds that were directly based on the COC model. Some preschool settings in Nova Scotia, too, have followed the COC model, which is even cited in the 1990 provincial guidelines. Other programs in Quebec and Ontario also have chosen to follow the High/Scope model. The Internet is a good source for information on many early childhood education theories and programs.

In line with Piagetian theory, the cognitively oriented model is based on the premise that children are active learners who construct their own knowledge from meaningful experiences. If you were to visit a cognitively oriented class, you would observe this philosophy in the environment, schedule, and activities, and in the children's and teacher's behaviour.

The Environment.   The environment is designed to be stimulating but orderly, where children can independently choose from a wide variety of interesting materials and use them in the manner they choose, as long as they do not hurt themselves or the environment. The classroom is divided into clearly defined work areas, each with a specific set of materials appropriate to that area. A cognitively oriented classroom contains a housekeeping, block, art, quiet, and large-group areas, although there might also be construction, music and movement, sand and water, and animal and plant work areas as well. There is an emphasis on real materials, such as dishes and tools, rather than toy versions. Accessible, uncluttered storage spaces in each work area are clearly labelled with silhouettes or pictures, facilitating cleanup and promoting a sense of order.

The Children.   Weikart's original program was designed for children from extremely deprived backgrounds. In addition to being deprived, most of the children were black and from single-parent families. The model has been adopted by many others, and is as likely to include middle-class children from advantaged homes and ethnic minority children as well as disadvantaged children. There is considerable interaction between children in a COC, and the encouragement of social skills is stressed in some applications of this model, such as Wright's UWO program.

The Teachers.   Teachers in the COC have a more structured role than those in the open and Montessori classes as the schedule described below suggests. Large-group circle times and small group lessons are structured into the program every day. In contrast to the Montessori classes, however, teachers let children use materials in whatever manner they wish.

The teachers work in teams, and the teacher-child ratio in Weikart's programs has varied from 1:5 to 1:8. However, Weikart and Schweinhart (1993) maintain that a ratio of 1:10 and a group size of 20 would be safe with trained teachers and 3-to-4-year-olds. The teachers are expected to become familiar with each child's developmental level, and to plan the child's program accordingly. Traditionally, the teachers' emphasis has been on intellectual challenges that will further development, rather than social development. However, in Wright's UWO program, social development was seen as equally important.

The Parents.   In Weikart's original program, parents were involved in biweekly sessions with a teacher and their child (or children) in their homes. During these sessions, the teachers aimed to show parents new ways to approach their children, and demonstrated how simple activities like cooking could be learning experiences. In addition, they tried to learn more about the child's family and culture in these visits so they could better meet the child's needs. Some adaptations of the COC, Wright's UWO project, for example, have not followed Weikart's parent program, and this may be a significant omission.

The Schedule.   The daily schedule is integral to the philosophy of the cognitively oriented program. Consistency helps children gain gradual understanding of time. The day is begun with a **planning time**, when children decide what activities they would like to participate in during the ensuing work time. A teacher helps each child individually think through what he or she plans to do, and then records the child's plans. A large block of time is then set aside for **work time**, during which children engage in self-selected activities, supported and assisted by the teachers.

After work time comes **recall time**, usually carried out in small groups, where children review their work time activities. This **plan-do-review cycle** is the heart of the cognitively oriented curriculum, helping children make deliberate, systematic choices with the help of the teacher. Additional daily periods include cleanup, considered a learning opportunity; a small-group time, which typically includes a teacher-planned activity that reinforces a cognitive concept; large-group time for stories, music, games, and other whole-group activities; outside time; and meals and nap, as appropriate to the length of the program day.

The Materials.   While there is no prescribed list of materials for a COC program, certain areas or centres are considered to form the core of the program: the block area, the house area, the art area, the quiet area, the construction area, the sand and water area, the music and movement or large-group area, the animal and plant area, and finally the outdoor play area (Hohmann et al., 1995). Each of these areas is richly furnished, much like the open class.

The block area, as an example, would include building materials, things to take apart and put together, and materials for filling and emptying. You might see blocks of several different sizes, tubes and boxes, Tinkertoys, interlocking materials, trucks and trains, small and large cars, and people and animals in the centre. Typically, the block area is located next to the housekeeping area; role play is common in both areas and children often want to use materials from each. The quiet area is filled with small manipulative materials and books. Some materials (e.g., beads, cubes, dominoes, and sound boxes) can be used for sorting and building, while others (e.g., pegs and pegboards, Lego blocks, Tinkertoys, and puzzles) are things that fit together and pull apart. Still other materials in the quiet area (e.g., nesting boxes and rings, and plastic pipe fittings) can be used for ordering and building.

The Curriculum.   Throughout the day, teachers focus on extending the cognitively oriented curriculum's **key experiences,** a set of eight concepts based on the characteristics and learning capabilities of preoperational children, as discussed by Piaget. The key experiences give the teachers a framework within which to observe each child's individual performance and support and extend children's self-initiated activities:

1. **Active learning** takes place when activities are initiated and carried out by children themselves. It involves learning through all the senses, manipulating and combining materials as a way of discovering their relationships, self-selecting activities and materials, and learning to use equipment and tools.

2. *Using language* is strongly stressed and encouraged through talking with others about meaningful experiences, describing, expressing feelings, having language written down by a teacher, and playing with language.

3. *Representing experiences and ideas,* according to Piaget the hallmark of the preoperational period, allows children to represent the world in nonverbal ways. Key experiences include such activities as recognizing objects through the senses, imitating actions and sounds, role playing, and drawing or painting.

4. **Classification** begins during the preoperational period as children note similarities and differences between objects. Children are encouraged to investigate and describe the attributes of things, sort and match objects, use objects in different ways, talk about characteristics that some things do not have, and distinguish between "some" and "all."

5. **Seriation**, the ability to arrange objects along some dimension, is promoted by having children make comparisons, arranging objects in order, and matching.

6. **Number concepts** are the basis for mathematical understanding and are built on many concrete experiences. To promote this concept, experiences are planned to encourage children to compare, count, and engage in one-to-one correspondence.

7. **Spatial relationships** are encouraged through assembling and taking things apart, rearranging and reshaping objects, observing and describing things from different perspectives, working with shapes, experiencing and representing the

child's own body, locating objects in the environment, and experiencing and describing relative positions and distances.

8. *Time* is a gradually acquired concept involving both understanding of time units and sequencing of events in time. Experiences that help children learn such concepts include signals for stopping and starting actions, experiencing and describing different rates of speed and time intervals, observing seasonal changes, discussing future events, planning, representing past events, and describing the order of events (Hohmann et al., 1995).

The cognitively oriented curriculum provides one illustration of how Piaget's theory has been put into practice. Central is the idea that children are active learners who develop appropriate concepts through interaction with the environment. Through a carefully prepared environment and the guidance of knowledgeable teachers, children attain a deeper understanding of the rules that govern the physical and social world (Hohmann et al., 1995; Weikart & Schweinhart, 1993).

● The Bereiter-Engelmann Model (DISTAR)

During the height of Head Start program development, several models based on behavioural theory evolved. One was developed by Carl Bereiter and Siegfried Engelmann in the 1960s, and it was labelled **DISTAR.** Like many of the models developed during that era, it was designed primarily to help children from poverty backgrounds gain some successful experiences that would diminish the likelihood of failure once they started elementary school. The Bereiter-Engelmann model is noticeably different from the other programs we have described, because it is based on some very different premises, both about how children learn and about how to best meet their needs.

DISTAR programs for children without special needs have not been plentiful in the 1980s and 1990s. However, DISTAR methods are increasingly being adopted by "hothousing" programs, and educational critics refer to the DISTAR research more and more frequently in their push for work-oriented, academic-based programs. Consequently, students and teachers in the 1990s need to be familiar with the model and the research on it, so they can respond to parents' queries and engage in the current educational debate in Canada.

Bereiter and Engelmann maintained that disadvantaged children, who were behind their more fortunate peers, needed not just enrichment activities, but a program that would *accelerate* their rate of learning. Such a program would not be well-rounded. Rather, the DISTAR program would emphasize the areas of development Bereiter and Engelmann thought were most relevant to school, and it would ignore other areas of development. Thus, the Bereiter-Engelmann program was designed to meet very specific, teacher-determined learning goals rather than to meet the needs of the whole child.

The Environment. In addition, the environment of the Bereiter-Engelmann model is quite different from that of other early childhood programs. The facility is

Reflective Exercise 3-1

Mr. La Vida, a single parent of 4-year-old Carlos, comes to you for advice. There is a history of language and reading disabilities in his family, and he is concerned as Carlos has some expressive language difficulties. He is trying to decide whether to send him to the DISTAR-type program or the Montessori centre in your community. He would like you to describe the strengths and weaknesses of each approach so he can make an informed decision. He reminds you that he also has extra time to spend with Carlos so he can supplement a program that does not meet all of his needs. You know Mr. La Vida is a committed and creative parent who is quite capable of supplementing the program.

arranged into small and large classrooms. Direct teaching activities are carried out in the small rooms, and the large room is used for less structured, large-group activities. A model floor plan suggested by Bereiter and Engelmann (1966) includes three small classrooms—named the Arithmetic Room, the Reading Room, and the Language Room—each furnished with five small chairs facing a chalkboard (and, presumably, the teacher). The most important feature of these small study rooms should be their acoustic properties, ensuring that they filter out any noise that would distract from lessons. They recommend that the rooms also be plain, to minimize distraction from the task at hand. A larger "homeroom" furnished with tables, a piano, and a chalkboard provides a place for snack and music times.

Bereiter and Engelmann also suggest that there be very few materials available to the children, mainly ones that will reinforce concepts taught in the lessons. They assume that the richness and variety of peer play and games, for example, will be readily available in the child's normal environment.

The Children.   Traditionally, the children in the Bereiter-Engelmann programs came from very deprived homes and they were eligible for Head Start programs. Subsequently, DISTAR methods have been adopted in some elementary schools in both Canada and the United States, and they serve children from more diverse backgrounds. DISTAR materials are now marketed for special education programs for children with language delays and disabilities, cognitive delays, and learning disabilities. These latter children come from a broad range of cultures, and socio-economic and ethnic groups.

The Teachers.   Bereiter and Engelmann (1966) suggest that elementary school teachers are more suited to teach in this model than teachers trained to work with young children. They comment on the training of early childhood educators:

[It] has provided them with a deeply ingrained bias against "forcing" the child in any way; the intensive preschool is premised on "forcing" the child. (P. 69)

Reflective Exercise 3-2

As a student in early childhood education, what do you think about Bereiter and Engelmann's comments on ECE professionals? What is your opinion of "forcing the child"? What happens if someone tries to force you to do something? Does forcing anyone ever really work? And, finally, what do you think David Elkind would say about the above quote?

The Parents. Traditionally, parents were not involved in the DISTAR model. However, in some of the special education applications of DISTAR methods, parents are asked to do supplementary work at home.

The Schedule. The daily schedule revolves around three fast-paced, no-nonsense, intensive 20-minute lessons in language, math, and reading, each involving five children and one teacher. These small group periods are interspersed with functional times for eating and toileting and a 15-to-20-minute music period. Music is also a direct instruction activity because it is used to reinforce language. Three teachers work with the children, each teaching one of the three subjects to each of the three groups of children.

The Materials. As noted above, there are few materials available to the children in a DISTAR program. Bereiter and Engelmann (1966) maintain that:

Sterilizing the environment is a firm requirement of the work-oriented preschool. Toys should be limited. … Paper, crayons, and chalk (but no paint) should be available. … Motor toys … are not necessary. (P. 72)

The materials that are available reinforce concepts learned in lessons. There are no housekeeping areas, no block areas, no creative art areas, and no practical life activities in this model. It is assumed that the richness and variety of peer play and games, for example, will be readily available in the child's normal environment. (One might question that assumption, however, given that the children are disadvantaged and their development is known to lag behind that of their middle-class age-peers.)

The Curriculum. The centre of this highly structured preschool curriculum is daily lessons conveyed through a direct instruction approach. The teacher presents carefully planned lessons, drills, and exercises designed to meet very specific goals. As noted above, these lessons are offered in just three academic areas—

language, math, and reading. Precise teacher questions that require specific verbal answers from the children are presented in careful sequence.

The teacher's enthusiasm is important in implementing this approach. Each lesson is designed to help the children master specific skills related to program goals. For example, language goals related to the use of plurals might be stressed one day in a language lesson, while the use of complete sentences, if-then statements, affirmative and negative statements, and polar opposites (big/little, up/down) would be covered in later lessons. Other topics in this prescribed curriculum include colour recognition and naming, counting to 20, recognition of letters, ability to rhyme, and development of a sight-reading vocabulary. Constant reinforcement, in the form of both praise and food, is used to motivate and encourage the children.

● The Reggio Emilia Model

In Chapter 2, we had the briefest of looks at the model that has emerged in Reggio Emilia when we discussed Loris Malaguzzi. You may recall that Reggio Emilia is a city in Italy where, over 25 years ago, the community began to establish a publicly funded system of early childhood education programs. The roots of the "Reggio approach" can be traced to the late Loris Malaguzzi, whose vision and guidance gave rise to these outstanding early childhood centres. Malaguzzi, in turn, drew upon the works of Dewey, Piaget, and Vygotsky. The centres established in Reggio Emilia serve children from 3 months to 6 years.

In the past decade, North Americans have become as intrigued with the "Reggio approach" as they were with Montessori's program in the second decade of the century. The exhibit of art and projects from Reggio, "The Hundred Languages of Children," has toured Canada and the United States since the late 1980s (Gandini, 1997b), and typically leaves most North American educators in awe. Lillian Katz (1997), an eminent early childhood educator, commented on how, over two decades, she had visited model early childhood programs in the United States, Australia, New Zealand, Germany, and many of the Open Schools in the United Kingdom, "but never [had] I seen provisions for young children as inspiring as those observed during my eight visits to Reggio Emilia" (p. 104).

The Reggio model draws upon Dewey's ideas about progressive, child-centred education and combines them with Piaget's constructivist approach and Vygotsky's social constructivism. As you know from the previous chapter, the Reggio child is viewed as an active and vital participant in constructing his/her own knowledge. In the Reggio model, the child is seen in relation to both teachers and parents, and relationships are interconnected and reciprocal. Children, parents, and teachers all have rights, and the well-being of one is connected to the well-being of the others.

An excellent resource on the Reggio model is Susan Fraser's (2000) book *Authentic Childhood* (Fraser, 2000). While we will provide an overview of the Reggio model here, students who wish to learn more about it and how it has been implemented in several centres in British Columbia should read *Authentic Childhood*. In addition, there are some excellent Web sites on the subject. The

Reggio Emilia model has been followed in varying degrees in other centres such as Loyalist College in Belleville, Ontario, and the St. Catharines Cooperative Child Care Centre in Ontario. In the A Canadian Professional Speaks Out box here, Alex Doherty describes the birth of the Reggio Emilia approach.

The Environment.   The physical space in Reggio Emilia is used to promote an inviting, esthetically pleasing, comfortable environment in which both human relationships and learning are central. The setting, full of children's work, conveys the close relationship of the children and teachers. Space is used in a manner designed to encourage communication and nurture relationships. Arrangements allow for places in which a child can work with a few children, a larger group of children, a teacher, or alone. Equipment, materials, and activities are arranged to invite exploration, discovery, and problem solving, and to offer many choices.

A Canadian Professional Speaks Out

THE BIRTH OF THE REGGIO EMILIA APPROACH

Alex Doherty, Director, Loyalist College Child Care Centre

The town of Reggio Emilia, in northern Italy, is located on an ancient Roman road, and the region is known mainly for its agriculture, cheeses, wines, and schools. The area was devastated in World War II. In the postwar period, women wanted to help rebuild the area after years under a fascist dictatorship and the devastation of World War II. An organized group, the Union of Italian Women (UDI), provided child care for working women, and empowered the women of Emilia Romagna, the region where Reggio Emilia lies, to declare the rights of young children and the rights of women. Almost as soon as the Germans retreated from Reggio Emilia at the end of the war, the women of Villa Cella, a borough of Reggio, decided to build a school from rubble. Parents and children gathered stones and sand from the river to make bricks, and they hauled wood from abandoned buildings. A young teacher named Loris Malaguzzi heard about the 1946 construction of this school on the outskirts of Reggio, and rode his bicycle there to take a look at the work in progress. In later years, he commented (Malaguzzi in Edwards, Gandini, & Forman, 1998, p. 42):

> ... the people had gotten together and had decided that the money to begin the construction would come from the sale of an abandoned war tank, a few trucks and some horses left behind by the retreating Germans.

When Malaguzzi told them he was a teacher, the people replied: "if that is, come and work with us." In Malaguzzi's words (in Edwards, Gandini, & Forman,

1998, p. 42), "it all seemed unbelievable: an idea, the school, the inventory consisting of a tank, a few trucks, and horses." The women assured him that they would build a school on their own, working at night and on Sundays. They had land donated by a farmer; bricks and beams could be salvaged from bombed buildings; sand was available in the river; work would be donated by all. Malaguzzi questioned them about money to run the school, and after a moment of hesitation, they replied "we will find it." Malaguzzi commented: "Women, men and young people—all farmers and workers, all special people who survived a hundred horrors—were dead serious" (Malaguzzi in Edwards, Gandini, & Forman, 1998, p. 42).

The school and the collaboration had begun—Villa Cella was the first of many schools formed in various parts of the town. Some were on the outskirts and some were in the poorest sections, but all were created and run by parents. In a short time, seven more schools joined the "school of the tank"; although a few early schools did not survive, most had the courage and strength to continue and prosper for many years. Even though there was little funding at any level for them, the perseverance of the parents and a high commitment level of the teachers sustained these preprimary schools.

The system of schools that began with women selling an abandoned army tank, several trucks, and a few horses went on to become perhaps one of the best-known early childhood programs in the 20th century. By 1997, the municipality of Reggio Emilia was operating 19 preschools or "scule dell infanzia," and 13 "nidi," or infant-toddler centres. The first foreign interest in Reggio schools was shown by delegations of visitors from Cuba, Bulgaria, Japan, Spain, Switzerland, and France. An intensive relationship with Swedish educators and researchers began in 1979, and an exhibit from the Reggio schools that had been shown municipally the previous year was sent to the Modern Museum in Stockholm. This exhibit, organized as a documentation of the children's work in Reggio Emilia schools, was received with great success. It was subsequently updated and now has toured the world as "The Hundred Languages of Children" in honour of a poem written by Malaguzzi. The exhibit has invited international exchange, and every year increasing numbers of people and educators from all over the world begin a relationship with the principles of Reggio Emilia from both the exhibit and annual delegations to the municipal schools. International awareness of the Reggio schools exploded in 1991, when they were identified by *Newsweek* magazine as among the best preschools in the world, and the Diana School in Reggio Emilia was identified as the best of all in the world. Since 1991, the interest from North America has become more intense, and yearly delegations to Reggio and collaborative interchanges with their schools are numerous. In September of 1994, we at the Loyalist College Centre for Early Childhood Education began our journey to develop the Reggio approach in a Canadian context—a program that you now know developed from the sale of one old tank and a few used horses and trucks!

Perhaps the atelier and the piazza would be the most striking elements of the environment for a North American. The atelier is just what the French word describes—an artist's studio or workshop. The *atelierista* is the art teacher responsible for the arts in the school.

The piazza is a central greeting and meeting place that facilitates encounters. It is close to the entrance of the school so parents will be encouraged to visit. The use of light, mirrors, exhibits, and natural materials also strikes North Americans—they find the visual aspects of the program stunningly beautiful, unlike what they have ever seen in an early childhood setting. The environment is designed to foster communication, interaction, and relationships as well as discovery, problem solving, and choices. Each centre is personal and family-oriented.

The atelier is used to document the children's work; transcripts of their discussions, photographs of their activities and representations of their projects are carefully arranged to document the process of learning in relation to various projects. These displays provide deeper insights to children, as they view and review their work and the work of their peers, and to teachers and parents, as they consider the process of learning of the children through these projects.

The Curriculum. Projects, in fact, are the central project around which Reggio Emilia's curriculum revolves. The project approach allows children, usually in small groups, to explore a concept or topic in depth. Projects can be short- or long-term, often lasting well over a month. Because there is no set schedule in Reggio Emilia's schools, children can work at a leisurely pace because they are under no time constraints in carrying out their projects. Often the representations of learning in projects are expressed in artwork; but, as Forman (1993) points out, children move from learning to draw to drawing to learn. Art is a vehicle through which children explore the properties of the concept or topic under study.

The subject or theme of projects can emerge from questions asked by children, ideas proposed by children or teachers, or everyday experiences. Thus, there is no preplanned curriculum beyond the general goals set by the teachers. Projects can revolve around most any topic, ranging from shadows, reflections, caves, and the city when it rains.

Forman cites an example of a project, in which children studied a pervasive feature of their community environment during spring—poppy fields. Children begin by drawing the subject, to start thinking about what poppies are like. Teachers and children communicate: they ask questions, examine each other's work, and consider the various aspects of life in a poppy field. After several days of discussing, drawing, and considering questions, there is a trip to a poppy field. The children have been immersed in poppies for several days now, and are ready to observe, compare, and ponder some of the questions they have asked. The earlier activity has prepared the children to learn about poppies in greater depth now. When they return to the classroom and again draw poppies, their creations are much more accurate and dynamic. They are, after all, based on careful redefinition of the subject or assimilation of new information. Immersion in a topic and a time frame for each project set by the interests of the children, not by the adults, allows for much greater depth of learning.

Tendig is not tally
is pricty & discovery

Another quite famous example of a project completed in a Reggio Emilia centre is *An Amusement Park for Birds* (Forman & Gandini, 1994) which is available in a video from Performanetics (19 The Hollow, Amherst, MA 01002, Fax (413) 253-0898). This project grew out of the children's interest in birds visiting the playground. During one spring, the children built a water source, a bird house, and an observatory for the birds (Gandini, 1997b). The following year, the teachers, the atelierista, and the pedagogista, an educator who specializes in teaching methods, asked the same children what they remembered from the previous year—lengthy discussions ensued and the children wanted to repair the previous year's constructions. Then one child suggested that they build an amusement park for the birds on the playground. In addition to the excellent videotape on this project, one that allows you to see a complex project unfolding, Fraser (2000, pp. 2–3) provides a rich description of the project if you are unable to see the video. The amusement park that ultimately was built had many wondrous things like waterwheels and fountains built by the children for the birds. The community also became involved: the local government provided a water supply to the meadow so the lake, fountains, and waterwheels the children built would work. Local volunteers helped place birdhouses at a height that would attract birds and parents provided many supplies. The mayor came to open the park and many community residents responded to the invitation in the local paper requesting the whole community to come to the grand opening. A fountain-shaped cake was served, and the event was a great success. — *leeng through others*

The Children. Children range from 4 months to 6 years of age. Infants and toddlers up to 3 years of age are in one setting, while 3-to-6-year-olds are grouped in another setting (Gandini, 1997a). All children stay with the same teacher and peer group for three years (0–3, 3–6). Children learn through peer exchange, negotiation, and dynamic communication.

The Teachers. Gandini (1997a, 1997b) has described the teachers in Reggio Emilia. Teachers always work in pairs so cooperation and collaboration between these pairs is the backbone of the Reggio system. Teachers act as resources for the children and learning partners with them when projects are under way. Teachers view themselves as researchers gathering information, and are engaged in continual documentation, observation, and discussion. Observation and listening are critically important in this model, and teachers have the role of researching and learning with the children and colleagues through questioning and dialogue. Learning is viewed as a spiral phenomenon, not a linear one, so ideas emerge before plans and preparations are made. Peer support, meetings, and discussions on all issues are critical. Teachers work 36 hours per week: 31 hours are spent in direct contact with children, and 5 hours are devoted to planning, meeting, and documentation time. The Reggio teachers' salaries are lower than those of elementary school teachers in Italy, and low when compared to North American standards. Benefits, however, are quite generous when compared to North American standards.

fours on fauly Dogamh

Reflective Exercise 3-3

In your placements in early childhood centres, how much time have teachers been given for planning? Find a copy of Harms and Clifford's (1998) *Early Childhood Environment Rating Scale—Revised* and review the section on adult needs. Discuss that section in relation to the Reggio Emilia model and several other models in the chapter.

Teachers have access to a pedagogista, who is a resource for teachers, parents, and community members. In addition, there is a psychologist who coordinates special education support for all teachers. All of the professionals in the Reggio Emilia centres hold the conviction that by working together they can offer the best experience for children.

In each preschool setting, as you know, there is an atelierista, a teacher trained in the visual arts, who has a special "classroom" or studio used by children and teachers. The atelierista is part of the team like the teachers, and works not just in studio but in the whole school to create the warm, beautiful, inviting team atmosphere. In all the Reggio schools, the teachers and the atelieristi work in concert, and this reciprocal relationship strengthens the skills of both groups of professionals (Gandini, 1997b). Art is not a separate subject but an inseparable, integral part of the cognitive/symbolic expression involved in the process of learning.

The Parents.   Parents are seen as an integral part of the program, and participate on the advisory committees that run each school (Gandini, 1997b). There is a welcoming atmosphere in every centre and adult-sized comfortable furniture for parents to sit as soon as they enter (Fraser, 2000; New, 1997). Central outdoor piazzas or courtyards are frequent meeting spaces for parents, teachers, and visitors, and several classrooms of children often will congregate there with their teachers (Fraser, 2000; New, 1997). Parent-teacher committee meetings are held at least once a month, and there are frequent meetings between parents and teachers to discuss ideas, child development, and curriculum, and simply to know one another better. Parents have the right to participate actively in the experiences of growth, care, and learning of their children, and parents' participation is encouraged and supported. New (1997, p. 228) notes:

> *Parent education programs in the United States [and Canada] rarely acknowledge the benefits to be gained when mothers and fathers are provided with support* and *treated as experts regarding their own child's development.*

Evening meetings with parents and teachers are well attended, often by community members as well as parents of children in the centres (New, 1997).

The Schedule.   Beyond a scheduled lunch and rest time (Fraser, 2000, p. 11), there is no set schedule of activities for the day in the Reggio Emilia centres, which are open from 8 in the morning until 4 in the afternoon for those not needing care during extended hours in the morning and afternoon (Gandini, 1997a). There is a general schedule that is flexible, which attends to children's sense of time and personal rhythms. A "full day provides sufficient time for being together among friends in a good environment and getting things done with satisfaction" (p. 19). Projects, the backbone of the program, do not start in a prescribed way, but rather evolve from chance events, interests, experiences, and discussions. Projects support learning by doing, and are evolutionary in nature. Questions, hypotheses, team collaboration, preparation, and documentation occur from project conception to completion. There are no restrictions on the amount of time a project might take—days or months are both acceptable.

The Materials.　The atelier contains a wide variety of tools and materials and examples of past projects (Gandini, 1997b). Wire, clay, paints, mirrors, cameras, and many types of paper and colouring tools, for example, are complemented by the atelierista. Videos, photographs, art media, and audio recordings are used for archival purposes and to document the process of learning, to evaluate children's experiences and interactions, to facilitate communication, and to display to the world a love of children and learning.

Research and Evaluation of Program Models

After learning about some of the program models in early childhood education, you are probably wondering if one model is better than another or if it makes any difference. Can you imagine how confusing it must be for parents not in the field to choose between models? The Partnerships box here does address some issues related to helping parents choose between programs. What we will do to help you decide about the strengths and weaknesses of the different models is to present the research on them, and ask: What does the available research tell us about the six models? Is there research on eclectic models that blend models? And are there any long-term follow-up studies—what happens to the preschool graduates in later years? First, however, several cautions are needed. While there have been many attempts to compare the effectiveness of different program models, the results are unfortunately not conclusive. Many variables can affect the outcome of these comparisons, and they have rarely been controlled in the available studies (Clarke-Stewart & Fein, 1983; Johnson, 1993).

To have a *valid* comparison of program models, you could not study, for example, children in existing programs who entered on a first-come, first-served basis; those children almost certainly would differ on a number of dimensions (e.g., family background, age, sex, ethnicity, etc.), other than the program model, and that would make the interpretation of results very difficult. What you would need to do for the study to be valid would be more like a lottery. You would have a list of 4-year-olds from a community, for example, whom you would *randomly* place in the different program models. Of course, that is highly unlikely to happen, as families have preferences about the location and type of program they select. Historically, such preferences and limited research funds have meant that most research on program models has been less than ideal.

Decisions about what to measure when you are comparing models are also difficult and subject to well-founded criticism. For example, if you measured children's achievement in reading and mathematics, you might expect to see the DISTAR model favoured, as it provides direct instruction in those areas. If, on the other hand, you were measuring creativity or social development, you probably would not think DISTAR "graduates" would be favoured in these areas. A more general problem is the difficulty of ensuring that the children in each program model are comparable in every way (e.g., family environment, age, temperament, sex, ethnicity, etc.). To date, there have been very few studies of even a single model that have successfully controlled for these variables, and none that have compared the preceding six models. In fact, much of the research in the field is addressing more fundamental questions, such as "Does early education matter?" and "For how long?" Nevertheless, there is some information available about the effectiveness of the different models and their relative strengths.

Partnerships

WHEN PARENTS ASK FOR ADVICE ABOUT CHOOSING A SCHOOL

When parents look for an early childhood program for their young child, their final decision may be based on a variety of criteria. For some parents struggling to make ends meet, affordability may be the most important consideration. Others may want a program that is convenient, near their home or place of employment. The major concern of some may be that their children be in a clean and safe environment where basic needs are met by caring adults. Other parents may be looking for an early childhood program that will lay the groundwork for later school success.

At some time, you may well be asked for advice by a parent who is trying to select the right school for his or her child. How do you advise a parent who asks, "Where do you think I should enroll Farzin?" It is generally best not to recommend one specific school to a parent because different programs meet different needs. You can, however, help the parent identify priorities to find a program that best meets both the child's and the family's needs. Which criteria are most important and which are not important? Parents may be concerned about cost, location, hours of operation, the credentials of the adults, the school's philosophy, the provision of lunch, and other such matters. Some telephone calls can then help the parent gather this information and develop a list of several potential programs.

Once the parent has some possible schools in mind, encourage her to visit them and spend some time observing. Help the parent identify quality indicators by which to evaluate each program. These should include a careful examination of child-adult interactions, activities, schedule, and the environment. Help the parent discriminate between a program that "looks" good and one that aims to meet the needs of each individual child.

Setting priorities, finding out which programs best fit these priorities, and observing will help parents in their decision-making process. Although such a process is time-consuming, spending a few hours to select the right program can save considerable time later. Such a process can help ensure that the child is in a program that is right for her or him.

● Comparisons of Program Models

While there are no studies that directly compare the six models you have considered, all but the Reggio Emilia model have been compared with some other programs. A bit of familiarity with these limited findings is worthwhile, especially for professionals who are frequently asked for advice on program selection.

Cognitively Oriented Curriculum, DISTAR, and Traditional Nursery School Models.   Weikart and Schweinhart (1993) describe a study that compared the effects of three program models—the DISTAR model, the Cognitively Oriented Curriculum, and the traditional nursery school model. The study is remarkable, not just because of its excellent methods, but also because it followed the children until they were 15 years old. All of the children were from extremely disadvantaged families, and most of them were black. After one year in the program, the IQs of the children in all three program models rose 27 points, from below-average to average. The DISTAR group made slightly greater gains only in the first year.

At age 15, however, the graduates of the programs did differ on self-reported delinquent acts. The DISTAR youths had higher rates of juvenile delinquency than those youths who had been in the other programs. In trying to account for this difference, the authors of this study speculated that children in the teacher-centred DISTAR program did not develop as great a sense of responsibility and initiative as those in the child-centred programs (Schweinhart, Weikart, & Larner, 1986b). Not surprisingly, proponents of the direct instructional approach have questioned these conclusions, and criticized the follow-up study's research procedures (e.g., Bereiter, 1986;

Courtesy of Yes I Can! Nursery School.

Engelmann, 1999; Gersten, 1986). Additional research would be needed to see if this is a persistent finding, but you would have to question the ethical issues involved in such a study in view of the available results.

Montessori, DISTAR, and Traditional Head Start Models.   Several studies, all initiated during the Head Start era, have compared Montessori, DISTAR, and Head Start programs that follow a traditional nursery school program (Chattin-McNichols, 1992; Lazar et al., 1982; Lindauer, 1993). Because these studies were an outgrowth of Head Start, all the children were from low-income homes, many were black, and many of the families had just one parent.

Louise Miller and her colleagues (Miller & Dyer, 1975; Miller & Bizzell, 1984) randomly assigned 4-year-old children to one of the model programs within their neighbourhood. After a year in these programs, children in all of the programs made gains on verbal intelligence scores. The gains of the DISTAR group were the greatest not only on the verbal intelligence scores, but also on a test of receptive language skills and on academic achievement measures. However, once the children entered school, the DISTAR group had the largest decline in IQ scores. By second grade, the Montessori children had the highest IQ, reading, and mathematics scores. Some of these gains were still present in sixth grade, and even in Grade 10. Changes in self-esteem and attitude may be relevant to these findings, but the reason why such gains would be more persistent for Montessori graduates remains a topic for discussion. The same study found that the levels of curiosity and inventiveness of the DISTAR children seemed lower than those of youngsters from the other programs, while the Montessori graduates had high curiosity scores until Grade 2 (Miller & Dyer, 1975; Miller & Bizzell, 1983).

Montessori, DISTAR, and Traditional Nursery School Models.   Dr. Merle Karnes compared 4-year-old lower-class children who attended Montessori, DISTAR, traditional nursery school, and community-integrated programs (Karnes, 1969; Karnes, Shwedel, & Williams, 1983). The community-integrated programs placed children eligible for Head Start funding into middle-class preschools. The 4-year-old DISTAR children made greater gains on mathematics tests after one year than Montessori graduates, and they continued to gain in their early school years. The children in DISTAR and nursery school programs also made greater gains on language measures than children in Montessori programs. However, after a year in grade school, the Montessori children made additional gains on IQ tests, and they were more successful in school, up to their Grade 10 year.

DISTAR and Montessori Models.   Bereiter (1967) studied the academic achievement of 3-to-4-year-old middle-class children in Montessori and DISTAR programs. The DISTAR children made significantly greater gains on reading, spelling, and arithmetic than the Montessori children during the one-year program.

Montessori Programs, Open Model, and Regular Public School.   Banta (1969) compared children from four different preschool/primary school combinations: Montessori preschool/Montessori primary, Montessori preschool/open primary, Head Start preschool/regular primary, and no preschool/regular primary. While there was a trend for the children in the two Montessori combinations to do better on verbal memory tests, the results were not significant. However, both Montessori groups had higher scores on a creativity test than children in the other program combinations.

Open and Formal Models.   Several British studies have compared the development of children in open programs with that of children in structured, teacher-centred, formal programs. Much of the research is observational, and does not focus on test scores. However, Silberman (1970) found that children from the open models did better than children in formal programs on measures of spoken and written language, drawing and painting, attention and memory, "neatness," ingenuity, and breadth and depth of extra-school interests. The general level of reading achievement also rose in Britain as the number of open classes increased.

Observational studies (Evans, 1975) have consistently noted the inventiveness and excellence in the arts in children in open programs. They also have noted high reading and freewriting skills, and similar strengths in mathematics. Nevertheless, these observational studies need to be supplemented with more empirical evidence for the superiority of the open model.

● Evaluations of Individual Models

Montessori Evaluations.   Montessori schools today vary considerably. Many, in fact, are a blend of the Montessori method and elements of traditional early childhood programs. Some studies have shown that Montessori children display greater task persistence and more independence than children from other programs; others report that they score lower on tests of creativity and language development (e.g., Chattin-McNichols, 1981, 1992; Elkind, 1983; Gettman, 1987; Lillard, 1973; Lindauer, 1993; Miezitis, 1972; Simons & Simons, 1986). Generally, there are no strong, consistent differences between children in Montessori programs and those in more traditional ones. However, several longitudinal studies reported above have found differences favouring Montessori graduates that persist into secondary school.

Open Model Evaluations.   There was very little controlled research on the open model, and most of it was observational in nature. Now the British system has changed dramatically as a national curriculum as been introduced. In Britain, like Ontario, mandatory government testing has been introduced so it is likely that the infant schools will become more formal (Curtis, 1994). Children in Britain are tested in the early primary years so the pressure for academic work is likely to find its way to the infant school. Unfortunately, the proponents of the open model do not have research available that supports the model's effectiveness—yet such research might well have led to a brighter future for open education.

Head Start Evaluations.   You have already considered some of the Head Start evaluations that involved comparison studies of different program models. Typically, the research showed that children in the program made gains in IQ and academic achievement scores. However, the so-called Westinghouse report (Cicerelli et al., 1969), a national study of the impact of Head Start, soon dampened the enthusiasm that greeted the early results. Apparently, these gains were short-lived, and disappeared soon after entry into elementary school when control children, who had not attended Head Start, caught up to the program graduates. Many criticisms of the Westinghouse report followed (cf. Lazar et al., 1982), that pointed to the inadequacies of the design, the measures, and the control groups used in the report. One group of critics, who formed the Consortium for Longitudinal Studies in 1975 (Lazar et al., 1982), had been involved in high-quality, research Head Start programs in the 1960s. They decided to pool their results from the 1960s and to conduct a long-term follow-up of the graduates who were between 8 and 18 years of age when the follow-up started.

In 1982, the Consortium for Longitudinal Studies reported (Lazar & Darlington, 1982) that early education programs had lasting effects on low-income children in at least four areas:

1. Children who had attended these programs did better in elementary school, and were less likely to fail a grade or to be placed in special education than matched controls.

2. Children who attended the programs had higher IQs and did better on achievement tests than their controls in their early school years.

3. In 1976, children who attended the programs up to ten years before were more likely than controls to cite their school and work accomplishments as reasons for being proud.

4. Participation in the programs had lasting effects on maternal attitudes. The mothers of program children were prouder of their children's school accomplishments than control mothers, and had higher aspirations for them, even when actual school performance was controlled for.

Of course, these results were welcomed by those who had supported early education, and they have had an ongoing, positive impact on the willingness of governments and foundations to support early childhood education. A more recent study completed by Zigler, Styfco, and Gilman in 1993 examined more than 200 follow-up studies of Head Start children. Like the Consortium, Zigler and his colleagues found that the socio-emotional development of the Head Start candidates benefited from program participation, as did their health status, their nutritional level, and their immunization rates. While the early cognitive gains made by the Head Start children were not maintained, these gains in areas related to physical and socio-emotional well-being may well translate into improvements in overall functioning. In fact, other studies (e.g., Zigler & Muenchow, 1992; Washington & Bailey, 1995) have also shown that fewer Head Start graduates than matched children without Head Start are in special education classes and fewer are institutionalized. Moreover, the Head Start graduates are more likely to attend college, hold jobs, and be productive citizens (e.g., Zigler & Muenchow, 1992; Washington & Bailey, 1995).

Cognitively Oriented Curriculum Evaluations. The Perry Preschool Project, launched by Weikart in 1962 in Ypsilanti, Michigan, followed the Cognitively Oriented Curriculum, and it was one of the studies included in the Consortium's database. As of the summer of 1993, the 123 children in the project have been followed until they were 27, and the results provide unequivocal support for the efficacy of early education (Berrueta-Clement, Schweinhart, Barnett, Epstein, & Weikart, 1984; Schweinhart & Weikart, 1985, 1993; Weikart & Schweinhart, 1993). At 19 years, graduates of the program were significantly better than matched controls in a number of ways. They were more likely to graduate from high school, attend a postsecondary institution, and be self-supporting at age 19. They were less likely to have been classified as mentally impaired, have been arrested, and be on public assistance. In addition, literacy levels were higher in graduates than controls at 19 years of age, and the program graduates spent significantly fewer years in school programs for children with cognitive disabilities.

A series of calculations looked at the initial cost of the preschool versus future money saved because of the reduced need for special education, welfare, and crime, as well as the future taxes the graduates would pay (Weikart & Schweinhart, 1993). Estimates suggest that the investment of $5000 per child per year in the preschool program resulted in a return of $28,000 per graduate to the taxpayers who would pay for special education, criminal justice, and welfare. Hence, the return from a high-quality program like the Cognitively Oriented Curriculum more than justifies the initial cost.

More recent results (Schweinhart & Weikart, 1993) report on the program graduates versus no-program controls at age 27 years, and these data are consistent with earlier findings. Schweinhart and Weikart were still able to find 95 percent of the graduates and matched controls at age 27, which is quite remarkable in itself. A series of interviews with the 27-year-old program graduates and their controls revealed the following statistically significant results:

1. Graduates have higher monthly salaries than controls. About 30 percent of the graduates earn over $2000 a month, but only 7 percent of the no-program controls do.

2. While 71 percent of the graduates completed Grade 12, only 54 percent of the no-program controls did.

3. Between age 17 and 27, 59 percent of the graduates received some type of social service, while 80 percent of the no-program controls did.

4. By age 27, 35 percent of the no-program controls had five or more arrests, while only 7 percent of the graduates did.

DISTAR Evaluations.   As you saw above, the DISTAR model has been included in a number of comparative studies that sought to examine the impact of this approach. Initial evaluations typically find that DISTAR children gain more than other children on IQ and achievement test scores. However, those gains decline quickly over the next few years. The only longitudinal data on the DISTAR graduates (Miller & Dyer, 1975; Weikart & Schweinhart, 1993), discussed in the section on comparisons between models, raised three concerns about them: (1) their greater drop in scores upon entry to public school, (2) their higher rate of adolescent delinquency, and (3) their lower curiosity and inventiveness scores. If these results are reliable, it would seem that the graduates pay a fairly high cost for the rapid gains they make on IQ and achievement tests. When these negative results are coupled with the impressive results of the long-term follow-ups on graduates of child-centred programs, it seems likely that programs like DISTAR may induce dependency on the teacher and a need for ongoing external reinforcement. In contrast, the less teacher-centred programs seem to be associated with children who have developed an intrinsic motivation to learn.

Reggio Emilia Model Evaluations.   To date, there has been no controlled research that the authors are aware of on the Reggio Emilia model. The evaluations have been observational in nature. Critics of the model can easily point to the abundant research on direct, formal models, and suggest that those favouring the Reggio model need to document the model's effectiveness.

Reflective Exercise 3-4

The artwork from both open-model and Reggio Emilia programs has drawn much praise worldwide. Compare and contrast the two models. Which features of both programs do you think contribute to the creativity exhibited by the participants? And why do you think the two models have attracted visitors from around the world?

We have explored some different early childhood education models, and we have discussed the research on the effectiveness of these models. Most of this research has been done in U.S. programs that enrolled low-income children, mostly black. Follow-up studies such as these provide evidence that high-quality early childhood intervention programs can and do make a difference. Let us now briefly examine what additional research tells us about the effectiveness of some other programs—some Canadian programs, some eclectic programs, and some programs for low-risk children.

Additional Research on Early Childhood Education

Mary Wright's (1983) UWO preschool was based on preserving "the best in the traditional Ontario preschool program, which had been developed in the 1940s at the University of Toronto's Institute for Child Study" (p. 353), and combining it with aspects of more recent Piagetian programs, such as the Cognitively Oriented Curriculum. Wright's program included both high- and low-income children, but financial constraints resulted in the presence of only the low-income children in the school follow-up study. All children made gains on ability, achievement, and social skill measures when they were in the program, and the gains were greater if they were enrolled for two years. In grade school, the low-income preschool graduates were less likely to fail and less likely to be placed in special education classes relative to matched controls. Moreover, they were viewed as better adjusted by their teachers than matched controls. Finally, there was a tendency for those low-income graduates who had spent two years in the program to do better than those who had only one year in a high-quality program.

Goelman and Pence (1990) have conducted a series of studies in British Columbia. They examined centre-based and family child care, the quality of the child's care at home and in the child care setting, and language development as a function of these variables. In the Victoria study, parents developed higher levels of friendship with family-based caregivers, but they had fewer negative concerns about centre-based care. This is consistent with the higher turnover rates that were found in family-based care. The providers of family child care generally had lower educational levels than centre-based teachers, but they were able to be more flexible about caregiving arrangements. Nevertheless, most of the home-based providers would have preferred to be employed in a different capacity. The unlicensed family homes were more likely to be of low quality than the licensed homes and centres in Victoria. In the low-quality homes, children watched more television than in the higher-quality settings, and their language development lagged behind that of children in licensed homes. However, caregiver training and the mothers' educational levels also were positively related to the language development scores. Moreover, those families with limited resources (e.g., single-parent families and ones with low income, little education, and lower-paying jobs) were more likely to have their children in low-quality, unlicensed settings. The Vancouver study followed the Victoria one, and concentrated on family-based care. Both the child's home and the care home were rated for quality, as were the parents and providers. The children's language was studied in both settings. The analyses confirmed the trends in Victoria. As you might predict, the quality of language and cognitive stimulation in both the child's own home and the care home was related to the child's own language development. The socio-emotional climate of the child's own family was also an important variable; it was directly related to cognitive stimulation in the child's home and the care home, and to language development.

Several studies in the United States that involved more eclectic programs have also added to our knowledge about the effects of early childhood education. For example, adolescents who had participated in the Syracuse University Family Development Research Program (FDRP) during their infant and preschool years were much like those who had participated in the Perry Preschool's Cognitively Oriented Curriculum. Most impressive was the highly significant difference in involvement in the juvenile justice system between these teenagers and a comparable (control) group that had not participated in an early intervention program. Not only had far fewer of the FDRP youngsters been involved in juvenile delinquency, but the severity of the offences, the number of incidents, and the cost of processing were far lower (Honig, 1993; Lally, Mangione, & Honig, 1988).

In addition, early intervention resulted in better school performance and lower absenteeism during adolescence for centre graduates than matched controls, especially for females. The teachers also rated the FDRP girls, relative to controls, as higher in self-esteem and self-control (Lally, Mangione, & Honig, 1988).

Additional studies have provided information on the effects of an early childhood program on middle-class children. Some studies have found that middle-class children in high-quality early childhood programs exhibit greater cognitive, language, and social competence than children without such experience (Clarke-Stewart, 1984; Howes & Olenick, 1986); others, however, have found greater levels of aggressiveness among children with child care experience (Haskins, 1985).

A study of infant day care, conducted in Toronto by William Fowler (1971, 1972, 1973, 1974, 1978; Fowler & Khan, 1974), found that middle-class infants and toddlers made very significant gains on ability measures. In fact, their gains were even greater than those of the lower-class children.

An influential U.S. study (Larsen & Robinson, 1989) followed children from advantaged families, those who had attended a high-quality preschool program, into third grade and compared them with children who had not had a similar early childhood experience. Results showed that, particularly for males, the early childhood program experience seems to be related to higher school achievement scores. Another study (Tietze, 1987), using a sampling of the general elementary school population of one state in Germany, found that children who had attended an early childhood program experienced greater school success than children who had not been in a preschool program (measured by retention and special education placement information).

One interesting variation of such investigations evaluated a sample of middle-class 8-year-olds in a state with minimal child care standards. The researchers (Vandell & Corasaniti, 1990) compared parents' and teachers' ratings of children who had been

Courtesy of Eglinton Public School.

in full-time child care since infancy with those of children who had experienced part-time or no child care. The youngsters with full-time child care histories were considered to have poorer peer relations, work habits, emotional health, and academic performance, and to be more difficult to discipline. The authors contrasted these findings to the positive results found in Sweden for children who had extensive child care histories in high-quality settings.

At this point, you have an overview of the different models and an understanding of the broad issues related to quality. Later in the text, in Chapter 11, we will return to the issue of quality and discuss the issues and additional studies on this all-important variable. Clearly more research can help us better assess the impact of early childhood education on all children, not only those in Canada and the United States. Many factors, including home experience and environment, quality of the program and teachers, and program philosophy, need to be taken into account. All such information will help us to better understand how we contribute to the lives of young children and to maximize their chance of success in the future. This information also can help us assist parents seeking advice on selecting a child care program.

Key Terms

absorbent mind
academic materials
active learning
activities
activity centres
auto-education
Bank Street model
British Infant School
child-centred
classification
Colour Tablets
competency-based program
conceptual materials
daily living
didactic
director
discovery
DISTAR
early childhood education models
eclectic approach
feral children
Golden Beads
in-service

integrated day
isolation of a single quality
key experiences
Malting House School
Movable Alphabet
number concepts
open education
Pink Tower
plan-do-review cycle
planning time
prepared environment
recall time
self-correcting
self-education
sensorial materials
sensory education
sensitive periods
seriation
Sound Boxes
spatial relationships
Tonal Bells
work time

Key Points

Application of Theories in Early Childhood Education

1. A number of human development theories have been applied to early childhood education through specific models.

2. Today there is great variation across Montessori programs. The traditional Montessori environment and materials include some unique features; the role of the teacher and the children's activities differ from those in other types of early childhood program.

3. Open education was developed in Britain and incorporates the ideas of Dewey, Piaget, and Freud. Teachers in the open model use the child's natural curiosity as the starting point for all learning. Open programs are child-centred and encourage discovery learning through activity centres.

4. Project Head Start was launched in 1964 and is the most ambitious, far-reaching early childhood program to date.

5. The Cognitively Oriented Curriculum, based on the theory of Piaget, revolves around activities that help children learn specific cognitive concepts.

6. The Bereiter-Engelmann model, DISTAR, based on behavioural theory, uses a direct instruction approach in which the teacher presents carefully planned lessons in three academic areas.

7. Recently, there is great interest in the early childhood education programs in Reggio Emilia, Italy. The Reggio programs include some unique features such as the atelier and the pedagogista. Theoretically, the program draws on the ideas of Dewey, Piaget, and Vygotsky. Teachers in the Reggio model use the child's natural interests as the starting point for all learning, and the project approach is followed. Projects are documented through the use of many media—paintings, photos, sculptures, and so on.

Research Support for Early Childhood Education

8. Research on early intervention programs have shown that they result in long-term, positive effects and cost benefits. DISTAR graduates usually make the greatest gains initially, but they experience the greatest decline in scores when they enter school.

9. Montessori graduates have retained gains in IQ and mathematics scores through to Grade 10.

10. Children in open programs have high reading and independent writing skills, and excel in the arts relative to children in formal models.

11. Long-term follow-up studies of Head Start and COC graduates show significant benefits that persist into adulthood.

12. The higher delinquency rate of DISTAR graduates remains a source of concern.

13. The UWO project has shown that similar positive changes in IQ and achievement scores, and in measures related to school success, are seen in Canadian children who attend high-quality preschool programs.

14. In Victoria, children in unlicensed family child care homes watched more television and had lower language scores than children in licensed homes.

15. Although there is far less research about the benefits of early childhood programs on middle-class children, some evidence indicates that high-quality programs can have a positive effect. For example, Fowler's Toronto-based study found that middle-class infants and toddlers made greater gains in a high-quality child care centre than their lower-class peers.

Key Questions

1. What are the strengths of the six program models? What are the weaknesses? Which program would you select for your children and why?

2. Visit a program in your community that conforms to one of the six models with a view to sharing your observations with your classmates. Does the program follow the model closely or is it somewhat eclectic? What three features of the program did you like the best?

3. Roopnarine and Johnson (1993) described 14 early childhood education models, including home-based and centre-based ones. The centre-based models could be placed in one of three categories: (1) Montessori models, (2) behavioural models, and (3) interactionist models. Where do the six models you have considered fit in this categorization and why? Which theorists have influenced each model?

4. The chapter discusses the higher delinquency rates of DISTAR graduates versus those in the COC and traditional nursery schools. Bereiter and Engelmann say the finding is unreliable because the original study had a poor technical design. You would have to do additional research to see if this result is reliable (i.e., reproducible). Discuss the ethical issues involved in conducting such a study in view of the available results.

5. In the Victoria study of family child care settings, children in low-quality homes watched more television and had lower language development scores than children in higher-quality homes. The children in low-quality settings also had more troubled, less affluent homes and their parents had less education. To what extent do you think television was a factor in their delayed language development? What other factors contributed to this delay? What recommendations would you make to the parents of the children in low-quality homes?

Chapter 4

Early Childhood Education in Canada

*T*his chapter will focus on the current state of early childhood education in Canada. Using a province-by-province approach, we will explore the following questions:

1. How and when did early childhood education evolve in each province and territory?

2. What regulations cover early childhood programs in each jurisdiction?

After considering the historical roots of ECE and its **regulation** in each province and territory, we will examine the similarities and differences in the **legislation** in these jurisdictions:

3. When was child care first legislated? Are child-teacher ratios specified in the legislation? Are there maximum **group sizes** or **centre sizes**? What are the ratios, group sizes, and facility sizes for (1) infants, (2) toddlers, (3) 3-to-5-year-olds, and (4) school-aged children? What are the space requirements in each jurisdiction?

4. When, if ever, were **teacher training requirements** introduced? What teacher education programs are available? The research, reviewed in Chapter 1, indicated that teachers with specific training in early childhood education and child development provided higher-quality care. Are we responding to this research in Canada?

5. What is the scope of licensed care in Canada? Are there enough licensed facilities to meet parental child care needs?

6. We will end the chapter by discussing recommendations about the role government should play in child care in the 21st century.

As a student in an introductory course, you probably will be most interested in the section on your own province or territory. However, you will probably want to see how the services, legislation, and/or teacher education programs in your area compare with others. Perhaps you plan to enter the profession, or have young children requiring care, or are thinking about relocating after you graduate. If that is the case, you perhaps are interested in learning about practices and alternatives in other parts of the country.

Canadian Child Care in Context: Perspectives from the Provinces and Territories (Pence, 1992), a two-volume work of almost 1000 pages, is an excellent source for information about child care across Canada that you may wish to consult. The publication was one component of the Canadian National Child Care Study (CNCCS). In that study, teams of authors from each province, the Yukon, and the Northwest Territories were asked to compile articles on their province or territory, the history of early childhood education (ECE) there, and current ECE regulations and practices. In addition, information on the scope of licensed child care and parents' child care needs and use was compiled for each province and territory. Those documents are an invaluable resource, but could not be fully covered in most ECE courses. Hence, they will be summarized below.

When the information for this chapter was assembled for the first Canadian edition of the this text, the task was quite challenging, as the World Wide Web was not available. In 1991, most institutions in the country that offer ECE courses willingly responded to the Canadian author's 1991 requests for information about their programs. In addition to their published data (Child Care, 1990), the Child Care Resource and Research Unit at the University of Toronto also shared unpublished data on child care in Canada that were presented in part at the Third National Child Care Conference in May 1993 (Child Care, 1993). Governments from across the country also responded to requests for information about their legislation for ECE programs. Thus, at that time, the collaborative efforts of many ECE professionals across the country and government officials made it possible to assemble this chapter on ECE in Canada and a related document (Young, 1993). A decade later, it is apparent that the Web has indeed made the country smaller when it comes to finding information about legislative practices and educational programs related to early childhood education in Canada. As students in ECE courses in the new millennium, you will be able to have a much broader perspective on the field in this country than virtually all of your predecessors. That perspective may subsequently influence your decision about where to pursue your career either as an ECE professional and/or as a parent of children requiring a high-quality program.

The Roots of ECE and Regulation of the Field

● British Columbia

Ritch and Griffin (1992) provided an overview of British Columbia, the third most populous province in Canada, for the CNCCS. Over half of British Columbia's three million people live in urban centres, and 50 percent of the people are concentrated in the Greater Vancouver area. The province has been ethnically diverse since the Canadian Pacific Railway was built in the 1880s; even in the early 1900s, Vancouver had the largest Chinese community in Canada. In recent years, British Columbia has seen a large influx of immigrants from the Pacific Rim as well as from the rest of Canada. Over 50 percent of the children in Vancouver come from homes where English is not the first language.

Traditionally, British Columbia had a resource-based economy with forestry, fishing, mining, and agriculture being its mainstays. However, the service-based industries now employ 70 percent of the workforce. Average incomes are high in B.C., and it continues to be one of the more affluent provinces.

Historical Overview.   Linda McDonell's 1992 article, *An Historical Overview of Child Care in British Columbia*, provides an excellent summary of developments in early childhood in the province from 1910 to the present. In 1910, the only early childhood facility was the City Crèche, located in a hospital in downtown Vancouver. The crèche was a facility where working mothers could leave their children for the day when they found work as domestics. The crèche closed at the onset of the depression, and nursery schools and private kindergartens did not appear until the 1940s in British Columbia. There were some family day care homes available to working mothers in the interim, mainly in Vancouver, where there was some concern about having high-quality substitute care. World War II led to an increase in day care facilities, but British Columbia did not have enough women working in war-related industries to qualify for federal funds.

The province led the country when it initiated the licensing of child care facilities 1937. By 1939, it had 20 licensed programs. The nursery school movement became visible in the 1940s, as did cooperative preschools, which steadily multiplied. Some private kindergartens also were established. There were 170 licensed programs in British Columbia by 1945, and concern was expressed about the need to establish standards for these facilities. In 1955, the province, responding to mounting pressure, added training requirements to the legislation, and the Faculty of Education at the University of British Columbia began to offer these courses. Trained early childhood educators became the norm in urban areas. However, despite considerable effort to offer courses in rural areas, few teachers in the remote areas of British Columbia were qualified, even in 1975. Training programs became more widely available during the 1970s and the early 1980s, and courses in infant and toddler care also were established.

In 1989, the regulations were revised so that centres could have programs for infants under 18 months of age (Griffin, 1992). Training requirements were also clarified. In addition, the maximum number of hours a child could spend in a centre per day was increased from 10 to 13. A review of the regulations was initiated in 1993 and changes were finalized in 1996 and 1997 (Child Care, 2000).

Regulation.   Early childhood programs in British Columbia are regulated by several different bodies (Child Care Resource and Research Unit, 1990, 1993; Griffin, 1992; McDonell & Griffin, 1992). School-based programs, including kindergartens (now known as Primary I classes), fall under the Ministry of Education. Non-school-based early childhood programs, including child care centres, family day care homes, nursery schools, out-of-school care, drop-in centres, and emergency child care centres, are governed by three ministries (Child Care, 1990; McDonell & Griffin, 1992). The Ministry of Social Development and Economic Security and the Ministry of Health are both involved in regulated child care in the province. The licensing of programs, inspections, certification of teachers, and approval of early childhood training programs all fall to the Ministry of Health.

The 1979 Community Care Facility Act and the British Columbia Child Care Regulations, as amended in 1990, 1996, and 1997, specify requirements for early childhood programs in the province (McDonell & Griffin, 1992; Griffin, 1992). **Teacher-child ratios,** group size, facility size, and teacher qualifications are regulated, but we will leave these issues until later in the chapter when we consider them from a national perspective. The revised regulations also contain an extensive account of appropriate programming for the young child's physical, intellectual, language, social, and emotional development.

● Alberta

The population of Alberta has almost quadrupled from 1921 to the time of the 1986 census, and that growth seems to have occurred primarily in the urban areas (Greenwood-Church & Crozier-Smith, 1992). While over two-thirds of the province's population were in rural settings in the 1930s, 80 percent of the population lived in urban settings in the 1980s (Greenwood-Church & Crozier-Smith, 1992). A large number of European immigrants moved to Alberta prior to World War I, giving the province a long tradition of ethnic diversity. While Alberta's fluctuating oil market has led to waves of immigration and emigration, the province has not experienced the significant increases in foreign immigrants witnessed by British Columbia and Ontario, for example.

Historical Overview.   *An Historical Overview of Child Care in Alberta* (Read, Greenwood-Church, Hautman, Roche, & Bagley, 1992) traces the development of ECE in Alberta until 1988, while Read (1992) discusses developments from 1988 until 1990. Child care has a comparatively brief history in Alberta where it was not generally available until the late 1960s. Until that time the few child care centres that existed were privately owned and received little attention from the government beyond routine fire and health inspections. With the advent of CAP in 1966, and

Alberta's Preventive Social Service Act in the same year, the onus was on the province to provide preventive, rather than custodial services, including child care. The province provided 80 percent of the funding to any municipality that opened a nonprofit child care centre, and the cities of Edmonton and Calgary quickly took advantage of the new funding agreement. Similar growth occurred in smaller urban centres, but the two major cities provided a model for ensuring high-quality programs. However, the municipal centres were primarily for children from low-income and single-parent families. As a consequence, profit-making child care continued to predominate in Alberta, and child care chains and franchises found the province a receptive home.

The first training programs for ECE teachers within the province were not instituted until 1970 when several two-year diploma courses and some extension courses were established. The demand for graduates of these programs increased after 1973 when the province finally agreed to provide funding for kindergarten programs offered by either the school boards or private nonprofit organizations.

Legislation governing child care licensing was not introduced until 1978, and only after the Alberta Association for Young Children (AAYC) had applied consistent pressure on the government to adopt and enforce standards. Interestingly, the standards were lower than those that Edmonton and Calgary had adopted from the Child Welfare League of America in the 1960s, and actually led to a decline in ECE standards, if not quality, in these two cities. Nonetheless, requirements for physical facilities, and child-teacher ratios were stated in the Social Care Facilities Licensing Act (revised in 1994) (Child Care Resource Unit, 1997). Training requirements were not included, however, much to the dismay of the AAYC. Group size requirements were added to the legislation in 1980, and teacher-child ratios were improved.

Inspections of child care facilities in Alberta after the 1978 Licensing Act seemed to be inconsistent and often cursory. Concerns about the inspection procedures and the continued lack of training requirements were expressed by a number of groups and even a commission of inquiry into child welfare during the 1980s. Moreover, the failure of the government to tie financial subsidies for child care centres to the quality of care in those centres was subject to criticism. Making subsidies contingent on strict conformity to the regulations typically is an effective method of ensuring compliance with the legislation. The ongoing barrage of criticism of the government's policies (and lack of policies), led by groups like the AAYC, finally led to the 1990 publication of *Alberta Day Care Reforms* (Alberta, 1990), which described changes implemented in revisions to the Act for 1995. In that document, the province outlined new training requirements. All supervisors of child care facilities to have completed a two-year diploma in ECE, or have equivalent education and experience, by September 1995; by September 1992, one of six teachers in an ECE centre had to have completed a one-year ECE certificate program. In 1994, the ratio changed to one in five, and then in 1995 to one in four. Teachers without those certificates had to complete an orientation course.

Centres that provide care for school-aged children have to be licensed so that they comply with fire, building, and zoning bylaws. However, they still do not have to conform to the teacher-child ratios laid down in the regulations. Kindergartens continue to be optional and many are housed in child care settings.

Regulation.   Because of ECE's recent history in the province, many of the current regulations in Alberta have been discussed above. In 1990, new regulations regarding teacher-child ratios, group size, and teacher qualifications were added to the Social Care Facilities Act (Read, 1992) and it was updated again in 1994 (Child Care, 2000). Teacher-child ratios and group size are not regulated for school-age children. According to the new regulations, the program must meet the children's physical, social, intellectual, creative and emotional needs. The revised requirements for teachers have been discussed above and, especially in view of the research on quality of care and teacher education, these regulations are welcome.

● Saskatchewan

Jean Nykyforuk (1992b) provides an excellent overview of this province in a 1992 article, "A socio-geographic overview of Saskatchewan." The province is vast, but its population is just over a million. While it is seen as a primarily rural province, over 60 percent of the population lived in urban centres by the time of the 1986 census. Like Alberta, Saskatchewan had a large wave of immigrants in the first several decades of the 20th century, and it again experienced growth after World War II. However, since 1987, with the slump in its economy, Saskatchewan has experienced a net loss in population. The province continues to be ethnically diverse, and also includes a large Aboriginal population. The province's economy is still tied to agriculture and mineral production, and manufacturing is secondary. Weather also remains a critical factor for Saskatchewan's well-being. The drought in the late 1980s had a marked effect on the province's economy.

Historical Overview.   Nykyforuk (1992a) also detailed the history of child care for the National Child Care Study in her article "An historical overview of child care in Saskatchewan." World War II did not have an impact on child care in Saskatchewan, as there were too few war-related industries for the province to qualify for the federal government's funding. It was not until the 1960s that a substantial number of women entered the workforce and began to need child care facilities. This growing need for child care, coupled with the financial assistance offered under CAP in 1966, led to a steady increase in the number of unregulated centres. Most were privately owned and operated as business ventures.

In 1969, the province enacted child care legislation, passing the Child Welfare Act. All advertised centres were to be inspected by a social worker who had the authority to close a centre; apparently this provision was not very effective. Several advocacy groups, including the Saskatchewan Day Care Development Committee, the Saskatoon Steering Committee, and the People for Child Care Action, were relentless in pressuring the government for improved legislation, more accessible child care, and larger government grants. In 1974, the government announced its intention to implement a new program and to increase funding.

Finally, in 1975, new regulations were passed, and significantly, they required that all licensed facilities (except those already in existence in 1975) be nonprofit organizations, run by a board that includes more than 50 percent of parent users of the centres. The regulations also included procedures and standards for licensing, requirements for centre size, and details of financing. Training requirements, however, were minimal, consisting of a 42-hour in-service program for centre-based teachers and nothing for family child care providers. Interestingly, nursery schools were exempt from the Act and not regulated by the province. Nykyforuk reports that 97 percent of all facilities were nonprofit by 1987.

A number of difficulties with the parent-board model have occurred, perhaps mainly because the boards did not have business training. In fact, the preschool-cooperative movement has found it necessary to develop training programs, which they offer every year for incoming board members.

The 1980 provincial review of child care services reported a number of difficulties, including the lack of any in-province training programs, other than the 42-hour government course. Both one- and two-year programs in early child development (initially, it was called the Child Care Worker Program) were established in 1981 at the Kelsey Institute in Saskatoon, which followed an outreach system to make programs available across the province through the community colleges.

Advocacy groups were active in Saskatchewan in the 1980s, seeking both expanded services and increased funding for child care. They also successfully lobbied against the Grant Devine government's 1984 intent to allow profit-making child care permissible. A provincial organization, the Saskatchewan Child Care Association (SCCA) was formed in 1988, to express concerns about the profession as well as advocacy issues. Nykyforuk (1992) suggests that the advocacy groups were needed as the government had not been increasing the number of licensed spaces, even though demand was increasing. As a consequence, a number of unlicensed, unregulated facilities sprung up, and the 1975 legislation did not limit the number of children who could be cared for in an unlicensed facility. While the unlicensed centres received no government funding, they also were not subject to the regulations.

In 1990, the Child Care Act was passed, replacing the 1975 regulations (Child Care, 2000; Dill, 1992). Under the new act, profit-making centres can be

Reflective Exercise 4-1

Assume that you have been hired to work in a cooperative preschool. Try to anticipate some difficulties you might encounter with a parent board.

established, but they must have parents on their boards. The legislation also insists that all centres be licensed, and it restricts the number of children who can be cared for in family child care homes whether or not they are licensed (Dill, 1992). In addition, the Act will permit centre-based care for infants. The regulations that accompany the Act now require supervisors of child care centres to have completed a one-year certificate program. Moreover, a wage enhancement policy was implemented in 1996.

In 1997, the province introduced an early childhood program for 3- and 4-year-olds at risk. Usually, these programs are run in conjunction with boards of education, although some are based with community groups.

Regulation. The 1990 regulations noted above introduced new requirements on centre size and group size as well as for the care of infants under 18 months. Nursery schools, however, are still not regulated. The new act requires programs to provide a developmentally appropriate environment. As noted above, supervisors now have to hold a certificate or its equivalent, but teachers only have to be over 16 years and take an orientation course within six months of being hired.

● Manitoba

Manitoba's population of 1,063,015 people in the 1986 census, 75 percent of whom live in urban settings, makes it the fifth most populous province (Stevens, 1992). Stevens (1992) provided an overview of the province for the CNCCS that helped to place child care in Manitoba in context. Manitoba's economy has shifted from total reliance on indigenous resources in the 19th century to dependence on the service industries (Stevens, 1992). Manitobans have a history of ethnic diversity, but they have not experienced significant immigration waves in recent years.

Historical Overview. Friesen, Humphrey, and Brockman (1992b) prepared an article, "An historical overview of child care in Manitoba," for the CNCCS that provided much of the following information on the development of the child care profession, facilities, and policies in Manitoba. Child care has a lengthier history in Manitoba than it does in the other prairie provinces, and can be traced back to the turn of the century when the Mothers' Association started advocating for the children of immigrants in Winnipeg. Several day care centres were established prior to World War I, and crèches sprung up over the years in communities where mothers worked for long shifts and volunteers identified a need for care. Church-based day cares were also involved in founding day nurseries when they perceived a need.

After World War II, child care services continued to evolve, and Friesen et al. (1992b) identify three periods of development that will be outlined below: (1) 1945–1974, (2) 1974–1981, and (3) 1982–present. Between 1945 and 1974, there was a steady increase in the number of child care facilities, and their growth became more marked when federal funds became available under CAP in 1966. Part-day nursery schools that offered enrichment opportunities for more affluent children and compensatory programs for the less fortunate also grew in number from the early 1940s. A laboratory nursery school was established at the University of Manitoba in 1943, during the period when the child study movement was flourishing. Licensing of centres was a municipal responsibility during this time, and the requirements focused on issues of health and safety, rather than curriculum, teacher education, group size, and teacher-child ratios. A series of government studies and briefs submitted to the government pointed up problems with the lack of consistent licensing standards as well as the lack of training programs in the province. A pilot training program was established at Red River Community College in the late 1960s. Then, in 1970, the University of Manitoba began a four-year program in Family Studies, while the University of Winnipeg introduced a three-year degree program in Developmental Studies in 1971. Friesen et al. (1992a) identify the years from 1974 to 1981 as the second period of development of child care services in the province. In 1974, the government began to fund its Child Day Care Program, and in the first year about 1500 spaces were included in this nonprofit program that was available to families eligible for subsidies. This new program apparently had more of a social service orientation than the previous programs, which had a welfare bias. While private centres that been in operation from 1974 through to 1977 were permitted to take subsidized children, up to 50 percent of their capacity, as of 1977, nonprofit spaces and family child care were generally favoured by the government's funding policies.

Licensing and inspections did not become uniform in Manitoba until 1982 when the new government introduced the Community Child Day Care Standards Act and Regulations. The Act also included standards for teacher training, teacher-child ratios, programming, equipment, health and safety, and behaviour management as well as requirements for the physical facility and fire safety. Funding for nonprofit organizations that had a parent-elected board was also outlined in the Act, and capital grants were made available. Teacher-training standards that had to be implemented in full by 1988 led to a rapid increase in the number of teachers who were knowledgeable in the area of child development. Between 1984 and 1988, the number of teachers who had completed a two-year diploma in ECE rose from 17 percent to 62 percent. The availability of funding for substitute teachers while untrained teachers upgraded their training in intensive programs presumably was a significant factor facilitating this rapid change. A competency-based assessment procedure was also introduced for people with experience in the field, but no formal training. Salary enhancement grants (SEG) for eligible nonprofit centres were introduced in 1986, partly in recognition of the educational requirements teachers had to meet, and partly in recognition of the negative effects of low salaries.

During the period from 1982 to 1988, the integration of children with exceptionalities also expanded and funds for the additional teachers required were made available. School-based child care also received capital allowances. In addition, the government demonstrated its interest in child care by working with the federal government to try to develop a comprehensive national system of child care.

The 1988 Manitoba Child Care Task Force demonstrated a continuing interest in the quality child care system the NDP government had begun to implement, and a number of the Task Force's recommendations were adopted. Although SEGs had been increased, teachers staged a one-day walkout from their centres in October 1989 to protest the still-inadequate salaries (Friesen et al., 1992a). The Manitoba Child Care Association, founded in 1974, accepted the government's plan to have a working group study the salary complaints, and in February 1990 the group's recommendations for short-term changes were adopted. SEGs were increased as was funding. Nonprofit workplace child care centres also became eligible for capital grants and a number of groups have taken advantage of the available funding, including the Assiniboia Downs Race Track Child Care Centre discussed in Chapter 1.

A Head Start type of program was also introduced in the late 1990s in Manitoba for 2-to-5-year-olds (Child Care, 2000). In addition, school-based programs are available for 4-year-olds in Winnipeg, but do not conform to the child care legislation.

Regulation.   Non-school-based ECE programs fall under the Ministry of Family Services in Manitoba, and the Community Child Day Care Act and Regulations mentioned above are the relevant pieces of legislation (Child Care, 1990, 1993, 2000; Friesen, 1992; Friesen et al., 1992a). The legislation on group size and teacher-child ratios is extremely strict and perhaps the best in the country, at least for centre-based care. A play-based program is described in the legislation, and, as noted above, teachers must meet training requirements.

● Ontario

Ontario, with close to ten million people, is the most populous province in Canada. Over 80 percent of the population is urban; 90 percent of the residents live in the small area of southern Ontario that makes up less than 10 percent of the province's land mass (Kyle, 1992d). Kyle (1992d) sketched an overview of social and demographic trends in Ontario that will help you place child care in its provincial context. Immigration to Ontario has been steady since World War II, and less than 50 percent of Ontario's population have British ancestors (Kyle, 1992d). In major urban centres like Toronto, as many as 40 percent of children in educational settings may not have English as a first language, and in some neighbourhoods there may not be any children with English as their native tongue (Kyle, 1992d). The needs of immigrant families, coupled with a high percentage of two-working-parent families, has led to a proliferation of early childhood programs: often both parents in immigrant families must work, and the families frequently require language classes.

Ontario also has close to 100,000 Aboriginals, more than any other province. However, Aboriginals constitute only 10 percent of the province's population. Special early childhood programs have been developed to meet the needs of Aboriginal children living on reserves and in some urban centres.

Young (1981) traced the development of ECE in Ontario through to the 1980s, and Irene Kyle (1992b), in her article "An historical overview of child care in Ontario," discussed more recent developments.

ECE has had a long, but fragmented history in Ontario. One of the first *public* kindergartens in North America, if not the first (Morrison, 1991), was established in 1871 in Ontario by Dr. J. L. Hughes (Stapleford, 1976). Dr. Hughes, who provided the impetus for the optional kindergartens, later became interested in child care as a consequence of discussions with Hester How, a public school principal (Stapleford, 1976). How had many pupils in her school who brought their preschool-aged siblings to school because their widowed or deserted mothers were working and unable to care for their children during the day. Hughes suggested the establishment of a crèche to care for these preschoolers, and thus, the crèche, which is now known as Victoria Day Care Services in Toronto, was opened in 1892. Unfortunately, the subsequent history of ECE programs in Ontario has not been marked by the coordinating force of people such as Dr. Hughes.

In 1885, again Ontario established itself as a pioneer in education when it passed legislation making kindergartens for 5-year-olds an integral part of the public school system (Fleming, 1971, vol. 5). However, it was not until after World War II that kindergartens became virtually universal in Ontario schools. Junior kindergartens are a more recent phenomenon in Ontario. In 1943, the first junior kindergarten for 3-to-4-year-old children was established by the Ottawa Public School Board (Young, 1981). Dr. McGregor Easson, the chief inspector of Ottawa public schools at the time, cited the positive effects that British and American nursery schools had on children's development as an explanation for these programs. Four years later, the Toronto Board of Education introduced a junior kindergarten program (Young, 1981) that was made available only to children from deprived environments (Fleming, 1971, vol. 6). Although the 1950 *Report of the Royal Commission on Education in Ontario* recommended that half-day, optional programs for 3- and 4-year-old children be established by the public school boards, the increase in the number of junior kindergarten programs throughout the 1950s was minimal (Young, 1981).

The establishment of ECE programs for children under 5 years of age, including nursery schools and child care centres, was much more sporadic and subject to the political and social pressures of the time than the establishment of kindergartens. Although the number of child care centres increased after the 1892 establishment of the crèche, and peaked during World War I, the 1920 Ontario Mother's Allowance Act, which provided unsupported mothers with sufficient funds to remain at home, resulted in a declining need for child care (Stapleford, 1976). In 1926, however, the St. George's School for Child Study, now the Institute for Child

Study, was established under sponsorship of the Department of Psychology of the University of Toronto with funds from the Laura Spelman Rockefeller Foundation (Fleming, 1971, vol. 5; Northway, 1973; Stapleford, 1976). The introduction of the study of child development at the university seemed to prompt a recognition of the educational aspects of care for children under 5. A number of half-day nursery schools that catered to middle-class children were established in subsequent years, and child care centres began to offer both education and care.

World War II marked a period of significant and rapid change for child care in the province (Stapleford, 1976). Mothers were needed to staff the war-related industries, and thus, the provision of extensive child care services became an urgent matter. A number of child care facilities were opened in response to this demand during the early war years (Stapleford, 1976). Early in 1942, a report of the Welfare Council of Toronto and District indicated that the available child care services were inadequate (Stapleford, 1976). Consequently, the Council pressured the provincial and federal governments to provide appropriate care for the children of employed mothers. By July 1942, the Dominion-Provincial Wartime Day Nursery Agreement, a cost-sharing arrangement, was negotiated, and Ontario established an advisory committee to direct efforts aimed at the rapid provision of day care. A wartime day nursery, which doubled as a demonstration and training centre for teachers, was in operation within two months (Stapleford, 1976). Parents paid fees covering approximately a third of the centre's costs, and the federal and provincial governments shared the remaining expense.

The province established a Day Nursery Branch in the Department of Public Welfare to promote and administer the establishment of additional "day nurseries," as they were called at the time. Dorothy Millichamp, the Assistant Director of the Institute for Child Study, was appointed to head the newly created Day Nursery Branch (Stapleford, 1976). By the end of the war, 20 day nurseries with 1200 children between the ages of 2 and 5 had been established throughout the province. Moreover, an additional 42 child care centres had been established in the public schools for 3000 children ranging from 6 to 14 years (Stapleford, 1976). These facilities for some 4200 children reflected an unusually strong commitment to the full development of each child, especially given the haste with which the centres were conceived and opened (Stapleford, 1976). In large part, the developmental nature of these centres is attributable to the influence that Millichamp and her colleagues at the Institute had on ideas of appropriate day care. However, many of the unsupervised day nurseries that opened during the early war years in response to the demand for child care facilities did not have the same commitment to high-quality care (Stapleford, 1976).

The end of the war marked the termination of federal government support for child care centres in the province. Contrary to popular expectation, the return of the veterans to the workforce did not mean that all the working mothers wanted to return to the home. Consequently, in 1946, the government passed the Day Nurseries Act, and became one of the first jurisdictions in North America to have both licensing and *inspection* of child care centres, and provincial and municipal sharing of the operating costs. By the end of 1947, there were 146 licensed centres in the province including 25 full-day and 139 half-day programs. Growth was slow throughout the 1950s, which is not surprising in view of Bowlby's assertion (discussed in Chapter 2) that short-term separations from the mother were comparable to being placed in a sterile orphanage. Once Bowlby's work was reassessed, confidence in child care grew, and by 1960 there were approximately 360 licensed day nurseries in the province (Stapleford, 1976).

The growth of preschools and child care centres in Ontario during the 1960s and 1970s was particularly rapid. By September 1980, a total of 66,998 children were enrolled in 1400 centre-based facilities licensed under the Day Nurseries Act (Ontario, 1981). Most spaces were for children 3 years and older; only 910 infants under 18 months and 2474 toddlers ranging from 18 to 30 months were in such centres in 1980. Junior kindergartens also multiplied in the 1960s and 1970s, and kindergartens were available in all school boards by the 1970s.

Given the lengthy history of ECE in the province, it is perhaps surprising to find that teacher education continues to be fragmented. Fleming (1971, vol. 5, p. 1), however, comments that Ontario has never been noted for the importance it has placed on the formal preparation of teachers. With the exception of the Institute for Child Study's graduate education and training program for nursery school and child care teachers, there were no facilities for the preparation of preschool teachers prior to the war. The provincially operated demonstration and training child care centre, established in 1942 to meet wartime needs, ceased operation shortly after the expiry of the War Measures Act.

In the years that followed the war, the primary impetus for the establishment of education and training programs for preschool teachers came from the Toronto Nursery Education Association (TNEA) (now the Association for Early Childhood Education, Toronto [AECET]) and subsequently the Nursery Education Association of Ontario (NEAO) (now the Association for Early Childhood Education, Ontario [AECEO]), which were founded in 1946 and 1950 respectively. The first success the Associations had was in persuading the government and Ryerson, now Ryerson Polytechnic University to establish an ECE program. Shortly afterwards the NEAO succeeded in convincing several universities to offer three-part extension courses for preschool teachers (Fleming, 1971, v. 5; Stapleford, 1976). Following successful completion of the first two sessions of these courses, students were given a letter of standing "recommending the holder as a student assistant" (Fleming, 1971, vol. 5, p. 17). Students who demonstrated their competence as teachers in a nursery school or child care setting for a period of a year, and completed the third part of the course, were then eligible to apply for NEAO certification. The NEAO, a voluntary professional organization, had instituted a voluntary system of certification to regulate the competence of the members of the profession. NEAO certification provided prospective employers with an effective means of identifying competent staff.

Since 1960, there have been a number of significant developments in terms of the availability of teacher education and training programs for early childhood educators in the province. In 1965, when the Ontario Colleges of Applied Arts and Technology were proposed, the NEAO saw them as educational institutions that

Courtesy of George Brown College.

could meet the growing demand for competent early childhood educators to staff the rapidly increasing number of child care centres and preschools in the province (Young, 1981). Early in 1966, NEAO representatives and Department of Education personnel began to prepare a series of guidelines for the development of ECE programs in the Colleges. In September of the same year, the first program opened at Centennial College and attracted far more applicants than enrollment capacity would allow. In 1967, an additional eight colleges that offered the ECE program were opened, and all had a capacity enrollment that year.

Despite the availability of trained teachers, the government continued to see child care as a welfare service, and professionals in the field grew more vocal. In the early 1980s, the Ontario Federation of Labour organized a child care conference, which led to the establishment of the Ontario Coalition for Better Day Care (now Child Care). The Coalition was very active in the 1980s, and eventually the Conservative government, in a pre-election package, announced a program that would increase funding and child care spaces. The defeat of that government in 1985 was followed by a Liberal/NDP coalition, then a Liberal majority in 1987, and then a surprise NDP government in 1990. These frequent changes in government have meant that some policies developed by one party were later questioned and implementation was delayed by another party. Nonetheless, there were some significant developments in this period.

The Liberal/NDP coalition developed a child care plan that became a reality in 1987 when New Directions for Child Care (1987, April 28) was included in the new government's Throne speech. This policy injected over 165 million provincial dollars into child care, and, clearly recognized it as a public service rather than a welfare benefit. School-aged programs were made a priority, and capital funding for child care centres in all new schools became available. Direct operating grants (DOGs) were given to all nonprofit centres in 1988 in an effort to improve teacher salaries, and later, 50 percent of the DOGs was given to profit-making centres.

Concerns about the quality of care, especially in profit-making centres, emerged during this period. A series of articles in the *Globe and Mail* (McIntosh & Rauhala, 1989) and the Provincial Auditor's Report in the same year pointed up inadequate enforcement of the regulations across the province, and subsequent Ministry initiatives have tried to rectify this situation. A shortage of trained teachers, due primarily to the rapid turnover of underpaid teachers in the field, is a continuing concern.

In 1990, funding for full-day kindergartens became available, and school boards were given a 1994 deadline for implementing junior kindergarten programs. Some large school boards, such as the Peel Board of Education, hastily established junior kindergartens after the announced deadline. They were just as hasty to terminate them when cuts in provincial funding for education were announced, and the impoverished Ontario government revoked its 1994 deadline.

In recent years, the Tory government commissioned the acclaimed *Early Years Study* by the Hon. Margaret McCain and Dr. Fraser Mustard (1999). This report documented the importance of the early years for brain growth and development, and showed a need for high-quality, accessible, and regulated child care. Although this led many to expect a massive cash influx into child care, this has not occurred. In Michelle Landsberg's (May 19, 2001) words, "In Ontario … [the] government has still got its thumb in its mouth as it toddles along, pulling its metaphorical 'little red wagon.'"

Regulation.   The legislation for Ontario has been outlined by Kyle (1992c, 1992d) and the Child Care Resource and Research Unit (2000). Two ministries are involved in early childhood education. School-based programs, including junior and senior kindergartens, are regulated by the Ministry of Education. However, child care centres housed in schools and all non-school-based child care settings, including nursery schools and parent-child resource centres, are regulated by the Ministry of Community and Social Services (COMSOC). The Day Nurseries Act and Ontario Regulation 262 specify requirements for centre-based and family child care in Ontario. The legislation outlines minimum requirements for the physical setting, teacher qualifications, teacher-child ratios, group size, nutrition, and safety in licensed facilities. The legislation also specifies that centres must provide appropriate programs that enhance motor skills, language, and cognitive and socio-emotional development.

The Education Act does not have comparable requirements regarding group size, teacher-child ratios, and indoor and outdoor space, nor do teachers have to have a background in ECE. As in Winnipeg, this leads to some serious discrepancies in the program requirements for 4- and 5-year-old children in the province. For example, a 4-year-old in a junior kindergarten may be in a class of 25 children with a teacher who has minimal experience with children of this age, while a 4-year-old in a child care centre would not be in a class with more than 16 children and two teachers, at least one of whom has studied young children in depth.

● Quebec

Carrière's (1992) article "A socio-geographic overview of Quebec" provides an overview of this distinct province in which more than 90 percent of its 6.5 million inhabitants are of French origin. While Quebec is the largest province physically, most of its population lives in the St. Lawrence Valley and 80 percent were in urban centres during the 1986 census. While pulp and paper production, mining, and hydroelectric power generation remain factors in the economy, manufacturing and the service sector have become major forces in Quebec. The province continues to be a destination for a number of immigrants, especially those from Asia, Central and South America, and the Caribbean. In the past five years, it also has become the Canadian leader in making quality child care accessible.

Historical Overview.   Desjardins (1992) provides a detailed account of the lengthy history of child care in Quebec, which dates back to the first half of the 19th century. Families moving into the cities to find work in new industries led to the creation of facilities to care for their children. As factory work by children under 12 did not become illegal until 1885, parents did not rely on older siblings for child care. Children's shelters, run by the Grey Nuns and the Sisters of Providence, were established in Montreal and some smaller locations as early as 1858. Over 60,000 preschoolers attended these centres between 1858 and 1922, but they in no way came close to meeting the need for child care in the province. Children under 2 years were not permitted to attend the shelters, and typically the eldest girl in a family left school at 10 or 11 to care for the younger children in her family. A labour journalist for *La Presse*, Jean-Baptiste Gagnepetit, campaigned against this practice and day care centres eventually received some government funding in the 1890s.

English-speaking mothers had even more difficulty finding care. Desjardins reports that the Montreal Day Nursery, founded in 1887 by wealthy volunteer women, was the only centre for English children in the 19th century.

Many of the shelters were closed early in the 20th century, while others became orphanages. With the advent of World War I, however, several child care centres were established, but orphanages became the more common form of care for single parents. Apparently, only a tenth of the children in orphanages in Quebec were real orphans. Despite recommendations by the Liberal government that child care facilities and junior kindergartens be funded during the Depression, the Duplessis government firmly refused to assist women who worked outside the home. World War II forced the government to abandon, at least temporarily, its view of working women as immoral, and six centres were opened in Montreal with federal funding. The Catholic Church, a potent force in Quebec society, denounced the child care centres, and most francophone women who worked during the war relied on informal methods of care. Duplessis closed the centres as soon as the war ended despite considerable protest, and unregulated, unsubsidized child care was the norm in the province throughout the 1950s. The city of Montreal had 27 private centres at that time, and a number of them offered a five-day residential program for children with working parents, so they could return to their homes each weekend. The Montreal Day Nursery also continued its service, and several religious groups offered help to needy children.

Despite the advent of CAP in 1966, the Quebec government remained steadfast in its opposition to child care by anyone other than parents, and it was not until the 1970s that any significant changes occurred. Federal government funding came through the Local Initiatives Program (LIP), a federally funded job creation program that provided "startup funds" for many child care programs throughout the country. In addition, the Perspectives Jeunesse or Focus on Youth program, another federally funded job creation program, targeted at youths, led to the creation of around 70 child care centres in Quebec, much to the dismay of the provincial government. When the funding stopped in 1973, occupations of government offices and street protests followed, pressuring Bourassa's Liberal government to develop a child care policy. The Bacon Plan, implemented in 1974, allowed needy children to be subsidized, but favoured for-profit centres as non-profit centres no longer received any public funds. Desjardins notes that 54 of the 70 nonprofit centres had to close for financial reasons several months after the Bacon Plan was implemented.

Pressure on the government to play a role in child care continued throughout the 1970s, and finally, in 1978, the government issued a policy statement on child care. The policy favoured parent choice of services, joint parent-government funding of child care, and additional options such as family child care and school-aged care facilities. In 1979, the government passed the Child Care Services Act and created a new government office, the Office des services de garde à l'enfance (OSGE), that now falls under the Minister for Women's Issues (i.e., Ministre déléguée à la Condition feminine) to deal with children's issues. The OSGE, among other responsibilities, was to ensure that quality child care was available, monitor centres, and improve teacher training.

The Act Respecting Day Care recognized five types of child care: the group child care centre (Garderie), family child care homes (Milieu familial), drop-off centres (Halte garderie), school-aged child care (Milieu scholaire) and nursery schools (Jardins d'enfant). Teacher training, teacher-child ratios, group sizes, and centre sizes were regulated, as were health and safety, equipment, and the physical plant. The Act and its regulations set standards for these facilities that have undergone substantial revisions in recent years, most recently in 1997 and 1998. Currently, an early childhood agency can offer both centre-based and family-based child care, but can have no more than 350 children in total under its care, a restriction that prevents the corporate growth in this field that our neighbours to the south have seen (cf. Chapter 1).

In 1996, in a precedent-setting move, the Quebec government announced that major changes were about to occur in early childhood policy. By 1997, they made regulated centre- and family-based child care accessible to all 4-year-olds for only $5 per day, and introduced full-day kindergarten for all 5-year-olds. It has been extended downwards since then—3-year-olds became eligible for the $5 programs the following year—and now all children under 4 years old are. Thankfully, they have not made this heavily subsidized service available only to working parents—families on social assistance, who often have children most in need of quality experiences, can also access it. Needless to say, this has led to massive expansion of licensed spaces, and an additional 85,000 licensed spaces are to be available in 2001.

Regulation.   The OSGE, a unique institution in Canadian child care, was a semiautonomous body that had the power to set standards and regulations for child care and to ensure the Act and its regulations were followed (Child Care, 1990; Fullum, 1992a, 1992b). It was replaced by the Ministry of Families and Children (MFE) in 1998 (Child Care, 2000), which is responsible for programs for children between 0 and 4 years old. School-aged programs fall under the Ministère de l'Éducation (ME) (Child Care, 2000; Fullum, 1992a, 1992b). Teacher-child ratios and group size are regulated, as is centre size. Teacher qualifications are also specified in the legislation. The MFE specifies that a High/Scope curriculum must be followed.

● New Brunswick

New Brunswick's population of 709,445 in the 1986 census made it the third-smallest province in the country (Gamble, 1992b). Joan Gamble (1992b), an ECE professor at Université de Moncton, prepared "A socio-geographic overview of New Brunswick" for the Canadian National Child Care Study. In the article, she provided an outsider with a picture of the province's economy and people. Almost two-thirds of the New Brunswick population are English-speaking, while a third of the population is French-speaking. The province also has close to 5000 Micmac and Maliseet Indians. The population is evenly split between urban and rural settings. While fishing, logging, trapping, and other resource-based occupations used to be central to the New Brunswick economy, service industries such as tourism, education, and governments are now the chief employers. The province is one of the poorer ones, and many young people have moved away during periods when jobs were plentiful in places like Alberta and Ontario. Women have moved into the workforce in increasing numbers, but the unemployment rate is chronically high.

Historical Overview. Gamble (1992a) also prepared "An historical overview of child care in New Brunswick" for the CNCCS. The history of child care, as we know it, is brief. During the first half of the century, the extended family was responsible for child care in the province. If one could not call on that informal network, the only option was to turn to the child welfare services. Prior to the 1950s, that usually meant allowing one's children to be placed in an orphanage, and those institutions were underfunded and of very questionable quality. Many served both children and adults who needed care. Large institutions for children in New Brunswick remained in existence until the mid-1970s, even though the research showing their negative effects on development had been available since the 1940s.

A number of unregulated child care centres were established in the 1960s and early 1970s in New Brunswick, and professionals in the field were becoming concerned about the quality of care in these centres. The formation of the Garde de Jour NB Day Care Association in 1973 was significant and the Association helped to accelerate changes in child care policies. In September 1974, the government proclaimed the Day Care Act, and teacher-child ratios and health and safety requirements finally became a reality. However, as we have seen in so many other jurisdictions, enforcement of the Act was sporadic, as there was only one supervisor to inspect all centres in the province. More comprehensive regulations were included in the 1980 Child and Family Services and Family Relations Act. The new legislation also differed in tone: child care was seen as a child development service, rather than a welfare issue.

Since 1974, excellent degree programs in education with a specialization in ECE were available at the University of New Brunswick and Université de Moncton, and some of the key experts in the field were graduates of these programs. However, college programs were needed. The Garde de Jour NB Day Care Association and other interested groups persistently urged the government to establish teacher training programs. Finally, several college-based training programs were established in the early 1980s. Subsequently, a competency-based program was developed for teachers with experience, but no formal training, so that they became eligible for an equivalency certificate. Then, in 1987, the Canada Employment Centre agreed to fund teachers in a part-time, formal training program, and many have taken advantage of this opportunity.

A number of significant developments in ECE occurred in the 1990s. For example, full-day kindergartens have become part of the school system, and government-funded early intervention programs became available. "Excellence in Education," a 1992 provincial government report, also recommended significant changes in teacher education.

Although the province still does not have any training regulations, a review of the child care legislation was initiated in 1992 (Child Care, 1993). Subsequently, a working group was established by the government in 1993 (Child Care, 1993), and teacher training, standardization of regulations, and wage enhancement grants were discussed by the group, but no changes occurred. In 2001, the government suggested there would be additional changes in the early childhood field so that it would meet the needs of young children and become more accessible. In addition, language programs for children in need would be introduced. The details of these changes, however, remain vague at this time.

The New Brunswick policy papers can be viewed on the Internet.

Regulation.   Lutes (1992) and Lutes and Gamble (1992) outlined New Brunswick's regulations for the CNCCS, and the Childcare Resource Unit (2000) recently reexamined it. School-based ECE programs fall under the Department of Education in New Brunswick, while non-school-based programs are under the Department of Health and Community Services. The 1980 Family Services and Family Relations Act and the 1983 Regulations 83–85 for the act contain regulations for non-school-based ECE programs. The 1985 Day Care Facilities Standards also apply to these programs. Centre size, teacher-child ratios, and group size are regulated in centre- and family-based ECE programs. The legislation does require centres to provide stimulating, developmentally oriented programs, but there are still no requirements for teachers, other than that they be 16 or older and willing to take training. As of 1993, primary staff had to be 19 and available to supervise staff under that age (Child Care, 1993, 2000).

● Prince Edward Island

Mullen (1992) provides an overview of Prince Edward Island, Canada's smallest but most densely populated province. The 1986 census found that close to 50,000 of the island's almost 130,000 people live in urban settings, while 70,000 live in rural, non-farm settings. The economy of Prince Edward Island has become far more service-based in the past 30 years, and service industries now employ two-thirds of the labour force.

Historical Overview.   Flanagan-Rochon and Rice (1992) documented the history of child care in the province for the CNCCS. Orphanages and informal mechanisms of child care, often involving relatives, were the norm in Prince Edward Island until the late 1960s when unregulated kindergartens developed, especially in the urban areas. Social workers saw these programs as potentially beneficial for disadvantaged children, and soon wanted full-day programs. Some federally funded, unregulated, unlicensed full-day programs were developed for children from impoverished families, and private operators opened centres in urban areas such as Charlottetown.

Significant growth in centre-based child care in Prince Edward Island was not seen until the mid-1970s. Nevertheless, concern mounted about the crowding, inadequate ventilation and lighting, and poor programming that characterized a few available settings in Charlottetown. In 1971, the provincial Department of Social Services assumed responsibility for regulating and funding child care. The province continued to fund several of the Head Start–type programs that had been federally funded until 1971, as well as the University of Prince Edward Island and Charlottetown child care centres. Moreover, they established a two-year ECE program at Holland College. Then, in 1973, Child Care Facilities Act was enacted, but it addressed only basic concerns like health and safety. However, the government initiated discussions about additional regulations with child care centre operators who, in turn, formed the Early Childhood Development Association (ECDA).

The ECDA gained prominence through a variety of public education programs and through ongoing submission of proposals for better regulations and training requirements to the government. They were instrumental in having the government undertake its 1983 *Study of Child Care Services in Prince Edward Island* which led to the introduction of teacher training requirements and other far-reaching revisions to the regulations for the act. The revised regulations were introduced in 1986 and the Child Care Facilities Act and the regulations were revised in 1987. The province, with the assistance of the federal government, funded a part-time program in ECE at Holland College for teachers seeking to upgrade their qualifications. The University of Prince Edward Island also introduced extension courses in ECE. As well, the government issued a long-range policy paper on child care and increased available funding. The Direct Funding Program, announced in 1987 and improved in 1990, not only allocates maintenance funds for centres but also provides operating grants with a portion designated for teachers' salaries (Flanagan-Rochon & Rice, 1992; Flanagan-Rochon, 1992a, 1992b). Consequently, salaries have increased substantially since 1987.

Regulation.   The Ministry of Health and Social Services is responsible for non-school based ECE programs, including kindergarten, in Prince Edward Island, while the Department of Education oversees school-based ECE programs

(Flanagan-Rochon, 1992a, 1992b). The five-member, multidisciplinary Child Care Facilities Board, which, by law, includes two ECDA members, is responsible for licensing and enforcement of the Child Care Facilities Act. The Coordinator of Early Childhood Services, the Assistant Coordinator, and their administrative assistant are resources for the board, and they act as inspectors in the province. They ensure that regulations related to group size, teacher-child ratios, centre size, and teacher training are followed. The curriculum must include group and individual activities, active and quiet play, and developmentally appropriate activities.

In 2000, half-day kindergarten programs were announced. They are being phased in over a three-year period and are play-based.

● Nova Scotia

Canning and Irwin (1992) prepared *A Socio-Geographic Overview of Nova Scotia* for the CNCCS. In 1986, 46 percent of Nova Scotia's 880,000 people lived in rural settings, but a large proportion of them live adjacent to urban areas where they work. Forestry, construction, mining, and fishing remain important in Nova Scotia's economy, but the service sector provides two-thirds of the available jobs. As the *Toronto Star* headline in July of 2001 read, one thing is "Still missing in Atlantic Canada: Wealth." While Nova Scotia may not be the poorest Atlantic province, unemployment rates are typically higher than the national average in Nova Scotia, even if they are lower than in the rest of the Atlantic region. The lack of employment opportunities forces many people to move to central and western Canada during economically bleak times, and this accounts for the relatively slow population growth. While more ethnically diverse than the other Maritime provinces, almost 90 percent of Nova Scotians are of British or French origin.

Historical Overview.   Irwin and Canning (1992b) documented the history of child care in Nova Scotia for the CNCCS. Child care was not regulated until 1967 when the Day Nurseries Act was proclaimed, and CAP funding did not become available until 1972. However, there were child care programs in the province before that time. Several centres were established in Halifax in 1910 for the children of working women, and orphanages became common institutions in the following decades. A centre for underprivileged children that charged ten cents a day for milk and snack was established by the Protestant Orphans' Home in Halifax in 1946, perhaps in an attempt to keep the children from becoming residents of their home. In addition to the child care centres opened by several orphanages, there were some generic Head Start programs, some parent-run programs, and a student-run child care centre operating on a nonprofit basis before licensing became a reality. In addition, some profit-making centres had been founded, sometimes by mothers who could not find adequate child care for their own children. Part-day preschool programs with an educational, rather than custodial, orientation, also were available for those who could afford them.

The 1967 Day Nurseries Act emphasized the importance of the physical environment for licensing, and did not address teacher training or curriculum.

However, a government committee looking at child care in the province just prior to the Act suggested that training programs were needed. The committee also suggested that CAP assistance be available only if children were in nonprofit centres, and that was adopted as policy. Part-time summer and evening ECE courses, organized by professionals in the field, were offered as early as 1968, and the program has continued since then, both with and without provincial funding. A Child Study option was established in Dalhousie University's Faculty of Education in 1970, and soon after, Mount St. Vincent University began a one-year diploma program in ECE and then a four-year degree program. The Nova Scotia Teachers' college also offers a two-year diploma course in child development through its Froebel Institute.

A number of child care centres were established in the early 1970s with the federal funding that was available through the Local Initiatives Program. Citizens involved in these centres pressured the province to continue funding these centres when LIP ended, and eventually received limited assistance. While additional assistance was offered in 1974 by the newly elected Liberals, they soon put a freeze on subsidized places that remained in effect until 1989. Centres were permitted to extra-bill on several occasions between 1975 and 1979 to keep solvent, and this led to an outcry about the lack of support for child care in the province. A task force was appointed in 1979 to look at financing, and improved funding, including yearly increments to the available subsidies, became a reality. Subsequently, a 1983 task force made far-reaching recommendations about teacher training, funding, infant care, and ECE-trained government employees. The teacher training recommendations, which required two-thirds of centre teachers to have ECE training by 1989, were accepted. Many of the other recommendations were accepted in principle, subject to the availability of federal approval of a cost-sharing plan. However, the federal approval did not materialize, and issues such as separate infant care standards and subsidies continue to be discussed. Nonetheless, the recommendations from government continued through the following years and the advocacy groups extracted firm promises only from the losing parties in the 1988 election.

Rural areas remained under-serviced, subsidized spaces remained frozen, teachers remained underpaid, and protest grew. Finally, in March 1990, 80 percent of the province's nonprofit centres closed. Teachers filled the legislative gallery, and the media focused on parental and community support for their demands for increased wages and better funding (Irwin & Canning, 1992a). Salary-enhancement grants were announced within days and the government created a Round Table on Day Care that was to review salaries, legislation, training, certification, and involvement of the private sector in child care by 1991. The Round Table released its interim report in April 1991, and 100 new subsidized spaces, fewer than were recommended, were created in 1992. The Round Table has become a permanent advisory council and continues to meet regularly.

On March 5, 2001, the Halifax *Chronicle-Herald* reported that the Nova Scotia announced $66 million in new spending on child care facilities and child development resources for infants and toddlers. In 2001, $6 million will be spent this year to provide additional training for child care workers and to improve their salaries. Given that Nova Scotia's 1500 child care workers earn an average $17,391 a year (Halifax *Chronicle-Herald*, March 5, 2001), the government recognized that recruitment and retention difficulties were related to the poor salaries. New non-profit child care centres also will benefit from the $66 million and be set up across the province.

Regulation.   The Day Care Services Section of the Department of Community Services is responsible for child care in Nova Scotia (Canning, Irwin, & Lewis, 1992; Irwin & Canning, 1992a). All facilities with four or more children are required to have licenses. The 1978 Day Care Act and Regulations, amended in 1984 and 1987, outlines requirements for licensed, non-school-based centres. Centre size, teacher-child ratios, and group size are regulated for most ages. Two-thirds of the teachers in a centre must have ECE training or the equivalent combination of experience and courses for those teachers working in centres prior to the change in the Act. The Act specifies that the program must be designed to stimulate development, and the 1990 *Guidelines for Operating a Day Care Facility for Children in Nova Scotia* note that a variety of models, including Montessori, the Cognitively Oriented Curriculum, and thematic approaches, are acceptable. New regulations are expected soon that will affect teacher qualifications and teacher-child ratios in centres as well as family child care (Child Care, 2000).

● Newfoundland and Labrador

Marc Glassman (1992a, 1992b) provided an overview of Newfoundland and Labrador's sociogeographic features for the CNCCS, and traced the history of child care in that context. In the 1986 census, 60 percent of the province's 568,349 people were found to be in urban areas. Only 2 percent of Newfoundland and Labrador's population have non-British, non-French origins. A small percentage of the population is Aboriginal, although the government has relocated Inuit communities in Labrador because of hydroelectric developments. Fishing, mining, logging, and their related industries remain important in the province's economy, and while the service sector accounts for a larger portion of the economy, it, in turn, depends heavily on federal transfer payments and government employment. The ongoing but troubled Hibernia oil fields project and the Churchill Falls hydro-electric project are viewed as possible means of enriching the economy of one of the poorest provinces.

Like the other Atlantic provinces, Newfoundland and Labrador had many people leave during the early 1980s, the boom years in central and western Canada, as employment was difficult to find at home. Newfoundland and Labrador has had the dubious distinction of generally leading the country in unemployment rates, lowest average income, and poverty statistics throughout the 1970s, 1980s, and 1990s.

Historical Overview.   As noted above, Glassman (1992a) has compiled the history of child care in Newfoundland and Labrador. The Day Care and Homemaker Services Act was not passed until 1975 when licensing and regulations for child care were introduced. Moreover, kindergarten was not available across the province until the 1973–74 school year. Several accounts suggest that a group of nuns operated a child care centre at the turn of the century in Renews, and unregulated kindergarten programs were available at least by the mid-1920s. Private preschool and kindergarten programs for fee-paying parents became more plentiful in St. John's between the 1940s and the 1960s, and workplace child care grew in St. John's in the 1960s. Play groups and generic Head Start programs also multiplied in the capital city during the 1960s. In addition, several child care centres and preschools were established in Labrador. It is interesting that the government prohibited care for children under 2 years in any licensed facility as of 1968, even though they did nothing about licensing existing facilities until 1975.

After a review of 1971 census data pointed up the great shortage of child care in Newfoundland and Labrador, the province launched a review committee in 1974. The committee's recommendations led to the enactment of the aforementioned child care act in 1975 and the Day Care and Homemaker Services Regulations in 1976. Although the Act seemed to emphasize the custodial aspects of child care and ignored teacher education, it did bring standards and licensing into being before more affluent provinces, Alberta, for example. Until 1980, subsidies were available only if children were in nonprofit child care, but it was then extended to include up to 50 percent of the spaces in any private child care centre in the province. Centres became more common in the St. John's area, but concerns still remain about the lack of facilities in the rural areas.

The province's Early Childhood Development Association (ECDA), founded in 1971, persisted in asking the government to implement regulations, teacher education programs, and funding policies that would enhance the quality of child care in the province. Many of their recommendations have been accepted, although the waiting period was often extended. As of 1989, supervisors of child care centres must have a one-year ECE certificate and a year of experience, or a two-year diploma or a degree in ECE, or a related degree (e.g., child development) and a year of experience. In addition, one teacher in programs with less than 25 children (two if there are more than 25) must have a year of supervised experience or training. The ECDA convinced Memorial University to offer a nine-course certificate program in ECE in the early 1970s, and it was extended to include a Corner Brook location. In 1980, however, the university

cancelled the program, assuming that what is now Cabot College and the Faculty of Education at Memorial would soon be offering two-year diploma and four-year degree programs in ECE respectively. Finally, in 1983, a year-long certificate program was established with Canada Employment and Immigration funding; the long-awaited two-year diploma program did not come into being until 1986. In 1988, both certificate and diploma programs were established in Corner Brook, some eight years after the university had cancelled the original program, fearing redundancy.

The issue of junior kindergarten was raised several times during the 1980s, by both teachers and government committees concerned about how unprepared many children are for kindergarten. The teachers were successful in reorganizing kindergarten programs to be more play-based and child-centred, but junior kindergartens are still not a reality in most school boards. Infant care, or the lack of it, also remains a concern; the province still does not permit licensed care for children under 2 years. The Association of Early Childhood Educators of Newfoundland and Labrador, founded in 1989, seems to have replaced the ECDA, and they, along with several child care advocacy groups, aim to ensure that affordable, high-quality child care is available in the province.

Regulation.   The Department of Social Services is responsible for ECE programs in the province, and a four-member Provincial Licensing Board oversees licensing and subsidies (Randell, 1992a, 1992). Nursery schools and preschools in private schools also fall under the Day Care and Homemaker Services Act, which means that ECE programs receive equal treatment lacking in some provinces, such as Ontario. The Department of Education oversees the curriculum in all ECE centres, kindergartens, and primary programs, and is represented on the Licensing Board. A full-time ECE consultant with the Department of Education develops programming standards and may inspect centres to see if they comply with them, at the request of the Licensing Board. The Department of Health is represented on the Licensing Board and is responsible for building, fire, health, and electrical code inspections. Finally, the Department of Career Development and Advanced Studies is responsible for postsecondary ECE programs.

Teacher-child ratios, group size, and centre size are regulated. Minimal teacher qualification requirements were in place for over a decade in a province that saw the first ECE graduates from a provincial institution only in 1988. In 1999, however, revisions to the act increased the requirements for teacher qualifications, introduced group size as a regulated variable, and introduced infant care (see the Government of Newfoundland and Labrador statutes on the Internet). The government recognized the significant impact that group size regulations would have on some operators and it is interesting to read how they will gradually phase in those changes, giving operators time to alter their facilities. If you would like to learn more about it, go to the government Web site and search for child care regulations.

● Yukon Territory

Mauch (1992c) describes this territory in "A Socio-Geographic Overview of the Yukon." Almost 75 percent of the territory's 30,000 residents are likely to live in Whitehorse, Faro, Dawson City, or Watson Lake. There is a large Aboriginal population, of whom the Inuvialuit are the best known. Around 25 percent of the population are native Canadians; in rural settings, they are usually the majority group. Mining and tourism are the major industries, and both are quite susceptible to fluctuations in the economy. Mining and tourism also attract a transient labour force that leaves the territory after earning high wages for a while. Single-parent families are especially common in the Yukon; 30 percent of all preschoolers, for example, live in single-parent families. The birth rate is high, exceeded only by that in the Northwest Territories. Moreover, over 70 percent of working-age females are employed. These characteristics of the Yukon's population have a number of implications for child care.

Historical Overview.   Linda Johnson and Mary Jane Joe (1992) have documented the history of child care in the Yukon and include a fascinating overview of Yukon life before the gold rush that would be good supplementary reading material. Prior to the influx of people that came with the discovery of gold, most Aboriginal and Native peoples led a traditional life, living in small bands and hunting and fishing for an existence. The extended family was a reality, there were few non-Natives, and major urban centres did not exist. The 1896 rush to the Klondike quickly ended the tranquillity. Schools were established in the Yukon with the arrival of non-Native parents, but Natives were excluded from them. In addition, they became foreigners in their own land, the wildlife and resources being disrupted by the newcomers. The rush came to a fairly abrupt halt in 1904, but the practices of the foreigners had become part of life for many in the Yukon. Native children were frequently sent to boarding schools run by missionaries (some of which are currently under investigation because of accusations of abuse), and uprooted from their families, language, and customs. In 1942, with the construction of the Alaska Highway, the population multiplied to almost six times its prewar size with the arrival of construction crews. Wildlife disruption, social disorder, and epidemics of non-Native diseases were pronounced. While growth slowed after the war, the population of 9000 was double what it had been in pre-Highway years, and urban centres started to spring up along the highway, further disrupting traditional ways of life.

Federal funding for schools was provided on the condition that Native children be allowed to attend them, and Native children were slowly integrated into public schools. Nonetheless, many of them were still residential because they were concentrated in larger towns and cities, and racism was a reality for most Native students (and adults) in these urban centres. Kindergartens were not available in the 1960s in the Yukon, but a generic Head Start kindergarten was opened in Whitehorse in 1968 with the aim of more gradually introducing Native children to English and school. The first child care centre opened the same year in Whitehorse. A subsequent boom that accompanied the opening of a zinc mine at Faro led to more demand for child care, and a number of child care centres and preschools opened in the early 1970s. However, there was no legislation, and any government funding for child care programs was on an ad hoc basis. Finally, in 1974, the Yukon child care association (YCCA) was formed, at the government's suggestion, and, in conjunction with the Department of Welfare, they began to draft legislation, arrange for inspections, draft funding policies, and lobby the politicians. While their proposals were ready by 1975, it took five years of persistent work before the government finally adopted the Day Care Act and Regulations. The legislation required centres with more than seven children to be licensed, and it laid down teacher-child ratios and maximum centre sizes. Funding for new centres had not been provided and standards for teachers had not been included, but some form of regulation was welcome.

In 1979, the Yukon attained a fully elected Cabinet and responsible government, and the politicians became more responsive and better able to respond to concerns. This change in governing procedures was associated with a number of improvements for child care in the Yukon, including a new subsidy program and a half-time staff position to help enforce legislation. The election of the NDP government in 1985 led to further changes. Standards were improved in revised legislation, a full-time coordinator for child care services was hired, and funding was increased. Startup grants and improvement funds also became available for group and family child care. Nevertheless, concerns remained. Most children in the Yukon were not in licensed child care and there were only three trained teachers in the territory. Most centres were in Whitehorse, while 50 licensed spaces were all to be found in other communities in 1987. A series of discussion papers followed the flurry of legislation and, in January 1989, the government released its policy paper, "Working Together: A Child Care Strategy for the Yukon." Substantial funds were made available, subsidies were increased, training programs established, and new legislation was promised. The new Child Care Act was passed in 1990.

Regulation.   Mauch (1992a, 1992b) outlined the relevant legislation for the CNCCS, and it was subsequently revised in 1995 (Child Care, 2000). Junior and senior kindergartens fall under the Ministry of Education in the Yukon, as do primary programs. Other ECE programs are under the jurisdiction of the Ministry of Health and Human Resources. In 1995, group size was added to the legislation as were requirements for teacher qualifications, phased in over five years (Childcare, 2000). It also specifies that centres provide experiences for children that will encourage development in all areas, but it does not yet regulate teacher qualifications. In the A Canadian Professional Speaks Out box, Sandra Beckman describes some of the issues related to child care for First Nations that are real concerns in the Yukon.

CHILD CARE ISSUES FOR FIRST NATIONS

Sandra Beckman, Yukon College, Whitehorse

The First Nations people make up one-fifth of the Yukon's population. There are four First Nations band-operated day care centres in the Yukon, as well as a First Nations family day home in an isolated northern community. Caregivers in the rural communities as well as the larger centres understand the need to include language, heritage, values, and learning styles of First Nations people in the day care programs.

At Yukon College, our mission statement mandates all programs to incorporate a native component as an integral part of courses, not just an add-on. The Council for Yukon Indians has developed a day care curriculum manual and curriculum resource guide entitled *Show Us the Way*, which is used in numerous day care centres and family day homes throughout the territory.

In a discussion of First Nations early childhood education, several points must be stressed:

1. A strong emphasis on verbal communication is vital; enriched programming is necessary to prepare First Nations children for our school system and increase success in postsecondary education.

2. There must be accessibility of child care training support for First Nations people wishing to enter the early childhood field. In the Yukon, this means offering courses in the rural communities to enable single parents and/or parents of young children to further their education without leaving their home or family. Yukon College has addressed this need, offering early childhood courses to various rural communities each term. Distance education will enable us to reach even more students.

3. Training for child care workers and administrators must recognize and provide programming for fetal alcohol syndrome and fetal alcohol effects. Agencies providing funding and/or support staff are overburdened, and rural day care centres cannot acquire or afford staff specifically trained in this area.

4. Strong, clear cultural role models are necessary. The caregiver is the most powerful part of the curriculum, providing consistent patterns that value First Nations history and traditions. This is evident in the remote family day home, where the operator provides opportunities for the children to observe meat drying, berry picking, smoking fish, and snaring rabbits.

5. Programming must include involvement from parents, elders, and the extended family. The First Nations day cares are extensions of the community.

(cont'd)

> ## CHILD CARE ISSUES FOR FIRST NATIONS *cont'd*
>
> Children develop a positive sense of identity, which in turn leads to increased self-esteem when they have clear cultural role models and learn how their heritage is related to the present.
>
> 6. Each band-operated day care, as well as the family day home, stresses the need to introduce the traditional language to the children. First Nations children in our child care centres need to be given the tools to adjust to non-native environments, yet should have ample opportunity to preserve and maintain their cultural traditions. The First Nations elders say the seed is the tree, the tree is the forest. Children are like the seeds of a tree. They contain not only the information of the one tree, but hold the potentiality of all the forests.
>
> To the parent(s), elder(s), and caregiver(s), each child is important. Although all children share some common characteristics, they believe each is a special being. It is the responsibility of the extended family, which includes the day care, to help each child reach his or her full potential.

● Northwest Territories

Cairns, Moore, Redshaw, and Wilson have described the sociogeography of the Northwest Territories (1992d), documented the historical roots of child care there (1992b), and reviewed legislation and training programs for the CNCCS (1992a, 1992c). The Territories are a vast expanse of land, and, prior to the sectioning off of Nunavut, the eastern part of the Northwest Territories, it covered four time zones! Still, the original Northwest Territories had a total population of just over 53,000 in 1988. While 25 percent of the people live in Yellowknife, and another 50 percent in the small communities around Great Slave Lake close to Fort Smith, the rest of the population is in very small communities and fluctuating locations. The Aboriginal people, including the Inuit, the Dené, and the Métis, make up 58 percent of the Territories' population. Hunting, trapping, and fishing are important both as sources of food and cash for the Aboriginal people, but municipal, provincial, and federal government positions account for 80 percent of the 18,561 employed people. Mining and oil production also are significant forces in the economy. The cost of living is high, especially in areas north of Yellowknife, where supplies are brought by air once a year.

Historical Overview.   The Dené and Inuit followed a traditional hunting-and-gathering way of life into the 1950s and 1960s, and child care, as we know it, was not an issue. However, moving to communities where their children could attend school has meant an end to that way of life for most of the Aboriginal people. Residential schools, established at the turn of the century, also disrupted life, as many children forgot their native language and some of their traditions and never learned others, such as parenting.

The first child care centres were not established until the 1970s, and government regulation and funding were not firmly in place until 1987. Limited subsidies were available from 1971, but funding centres was not seen as a government concern. Short-term funds, including the federal LIP grants, were often used to set up centres, and parents and communities struggled to keep budgets low and the centres affordable. In one centre, "bare bones" budgeting meant that teachers even brought bones from home to make soup each day! The Pairivik centre in Iqaluit (then Frobisher Bay) was established 1971 by Inuit women who were working and returning to school. The centre was bilingual, and children attended on a drop-in basis, which was consistent with community needs; sometimes they would attend for several months, then leave to visit relatives in another area, and then return for several months again. A similar facility opened in Baker Lake, but received less government funding. Organizations such as the YWCA and companies such as the Nanisivik Mine also opened centres to meet the needs of working parents. A number of centres also were established in the early 1970s with LIP funding in far-ranging locations, including Fort Simpson, Pangnirtung, Inuvik, and Coppermine.

In 1976, the government adopted a subsidy policy, but avoided regulating and licensing policies. In 1980, the policy was changed so that funds were made available to eligible families, rather than centres with eligible children. This revision would make child care services more readily available to families in small communities that did not have centres. While this did allow parents to find family child care homes and babysitters, it led to the closing of the Yellowknife YWCA centre, which had previously received deficit funding. A group of parents took over the centre, which continues to operate. Several private facilities were opened in the early 1980s, and a prekindergarten centre was opened in Fort Norman with funding from the National Native and Drug Abuse Program.

The second national child care conference in Winnipeg in 1982 was a significant event for child care in the Northwest Territories. A number of delegates from the territory attended, and ultimately they formed the N.W.T. Child Care Association (NWTCCA). They were concerned about the lack of regulations, but knew that strict rules would prevent centres from opening in many small communities. They developed voluntary standards for Yellowknife and shared them with small communities. Subsequently, a discussion paper stimulated the government to fund a family child care program in Yellowknife, and eventually to review child care needs as public demand for services was growing in small communities and Yellowknife. Finally, in 1988, the Northwest Territories Child Day Care Act and the Child Day Care Standards Regulations became law (Cairns et al., 1992a, 1992c), and all of Canada had child care legislation. The Act covered licensing, health and safety, teacher-child ratios, nutrition, and space. Teacher education was not covered, as there were no available programs. However, significant progress has been made in this area since 1988.

Since the late 1980s, professionals in the Northwest Territories are emphasizing the development of culturally appropriate child care practices and culturally appropriate teacher education practices for people in that vast expanse. The geography of the Territories poses special problems for inspection and monitoring,

and for professional development as many communities are accessible only by plane. In 1989, the government introduced startup, maintenance, and operating grants for nonprofit centres and homes, and Cairns et al. (1992d) report there were requests for funding for over 400 new spaces.

Regulation.   The Department of Education, Culture, and Employment's Child Day Care Section administers the Northwest Territories Child Day Care Act, and two inspectors are responsible for all licensing and monitoring of group and centre sizes, and teacher-child ratios. Programs are to facilitate development and reflect the ethnic and cultural backgrounds of the children. Currently, teachers are required to be only 19 years of age, and they must supervise any support staff under 19. The children's cultural background also is to be reflected in staffing patterns. In nonprofit programs, parents must compose at least 51 percent of the Board members. Profit-making programs must also specify how they will involve parents.

● Nunavut

The territory of Nunavut was just created in 1999 and was previously part of the Northwest Territories. The land that became Nunavut had been populated by the Inuvialuit for centuries and the new territory was proposed as part of the settlement of their justified land claims for that territory. In order to have legislation in place on April 1, 1999, the day Nunavut came into being, the majority of the N.W.T. statutes were duplicated, although some were specifically created by the Northwest Territories for Nunavut. For this reason, the similarities in the history and regulations of both Nunavut and the Northwest Territories are still quite pronounced.

Current Practices and Future Directions in ECE in Canada

Clearly, there are many differences in the history of early childhood education across Canada. Some of the variations reflect the sociogeographical and political differences that mark the country. For example, the "have not" provinces generally have been slower in to fund programs. However, that is not always the case. Alberta, for example, despite its wealth, was most reluctant to acknowledge ECE as a provincial responsibility. If it were not for the persistent demands of professionals, parents, and other advocates for regulations and training, that province would likely still be without legislation.

In some jurisdictions, early childhood programs have been available for over a century, while they are quite recent developments in others. The provinces with more progressive legislation (e.g., Manitoba) have generally had early childhood programs in place for a long time. This lengthy history generally leads to higher standards for teacher education. In addition, the regulations for early childhood programs differ greatly across jurisdictions, and sometimes even within them. Nevertheless, at least every province and territory now has some form of regulation. Moreover, since the first Canadian edition of this text was published in 1994, there have been very positive changes in a number of jurisdictions. Notwithstanding this progress, students and professionals in the field will have to continue to advocate uniform national standards for early childhood programs.

● Teacher-Child Ratios, Group Size, and Centre Size in Canada

The research on quality in early childhood programs, discussed in the first chapter, showed teacher-child ratios and group size to be important variables in defining high-quality programs. The specific group and centre sizes and the teacher-child ratios for each Canadian jurisdiction are outlined in below. As you know from Chapter 1, legislative definitions of terms such as "infant," "toddler," and "preschooler" vary across the country, but some generalizations are possible. Exhibit 4-1 summarizes the Canadian legislation. As you can see, the legislation does not yet ensure we provide licensed programs with the best ratios, and the most favourable group sizes throughout the country. Group size is still not regulated in Nova Scotia, Nunavut, and the Northwest Territories. The required teacher-child ratios in some locations are also quite low.

The regulations on teacher-child ratios, group size, and centre size are anything but consistent across the country.

Exhibit 4-3 shows the regulations for Canadian toddlers. In some locations, the group size is greater than the recommended size and the teacher-child ratios are not in line with those suggested in the National Statement on Quality Child Care. The teacher-child ratios specified in the regulations for 3-to-5-year-olds (see

---

Reflective Exercise 4-2

In Exhibit 1-5 in Chapter 1, you saw the teacher-child ratios recommended in the National Statement on Quality Child Care (Canadian Child Day Care Federation, 1991). Compare Exhibits 4-2, 4-3, 4-4, and 4-5 with those recommendations. Which jurisdictions are doing best? Where would you be concerned?

EXHIBIT 4-1 *Legislation of Child Care, Coverage of Ratios, and Group Size in the Current Regulations*

Province or Territory	Date of First Legislation	Are Ratios Regulated?	Is Group Size Regulated?
British Columbia	1937	Yes	Yes
Alberta	1978	Yes	Yes
Saskatchewan	1969	Yes	Yes
Manitoba	1982	Yes	Yes
Ontario	1946	Yes	Yes
Quebec	1979	Yes	Yes
New Brunswick	1974	Yes	Yes
Prince Edward Island	1973	Yes	Yes
Nova Scotia	1967	Yes	Yes
Newfoundland and Labrador	1975	Yes	No
Yukon Territory	1975	Yes	No
Nunavut	1999	Yes	No
Northwest Territories	1988	Yes	Yes

SOURCES: Child Care (2000); Young (1993b, 2001).

EXHIBIT 4-2 *Teacher-Child Ratios and Group Size for Centre-Based Care—Breakdown by Province for Infants[1]*

Province or Territory	Ratios for Infants	Group Size	Centre Size
British Columbia	1:4	12	NA
Alberta	2:6[2], 2:8	6[2]–8	80
Saskatchewan	1:3	6	90
Manitoba	1:3[3], 1:4	6[3]–8	70
Ontario	3:10	10	NA
Quebec	1:5	15	80
New Brunswick	1:3	9	60
Prince Edward Island	1:3	6	50
Nova Scotia	1:4	10	60

EXHIBIT 4-2 *cont'd*

Province or Territory	Ratios for Infants	Group Size	Centre Size
Newfoundland	1:3	6	50
Yukon Territory	1:4	8	64
Northwest Territories	1:3[2], 1:4	6[2]–8	NA
Nunavut	1:3[2], 1:4	6[2]–8	NA

[1]In eight of the thirteen provinces and territories, infants are defined as being between 0 and 18 months of age (see Chapter 1 for definition).
[2]Infants under 12 months.
[3]1:3 and group size of 8 if in separate age groups; if group has 12-week-olds through 2-year-olds, the 1:4 and group size of 8 applies.
NA: Not applicable.

SOURCES: Child Care (2000); Young (1993b, 2001).

EXHIBIT 4-3 *Teacher-Child Ratios and Group Size for Centre-Based Care—Breakdown by Province for Toddlers[1]*

Province or Territory	Ratios for Toddlers	Group Size	Centre Size
British Columbia	1:4	12	NA
Alberta	1:4–1:6	8–12	80
Saskatchewan	1:5–1:10	10–20	90
Manitoba	1:4–1:6	8–12	70
Ontario	1:5–1:8	15–16	NA
Yukon Territory	1:6	12	64
Quebec	1:8	30	80
New Brunswick	1:3–1:5	9–10	60
Prince Edward Island	1:3–1:5	6/NA	50
Nova Scotia	1:6	18	60
Newfoundland	1:3–1:5	6–10	50
Northwest Territories	1:4–1:6	8–12	NA
Nunavut	1:4–1:6	8–12	NA

[1]Canadians seem to have difficulty with the term *toddler*; there are three different definitions across nine jurisdictions, and another four avoid the term. We will use the most common definition: toddlers range from 19 to 35 months of age. When there are several entries in a column, it is because that jurisdiction has cut-offs that do not conform to the definitions.

SOURCES: Child Care (1990, 1994, 2000); Young (1993b, 2001).

Exhibit 4-4) are closer to those being advocated in most areas, but the regulated group sizes are not ideal in some provinces. Moreover, group size, which has such a pronounced impact on the quality of care, is still not regulated in all locations.

While we have made great strides in improving the quality of licensed early childhood programs in the country, especially with the advent of CAP in 1966 and the wider availability of licensed child care that accompanied CAP funding, our regulations still have a distance to go. This is especially true now with the cessation of CAP funding and current economical and political stresses placed on the Canadian family, leading to a greater need for quality child care. Advocates for

EXHIBIT 4-4   *Teacher-Child Ratios and Group Size for Centre-Based Care—Breakdown by Province for Children 3 to 5 Years[1]*

Province or Territory	Ratios	Group Size	Centre Size
British Columbia	1:8[2]–1:10	20	NA
Alberta	1:8–1:10	16–20	80
Saskatchewan	1:10	20	90
Manitoba	1:8–1:10	16–20	70
Ontario	1:8	16	NA
Yukon Territory	1:8–1:10	16	64
Quebec	1:8–1:10	30	80
New Brunswick	1:7[3]–1:12	14 >3 yr.; 20 >4 yr.; 24 >5 yr.	60
Prince Edward Island	1:10	NA	50
Nova Scotia	1:8[2]–1:12	NA	60
Newfoundland	1:8	16	50
Northwest Territories	1:8–1:9	16–18	30
Nunavut	1:8–1:9	16–18	30

[1]Some jurisdictions have different requirements for children of the same age, depending on the type of facility they attend. See the notes below for clarification.
[2]The more favourable ratios are for full-day programs.
[3]The 1:7 ratio is for 3-year-olds, while 1:12 is for 4-year-olds.

SOURCES: Child Care (2000); Young (1993b, 2001).

young children across the country continue to express their concern about this failure to provide the optimum environment for young children.

When you study Exhibit 4-5, you will have comparable concerns about the ratios and group sizes for children who are 5 years and older. Similarly, inspection procedures and the regulations related to the physical facility are highly variable across the country. For example, there is wide range of requirements regarding the actual amount of space each child needs. You may wonder why 2.75 m^2 is adequate indoor space in some locations (see Exhibit 4-6), while others need 5 m^2 per child, and the same question applies to outdoor space.

EXHIBIT 4-5 *Teacher-Child Ratios and Group Size for Centre-Based Care—Breakdown by Province for Children 5 Years and Older[1]*

Where	Ratios for Over-5-Year-Olds	Group Size	Centre Size
British Columbia	1:10–1:15[3]	20–25 [3]	NA
Alberta	1:10[2]	20	80
Saskatchewan	1:10–1:15[3]	20–30[3]	90
Manitoba	1:10–1:15[3]	20–30[3]	70
Ontario	1:12–1:15[3]	24–30[3]	NA
Yukon Territory	1:8–1:12[3]	24	64
Quebec	1:15	30	80
New Brunswick	1:12–1:15[3]	24–30[3]	60
Prince Edward Island	1:12–1:15[3]	NA	50
Nova Scotia	1:15	NA	60
Newfoundland	1:12–1:15[4]	24–30[4]	50
Northwest Territories	1:10	20	NA
Nunavut	1:10	20	NA

[1]Some jurisdictions have different requirements for children of the same age, depending on the type of facility they attend. See the notes below for clarification.

[2]There is no legislation for children over 6 years.

[3]The more favourable ratios and group sizes are for full-day programs for 5-year-olds.

[4]The more favourable ratios and group sizes are for children under 84 months, while the others are for 7-to-12-year-olds.

SOURCES: Child Care (2000); Young (1993b, 2001).

EXHIBIT 4-6 *Summary of Space Requirements in Child Care Settings in Canada*

Province or Territory	Indoor Space	Outdoor Space
British Columbia	3.7 m^2	7 m^2
Ontario	5 m^2	5.6 m^2 & fence
Alberta	3 m^2	<19 mos.: 2 m^2 & fence; >19 mos.: 4.5 m^2
Manitoba	3.3 m^2	7 m^2 & fence
Saskatchewan	3.7 m^2: infants; 3.25 m^2	7 m^2
Quebec	2.75 m^2	4 m^2 & fence
New Brunswick	3.25 m^2	Fenced & drained
Nova Scotia	2.75 m^2	5.46 m^2 & fence
Prince Edward Island	3.5 m^2	7 m^2 or park near
Newfoundland and Labrador	3.3 m^2	Drained/Safe/ Approved by Ministry
Nunavut	2.75 m^2	5 m^2
Northwest Territories	2.75 m^2	5 m^2
Yukon	4 m^2	5 m^2, fenced & drained

SOURCE: Young (1993b, 2001).

● Regulation of Teacher Training and Program Availability

The research we discussed in Chapter 1 found that teacher training and knowledge of child development were excellent predictors of high-quality care. However, the Canadian legislation governing child care does not consistently reflect this research finding. Exhibit 4-7 summarizes the regulation of teacher qualifications and the **availability** of training programs in the country, while Exhibit 4-8 shows the types of available training programs, and the legislative requirements for knowledge of child development and experience. By 1989, teacher education programs were in place in all of Canada, but some jurisdictions still do not require teachers to be trained. Furthermore, many do not require knowledge of child development. On the more positive side, individuals in remote locations who rarely had access to educational programs can now study for diplomas and degrees more readily as distance-education programs such as those at Arctic College and Athabasca University are accessible thanks to e-mail and the World Wide Web.

Of course, the regulation of teacher qualifications and the availability of post-secondary educational programs are closely related, as Exhibit 4-7 suggests. In some locations (e.g., B.C., Manitoba, & P.E.I.), changes in legislation seem to have stimulated the provision of ECE training programs on a broader basis. In other locations, Alberta and Quebec, for example, teacher training programs have pre-dated legislation by a number of years. In these latter cases, a lengthy history of governmental reluctance to be involved in child care—if not full opposition to it—seemed to be a factor in the long wait for legislation. In yet other locations such

EXHIBIT 4-7 *Legislation of Teacher Qualifications and Availability of Teacher Training*

Province or Territory	When Was Teacher Training Required?	When Was Teacher Training Available?[1]
British Columbia	1955	1955
Alberta	1995	1970
Saskatchewan	1989	1981
Manitoba	1982	Late 1960s
Ontario	1960	AECEO programs: 1960; college programs: 1967
Quebec	1985	1960s
New Brunswick	—	Early 1980s
Prince Edward Island	1986	1987
Nova Scotia	1989	Early 1970s
Newfoundland	1989	Short-lived program: 1970s; widely available programs: 1986
Yukon Territory	1997	1989
Nunavut	—	1988
Northwest Territories	—	1988

— No "real" requirements in place in 2001.

[1] The founding dates of the few Canadian university-based programs (e.g., Institute for Child Study—1926), founded during the era of the child study movement (see Chapter 1), are not included here.

SOURCE: Young (1993b, 2001).

EXHIBIT 4-8 *Summary of Teacher Education Programs in Canada*

Province/Territory	One- and/or Two-Year Programs	Degrees	Child Development	Experience
British Columbia	Both	Yes	1 teacher per group & supervisor	Supervisor & 1 teacher per group
Alberta	Both	Yes	Supervisor & 1 of 4 teachers	Supervisor & 1 of 4 teachers
Saskatchewan	Both	Yes	Supervisor	Supervisor only
Manitoba	Both	Yes	Supervisor and 2/3 of the staff	Supervisor
Ontario	Two-year only	Yes	1 teacher per group & supervisor	Supervisor & 1 teacher per group
Quebec	Both	Yes	2/3 of the staff	2/3 of the staff
New Brunswick	Both	Yes	None required	None required
Prince Edward Island	Two-year only	No	Supervisor & 1 teacher	Supervisor
Nova Scotia	One-year diploma and post-diploma courses	Yes	Supervisor & 2/3 of the staff	Supervisor & 2/3 of the staff
Newfoundland	Both	Yes	Supervisor (post-1989) and 1 teacher per group	Supervisor
Yukon Territory	Two-year with distance education	Yes	30% of the staff at Level II (1-year); 20% at Level III (2-year)	50% of the staff
Northwest Territories	Both with distance education	No	None required	None required
Nunavut	Both with distance education	No	None required	None required

SOURCE: Child Care (2000); Young (1993b, 2001).

as Newfoundland and Labrador, the Yukon, and the Northwest Territories, how-ever, programs did not become "readily available" until the late 1980s—and "readily available" in these locations may still be thousands of kilometres away. Understandably, these jurisdictions have been reluctant to implement training requirements when local programs have just recently become available. Newfoundland and Labrador and the Yukon are phasing in requirements. Presumably, initiatives like those seen in Manitoba, coupled with a gradual phasing-in of teacher training requirements as in the Yukon, would encourage the maximum number of individuals to enroll in the courses.

You will probably be surprised, especially as a student in the field, to see in Exhibit 4-8 that many Canadian jurisdictions do not require all teachers to be knowledgeable about child development, despite the available research. Moreover, the failure of many legislators to recognize the value of experience is a concern. In three jurisdictions, no one in an ECE program has to be experienced in the field. In another four jurisdictions, only the supervisor has to have experience in the field. While the supervisor is important in a program, quite frequently she or he spends a large proportion of time doing administrative tasks and relatively little in direct contact with the children. Clearly, as Canadians, we still have to make a number of changes in our legislation, if we want high-quality programs to be the norm in this country.

● Scope of Licensed Child Care in Canada and Parental Needs

Another challenge emerges when you look at the number of licensed child care spaces in Canada (Child Care, 2000; National Child Care Information Centre, 1991; Pence et al., 1992) for each jurisdiction, summarized in Exhibit 4-9. Those numbers are minute relative to the number of 0-to-12-year-olds who have working mothers, as the Exhibit shows. They are also minute if you look at the number of 0-to-9-year-olds requiring some form of care according to the CNCCS data in the early 1990s (see Exhibit 1-1, Chapter 1). More troubling still is the fact that even more Canadian children are expected to need care in the future. More and more families are expected to have both parents working, so fewer children will be cared for at home. A corresponding increase in the availability of licensed programs would be welcome, but very few jurisdictions have increased the number of regulated spaces—though Quebec has set a significant precedent. Perhaps a national child care policy will be required before we see more readily available licensed ECE programs and fewer children in poor-quality care and fewer with the proverbial latchkey around their necks. While licensed and regulated care is expensive, many parents want the assurances that licensing brings with it. They know that a licensed program in a centre or home is inspected, and that it must conform to a set of regulations. They want some guarantee that their children are receiving high-quality care and education while they work. And they do not want to spend their time at work worrying about the well-being of the children.

EXHIBIT 4-9   *Scope of Child Care in Canada and Needs of Parents*

Province or Territory	Number of Children 0–12[4] Years	Children 0–12 with Working Mothers[4]	Number of Children 0–9 Years in Some Form of Care[1]	Number of Licensed Centre-Based Spaces[1,2,3,4]	Number of Licensed Family Child Care Spaces[1,2,3,4]
British Columbia	640,000	402,000	283,300	51,621	17,357
Alberta	532,200	358,000	272,300	40,528	6,505
Saskatchewan	182,200	124,000	112,600	4,889	2,235
Manitoba	195,700	132,000	103,000	17,001	3,489
Ontario	1,973,600	1,320,000	909,400	159,090	18,000
Yukon Territory	NA	NA	NA	891	416
Quebec	1,172,400	749,000	569,400	0–5 yr.: 60,541; 5–12 yr.: 92,700	21,761
New Brunswick	119,100	75,000	59,300	9048	156
Prince Edward Island	24,200	18,000	12,300	3,678	39
Nova Scotia	152,000	97,000	79,600	10,994	169
Newfoundland	86,200	49,000	44,900	4,275	0
Northwest Territories	NA	NA	NA	913	232
Nunavut	NA	NA	NA	206	NA

NA: Not available.

SOURCES:
[1]Pence (1992b).
[2]National Child Care Information Centre, Child Care Programs Division (1991).
[3]Young (1993b, 2001).
[4]Child Care (2000).

The *National Statement on Quality Child Care* (Canadian Child Day Care Federation, 1991) discussed child care as a partnership between parents, professionals (and their associations), training institutions, and all levels of government. That statement continues to provide an outline of the role government should play in child care in this country. Government:

- *encourages a variety of flexible delivery models to meet the diverse needs of families*

- *recognizes current research and social policy issues as the foundation on which licensing standards are built*

- *employs individuals within the licensing body who have completed recognized advanced professional training and experience related specifically to the field*

- *provides information to enable parents to make meaningful choices regarding quality care*

- *ensures that quality care is accessible and affordable*

- *coordinates various departments and levels at the municipal, regional, provincial/territorial and national levels to ensure quality child care. (P. 15).*

In the light of the current state of affairs in Canada, which you have considered in this chapter, it would be difficult not to conclude that governments at all levels have a major challenge ahead if they hope to meet these objectives. As professionals entering the field, you will have to keep legislators reminded and concerned about these objectives.

Key Terms

availability	regulation
centre size	teacher-child ratio
group size	teacher training requirements
legislation	

Key Points

1. The history of early childhood education in each province and territory is reviewed.

2. Similarities and differences in the history of early childhood education in each province and territory are reviewed.

3. The date when child care was first legislated in each jurisdiction is related to the legislation on teacher-child ratios, group sizes, and centre sizes.

4. Ratios, group sizes, and facility sizes for different age groups are compared.

5. The requirements for indoor and outdoor space for each jurisdiction are considered.

6. Teacher training requirements in each jurisdiction are considered and the availability of teacher education programs is discussed. The research on teacher education we reviewed in Chapter 1 is related to these findings.

7. The scope of licensed care in Canada is outlined, as is parental need.

8. Recommendations about the role government should play in child care are outlined.

Key Questions

1. Compare the history of ECE in your province or territory to that of two other jurisdictions. Then relate those differences to any corresponding differences in the regulations and training programs in each location.

2. Formulate your recommendations for improving the quality of ECE in your province or territory in the 21st century.

3. Review the CNCCS findings on the child care options parents report using in your province or territory. If you were in government, what changes would you recommend? Which child care arrangements concern you and why?

4. Pence's (1992) publication, *Canadian Child Care in Context: Perspectives from the Provinces and Territories*, contains bibliographies that list publications relevant to ECE for each province and territory. Study the bibliography for your location and select one article for study.

Part 2

Who?

Early childhood education is made up of different people. In Part 2 we will explore the who of this field by examining the characteristics and needs of the children, their families, and their teachers.

- In Chapter 5, **Children and Their Families,** the characteristics, commonalities, and uniqueness of young children will be considered. Then we will turn our attention to parents and other family members. They are the ones with whom early childhood educators share the responsibility for raising young children.

- In Chapter 6, **The Early Childhood Educator,** we will look at the different roles of those who work in early childhood programs. We will also focus on early childhood education as a profession, and critically consider some issues educators in the field face today.

Chapter 5

Children and Their Families

*A*t the heart of early childhood education are young children. All the topics we will discuss in ensuing chapters are aimed at gaining a better understanding of children and how, together with their families, we can best meet their needs. Although our focus will be on children, it is always important to keep in mind that they must never be seen in isolation, but rather as part of a family system that provides context and identity through its lifestyle, culture, heritage, and traditions.

Knowing the families of children in an early childhood education program is often as important as knowing the children. Children are integral members of their family systems, and, conversely, family values and culture are an inseparable part of children. Families who choose an early childhood education program are sharing or allocating some of the responsibility for socializing their children with the teachers in the program they select. Children need to feel there is continuity between their home and school experiences, and that continuity can best be assured through a carefully fostered partnership between the family and the early childhood program (Powell, 1989).

In this chapter we will take a closer look at children, their families, and the techniques that help cement a strong bond between home and school, by considering the following questions:

1. In what ways are young children alike? We will examine three issues in the discussion of similarities between children:

   • "Profiles" that identify typical traits shared by the majority of children of different ages

   • The need of all children for positive self-esteem

   • The need of all children for play as a way of learning about the world

2. We will then examine factors that contribute to the wonderful diversity among children. Inborn traits such as temperament will be discussed, and external factors that contribute to differences between children, including culture, language and dialect, and social class, will be considered.

3. Then, we will consider a brief overview of family systems theory as a way of viewing the family as a dynamic unit.

4. The Canadian family has undergone many changes recently. We will consider some of these changes by looking at the following:

   • Variety in family forms

   • Other factors that contribute to family diversity

   • Families in poverty

5. Families have specific needs that the early childhood program can address. We will consider issues related to family needs, including:

   • The needs of adults in a unique stage of development, separate from their children's development

   • The need to feel empowered, in control of their lives

   • Coordination of the needs of the family with the early childhood program

6. Two-way communication between families and the early childhood program is an important element in providing consistency for children. We will examine the following methods of communicating with parents:

   • Communicating with individual parents informally, on a day-to-day basis, and formally, through conferences and home visits

   • Communicating with groups of parents, through written communiqués, bulletin boards, and meetings

7. Families can be involved in the early childhood program in a number of ways—as resources, in the classroom, and as decision makers

8. One function of the early childhood program is parent education, which can take a variety of forms.

Children

Recognizing Similarities

Children are wonderfully engaging and winning in part because of the freshness with which they approach all experiences. Most children possess a sense of trust that the world and the people in it are friendly and kind, and they will tackle that world with joy and enthusiasm. The amount of information that children learn in the first few years of life is unparalleled in later learning. At no other time in life will there be such zest and liveliness toward acquiring skills and knowledge.

Our task in working with young children is to provide an environment in which this enthusiasm is nurtured and sustained rather than subdued or even destroyed. Preschoolers are eager to learn, but such eagerness can be battered down if they are frequently overwhelmed by developmentally inappropriate experiences. This awesome responsibility on the shoulders of early childhood educators can be met through careful and sensitive study and understanding of the characteristics and needs of young children.

● Age-Related Similarities Among Children

Although each child is unique, all children nonetheless have much in common. All children share the need for nurturing and trustworthy adults, for stability and security, for increasing **autonomy**, and for a sense of competence and self-worth. Similarly, there are common attributes and skills that characterize children at different ages during the preschool years. In the course of normal development, children reach developmental milestones in a fairly predictable manner and within a reasonable time range (Allen & Marotz, 1994). For that reason, you can make checklists or normative tables that describe the typical features of children at different ages within each developmental domain. Arnold Gessell, in fact, spent his life developing normative tables. More recently, Allen and Marotz (1994) published a book with profiles of typical children from birth to 8 years that you may wish to consult. The Toronto Board of Education's *Observing Children* looks at the typical child from 2 to 13 years and is also a valuable resource.

Note that milestones are different from theories about how children learn. Milestones are a list of observable skills (e.g., walking). A theorist's job is to propose how the child reached these milestones (remember our discussion on genetics versus environment).

While a comprehensive summary of developmental norms is beyond the scope of this text, a brief overview of some developmental characteristics of children in the early childhood period is appropriate. Keep in mind that knowing what to expect of children is different than pushing children to reach milestones before they are ready. Hence, part of your job is knowing the individual children—where they've been, where they are, where they need to go, and how to appropriately guide them as they make their way there. This text emphasizes programs for children between 2 and 5 years of age but also provides an overview of infant and toddler programs as well as primary-school programs. However, students interested in working with infants, toddlers, and primary-school children will need to seek additional resources that discuss in more depth the development of children of these ages and programs for them. Following is a simplified compilation of what children tend to be like at these ages. Again, how they came to be this way is a different story.

Infants (birth to 12 months).   Early childhood programs for infants under 1 year were rare until the 1960s when a number of research-oriented programs were established to determine the effect of high-quality programs on infant development (Fein & Fox, 1988). While there still is considerable controversy about some of the findings, the weight of the evidence suggests that high-quality programs are beneficial even in the first year of life, especially for those from disadvantaged homes.

The first year of life is characterized by constant change and many significant firsts (Fogel, 1991). Infants grow very rapidly and develop many physical skills in a short period of time. They learn to control their heads, and they begin to smile, roll over, and sit and then to crawl and creep. At birth, babies' movements are mostly reflexive and they are unable to manipulate objects. But by the time babies reach their first birthday, their caregivers are kept busy childproofing the environment by placing dangerous objects out of reach and watching as independence in eating finger foods and drinking from a cup begin to emerge. In fact, the first year is quite challenging for caregivers as their charges have developmental needs that alter almost from one day to the next.

Differences in temperament become evident early in the first year of life (Thomas, Chess, & Birch, 1968). Some infants are active and regular, while others are much quieter, and still others have an unpredictable schedule. Infants also differ on the approach-withdrawal dimension. Some approach new people, foods, and experiences with enthusiasm, while others tend to withdraw from or be upset by novelty. Some are very adaptable and responsive. Others may scream at any schedule disruption but sleep through a parade. In a group setting in particular, you will notice that some infants seem to fuss and cry much of the time, while others seem happy most of the time. These inborn characteristics demand that those caring for infants learn about the temperaments of those in their care and adapt their behaviours to meet the individuals' needs. Thomas et al. (1968) and Chess & Thomas (1987) referred to this as a "goodness of fit" between the child's and the caregiver's temperaments. Recognizing differences in our temperaments helps us adjust to make the fit a positive interaction in all of our relationships. A regular baby may adapt to a schedule that has some consistency, but the irregular baby will need a highly flexible schedule. A more active baby will respond to a program that offers a wide range of activities, but the tranquil, quiet baby will not try all of the activities.

clam
lean a tranq life

One-Year-Old Children (1 to 2 years).   While the first year of life is characterized by many rapid changes, the second year of life has its own excitement. Usually, children begin to take their first toddling steps between 12 and 15 months of age. Moreover, language begins to emerge and develop rapidly during this time; the use of speech is a characteristic that makes humans unique. The fact that these two major human traits develop without direct teaching often makes people take these accomplishments for granted, but it would be difficult to find a youngster who was not delighted with these new skills. Suddenly, with hands free, a child can explore the world with extra zeal. Having some language skills, a child can communicate pleasure and displeasure more easily. Of course, discussing whether walking and talking are learned behaviours or biological traits would make an interesting class debate!

In the second year, the child is quite egocentric and relates to adults better than to children. Early in the second year, children are usually willing to agree to adult requests and to receive adult assistance, but as they approach their second birthday, refusals to cooperate and a strong desire to "do it myself" become more frequent. It is important to remember, no matter how hurried we become, that the child's need and desire to master a task alone must be honoured if we hope to foster self-esteem and a developing sense of autonomy.

Usually one sees the beginnings of pretend play during the second year, and it becomes more complex as the child's abilities to communicate with others and to understand their requests improve. Storybooks become of greater interest, and the child's attention span slowly increases, even if it remains very short by adult standards. Most play is action-oriented, and a sense of ownership—often expressed by a loud "Mine!"—becomes apparent. Building with blocks, scribbling, and matching objects interest the child in the second year, and most activities are approached with vigour and delight.

Two-Year-Old Children.   It is true that 2-year-olds, with their limited self-control, may well express their growing independence and self-assertiveness by grabbing a desired toy from a peer or by throwing a tantrum. Tantrums, in fact, are common among 2-year-olds, and reflect, in part, their limited verbal skills, which often do not allow them to express what they want. Two-year-olds are also inept at delaying gratification; they do not have the ability to wait for something they want "right now" (Allen & Marotz, 1994; Ames, Gillespie, Haines, & Ilg, 1980; Bredekamp, 1987). Moreover, they are just beginning to acquire some social skills, and tend to play side-by-side with peers rather than interact with them.

While these trying characteristics are typical of 2-year-olds, this transitional stage is inspirational to behold. Curiosity is boundless in 2-year-olds, and the world is their oyster to explore, savour, and enjoy. Two-year-olds undertake many activities for the sheer pleasure rather than to reach a goal. Running is enjoyed in itself rather than as a means of getting somewhere fast; painting means involvement in a sensory process rather than an interest in producing a picture. Activities are also undertaken with enormous enthusiasm. Two-year-olds wholeheartedly throw themselves into activities, whether painting, squishing play dough, pouring sand and water, or reading books. They particularly enjoy sensory experiences, using touch, taste, and smell, as well as sight and sound. Two-year-olds are notorious for their desire to repeat, using newfound skills over and over again. This desire is normal and should be encouraged, for it builds competence and allows children to fully assimilate skills before moving on to new ones.

During this year, most children increasingly gain body control: they are more self-assured about walking, their running no longer has a baby stagger, and their newfound finger control allows them to put together simple puzzles or paint with a brush. At the same time, they experience tremendous language growth. Their growing vocabulary, sentence length, and grammatical forms open up all sorts of possibilities because of this increased communicative competence. Self-help skills are also improving, including the achievement of toilet training for the majority of children during this year. Just as important as learning motor, language, and self-help skills is the process of gaining independence through this mastery.

Teachers of 2-year-olds need to provide a supportive, consistent, and safe environment in which rapidly growing skills can be practised and mastered. Frequent and enthusiastic praise conveys that adults value the acquisition of skills. Gentle guidance acknowledges children's growing sense of self while helping them develop self-control in relation to others (Bredekamp, 1987). Visit the Web site of Zero to Three for more information on the first three years of life.

Three-Year-Old Children.   Three-year-olds have truly left babyhood behind, not only in appearance—with the loss of baby fat—but also in added skills. Increased balance and control are evident in large motor, fine motor, and self-help areas. Three-year-olds like to use their new skills by being helpful and wanting to please adults. Their added competence does not mean that they won't occasionally have accidents or revert to earlier behaviours when upset, but overall their characteristic way of responding to school experiences is with enthusiasm and enjoyment.

By age 3, children's speech is intelligible most of the time and consists of longer sentences. Language becomes much more of a social and cognitive tool. Three-year-olds engage in more extensive conversations, talking with and not just to people, and they delight in both answering questions and asking them. In fact, 3-year-old children are usually bursting with questions, constantly asking why, what for, and where about everything imaginable. Three-year-olds can ask questions on topics not covered in encyclopedias, *The Guinness Book of World Records*, or *The Farmers' Almanac*! Vocabulary continues to increase dramatically, and grammar becomes more accurate.

This greater language facility helps increase peer interaction among this age group. Three-year-olds are much more socially aware than younger children, and their make-believe play, which they began in the previous year by imitating simple personal and home routines, at times includes several children. Short-lived friendships begin to form, and children will play with one another as well as near one another. Social problem-solving skills are just beginning to emerge. With guidance, 3-year-olds may share and take turns, but they still find such behaviours difficult (Allen & Marotz, 1994; Ames, Gillespie, Haines, & Ilg, 1980).

Teachers of 3-year-olds need to respect the growing skills and competencies of their charges without forgetting just how recently they acquired them. It is important to maintain patience and good humour, remembering that the enthusiasm with which 3-year-olds use these skills is not always matched by accuracy and speed. Because 3-year-olds enjoy helping as well as practising self-help skills, such behaviours should be promoted and valued. The emerging social skills of 3-year-olds should be encouraged in an atmosphere where social exploration is safe and where playing alone or not giving up a favourite toy is also acceptable (Bredekamp, 1987).

Four-Year-Old Children.   Four-year-olds have achieved a maturity and competence in motor and language development that leads them to assume a general air of security and confidence, sometimes bordering on cockiness. It is a time of "constantly testing limits in order to practice self-confidence and firm up a growing need for independence" (Allen & Marotz, 1989, p. 87).

Four-year-olds seem to be in perpetual motion, throwing themselves wholeheartedly into activities. They have mastered the basics of movement and now eagerly embellish on these. Climbing, pedalling, pumping on a swing, jumping over and off objects, and easily avoiding obstacles when running are routine, and all contribute to greater flexibility and exploration in play. Showing off new physical stunts—or trying to—is a favourite pastime. Improved muscle coordination is also evident in more controlled use of the fingers, such as in buttoning, drawing, and cutting with scissors. In addition, many self-care activities have become routines rather than the challenges they were at earlier ages.

If increased competence leads to noticeable embellishments in motor activities, this is even more evident in the language area. By age 4, most children's language usage has become remarkably sophisticated and skilled. This accomplishment seems to invite new uses for language beyond communication. Four-year-olds love to play with language, using it to brag, engage in bathroom talk, swear, tell tall tales, and make up silly rhymes. And, if you can imagine, 4-year-olds are even more persistent than 3-year-olds in asking questions.

For 4-year-olds, peers have become very important. Play is a social activity more often than not, although 4-year-olds enjoy solitary activities at times as well. Taking turns and sharing become much easier because 4-year-olds begin to understand the benefits of cooperation. Their imaginative variations of movement and language skills extend into group play, which is usually highly creative, ingenious, and touched by their sense of humour.

Teachers of 4-year-olds need to provide an environment in which children have many opportunities for interactions with one another, with adults, and with a wide selection of appropriate and stimulating materials. Because of their heightened social involvements, this age group needs consistent, positive guidance to help develop emerging social skills, for instance, in sharing, resolving conflicts, and negotiating (Allen & Marotz, 1994; Ames, Gillespie, Haines, & Ilg, 1980; Bredekamp, 1987).

Five-Year-Old Children.   Five-year-olds are much more self-contained and controlled; they have replaced some of their earlier exuberant behaviours with a calmer, more mature approach. They are competent and reliable, taking responsibility seriously. They seem to be able to judge their own abilities more accurately than at earlier ages, and they respond accordingly.

Five-year-olds' motor activities seem more poised, their movements more restrained and precise than ever before. There is also greater interest in fine motor activities as children have gained many skills in accurate cutting, gluing, drawing, and beginning writing. This interest is spurred by the new desire to make something rather than merely to paint, cut, or manipulate the play dough for the sheer enjoyment of these activities. The self-reliance of 5-year-olds extends to assuming considerable responsibility for self-care as well.

Language has also reached a height of maturity for this age group, exhibited through a vocabulary that contains thousands of words, complex and compound sentence structures, variety and accuracy in grammatical forms, and good articulation. Language increasingly reflects interest in and contact with a broadening world outside the child's intimate family, school, and neighbourhood experiences. The social sphere of 5-year-olds revolves around special friendships, which take on more importance. By age 5, children are quite adept at sharing toys, taking turns, and playing cooperatively. Their group play is usually quite elaborate and imaginative, and it can take up long periods of time (Allen & Marotz, 1994; Ames et al., 1980).

Teachers of 5-year-olds, after providing a stimulating learning environment and setting reasonable limits, can expect this age group to take on considerable responsibility for maintaining and regulating a smoothly functioning program. Five-year-olds need to be given many opportunities to explore their world in depth and assimilate what they learn through multiple experiences. One way in which children can discuss, plan, and carry out ideas stimulated by their experiences is through group projects (Katz & Chard, 1993). There are several valuable Web sites for teachers and parents of kindergarten-aged children.

Primary or School-Aged Children.   Children from 6 through 8 years of age are usually in Grades 1, 2, or 3. These are known as the "primary grades" in most provinces, and attendance at a formal school or an approved alternative is no longer an option at this stage in a child's life. Unfortunately, the years from birth to 5 seem to receive more attention from the early childhood field, despite the fact that primary-grade children still share many of the developmental needs evident in the earlier years.

The pressure-cooker, skill-oriented primary programs that have become more common in recent years fail to recognize the need of children aged 6 to 8 to play and to experience success. Moreover, such programs do not reflect an understanding of the developmental unevenness that typifies children of this age. Just because Jimmy's gross motor skills are at a 7-year-old level, it does not follow that his fine motor and language skills are at the same level. The situation can be even worse for those primary-grade children who have late birthdays relative to the majority of children in their class. Too often, subject- and skill-oriented teachers forget that some children in the class may be almost a year younger than others. At this stage in development, a year is a very long time, and it is unreasonable to assume that children who vary in age by almost a year should be achieving at the same level. Susie may be working at a beginning Grade 1 level in reading while Mario is at a late Grade 1 level; even though Susie may seem behind to the teacher, the fact that Susie is one year minus a day younger than Mario needs to be considered. The fact is that both Susie and Mario may be working at an age-appropriate level.

Certainly, physical growth has slowed down in 6-to-8-year-olds, relative to preschoolers, but basic skills still need to be refined, and children of these ages need active play on a regular basis. Primary-level children are boisterous and enjoy roughhousing, even though there is a risk of injury. Balancing stunts, including riding a two-wheeler and acrobatics, are challenges that are tackled with enthusiasm, but fatigue and hunger may follow.

Peer pressure and a need to be accepted become more marked during these years, and play has a highly social quality. While the 6-year-old has best friends for short periods of time, friendships become more enduring and more important for the 7- and 8-year-olds. However, 6-, 7-, and 8-year-olds have rigid gender-role stereotypes, are quite discriminatory, and rarely form close friendships with a member of the opposite sex. Nonetheless, they begin to test behaviours, things, and ideas with friends that they will later have to test in the wider world. The peer group will slowly increase in importance up to the adolescent years, when it will become a more important reference group than the family.

Simple competitive sports become a possibility during the primary years, but they are not without friction. Impatience, a lack of persistence, and complaints are not infrequent, but sensitivity and cooperation also increase during these years. As children approach 7 and 8 years of age, they become less egocentric, and logical thinking processes begin to emerge. A sense of morality also starts to develop along with an increasing understanding of rules.

Children in the primary grades like to chatter, but they talk with people rather than to them. Vocabulary growth is slower than it was during the preschool years, but it still increases steadily. The mechanical aspects of speech are not fully mature, and irregularities should not be a concern. However, the ability to appreciate the subtleties and the humour of language increases rapidly during this period, as many parents and teachers know. Riddles, puns, and knock-knock jokes are shared with delight.

Reading and writing usually begin—and are sometimes mastered—during this period, but reversals of letters and numbers are common. Mathematical concepts proliferate, and sequencing skills and storytelling abilities improve dramatically. Planning, sorting, classifying, and collecting are enjoyed, as are real gadgets like radios and cameras. Attitudes toward school as well as toward themselves are being formed at this time, so teachers and parents must ensure that primary-level children experience success on a regular basis.

● Need for Self-Esteem

One thing shared by all children is the need to feel good about themselves. Young children are beginning to form a **self-concept**, perceptions and feelings about themselves gathered largely from how the important people in their world respond to them. One aspect of self-concept is **self-esteem**, children's evaluation of their worth in positive or negative terms (Greenspan & Greenspan, 1986; Essa & Rogers, 1992; Marshall, 1989; Samuels, 1977). Such evaluation can tell children that they are competent, worthwhile, and effective or, on the other hand, that they are incapable, unlikable, and powerless. It is particularly noteworthy that children who feel good about themselves seem to be more friendly and helpful toward peers (Marshall, 1989).

A healthy self-concept is vital to all areas of a child's development. Although readiness in the natural progression of development is triggered internally and furthered by appropriate external stimuli, successful mastery of new learning also depends on a child's feelings of competence and ability to meet new challenges. **Perceived competence** reflects the child's belief in his or her ability to succeed at a given task (Marshall, 1989). Successful experiences result in self-confidence, which, in turn, boosts self-esteem. Thus, many appropriate yet challenging experiences help the child feel successful, confident, and capable (Essa & Rogers, 1992).

The child needs to feel competent and able to face challenges, as well as have a sense of **personal control**—the feeling of having the power to make things happen or stop things from happening. When children generally feel that what happens to them is completely out of their hands, particularly if what happens is not always in their best interests, they cannot develop this sense of control and will tend to see themselves as helpless and ineffective. All children need opportunities to make appropriate choices and exercise autonomy to begin to develop the perception that they have control, which also contributes to their emerging sense of responsibility for their own actions (Marshall, 1989).

The early years are crucial in the development of self-concept, since it forms and stabilizes early in life and becomes increasingly resistant to change (Samuels, 1977). Above all, children's positive concepts of themselves reflect healthy parent-child relationships that are founded on love, trust, and consistency. Then, when early childhood teachers enter young children's lives, they also contribute to the formation of that concept.

At the same time, if a child comes to school with a history of abuse or neglect, the teacher's contribution of offsetting positive experiences can help nurture self-esteem. Teachers strengthen children's positive self-esteem if they are sensitive to each child as an individual and to the needs of children for affection, nurturing, caring, and feelings of competence. Thus, teachers who understand children, know their characteristics, respond to them, and know how to challenge them in a supportive manner contribute to this positive sense of self. In essence, everything the early childhood teacher does has an impact on the children's self-concepts.

Reflective Exercise 5-1

Pair off with one of your classmates. One of you will tell the other one of something difficult you recently did (e.g., learning to ski, memorizing terms for a chemistry exam, etc.). The second person, in listening, first provides encouraging feedback (e.g., "I know you must have done well; you are so capable!"). Then the first student repeats the story while the second student gives negative feedback ("I bet you couldn't do it!" or "You seem like such a klutz!"). After this, reverse roles and repeat the exercise. After you have finished, explore and discuss your feelings in this exercise. Then, as an entire class, consider this discussion in the context of young children.

● Need for Play

Another thing that children have in common is the need for play, which serves as a means of learning about and making sense of the world (Rubin, Fein, & Vandenberg, 1983). But more than that, play is essential to all aspects of children's development. "It is an activity which is concerned with the whole of his being, not with just one small part of him, and to deny him the right to play is to deny him the right to live and grow" (Cass, 1973, p. 11). Play promotes mastery as children practise skills; it furthers cognitive development as thinking abilities are stretched; it involves language, encouraging new uses; it involves physical activity; it helps children work through emotions; its inventive nature makes it creative; it is often a socializing event; beyond all that, however, it provides a way for children to assimilate and integrate their life experiences. In no way is play a trivial pursuit; rather, it is a serious undertaking necessary to healthy development for all children (Almy, Monighan, Scales, & Van Hoorn, 1984).

Although the different types of play will be discussed in more detail in Chapter 7, it is worth noting at this point that, with age, children develop increasing social and cognitive skills that influence their play. If you are aware that play changes with age, it helps you to have appropriate expectations for young children in an early childhood program and to engage in their play. For instance, a 10-month-old engages in simple games like peek-a-boo, whereas several 5-year-olds may collaborate to build a rocket ship in the block centre. As a teacher, you are more likely to initiate play sequences with infants and toddlers. With older children, however, you probably will not initiate many play sequences; rather you would structure the environment to facilitate the child's play. Children between 3 and 5 years, for example, need sizable blocks of time to engage in self-selected play, both indoors and outdoors, and many open-ended materials that lend themselves to exploration and mastery (e.g., play dough, sand and water, building blocks). In addition, time, space, and materials that lend themselves to social play should always be available (including dolls, dress-up clothes, and blocks). However, organized games with rules, particularly competitive games, are beyond the ability of most preschoolers to understand and should not be part of the early childhood program.

Reflective Exercise 5-2

Think back to your earliest memories of play. What makes play memorable for you. The location (a tree house, neighbour's back yard, park)? Special playmates? Special play materials or toys? What did you learn from their play? Having read about the importance of play, do you have new insights in thinking back over your own childhood play experiences?

● Respecting Differences

Infants and young children have many characteristics in common and certainly share basic needs for affection, acceptance, consistency, respect, and appropriate challenges, yet there are many variations among children. The profiles of infants, toddlers, preschoolers, and primary-level children presented earlier reflect many common characteristics of these ages, but they rarely describe any one child. While falling within the normal range of development, each child possesses a unique blend of attributes that makes him or her one of a kind. The A Closer Look box here examines the concept of inclusion in the classroom. Inclusion is a concept that promotes the recognition of and respect for similarities and differences, or diversity, among children. Diversity includes factors such as the physical, intellectual, social, emotional, linguistic, creative, cultural, and financial. The concept of inclusion upholds all children's fundamental rights to access services and to grow and learn to their maximum potential.

A Closer Look

THE CONCEPT OF INCLUSION: CHILDREN WITH DIVERSE NEEDS

Some children are born with or acquire conditions that place them outside the typical range of development for their age. They might have a developmental delay, meaning that they accomplish tasks in one or more developmental areas at a considerably later age than their peers. Some children are considered at risk for delay, with a significant probability that problems will occur because of adverse environmental factors such as poverty or low birth weight. With appropriate help, children who have developmental delays may well catch up to age norms. Other children may have an impairment, indicating development that is in some way different (not just slower) from that of most children. Children with hearing, visual, intellectual, or motor disabilities are part of this category. Similarly, children have different learning styles, behaviour patterns, temperaments, emotional and social needs, stressors, experiences, and cultural, religious, and financial parameters that need to be addressed.

We'd like to propose that all children have special needs. These needs are diverse yet equally important. We recognize that they require different approaches. Accepting and welcoming diversity among children means we can accept and welcome it into our schools and classrooms. Understanding diversity means reducing misconceptions and fears we might have about it. This is the first step toward an inclusive classroom—one that embraces all children and provides for their unique needs.

Children's differences reflect both inborn and external factors that have molded who they are. Some children are born with an easygoing temperament; for instance, they have a moderate activity level, a predictable schedule of sleeping and eating, and a positive attitude toward, and curiosity about, new experiences. Other children have more difficult temperaments and are, for example, more irritable, unpredictable, and difficult to calm down (Thomas, Chess, & Birch, 1968; Chess & Thomas, 1987). Although children are born with such temperamental characteristics, these gradually tend to affect the adults around them so that parents and teachers may begin to think of children as difficult or easy, thereby expecting and reinforcing these behavioural traits. In turn, then, adults' perceptions of children contribute to children's self-perceptions.

A child's individuality is also shaped by the family. In most cases, the family is the most potent force in the young child's life. Consequently, it is important that early childhood educators endeavour to learn as much as possible about the families of young children. We must consider how to develop programs that respect and value the differences in the cultural, ethnic, religious, linguistic, and economic backgrounds of children's families. Early childhood teachers need to be sensitive to family diversity and genuinely value different cultures and backgrounds. Children mirror their primary environment—their home and family—as, of course, they should. If teachers, either consciously or unconsciously, put down, ignore, or negate what children experience and learn at home, they will convey that the family, including the child, is in some way inferior and undesirable. What a detrimental impact this would have on children's self-concepts!

● Inclusion

One of the provisions often made is that children with disabilities be placed in the "least restricted" environment. First, this description itself implies restriction. A description with a more positive connotation such as "most enriching" would be more suitable (Spodek & Saracho, 1994). Second, we need to remember that children should be afforded the most enriching environment. A classroom, school, community, and government that support the diversity of children—whether developmental, cultural, racial, or financial—support the concept that all children belong to, and benefit from, being together.

Initially inclusion, formerly called integration or mainstreaming, meant that children that had been kept at home or institutionalized could be physically integrated (i.e., attend a segregated classroom within a school for typical children). This model is still prevalent today even though the champions of inclusion are clear: inclusion means inclusion in every respect. In this sense, inclusion is looked upon as a human rights issue, not an education issue, in that it specifies children's rights to be included and to have access to the same learning opportunities and experiences as their peers, with their peers, in their own neighbourhood. It also affords parents the right to choose. Some parents still choose segregated programs feeling these best meet the needs of their children, but the point is they were provided with options. In the past, segregation was the only option available.

Helping parents make informed choices, providing a range of options that includes inclusion, and providing the necessary supports to implement the chosen option are critical to the success and acceptance of an inclusionary model. This concept has led to the expansion of inclusion—the integration of children with special needs into regular programs. Inclusion is certainly not new, having informally been part of many early childhood programs throughout this century.

An inclusive program is founded on the premise that young children, whether disabled or not, are much more similar than different (Wilderstrom, 1986). Children with special needs can benefit from a good inclusionary program by experiencing success in a variety of developmentally appropriate activities, through contact with age-mates who can be both models and friends, and by exposure to the many opportunities for informal incidental learning that take place in all early childhood programs (Deiner, 1993). At the same time, children with no disabilities benefit from inclusion by learning that children who are in some way different from them nonetheless have far more commonalities than differences (Karnes & Lee, 1979). An increasing number of young children with disabilities are enrolled in early childhood programs (Wolery et al., 1993).

Although inclusion has many potential benefits, the benefits do not happen automatically. In other words, inclusion does not simply mean enrolling children with special needs in an early childhood program. Careful planning, preparation, modification, evaluation, and support are necessary for successful inclusion. Early childhood educators, because they know a great deal about children and how best to work with them, have many skills needed for working with children with disabilities. However, placement of children with special needs in early childhood classes also requires teachers to learn some additional skills. It often means having to acquire and use new teaching strategies, new terminology, and different evaluation tools. It also involves working with a wider range of professionals (e.g., speech and physical therapists or psychologists) and more focused involvement with parents. In addition, early childhood educators may find themselves with unexpectedly strong emotional reactions such as pity for the child, anger that the child has to suffer, fear of the disability, or self-doubt in their own abilities, which they must face and resolve as fear and ignorance prove to be the major blockers to inclusion. One of the keys to successful inclusion is to view each child, whether disabled or not, as an individual with unique characteristics, strengths, and needs. This involves an attitude that sees a child, not a child with Down syndrome or a child who is blind or a child who stutters. For example, Ted may have Down syndrome, but he loves to paint, enjoys listening to stories at group time, and gives terrific hugs. Similarly, Noni's visual impairment does not diminish her enjoyment of the sand table, her budding friendship with Connie, or her ability to make others laugh through her language play. And Manuel, while often tripping over his words, can throw and catch a ball accurately. Many times he is the one who notices a colourful butterfly passing or the first buds of spring, and he has a totally winning smile. Working with a group of children means recognizing, encouraging, and building on each child's strengths. In this way, children's self-concept and self-assurance are boosted so they can meet the challenges posed by their disabilities. Early childhood education principles are based on knowledge of child development, learning, and developmentally appropriate practices using a team approach. This makes early childhood education somewhat intrinsically inclusive in that it recognizes and addresses the developmental range of children and the need for programs to accommodate this.

It is beyond the scope of this text to discuss in depth such topics as characteristics of children with special needs, appropriate teaching methods, testing and assessment tools, interdisciplinary team models, legislation, and the unique needs of children at risk, or the parents of children with disabilities. This field combines the traditional skills of teachers of young children with those of special educators, therapists, and medical personnel. Most early childhood educators, however, will inevitably find themselves in one of the following situations:

1. One or more children with special needs will be included in their class.

2. They will have concerns about a child who seems to experience consistent difficulties in one or more areas of development.

3. They will be members of a team that supports and represents the child and family through their decision-making processes.

Communication within the team makes all team members informed, responsible, and accountable to the concept and process of inclusion. It is important that teachers work with parents and specialists to make the inclusion experience successful. Likewise, teachers concerned about a child's functioning need to document their concerns and discuss them with the parents, as well as offer some concrete suggestions, for instance, about how to begin the referral process so the child is seen by an appropriate specialist. For these reasons, it is important that teachers of young children seek basic information about the characteristics of children with special needs, their families, and the importance of providing an inclusive environment for all children. Now let us look more closely at these families to which children belong.

Families

While children are central in early childhood education, their families are equally important. Children are integral members of their family systems, and, conversely, family values and culture are an inseparable part of children.

Courtesy of George Brown College.

Families are also at the core of early childhood education because the early childhood staff shares with families the responsibility for socializing young children. It is important to provide for children a sense of continuity between home and school experiences, which can best be assured through a carefully fostered partnership between the family and the staff (Powell, 1989). This relationship implies mutual respect and equal power regarding ownership of rights, roles, and responsibilities of everyone involved.

Families—A Theoretical Perspective

Just as it is imperative that you be familiar with developmental stages of early childhood educators and of children, it is equally important to understand family functioning from a theoretical and developmental perspective. The **family systems theory** provides a useful approach to understanding the family as an ever-developing and changing social unit in which members constantly have to accommodate and adapt to one another's demands as well as to demands from outside the family. This theory provides a dynamic rather than static view of how families function.

From the perspective of the family systems theory, the influence that family members have on one another is not one-way but rather interactive and reciprocal. This interaction causes changes in the individual, between individuals within the family, and between the family and others. It is impossible to understand the family by gaining an understanding of just its individual members because the family is more than the sum of its parts. It is necessary to view its interaction patterns and the unspoken rules that govern the members' behaviours. As in any healthy relationship, healthy families work well together, communicate often, are able to make effective decisions, and can handle change. In addition, understanding the family means looking at its functioning within the larger context, for instance, the extended family, the community, and the neighbourhood. The early childhood centre becomes part of that larger context in which families function (Bronfenbrenner, 1986; Walker & Crocker, 1988).

Each individual's development occurs in a broader ecological context, within different but overlapping systems. This is called the *ecological model*, since it looks at the ecosystems or habitats that the individual grows in, affects, and is affected by. The **microsystem** is the most immediate system that affects the individual; it could be the family, classroom, or workplace. These components of the microsystem are linked together in the **mesosystem** through such relationships as parent-teacher interaction or employment practices that affect the family (e.g., employer-supported child care or maternity leave benefits that make up any difference between the employee's regular salary and unemployment insurance benefits).

The **exosystem** includes broader components of the neighbourhood and community that affect the functioning of the family, for example government agencies or mass media. Finally, the broadest system to affect families is the **macrosystem**, which includes cultural, political, and economic forces (Bronfenbrenner & Crouter, 1983). From such an ecological perspective, the child and family are seen more clearly as part of and affected by many other systems, each of which influences their development and functioning.

Perceiving children and families as parts of various systems helps us to avoid seeking simple explanations and to acknowledge the complex interactions that often underlie children's and parents' behaviours. We must take time to look at the many factors affecting behaviour before jumping to conclusions. It is also important to recognize that families and schools interact to affect children's development in myriad possible directions (Goelman, 1988). This perspective makes good communication between home and school an imperative, not a choice. Finally, a systems approach helps us see the interrelatedness of all aspects of children's lives. We simply cannot assume that the child's home exists in one isolated compartment, while the school is in another. In the same way, we cannot presume that families' lives can be segmented into isolated facets.

The Changing Canadian Family

The family is and always has been the most important element in most children's lives. The family is where children experience the emotional and physical care and sustenance vital to their well-being. But the family has no simple definition or boundaries. Several decades ago, most Canadian children might have been part of a traditional family—working father, housewife mother, and two or three children. However, as we saw in Chapter 1, that image of the traditional family is the exception rather than the rule in Canada in 2000s.

Family Forms

Of course, the nuclear family—a married couple with children—is still the prevalent family form, but no longer is it virtually the only family form one encounters as a child or an adult. Today many Canadians live common-law—the number of common-law relationships has steadily increased over the past decade (Statistics Canada, 1997, Oct. 14). Moreover, data from the 1996 Canadian census show that both the number of single-parent families and the number of never-married individuals reported in census data has continued to increase (Statistics Canada, 1997, Oct. 14). Almost 20 percent or 1 of every 5 children in Canada live in a single-parent family in 1996! Single-parent families are most frequent in Quebec, the Yukon, and the Northwest Territories, and least frequent in Alberta (Statistics Canada, 1997, Oct. 14). Some children still live with an extended family of grandparents, uncles, aunts, cousins, and many other relatives who are in frequent, close contact, and this appears to be a pattern preferred by those new immigrants to the country who can afford to bring the extended family to Canada.

The Vanier Institute of the Family has excellent resources on the Canadian family. See their Web site for more information.

With these changes in the family come changes in the definition of "parent" as we have traditionally understood the term. Nowadays, children may have one, two, or more parents: these may be the biological parents, stepparents, adoptive parents, legal guardians, or foster parents. When parents divorce, children may live with the same single or remarried parent all of the time, may alternate between two parents who have joint custody, or may see the non-custodial parent for brief times during weekends or holidays. For some children, grandparents or other relatives take on some of the functions of parents, especially when teenage parents are involved. Some divorced parents find alternative living arrangements, perhaps moving back in with their own parents, sharing housing with another adult or single parent, or joining a group housing arrangement. This is known as the *blended family*. Because of divorce and remarriage, today's children may also acquire various natural and adoptive brothers and sisters, as well as half-siblings, stepsiblings, or unrelated "siblings" in less formal family arrangements. In larger urban communities, in particular, it is also becoming more common to find children living with a gay or lesbian parent, the parent's mate, and often the children of that mate. While most individuals would not have been open about such a relationship two decades ago, they are becoming a more visible segment of society. Similarly, there may be a single-wage earner, dual-wage earners, or no-wage earner creating new family forms and varieties of care arrangements unfamiliar in past generations.

Whatever the family form, a wide range of people can make up a child's network of significant family members, as defined by emotional as well as legal ties. It is necessary, as a teacher of young children, that you also consider and acknowledge the unrelated but significant people as part of a child's family. Anyone who is important in the child's mind should be considered as important by you as well.

It is also vital that you are aware of legal restrictions that might affect children's relationships with adults in their lives. You should ensure that such information is accurately and promptly recorded in your files. During some divorce proceedings, for example, one parent may file a **restraining order** against the other, legally limiting or forbidding contact with the child. Although such situations are usually upsetting for everyone involved, it is necessary to be aware of and make appropriate provisions for complying with any legal action. As a professional, you are bound by the restraining order, even if you are not in agreement with it. Other legal terms such as "joint custody," "access," "supervised visits," and "joint guardianship" need to be understood by staff, and the entire centre needs to take ownership of the knowledge and the well-being of the child. A child care centre is busy and chaotic, often making use of supply staff, parents, and guests. Having a release form on file at the school is one important way of ensuring that only authorized persons pick up the child. After all, the majority of child kidnappings are committed by a divorced parent who does not have custody of the child (Sheldon, 1983). In the A Canadian Professional Speaks Out box, Barbara Young, a Kelowna-based lawyer, describes the experiences she has had with "abductions" of children from an early childhood program by the non-custodial parent, and outlines some cautionary measures. These include erring on the side of caution since "no responsible parent will begrudge your taking a little extra time to ensure that his or her child is safe and is leaving with a person of authority" (Essa & Young, 1994, p. 134).

Family Variations

Not only is there great variation in family form and composition, but other characteristics differentiate families as well. Some of these include economic, racial, cultural, ethnic, religious, linguistic, and geographic factors. The many ways in which families vary can affect not only family customs and traditions but also more fundamental issues, such as defining values and relationships (Jenkins, 1987). In some cases, a family's uniqueness includes a mixture of cultures,

---

A Canadian Professional Speaks Out

CUSTODY DISPUTES AND PICK-UP AUTHORIZATION

Barbara Young, Kendall & Penty Law, Kelowna, British Columbia

Most students reading this book will recall hearing or reading about at least one incident of child abduction either by strangers to the child or by a relative or parent of the child.

As early childhood educators you will have children in your centre whose parents are either separated from each other or who are divorcing. This is a stressful and unhappy time for everyone in the family and it will raise concerns for you as the professional responsible for the security of the child during school hours.

There are unfortunate incidents in which parents may give more priority to their legal disputes than to their concerns for the well-being of their children. There have been situations in which a parent not entitled to visit a child has taken that child without the other parent's knowledge or consent by convincing the teacher that it is all right for him or her to do so. This unauthorized removal of the child may place the child at risk and will, of course, cause a great deal of anxiety for everyone until the child is returned.

Your centre must have a policy for ensuring that each child leaves the centre with a person authorized to transport him or her. Under normal circumstances both parents have that authority and can legally assign another person such as a nanny, grandparent, or friend to pick their child up from school.

In a divorce situation the concept of legal authority over the child is complicated somewhat. When parents live together and raise children together they both have equal legal authority to make decisions about a child's upbringing, physical care, and control. Once parents have separated, they may have a written separation agreement or court order that grants "custody" of the child to one parent. That means that that parent has the legal right to make decisions related to the child's physical care and well-being. If the parents have "joint custody," then the situation is much like it was before their separation and they both have the authority to make decisions about the day-to-day care of the child.

The parent who does not have custody of the child will almost always have the legal right to visit with the child and to obtain information about the child's schooling and health. The right to visit the child is called "access." This parent may also have the rights of "joint guardianship," which does not enable that person to make the day-to-day decisions about the child's care but does permit that parent to have access to information about the child's health care education and religious upbringing and to be consulted by the other parent on decisions related to those and other major issues affecting the child's upbringing.

The ECE centre should have a policy of only allowing the child to leave the centre with a parent or authorized person known to the teachers or with a person who has the parents' written authority to remove the child from the centre. As a policy of registration, the centre should have signatures of the child's parents or guardians on file, and it would be preferable to have a photograph of the parents or people usually responsible for transporting the child. In this way temporary teachers and new staff will have a way of knowing whether or not the adult who comes to get the child is authorized to take the child with him or her.

To be on the safe side the ECE should always rely on the advice of the custodial parent regarding the transporting of children and the giving out of any information about the child.

A good rule of thumb when setting up a policy for the security of your children in the ECE is to err on the side of caution. No responsible parent will begrudge your taking a little more time to ensure that his or her child is safe and is leaving with a person with authority.

As professionals interested in the child's education development and security, you will find it advisable to remain neutral with respect to the matrimonial disputes of your students' parents whenever possible. You may decide to have a policy, as many schools do, of denying requests for letters supporting one parent's parenting ability over that of the other. These requests will certainly be made and do compromise your professional neutrality as the child's educator, which is our prime area of responsibility. In addition, it exposes you to the risk of being subpoenaed to court to be a witness in a custody trial.

There is, of course, an exception to this general rule of remaining neutral, and that is when you believe that a child is in danger of either physical or sexual abuse. You have a legal responsibility to report your concerns to the authorities and if necessary to complete your obligation by testifying at a trial investigating the complaints of abuse.

religions, races, and generations. The teacher can learn about characteristics of various cultural, racial, or religious groups by reading, but it is very important to avoid making large-scale generalizations about a family on the basis of group traits. Families are complex, and only through genuine interest can a teacher get to know them well. Effective and frequent communication helps the teacher become aware of family attributes that can affect the child and family as participants in the early childhood program.

Increasing numbers of families of varied cultural, ethnic, and religious backgrounds are finding the need or making the choice to enroll their children in early childhood programs. It is of utmost importance that teachers be sensitive to differences in values, cultural expectations, and child-rearing practices. Effective communication is the key to promoting and achieving mutual understanding between families and centres which, in turn, help provide a consistent, positive experience for the children. Two excellent Canadian resources are Chud and Fahlman's (1995) *Honouring Diversity Within Child Care and Early Education*, and Shimoni and Baxter's (1996) *Working with Families: Perspectives for Early Childhood Professionals*. An additional resource is Gonzalez-Mena's (1993) *Multicultural Issues in Child Care*, in which she describes the sleeping, eating, and play practices of different cultural groups.

Families in Poverty

Poverty, as one factor in the lives of many families, bears closer scrutiny. Canada's Aboriginals stand out as being among the poorest people in the country. Poverty is also far more frequent in single-parent families (Pence, 1992b).

Reflective Exercise 5-3

Divide your class into three groups and have the respective groups look at the sleeping, eating, and play practices Gonzalez-Mena (1993) describes. Have each group share their findings with the class. Then, in the following class, discuss how you might react to some of the cultural differences. Value differences between teachers and parents are inevitable, as Janet Gonzalez-Mena (1997) has noted, and you should anticipate them as just part of your role. Differences that stem from cultural differences in certain practices, sleeping for instance, can be resolved. Nevertheless, teachers have to compromise on some of these issues. While a child care practice such as toilet training can be a source of conflict, you can also have rich discussions about such an issue, and by discussing it with parents, you, as the teacher, may gain a better understanding of the roots of these cultural differences even if you might not use the same approach.

A number of Canadian early childhood education programs have been aimed at helping economically disadvantaged families. Children who live in poverty often, but not always, have greater needs than children from more advantaged homes, as do their parents. Poverty does not pose a problem for children who have competent, stable parents who meet their needs. However, a variety of problems, including psychological instability, marital breakdowns, violence, and alcoholism, for example, are more common in poverty-stricken homes. Children from troubled disadvantaged homes are likely to exhibit delays in their cognitive and language skills, in their socio-emotional functioning, and in their physical development. They present a special challenge to early childhood educators. Nevertheless, teachers in high-quality early childhood programs can have a significant and lasting impact on the lives of disadvantaged children and their families. Rigorous research has shown that these high-quality early childhood programs, particularly those in which family support has been included, have a dramatic effect not only in terms of children's later school achievement but also on their families (Chafel, 1990; Consortium, 1983; Seitz, Rosenbaum, & Apfel, 1985; Zigler & Freedman, 1987; Doherty-Derkowski, 1995).

Teachers in quality settings also have an impact on the lives of families that are more fortunate. Many affluent families have a variety of concerns and difficulties such as illness, marital discord, substance abuse, and work-related problems. Other families are faced with fewer difficulties, but still welcome and profit from a supportive relationship with their children's teachers.

● The Needs of Families

The fact that a child is enrolled in an early childhood program indicates that the family has a need that the program is able to meet. The most common and certainly the most obvious family need is provision of child care while the parents are at work. The growth of child care centres and family child care homes over the past three decades has been in response to the dramatic increase in the number of working single-parent and dual-income families.

But beyond the overall need for responsible and knowledgeable adults to provide care for children while their parents work, families have other needs that the early childhood centre can help meet. Some of these needs concern helping the parents, as individuals, meet the demands of their multiple roles. Others revolve around coordination of home and school routines and practices. One note to keep in mind: although it would be ideal if early childhood educators could meet everyone's needs—children's, parents', co-workers'—sometimes this is just not possible. Setting realistic goals within the particular early childhood education work setting can help establish priorities.

Parenthood

We typically view parenthood from the perspective of children's development and how parents facilitate, support, and promote it. Rarely is parenthood seen from the viewpoint of parents and their needs. Erik Erikson (1963), whose theory of human development was one of the first to span adulthood as well as childhood, believed that the most important need of the mature adult in the stage of **generativity** is to care for and nurture others. The tasks of this stage are often carried out in parenthood, through which the adult is concerned with meeting the needs of the next generation. Implied in this process is growth of the adult as an individual, which is separate from the nurturance extended to children. This acknowledgment of adulthood as a period of continued development has been advanced in recent years by other writers (i.e., Gould, 1978; Levinson, 1978; Sheehy, 1976).

Parenthood as a distinct process has also been examined in greater depth. Ellen Galinsky (1981), after extensive research and interviews with scores of individuals, suggested that parents change and develop in their roles, just as children do, by moving through six stages of parenthood. Each stage involves issues to be faced and a crisis that the parent has to resolve successfully. The parents of an infant are in the nurturing stage, forming a strong attachment and integrating this new member into the family unit. The parents of a young preschooler are enmeshed in the **authority stage**, defining rules and their own roles. Toward the end of the preschool years, parents enter the **interpretive stage**, in which they are confronted with the task of explaining and clarifying the world to their children.

Galinsky was particularly concerned with the "images" that parents create, images of what they expect the child to be like before it is born, images of how they and their children will act and interact, or images of the loving relationship they expect. These images, especially what they wish to recreate or what they would like to change, emerge from parents' past experiences. Often, however, images and reality are different. Growth occurs when parents modify images so they become more consistent with reality or adjust their behaviour to come closer to the image.

Galinsky emphasized that parents frequently feel their responses and emotions are unique, and are unaware that other parents also experience them. Yet, as she pointed out, during each of the stages of parenthood, parents face predictable issues and strong emotions. It helps parents to discuss and recognize their shared experiences as well as to have opportunities to observe the behaviour of others' children. It is also helpful when professionals explain common reactions and feelings, for instance, to a child's first day at school. In working with children, then, it is very important to acknowledge that parents undergo personal development that parallels their children's growth but has separate issues and conflicts that need to be resolved.

Empowerment, Partnerships, and Advocacy

When parents feel confident and competent in their abilities as mothers and fathers and members of the larger community, their children benefit. Unfortunately, some parents feel that they are powerless in controlling what hap-

pens to them and to their children. Early childhood programs can fill a crucial need for families by promoting **empowerment**, a sense of control or power over events in one's life. This is particularly important as families deal with a variety of agencies and professionals, for instance, school, welfare, and political systems.

Parental empowerment has been a direct aim or an unexpected outcome in some programs designed for low-income families (Cochran, 1988; Ramey, Dorvall, & Baker-Ward, 1983; Seitz et al., 1985). As cited in one report of such a program, "Intangible but crucial shifts in attitude took place in parents who were often severely demoralized at the start" (Nauta & Hewett, 1988, p. 401). Parents began to see that they could have an impact. Professionals can use a wide variety of techniques to help parents attain this sense of control, including approaches described in a number of excellent publications, for instance Alice Honig's *Parent Involvement in Early Childhood Education* (1990).

One of the forces behind the concept of parental empowerment has been the move toward viewing parents and teachers as equals. This relationship, with mutual respect and an equal balance of power regarding decision making, can be called a partnership. Not too many years ago, the pervasive attitude was that professionals were experts whereas parents were the passive recipients of their expertise (Powell, 1989). Such a view does not provide parents with the security that they know their child best and that they should be full participants in any decisions that affect the child. As equal partners, both parents and teachers need to be treated with respect, their opinions should be asked for and taken seriously, and both partners must be involved in decisions about the child. Often parents need to be encouraged to advocate for their children and need to feel they have an ally, not an adversary, in the school. Part of the school's role is to educate the parents on and appreciate the parents' role in the advocacy process. Understanding the concepts of communication and relationships helps raise parents' awareness about their rights and responsibilities in their role as empowered equals. In addition, when early childhood professionals and parents share child development information, both have tools with which to make informed decisions about the children's needs. Thus, involving, consulting and collaborating with, and providing relevant education for parents and teachers can have a far-reaching impact by helping both recognize their own importance, competence, and integral and mutual role in the child's quality care (Swick, 1994).

● Coordinating Needs and Programs

Helping parents reach their potential as effective adults may be a goal in some programs that work extensively with families, particularly those from impoverished backgrounds. In all early childhood programs, there are additional points of contact between parents and teachers, at times revolving around seemingly mundane matters but nonetheless important. A flexible, good-humoured attitude can help establish and maintain positive home-school relationships.

Parents' busy lives or unforeseen events are sometimes at odds with the schedule and routine of the early childhood centre. For instance, one mother expressed concern that the centre's afternoon snack, provided at 3:30, was served too late and that the child was not interested in dinner at 5:30. Another parent preferred that her child not take a nap at school because when he slept during the day, he was just not ready to sleep at home until quite late in the evening. Other problems (e.g., car trouble, a traffic snarl, or unexpected overtime at work) may keep a parent from arriving until after the centre has closed.

All of these situations can cause conflict but also provide an opportunity to evaluate what is best for the child, the parents, the other children, and the teachers. Sometimes such predicaments can be resolved fairly easily, but there are times when the needs of the child, the parent, and the school directly conflict. For instance, there is no simple solution as to whether a child should take a nap, particularly when he appears to need it, or not take a nap because a delayed evening bedtime keeps his mother from getting the sleep she needs. Teachers must carefully weigh their own professional judgment of what is best for the child, taking into account the child's need for sleep, the potential effect of being sleepy and cranky on the ability to function well at school, and the fact that the child would be treated differently from the other children by not napping. One way of resolving such conflicts—whether they involve naps, snacks, or pickup time—is communication, our next topic.

● Communicating with Families

Effective, positive communication is the key to any successful relationship, especially with families, and is vital to providing a consistent and congruent experience for young children. There is no simple formula for ensuring that such contact does, indeed, take place. But ensuring that it does take place is a right, role, and responsibility of both family and teachers. Families are an excellent resource and advocate not only for their children but also for child care in general. As partners, we rely on and trust each other to take ownership of children's overall positive growth and development and to effectively communicate in order to achieve this. Each family is unique and brings to the early childhood program distinctive strengths and needs. Just as the teacher deals with each child as a unique individual by employing a variety of teaching and guidance methods, so must a flexible approach be maintained in communicating with families to meet their individual requirements.

Communication with families should be viewed as a way to foster between the teachers and the family a bond that enhances the child's experiences in both school and home settings, and not simply as an opportunity to report inappropriate behaviour. Even if inappropriate behaviour is among the topics discussed, meetings and case conferences about individual children should be supportive and affirm the child's and family's strengths. Parents should leave such meetings feeling they have learned something, have contributed as an equal partner in the relationship, and would like to return.

Of course, formal meetings and conferences are not the only way to communicate. There are many bits of information that need to be shared by teachers and the family. For instance, both sides will benefit from discussing the child. In addition, there is often more general information about various aspects of the program that must be shared with families. The type of information to be conveyed often determines the communication method used. Communication, as we will discuss, can be carried out using both individual and group methods. Most early childhood centres utilize a combination of these approaches. However, parents and teachers should feel equally comfortable in initiating and requesting communication, be it a formal meeting or an informal chat.

● Individual Communication Methods

The best way to get to know each family is through interaction and contact with individuals. Informally, such contact can take place daily, for instance, when children are dropped off and picked up from school. More formally, scheduled conferences between teacher and parents or other family members provide an avenue for exchange of information.

● Informal Contact with Families

Daily Exchanges.   At the beginning and end of each day, at least one teacher should be available to exchange a few words with family members who drop off or pick up their children. Such informal interactions can make teachers more sensitive to the needs of children and families, can establish mutual trust, can convey a feeling of caring and interest to parents, and can heighten parents' involvement in the program. A recommendation from the 1980s still is relevant: "By being open, receptive, and chatty, teachers encourage parent interest and commitment" (Reiber & Embry, 1983, p. 162).

Notes and Phone Calls.   Because frequent school-family contacts are important, it makes sense to structure the schedule so that staff are free to participate in such exchanges (Tizard, Mortimer, & Burchell, 1981). The informal dialogues at the start and end of the day tend to be the most pervasive form of family involvement in early childhood programs (Gestwicki, 2000), especially those primarily involving working parents. In programs where children arrive by bus or come in car pools, the teacher needs to make an extra effort to maintain contact with parents, for instance, through notes or telephone calls (Gestwicki, 2000).

Some schools send home "happy notes"—brief, personalized notes that share with the parents something positive that happened during the day (Bundy, 1991). Telephone calls provide a comfortable way of talking to parents, particularly if the calls are made often enough and not only when they signal a problem.

Open-Door Policy.   Parents should always be welcome at the school. They have entrusted the care of their child to you. Working parents need a link to the children and need to spend whatever time they can with their children. In addition, the more time you spend together, the more you begin to understand and appreciate each other's needs. Parents are an excellent source of information, comfort, and strength. As partners, you share the responsibilities of caring.

● Formal Contact with Families

Informal daily contacts between teachers and family members can create a mutually respectful and non-intimidating atmosphere. When teachers and parents feel comfortable with each other, communication will more likely be honest. In addition to such day-to-day encounters, more formal opportunities should be structured, when a sizable block of uninterrupted time is set aside for in-depth discussion. Such formal contacts can take the form of a **parent-teacher conference** or a home visit.

Parent-Teacher Conferences.   This is a regularly scheduled meeting that can satisfy different objectives. It can focus on getting acquainted; sharing information about the child and presenting a progress report; or, at the initiation of either teacher or parents, solving problems or discussing specific issues (Gestwicki, 2000). Conferences often have negative connotations for the participants, who may view them as a time to share complaints and problems, perhaps even as a last resort when all else fails. But routinely scheduled conferences should be positive, affirming, and supportive. Parents of children with exceptionalities often need to conference more frequently, but they usually have a very positive attitude toward such conferences as they act as a resource in helping them to meet their child's needs.

A conference should never be an impromptu event. Both the teacher and the parents need to be well prepared, reviewing relevant information and thinking about how best to present it. In fact, preparing for conferences should be an ongoing process, beginning when the child first enters the program. Being ready with some anecdotes to support what you tell the parents helps convey to them that you know their child well. It is also important to think through what questions you might want to ask of the parents to help you to better understand and work with their child.

Equally importantly, you should facilitate a relaxed and easy forum for conversation. Sometimes sharing something with the parents, for instance, a picture painted by the child or a favourite recipe for play dough, contributes toward creating a positive atmosphere. The Partnerships box presents some helpful strategies to use when conducting a parent-teacher conference, suggested by Carol Gestwicki in her valuable book, *Home, School, and Community Relations: A Guide to Working with Parents* (2000).

Partnerships

HELPFUL STRATEGIES FOR PARENT-TEACHER CONFERENCES

1. Use common, not technical, terms. Avoid jargon that is not readily understood by someone unfamiliar with child development terminology. Don't tell the parents, "Halie functions one standard deviation below her age norm in fine motor development," when you could convey the message by saying, "Halie is still learning to cut with scissors and string small beads; we've been working on such tasks."

2. Use an egalitarian, not an authoritarian, approach. Parents can easily be put off when confronted with a teacher who is the expert and knows it all, telling them what they "should," "have to," or "must not" do. An authoritarian approach conveys that only the teacher is right and, by implication, the parents are wrong. Nothing prevents give-and-take discussion more quickly!

3. Provide an objective evaluation of the child. Teachers have to be sensitive to how closely parents' self-esteem is tied to their children. When a teacher seems critical of the child, the parents may quickly feel hurt and defensive. This does not mean that you should avoid sharing your concerns about the child. This can be better accomplished, however, by providing the parents with objective descriptions of the child's behaviour rather than by using labels and negative words. Examples of words to avoid include "problem," "immature," "hyperactive," and "slow."

4. Provide privacy and maintain a professional tone in conversations. It is important to ensure confidentiality in all information about children and families. A parent-teacher conference should never include discussions about other children and parents. Such talk can only make the parents wonder what the teacher might say about them.

5. Provide alternatives rather than answers. Problem situations, shared by parents, are seldom simple and easily solved, because the teacher cannot know all the complexities. Furthermore, there are usually many possible ways of dealing with problems. It is important to ask the parents what they have tried and what has worked for them. In addition, it is helpful to provide alternatives for parents. You might provide several suggestions that have "worked for other parents" or that "we've tried in the classroom" as ideas for the parent to consider. When parents come to their own conclusions and chart a course of action, these suggestions are much more likely to be effective.

6. Take your time in approaching solutions. It is not realistic to expect that complex problems can be solved during a parent-teacher conference (Gestwicki, 2000). The teacher may suggest that both she (or he) and the parents take time to observe before jumping to premature conclusions.

7. Be sure to check back with the family to see if the suggestions are working. If they are not effective, meet again and formulate new strategies. If they are working, continue to provide support and feedback.

Home Visits.　**Home visits** share some of the same objectives and procedures as parent-teacher conferences, but they contribute some added benefits as well. A teacher who visits a family at home conveys a sense of caring and interest in the child's world beyond the classroom. Children are usually delighted to introduce their room, toys, pets, and siblings to the teacher and feel very special that the teacher is visiting them at home. Parents can observe firsthand the interaction between the child and the teacher, and may become more relaxed with the teacher who has shown this special interest. In addition, teachers can observe firsthand the family's home environment and parent-child interactions in order to better understand the child's behaviour. In some instances, especially once a sense of trust has been established, home visits can become an extremely important source of support (e.g., for teenage parents). Parents with children who have special needs often prefer home visits as they cause less disruption to the other children in the family (Allen, 1988).

Although there are very important benefits in conducting home visits, they are also quite time-consuming and may (though certainly not inevitably) intimidate the parents. On the other hand, a teacher from a suburban home may be intimidated by visiting an inner-city home. A teacher's commitment to learning as much as possible about the children in the class and their families must be weighed against other factors, including perceived risks to the teacher, comfort level of the parents and teacher, and time. There are instances when meeting at the centre or school, for example, is preferable or when it is necessary for a colleague to accompany you to the child's home for support and an additional source of information.

Communication Book.　Some programs send a communication book back and forth with the child daily between home and school. Teachers can write about the child's day while parents can write about exciting news, sleep patterns, anecdotes, or influential events that might lend insight into the child's behaviour for that day. It is important to remember that it is not mandatory for parents to write in the book daily but that it is there as a tool if they need to use it. This type of communication system is especially worthwhile with infants and toddlers who are not able to go home and report the day's events to their parents.

● When Problems Arise Between Parents and Teachers

Ideally, parents and teachers cooperate fully to provide positive experiences for children at home and at school. Unfortunately, there are times when this ideal is not always realized. In fact, parent-teacher disharmony is quite common (Galinsky, 1990; Gonzalez-Mena, 1993). Parents and teachers may disagree, particularly when they feel rushed and tired or when they are preoccupied with other aspects of their lives. In addition, both may harbour some unacknowledged negative feelings, for instance, disapproval of working mothers, jealousy or competition for the child's affection, or criticism of the other's child guidance approach (Galinsky, 1988, 1990). Although the child provides a common bond between parents and teachers, there are many other factors that affect their moods and impinge on their interactions. The job stress experienced by parents as well as by teachers can certainly spill over into the brief contact between them as children are dropped off or picked up at school during what Ellen Galinsky called the "arsenic hour" (1988). In addition, teachers sometimes resent certain parents. For example, there may be parents who convey the impression that they do not value the teacher and his or her work. In other cases, the teacher may feel that she or he is the only person who is an advocate for the child. There also is the case of the parent who is always late picking up the child from the centre.

Galinsky (1988) offered some concrete suggestions for working more effectively with parents. She suggested that when teachers become upset with parents, it is often because teachers' underlying expectations are somehow not realized; teachers need to examine whether their expectations are realistic. Similarly, teachers should scrutinize their attitudes toward the parents, looking for hidden resentments or prejudices. Teachers also need to make an effort to see the situation from the parents' point of view, asking themselves how they might feel if they were in the parents' shoes.

It can be very helpful for teachers to develop a support system, whether within their own program or even outside of it, which allows them to express and explore their feelings in an accepting and safe atmosphere. Teachers must also recognize and convey to parents the limits of their role. This includes being familiar with community resources to which parents can be referred when a problem is beyond the scope of the teacher's role and expertise. Parents also need support, and sometimes, establishing a school parent support group gives them the necessary outlet they need to calm fears and ease pressures.

There is no simple formula for effective parent-teacher communication. The parent-teacher relationship is founded on trust and respect, which grow out of many small but significant daily contacts. Greeting parents by name, writing personalized notes, making phone calls to parents whom the teacher does not see often, being sensitive to parents' needs, and sharing brief, positive anecdotes about their children all contribute to a good relationship (Morgan, 1989).

● Group Communication Methods

In addition to personalized, individual contact between parents and teachers, early childhood programs generally also utilize other communication methods for getting information to the parents as a group. These methods can serve a functional purpose, for instance, to let parents know that the school will be closed Monday when Canada Day falls on a Saturday. They may also take on an educational role, for example, to give parents insight into an aspect of child development. We will review four such methods: physical environment, written communiqués, bulletin boards, and meetings.

● Physical Environment

Setting the stage for communication is the first step. If parents feel comfortable in the school, they will be more likely to voice concerns, make suggestions, participate, or praise. An inviting atmosphere and welcoming tone is so important. Are there people smiling and greeting parents? Is there a parent information board at the front door? Is there adult-sized furniture where they can relax? A family achievement wall of fame? A calendar of social events and pictures of prior events? Is time always available to meet with parents? Are parents regularly invited to events and meetings? Parents are an integral, vital, and key component to the program. Using the principles of invitational education (Purkey & Novak, 1996; cf. A Canadian Professional Speaks Out, Chapter 6), you can make the centre an inviting place where adults want to be, where they have no concerns about comfort and acceptance. Even parents who have never been comfortable in an educational setting before realize that some centres are indeed "the most inviting place in town."

● Written Communiqués

Newsletters, memos, or other written material can be an effective way of getting information to all families—as long as the parents are literate—and the note does not fly away when Guzmayadi gets off the bus! Written communiqués can provide parents with an overview of current events in the program (e.g., hatching of duck eggs), and thus facilitate parent-child discussions about the program (and possible expertise on ducks from a parent).

It is, of course, important to match written information to the reading abilities of the parents. If many or all of the families in the program are non-English-speaking, for instance, communiqués should be written in the parents' primary language. In larger communities with a high percentage of immigrants, translation services, if not available through a parent, are often available through an ethnic group's cultural association. Community social workers and psychologists also have access to a list of translators. It is also important that all such materials be neat, attractive, and accurately written. A sloppy, misspelled, and ungrammatical letter conveys that the teacher does not care enough about the families to produce a thoughtful document. Today many schools have access to a computer, which makes it simpler than ever to compose attractively arranged letters or newsletters, check the grammar and spelling, and incorporate graphics. Other factors to consider are the type and size of print, amount of print, visual effects, type of paper (is it recycled, supporting the school's stated environmental policy?), use of colour, and so on. These factors signify time, effort, care, and professionalism.

Many programs produce a regular newsletter that may contain announcements, news of what the teachers have planned for the upcoming time period, new policies, relevant community information, child development research summaries, columns by local experts, and other information of interest to families. A newsletter is only effective if it is read. Thus, its length, the information included, and the writing style need to be carefully considered.

Another form of written communication that can convey a great deal of information to parents is a school handbook, which parents are given when they enroll their children in the early childhood program. Such a handbook should contain relevant information about school policies and procedures, fees, hours of operation, holidays, sick child care, birthday routines, and other important matters. In addition, it should include a clear statement of the school's philosophy (Bundy, 1991).

● Bulletin Boards

Bulletin boards can be either a useful means of conveying information or a cluttered mass of overlaid memos that no one bothers to look at. To be effective, a bulletin board should be attractively laid out, feature contents that are current, and have items that do not compete with one another for attention. Further, if family members know that only current and important items will be posted on a specific bulletin board, they are more likely to pay attention to it.

Bulletin boards can be used for a variety of purposes. They can be informative, for instance, letting parents know that the children will be taking a field trip the following week or that a child in the group is home with chickenpox. Many centres include a notice of the day's activities on a bulletin board, which lets parents know the highlights of their child's day.

Bulletin boards can also be educational, conveying relevant information in a way that appeals to those who look at it. At one centre, for instance, the teachers wanted to follow up on comments from several parents that their children were just scribbling rather than drawing something recognizable. The teachers wanted to help parents understand that children's art follows a developmental pattern. They matted selections of the children's pictures, arranged them attractively on bulletin boards organized by the children's ages, and interspersed the pictures with quotes from experts on children's art. The pictures supported the quotations, thus conveying the messages that children gradually move toward representational art and that there are common steps children go through in their development of art. Many parents commented on how helpful they found this bulletin board information. It proved to be a most effective teaching tool.

In another centre, a Canadian cooperative nursery school, the teacher became concerned when she noticed that some parents were not using seat belts for their children when on a trip to the sugar bush, even though they are mandatory. An inviting bulletin board display on the merits of seat belts was her diplomatic approach to this concern.

● Meetings and Other Group Functions

Group gatherings can provide another effective way of reaching family members. Such functions can take the form of meetings, the traditional forum for formal **parent education**, or they can be social. In addition, parent discussion groups may be part of the early childhood program. When planning any kind of group function, however, keep in mind that family members are busy people who will weigh the benefits of attending a school program against other demands on their time. In fact, for some parents the pressure of one more thing to do might be so stressful that it would outweigh the advantages of the program. Because each family's needs are different, the early childhood program must facilitate communication with parents in many different ways and be prepared to individualize ways of meeting these needs.

If the supervisor and teachers feel that parent meetings can serve a positive function in meeting the needs of some of the families, they must ensure that what they plan will interest potential participants. One way to assess what might be relevant to parents is to conduct an interest survey. A brief form can solicit preferences about topic choices, time and day, and type of meeting. If the teachers or the supervisor plan parent functions without input from the parents, these functions may well fail to match the interest of the parents and result in very low attendance (Gestwicki, 2000). Also, parents are often more likely to come to a meeting if a meal or snack is included and if child care is provided. On the other hand, keep in mind that if children have already spent nine or ten hours at the centre, adding two evening hours may be more than is reasonable.

Parent get-togethers may feature a speaker with expertise on a topic of common interest, or they may revolve around discussion led by a facilitator. It is important to remember that parents' shared experiences are a valuable source of information and support (Kelly, 1981). Thus, if the main part of the program includes a speaker, time should also be allocated for discussion.

One particularly enjoyable way of presenting some topics is to illustrate them with slides or videotapes taken of the children at the school. Such subjects as children's play, social development, or developmentally appropriate toys can be enhanced with such visuals. In addition to gaining insight into an aspect of their children's development, parents will feel great pride in seeing their youngsters depicted on the screen.

Small groups are generally more effective than large groups in encouraging participation (Gestwicki, 2000). A common interest can also create a more intimate atmosphere for a meeting, for instance, involving parents whose children will enter kindergarten the following year or just the parents of children in one class rather than those from the entire early childhood centre.

Some centres generate considerable enthusiasm for social events during which parents and teachers have the opportunity to exchange information in a relaxed atmosphere. These can include holiday parties, meals, or an open house, and they can involve all family members. One university program sponsored a potluck dinner for families, staff, and student-teachers every semester. Prearranged seating assured that student-teachers sat with the families of children they were observing. This event attracted almost all of the families and proved to be enjoyable as well as valuable for all involved.

Family Involvement

We have been discussing various ways in which communication between teachers and families can be maintained. However this communication takes place, it implies involvement on the part of the family. Let's look at family involvement in more detail. Later, the A Closer Look box examines the parents' role in the early childhood environment.

Family involvement in the early childhood program is a multifaceted concept, embracing a wide range of options and levels. It can mean that parents and other family members are passive recipients of information; parents may be more intensely engaged by serving as volunteers in the program; or, at an even more complex level of involvement, they can be participants in the decision-making process of the program (Honig, 1979). Whatever the level, however, ample research has shown that such involvement has positive benefits for both children and families (Becher, 1986; Gestwicki, 2000; Powell, 1989).

The family-centred model encompasses all aspects of involvement and acknowledges the family as the focal point of care. Remembering that the family is a system, the advocates of this model focus on empowering and strengthening the family as a whole. Early childhood educators using this model go beyond just linking or directing families to employment agencies, social service agencies, or support groups. They help provide and coordinate services and become members of the family's interdisciplinary team.

There is a reciprocal relationship between the family and the early childhood program, each providing support and help to the other as they are able. Family involvement will vary according to each family's ability to contribute and to its needs. Some families invest a great deal of their time and energy in the program, whereas others need all their resources to cope with the stresses they face. Some families support the program by participating in and contributing time to various school activities; others seek support from the program in facing their personal strains. As a teacher in an early childhood program, you will need to be flexible to be able to recognize each family's capabilities and needs and to set expectations or provide support accordingly. While this may seem like a formidable task early on in your studies, the qualities that drew you to the early childhood profession, coupled with the knowledge and experience you acquire during your studies, will help you to be sensitive to each family's needs.

You will also find that you can involve families in your program in a variety of ways. For example, you might involve family members as resources, as volunteers in the classroom, and/or as decision-makers. Regardless of the extent or type of involvement, an involved parent is a far greater asset to the program than an uninvolved one, since planning, implementing, and evaluating becomes a team effort. A comprehensive family-centred model utilizes all these approaches, making the family the focus, rather than the program.

Families as Resources

Family members have many talents and abilities to contribute to the program. Many early childhood programs invite parents or relatives to participate on occasions when their job skills, hobbies, or other special expertise can augment and enrich the curriculum. For instance, a teacher may invite Ronnie's mother, who is a dentist, to help the children understand the importance of good dental hygiene and care; the teacher may take the children to visit the bakery owned by Annie's uncle, because the class is discussing foods; she can ask Carmelo's father to show the children how he makes pottery; or she may invite Ivan's mother and new baby brother when the class talks about babies and growing up. All family members—parents, siblings, grandparents, other relatives, and even pets—can be considered part of the program, extending its resource base.

Family members can also help out with maintenance and construction tasks that are part of the program. In some early childhood programs, especially parent cooperatives, parents routinely take home the dress-up clothes and other classroom items to wash or clean. In others, regularly scheduled cleanup days bring teachers and family members to the centre on specified weekends to deep-clean the facility, materials, and equipment. Family members with carpentry skills may construct or repair equipment. Others may develop learning materials and games at home that will expand the activity options available to the children.

There are other ways in which family members can serve as program resources. For instance, they can help orient new families to the early childhood program, serve as role models, and provide support to other families. Their suggestions and ideas can enrich the program. Family members can also be extremely effective in providing local and provincial support for legislation that affects children and families, and can help provide program visibility in the community if the school is seeking outside funding. Family support can be a potent force in maintaining a high-quality early childhood program.

Family Members in the Classroom

Family members may also volunteer as teacher aides. Programs such as parent-cooperative preschools require parent involvement on a regular basis. Some programs modelled after Project Head Start also require that parents spend time in the classroom, although forced participation can be counterproductive (Honig, 1979; 1990). In most programs, particularly in child care centres, parents participate occasionally or not at all because parents are usually working while their children are at school. Some teachers relish such involvement; others feel skeptical and reluctant, fearing a clash with the parents' child-rearing practices, feeling stress about being under constant observation, or worrying that the children will get overexcited (Gestwicki, 2000).

Having parents in the classroom can have many benefits for children, parents, and teachers. Children can benefit from having their parents participate in the classroom, feeling pride and a sense of security as they see their parent(s) working together, and respecting and valuing each other's contribution (Gestwicki, 2000). For parents, such firsthand experience can provide insight into how their children spend their time at school, a basis for observing their own children in relation to age-mates, and a chance to note guidance techniques used by teachers. Teachers can benefit from the support parents offer, the added pair of hands that can expand activity possibilities, and the opportunity to gain insight into parent-child interactions (Gestwicki, 2000). There are, however, some consequences of having parents in the class that teachers and parents should expect.

The full-time teachers in parent cooperatives perhaps have the most experience with parents in the classroom as the staffing schedule includes a rotating staff of parents. Teachers in cooperatives often comment that children behave differently when their own parents are there as helpers, although this change is most pronounced on the first few occasions when a parent is present. It is important to forewarn parents that child's behaviour may be different when one or both of them is present as their child's behaviour on the day they visit may become a concern for them. Some children, for example, develop new bravado if Mom or Dad are there—the usually gentle and quiet child may become aggressive and loud; the independent child might become clingy and whiny.

● Family Members as Decision Makers

Some programs ask parents to serve on an advisory or a policy board. Some university-based programs, for instance, invite parents to participate in parent advisory councils. Many not-for-profit child care or preschool centres also require a governing board of which parents are members. Effective decision-making boards can promote a true partnership between families and the school program (Dunst & Trivette, 1988), providing support for the school, empowerment of parents, and increased mutual understanding.

● Adult Education and Lifelong Learning

All forms of family involvement potentially serve an educational function, since parents have the chance to gain insights into their children's development and the school's program. Often, however, early childhood programs provide specific parent education aimed at enhancing parent-child relations and improving parenting competence. Given the numbers of children who grow up in abusive homes and in poverty, some professionals even consider that high-quality parent education programs should be mandatory to prevent needless impairment of children through abuse, neglect, and deprivation (Anastasiow, 1988). Evaluation of many parent education programs aimed at economically disadvantaged families has indicated that such programs can be very effective, although much still remains to be learned through systematic research (Clarke-Stewart, 1983; Powell, 1986). In addition, there is limited evidence that parent education enhances the parenting skills of middle-class families as well (e.g., Harris & Larsen, 1989), although the anecdotal evidence from Reggio Emilia suggests this involvement is very important.

A Closer Look

PARENTS' ROLE IN THE EARLY CHILDHOOD ENVIRONMENT

Parents can be active participants in matters related to the early childhood environment. To begin with, the parents' choice of a preschool or child care centre can be viewed as part of an environmental decision. Early childhood facilities, as part of a larger environment, contribute to and reflect the total character of their community. Often children's programs mirror the community's purpose and ethnic or cultural characteristics. For instance, there are distinct differences in an inner-city centre, an employer-supported program located on the premises of a factory, a suburban child care facility for dual-income parents, or a bilingual preschool in a predominantly immigrant community. By enrolling their children in their community's early childhood facilities, parents lend support to the wider community (Berns, 1989).

In addition, parents can contribute in a variety of ways to selecting, modifying, or maintaining various aspects of the environment. Some programs have advisory or policymaking parent councils that may be involved in decisions about major purchases or construction. Parents also often have a strong commitment to their children's program and are willing to spend a few weekend hours helping to paint, clean, varnish, or construct. Many parents contribute to their child's centre by making learning materials or contributing throwaways that children can use for creative activities. As in all areas of the early childhood centre's functioning, parents can be a tremendous resource in matters related to the environment.

The scope of parent education programs is not easy to capture in a single definition because there is great diversity in the field. Douglas Powell (1986) spelled out some of the contrasts in parent education:

> *Some programs focus on family-community relations while others teach parents how to stimulate a child's cognitive development. Some programs prescribe*

specific skills and styles in relating to young children. ... Some programs are highly structured while others let parents select activities they wish to pursue. In some programs the staff serve as child development experts while other programs adhere to a self-help model with staff in non-directive facilitator roles. There are important differences in the use of professionals, assistants, or volunteers, program length (weeks versus years), and program setting (group- versus home-based). (P. 47)

Parent education can take many forms. Often informal, one-to-one interactions at pickup and drop-off times are valuable, especially because they are tailored to the individual. Parent get-togethers or meetings are another frequently used forum. The content of such programs can vary widely, depending on parents' interests and needs. Christine Cataldo, in her book *Parent Education for Early Childhood* (1987), suggests a wide variety of subjects. Popular topics often revolve around children's development, including characteristics and common problems of various ages. Other topics can focus on various aspects of caring for children, for instance, nutrition, health and fitness, self-care and protection, and selecting child care services. Family composition, challenges, and crises offer many program possibilities as well. Children's play and appropriate toys provide other topic choices of interest to parents. In addition, most parents are concerned with issues related to children's behaviours, discipline, guidance, fears, sexual development and interest, personality development, and self-esteem. Finally, the family's involvement in and promotion of children's education include many areas of interest to parents.

Programs can be presented by the early childhood staff, based on their own expertise, or by local resource persons. It is important that presenters be well informed on the topic chosen and that they provide accurate information. In addition, a variety of packaged parent education materials are also available. Such packages may include extensive manuals and provide the facilitator with all the necessary resources to conduct the program. Two popular examples of such parent education programs that focus on development of child guidance skills are Parent Effectiveness Training (P.E.T.) (Gordon, 1976) and Systematic Training for Effective Parenting (STEP) (Dinkmeyer & McKay, 1976). A final note is that there is a wide range of education levels among parents at centres. As well, many parents are also students. These diverse and rich facets of parents' lives should be recognized, respected, and supported.

Key Terms

autonomy vs. shame and doubt	family systems theory
authority stage	generativity
empowerment	home visits
exosystem	interpretive stage
family involvement	macrosystem

mesosystem
microsystem
parent education
parent-teacher conference
perceived competence

personal control
restraining order
self-concept
self-esteem

Key Points

Children—Similarities

1. The early childhood educator's understanding of child development is vital in providing a supportive and developmentally appropriate program for young children.

2. Positive self-esteem is a need shared by all children and is fostered by adults who convey to children that they are competent and worthwhile.

3. Children's perceived competence reflects their belief in their own ability to be successful; such self-confidence contributes to positive self-esteem.

4. Children who have a sense of personal control and a feeling that they can make things happen see themselves as effective, which also contributes to self-esteem.

5. Play provides many opportunities for children to practise skills, stretch thinking abilities, work through emotions, socialize, and be creative.

Children—Differences

6. Children have inborn temperaments that contribute to individual differences. Some children are basically easygoing, whereas others are difficult.

7. Children's uniqueness also derives from the cultural, ethnic, religious, or economic background of their families. These differences will be discussed in greater detail in Chapters 13 and 14.

Families—A Theoretical Perspective

8. Family systems theory views the family as a dynamic, constantly changing system that interacts with other systems, for instance, those within the community.

The Changing Canadian Family

9. There is no simple or single definition of the family because families come in many forms. Families also differ on the basis of economic, racial, cultural, ethnic, religious, language, and geographic factors.

10. An estimated one-fifth of Canadian children grow up in poverty, a relevant factor in many early childhood programs.

The Needs of Families and Parenthood

11. One of the most important needs of working parents is for high-quality, reliable care for their young children.

12. The Canadian family is changing very rapidly, and this often adds to a teacher's responsibilities (e.g., poverty and legal problems of the parents).

13. It is important to acknowledge that parents undergo personal development which parallels their children's growth but that they have separate conflicts and issues which need to be resolved.

Communicating with Families

14. Teachers and parents need to work closely to determine what is best for the child and the family. This is accomplished by effective, positive communication.

15. When problems arise, teachers need to develop a support system that allows them to express and explore their feelings in a safe and accepting atmosphere.

16. There are many ways to avoid communication problems (e.g., parental bulletin boards, parent lounge, parent associations and support groups, newsletters, handbooks).

17. Extended families (including pets) can have positive benefits for the children as well as the family.

18. Parental education is important at the centre and can include not only children's development but also nutrition, self-care, fitness, and selection of childcare services.

Family Involvement

19. Family involvement in the early childhood program has positive benefits for children, families, and the school.

Key Questions

1. Observe several children of the same age. These might be children you work with and know well or children that you are observing for the first time. What traits do they share? How are they similar? Can you draw some conclusions about children of that particular age?

2. Think about these same children and describe what makes each unique. How do they differ? Do you have any indications about what factors underlie these differences?

3. As you observe children, identify a child who appears to be self-confident. How does the child express this confidence? Do you see a difference between this child and another who seems less assured?

4. Think of your own family history. How has your family changed over the past two (or three or four) generations? Consider maternal employment, divorce, closeness to extended family, and other factors. Compare your family with that of other members of your class.

5. Sometimes the needs of families conflict with those of the program. Which elements of the early childhood program could pose a potential conflict? How might these be resolved? Read the Ethics Commission's "Ethics Case Studies: The Working Mother" in Young Children, November 1987, page 16, for insight into the suggestions of professionals to resolve such a conflict.

6. Visit an early childhood program. What evidence of communication with parents do you see? Look at bulletin boards, notes, pictures, and other written material. What kind of interaction do you notice between parents and teachers? What "messages" about the school's concern for parents do parents get from this communication?

7. Ask several parents whose children are enrolled in an early childhood program about their contacts with the teachers and the program. What is their overall attitude about contact between home and school? Do they feel it is important or not important, positive or negative, present or absent, supportive or lacking in support? What do they expect from the teachers? Do they feel that communication between parents and teachers is important for their children?

8. How can parent involvement benefit the early childhood program? List some concrete ways in which parents might contribute to the program.

Chapter 6

Oct 23.03

The Early Childhood Educator

This chapter is about you and your entrance into a very significant, but perhaps undervalued profession that is both old and virtually in its infancy. What does it take to be both a nurturer and a teacher? As a quality early childhood educator, you will find you have to be a jack of all trades—but you are the master of one: you know children. Nevertheless, you will be expected to have talents and skills that you may not even have tried before! One day you are a fundraiser and an expert on caring for the frogs Guido brought to the centre. Then, lo and behold, the next day the job you are a specialist on diaper rash as well as the "fill-in" cook as the real cook went home sick. The following day, you deal with a child who is anaphylactic for peanuts who sat next to Emilia on the bus when she ate M&Ms. Two days later, you have even more talents than you could ever have anticipated: you are a carpenter, fixing the outdoor shed, and a professional, attending a conference on children with special needs. The list of roles and tasks that a teacher is expected to assume is probably infinite, and no text or course can begin to predict what you may be called upon to do. But suffice it to say there is never a dull moment in this field.

This chapter will focus on you not only as a teacher, but as an individual, as a caregiver, and as a member of a profession. Before turning to the professional skills you will need, let's remind ourselves that early childhood educators are people too—with lives and needs, with joys and sorrows. All people need to care for and be cared about. Recognizing your own strengths and needs together with those of others will help you to become a happy, healthy, and successful teacher. As a teacher in an early childhood education program, you will be challenged to integrate knowledge about many things, such as:

1. What you know about child development

2. What you know about the importance of families

3. What you know about creating a healthy and stimulating environment

4. What you know about planning a child-centred curriculum

5. What you know about appropriate and nurturing guidance

6. What you know about providing the best possible care and education for young children

The Early Childhood Educator

Before continuing our discussion of early childhood educators, it is important to clarify terminology. No universally accepted categories and titles define those who work with young children, although several have been proposed. Often labels conjure up stereotypes and do not reflect different educational and experiential backgrounds found in the field (Phillips & Whitebook, 1986).

In keeping with our Canadian profession, we will use the term *early childhood educator*. Other terms, particularly **teacher**, **caregiver**, and **child care worker**, will

also be used interchangeably. Traditionally, *caregiver* has meant someone who cares for the physical and emotional needs of the child, whereas *teacher* denotes an educational function. "However, this distinction is not a particularly clear one, for the line between education and nurture in the early years is not a distinct one" (Spodek & Saracho, 1982, p. 401).

Certainly the early childhood teacher cares for and the caregiver teaches young children. Have you met an early childhood educator who has not tied shoelaces, wiped noses, or dried tears? And have you met an early childhood educator who has not helped children learn how to zip coats, assemble puzzles, or share? Teaching and caregiving functions are related to the point where a distinction is impossible to make (Willer, 1990). In a classic work, Almy (1975) summarized it this way:

> The early childhood educator role may be seen as that of "double specialist" in a variety of ways: In teaching young children and in assessing their development and learning; in working with children and in working with adults; in thinking concretely (maintaining insight into the child's thought) and thinking formally, in practice as well as in theory. (P. 28)

Qualities of the Early Childhood Educator

If asked what qualities a good teacher of young children should have, most of us would come up with an intuitive list of characteristics. Research, however, is not particularly clear-cut in showing a consistent relationship between teacher effectiveness and personal qualities. This is partly due to problems in the methodology of such research, inconsistency in what is being measured, difficulty in distinguishing between teaching style and teaching techniques, and even lack of agreement about what constitutes good teaching (Feeney & Chun, 1985; Katz, 1984a). Certainly, those who care for children need qualities beyond liking babies.

Some clues about what makes a good teacher of young children can be gleaned from early childhood educators and researchers based on their experience and insight. Almy et al. (1984) and Balaban (1992) list several qualities, some of which are included in the following list:

- Patience
- Warmth
- Nurturance
- Energy
- Maturity
- Openness to new ideas
- Ability to move between concrete and abstract thinking

- Ability to anticipate and plan
- Ability to provide an interesting environment
- Ability to elicit language
- Ability to problem-solve
- Playfulness
- Ability to see things from the child's point of view

Good teachers are able to:

- Protect
- Listen
- Observe
- Comfort
- Cope

- Facilitate social interactions
- Guide parent-child separation
- Care for the whole family
- Smooth "jangled feelings"
- Understand

You would certainly want to add many of your own characteristics to this list. Here are a few to think about:

- Gentleness
- Respectfulness
- Intrinsic motivation
- Optimism
- Sincerity
- Inquisitiveness
- Humour
- Openness

- Fairness
- Sensitivity
- Ability to communicate
- Reliability
- Reflectiveness
- Resourcefulness
- Empathy
- Ability to advocate

Your qualities are not something you have, but something that make you who you are. You will find it difficult to separate your personal and professional qualities because they are intertwined. What is important to note is that a good teacher is able to identify his/her qualities, strengths, and needs as well as those of others. Knowing your **learning style** and that of others you interact with will help you to understand, adjust, and contribute to positive, healthy interactions. You should be able to assess, implement, evaluate, and accommodate differing learning styles as they affect you and the others in your midst—the children, families, colleagues with whom you work, and the communities in which you work. According to Adler (1993) the best teachers are those who "are able to systematically reflect on their own teaching" (p. 160) or, in other words, engage in reflective practice. Flexibility is second nature to good teachers. But there really is no simple or single definition of a good teacher of young children. In a summary of six in-depth interviews that searched for a definition of the "good preschool teacher," Ayers (1989) concludes that there is a "kaleidoscope of possibility, for there are endless good preschool teachers" (p. 141).

What does distinguish teachers, according to Katz (1984b), is their professionalism, the way they use their knowledge and standards of performance. Teachers possess advanced knowledge in child development and early childhood education that they apply when they have to make judgments and decisions on a moment-by-moment basis. At the same time, they also share with other professionals a commitment to maintaining the high standards set by the profession through its organizations. The ideal early childhood professional is well paid and knowledgeable and demonstrates high-quality performance, which results in better outcomes for children (Willer & Bredekamp, 1993, p. 64).

Professionalism

This book stresses the importance of the early childhood years, early childhood education, and your role as an early childhood educator. To fully realize that importance, however, you must see yourself as a member of a profession. A profession is different from a job by virtue of certain characteristics. These include:

- A core knowledge base involving philosophical and theoretical principles

- Standards of practice that stem from that knowledge base (Katz, 1988; Vander Ven, 1986)

- A defined code of ethics

- Specialized training founded on that knowledge base

Those who have written at great length about early childhood professionalism, recognizing that there are many inconsistencies and problems to be faced, do not always agree to what extent the field meets the criteria of a profession. Increasing dialogue through conferences and written works has helped to sharpen the focus on relevant issues, for instance, low pay and shortage of qualified early childhood teachers, and on strategies for combating these. Nonetheless, the expanding concern about professionalism, evident at both national and local levels, should propel early childhood education toward its goals, which include a better definition and greater focus.

Although, in many ways, the early childhood field has moved toward professionalization, there is concern that professional status is not universally acknowledged by those who work in the field or by the public at large (Childcare, 2000; Dresden & Myers, 1989; Radomski, 1986; Silin, 1985). Two Canadian studies of child care workers are relevant:

1. *Caring for a Living* (Canadian Child Day Care Federation & Canadian Day Care Advocacy Association, 1992), a study completed in the early 1990s

2. *You Bet I Care!: A Canada-Wide Study On: Wages, Working Conditions, and Practices in Child Care Centres* (Doherty, Lero, Goelman, La Grange, & Tougas, 2000), a study completed in 2000

In this chapter, we will touch on some of the issues raised by these studies, and then return to them in the final two chapters where we will consider the issues in greater depth. The two Canadian studies asked similar questions of early childhood educators, though the scope of the 2000 research was greater, and both raised concerns about the status of the profession that you have chosen. It is clear there is much room for advocacy in this field—for advocating on behalf of a profession that is so critical to infants, toddlers, and young children in Canada.

What can we learn from these two studies? The 1992 study found that 7 out of 10 early childhood educators had postsecondary degrees or diplomas, as opposed to 4 out of 10 workers in the general Canadian workforce. By 2000, that percentage had increased to 8 1/2 out of 10 early childhood educators. Clearly, the profession has well-educated workers. And what are the wages for these well-educated professionals? In the early 1990s, the salaries of the teachers were well below the average wage for Canadian industrial workers. In fact, the 1992 report indicated that someone working in a warehouse, a position that generally requires less skill, education, and responsibility, earned 58 percent more than the average teacher in a non-school-based early childhood program! In the more recent study, the average wage nationally was comparable to that of parking lot attendants, although there is considerable fluctuation in salaries regionally.

Reflective Exercise 6-1

How do you react to these comparisons of early childhood educators and warehouse workers and parking lot attendants? Do you think these occupations were selected for shock value? What do you think your class could do to enhance the status of the profession?

In 1992, most of the Canadian teachers surveyed (84 percent) felt that their profession was not valued by the general public. "It's a bit of a Catch-22: for not only are staff paid poorly, they believe the value of the work they perform is neither acknowledged nor appreciated. And until they are paid higher wages, these perceptions are unlikely to change" (Canadian Child Day Care Federation & Canadian Day Care Advocacy Association, 1992, p. 1). In 2000, 95 percent of the educators surveyed reported they made a difference in children's lives, and about 85 percent found the work made good use of their skills and was stimulating and challenging. Despite that level of satisfaction and challenge, approximately 75 percent of the teachers and supervisors reported that poor pay and lack of opportunity for promotion were the most negative aspects of the job. As in the 1992 study, the educators thought the public undervalued the profession—although some noted that other professionals respected their work. Changes in salary levels and the public perception of the profession are definitely needed in this country. As a student entering the profession, you and your classmates are most likely to effect these long-overdue changes!

As students embarking on a career in early childhood education, you and your classmates are in a unique position to develop from the start a sense of professionalism that is furthered by every course you take, every day you spend with children, and every conference you attend. Your competence and recognition of the importance of their role will enhance not only your work with children and families, but also your contributions to the early childhood profession. Early childhood education teachers who have a clear concept of who they are, what they do, and the importance of their role are quite effective in educating the public. Now let's look again at those four aspects of professionalism—core knowledge, standards of practice, ethics, and training.

● Core Knowledge Base of the Early Childhood Education Profession

As in any profession, such as law or medicine, there is a **core knowledge base** from which early childhood educators draw. This helps define us as professionals within our field and evaluate our effectiveness. It gives us a framework within which to work and serves as a springboard for improvement.

The following, adapted from guidelines established by the National Association for the Education of Young Children (Willer & Bredekamp, 1993, p. 64) and supported by the Canadian Association of Young Children, outlines the exclusive knowledge base and competencies unique to the early childhood education program. An early childhood educator must:

• Understand child development and demonstrate the implication of this knowledge in practice

• Provide an environment that is safe, healthy, nurturing, consistent, and secure for all so that trust is promoted

- Observe and assess children's behaviour in order to plan, individualize, and evaluate children's learning, your own teaching practices, and the curriculum

- Plan, implement, and evaluate developmentally appropriate curriculum that will enhance all facets of children's development—physical, intellectual, creative, linguistic, emotional, social, and moral, to name a few

- Guide children by establishing and facilitating supportive relationships

- Foster and maintain positive and productive relationships with children, families, centres, communities, and your own and other professions)

- Support the development of individual children, recognizing that children are best understood in the context of family, culture, and society

- Model an understanding of the early childhood education profession by making a commitment to professionalism

A person never stops the process of becoming a professional because she/he is always adding to her/his core knowledge base and skill level. Ongoing **professional development** is a part of lifelong learning and of personal and professional growth and development.

Developing Your Philosophy.   It would be difficult to work with young children in an appropriate way without a belief system that dictates how you interact with people. A philosophy is a statement of beliefs and is reflective of your value system, and a philosophy of teaching often is based on theories that can be guided by research. Just as an organization often has a *mission statement*—a statement of what it believes and hopes to accomplish that determines the way it conducts business—so you have a philosophy and values that determine your actions. Philosophies and mission statements and values and beliefs also hold you accountable to your intentions and imply a plan of action. The Reggio Emilia model (discussed in Chapter 3), for example, is a recent example of a *comprehensive* and *inclusionary* approach to child care as it involves the entire community in the development of a system of "early childhood services *based on a common value system* [italics added] and pedagogical philosophy" (Pence & Moss, 1994, p. 173).

You will also find that experience affects your philosophy. Though the basic premises or foundation of your philosophy may never change, your philosophy will become more comprehensive with experience and knowledge. Examples of philosophical statements might include common ideas or beliefs about children such as "I believe all children can learn" or "I believe all children have the right to **inclusive education**" or "I believe all children learn through play." You can also see by now that people hold different belief systems that will conflict with your own. Think of the opposite statements of those just given. What if educational policymakers believed children with special needs could not learn? What if a parent in your program believed children should not play? Their beliefs determine their actions just as your beliefs determine your actions.

Courtesy of Yes I Can! Nursery School.

That is why having evidence that supports your beliefs is important. Being able to explain, state why, or give a rationale for what you believe helps others understand your actions. Hence, a parent night focusing on the importance of play or a policy stating why your program is inclusive of all children will help people accept what, why, and how you do things. Communicating your philosophy is very important.

One way of communicating is through actions. We've all heard the saying that actions speak louder than words. A belief statement can be transformed into an action statement and into actions. For instance, a teacher might say, "I believe all children should be treated with respect," but her action of pulling a child up by the arm or yelling at the child does not support what she says. Your actions must also reflect your beliefs. In other words, you must practice what you preach.

So how do you go about developing your philosophy? You probably already have a good philosophical base. Write it out in "I believe…" statements. Write an action statement of "I will" for each belief statement. For each statement you make, find research that supports it. As you learn and gain more experience throughout your career, continue to refine your philosophy. You must always have a reason for what you do and be able to explain it to others. Just as your philosophy shapes you, so you shape it. It will reflect your growth and development as an early childhood educator and guide your practice. It will help you keep sight of why you entered this wonderful field in the beginning. Remember, in the spirit of childhood, never stop asking why!

● Standards of Practice—Rights, Roles, and Responsibilities

As a member of a profession, and as a person, you are entitled to certain rights and privileges as well as justice and fairness. Similarly, as a professional, there are many roles or functions that you are expected to perform. In the profession, the parts you play and the rights offered to you imply certain responsibilities on your part—duties, skills, and actions that you must carry out in a manner for which you are held accountable. When you meet those expectations, your honour and that of your profession is established and strengthened.

Rights of an Early Childhood Educator. As an early childhood educator, you have the right to:

• Belong to a professional organization that advocates on behalf of its members, promotes the profession, conducts business in a positive, supportive, effective, responsible, and ethical manner, and collects, develops, and disseminates current information about the field to its members

- Access ongoing training and development that will enhance your effectiveness in working appropriately with children

- Have a written job description, a policies and procedures manual, training, and a contract

- Have an evaluation process that is open and fair, and is followed with opportunities for field work and professional development that help you meet recommendations and expectations outlined in the evaluation

- Receive pay that is commensurate with your degree of education and training, your core knowledge base, your responsibilities, and community expectations

- Be recognized as a valued, respected, and credible partner in a reciprocal and mutually beneficial system of government

- Belong to a work environment:

    i. That is safe, nurturing, and healthy

    ii. That encourages, promotes, and supports the development of relationships, communication, and professional development

    iii. That recognizes and respects the needs, diversity, confidentiality, and privacy of its staff—in tandem with human rights and labour regulations

    iv. That encourages freedom of speech in the assumption of democratic practice

Roles of an Early Childhood Educator. As an early childhood educator, you are expected to be:

- A professional
- A nurturer
- A caregiver
- A teacher
- An advocate
- An employee
- A colleague
- A member
- A partner
- A learner
- An individual with specific strengths and needs in the context of your own family, culture, and society

Responsibilities of an Early Childhood Educator. Your responsibility is ultimately to understand and implement the core knowledge base previously discussed. This is a serious task with powerful consequences that affect the lives of many people. Your responsibilities are linked to each of your roles, since each of your partners (i.e., children, families, colleagues) also have rights that must be recognized, respected, and addressed. By now you can see the importance and interrelatedness of a **systems approach** in the workplace and how impossible it would be to acknowledge only isolated elements of a system. Issues of philosophy and practice must be considered when viewing a system. A system has many parts that must work both dependently and independently to keep the system working. Thus a system is dynamic or fluid—it is always moving, changing, and adjusting—and needs components that are both flexible and adhesive to keep it malleable yet in tact. Communication is the substance that bonds the elements and the people of our profession.

● Ethics

One of the hallmarks of a profession is its recognition of and adherence to a **code of ethics**. Such a code embodies guidelines for behaviour, facilitates decision making, and provides the backing of likeminded professionals when the practitioner takes a "risky but courageous stand in the face of an ethical dilemma" (Katz, 1988, p. 77). In recent years, a number of provincial organizations have developed codes of ethics governing the profession. For example, the Canadian Child Care Foundation has a code of ethics that is based on the Code of Ethics developed by the Early Childhood Educators of British Columbia (ECEBC).

Some provinces as well as British Columbia, such as Prince Edward Island and Ontario, have developed their own codes of ethics (e.g., the Association for Early Childhood Educators, Ontario). To view two provincial codes of ethics, one from the Early Childhood Development Association of Prince Edward Island and another from the Association of Early Childhood Education, Ontario, go to the Canadian Child Care Federation's Web site. Click on affiliates to access the P.E.I. and Ontario Associations' Web pages; both have their code of ethics available online whereas most other associations charge for a hard copy.

Smaller and newer provincial associations often adopt codes of ethics from other provinces rather than reinventing the code. For example, the Saskatchewan Child Care Association (SCCA) is relatively new so they adopted British Columbia's code. This reflects a dedication to professionalism for such a young organization. Since codes consume a great deal of time and resources to develop, the SCCA wanted to ensure it had a code of ethics clearly outlined from the beginning. This helped to establish its credibility as an agency for its members and as a spokesperson for the field and the children in its care.

Codes of ethics recognize that many of the day-to-day decisions made by those who work with young children are of a moral and ethical nature. Early childhood educators, for instance, may find themselves in situations with conflicting values in which it is not clear whether the rights of the child, the parents, the school, other children in the program, or the teachers are most important (Feeney, 1988b). A code of ethics provides common principles for dealing with such dilemmas, principles based on the value of childhood as a unique stage of life, on knowledge of child development, on appreciation of the importance of family and cultural ties, on respect for the dignity and value of children and adults, and on helping individuals reach their potential through trusting, positive relationships.

Because children are particularly vulnerable, those who work with them have an important responsibility that is supported and defined by a code of ethics (Feeney & Kipnis, 1985). As you enter the early childhood education profession, it is important to learn about the code of ethics followed in your area. If you are in a jurisdiction that does not yet have a code, you should familiarize yourself with one or more from other jurisdictions and perhaps help the professional association in your province or territory to develop one.

● Training and Regulation in Early Childhood Education

Many individuals contribute toward providing a good early childhood education program, or system, through their levels and types of expertise. Such expertise stems from different types of training. In addition, a variety of regulations and quality controls apply to early childhood programs and the personnel who staff them. The range of training options and requirements varies greatly across the country, as do the regulations governing early childhood programs.

Academic Teacher Training Programs. Because you are reading this text, you are most likely involved in an academic early childhood education program whose aim is to prepare qualified teachers and directors of programs for young children through a combination of course work and practicum experiences. As you know from Chapter 4, such programs exist at the college, university, and post-graduate levels. In more advanced programs, greater depth and more theoretical and research knowledge become increasingly important. You are entering a field of exciting growth, change, and recognition that has taken centuries to evolve and only decades to explode.

As we noted above, Canadian early childhood educators are well educated themselves. The situation is comparable in the United States where two-thirds of teachers and more than one-half of assistant teachers have taken at least some early childhood or child development course work (Whitebook, Howes, & Phillips, 1989). Many colleges and universities across Canada have reciprocal agreements. These may be called "fasttracking," "equivalency," or "direct entry." These allow students with child studies degrees to enter the second year of a college's early childhood education program or a student with an early childhood education diploma to enter the second year of a child studies degree program. Some professional organizations also grant equivalency—a diploma equivalent to an early childhood education diploma and recognized by that province's ministry governing early childhood education college programs—to individuals who have a unique combination of experience and education (e.g., someone trained in another country). With such a diverse and highly trained group of individuals working in the early childhood field, you would expect the profession to be viewed with considerable respect. However, early childhood teachers do not feel their work is held in high regard by the Canadian public, and they are trying to better this situation through their professional endeavours.

Careers in Early Childhood Education

Typically we think of anyone trained in early childhood education as working in a child care centre. However, there are many other jobs available to early childhood education personnel. They include directors, teachers, assistants, resource teachers, home visitors, therapy assistants, and early intervention specialists. People with these positions work in many varied settings such as the following:

- Elementary schools assisting a teacher
- Special needs classrooms
- Treatment centres
- Hospital
- Recreation programs
- Homes with children with special needs
- Agencies (e.g., infant stimulation)
- Associations for community living
- Child welfare agencies
- Drop-in centres (e.g., at a shopping mall)

In the future, more Canadian boards of education will probably have early childhood educators working in partnerships with teachers in junior and senior kindergarten classrooms. And if you are an **entrepreneur** who wants open your own school, or design your own materials, or promote your own methods, these careers are also possible. You will have to investigate your province's and city's legislation, professional organizations, training programs, and business opportunities and incentives.

Regardless of the setting in which you work, you must strive to make it welcoming and supportive. In the A Canadian Professional Speaks Out box, John Novak and Pam Rogers examine this concept of invitational education.

Teachers' Developmental Stages

Just as children are considered to progress through developmental stages of growth and development in many domains, so teachers progress through stages as they grow professionally gaining knowledge, training, skills, and experience. Katz (1977) concludes that each of these stages has unique developmental tasks and training needs. It is helpful to realize that others begin their teaching experiences with similar feelings of inadequacy or anxiety and that these evolve into more advanced stages as competence develops.

INVITING SUCCESS IN EARLY CHILDHOOD EDUCATION

John M. Novak and Pamela Rogers, Brock University, St. Catharines, Ontario

Of the many things young children learn, perhaps the most important is the picture they develop of who they are and how they fit into the world. This highly personal portrayal of existence and possibilities is called the self-concept. We see it as key in the development of each child's intellectual, psychological, social, moral, and physical potential. Children who believe in their personal worth and possibilities are more likely to engage in and sustain activities and relationships that call forth a greater realization of their potential. A vital question then for educators of young children is, "What can we do to promote the development of a positive self-concept?"

We believe that we do not have direct access to another's self-concept. Rather, because an individual's self-concept is personally constructed through the messages received, interpreted, acted upon, and evaluated, our role as educators is to be message designers and implementers. Thus, if we take self-concept to be the core of future development, our educational responsibility is to construct and extend signal systems that invite children to see themselves as valuable, able, and responsible learners who can behave accordingly. We call such an approach to child development **invitational education** and feel that it offers a systematic and morally defensible approach for working in early childhood education.

Invitational education is a perceptually based self-concept approach to teaching, learning, and caring that is centred on the following five principles:

1. People are able, valuable, and responsible and should be treated accordingly.

2. Education should be a cooperative activity.

3. Process is the product in the making.

4. People possess untapped positive potential in all areas of human endeavour.

5. Potential can best be realized by places, policies, processes, and programs specifically designed to invite development, and by people who are intentionally inviting with themselves and others personally and professionally.

Educators using these principles as an operating stance work together to make their centre or school "The Most Inviting Place in Town." Focusing on the development of caring interpersonal practices, nurturing environments, person-centred policies, and engaging programs, invitational educators aim to create an institutional culture that enables all involved to more fully relate, assert, invest, and cope. To assist educators in developing and sustaining inviting environments, several books have been written, and International Alliance for Invitational Education (with a Canadian Centre) has been formed, and a rating scale for early childhood education constructed.

- *Stage 1: Survival.* Beginning teachers' main concern through the first year or so of teaching is usually focused on whether they will survive. The realization of the great responsibility they have for the group of children, and the discrepancy between the success they expect and the reality of the classroom, result in anxiety and feelings of inadequacy. In general, they are acquiring information about what children are like and what can be expected of them. At this stage, the teachers' main need is for support, encouragement, and guidance, provided on-site as required.

- *Stage 2: Consolidation.* Having recognized that they can indeed survive, teachers begin to focus on specific tasks. As they consolidate the information gained from their first year or two, they move their attention more specifically to problem children or to situations that deviate from the general norm. Their needs at this time are for continued on-site training that supports exploration of alternatives to deal with problem situations.

- *Stage 3: Renewal.* By now, teachers in their third or fourth year begin to seek some new approaches and ideas as they tire of the way they have been doing things for the past several years. The search for renewal can be met through meetings with colleagues, professional organizations and conferences, professional books and journals, and visits to other programs.

- *Stage 4: Maturity.* This final stage is reached by different teachers at different points and represents a coming to terms with themselves and their profession. Now they ask deeper and more abstract questions, looking at the broader implications of their work in the context of the larger society. Their experience makes these questions more meaningful. Mature teachers need opportunities to read widely, interact with others, and participate in seminars and other forums where such questions are addressed by others searching for similar insights.

Reflective Exercise 6-2

Reflect on your first few days of practice teaching. Did you have concerns about survival in the field? Discuss the survival aspect of practice teaching as a class.

Staffing in Early Childhood Programs—Relationships and Team Building

The people—or **human resources** if you are in a large organization—who make up the early childhood program are a system in their own right. That system, of course, affects the systems it interfaces with—the children, the families, the community, the field. The early childhood educator works within this system along with others who share the tasks of the program. Staff members, from the supervisor or director to the custodian, contribute toward making the program successful, the lives of children important, and the profession of early childhood education respectable. Many different staffing patterns exist and work successfully; variables like the type of facility, its size, the guiding philosophy, and the funding source all can affect which staffing model is selected. For example, a half-day preschool attended by 15 children may, for instance, be staffed by one owner/teacher and one additional teacher. On the other hand, a nonprofit child care program in which 160 children are enrolled might involve a board of directors, a director, a curriculum coordinator, a parent coordinator, 12 senior teachers, 28 full- and part-time assistants, a variable number of **volunteers**, a secretary, a cook, a custodian, a list of substitute staff, and various **community professionals** who serve as resource persons. Exhibit 6-1 schematically illustrates the staffing patterns of these two hypothetical programs.

The distribution and allocation of responsibility also varies in different programs. Some have a hierarchical structure, fashioned as a pyramid, in which power trickles down from the top and each level in the structure reports to that above. Thus, in some classrooms that follow this model, one teacher is designated as the senior teacher or teacher supervisor, and other teachers work under her or him, following the senior teacher's direction and guidance.

Yet, in the early childhood field, there is often an alternative to this pyramidal structure because of the strong interdependence and interconnectedness between teachers, who frequently make decisions by consensus. This can be depicted as a web, which allows for more flexible and dynamic relationships than the hierarchical model, in which the power structure tends to be static and individuals' responsibilities depend on their position in the structure (Dresden & Myers, 1989). More recently, the term career lattice has been suggested as an appropriate symbol for the uniqueness and diversity that is seen in early childhood more than in most fields (Bredekamp & Willer, 1992). A lattice allows for both horizontal and vertical movement between positions, with each position having an accompanying level of education, pay, experience, and responsibility (Bredekamp & Willer, 1992).

The notion of **team teaching** also been common in early childhood settings for many years—as in Reggio Emilia, classes are co-taught by team teachers who share responsibilities. Team teaching is based on a relationship of trust and communication among the teachers, something that takes time to build. A good team finds

EXHIBIT 6-1   *Staffing Patterns*

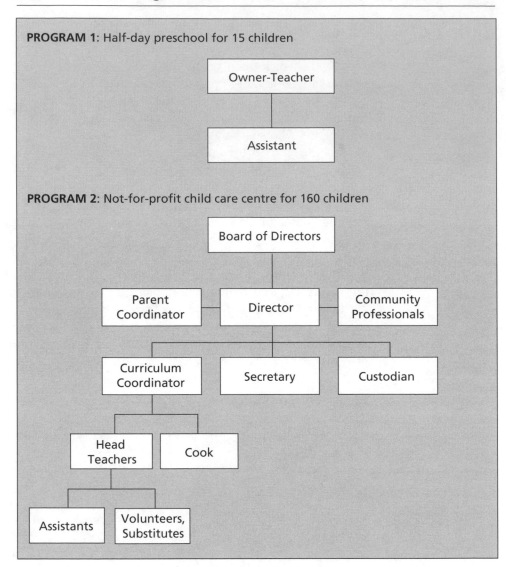

PROGRAM 1: Half-day preschool for 15 children

Owner-Teacher

Assistant

PROGRAM 2: Not-for-profit child care centre for 160 children

Board of Directors

Parent Coordinator — Director — Community Professionals

Curriculum Coordinator   Secretary   Custodian

Head Teachers   Cook

Assistants   Volunteers, Substitutes

many bonuses in this relationship such as added flexibility, creativity, problem-solving capabilities, and focus on what each member of the team enjoys most or does best. In addition, the collaboration between teachers provides the children with a model for cooperative behaviour (Thornton, 1990).

Whatever administrative structure you encounter as a student and as new professional, it is important to inquire *at the outset* about the lines of responsibility in terms of providing direction, feedback, evaluation, and resources. By learning the lines of authority and communication, teachers in a program will know whom to seek out for instructions and information, with whom to discuss problems, and where ultimate responsibility for various decisions lies. Smooth functioning depends on a clear understanding of these responsibilities, the lines of communi-

Courtesy of Play and Learn.

cation, and cooperation among the staff (Click & Click, 1990; Click, 1995; Sciarra & Dorsey, 1990). We will now briefly examine some of the positions and their responsibilities held by staff members in early childhood programs.

● Director and/or Supervisor

Directors and/or **supervisors** perform a variety of tasks, depending on the size and scope of the program. Very large centres may have both an administrative director and an assistant director. While the director would play an administrative role, the assistant would have more direct involvement with the children as well as some supervisory responsibilities. In smaller programs, the director may double as a teacher and supervisor for part of the day. Traditionally, the director is responsible for financial, personnel, policy, and facility decisions; provides community linkages; handles licensing and regulation; and is the ultimate decision maker in the chain of responsibility in all matters that pertain to the program. In addition, the job description often involves staff selection, training, monitoring, and evaluation. In programs that depend on grants and other outside sources of funding, the director may spend much time writing proposals and meeting with influential decision makers. Directors often have additional training beyond their ECE diploma or degree. Still, you may find the director with a toilet plunger one day, a child with a scrape in need of a bandage the next, and a crying parent the next—the director has to be ready to be a plumber, a nurse, and a counsellor when necessary, as he or she holds the ultimate responsibility for what happens!

● Resource Teacher

Many communities and, in fact, many centres have a resource teacher on staff to assist in the inclusion of children with special needs into programs. This position requires additional qualifications too—often a one-year certificate or diploma following the two-year Early Childhood Education diploma. The resource teacher's role is exactly what it seems—to be a resource. It is not his or her job to take over the programming or the disciplining for the children with special needs. It is, instead, to help train all staff in understanding and therefore accepting the principles of inclusion. By educating and training each and every person involved—the teachers, the parents, the cook, the custodian, the other children, and the volunteers—everyone has ownership of the success of inclusion. By increasing the knowledge and confidence of the team, fear and ignorance—two of the biggest barriers in working effectively with children with special needs—are reduced. Everyone becomes a competent and proficient team member and advocate, thereby creating a positive, supportive environment which fosters the overall development and endless potential of each and every individual within it.

Some provinces have associations of resource teachers. In Ontario, for example, the association is called Early Childhood Resource Teacher Network of Ontario.

● Home Visitors

Infant stimulation (or education) workers are often people with their Early Childhood Education certification. They belong to a team, which includes speech, physical, and occupational therapists, that helps develop a program for the child with special needs once he/she arrives home from the hospital. The infant stimulation worker visits the home on a regular basis, helping the parents work with their child from newborn to 2 years. Special needs children may also attend a centre-based program part time. Due to the high medical needs of these children, these programs are often funded by ministries of health, or jointly by health, social services, and education ministries. Home visits are often part of the centre or program mandates for itinerant resource teachers (those who travel from centre to centre from a base centre or agency). This helps bridge programming from home to school or home to community and provides families with additional support systems. Early childhood educators have also held positions as child care workers for children's aid societies. They have also acted as therapy assistants carrying out the therapy programs developed for children with special needs by speech, physical, occupational, or psychosocial therapists.

Early childhood educators have also been trained as early intervention specialists, assessing children's developmental progress throughout their specialized programs, or as special needs workers at homes through such agencies as Community Living. Communication of all team members, together with families, is essential to the family's overall well-being and the child's growth and development.

● Teaching Staff

Those who work directly with children may hold a variety of titles, and these titles vary from one Canadian jurisdiction to another. Staff composition varies greatly with the actual physical layout of a program and group size. Group-size regulations vary greatly across the country, and they affect the staffing structure. In locations that have strict group-size regulations, you would usually find two teachers per room. In another setting, however, you may find a large open room with four or five teachers present, while only one teacher may be in yet another setting. Nevertheless, certain roles are relatively common across the country. We will look at two common teaching positions in more depth—the senior teacher and the assistant teacher. We will also examine a team teaching approach to the role of the teacher.

● The Senior Teacher

In many jurisdictions that require teacher training, the teacher with more education and experience acts as the **senior teacher** when there are two or more teachers in a room. However, the titles used vary greatly not only from province to province but also even within cities. Typically, the more senior teacher, **lead teacher**, team leader, coach, or mentor is responsible for coordinating the planning and implementing of the daily program. This involves knowing each child and family well and individualizing the program to meet each one's specific needs; responsibility for the physical environment of the classroom, setting up equipment, rotating materials, and ensuring a good match between what is available and the children's skill levels; maintaining records for the children in the class; initiating and maintaining family interactions, both informally at the start and end of each day and formally through conferences or meetings; and facilitating an atmosphere of communication and support with other staff members who work in the class by providing direction, guidance, and feedback.

● The Assistant Teacher

In many settings, one or more teachers function in an **assistant teacher** role. Assistants have a variety of titles within a municipality, and the range of titles is greater when you cross provincial and territorial boundaries. Some terms that are used include "auxiliary teacher," "associate teacher," "small-group leader," "aide," and "helper." In the assistant role, the teacher works with the senior teacher to provide a high-quality program for the children in the class and their families. Frequently the assistant has less education and experience than the senior teacher, but this is not always the case. Depending on the assistant's skill level and experience, this teacher may share many of the senior teacher's responsibilities, for instance, participating in curriculum planning, leading large- and small-group activities, being involved in parent interactions, and arranging the environment. Because of the assistant teacher's close working relationship with the senior teacher, open and honest communication and mutual respect are vital between the two. In some schools, an assistant teacher may serve as a floater, moving among classrooms to help with special activities or during specific times of the day. Some colleges offer an early childhood assistant (ECA) certificate program that runs as a one-year rather than the typical two-year early childhood education program.

● Team Teaching

In many settings, the senior teacher position does not exist; teachers work as a team, under the direction of the program supervisor and/or director. Mary Wright's (1983) University of Western Ontario program, for example, had a program director (Wright), who also had teaching responsibilities at the university level, and four highly qualified teachers. One of the teachers was the supervisor of the school, while a second one was the assistant supervisor. The four teachers rotated through four different teaching timetables, one per week, which Wright describes in great detail in her very readable text (Wright, 1983).

The team teaching approach allows each teacher to interact with all the children and to work in all areas of the program. It also maximizes the children's flexibility, since each area is supervised by a teacher, allowing the children to move freely from one activity to another. Finally, the teachers experience more variety in their work with this approach, and no one individual is always stuck with the less appealing duties (e.g., paint cleanup and washroom duty).

● Volunteers

Some centres use volunteers to help with various aspects of the early childhood program. Volunteers can include parents, student teachers or interns, members of volunteer organizations, foster grandparents, and other interested community members. To use volunteers most effectively, however, there has to be a well-planned orientation, training, and monitoring component that helps the volunteer understand the program, its philosophy, and its operation. Volunteers, as much as any other component of your program, are a reflection of your program and are advocates for it in the community. They must be as well versed and as much an integral and equal team member as any paid personnel. Although volunteers can provide a wonderful additional resource to a program, the reality is that volunteers are not as plentiful as the potential need for them.

● Support Staff

Depending on the size and scope of the centre, some people usually serve in a support capacity. These might include (although they certainly are not limited to) people involved in food preparation, maintenance, and office management. They, too, are essential and equal team members who must clearly understand the centre's mission statement, program goals, policies and procedures, the principles of inclusion, developmentally appropriate practices, and the key concepts of early childhood education. **Support staff** are in contact with children and families each day and must reflect and advocate the standards the profession demands. This reflects the true impact of the need for and role of effective communication, team problem-solving skills, solid organizational restructuring, training, evaluation, and accountability.

Large programs often have a cook who is in charge of meal preparation, shopping, and sanitation and maintenance of the kitchen. The cook may also plan meals, if that person has an appropriate background in nutrition, or may participate in classroom cooking projects. A dietician may serve as a consultant to the program to ensure that children's nutritional needs are appropriately met through the program's meals. In smaller programs, particularly those not serving lunch or dinner, the teaching staff or director may take responsibility for snack planning and preparation.

One of the most important yet difficult tasks of any centre serving busy and active young children is maintenance. Daily cleaning, sweeping, vacuuming, sanitizing, and garbage disposal are vital, though usually unpopular, functions. Large programs may have a custodian as part of the staff, whereas others hold contracts with a janitorial service. Often the expense of a maintenance crew or custodian has to be weighed against other important needs, and the teaching staff may find that its responsibilities include many maintenance chores. Most centres compromise by having the staff maintain cleanliness and order, while a cleaning service is responsible for intermittent deep cleaning of the facility. Other support staff take care of office needs. Large programs often have a secretary who maintains records, answers phone calls, manages typing needs, and may handle some accounting tasks. In smaller programs, such tasks may fall to the director. Some programs may employ a part-time accountant or have a receptionist in addition to the secretary. Programs that are part of or housed with other agencies may share custodial and secretarial staff.

● Board of Directors

Particularly in nonprofit centres, some type of policymaking governing board holds the ultimate responsibility for the program. This board of trustees or **board of directors** may be a very powerful force, making all pertinent decisions that the director then carries out, or it may be only a nominal group that gives the director responsibility to make these decisions. Ideally, a board of directors' role falls somewhere between these extremes (Sciarra & Dorsey, 1990). Boards of directors are usually made up of program parents and community members who come from a variety of spheres of expertise and influence, most of which are not likely to be related to early childhood education. It is wise, however, to include one child development expert on the board. The director serves as a liaison, helping the board understand the rationale for decisions made on the basis of child development knowledge, while utilizing the expertise of board members in areas in which the director is not so well versed. Boards can be very effective, for instance, in fiscal management, fundraising, construction and expansion projects, or lobbying for children's rights.

● Community Professionals

The resources of a centre can be expanded through other professionals in the larger community, for instance, health and mental health professionals, social workers, speech pathologists, occupational therapists, and physiotherapists. In some programs, especially those involving subsidized children, families may be referred to the early childhood program by a community agency. In these cases, the program and referring agency frequently work together to maximize the help provided to the child and family. In other cases, the early childhood program may help connect families with community agencies and professionals to provide needed services. It is important for teachers to recognize the "boundaries of their own professional expertise" and know when other professionals need to be consulted (Sciarra & Dorsey, 1990, p. 369).

Coordinating and supporting staff to create an atmosphere of caring is difficult yet rewarding. Effective communication through team problem solving, solid organizational structure, training, and evaluation creates a sense of unity and trust that translates into accountability. Everyone shares in the responsible, professional, and successful operation of the program. In the A Canadian Professional Speaks Out box, team building and collaboration are expanded upon.

A Canadian Professional Speaks Out

TEAM BUILDING AND COLLABORATION

Pamela Nuttall Nason, Professor in Early Childhood Education, University of New Brunswick

Working directly with preschool and primary children has, without a doubt, been the most deeply satisfying work that I have done in my career as an early childhood educator. This work with children has also involved collaborating with parents and other professionals—to ensure the greatest possible continuity of education and care for the children I served. Though I understood this collaboration to be an essential aspect of my job, I often felt a bit insecure about the role I ought to be playing with parents and other professionals—speech therapists, public health nurses, doctors, and social workers—all of whom invariably spoke with great clarity and authority. They sounded so much more sure of themselves than I ever felt. Often I left interdisciplinary meetings where provisions for an individual child were being discussed feeling, somehow, that I had adequately represented neither the child's needs nor my professional capacity to meet those needs.

It was not until I participated in the New Brunswick Maternal Literacies project that I discovered working with parents and other professionals to be a pleasure comparable to that of working directly with the children. The New Brunswick Maternal Literacies project, a collaborative action research project funded by the Social Sciences and Humanities Research Council under the category of Women and Work, involved primary teachers, mothers, graduate students, and university professors working together over a two-year period to promote positive literacy interchanges between home and school. We wanted in particular to document and honour the literacies that rural mothers teach to their children and to find workable ways to integrate these maternal literacies into schooled literacies.

Our collaborative research involved regular meetings between parents and professionals—just the sort of meetings I had come to dread earlier in my career! But Lissa Paul, my colleague at the University of New Brunswick and a co-investigator in this project, was unconcerned. A feminist scholar of children's literature, she knew how to make room for everyone's voice. We adopted a rotating chair for our meetings; everyone had the opportunity to preside once or twice. We took turns at setting an agenda. We sat in a circle so no one would be "head" of the table. We chose a lounge to meet in rather than a more formal meeting room and determinedly replaced "discussion" with "conversation," respecting no one as the "expert" but honouring the expertise and experience of everyone. We dispensed with formal titles, which might imply a hierarchy. We preserving everyone's dignity, and made sure that no one's viewpoint was privileged, was paramount. Collectively we saw to that. We chatted, gossiped, and laughed our way through our monthly day-long meetings, and at the end of each, without having made a single formal resolution, we always came up with wonderful plans for the coming month. When we parted we felt good about the contributions we had made. And perhaps more importantly, we parted as friends.

When it came to publishing our research, it was Lissa who suggested that teachers, mothers, graduate students, and professors all write from their own perspective, in their own voice. Instead of writing about mothers and teachers, as academics typically do, Lissa and I wrote with them (Blake, Christine, Fulton, Gorham, Graham, Kershaw, Leavitt, Nason, and Paul, 1995; Gorham and Nason, 1997). And when we presented papers at academic conferences—the Learneds in Montreal and the Atlantic Educators conference in St. John's—everyone spoke their own part. These practices enabled me to find my voice, and I now take immense pleasure in collaborating with other adults for the betterment of young children.

Sources: Frankie Blake, Maria Christine, Winnifred Fulton, Peter Gorham, Marilyn Graham, Janet Kershaw, Midge Leavitt, Pam Nason, and Lissa Paul, "The pig's tale: Exploring maternal literacies," *Primary Teaching Studies* (London: University of North London Press), 9(1995)2; Peter Gorham and Pam Nason, "Why make teachers' work more visible to parents?" *Young Children*, 52(1997)(5).

Teacher Evaluation

Canadian early childhood teachers, on average, find great job satisfaction in their profession, which compensates for some of the dilemmas facing the field. In both *Caring for a Living* (Canadian Child Day Care Federation & Canadian Day Care Advocacy Association, 1992) and *You Bet I Care!* (Doherty et al., 2000), it was noted that the nature of the work and the opportunity to make a difference in the lives of children is the silver lining (Canadian Child Day Care Federation & Canadian Day Care Advocacy Association, 1992, p. 1) in early childhood education. The opportunity to contribute to and observe the development of their young charges provides a great source of pleasure to early childhood educators. Undoubtedly, those of you who are planning to enter this profession will be happy to know it brings such rewards to its members.

Satisfaction is, however, combined with many other factors. Is the pay satisfactory? Do I have a voice? Can I see progress? Do I feel respected? Am I making a difference? Am I growing as a professional? Self-evaluation is critical to personal and professional development. As well, credible professions will be accountable to their mandate by ensuring that both their program and their teachers are evaluated on a regular basis. This evaluation should be done in the spirit of learning and for the purposes of improvement for the benefit of all parties concerned—teachers, children, parents, colleagues, and the community. Results of evaluations need to be shared and discussed and written action plans agreed upon and maintained by all those involved. Often professional organizations such as provincial early childhood education ones have an accreditation process for teachers. Self-improvement is important. But recognizing that self-nurturing is vital is more difficult for those who tend to spend their career giving. As we mentioned earlier, self-care is as much a responsibility as it is a right. Caring for your needs means you are far more effective in caring for others. Being aware, being open, and being communicative—asking, listening, sharing, watching—show you are capable of both teaching and learning.

Professional Organizations

One sign of a profession is the existence of organizations to which members belong and of professional journals that members read. Such organizations and their literature provide members with support and a sense of common interest and purpose. In Canada, early childhood educators have several pertinent organizations and journals at the national level; many more are found at the provincial and territorial levels. In addition, numerous organizations focus on more specialized groups, for instance, those involved in for-profit child care, Montessori, church-sponsored programs, home-based care, early childhood special education, and others. We will briefly discuss the major national organizations, and also one influential American organization. The 1992 study *Canadian Child Care in Context: Perspectives from the Provinces and Territories* (Pence, 1992a) contains an extensive list of the professional organizations in each Canadian jurisdiction. Some of these are summarized in the following list.

Courtesy of Play and Learn.

● Canada

1. The Canadian Child Care Federation (CCCF) (formerly the Canadian Child Day Care Federation or CCDCF) or Fédération Canadienne des services de garde à l'enfance (FCSGE) has a recent history. Although the idea for a national organization was formulated in 1983, it was not until 1987 that the CCDCF received federal funding and opened

an office in Ottawa. In 1993, the CCDCF changed its name. CCCF publishes a research journal entitled *Visions* and a quarterly bilingual magazine entitled *Interaction.*

The CCCF aims to improve the quality of child care in Canada by providing services to those in the field. It supports provincial and territorial organizations, and aims to provide information and services to professionals in the field. National conferences, regional workshops, a quarterly magazine (*Interaction*), information sheets, and a speakers bureau are among the services the federation offers. The CCDCF also developed the national statement on the quality of child care. In addition, the federation addresses issues related to the training and education of people entering the field. To learn more about them, see their Web site.

2. The Child Care Advocacy Association of Canada (CCAAC) (formerly Canadian Day Care Advocacy Association), founded in 1983, aims to make high-quality, affordable, nonprofit child care accessible to all Canadians who need it. It is funded by the Secretary of State and run by a nonprofit volunteer board.

3. The Canadian Association for Young Children (CAYC) includes a diverse range of members concerned with the overall development and care of children up to 9 years of age. It also mandates working toward quality practices and programs, providing professional growth and development, providing information on children, and coordinating efforts of all groups whose focus is children. The CAYC publishes *Canadian Children* semiannually. See their Web site.

4. Canadian Council for Exceptional Children (CCEC). The council advocates for the needs of children who face challenges in many areas of learning and development. It has an extensive network of provincial and local chapters, publications including journals (*Exceptional Children*), magazines (*Teaching Exceptional Children*), newsletters, and resource materials. It has numerous subdivisions, one of which is called the Division for Early Childhood (DEC). Its provincial, national, and international (U.S.) membership attend annual conferences that are an excellent forum for professional development.

5. Although not an association, the Child Care Resource and Research Unit at the University of Toronto is an excellent source of information regarding Canadian research, statistics, legislation, projects, and issues surrounding child care in Canada. Their Web site, well maintained and up to date, is one of the best resources for Canadians in early childhood education.

● United States

The National Association for the Education of Young Children (NAEYC), the largest early childhood education organization, is a powerful voice for children, families, and teachers in the United States. NAEYC's primary goal is to make high-quality care available for all children (NAEYC, 2001 [on-line]). NAEYC aims to improve quality in three ways:

- NAEYC creates professional development opportunities and resources. In addition, the organization sets and promotes standards of professional practice such as Developmentally Appropriate Practice policies and texts. These resources are all designed to facilitate improvements in both the professional practice and working conditions.

- NAEYC aims to improve public understanding, and increase support and funding for high-quality programs through their public policy initiatives, public awareness activities, and speaking engagements.

- NAEYC aims to build and maintain a strong, diverse, and inclusive organization, as that is how the other goals will be achieved.

NAEYC seems to be meeting with success; in 1991, membership was 77,000, and it is 103,000 in 2001. NAEYC holds the largest early childhood annual conference attended by more than 25,000 early childhood education professionals yearly. The NAEYC also has an extensive series of publications that are invaluable to professionals in the field, including the bimonthly journal *Young Children* and more than 80 books and other resources. At present, our Canadian organizations are not as well developed as the NAEYC and do not yet have a comparable range of publications. Canadians frequently turn to the NAEYC for additional resources they require.

Reflective Exercise 6-3

Visit the NAEYC Web site and discuss the resources that are available on-line.

● Benefits of Student Memberships

As a student entering the early childhood profession, you should consider becoming a member of a professional organization. Most of the organizations have a student membership option, which costs considerably less than the regular membership. By becoming a member, you can keep abreast of new developments, have the opportunity to meet and participate in a support network with others in the same field, and attend workshops and conferences at the local, provincial, and national level. In fact, you may even be eligible for the CCCF's travel subsidy which would help you attend its national conference. (If you attend the conference, you can suggest to the instructor who assigned this text that you will do a conference report and/or seminar in place of another course assignment.) The contacts you make as a student can be very helpful when you are seeking a position in the field; professionals hiring in the field typically prefer to hire someone they know has been active in their association rather than a total stranger. If you need additional information about the organizations in your community and province, ask your instructor or professionals you know to elaborate on the available associations. The abovementioned Web sites for the Child Care Resource and Research Unit and the Canadian Child Care Federation both retain an extensive, updated list of associations and addresses.

Key Terms

assistant teacher	invitational education
board of directors	lead teacher
caregiver	learning style
child care worker	professional development
code of ethics	senior teacher
community professionals	supervisors
core knowledge base	support staff
directors	systems approach
entrepreneur	teacher
human resources	team teaching
inclusive education	volunteers

Key Points

1. You must recognize your own strengths and needs and how these relate with others' to create positive, healthy relationships.

2. Early childhood educators are nurturing caregivers as well as teachers.

3. The system of early childhood education is a holistic organizational structure defined by individuals who are connected to it.

4. This dynamic system uses communication and relationships to promote the team or partnership and its philosophy.

5. Professionalism is based on four criteria: core knowledge base, standards of practice which include rights, roles, and responsibilities, a code of ethics and training, and regulation in early childhood education.

6. Teachers progress through developmental stages.

7. Early childhood educators contribute to and observe children's development while also making appropriate evaluations that hold them accountable to their professional responsibilities.

8. By knowing the risks, issues, and challenges that face them professionally, early childhood educators are motivated and prepared to enter the profession equipped with a solution-oriented attitude.

9. There can be a variety of staffing patterns depending on the type, size, and philosophy of the program as well as its funding source.

10. The size and complexity of a program will affect the size and complexity of the staffing pattern. Early childhood programs can have various structures of staff authority and responsibility.

11. The role of the director will depend on the size and nature of the program.

12. In many programs, senior teachers and assistants, each with distinct responsibilities, are identified.

13. Most early childhood programs, depending on their size and scope, have some support staff who help with the maintenance and functioning of the program.

14. Some programs utilize volunteers, have a board of directors who are involved in the decision-making process, and call on community professionals to expand the services of the program.

15. Professional organizations are important bodies for effecting real change in the child care profession. Membership is important if you wish to advance the profession.

Key Questions

1. Talk to several teachers of young children. What do they view as the most rewarding parts of their jobs? What most frustrates them? Compare their answers with your own goals and expectations.

2. Review the section on team teaching. What are the advantages of such an approach? What are the disadvantages? Compare this approach to the one used in the program(s) where you have observed and/or had a practice teaching placement.

3. What are the advantages of belonging to a professional early childhood organization? Review several issues of such professional journals as *Interaction*, *Vision*, and *Young Children* to get a sense of what organizations like the CCDCF, the CCAAC, and the NAEYC have to offer.

4. Some professional organizations in Canada have been active in developing codes of ethics for the profession and in advocating improved salaries and working conditions. Review their newsletters to see what kind of issues are being discussed.

5. Visit two child care centres in your community and compare and contrast their administrative structures.

Part 3

How? The Basics

We will now turn our attention to the basic hows of early childhood education. In Part 3, we will examine the following fundamental components of high-quality early childhood education programs:

- Chapter 7, **Play and Developmentally Appropriate Practice**, will examine some of the basic constructs in early childhood education programs, including:

  1. The role of play and its importance

  2. The implementation of developmentally appropriate practices

  3. The importance of a curriculum that does not encourage bias or stereotypes

  Some basic components of that curriculum and planning guidelines will then be addressed.

- Chapter 8, **Guidance: Routines, Group Activities, and Behaviours**, will look at a number of important aspects of the early childhood program. Guidance suggestions for routines, transitions, and group activities are provided to help the teacher work effectively with the class as a whole. We also discuss the principles and strategies that teachers use in directing young children's behaviour. These general principles and strategies are important in helping children meet appropriate expectations.

Courtesy of Eglinton Public School.

Chapter 7

Play and Developmentally Appropriate Practice

*A*s you know from Chapters 1 and 3, high-quality programs that combine the best of several different approaches have been successful, and you may well want to select different components from different models when you design a program. In keeping with this **eclectic approach**, this text presents and combines many perspectives. Nonetheless, the basic premise of the authors is that all quality programs provide and support a play-based curriculum that nurtures children and their development.

In this chapter, we will examine **play**—the child's way of actively learning about and making sense of the world—and developmentally appropriate practice. A program that combines play and developmentally appropriate practice is one that nurtures and frames children's emotional development and well-being.

The Relationship Between Play, Guidance, and Emotional Development

Play is the cornerstone of quality early childhood education programs, because it is a universal among children and provides the foundation of developmentally appropriate practice. The whole child will develop in a child-centred, play-based program or curriculum that is appropriate to the child's developmental level and individual history. While the child's cognitive skills are the focus of a work-oriented, teacher-centred, accelerated learning program, good teachers would ask, "At what cost?" Teachers in quality early childhood education programs want to see the child grow in all developmental domains. They want to provide a program that supports the development of the child physically, intellectually (cognitively), creatively, linguistically, emotionally, and socially. And they are willing to prepare,

Courtesy of George Brown College.

organize, and regularly evaluate an environment that is rich with opportunities that encourage child development based on learning through play.

Play is the vehicle through which children learn, and the focal point for children's interactions. A play-based curriculum is one that also provides **guidance**. Teachers do not teach "play" as a subject, but help children to find ways to solve problems encountered in play and to elaborate upon and extend the discoveries they make.

Your Role as Nurturer

In the introduction, we noted that three basic components are integral to all high-quality adult-child interactions: developmentally appropriate practice, a play-based curriculum, and positive guidance from adults. The nature of a child's play is determined in part by the child's developmental level, but it also is shaped by the environment and by the people—children and adults—in that environment. Trusting and kind adults who provide an appropriate and safe play setting enhance a child's development, and guide the child in interactions with other children, with adults, and with the environment. As an early childhood educator, your job is to provide an appropriate environment for play and guidance in that setting—*how you go about doing that is everything to children*. It sets the tone of your relationships with children—either strengthens or weakens them, establishes trust or mistrust, encourages or hinders independence, and fosters or crushes self-esteem, all of which are components of emotional development.

Above being a teacher or a caregiver or a specialist, you are a nurturer, someone whom children depend on for their well-being in each of the developmental domains—physical, intellectual, social, emotional, linguistic, creative, behavioural, and spiritual. You can be a nurturer in any type of program in any environment. Children play anywhere and where they play, they generally require non-intrusive, empowering strategies to help them to discover, gather, and utilize information and to problem-solve in a positive, productive, and supportive manner. Children rely on our dependability. They trust we will be there, that we will not harm them, that we will encourage and reassure them, that we trust them and realize their potential contribution, and that we will help them gain their confidence to discover, explore, and make sense of everything a safe world has to offer.

Emotional Development

A. F. Lieberman, in *The Emotional Life of the Toddler* (1994), emphasizes that the nurturing role of the early childhood educator is the most important. This is based on the belief that healthy emotional development is the foundation upon which all other development depends.

Healthy emotional development encompasses six milestones, according to Greenspan and Greenspan (1986). A child's inborn temperament coupled with the quality of the interactions children experience at each stage support children in their attainment of the following six milestones.

1. *Self-Regulation and Interest in the World—"Developing a Sense of Security."* Children can organize and cope with all the new stimuli and sensations the world has to offer.

2. *Falling in Love—"Developing a Sense of Attachment."* Children demonstrate an interest in the human world and take great pleasure in personal interactions. They enjoy the world, smiling, cooing, watching, kicking, reaching, and listening.

3. *Development of Intentional Communication—"Developing a Sense of Trust."* Children gain an awareness that they can express needs in many ways through actions and sounds, and that they can expect these needs to be met by caring adults.

4. *Emergence of an Organized Sense of Self—"Developing a Sense of Independence."* Children understand that they can have an effect on the world. They take initiative, explore, express themselves, assert needs, and gain a sense of autonomy, empowerment, pride, and confidence as they develop a positive self-concept and high self-esteem.

5. *Developing Emotional Ideas—"Developing a Sense of Empathy."* Children explore and practise, through pretend play, ways to identify, label, manage, and use the many new emotions and ideas about emotions they observe and experience.

6. *Emotional Thinking: The Bases for Fantasy, Reality, and Self-Esteem—"Developing a Sense of Self-Control."* Children develop interpersonal (between people) and intrapersonal (within self) skills to identify, express, and manage emotions. They understand the relationship between feelings, behaviour, and consequences and interact in socially appropriate ways.

As we read in Chapter 2, Erik Erikson's theory of child development was also seated in emotional growth. Children need to develop a sense of trust and security by having their needs met consistently, predictably, and positively. They need to develop a sense of autonomy through encouragement and opportunities for **exploration**. Children also need to develop a sense of initiative whereby they feel safe in expressing their ideas, taking risks, and making mistakes.

Abraham Maslow (1965) felt that the overall goal of development was to achieve self-actualization, which simply means realizing one's potential. Five basic needs must first be met. Maslow called this a hierarchy of needs, because one level of needs had to be satisfied before moving to the next level. First, essential physical needs such as food and sleep must be satisfied. Maslow felt that fulfillment of emotional needs such as a sense of safety, security, belonging, and affection comes next. Only when these emotional needs are realized and met can children develop high self-esteem—a sense of personal worth and value and a positive self-concept.

Children's self-actualization—applying their knowledge and abilities confidently and appropriately—is only possible once their basic physical needs are met, they feel safe, secure, and loved, and they view themselves as worthy, competent, and responsible.

As an early childhood educator, you recognize that your role includes fostering healthy emotional development in children. Exhibit 7-1 lists both signs of healthy emotional development and examples of ways to foster this development. This chapter and Chapter 8 present many guidelines to help you to foster play, to provide an appropriate environment, and to provide positive guidance—if you can do those three things, then you are simultaneously ensuring the healthy emotional development of the children in your care.

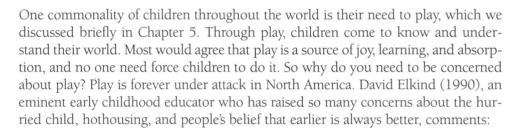

One commonality of children throughout the world is their need to play, which we discussed briefly in Chapter 5. Through play, children come to know and understand their world. Most would agree that play is a source of joy, learning, and absorption, and no one need force children to do it. So why do you need to be concerned about play? Play is forever under attack in North America. David Elkind (1990), an eminent early childhood educator who has raised so many concerns about the hurried child, hothousing, and people's belief that earlier is always better, comments:

> *The major victim of the earlier is better ideology has been the play of infants and young children. ... Play is a bad word. Given children's sponge-like abilities to learn, the purported rapidity of brain growth, and the time-limited nature of this window of opportunity, play is extremely wasteful of time that might be put to more important and more long-lived activities. ... Childhood is a period for work, not for play. (Pp. 4–5)*

Early lessons in almost everything become more and more prevalent, and the value of play is being questioned by more and more parents and members of the public. This places additional demands on teachers in early childhood education programs. They not only have to decide what to include in their programs, but also they have to be able to give cogent reasons for their practices to others. Far too frequently, teachers have adopted play-based program models without knowing why the approach was valid, and then they have been unable to articulate the reasons why they have play as a central feature in the curriculum (Monighan-Nourot, 1990). Teachers in play-based programs need to be familiar with the research on play and its effectiveness.

● Theories of Play

Theories of play have proliferated over several centuries (Berlyne, 1969; Bruner, Jolly, & Sylva, 1976; Gilmore, 1971; Rubin, 1982; Rubin, Fein, & Vandenberg, 1983), and Canadians have been among the leaders in play research for a number

EXHIBIT 7-1   *Positive Emotional Development*

Indicators of Positive Emotional Development in Children

- Express self through play
- Express their creativity
- Exert independence
- Problem-solve
- Investigate
- Experiment
- Make decisions
- Take risks and accept mistakes
- Make good judgments
- Question
- Help others
- Respect others
- Feel safe in asking adults for help, clarification, and guidance
- Display competence
- Take responsibility
- Show initiative

Fostering Emotional Development

- Model calmness in our approach—show self-control
- Be reasonable
- Provide a safe and secure environment that provides challenges and successes
- Show that we trust and can be trusted
- Model fairness in our methods
- Help to solve problems and clarify issues
- Display accuracy in determining intent of children's behaviour
- Model a respectful attitude of children as people
- Foster and protect children's self-esteem
- Be a positive role model for communication, interpersonal skills, and problem solving
- Genuinely enjoy the children
- Show understanding and tolerance of children's mistakes
- Be flexible
- Include children in the decision-making process
- Believe children to be capable
- Afford children the same rights and opportunities as any person
- Provide a range of appropriate choices
- Show unconditional acceptance (no bribes, bargains, or ifs)
- Provide time and be flexible with our limits and routines to accommodate for individual differences and interest
- Show that we will help solve problems in a fair and mutually beneficial way
- Demonstrate that we are credible—we know about children and we know what we are doing
- Be dependable and reliable
- Be comforting
- Show admiration, affection, approval, acceptance, and pride
- Be encouraging
- Listen
- Create a beautiful environment with the children

of decades. In fact, three of the researchers in the foregoing list of references, Berlyne, Gilmore, and Rubin, have been based at Canadian universities. (The first two worked with Piaget in Geneva and at the University of Toronto, and Rubin worked at the University of Waterloo.) Most researchers (e.g., Rubin et al., 1983) agree that early play theories fall into four categories:

1. *The surplus energy theory.* Play is a mechanism for burning off excess energy.

2. *The relaxation and recreation theories.* Play meets an adult's need for relaxation after a hard day's work.

3. *The practice theory.* Play allows children to practise adult activities.

4. *The recapitulation theory.* Children are the link in the evolutionary chain between animals and adults. In play, children go through or recapitulate all the steps humans passed before reaching their current evolutionary stage.

Roots of these theories can be found in 20th-century play theories, but all the early theories have been the subject of serious criticism and found lacking in a number of ways (Rubin et al., 1983). More recent theories of play have placed less emphasis on why people play and more on the actual process of play.

A comprehensive review of recent theories of play is beyond the scope of an introductory text. However, the views of Freud, Piaget, and Vygotsky on play merit consideration, especially because they have had considerable influence on early childhood education.

● Freud's Theory of Play

According to Freud, play has anxiety-release and wish-fulfillment functions. Play allows the child a release from the real world and the opportunity to express impulses and wishes that are not acceptable in the real world. In that sense, play is healing, as it permits children to relieve frustration and express their emotions. Play therapy evolved from the Freudian view of play, and it remains a common and powerful tool in therapeutic and hospital settings.

● Piaget's Theory of Play

One of Piaget's (1951) earlier works, *Play, Dreams, and Imitation in Childhood*, concentrated on play, including that of his own children. Piaget saw play as pure assimilation (see Chapter 2 on Piaget to refresh your memory about the terms he used). In play, the child assimilates a person, an event, or an object into current schemes or ways of thinking. Piaget also noted that play changes with age.

1. *Practice play.* In the sensorimotor stage of development (birth to 2 years), play is physical, not symbolic. **Practice play** is the term Piaget used to describe the repeated actions of the infant. Whether sucking, banging, or dropping an object, the infant repeats the behaviour that once was difficult and takes

pleasure in mastering the skill. As motor development, such as the ability to grasp, bring hands to mouth, and reach, become refined, babies use practice, trial and error, and experimentation to gain control over the environment.

2. *Symbolic play*. As children enter the preoperational stage (2 to 7 years), **symbolic play** becomes possible as the child can mentally represent objects, events, and people. For instance, a block becomes an iron, a bowl becomes a hat, or a tube becomes a microphone. This is why simple materials with their limitless possibilities are far more appropriate than absolute toys with a single purpose. **Pretend play** is common during this period, and it becomes more social in nature, progressing from solitary to group pretend play.

3. *Games with rules*. **Games with rules** become possible once concrete operations (7 to 11 years) are achieved and children initiate an interest in organized games with simple rules. The rules become more complex as the child's cognitive capacities become more advanced.

Vygotsky's Theory of Play

Vygotsky (1976), the Soviet psychologist we discussed in Chapter 2, died before he completed work on his theory of mental development. Nevertheless, his work on play in preschoolers has had a significant impact on research involving pretend play (Rubin et al., 1983). Like Freud, Vygotsky saw the emotional side of play, "the imaginary, illusory realization of unrealizable desires" (1976, p. 539). Like Piaget, he also saw the cognitive side of play—play was conscious or mental activity that was not present in infants and animals. Like other aspects of mental development, play initially demands action, but later it becomes imagination:

> The old adage that child's play is imagination in action can be reversed: we can say that imagination in adolescents and schoolchildren is play without action. (1976, p. 539)

Imaginary play did not emerge until around 3 years, according to Vygotsky, as younger children were too constrained by reality. For example, a child of 2 years will not and cannot say "I am standing up," if the child is really sitting down. Similarly, the child cannot say "It is snowy," if looking out the window on a sunny, summer day. A word or an action cannot be separated from the real object or action. As the child approaches 3 years, however, thought becomes possible without objects and actions, and words can be freed from objects and reality. The child can talk about standing while sitting, and about snow while in the sun. What facilitates this change is the ability to use one object (e.g., a stick) for another (e.g., a horse), or one action (e.g., stomping feet on the floor) for another (e.g., being a train). In the horse example, the stick is a pivot or tool that severs the meaning of the word *horse* from a real horse. Once the child understands that a stick can be called a horse, the child can also understand that a word is separate from an object. At first, props or pivots have to be quite similar to the object they represent (e.g., a file folder could not be a horse), but gradually similarity becomes less of an issue. (Research has provided strong support for this contention.) The child becomes able to manipulate *meanings* and that is critical for mature thought. So, for Vygotsky, play is the source of development and a major factor in language development.

What Is Play?

No doubt you have heard that old, familiar saying that play is children's work. Though children would certainly not consider it work, they do realize it takes considerable energy, effort, and thought, and they do expect us to recognize and respect these efforts. This adult frame of reference does help us see children as engaged in meaningful activity. The image of the little scientist helps some adults understand what it is children actually do as they play. Children, like all people, have many natural roles as they play—teacher, mentor, leader, manager, friend, confidant, learner. These actual roles are combined with the pretend roles children try on to gain insight and gather knowledge. As you will see, our primary role in play and guidance is to help children recognize and gain these insights to expand their knowledge base, not by telling or by continually questioning or by forever pointing out the obvious, but by careful observation, documentation, evaluation, and, most of all, timing. The methods we use—labelling, elaborating, demonstrating, and challenging; the reasons we use them—to encourage, prompt, support, empower, and nurture; and how we use them—with a calm voice, at the child's level, respectfully, sincerely, confidently, and warmly—are equally important in facilitating and guiding play in order to foster healthy, emotional development.

Charlesworth (1987) described play as a sequence of four activities young children engage in when they encounter new objects and situations. These include:

- Exploration—an investigation of the situation

- Manipulation—familiarization with features and properties

- Practice—experimentation

- Repetition—mastering skills relative to the object/situation

Children do this wherever they are, without fancy toys. In many ways, children create their own learning environment—the environment they see is not as important as the environment they hear and feel. Our role is to create, through our actions and words, an atmosphere of warmth and security where children feel perfectly at ease doing what they do best—play.

Courtesy of George Brown College.

● Definitions of Play

Definitions of play have abounded over the years, with the most satisfactory ones focusing on play as an attitude. Children and adults enter into play with an attitude or psychological disposition or set, as the psychologists call it, that is different from their attitude when they work or study. That attitude distinguishes play from other forms of activity. A child who is playing has different intentions than one who is not. Rubin and his colleagues (1983) have outlined characteristics of play which theorists from different perspectives agree upon:

1. Play is intrinsically motivated: it comes from within the child and is not induced by needs for food or company, social demands, or promises of rewards.

2. In play, children focus on means, not ends. In play, the end product is not important. Pleasure comes through the process of playing.

3. Play is more than exploration: play occurs with familiar objects, while exploration occurs with unfamiliar ones. In exploration, a child says, "What can this object do?" but in play, the question becomes, "What can I do with this object?"

4. Play is an "as if" activity: it involves pretending and has non-literal qualities.

5. Play has no externally imposed rules, whereas games do.

6. Play requires active involvement, whereas daydreaming does not.

7. Play is emergent and novel, not predetermined or scripted.

● Play as Creativity

Given these characteristics, play can also be viewed as synonymous with creativity (discussed more in Chapter 10). Children approach their environment in unique and novel ways on their own initiative. They invent, discover, form hypotheses—in essence, they utilize scientific methodology. In so doing, they gather and construct knowledge. Children need an environment that does not restrict their creative nature. A restrictive, authoritarian environment can be frustrating and stressful to children as it inhibits and confines their natural drive and instinct to explore. Torrance (1963) argued that children's diminishing outward show of creativity and increasing conformity was a people-made rather than developmental phenomenon. Our progressively structured system of school environments gradually extinguish, or at least divert inwards, children's natural tendency to be creative thinkers. It appears that children give in to the pressures of conformity. (We might wonder whether our attempts to socialize might better be replaced with attempts not to socialize.) You will see that guidance plays a pivotal role in facilitating and supporting children's drive to discover.

Overview of Play: Play from Infancy Through to the Early School Years

● Play in Infancy

Teachers working in settings that include infants and older preschoolers will tell you that their role in play differs substantially with the age of the child. In a preschool setting, for example, extended periods of time are allotted for self-directed play, whereas infants play for much shorter periods of time. Younger infants also spend much of their day involved in caregiving routines, such as feeding and changing. Play with infants often evolves during these caregiving sequences. The infant in the sensorimotor period of development also needs abundant opportunities to actively explore the environment—looking, smelling, tasting, banging, moving, listening, and shaking. Of course, arranging the environment so that sensorimotor play will occur is the responsibility of the caregiver. Teachers also are important facilitators of infant play, and they will be more likely to initiate play sequences with the very young than they would be with preschoolers.

To date, most studies of infant play have been descriptive in nature (Rubin et al., 1983). Most play during the first year is with single objects; the infant applies a sensorimotor action to the object. This type of play diminishes rapidly between 7 and 18 months, dropping from 90 percent of all play sequences to 20 percent. Symbolic play with objects (e.g., drinking from an empty cup) shows a marked increase between 11 and 18 months in a wide variety of settings and cultures.

The games parents play with infants also have been the subject of a number of investigations (Rubin et al., 1983). Parents initiate a number of play sequences (e.g., peek-a-boo, tickling, hiding), and infants coo, smile, and laugh in return. In the first few months of life, play is more likely to involve tactile, visual, auditory, and motor stimulation as opposed to toys. However, infants as young as 2 months respond to a responsive toy and try to maintain the stimulation. There is some suggestion that the language used in parent-infant game sequences introduces turn-taking conversational rules and social interaction.

The quality of play changes rapidly in the second year, and sensorimotor schemes are used less frequently. Pretend play with objects such as toy cups, spoons, and pillows becomes more frequent. These sequences also come to involve others rather quickly; rather than self-feeding, the toddler will feed a doll, a parent, or a caregiver. Initially, this form of play involves an isolated event, but complex sequences soon emerge. These sequences are related to familiar activities such as cooking, feeding, phoning, and changing. Substitute objects, rather than realistic objects, usually enter into play around 18 or 19 months, but the substitute needs to have some similarity to the real object for some months to come.

Around 2 years, the toddler uses substitute objects more freely, and they contribute to an increase in the diversity of pretend-play sequences. Pretend play becomes more social in the third year as the following section indicates.

● Play in the Preschool and Early School Years

Mildred Parten (1932) provided one of the landmark studies on play. Her work, still considered valid today (Sponseller, 1982), categorized young children's social play. She found that between 2 and 5 years children move from being asocial in their play to being associative. Although children at later ages engage in earlier forms of play, particularly solitary play (Hartup, 1983a), their play is typically more complex than it was when they were younger. Parten's six categories of social play are outlined in Exhibit 7-2.

Other researchers have viewed play from a different perspective. For instance, Sara Smilansky (1968) proposed play categories based on children's increasing cognitive abilities and measured by how children use play materials. This view is complementary to Parten's classifications, because it focuses on a different aspect of play. Smilansky's categories are also highlighted in Exhibit 7-3.

Rubin (1977, 1982) found that both Parten's and Smilansky's categories were necessary to understand some elements of play observed in preschool settings in the Waterloo area. For a series of studies on play, he combined the two categories in the tabular format shown in Exhibit 7-4. This table is often adopted by early childhood educators who wish to evaluate the types of play occurring in their programs.

● Pretend Play

The development of positive social traits is fostered in a variety of preschool activities and learning centres, but it is perhaps most naturally facilitated in pretend play. In pretend play, children use symbols such as words, actions, or other objects to represent the real world; in pretend play, they expand this symbolic play to include other children (Fein, 1979; Smilansky, 1968). Theorists and researchers have postulated a relationship between pretend play and the development of social competencies. For instance, through such play, children have many opportunities to learn about social rules by taking on someone else's identity and enacting common situations, and by negotiating with peers when conflicts arise (Doyle & Connolly, 1989). Although research has found that not all children engage in pretend play (Christie, 1982; Smilansky, 1968, 1990), a number of programs have been successful in teaching young children how to do so.

The first of the series of pretend-play training studies was carried out in Israel by Sarah Smilansky (1968). She helped children from deprived backgrounds learn skills required in role taking, use of symbols, social and verbal interaction, and persistence. The level of teacher intervention depended on the skills and needs of the children. If children had very limited skills, the teacher facilitated pretend play by participating in the children's play directly. As children became more adept, the teacher became less obtrusive, taking on the role of an outside observer who made suggestions to enhance play rather than being a participant.

EXHIBIT 7-2   *Parten's Categories of Social Play*

Type of Play	Definition	Example
Unoccupied behaviour	The child moves about the classroom going from one area to another, observing but not getting involved.	Sebastian wanders to the blocks and watches several children work together on a structure. After a few seconds he looks around, then walks over to the art table, where he looks at the finger-painting materials briefly but does not indicate a desire to paint. He continues to wander, going from area to area, watching but not participating.
Solitary play	The child plays alone, uninvolved with other children nearby. Children at all ages engage in this type of play, although older children's solitary play is more complex (Almy et al., 1984; Rubin 1977).	Soon Yi works diligently at building a sand mountain, not looking at or speaking with the other children who are involved in other activities around her.
Onlooker play	Quite common among 2-year-olds, this type of play involves watching others nearby at play, without joining in.	Rajeef stands just outside the dramatic-play area and watches a group of children participate in doctor play using various medical props.
Parallel play	Children use similar materials or toys in similar ways but do not interact with one another.	Kalie alternates red and blue Lego blocks on a form board while Terrance, sitting next to her, uses Lego blocks to build a tall structure. They seem influenced by each other's activity but neither talks to the other nor suggests joining materials.
Cooperative play	This play, typical of older preschoolers, is the most social form and involves children playing together in a shared activity.	On arriving at school one day, the children find an empty appliance box in their classroom. At first they climb in and out of the box, but then a few of them start talking about what it might be used for. Jointly they decide to make it into a house, and their discussion turns to how this could be accomplished. While continuing to discuss the project, they also begin the task of transforming the box, cutting, painting, and decorating to reach their goal. It takes several days, but the children together create a house.

EXHIBIT 7-3 *Smilansky's Categories of Cognitive Play*

Type of Play	Definition	Example
Functional play	This repetitive, motor play, characteristic of infants and toddlers, is used to explore what objects are like and what can be done with them.	Clark picks up a block, turns it, and looks at it from all sides. He bangs it on the floor, then picks up another block with his left hand and bangs the two blocks together. He alternates striking the blocks against each other and on the floor.
Constructive play	This involves creating something with the play objects.	Clark uses blocks to construct a tower. His activity now has a purpose.
Dramatic play	The child uses a play object to substitute for something imaginary.	Clark takes four blocks, puts one on each of four plates placed around the table, and says, "Here is your toast for breakfast."
Games with rules	These involve accepted, pre-arranged rules to play. This stage is more typical of older children.	In kindergarten, Clark and a group of peers play the game "Blockhead," agreeing on the game's rules.

EXHIBIT 7-4 *Play Rating Sheet Using Rubin's Combination of Smilansky's and Parten's Categories*

Type of Play	Solitary Play	Parallel Play	Group Play
Functional play			
Constructive play			
Dramatic play			
Games with rules			

In many cases, children assist peers who are not as skilled in entering pretend play. For instance, 4-year-old Felix most often engaged in onlooker behaviour during child-selected activity times, usually standing on the outskirts of social groups. One day in November, Yasmine, age 5, deftly included Felix, who stood at the edge of the housekeeping corner observing a family group prepare dinner. The participants had assumed all the obvious roles, including that of family dog. The mother, Yasmine, took Felix by the hand, led him to the play oven, and declared, "You can be the turkey." She helped Felix fit himself into the oven and closed its door. A few seconds later, she opened the door, checked Felix's done-ness by squeezing his thigh, and declared, "Turkey's done!" Everyone gathered around as the turkey was helped out of the oven. Felix's big grin testified to his delight at being assigned such an important role! Discussions ensued about children never getting into a real stove, fridge, and so on, for which the teacher checked, by listening, observing, and probing for prior, current, and new knowledge on the subject. In this way, the teacher identified those concepts that needed further guidance and discussion.

Most young children engage in dramatic pretend play naturally; however, such play should also be purposefully encouraged and enhanced in all early childhood settings. Every early childhood classroom should have an area set aside and equipped for dramatic play. Most commonly, dramatic-play props and children's engagement in dramatic play will centre on housekeeping because home-related roles and activities are most familiar to young children. Children re-create and enact what happens at home: meal preparation and consumption, bedtime routines, visitors, child rearing, even arguments. Home-related kitchen, living room, and bedroom items, as well as a selection of dolls, dress-up clothes, and mirrors, stimulate children's creative and social engagement in housekeeping play. Materials for younger preschoolers should be realistic, whereas they should be more abstract for older preschoolers, to encourage pretending (Fein, 1982). Children can be further encouraged to broaden their concepts and dramatic play through displays and pictures of people of all ages and different ethnic groups engaged in common household activities.

Dramatic play can also revolve around any other theme familiar to the children. Health care, shopping, and recreation are usually particularly relevant to young children because they invariably have visited the doctor, grocery store, or park. Children will also enact favourite book, television, or movie roles and stories. Ensuring children are familiar with a topic through concrete, firsthand experience before they engage in dramatic play also helps enhance their experiences. Ideally a program should have both a home centre and a dramatic-play centre. If this is not possible, placing appropriate props for use in the dramatic-play area following a field trip, for instance, can help children assimilate and integrate information from the trip.

You should make dramatic-play kits available for children to integrate into the home centre rather than imposing a theme on the centre. Themes sometimes serve to restrict or impose play on children (e.g., children feel they must play "grocery store" because that is what is available). Without the choice between a home centre and a dramatic-play centre, themes may actually rob the children of the value of the home centre where they often need to recreate circumstances to work them out. Kits, on the other hand, can be taken off the shelf as needed by the children. As well, number limits in the centre are usually not necessary. A more appropriate limit states that if everyone is cooperating, everything is fine!

● Research and Value of Play

Research on pretend play has consistently found that this type of play increases with age in middle-class children from intact families, and it becomes more interactive with age. However, solitary pretend play decreases between 3 and 5 years and then increases again around age 6 (Rubin et al., 1983). Parallel pretend play remains frequent throughout the preschool years. A number of studies (Rubin et al., 1983; Shefatya, 1990) have suggested that pretend play is delayed and/or less mature in children from lower-income backgrounds. Some of these studies have not been well controlled, and the differences may not be as great as was once suspected. Nevertheless, across several cultures, children who have parents with less formal education engage in less pretend play than children who have parents with more formal education. Children who watch a great deal of television also are less likely to engage in pretend play, and there is some suggestion that divorce reduces the occurrence of pretend play, especially in boys. Large toys that accommodate pretend play themes (e.g., a horse, a car) seem to produce more pretend play, as do more creative playgrounds.

Rubin and his colleagues (1983) and Smilansky (1990) also have reviewed the extensive literature on the effects of play on development, but the literature is clouded with methodological difficulties. The evidence suggests that **problem solving**, story making, classification skills, and scores on intelligence tasks are positively correlated with pretend play. Tutoring in pretend play has also been investigated (Rubin et al., 1983; Smilansky 1990) and found to lead to both an increase in pretend play in the class, improvement in related cognitive skills, and an increase in social participation. As peer interactions are significant influences on cognitive development, the increase in social participation may have far-reaching effects.

Smilansky (1990) noted that 12 independent studies, conducted over a 16-year period, have shown positive benefits from adult intervention in pretend play. The interventions were meant to improve and extend the play, not to make it adult-dominated. Subsequently, she conducted a survey of 120 preschool and kindergarten teachers in the United States and Israel to see if these results affected educational practices. While 100 percent of the teachers had a playhouse corner in their programs, 90 percent of the teachers did not expect all children to play there during the week, and none of the teachers assessed the children's play in that area. In fact, none of the teachers remembered any course that covered pretend play, and 90 percent of them did not think pretend play helped prepare children for school. Moreover, 50 percent of the teachers never intervened in pretend play, and another 30 percent only encouraged and facilitated pretend play. This gap between research and practice concerned Smilansky, who maintained that the cognitive learning potential of pretend play is being overlooked in many classrooms. Other teachers believe that provision of a proper setting and environment plus encouragement is sufficient for the child to grow. They look on intervention in sociodramatic-play activity with suspicion (Smilansky, 1990, p. 40).

Smilansky recommended a fundamental change in attitudes and pointed to teacher education as the force that can lead to such a change. With knowledge about the importance of pretend play, and appropriate assessment and intervention techniques, teachers are likely to make much greater use of this untapped resource. Wright (1983), for example, demonstrated that changes in the theme of the dramatic-play centre (e.g., a store, hospital, hairdresser, and barbershop) led to increased use of the centre, especially by older children. A study by Marcotte and Young (1992) in Hamilton, Ontario, also found that a switch in the dramatic-play centre's theme was associated with a substantial increase in language use in the centre.

Smilansky (1990) and Rubin et al. (1983) have documented many studies that have demonstrated the value of play in the life of the young child. Teachers who are aware of this literature are able to defend play-based, developmentally appropriate programs and resist the push for academics.

● A Note on Superheroes

Though superhero play has been criticized, proponents of this type of play emphasize the fact that children emulate the noble qualities in superheroes and strive toward these values and images. Kostelnik, Whiren, and Stein (1986) pointed out that children benefit from these play experiences in many ways:

- Children are empowered.

- Children experience positive emotions (e.g., courage, strength, pride, glory, and wisdom in doing something good).

- Children gain confidence in themselves and adults.

- Children experience and imitate clear models of good behaviour and strive toward these roles.

- Children practise problem solving, decision making, conversational skills, and cooperation.

- Children can role-play in a safe environment.

Saltz, Dixon, and Johnson (1977) introduced thematic fantasy play to help children act out fantasy characters. Saltz and Saltz (1986) found that this play activity improved children's performance across social, emotional, and cognitive domains. As early childhood educators, we need to remember that children can learn good things through imitation and observation. Children usually want to play the good guys. They can choose what aspects they will learn. Conversely, they ignore aspects that are above their thinking, experience, or interest level. We provide dramatic play as an outlet for children to solve problems they have seen, heard, or experienced, yet we often preclude them from exploring selected aspects of these problems through play by assuming we know what the problems are.

How will we learn what hidden experiences or fears the children have if we impose biases on what they are able to express through play? Where, then, is the safe outlet for experience of fears, anxieties, and confusion? How can we guide what we cannot observe? We need to be aware that implementing blanket policies (e.g., no play involving pretend use of guns) may prevent children from showing us what we need to know since we cannot possibly know ahead of time what children need to express to us. Carlsson-Paige and Levin (1992) wrote an excellent guideline entitled "Who's Calling the Shots?" that deals practically with both sides of the debate concerning children's fascination with war play and war toys.

To guide, among other things, means to help children understand, to pose questions, to clarify and confirm, to help them research and investigate, and to provide information to help identify and work through problems and fears. Our curriculum should enable children to show what they know. Only then can we adequately and effectively guide them.

● Cooperative Games

One prosocial goal that early childhood educators cite for young children is cooperation, the force that unites people into working together toward a common objective. Games can be easily adapted to keep the element of fun while minimizing competition. For instance, the game of musical chairs can be changed so that all the children share the decreasing number of chairs, until everyone is piled on (and around) the last chair.

Terry Orlick (1978a, 1978b, 1982) first turned our attention to the destructive outcome of some competitive games and proposed cooperative games as an alternative. The rationale for cooperative games is not just the avoidance of situations in which most of the participants lose but is much broader, extending to a general concern for the quality of life, emphasis on peace and harmony, and decrease in societal aggression.

Activities involving two or more players can be considered cooperative if one or more of the following is involved: shared goals, joint decision making, shared ideas and materials, negotiation and bargaining, coordination of efforts to meet goals, and evaluation of progress toward goals (Goffin, 1987). Although Orlick recommended organized group games as a vehicle for promoting cooperation, this trait can be encouraged in more indirect and less structured ways as well.

Classroom space can be organized to encourage interactions, and ample time blocks can be allocated for child-selected play. Cooperative endeavours may well require more space and more time than activities in which children act alone. In addition, materials should be selected for their cooperative properties. Open-ended materials such as dramatic-play props, blocks, water, sand, and puppets particularly promote cooperation.

● Guidance

Certainly, understanding that children need to play, and knowing what play is, are major steps toward providing a quality program. Your role in guiding children's play is inextricably linked to your role in guiding children. The principles that govern our interactions with children apply throughout the day. In fact, the principles of guidance are, in many ways, the early childhood education program. If you adhere to principles that guide and nurture, foster and support, empower and enhance, then you also subscribe to concepts indigenous to human rights—concepts such as fairness, equality, diversity, and justice. If the principles are practised, the concepts will emanate from your program and the children.

As you are well aware, you could not go through a day of play-centred learning without a few occasions where misunderstandings and conflicts arise as children play to assert themselves, to figure things out, to gain a sense of achievement. Your role of guiding children in their development in a manner that keeps their self-esteem intact yet enriches the learning experience is a delicate yet fundamental one. As soon as you interact with children, you have an impact on them. There are two possible outcomes. This impact can be negative and debilitating or positive and nurturing. The goal of guidance is to nurture children's emotional development while helping them grow and learn as they play and interact with others.

Appropriate Practices in Early Childhood Education

In the foregoing section, we have examined play and your role in nurturing and guiding the child's emotional development. But we have not yet examined the foundation upon which the child's daily life is built. The program model you choose, fancy toys, and a beautiful setting are all for naught if your stance—the way you interact with children—is inappropriate. Equally important is the inter-action between child and program, for which you are the link. In this section, we will discuss the concept of appropriate practices in early childhood education, but we will not prescribe a program outline with schedules, routines, and environments laid out like a recipe. The wording "appropriate practices" in the heading above was selected instead of the more frequent "developmentally appropriate practices" so as to broaden the scope of our discussion. At times, however, we do retain the term "developmentally," since the term is used widely in the field itself. (In the A Closer Look box in this chapter we feature developmentally appropriate programs in transition.) The notion of appropriate practices applies to many pro-grams, and we hope that you will gain a feel or sense of this ideal in this section.

Courtesy of Yes I Can! Nursery School.

Appropriate practices should include a commonsense approach to child care. Common sense dictates that you pay attention to the environment. Knowledge about child development, play, and learning help you determine what is appropriate for the environment. Is the room too hot or cold? Too light or dark? Too noisy or quiet? Is there time for privacy? For conversation? For outdoor play?

Think about your own situation. You come to a particular program setting—college or university. The setting is based on a particular model—adult learning. You choose a particular program—early childhood education. The teachers use their knowledge of adult learners when they engage in particular practices. These include setting up the physical environment, designing a schedule, and choosing activities (e.g., individual, small-group, large-group) and materials. Do you feel these practices were designed with your learning and developmental needs in mind?

In high-quality early childhood programs, "developmentally appropriate" means they meet the following criteria:

- The program is age-appropriate for the children it serves.

- The program is adapted to be *individually appropriate* for each child it serves. Every child in the program is different, and the program is responsive to developmental, temperamental, familial, cultural, and ethnic differences.

- The program promotes inclusion.

- The program provides adequate time for various pursuits. Children need time in a program—time to be alone, time to be with others, time to reflect, time to be noisy, time to be children. In planning a program, you will want to provide time for self-directed activity, indoor and outdoor play, group activities, meals and/or snacks, and napping in a full-day program. You will want to allow time to get outerwear on and off, but you do not want a child to be bored while waiting for others to get their outerwear on or off. A child's needs for time vary with the developmental level and history of the child.

- The program provides variety and choice.

- The program offers different experiences at varying levels of difficulty. Both self-selected and teacher-directed activities have value, but there must be a balance between them.

- The program provides flexibility and predictability. Striking a balance between versatility and stability is an ongoing challenge for teachers.

- The teachers, together with children and parents, plan the program, choose resources, and organize the environment so that play-based, child-centred learning will occur.

- The program should be evaluated on a daily basis. Evaluation is multidirectional and includes the children.

● Developmentally Appropriate Programs

By the mid-1980s, the "earlier is better" ideology had led to the establishment of increasingly academic kindergarten programs in many parts of the United States. The National Association for the Education of Young Children (NAEYC) opposed this move to direct instruction and maintained that play-based programs, in which children were active learners, were more developmentally appropriate. To support its position, it produced and subsequently expanded *Developmentally Appropriate Practice in Early Childhood Education Programs Serving Children from Birth Through Age 8* (Bredekamp, 1987). This document generated considerable discussion. It also generated a number of changes to more **developmentally appropriate practices**, even at the elementary school level (e.g., Scales, Almy, Nicolopoulou, & Ervin-Tripp, 1992a; Smith, 1991). In 1997, NAEYC released the second edition of this document (Bredekamp & Copple, 1997). The document is as relevant in Canada as it is in the United States. A full discussion of the policy is beyond the scope of an introductory text, but the key points merit our attention. In addition, there are excellent resources on the topic, such as Carol Gestwicki's 1999 book, *Developmentally Appropriate Practice*.

Just what do these policy papers say? In 1987 the concept of developmental appropriateness had two components: *age-appropriateness* and *individual appropriateness*. The concept of age-appropriateness may already be somewhat familiar, especially if you have studied child development or developmental psychology. Bredekamp (1987) offers this definition of age-appropriateness:

> *Human development research indicates that there are universal, predictable sequences of growth and change that occur in children during the first nine years of life. These predictable changes occur in all domains of development—language, physical, emotional, social, and cognitive. Knowledge of typical development of children within the age span served by the program provides a framework from which teachers prepare the learning environment and plan appropriate experiences. (Pp. 3–4)*

The concept of individual appropriateness is perhaps less familiar:

> *Each child is a unique person with an individual pattern and timing of growth, as well as individual personality, learning style, and family background. Both the curriculum and adults' interactions with children should be responsive to individual differences. Learning in young children is the result of interaction between the child's thoughts and experiences with materials,*

ideas, and people. These experiences should match the child's developing abilities while also challenging the child's interest and understanding. (Bredekamp, 1987, pp. 3–4)

In the 1997 document, this concept of individual appropriateness was subdivided to elaborate on the importance of social and cultural contexts as well. The policy continues with many examples of both appropriate and inappropriate practices for early childhood programs for newborn-to-8-year-old children. The policy also comments on play: "Children's play is a primary vehicle for and indicator of their mental growth. ... Therefore, child-initiated, child-directed, teacher-supported play is an essential component of developmentally appropriate practice" (Bredekamp, 1987, p. 4; see also Bredekamp, 1997, p. 14). Additional NAEYC publications include *Developmentally Appropriate Practice in Early Childhood Programs Serving Infants* (1989a) and *Developmentally Appropriate Practice in Early Childhood Programs Serving Toddlers* (1989b). They deal with the special needs of the very young. Below we look at age-appropriateness and individual appropriateness in more detail.

● Age-Appropriate Programs

Developmentally appropriate programs support children in their natural propensity for play rather than just teaching them directly. This is a delicate balance. Some studies show that simply leaving children to their own devices is detrimental to development. For instance, children in orphanages (Skeels, 1966) who experienced severe environmental deprivation acquired developmental delays. More recently, a similar situation in Romanian orphanages was brought to our attention. Yet placing children in direct instruction programs that are beyond their developmental level in order to boost their IQ also creates stress and is detrimental to development, as pointed out by at least four well-known childhood experts of our time: Elkind (1986), Brazelton (1992), White (1968, 1975), and Greenberg (1988). Certainly the extremes of any practice are inappropriate. Similarly, taking sides or ignoring the virtues of opposing methodologies is equally worrisome. Simply teaching or simply playing is not enough. Developmentally appropriate practice "recognizes age-related human characteristics that permit general predictions within an age range about what activities, materials, interactions or experience will be safe, healthy, interesting, achievable and also challenging" (Bredekamp, 1997, p. 9).

Perhaps one of the most important statements to come out of the NAEYC revision of 1997 is the recommendation (on page 23 of the document) to move from an either/or to a both/and way of thinking, as we did originally with the nature/nurture controversy. Hence, whole language or phonics becomes whole language and phonics. Many ideas can be compatible and effective in combination: play-based and direct instruction; routine and emergent curriculum; integrated theme and content area study; choice and limits—to give just a few examples. Balance is achievable and acceptable within the framework of "developmentally appropriate" and "high-quality."

● Individually Appropriate Inclusive Programs

A good early childhood program is intrinsically inclusive of all children because it accommodates a range of developmental, cultural, familial, social, financial, religious, and ethnic needs. A good early childhood program's "freedom within structure" environment is flexible enough to adapt to all children, and it has staff trained in child development, stages of play, and guidance so that they too can adjust their approaches for every child. The concepts of empowerment, respect, age and individual development, opportunity, and nurturing lend themselves to accepting children with a wide range of needs. As well, since we subscribe to the team and transdisciplinary approach, we know we have many resourceful partners to help us in embracing diversity.

Ignorance or indifference are certainly not the same as acceptance. Sensitivity to and awareness of individual differences are important. Fairness means you recognize these individual needs and address them. In order to provide an anti-bias, multicultural, inclusive program, teachers must be knowledgeable as to the implications of an activity to ensure that their program meets the needs of the children and families it serves and that it sets an example for the generations to come.

The concepts of *anti-bias, multicultural, inclusive education* (Derman-Sparks & Ramsey, 1993) will be apparent in every high-quality educational program. These programs actively confront—or proactively avoid—exclusion, prejudice, stereotypes, and the "isms" and phobias, including racism, sexism, and homophobia. The diversity of children and families in the program is respected and reflected throughout the program, the day-to-day environment, staffing, provision of opportunity, and all activities. Inclusion is a common thread, a philosophical base, that permeates every facet of the program. It is not represented by a special day, a unique toy, or a learning centre or a circle; it is a fundamental component of the program. This concept is so crucial to appropriate practice that Ruth Fahlman's A Canadian Professional Speaks Out box and the Partnerships box focus on it in more depth. Many Web sites have interesting suggestions for multicultural activities.

A Canadian Professional Speaks Out

ANTI-BIAS EDUCATION: A PERSONAL AND PROFESSIONAL CHALLENGE FOR EARLY CHILDHOOD EDUCATORS

Ruth Fahlman, West Coast Child Care Resource Centre, Vancouver

For many early childhood educators in Canada today, anti-bias education is a new and challenging topic. For some educators, anti-bias, human rights, and social justice concepts and goals may seem far removed from the ECE environment. For others, working with young children is both a vocation and an avenue for political action, "for making a better world."

(cont'd)

ANTI-BIAS EDUCATION *cont'd*

Whatever our current personal perspective, it is important to consider that what we choose to do or not to do has consequences for children in their immediate environment and in the long term. Do we intervene effectively when children or adults reveal bias or prejudice? Do we select materials for our program that portray and reflect human similarities and differences positively? Do we introduce developmentally appropriate experiences for exploring individual and group rights and responsibilities? When making choices that relate to anti-bias ECE practice, we are challenged to examine our actions, and to clarify how these actions reflect our values and support our goals.

As we review our own practice, we are engaging in some of the processes that are, ultimately, at the heart of anti-bias education: namely, reflection, action, and evaluation. In turn, we can also encourage children to explore anti-bias issues by considering such questions as, "What do we think is important about sharing and getting along with everyone?" (reflection), "What can each of us do to take care of ourselves and treat each other fairly?" (action), and "What areas of our own behaviour do we want to improve?" (evaluation). Questions like these promote children's connection with issues such as respect, fairness, and inclusion through action-oriented self-awareness, personal responsibility, and problem solving.

As we encourage these understandings and abilities in young children, we provide the foundation for their later consideration of broader social issues such as, "How do people share wealth and privilege, and get along without resorting to violence and war?," "What can individuals, organizations, and governments do to share more fairly and resolve differences more effectively?," and last, "How well are we, as a human family, dealing positively and creatively with our similarities and differences?" In considering these questions, we can see the links between the social challenges for children in the preschool environment and the challenges faced by society as a whole.

For early childhood educators, then, we return to consideration of how much or how little of an anti-bias approach we choose to implement within our programs. Some of us may feel that our knowledge is inadequate or that we lack the skills for addressing issues such as stereotyping or discrimination. We may also have ambivalent feelings about exploring some areas or aspects of anti-bias with young children—perhaps we are comfortable talking about special needs, but feel less so about sexual orientation or poverty or religion. Such hesitations or concerns are valid and may be addressed through professional development and peer support. Yet when deliberating on the need to change our attitudes, knowledge, and practice, we should always consider the consequences of what we do or not do with children. Is not self-awareness, personal responsibility, and problem solving in the social sphere as important, or more important, than anything else we teach children? If we do not model how to reflect, act, and evaluate in relation to anti-bias issues, how and when will children learn these skills?

As individuals within a diverse society, and as educators guiding young children, it is important that we consider carefully our values and goals, and how they relate to anti-bias education. Many resources and options are now available for instructing developmentally appropriate anti-bias concepts and content within ECE settings. For early childhood educators committed to human rights and social justice goals, implementation of anti-bias ECE is one way to act on these values, thereby helping young children "begin well in the beginning" to identify with and protect the rights of the whole of the human family.

Partnerships

REFLECTIONS OF FAMILY CULTURE AND VALUES

Communication with parents is particularly important in clarifying home and school values about socialization and about children's cultural and racial identities. Although the school is responsible for conveying to parents what values it tries to instill in the children through the curriculum and guidance techniques, the school also is responsible for obtaining similar information from parents about what they value for their children. Teachers need to be sensitive to the many variations among families of different cultures, and they must be particularly aware of their own attitudes and biases. It is easier to convey positive messages to a family with whose parenting style and values you are familiar with and agree with than it is to understand and accept an approach different from your own.

Another reason that good parent-teacher communication is vital is to avoid making assumptions about children's home life based on cultural generalizations. There are wide variations within cultural groups. In addition, individual families' adaptation to Canadian culture will also affect their lifestyles and customs. One child care centre director, for instance, hired one of the parents to help with meal preparation. When this mother, who had recently come from Colombia, asked the director to explain the "tacos" on the menu, the director was taken aback, assuming that anyone from Central or South America would know what they were. As she quickly learned, Central and South America represent many countries with diverse and individual foods and customs.

Teachers can gain much information from parents about cultural and ethnic backgrounds and values. For instance, it is important to have the child's full name, the name the family uses, and the correct pronunciation. In some cultures such as the Vietnamese, the correct order in giving a name is last name first, followed by first and middle names (Morrow, 1989). Also some Asian families give a child one name to be used in public and another to be used at home. It is important, therefore, to have accurate information about what name to use in speaking to the child.

Also gather information about the child's family, special friends, pets, or any other people or objects that are important. This will help facilitate discussions and provide ways of involving what is closest to the child. In addition, obtain information about holidays and other special cultural, religious, or family celebrations, including when they are observed, their purpose, and how the children are involved. This will help incorporate cultural activities that are meaningful (*Culture and children*, 1985).

Some teachers may face an additional challenge if some of the families whose children are enrolled in the program speak a primary language other than English. In some communities with a large population from another culture, early childhood programs may have teachers who speak the language of this group and can either facilitate communication or provide a bilingual program. This is often not the case, however. It is important to help children, parents, and teachers communicate. One way is for teachers and even other children to learn some common words and phrases that can help the child begin to integrate into the class. While children may quickly learn enough English to function effectively at school, their parents generally will not acquire the new language as rapidly, and communication with the school could be a problem.

Because communication between home and school is so important, the school can do several things. Finding an interpreter who can facilitate occasional parent-teacher meetings can be helpful. If there are older siblings, they are natural interpreters who can be asked to assist. You might also offer to locate an ESL (English as a second language) program if the parents are interested in improving their acquisition of English. For everyday interaction, try to learn and use a few common words and phrases in the family's language: this can convey your desire and willingness to communicate. If nothing else, your quaint pronunciation attempts will bring a smile to the parent's face and create a sense of shared effort.

Finally, Derman-Sparks (1989), in *Anti-Bias Curriculum*, suggested that in addition to open communication in which values and ideas can be shared by parents and teachers, the school can provide accurate information to parents about the development of children's sexual, racial, and ethnic identities and attitudes. A series of parent group meetings can inform and invite discussion about such topics as gender identity and sexism, the creation of non-sexist environments, the development of racial identity and awareness, the creation of anti-racist environments, and evaluation of children's books for sexist and racial stereotypes. Such groups can help parents gain information about the school's philosophy, help teachers attain insight into parents' values and attitudes, and provide parents with strategies for anti-biased socialization of children.

Developmentally Appropriate Environment

Take a moment to think about a place where you enjoy spending time. What are its appealing features? Is it relaxing and soothing, stimulating and exciting, thought-provoking and challenging, orderly and methodical, comfortable and homey, or colourful and bright? Now think about a place that you do not particularly like, and consider why it is unappealing to you. It may be that this place is boring, messy, stark, disorganized, dark, or uninviting. Think about spending all

Courtesy of Play and Learn.

day in each of these places. What feelings and attitudes does each place evoke? How do you think you would act and react in each place? Can you draw some conclusions about how and why the environment affects you?

According to research, when children are in a particular **behaviour setting**, they behave in a manner appropriate to that locale, following what might be viewed as unspoken rules. Kounin and Sherman (1979) observed the following:

It is apparent that preschoolers behave "schoolish" when in a preschool. They are diligent creatures who spend 95 percent of their time actively occupied with the facilities provided and they deal with the facilities appropriately. They do all of these things in a sort of unwritten private contract between themselves and the setting they enter: teachers and peers infrequently exert any pressure to either enter or leave these settings. (P. 146)

Such research underscores the importance of providing an environment that supports development and learning. If children's engagement in activities is largely prompted by the environment, then it is incumbent upon teachers to provide the most appropriate setting possible.

The quality of the environment has an impact on the behaviour of both children and adults who spend time in that space (Kritchevsky, Prescott, & Walling, 1977). "Arrangement, organization, size, density, noise level, even the color of the classroom directly and indirectly invite a range of behaviors from children and teachers" (Thomson & Ashton-Lilo, 1983, p. 94).

More than a room's fixed features (i.e., room size, room shape, acoustics, storage, shelving units), it is the movable elements that allow you to arrange a well-planned, developmentally appropriate environment for children. Placement and grouping of **equipment** and furnishings communicate many messages. They convey the purpose of spaces, set limits on behaviour, establish boundaries, invite possible combinations of play through juxtaposition of areas, and encourage quiet or active involvement. Research has provided some guidelines for maximizing the effective use of space.

Phyfe-Perkins (1980), in a review of studies that examined the effect of physical arrangements on children's behaviour, proposed some helpful principles:

- Children in full-day care need privacy; thus, places where children can be alone should be provided in the environment.

- Soft areas such as beanbag chairs, pillows, or rugs allow children to snuggle and find comfort if "adult laps are in short supply" (p. 103).

- Small, enclosed areas promote quiet activities and interaction among small groups of children.

- Physical boundaries around areas can reduce distraction, which, in turn, increases attention to activities.

- Large spaces allow for active, large-group activities that are more boisterous and noisy.

- Clearly organized play space and clear paths can result in fewer disruptions and more goal-directed behaviour.

Exhibit 7-5 elaborates on guidelines for organizing classroom space.

EXHIBIT 7-5   *Guidelines for Organizing Classroom Space*

1. The room arrangement should reflect the program's philosophy. If the program's aim is to foster independent decision making, self-help skills, positive self-concept, social interaction, and more child-initiated than teacher-initiated activities, this should be promoted through room arrangement.

2. Keep in mind the children's ages and developmental levels. As children get older, provide more choices, a more complex environment, and greater opportunity for social play. For young preschoolers, it is best to offer a simple, uncluttered, clearly defined classroom with space for large motor activity.

3. Any environment in which children as well as adults spend blocks of time should be attractive and esthetically pleasing. Thought and care should be given to such factors as the arrangement of furnishings, use of colours and textures, and display of artwork. Plants and flowers added to the classroom can enhance its attractiveness.

4. If children are encouraged to make independent choices, then materials should be stored at a level where children can easily see, reach, and return them.

5. If children are to develop self-help skills, toileting facilities and cubbies for coats and boots should be accessible to them. Access to learning materials also contributes to development of self-help skills.

6. If the program supports a positive self-concept in children, then there should be individual places for children's belongings, for their projects or art to be saved, and for their work to be displayed.

7. If development of social skills and friendships is encouraged, then the environment should be set up to allow children to participate in activities with small groups of other children without undue interference or disruption.

8. If children are to have many opportunities to select and direct their own activities, then the environment should be set up to offer a variety of activity choices.

9. There should be places for children to be alone if they so wish. Quiet, private spaces can be planned as part of the environment (e.g., a corner with large pillows, a cozy spot in the library area, a designated rocking chair with cushions).

10. There should be soft places in the environment where children can snuggle and find comfort.

11. An environment set up into learning centres should have clearly marked boundaries that indicate the space designated for each given area. Storage shelves and other furnishings can be used to define the edges.

12. Paths to each area should be clear and unobstructed. Children are less likely to use areas that are hard to reach.

13. A pathway to one area should never go through another activity centre. This only interferes with ongoing play and can cause anger and frustration.

14. Doorways and other exits should be unobstructed.

15. Quiet activities should be grouped near one another, and noisy ones should be placed at some distance from these (e.g., the block centre should not be next to the book centre).

16. Group those activities that have common elements near one another to extend children's play possibilities. Blocks and dramatic play are often placed next to each other to encourage the exchange of props and ideas.

17. Provide areas for individual, small-group, and large-group activities by setting up different-sized centres.

18. Some areas require more space than others (e.g., block play is enhanced by ample room to build and expand block structures).

19. The sizes of various learning centres will, to some extent, convey how many children can play in each area and how active that play should be. Small, cozy areas set natural limits on the number of children and the activity level, whereas large areas send the opposite message.

20. Decrease noise level by using carpeting or area rugs in noisy centres (e.g., block centre).

(cont'd)

EXHIBIT 7-5 *cont'd*

21. Place messy activities near a water source.

22. Place activities that are enhanced by natural light near windows. Ensure that all areas are well lit, however.

23. Place tables and chairs in or near centres where tabletop activities are carried out (e.g., art and manipulative areas). Tables scattered throughout the room can take on an added use during snack time.

24. Consider multipurpose uses for space, especially where room size is restricted. When your room allows for a limited number of areas to be set at any one time, some of these might be used for more than one activity (e.g., the area designated for large-group activities might also be the block centre, music centre, or place set aside for large motor activity).

25. Some learning centres may not be part of the classroom on a daily basis. Such centres as woodworking, music, or cooking may be brought into the classroom on a less frequent schedule or may be rotated with other areas for specified periods of time.

26. Be flexible in the use of space and open to rearranging it. As children mature and their interests change, so should the centres. Also, if repeated problems arise, try solving these by rearranging the environment.

27. Safety should be an overriding, primary concern in setting up an environment for young children.

● Impact of the Environment on Children

"Developmentally appropriate" does not mean sterile, clean, or filled with expensive toys. Earlier we said that an environment devoid of materials or people with which to interact can result in serious developmental delay. Conversely, a beautifully planned and decorated environment, though it presents more opportunities for exploration and is appealing to the senses, can become developmentally inappropriate when combined with poor guidance, strict schedules and routines, or direct instructions.

Each province and territory has its own legislation regarding environment, yet it only sets out minimal standards that can be improved upon. In addition, the Early Childhood Environment Rating Scale (Harms & Clifford, 1998) is one instrument that assists teachers in beginning to assess some aspects of the developmental appropriateness of their centre. While this tool is based on normative practices (Varga, 1997) and thus is somewhat culturally specific, it is widely used since it is one of the first and the best tools for assessing the environment.

The early childhood environment should support the development of children. It has a direct effect on how children behave toward one another. Positive peer interaction is promoted when children are not crowded, when an ample number and variety of items are available, and when socially oriented materials are provided. Classroom arrangement and careful selection of materials also foster cognitive development by providing opportunities for children to classify, find relationships, measure, compare, match, sort, and label (Weinstein, 1987). The environment also enhances both fine and gross motor development through a range of appropriately challenging equipment and materials.

Children's growing sense of independence is supported when they can confidently and competently use equipment and when space and materials are arranged so that they can see what is available and make autonomous choices. At the same time, children develop a sense of responsibility when the environment makes it clear how and where materials are to be returned when they finish using them. Children are more productively involved in activities when the purpose of classroom spaces is clearly defined and when materials are developmentally appropriate (Phyfe-Perkins, 1980; Thomson & Ashton-Lilo, 1983). Children are more likely to follow classroom rules when the environment reinforces these; for instance, if it is important for reasons of safety that children not run inside, classroom furnishings should be arranged in a way that makes walking, rather than running, natural.

The environment also enhances children's self-esteem when it is designed with their needs and development in mind, when it provides space for personal belongings, and when it promotes competence by allowing children to function independently yet safely (Weinstein, 1987). In addition, the environment should convey a sense of security and comfort through a friendly, warm, and inviting atmosphere and through soft elements such as beanbag chairs, carpeting, or sling swings (Jones & Prescott, 1978; Weinstein, 1987).

Reflective Exercise 7-1

Mr. and Mrs. Jones want their 3-year-old daughter, Brianna, to excel in life. They want to enroll her in an academically oriented ECE program, as well as ballet, swimming, and Japanese. Mr. and Mrs. Jones know you are an expert in the field, so they come to you for advice about how to find the best academic program in town. Discuss their wishes with them in the context of what you know about the importance of play for young children.

● Impact of the Environment on Teachers

When the environment is set up to maximize children's development, prevent problem behaviours, and promote appropriate behaviours, teachers' well-being is indirectly supported. More directly, teachers' jobs are made more pleasant if they work in esthetically pleasing surroundings, if they have a designated space where they can relax and plan, and if their needs are generally taken into consideration

(Thomson & Ashton-Lilo, 1983). Both personal comfort and professional needs should be supported (Harms & Clifford, 1980). Environmental factors such as temperature, light, colour, sound absorption, ventilation, and spatial arrangement can facilitate or hinder staff in carrying out their jobs (Jorde-Bloom, 1988a). Thus, a carefully arranged environment can help prevent teacher burnout by supporting teachers' goals for the children and by making the work site a pleasant place to be.

Developmentally Appropriate Equipment

Early childhood equipment refers to furniture and other large items that represent the more expensive long-term investments in an early childhood facility. Materials refer to the smaller, often expendable items that are replaced and replenished more frequently. Because equipment can be expensive, its acquisition requires considerable thought. Exhibit 7-6 lists basic equipment and materials that should be included in a classroom for preschool-aged children.

● Criteria for Selecting Equipment

We remind you that a list of commonsense questions is a far better guide than an actual list of specific equipment. Some important questions to ask when selecting equipment include the following:

• Does this piece of equipment support the program's philosophy?

• Is the equipment appropriately sized for the children?

• Is the equipment safe?

• Is the equipment durable?

• Is there room for this equipment?

• Can the equipment be constructed rather than purchased?

• Is the equipment esthetically pleasing?

• Is the equipment easy to clean and maintain?

• Will it accommodate everyone?

• Is it compatible with the concept of diversity?

● Computers

Over the past 15 years, early childhood programs have been investing in the purchase of computers and **software** for children's use. A growing number of people have achieved **computer literacy**. In other words, they are knowledgeable about and capable of using a computer. It is often argued that young children are entering a world in which familiarity with computers will be a prerequisite for effective functioning. Therefore, exposure to computers and development of some basic computer skills should be part of early childhood programs.

NAEYC released its position statement "Technology and young children ages three through eight" in 1996 in response to this trend. Various concerns have been raised about the developmental appropriateness of using computers with young children (Barnes & Hill, 1983). However, research shows that young children are quite competent in using the symbols of computers appropriately (Clements, 1987). When computers first became widespread in early childhood education, an often-heard concern was that their use would be at the expense of peer interaction. This fear has been dispelled by a number of studies that document the positive effects of computers on socialization and cooperation (Essa, 1987; Swigger & Swigger, 1984; Ziajka, 1983). Another concern has been that the computer could decrease participation in other activities, but research has shown that it augments rather than replaces other centres (Essa, 1987).

The computer should be viewed as neither good nor bad, but rather a tool similar to the many other educational resources used by children. It is the wisdom of the teachers, who structure the conditions and setting in which computers are used and who select the software, that makes such activities relevant and worthwhile (Clements, 1987; Haugland & Shade, 1990).

Acquiring a computer for children's use necessitates the purchase of software, the set of instructions that direct the computer to perform an activity (Davidson, 1989). Software, which is usually stored on a disk that is inserted into the computer, is available through a variety of commercial sources. More and more software packages for young children are being developed and put on the market, offering a confusing choice to a novice software buyer. Haugland and Shade (1990), in assessing more than one hundred software packages, suggested using the following criteria for judging developmental appropriateness:

1. *Age-appropriateness.* The concepts taught and methods presented show realistic expectations of young children.
2. *Child control.* The children, as active participants, not the computer, decide the flow and direction of the activity.
3. *Clear instructions.* Verbal or graphic directions are simple and precise. (Written instructions are not appropriate.)
4. *Expanding complexity.* Software begins with a child's current skills then builds on these in a realistic learning sequence.
5. *Independence.* Children are able to use the computer and software with a minimum amount of adult supervision.
6. *Process orientation.* The intrinsic joys of exploring and discovering are what engage children on the computer. Completed work is not the primary objective and extrinsic rewards are unnecessary.
7. *Real-world models.* Objects used in software are reliable models of aspects of the world.

8. *Technical features*. Children's attention is better held by high-quality software, with colourful, uncluttered, animated, and realistic graphics, realistic sound effects, and minimal waiting times.

9. *Trial and error*. Children have unlimited opportunity for creative problem solving, exploring alternatives, and correcting their own errors.

10. *Transformations*. Children are able to change objects and situations and see the effects of their actions.

Developmentally Appropriate Materials

In addition to the more expensive equipment, an early childhood classroom requires a rich variety of play and learning materials. This includes commercially purchased items such as puzzles, crayons, or Lego blocks; teacher- or parent-made games and manipulatives; commercial or teacher-assembled kits that contain combinations of items for specific dramatic-play themes or flannel-board stories; and donated scrap materials for art or construction activities. Review the recommended basics for an early childhood program listed in Exhibit 7-6.

● Criteria for Selecting Materials

More than ever, a great selection of early childhood materials is commercially available. Toy and variety stores and catalogues, display variously priced toys and games that often promise to educate fully or entertain young children. In selecting learning and play materials, the following specific criteria must be met to ensure their suitability for young children:

1. *Developmentally appropriate*. Materials should match the stage of development of the children. Infants need toys that are responsive to sensorimotor actions: mobiles to see and bright, durable books and pictures. Toddlers and very young preschoolers just mastering language and locomotion will benefit from play items that encourage vocabulary building, promote a sense of balance, exercise fingers, and feed their burgeoning sense of independence. Older preschoolers, on the other hand, need materials that utilize their more refined skills in all areas of development. All preschool materials, however, should actively involve children, be interesting, and be safe.

2. *Active*. Young children need materials that promote interaction. They quickly get bored with items that require no action on their part. All early childhood materials should promote active involvement and exploration.

3. *Open-ended*. Among the most popular and most frequently used materials are open-ended toys, ones that can be used flexibly and do not dictate how they are to be used. Not all materials in the early childhood program will be open-ended (e.g., puzzles have only one outcome), but the majority should be.

EXHIBIT 7-6 *Basic Equipment and Materials for a Preschool Classroom*

A classroom for 16 to 20 young children should include, but not be restricted to, the following equipment and materials:

Equipment	Materials	
Basic Furniture	3–4 tables that seat 6–8 each (round, rectangular, or both) for meals and activities, as needed 24–28 chairs 1 rocking chair	16–20 cubbies, one for each child, to store personal belongings Beanbag chairs, pillows Bulletin boards
Dramatic-Play Centre	1 small table 2–4 chairs 4 appliances 1 large mirror 1 ironing board 4–6 dolls, different ethnic groups, both sexes 1 doll bed or crib	Dress-up clothes, both men's and women's Empty food containers Set of dishes, pots/pans Telephones Doll clothes, blankets Dramatic-play kits for selected themes
Art Centre	2 easels, two-sided 1 storage shelf	Variety of paper, paints, crayons, scissors, glue, collage materials, and clay materials
Block Centre	1 set unit blocks, 250 to 300 pieces, 12 shapes 1 set hollow blocks 1 set cardboard blocks	3–6 large wooden vehicles Various props, including animals, vehicles, people, and furniture
Manipulative Centre	1 storage shelf with individual storage bins	Wide variety of puzzles, pegboards, construction toys, parquetry, beads, and lotto and other games
Sensory Centre	1 sand and water table	Variety of props such as deep plastic bins, funnels, scoops, hoses, measuring cups, water wheels, containers, and shovels

(cont'd)

EXHIBIT 7-6　*cont'd*

Equipment	Materials	
Language Centre	1 bookshelf	Wide variety of books
	1 large flannel board	File of flannel-board stories
	1 tape recorder	Writing materials
	1 puppet theatre	Variety of puppets
Science and Math Centre	Animal homes, such as aquarium or cages	Animals
	Plants, garden supplies	Variety of math materials such as attribute blocks, Cuisenaire rods, calendars, and timers
	Wide variety of natural materials found in nearby environment	Variety of old mechanical objects to take apart, such as clocks, watches, cameras, and locks
	Variety of scientific instruments, such as microscopes, magnifiers, magnets, and thermometers	
Music Centre	1 record player	Storage unit for instruments
	1 set rhythm instruments	Variety of records/tapes
	1 autoharp	Props for movement activities, such as scarves or streamers
	3–4 tonal instruments such as xylophones or bells	
Woodworking Centre	1 woodworking bench with vise	Soft wood scraps
	1 set tools	Thick Styrofoam sheets
	1 tool storage unit	Variety of nails, screws
Outdoor Equipment	Gross motor equipment that allows children to slide, climb, swing, hang, balance, and crawl	Sensory materials such as fine-grained sand and access to water (in appropriate weather)
	8–10 wheeled vehicles: tricycles, wagons, and scooters	Movable equipment such as crates, planks, cardboard boxes, and tires
	A playhouse or other space for quiet or dramatic play	Balls, ropes, parachute

Note: This suggested equipment and materials list is by no means exhaustive. Many other items could and should be added, selected to suit the program, children, and staff.

4. *Feedback-oriented.* As children interact with materials, they should receive feedback on the success of their actions. A completed puzzle tells the child that the pieces have been fitted together correctly; when their bridge stays up, the children know that the blocks were stacked successfully; when there is a place setting for each of the four children at the table in the home centre, they know that they have matched children and dishes appropriately.

5. *Multipurpose.* Materials or combinations of materials should suggest many possibilities for play. Children's problem-solving skills and imaginations will be enhanced by multipurpose materials. Children of different skill levels should be able to use materials successfully.

6. *Safe and durable.* Items purchased for children's use should be sturdy and constructed from high-quality material. Preschoolers should not be given toys that require electricity. All materials should be checked regularly for loose parts, sharp edges, splinters, or chipping paint. All materials should be non-toxic and age-approved.

7. *Attractive and esthetically pleasing.* Materials should be appealing and inviting. Colour, texture, and appearance should be considered when choosing materials in the same way you consider them when redecorating a kitchen.

8. *Not stereotyped.* Materials should encourage a sense of equality and inclusion rather than reinforce sexist, racial, or cultural stereotypes.

9. *Diverse.* A wide variety of materials that cater to different interests and that meet all developmental needs is necessary. There should be ample materials to develop fine and gross motor skills, to exercise cognitive processes, to promote language use, to encourage socialization, to provide outlets for emotional needs, and to invite creativity. Although variety gives children divergent ways through which they can develop skills, there should also be more than one of some items. This is particularly important with infants and toddlers. However, younger preschoolers, who have not yet mastered the art of sharing, especially need the assurance of multiples of some items.

● **Teacher-Made Materials and Resources**

Some of the best early childhood materials are not purchased commercially but constructed as projects by teachers, parents, and/or children. Homemade toys are often tailored to fit the specific interests or needs of the children. Many resource books offer excellent suggestions and instructions for games and materials that enhance cognitive concepts, fine or gross motor skills, and language development (Baratta-Lorton, 1979; Debelack, Herr, & Jacobson, 1981; Linderman, 1979).

Projects evolve daily and require planning and collecting information through collaboration of teachers and children. Teachers and children can also develop and organize classroom resource materials to facilitate planning and programming. One helpful resource is the dramatic-play kit, which contains a collection of props for common dramatic-play themes. Contained in individually labelled boxes, dramatic-play kits can include some of the suggestions below.

- *Health theme*. Bandages, empty syringes, hospital gowns, stethoscope, bandages, empty medicine vials, and similar items donated by local doctors, hospitals, and other health-care providers.

- *Bakery theme*. Rolling pins, cookie cutters, baking pans, muffin liners, and aprons.

- *Self-care theme*. Small mirrors, combs, toothbrushes, hair rollers, empty shampoo bottles, and other cosmetic containers.

- *Grocery store theme*. Empty food containers, cash register, cash register tapes, bags, and play money.

- *Plumbing theme*. Taps, connectors, lengths of ABS piping, plugs, wrenches, and a hard hat.

It is worthwhile to note that many typical early childhood education programs set up the dramatic-play centre in a theme often arbitrarily chosen by the teacher (e.g., the grocery store). Current practice is moving toward involving the children in deciding on a relevant theme, by recognizing key experiences arising daily or by keeping dramatic-play kits available for children to take off the shelf and use at any time. Numerous community resources can be tapped for useful materials. It is a good idea to canvass your community for possible resources to complement whatever marvellous ideas you and the children decide to pursue.

● A Note About Learning Centres

Traditionally, indoor space is often organized into **learning centres** (also called interest or activity areas), which combine materials and equipment around common activities. Learning centres can include art, manipulatives, dramatic play, sensory experiences, blocks, music, science, math, computers, books, language arts, woodworking, cooking, and a variety of other areas that fit the unique interests, developmental needs, and characteristics of a group of children and teachers (Essa & Rogers, 1992).

Learning centres allow children to make choices from a range of available, developmentally appropriate activities. In the field of early childhood education,

---

Reflective Exercise 7-2

What are some of the unique features of your community? Which would interest young children? Think of several ways in which your community can be the basis for relevant learning for preschoolers.

there have recently been modifications to this concept. We now include children in the design of these centres by inviting them to choose materials that would make the centres more enjoyable. Historically, each centre has been independent of the others. For example, we would say, "Go to the math centre to do math." This felt off-kilter to us as teachers because we knew that every other centre (e.g., blocks, language, construction) also supported math concepts. As early childhood educators, we supported the concept of an integrated curriculum, yet our centres existed separately from one another rather than being interconnected. When children play at home, they rarely go to a block centre or a math centre or a language centre. Rather, they access materials from their environment, then engage in their activity—cooking, building, drawing, recording, pretending—on the basis of projects that have evolved from their play, ideas, and discussions. Children might decide, "Wow, let's make a birdhouse!" and then ask "What do we need?" and then begin to plan.

With these modifications, learning centres can be seen more as storage centres, areas that house particular materials that children can access—paper, pencils, dress-up clothes, masking tape, a tape recorder, and so on. Hence, children don't go to the art centre to use clay to make a dinosaur on a particular day because that is the teacher-designated art activity. Rather, clay is available as a tool or medium if the children need to design or make something to enhance their idea, play, or project. The computer is set up not just with a predetermined software program such as Sticky Bears but is there as a resource if the children want to design a fort or write a song. Writing utensils are used in many areas of the program for recording, planning, and drawing. In this sense, the teacher uses principles to guide the children through the day as their ideas emerge rather than imposing her or his ideas on the children through planned themes. We will elaborate more on this idea at the end of this chapter and in Chapters 9 and 10 when we discuss curriculum.

Developmentally Appropriate Schedules

Obviously the schedule in a program will vary with the children's ages, their developmental histories, and the length of the day. This, too, is legislated by province to ensure that adequate time is allotted for children to rest, eat, play, and toilet. Unfortunately, legislation, despite its good intent, sometimes negates the purpose of developmentally appropriate programming as it regulates choice, flexibility, and the concepts of child-centredness and individual appropriateness right out the centre door. Teachers have to use caution. Schedules of convenience are as detrimental as limits of convenience (see Chapter 6). Children are learning to pay attention to their internal clocks and their private voices and to make decisions and voice them. Very early on, children know when they have to go to the bathroom, are hungry, and are tired. Just like you, they need time—down time, social time, planning time, time to finish, time alone—and they need space. Imagine how frustrated we would make them if we spent every minute of the day telling them when, where, and what to do and how to do it!

Of course, infants and toddlers have unique needs, as any parent or teacher who has been with them knows. It is somewhat more difficult to determine what they are communicating to us. Rarely do they have predictable schedules. While time must be allocated for feeding, changing, and sleeping, the very young will always be somewhat unpredictable in their needs. Familiar teachers need to respond to them in a consistent manner and realize that the child's schedule will change in short order.

Programs for older preschoolers and school-aged children are more likely to have a general schedule in mind. Obviously, the outline of the day for a 2- or 3-hour preschool program will differ from that of a 9-to-11-hour child care centre program. But it is not only the difference in the number of hours but also the needs of the children that distinguish schedules for these two types of programs.

In planning the course of a typical day in an early childhood program, teachers typically allot times for self-selection, group activities, routines, and transitions. Children and their parents are greeted when they arrive and bid farewell at the end of the day. Both the indoors and outdoors are used whenever possible, and there is a balance between quiet and active times, and between group and individual times. The teachers know their responsibilities and thus ensure that no area of the program is unsupervised. However, they should in no way be rigid about their schedule.

A flexible daily schedule does provide security because it gives the day a predictable order. Children need predictability, and they soon know the general outline of the day. Thus, a schedule can give form without dictating exactly what happens each minute. A schedule is simply an outline of a typical day that can be changed when children's interests and needs point to a need for change. For example, if children want to watch a large cement truck that comes into view just as the group is about to go indoors, the teachers should extend the outdoor period. If new materials are attracting considerable attention, activity time is extended. If it has been raining relentlessly for two weeks and today is a beautiful, sunny day, plan to spend a large portion of the day outside so everyone can enjoy the nice weather. Similarly, if, despite your best efforts, the children are restless and uninterested in your group activity, shorten the time rather than allow a negative situation to develop. In other words, use cues from the children—and your judgment—to adapt the schedule if it will improve the flow of the day and better meet the needs of the children. You might also ask the children what changes in the schedule they would suggest. Their insights will surprise you! And if the chickens start to hatch when you are about to read a story, always forget the story!

You will make appropriate age adjustments in your typical day. For example, you will extend the number of choices available for older children, who also are able to make some transitions as a group. With school-aged children, you also will have more teacher-initiated activities and they will usually last for a longer period of time. The materials you select will be developmentally appropriate as well. You may read a short story to an infant but read the same story and sing a song with several toddlers. Preschoolers who have some experience in the program may want to sing several songs after a more complex story, but on some days they will not. Kindergarten and primary-level children may spend even longer times with the group.

Some large early childhood centres present special challenges because they have multiple classes that share some facilities. This can put some constraints on your flexibility but still allows for some latitude, especially when the team plans together rather than for individual classes. The self-contained parts of the program, such as activity or group time, can and should still be adapted freely.

As teachers, you will review the day's events and make adjustments on a regular basis. You will realize that schedules have to be tailor-made by teachers who know the needs of the children in their care. While the main scheduling consideration for child care centres is the needs of the children, the schedule must also take your needs into account. Early childhood teachers spend long and difficult hours working with their young charges, a job that can be both tiring and energizing, frustrating and rewarding. As a complement to the schedule you develop for the children, you need a schedule that provides rest, rejuvenation, and planning time for the adults. When the needs of the adults are considered, the children's needs will be better met, and teacher burnout is less likely to occur.

A Closer Look

DAVID AND RITA

David's parents enrolled him in a 9-to-noon preschool program sponsored by the city recreation department so that he could have an enriching social and learning experience. He typically gets up at 7:00, eats breakfast with his parents before his father leaves for work, plays alone or with his younger sister Tina for an hour or so, then gets dressed. At 8:45 his mother drives David to the nearby recreation centre, where he spends the morning in play and activities. At noon he goes home and eats lunch with his sister and mother. While Tina takes her nap, David and his mother often read or play together. After David's sister awakes, they pass the afternoon with errands, a trip to the grocery store, play, television watching, or a visit to a neighbourhood friend. Dinner is served around 6:00, then a television show on some evenings, a bath with Tina, a story read by David's father, and bed by 8:00.

Rita, who lives with her mother and two older sisters, has been at her child care centre since she was six weeks old because her mother has always worked. Rita gets up at 6:30, gets dressed with help from one of her sisters, and is out of the house by 7:15. Sometimes she does not eat breakfast because she is just not hungry yet; sometimes she munches on a piece of toast in the car. On the way to the child care centre, they drop off Rita's sisters at a neighbour's house, where they stay until it is time to go to their elementary school. Rita gets to the child care centre, sponsored by a church near her mother's workplace, by 7:45. Her day is spent in planned activities, play, meals, and nap at the centre until her mother picks her up around 5:30. They pick up her sisters, sometimes stop at the grocery store or at McDonald's, then get home around 6:30. While dinner is being prepared and after dinner, the girls watch television. After a bath, Rita is usually in bed by 9:00.

David's preschool program and Rita's child care centre serve different functions and meet different needs for these two children. David's preschool experience is an interlude in his day, most of which is spent at a fairly leisurely pace in his home with his family. It offers what cannot be provided by his family—opportunities for social interaction with peers, development of group skills, exposure to stimulating new ideas and activities, and group guidance from knowledgeable adults.

Rita, on the other hand, spends relatively little time at home, and often that time is busy and rushed. Rita's program also provides many opportunities for socialization with peers and for learning. But the child care centre, where Rita spends the majority of her waking hours, by necessity must also meet more of her physical requirements, for instance, for food and rest. It must also provide more for her emotional well-being by providing a nurturing climate in which she feels warmth, security, and recognition as a unique individual, not just a member of the group. In many ways, the child care centre replaces rather than augments part of Rita's home experience. Thus, when setting a schedule, whether for a preschool or a child care program, the central concern must be the needs of the children.

Reflective Exercise 7-3

You probably know children such as Rita (see the A Closer Look box), ones who spend most of their day in a child care centre. How can you best meet her needs? In what ways could the schedule accommodate to Rita's needs?

Components of the Developmentally Appropriate Program

Most early childhood programs contain some fairly standard elements. How these components are arranged and how much time is allocated to them reflect the ages and individual histories of the children, and the teachers' philosophy and goals. It would be absurd for an infant program to allocate large blocks of time for self-initiated play, but this would be a standard feature in developmentally appropriate preschool and primary programs.

The philosophy and goals of the program should reflect a respect for the child's growing independence, increasing decision-making skills, and ability to draw what is valuable from the day's experiences. The teacher facilitates play, structures

the environment, and supports children's choices. The teacher offers group activities for older children, recognizes that some children are not yet ready for them, and supports projects that emerge from children's creative thinking. The teacher also keeps groups small and has faith in children's ability to learn and flourish in a well-planned program. Planning does not mean deciding on all the activities to offer the children but on preparing to support and follow through on things that arise during the day.

Let us now examine standard components of the early childhood programs for preschool and school-aged children. (If you intend to specialize in infant care, consult additional resources.)

● Activity Time

In many programs, **activity time** is also called self-selected learning activities, free play, play time, learning centre time, or other, similar names suggestive of the fact that children make choices about the activities in which they engage (Hohmann, Banet, & Weikart, 1979). A wide variety of well-planned activities or opportunities from which children can design projects should reinforce and support the objectives of the curriculum. Each day should also provide multiple opportunities for development of fine and gross motor, cognitive, creative, social, and language skills.

Early studies confirmed the importance of an adequately long time block for self-selected play. Christie, Johnsen, and Peckover (1988) compared 4-and-5-year-olds' social and cognitive levels of involvement in play during 15-and-30-minute free-play periods. They found that when the play period was longer, children engaged in more mature play. More specifically, in the longer play period, children engaged in considerably more group play than parallel or solitary play; in the shorter period, there was more onlooker and unoccupied behaviour. During the longer play period, there was significantly more constructive play, in which objects were used to make something.

Beginning teachers are often concerned that they are not active enough during activity time or free play, but being a careful listener and observer is not being idle. Try to think of this time as an opportunity to respond to child-initiated learning opportunities. When you are simply looking and listening, you are learning more about the developmental status of the children you observe. Your demeanour says that you are always approachable and that you are ready to guide children into productive activities and help them resolve disagreements. At other times, you engage in quiet, informal conversations with children, but you do not distract busy players. Your relationships with the children are strengthened, and their self-esteem is enhanced because you let them discover solutions to their problems, rather than provide them.

When planning the activity time block, you should consider safety and adequate supervision. Some activities require close attention by an adult, while others can be carried out relatively independently by the children. Such activities as cooking and woodworking require constant teacher attention. Water and sand play, other sensory activities, messy media, and blocks also need to be monitored on an ongoing basis.

Children can be involved in planning their time. This can include timelines, materials, evaluation methods, accessing resources, and procedures that might require the teacher's guidance. New teachers tend to want to limit the number of children in centres, but this often causes more problems than it intended to avoid. Children cooperate and solve problems quite readily when the environment enables them to do so.

For each activity time block, it is important to consider the balance between activities that should be closely supervised and those that are more self-directed, particularly in relation to the number of adults available in the class. It can be easy to lose sight of safety needs in an effort to provide a wide variety of interesting and stimulating activities.

● Large-Group or Circle Activities

Most programs include one or more times when all of the children and teachers gather together. **Large-group times** such as circle time, which originated with Froebel, can be used for many purposes. Some teachers tend to use it in the same way day after day, and others use such times to meet various objectives. Some programs have several group times, each serving a different purpose. Examples include times for stories, music, and movement; sharing time, when children bring something special from home or present projects, ideas, or feelings; and times to share news with their peers.

Group times help the teacher meet a wide variety of objectives. For instance, they provide an excellent opportunity to introduce new topics and explore new materials, or to probe the children's comprehension of concepts and information (Essa & Rogers, 1992). They can also be used for discussions, stories and books, songs, finger plays, movement, socialization, poetry, games, dramatizations, sharing, relaxation exercises, planning and review, calendar or weather activities, and a host of other activities often carried out with the whole group (McAfee, 1985).

From interviews with and observations of early childhood teachers, McAfee (1985) found that the most popular and frequently observed circle activity was reading of books or stories, then music. As well, sharing time or "Show and Tell" was observed quite regularly, whereas other types of activities were seen relatively infrequently or not at all.

Group times are usually teacher-initiated and -led, although teachers always seek children's input. However, older preschoolers enjoy and are very competent in leading group activities, for instance, "reading" a familiar book, leading songs, and moving the group into transitions. Such opportunities to take over group leadership should, of course, never be imposed and should be conducted as the child chooses. You can find a variety of children's songs on the Internet to share with your class.

When guiding large-group (and small-group) activities, it is important to remember how children learn and what constitutes developmentally appropriate group activities. Children, as active learners, will gain more from activities that allow for their input, include active involvement, and encourage flexible problem solving. Asking children to answer questions for which there is a right or wrong response does not support their developmental needs and their growing self-esteem.

Teachers often become overly concerned on the logistics of circles such as requiring all children to come to circle simply because it is circle time or insisting everyone sit on their bottoms. The guidelines, instead, should say: We trust you will get comfortable, respect your neighbour, and respect whoever is talking. So as long as children are following the "no hurt" rule, lying down should not be prohibited. The objective is for them to enjoy circle time without bothering anyone else. Our messages should give children the benefit of the doubt and convey trust.

● Small-Group Activities

With infants and toddlers, the group size must be very small for most activities. For preschoolers and school-aged children, who are usually in larger groups, programs need to include a **small-group activity time** during which five or six children work with one teacher. This can be handled by staggering small groups throughout the program day or by having each teacher take a small group during a designated small-group time block. Usually such times focus on specific concepts and materials and are geared to the abilities and interests of the children in the group (Hohmann et al., 1979; Wright, 1983). Children should not be grouped by developmental level for activities. Hohmann and colleagues recommend that small groups represent a cross-section of the classroom population to promote cross-learning. In a small-group setting, the teacher has an opportunity to pay close attention to each child. As you might expect, careful planning is crucial for successful small-group activity times. In addition, children should be able to choose not to attend small-group activities.

● Outdoor Activities

Outdoor play should be a large part of the daily schedule. Some adults think of outdoor play merely as a time for children to expend excess energy and for teachers to take a rest. But outdoor time contains far too many valuable opportunities for learning and development to be dismissed in this way, as the open-model schools have so aptly demonstrated. When you think of outdoor play as an integral part of the early childhood experience, it becomes natural to allocate a large period of time for it. Outdoor time still requires planning in the same way that indoor activity does, and it involves the same kinds of teacher-child interactions.

Just as during activity times, the teacher's role when outside includes setting up a stimulating and safe environment, providing for each child's individual needs, guiding children's behaviour, providing a variety of experiences, taking opportunities to teach concepts, and encouraging exploration and problem solving. An important skill that you, as the teacher, should develop is the ability to scan, to keep an eye on the entire outdoor play area. It is particularly important to pay attention to the fronts and backs of swings, slides, climbing equipment, tricycles and other wheeled toys, and the area in and around the sandbox.

Time for outdoor play may be affected by the weather, although the weather should never be used as an excuse for not going outside. Children do not catch cold from playing outside in the winter, and rain can be glorious. Children thoroughly enjoy the snow or rain, and proper dress is all that is required. Nevertheless, there are times in most areas of Canada when frostbite or heat stroke will be a concern. Outdoor time can work well as a free-flow system if teachers, rather than groups, are assigned to the playground.

If inclement weather does prevent the children from enjoying outside time, gym time and games should be available so children can expend energy. Many schools have a selection of large-motor equipment, such as tumbling mats or indoor climbing apparatus, to use on rainy days, but these should be available every day since physical activity is central to overall health and development.

Finally, teachers often consider the school playground as the limit of outdoor experience, but walks, parks, nature trails, farms, hikes, swims, and beaches are all valuable outdoor experiences. Common safety sense should prevail, including permissions, emergency information, enough adults including parents, a first-aid kit, an attendance list, an emergency plan, assigned tasks and children, proper equipment, drinks, spare clothes, and a discussion with the children about safety and expectations in your usual calm, empowering way.

The Benefits of Outdoor Play.   The outdoor area and the time children spend outdoors should be integral parts of the early childhood program because of their many inherent values. Lovell and Harms (1985) summarized some of the educational and developmental objectives that well-planned outdoor activities in a well-designed, safe playground can meet:

1. Age-appropriate equipment should facilitate a wide range of **gross motor activities** at different levels of challenge, including balancing, throwing, lifting, climbing, pushing, pulling, crawling, skipping, swinging, and riding.

2. **Social skills** such as sharing, cooperating, and planning together can be encouraged by such equipment as tire swings, on which several children can swing together, wide slides, or movable equipment with which children can build new structures.

3. Activities and equipment should also enhance **development of concepts**, for instance, understanding spatial relations (e.g., up and down, in and out, under

and over, low and high) and temporal relationships (e.g., fast and slow; first, second, and next).

4. Problem solving that involves both physical and social skills should be encouraged as children figure out how to move a heavy object or how to share a popular item.

5. Children can learn about their natural world by **observing**, helping to care for plants and animals, noting seasonal and weather changes, and learning about environmental concerns.

6. A variety of activities carried out outdoors, such as art, woodworking, or music, can enhance **creative development**.

7. Children can try out and **experience** various adult roles through dramatic play, for instance, recreating the fire station, gas station, or airport.

8. In addition to stationary equipment, movable components such as planks, climbing boxes, and ladders allow children to create new and different possibilities to enhance their motor, social, language, cognitive, and creative development.

9. Exploration and **increasing competence** help children develop positive self-image and independence.

● Routines

Routines are regular, predictable behaviours that are repeated every day—or almost every day—in early childhood programs. They include arriving and departing, cleaning up the playroom and the playground, transitions, and personal care routines. How you approach personal care will vary greatly with the children's ages but will include eating, resting, washing, and toileting. Routines can provide valuable learning experiences, and they are also important for children's well-being. While routines are regular behaviours, it is important to remember that their timing should never be carved in stone.

● Cleanup

With infants and toddlers, there is a constant balancing act in how much tidy-up is required to ensure safety, and encourage independence yet maintain a relaxed, low-key setting. With age, children are more likely to put toys away after they are finished with them. Gentle reminders about your class discussions on why cleanup is necessary are usually enough. Older children also are quite willing to assist in tidying up large toys like blocks. Children also enjoy helping to put outdoor toys in the storage shed. Since children need warning, cleanup should not be sprung on them.

● Meals and Snacks

Sharing food provides a unique opportunity for socialization, learning, and fun. Thus, almost every program includes at least one snack, if not several meals. Children can assist in every aspect—meal planning, shopping, preparation, delivery, setup, serving, and cleanup. Discussions of fitness, nutrition and "Canada's food guide to healthy eating" (Health Canada, 2001), gardens, and anatomy can surround this activity. Children's involvement piques their interest, generates questions and ideas, and identifies interests, experiences, and prior knowledge while developing skills in all areas. The timing of meals, however, should be dictated by the children's needs, not by a rigid schedule. If it appears that some children get to school having had breakfast several hours before or not having eaten breakfast at all, then an early morning meal should be available. Snacks should be available for a period of time and children be allowed to eat as they feel the need to refuel. Having snack at a set time is unnatural and does not allow for individual differences or choices. Snacks should, of course, be self-serve and nutritious and offer variety.

Timing of lunch will depend on the ages of the children, the length of time they are at the centre, and when morning snack was served. Younger preschoolers may need lunch at 11:30 a.m. and be ready for a nap by noon. How much time is allocated for eating will depend on the children in the group and the type of meal. Generally, however, 15 to 20 minutes for snacks and 20 to 30 minutes for lunch is adequate. Most children can comfortably finish a meal in this period of time.

In any given class, you will find children who are vigorous eaters, enjoying whatever is served, and others who are picky and selective. Even individual children will vary considerably in appetite from day to day or meal to meal, just as you do (Alford & Bogle, 1982). Let's look at some suggestions for encouraging good eating habits and for dealing with some eating problems.

- A relaxed, comfortable atmosphere is vital to good eating. Eating is a time for sharing and talking.

- Teachers should sit and eat with the children during all meals.

- Children should never be forced to eat a food, but they should be encouraged to try all menu items since food preferences and aversions are formed at an early age.

- Involve children in the mealtime.

- Children should be allowed to be as independent as possible at mealtimes.

- Teachers should not serve the meal. "Family style" means children must use their language (e.g., "Please pass the potatoes") and make decisions about what and how much to eat. Drinks should accompany meals; everyone needs to wash down the occasional mouthful.

- It is important to be aware of foods that put young children, especially those under the age of 3, at risk of choking and food allergies.

- Always have the children wash their hands before eating.

- Be sensitive and accommodating to cultural and religious food variations.

● Nap or Rest

In full-day programs, children should have time for sleep or rest during the middle of the day, usually sometime after, though not immediately following, lunch. Allocating one to two hours for this time is usually enough (see Chapter 9 for a more detailed discussion). Also be aware of your local regulations for rest time, because some jurisdictions include specific requirements.

● Transitions

The times between activities are as important as the activities themselves. Failing to plan how children will get from one area to another—from group to the bathroom to snack, or from activity time to putting on coats to going outside—can result in chaos. We will discuss transitional techniques in more detail in Chapter 9.

Guidelines for Program Planning

These components of the early childhood day—activity time, large-group activities, small-group activities, outdoor activity, cleanup, meals, nap or rest, and transitions—can be combined in your program in a wide variety of ways. Let's examine some guidelines that will help in planning an effective program.

● Alternating Active and Quiet Times

Children need time both to expend energy and to rest. A useful rule in planning is to look at the total time in terms of cycles of activity and rest, boisterousness and quiet, energy and relaxation. Categorize the descriptions of time blocks listed in your daily schedule in terms of active (e.g., activity time, outdoor play, large-group activities that involve movement) and less active times (e.g., story, small-group activities, nap, snack).

In applying this guideline, think about providing the opportunity to be physically active after quiet times and to slow down after active involvement. Also consider the total consecutive time that children are expected to sit quietly. If you planned to have children sit at a large-group activity from 10:00 to 10:20, then move into a small-group activity from 10:20 to 10:35, and then have snack until 11:00, you would be courting chaos, if not disaster. Young children need periods of activity, and that plan has children shifting from one relatively inactive period to another for a full hour. Similarly, when children have been engaged in active exploration, a quieter time should follow. One caution: do not expect children to move immediately from very active involvement, such as outdoor play, to being very quiet, such as nap time. For such times, plan a more gentle transition that helps children settle down gradually. Usually, young children come to understand the parameters, limits, and basic rules quite quickly so they move from place to place as their interest changes or as they finish what they were doing.

● Balancing Child-Initiated and Teacher-Initiated Activities

In quality early childhood programs, most of the day consists of large time blocks in which children can make decisions about the activities in which they will participate and how they will carry them out. Most programs also include times when teacher-directed group activities are available. Most of the day's activities should, however, be child-selected and allow children to move from activity to activity at their own pace (Miller, 1984). Typically, activity time and outdoor time accommodate child initiation, whereas small- and large-group times involve teacher initiation. Some functional activities, such as snack, meals, and nap, also require some teacher direction, but meal and snack times also include opportunities for children to make choices.

Developmentally appropriate programs emphasize child-initiated, child-selected, and teacher-supported activities. When young children are allowed to decide how they will spend their time, they develop qualities such as autonomy, judgment, independent decision making, social give-and-take, initiative, exploration, and creativity. In addition, children develop a reasonable amount of compliance, they understand the rules of group behaviour, and they accept the authority and wisdom of their teachers in safety-related issues. Generally, if teachers convey respect for and trust in the ability of children to make appropriate decisions, children will reciprocate with enthusiastic participation in teacher-initiated, developmentally appropriate activities that engage their interest. Teachers who trust the children's abilities, of course, also allow children to leave group activities that do not interest them.

● Activity Level of the Children

By nature, young children are active and must have many opportunities for expending energy. Some children, however, are more active than others. And, on average, boys are more active than girls (Maccoby & Jacklin, 1974). Occasionally, you will find that you have a group in which a large portion of the children is particularly active. If this occurs, a schedule that has worked for you in the past may not serve as well because the needs of the children are different. In such a case, adjusting the schedule and the classroom arrangement and the types of activities planned will help the class run more smoothly. You might, for instance, carry out some activities, which are traditionally indoor ones, outside and plan either a longer or an added outdoor time block.

Developmental Level of the Children

As children get older, their attention span noticeably increases; thus, your daily schedule should reflect the group's ages and developmental levels (Miller, 1984). For older preschoolers, plan longer time blocks for small-group, large-group, and activity times. On the other hand, younger preschoolers require added time for meals and nap. With even younger children, you may also want to schedule regular times for toileting, for instance, before going outdoors and before nap. And with infants, you would want to check diapers and have bottles available before going outdoors.

The length of time you devote to large-group activities can be problematic. The time allocated to such activities will depend on the ages and attention spans of the children, but it also depends on the length of time they have been in the program and on their activity level. At the start of the year, 5 minutes may be long enough for young preschoolers, but they may want to participate in a large-group activity for 15 minutes later on. Children entering kindergarten, with previous experience in an early childhood program, may be interested in spending 20 minutes in a group, whereas children new to a group experience may lose interest after 5 minutes. Children of all ages can, of course, sit for a longer period of time if the activity captivates their interest; but, generally, a well-paced, shorter group time is more rewarding for all. As the program year progresses, reassess the length of group time and adjust it according to the children's interest.

No matter how long or short the attention spans are in your group, it is important to remember that young children need to be *actively involved in problem solving*. A group time that just entailed listening to the teacher would not be a source of learning for young children.

Group Size

Group size may also influence your planning. A general rule of thumb is to keep groups as small as you can. If you happen to be in a province or territory that does not have group-size regulations—or has less-than-ideal ones, try to arrange the program so that the children are in smaller groups as much as possible. For example, while one group is outdoors, another group is indoors. When some children are involved in self-selected activities, offer a music activity or read a story for those who are interested.

Family Groupings

Of course, if you are in a program that has family groupings, the mix of ages will influence the length of your group activities and your program planning. You will also need to provide either a wider range of activities or variants of the same activity so that there is a selection of developmentally appropriate materials.

Arrival of Children

How children arrive and leave the centre—whether over staggered periods of time or at about the same time—has to be taken into account in planning. In most full-day programs, the early morning period, until most or all of the children are at the centre, and the late afternoon period, when children start leaving for home, require some special considerations. The arrival or departure of children makes carrying out teacher-initiated activities difficult because the teacher and other children are interrupted frequently and because the arriving or departing children will not get the full benefit of the teacher-led activity. Thus, self-selected activities, in which children can control engagement and disengagement, should be available during such times.

Seasonal Considerations

In geographic locations where the weather varies considerably from season to season, you may want to adjust the schedule according to the time of year. For instance, during winter in northern Alberta and the Yukon, it would be difficult to keep to a schedule that contains three outdoor time blocks when each involves helping children get into their snowsuits, boots, mittens, and hats and then getting them out of such clothing at the end of the outdoor time. At the same time, a lengthy outdoor time is inappropriate when the temperature is well below freezing, when the wind chill is great, or, for that matter, when it reaches 34 degrees Celsius. Yet once spring arrives and the temperature is balmy, the schedule should allow for longer outdoor time. The weather can certainly affect your schedule, so a flexible approach and attitude are important when working with young children.

"Wasted Time"

Keep in mind that when children spend most of their waking hours in an early childhood program. It is, therefore, particularly important to assure that their daily experiences are meaningful. Davidson (1982) observed time use in child care centres and found that, when considered cumulatively, a considerable amount of time each day—often well over an hour—was wasted. She found wasted time particularly during routine activities such as lunch, nap, transitions, and special or unexpected occasions. Wasted time, Davidson suggests, can lower self-esteem, encourage children to behave inappropriately, and make it more difficult for them to learn to value and use time wisely. Davidson found that the causes for ill-used time included poor organization, inadequate equipment or space, not enough teachers for the number of children, lack of respect for the children, and inappropriate activities.

One clarification should be made. The wasted time described by Davidson revolves around times that force inactivity on children. Children, however, may *choose* times when they do not engage in activity, stand at the periphery to observe, or seem to be daydreaming. Such times represent a self-selected rest from activity, rather than imposed inactivity.

Some realities of early childhood programs (for instance, less than an ideal number of teachers, too large a group size, and/or inadequate space) are beyond the teacher's control. Nevertheless, teachers who are caring and concerned about the needs of the children and plan an age-appropriate program are on the right track. Additional attention and sensitivity to times in the schedule during which waiting and idle inactivity could occur will help improve the program. Moreover, how you handle these routines can make a major difference. For example, snowsuit time can be a time for conversation, singing, and developing self-help skills. Children who wake up early from a nap could look at a book with an adult, or by themselves, if they are old enough. Lunch time is often rich with opportunities for socialization and conversation, and learning about and enjoying foods.

Partnerships

DEVELOPMENTALLY APPROPRIATE PROGRAMS
IN TRANSITION

Although developmentally appropriate programming has been the accepted practice, Varga (1997) pointed out some consequences if we keep our view too narrow. She warned that we do not want to become so absorbed in the notion of childhood that we forget children have characteristics of people as well. Children disagree; they have opinions; they need space. So often we create conflicts and power struggles with children by imposing on them time limits and transitions that make no sense save because the schedule says this is what we do now. Developmentally appropriate programming strives to respect the nature of the child through a child-centred curriculum. However, programs border on overdirection and disempowerment by imposing schedules and routines on children's personal time—when they eat, sleep, and toilet.

Spatial arrangements are made by the caregivers, themes are imposed, materials are determined off limits on certain days; a limited range of developmentally appropriate materials—often unrelated to the real world—are offered or allowed, and there is confined space without freedom of movement within and between indoors and out. Child-centred play and decisions can be made only within the confines of a self-contained learning centre and a set time with no room for suggestions or projects to emerge—and all this under the constant vigilance of the teacher.

Remember what play was really like? Parents ensured a safe environment; and there were all kinds of stuff to explore, play with, and discover in the house, the basement, your room, and your backyard. You could come and go within those boundaries: read in your room, build a fort, play school, dance to music, or plant a garden. It felt like all the space belonged to you, and you felt free and safe to travel within it. You would dream up little projects every day, and parents were there to help you find where to look and to ask the right questions. They didn't interfere in your play or private time but worked for hours on projects you created together. You knew there were limits and consistency and a proper place for things, that you had to ask about certain things, and that there were problems to solve. You helped choose your own markers, had your own art kit, and decided when you were sleepy and hungry.

The programs of the new millennium will strike a balance between old concepts and the new. We are beginning to recognize the need to value children as competent individuals without pushing them too early to learn academically or leaving them completely abandoned. Recognizing learning as a relationship that develops from interactions will no doubt help.

Key Terms

activity time
behaviour setting
computer literacy
developmentally appropriate practices
eclectic approach
equipment
experience
exploration
games with rules
guidance
hierarchy of needs
increasing competence

large-group times
learning centres
observing
play
practice play
pretend play
problem solving
routines
small-group activity time
social skills
software
symbolic play

Key Points

1. A teacher is also a nurturer in each of the developmental domains—in any program, in any environment.

2. Healthy emotional development encompasses developing a sense of security, attachment, trust, independence, empathy, and self-control (Greenspan & Greenspan, 1986).

3. Children discover their world through play. Therefore, it is important to be familiar with research on play and its effectiveness (e.g., Freud—emotional; Piaget—cognitive; Vygotsky—social).

4. Our progressively structured system of school environments may gradually extinguish, or at least divert inward, children's natural tendency to be creative thinkers.

5. Pretend play, thematic fantasy play (superheroes), and cooperative games together act to produce a general concern for life, an emphasis on peace and harmony, and a decrease in social aggression by providing positive alternatives.

6. Developmentally appropriate programming suggests supporting children in their natural propensity for play and not just teaching them directly. This is a delicate balance.

7. The diversity of children in the program and their families is respected and reflected throughout the program, the day-to-day environment, the staffing, and all activities.

8. To encourage responsible behaviour from the group, help the children to make some of the rules, thereby creating ownership of their world.

9. A pleasant, safe, well-planned environment for both children and teachers will produce long-term positive effects on how children and teachers interact with one another.

10. Equipment selections should support the program's philosophy, be appropriately sized, safe, and easy to maintain, and respect the concept of diversity.

11. By including the children in the design and theme of learning centres, you enable children to make choices from a range of developmentally appropriate activities and materials.

12. A flexible daily schedule provides security and predictability but also allows for the unexpected.

13. The developmentally appropriate program includes diverse elements (i.e., indoor and outdoor time, small-group and large-group activities, routines that provide valuable learning experiences).

14. Program planning reflects the needs of all the children and includes different levels of activity that teach the children problem-solving techniques.

15. Routine activities create time for conversations, singing, and developing self-help skills when used creatively.

Key Questions

1. Visit an early childhood program and observe the children at play. Look for examples of the types of play we discussed in this chapter. Do you see a relationship between age and type of play?

2. Observe the dramatic-play area in an early childhood centre and record the types of play you see. Also watch to see if there is any teacher involvement in the play. Do you agree or disagree with what you saw? Relate your observations to Smilansky's concerns.

3. Visit an early childhood program and look at its program. What elements are included? Does the program seem developmentally appropriate by taking into account the needs of the children? Does it provide the kind of balance discussed in this chapter? Would you change anything in this program? Why or why not?

4. Using your knowledge of how children learn best, consider the issue of child-initiated versus teacher-initiated activity. Do you agree with the author that there should be ample time for children to make decisions and exercise independence, or do you think more teacher control is important? Note that not everyone agrees on this question. Discuss it with others in your class and consider both sides.

5. What are your memories of your earliest school experiences? What kinds of activities were involved? Can you glean from your recollections what type of curriculum your preschool or child care or kindergarten teacher might have been following?

Chapter 8

Guidance: Routines, Group Activities, and Behaviours

When we discuss guidance of children's behaviours, we are not just considering what we expect of them today, but also looking at the beginning of a lifelong process. Even though it is a cliché, today's children *are* tomorrow's adults. In that context, guiding the behaviour of young children takes on an important and delicate meaning. Every time you respond to an infant's cries, to a toddler's request for help, and to two toddlers' struggle over a toy, these children are learning about human responses. Every time you help a child to look at his or her behaviour and to evaluate its appropriateness, you are empowering the child, helping the child along the road to self-discipline and self-control. Every time you give older children direction, ask their help, help them prevent or solve a disagreement, or convey your expectations to them, you are affecting not just their immediate behaviour but also their future behaviour. You are, in essence, contributing another grain to the growing hill of such grains that is becoming the child's character.

In a well-managed classroom, children and teachers are involved, busy, happy, organized, and smoothly functioning, working within a flexible schedule and curriculum. Infants and toddlers will become familiar with the routines that are such an integral part of their curriculum. Older preschoolers will be learning what is expected and will come to behave according to those expectations. School-aged children who have had consistency in their lives will readily adapt to the group expectations, but children with less positive experiences may need extra time. The classroom atmosphere is one in which the children are continually learning to be responsible for their own and the group's behaviour. Such a classroom does not just happen, however. Teachers set the stage through their guidance techniques.

1. We will begin by discussing the differences between guidance and discipline, and then look at the kinds of behaviours we expect of children, and how to select a personal guidance approach.

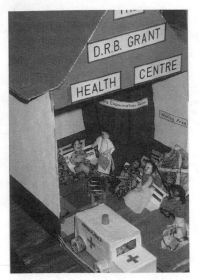

2. Then we will look at four routine times: arrival at school, meals, toileting, and sleep. All four have strong emotional significance for the child and need sensitive handling by the teachers.

3. We will examine how the developmental appropriateness of expectations and activities affects behaviour.

4. Transitions, those times when children move from one activity to the next, deserve special attention.

5. Then we will look at occasions when the out-of-the-ordinary happens, either planned—such as a field trip—or unplanned—for instance, an accident.

6. One of the biggest challenges you will face when beginning to teach is knowing where to draw the line between behaviours that fall within the normal range and behaviours for which professional help should be sought.

7. We will also talk about how other variables affect behaviour in both subtle and direct ways, and then consider a variety of guidance techniques and when these are used most effectively.

Guidance and Discipline

We will be using the word "guidance" throughout this chapter. Before continuing, let's briefly examine this word and differentiate it from some other, related ones. One definition of **guidance** in Webster's *Dictionary* is "the act of directing ... to a particular end." This implies, as we discussed earlier, that guidance is an ongoing process and that techniques must be congruent with the kind of people you want children to grow up to be. Guidance is also related to discipline, which, unfortunately, for too many adults, connotes a reaction to a misbehaviour by the child who did not follow the rules (Morrison, 1988). The word **discipline**, however, comes from the Latin word meaning learning or teaching, and, in early childhood education, we need to focus on this positive aspect of discipline. **Positive discipline**, or guidance, helps children achieve self-discipline (Gordon & Browne, 1993); it is an empowering force, not a negative one.

Undoubtedly, you will meet parents who equate **punishment** with discipline. But punishment has a whole series of difficulties associated with it. For example, it emphasizes what the child should not do, without giving any indication of what the desired behaviour is; it is a one-time rather than an ongoing occurrence; it focuses on obedience rather than on development of self-control; it undermines self-esteem; and it makes a decision for the child rather than allowing the child to think through a solution (Gartrell, 1998; Gordon & Browne, 1993; Marion, 1999; Miller, 2000; Reynolds, 2001). In addition, physical punishment may, in fact, increase undesirable behaviours such as aggression (Maccoby & Martin, 1983;

Marion, 1999; Patterson, 1982) because it models the very behaviour it is intended to discourage. Early childhood experts discourage punishment because of its *long-term ineffectiveness* in changing behaviour. Children will also learn to dislike and avoid those who punish them (Gartrell, 1998; Gordon & Browne, 1993; Marion, 1999; Miller, 2000; Reynolds, 2001; Sheppard, 1973). Positive discipline has none of these difficulties, and it preserves the child's self-esteem.

What Behaviours Do We Expect of Young Children?

Parents and early childhood educators in general hope to help develop children who are friendly, sociable, responsible, helpful, cooperative, and considerate, and who acquire a conscience (Gartrell, 1998; Moore, 1982; Reynolds, 2001). Such a range of behaviours, however, does not emerge without thoughtful and consistent guidance from parents and teachers (e.g., Gartrell, 1998; Gordon & Browne, 1993; Hildebrand & Hearron, 1999; Marion, 1999; Miller, 2000; Reynolds, 2001).

Among the qualities of children that parents and teachers often value is an ability to care about others, to share willingly, to be altruistic and empathetic, and to be understanding of the needs of others. Such prosocial behaviours are most likely to appear in children who live in a nurturing environment, where understanding and caring are modelled, where responsibility is expected, and where **inductive reasoning** is used (Mussen & Eisenberg-Berg, 1977). Induction involves an approach in which adults help children see the **consequences** of their behaviour on other people through logic and reasoning.

One correlate of prosocial qualities in children appears to be development of self-control. This, in turn, leads to self-regulation, in which the child's judgment about the situation dictates the response (Kopp, 1982). Internal rather than external control is critical, for it means that the child does what is right, not because she or he might be rewarded (or punished), but because she or he knows this action is the morally responsible thing to do. Development of inner control, a long process tied to the gradual evolution of ego strength and moral judgment, is fostered through many opportunities for the child to make decisions and to experience the consequences of those decisions (Kamii, 1984). And, of course, one would not expect to see any signs of inner control in the very young. Nevertheless, it is during those earliest years that the foundations for self-regulation are constructed (e.g., Gartrell, 1998; Gordon & Browne, 1993; Marion, 1999; Miller, 2000; Reynolds, 2001).

A climate in which such opportunities are offered is *child-centred and nurturing, respectful of the child's growing autonomy*. Adults in the child's world are careful to use inductive reasoning, focusing on explanations that stress the rights and feelings of others rather on punitive admonitions or restrictions (Honig, 1985a, 1985b; Maccoby & Martin, 1983). Thus, the child is told, "It really makes Ingrid feel unhappy and hurt when you tell her nobody likes her," rather than "Don't you say that, you selfish brat!"

In an article titled "Obedience is not enough," Constance Kamii (1984) differentiates between **morality of autonomy**—based on an inner sense of integrity—and **morality of obedience**—based on doing what one is told to do. To achieve morality of autonomy, children need, from an early age, many opportunities to develop a sense of personal values. The development of values comes from the opportunities to exchange viewpoints with others and opportunities to make decisions.

An interaction style between adult and child, in which *the child is given a reason for what the adult expects*, has also been shown to produce children who are socially competent; have positive interactions with peers; and are self-controlled, assertive, self-reliant, generally happy, and explorative (Baumrind, 1967; Marion, 1999). The adult engages in verbal give-and-take with the child, provides opportunities for decision making, and is consistent in setting and enforcing rules and expectations (Baumrind & Black, 1967).

Research supports the fact that the process of child rearing and child caregiving is tied to the characteristics that the child displays. A consistent, loving, firm, reasonable, inductive environment helps lead to children who are morally responsible, considerate of others, independent, and assertive. These findings give direction to early childhood settings, which are partners with parents in the process of child rearing.

Factors in Selecting Guidance Techniques

But where will you begin? What approach or approaches to guidance should you use? Some guidelines may help you select an approach to working with young children.

First, try to think through your own values and expectations as they relate to the care of infants and young children. Do this in the context in which you were reared, because your own background will affect your views. If you were raised in a family that used firmness and fairness, you will most likely bring your own experiences to the task of guiding young children. If your family was authoritarian—you were expected to follow rules because someone bigger than you said these were the rules—then you will need to examine whether you carry this attitude into your work.

Self-understanding is very important in working with young children; if you acknowledge your strengths and identify areas you might want to change, you will

Reflective Exercise 8-1

As a class, discuss how child rearing has changed since you were young. Weigh the pros and cons of these changes.

emerge with a more solid foundation. As you examine your own values, keep in mind your aim in working with the children whose parents have entrusted them into your care. Guidance is a long-term process, contributing to the evolution of children into adults. If the aim is to develop caring, competent, self-directed adults, this process begins early in life. What matters is that the guidance principles applied are congruent with the desired outcome.

Good early childhood educators generally follow an **eclectic** approach to guidance, and, in so doing, hope to empower the child with self-discipline and problem-solving skills. Developing a personal style of guidance takes time, and it may well change over the years of your professional involvement and development. What is important is that you be comfortable with the guidance approach you use because it is effective and supports children's development in a positive, nurturing manner.

Some examples of how to provide guidance at particular times of the day and for particular problems follow below. The following discussion, coupled with the experience you acquire in your field placements, should help you on the road to developing your own guidance strategies. And perhaps there is no better place to start than the beginning of the day in the early childhood program.

Partnerships

WORKING TOGETHER WITH PARENTS TO SOLVE BEHAVIOUR PROBLEMS

Parents often seek out teachers' advice or support when they deal with their children's misbehaviours. It is, however, important to keep in focus the concept of guidance as an ongoing, positive process and to convey this philosophy to parents. Let parents know that your approach to guiding children is primarily concerned with helping them develop inner control and self-direction rather than merely a matter of dealing with problems. Many adults think of working with children in terms of discipline; however, you can help parents see guidance more broadly by framing your philosophy in terms of laying a foundation for lifelong patterns of creative problem solving, positive interactions, and concern for the needs of others.

When parents approach you about a behaviour they find troubling—or you approach them—it is important that effective communication, based on mutual understanding, take place. It is critical to recognize that a child cannot be viewed in isolation, solely within the context of the hours spent at school. What happens during the other hours, the people with whom the child interacts, the quality of these interactions, and the overall quality of the lives of these other people all affect the child. Thus, to understand the child well, you must also get to know the other important people in the child's life; the most basic way to do this is through frequent, informal, positive contacts (Herrera & Wooden, 1988). Individual families have unique characteristics, including their way of guiding their children. Many factors, such as the way the parents themselves were raised, and their culture, will have an impact. Knowing the family and having a trusting relationship will be beneficial if a behaviour becomes a concern.

Morgan (1989) recommends that when parents bring up concerns about their child's behaviour it is helpful for you, as the teacher, to keep certain points in mind. For instance, never forget the depth of the emotional investment parents have in their children and acknowledge underlying feelings, such as anger, defensiveness, or frustration. One underlying message may be a parent's need for reassurance that he or she is a good parent; whenever appropriate, provide sincere feedback. Also recognize that parents may have different values and beliefs about appropriate guidance, for instance, in relation to spanking. Acknowledge the parent's view in a nonjudgmental manner, while stating your philosophy. If suitable, you may use such an opportunity to help the parent explore an alternative method of guidance. Finally, clarifying a parent's misconception about child development can be reassuring and can help parents see a child's behaviour in better perspective.

Arrival at School

The transition from home to school that typically occurs first thing in the morning has to be considered carefully. Leaving their parents for the day can be very difficult for children, although going to a place that the child enjoys can ease the arrival process. Nonetheless, the security of each child's **attachment** to the mother or significant will have an impact on the arrival/farewell process. Children who are most distressed at separation often show signs of anxious attachment as well (Fein & Schwartz, 1982). Feelings of **separation anxiety** are not uncommon in preschoolers, although they are more prevalent in younger children (Papalia, Olds, & Feldman, 1999; Hinde, 1983). Other factors, particularly what happened at home as a child was getting ready that morning, also have an impact.

It is worth thinking through the arrival procedure and individual children's reactions and needs. Especially in a child care setting in which many children will be spending a large portion of their waking hours and where they arrive at different times of the morning, it is best to provide a low-key opening for the day. A few quiet activities, some soft music, and *available teachers* to ease anxiety or welcome enthusiastic children can help the day get off to a good start (adequate teaching staff is critical for such an enthusiastic welcome). This allows Jesse to sit quietly in a teacher's lap with his thumb in his mouth until he feels fully awake;

lets Katrina take her father to check on the guinea pig babies she has been talking about since their birth last week; provides time for Thui's mother to spend a few minutes until Thui gets involved in an activity; or gives Larry's mother a chance to tell the teacher that her husband was in an auto accident the previous day and that Larry might be upset.

In any program, provision must be made for a teacher to welcome each child and parent individually. It is reassuring to a parent on parting from his or her child to know that someone is aware of and pleased about the child's presence at school. Similarly, children need to know that the teacher is glad to see them and is looking forward to mutual enjoyment during the day. This time also provides a chance for the parent to share pertinent information, which might affect the child's behaviour that day, with the teachers. Morning is not, however, a time for the teacher to bring up concerns with the parent.

● Morning Health Check

Many schools use this early morning greeting as an opportunity to give each child a health check, before the parent rushes off to work. This conveys their interest in the children's health and their concern that ill children not remain at school. A quick visual inspection of the child can tell you whether the child appears unusually listless, has dull or heavy eyes, is developing a rash, has a runny nose, or looks flushed. A hug or touch is an important part of a welcome for young children, in particular, and, at the same time, it lets you know if the child has unusually warm skin.

If you suspect that a child is ill, discuss this with the parent and help find an alternative child care arrangement, if necessary. Working parents often find it difficult to cope with ill children, but a child who is sick should not be allowed to remain at school, both for the well-being of the child and for the health of the other children. Some communities have sick-child care arrangements, of which parents should be apprised early in the school year. Your school might also have a list of people willing to come into the home of a family with a sick child.

● The New Child at School

A special example of arrival at school that often causes great anxiety for both children and parents is the initial entry into the program. This experience can be traumatic, fraught with the unknown. It is difficult for a child who thinks concretely to conjure up a mental image of what school is—without an image, the idea of school can be very frightening. Therefore, the child must have the chance to gradually become familiar with school, with the security of the parents nearby, rather than being thrust into a first day with no introduction or transition.

Ideally, a new child should visit the school with a parent before her or his first day. After this visit, the child can stay for a short period while the parent leaves briefly, which can help the child realize that she or he has not been abandoned. After that, the parent can be encouraged to stay a few minutes at the beginning of the first few days, as the child needs additional reassurance. If such an arrangement cannot be made because of parents' work schedules, urge the parents to allocate a little extra time at the beginning of those first few days.

One designated teacher should be available to welcome and spend some time with a new child. It is good for the child to have a reliable adult to turn to with questions or concerns, although this should not be allowed to turn into a clinging relationship. This teacher also should be prepared to deal with the child's fears, anger, or tears, if necessary.

Other children, those who are veterans of the program, often help ease the new child into the centre. You might facilitate this by introducing the newcomer to another child who can show that child the classroom. As children get older, peers become increasingly more important in supporting separation from mother (Gunnar, Senior, & Hartup, 1984; Papalia et al., 1999). For some children, a classroom pet can help ease the anxiety of the new school experience.

The first few days at school can be difficult for the new child, the parents, and the teachers. This experience can be even more disconcerting, however, when not just one new child but many or all of the children, starting a new school year, find themselves in unfamiliar surroundings. In such a case, it is best to encourage parents to stay with anxious children. Another approach is to plan a phased-in start to school, with only a few new children beginning at a time.

Meals and Eating Behaviour

Meals are an important element of the early childhood program because they fulfill not only a vital physiological need, but also social and emotional needs. Care and thought must be given to menu planning, whether children will be eating a single, daily snack in a preschool program or breakfast, lunch, and two snacks in a child care program. Young children take in relatively few calories, yet they need a wide range of **nutrients**; thus, foods that maximize nutritional value should be selected. Meeting children's nutritional needs is particularly important because many of today's parents do not do so as reliably as parents of past generations (Rothlein, 1989).

● Providing Nutritious Meals That Children Will Eat

Perhaps infants are the easiest children to feed! At least, before solid food is introduced, they do not have strong likes and dislikes. And they are easiest to feed if their nursing mother visits the program for feeding times, as many do when the centre is close to work. Finicky appetites arrive in most children with the introduction of solid food. It is especially challenging to meet toddlers' and preschoolers' nutritional needs, because these children are often extremely choosy eaters. School-

aged children tend to have developed a liking for more foods, so they are easier to please. Let's look at some guidelines that can be helpful in providing nutritious foods that children will eat.

- *Provide variety.* A month-long menu helps to ensure variety.

- *Take advantage of fresh seasonal fruits and vegetables.* Fruits and vegetables provide important nutrients, enjoyment, and opportunities for learning. Not all children have had the chance to see that peas do not grow in freezer packages or cans but come in pods!

- *Offer simple foods.* Most young children prefer unmixed, readily identifiable foods.

- *Introduce children to new foods carefully.* Children are leery about new foods. Introduce only one new food at a time, and serve it with familiar foods. Talk about the food's colour, texture, shape, and taste, but do not force tasting.

- *Give special names to dishes sometimes, which adds to the fun of eating* (Lambert-Lagace, 1983). "Ants-on-a-log," celery sticks with peanut butter and raisins, are a favourite at many schools.

- *Offer finger foods when possible.* Infants and toddlers love to play with their food and manage it themselves. Older children also enjoy finger foods, like pizza, hamburgers, and "ants-on-a-log."

- *Limit sugar in the foods you provide.* Sugar leads to dental caries and provides empty calories, quickly satiating children's small appetites. Avoid foods with added refined sugar, such as processed desserts, canned fruits, soft drinks, or punch.

- *Provide healthy snacks that contribute to the daily nutrient intake.* Cheese, whole-grain crackers or toast, fresh fruit and fruit juices, and yogurt popsicles are a few simple, yet nutritious snack ingredients that children enjoy. Consult *Canada's Food Guide* when planning snacks, and keep it posted in the centre's kitchen.

- *Time meals carefully.* Children's capacity is small, so relatively frequent meals with small servings are best (Alford & Bogle, 1982). Snacks should be served at least two hours before a meal (McWilliams, 1986).

- *Vary the location of meals now and then.* An occasional picnic (e.g., on blankets in the playground or at a park) can add to the enjoyment of eating. Even a picnic on a blanket in the classroom provides a change from routine, and a buffet- or cafeteria-style meal adds variety (Endres & Rockwell, 1980).

- *Be sensitive to children's cultural food preferences and religious restrictions as you plan meals.*

● Encouraging Healthy Eating Habits

In any given class, you will find children who are vigorous eaters, enjoying whatever is served, and others who are picky and selective. Even individual children will vary considerably in appetite from day to day or meal to meal (Alford & Bogle, 1982). Let's look at some suggestions for encouraging the formation of good eating habits and for dealing with some eating problems.

- A relaxed, comfortable atmosphere is important to good eating.
- Teachers should sit and eat with the children during all meals.
- Children should never be forced to eat a food, but they should be encouraged to taste all menu items.
- Food preferences and aversions are formed at an early age.
- Involve the children in mealtime.
- Children should be allowed to be as independent as possible at mealtimes.

Be aware of foods that are a choking risk. Problematic foods are hard, slippery, or of a size that can plug up the throat, such as raisins, carrots, or grapes (Pipes, 1989a).

● Problem Eating Behaviours

Some children are finicky eaters. Innate as well as learned preferences seem to play a role in developing food habits (Trahms, 1989). In some cases, children are picky eaters because they have learned that such behaviour gets them attention (Essa, 1995). By not focusing on children's eating behaviour in your conversations, you take away that attention while directing it to something more pleasant.

Overweight children pose a special concern because of long-range social and health problems associated with obesity. It

Courtesy of George Brown College.

is very likely that obese children will become obese adults, so early intervention is crucial (Pipes, 1989b). Overweight children need to both reduce their food intake and increase their activity level. All children will benefit from a healthy, low-sugar, low-salt menu.

Toileting

Toileting is important because it helps children become more independent and establishes habits of good hygiene. Toileting takes on particular significance in groups of toddlers and young preschoolers, who are in the process or have recently mastered bowel and bladder control. Even with older preschoolers, it is good to remind ourselves that these children were still in diapers just a couple of years ago!

Before toileting becomes a matter-of-fact routine of life, young children may go through a period when they are especially interested in the acts of urinating and defecating and everything that surrounds them. Young preschoolers may enjoy flushing the toilet repeatedly, watching others sit on the toilet, or talking about their accomplishments. It is best to react in a matter-of-fact way that acknowledges the child's interest but does not convey shame or self-consciousness about these natural bodily functions.

Some young preschoolers mastering bladder control need reminders to go to the bathroom. Watch for wiggling and holding behaviours which indicate a need to urinate. Some young children delay going to the bathroom for fear of losing their activity—tell children you will "hold" their place at the play dough table, for example, or protect their block structure until they return.

Many schools have a common bathroom for all children, not separating boys from girls. This provides a setting in which children can observe and note sex differences without any attending mystery or fuss.

● Toilet Accidents

With young children, toilet accidents are inevitable. Children who have just recently mastered bladder and bowel control may not yet have the timing worked out. Older preschoolers will also have periodic accidents that are *not* a cause for concern or shame. Teachers must handle toilet accidents gently and sensitively.

Children react differently to these accidents. For some, an accident is embarrassing and upsetting, whereas others will find it a minor irritant at most. *In neither instance should a child ever be lectured, shamed, or chastised for a mishap.* Accidents should be handled in a matter-of-fact manner that does not call attention to the child and conveys acceptance of the accident as "no big deal." Having a supply of extra underwear, pants, and socks available in case of accidents helps it not to be a big deal. Always ask parents to leave extra labelled clothing for accidents. When a child has an accident, give the child a change of clothes and provide privacy for changing to avoid embarrassment and/or ridicule. Keep a stock of plastic bags for storing soiled clothes.

Clothing may contribute to accidents—preschoolers have to be able to get their clothes off easily and quickly. Small buttons, overalls, belts, and back fasteners can frustrate a child trying to undress to use the toilet. Simple clothes with elastic waistbands are the easiest for children to handle. Sometimes children will suddenly have repeated accidents long after they have achieved toileting independence. Is there a reason for this behaviour? Could the child have a bladder infection? Is the child reverting to younger behaviour after the birth of a new sibling? Is the child using accidents to get attention? Each of these reasons will require a different approach. A Closer Look relates the case of a 4-year-old child whose sudden accidents baffled both her parents and her teachers.

A Closer Look

SHIRLEY'S "ACCIDENTS"

When Shirley was 4, her parents, Dan and Alene, decided to get divorced. For the first time in her life, Shirley's father did not live at home with her. About a month after Dan moved out, he was involved in an accident at work. Alene got a phone call early one Saturday morning that Dan was in the emergency room of the local hospital. She and Shirley went immediately to the hospital.

Since they had left home in a hurry, Shirley and Alene had not had breakfast. After 2 hours of waiting with Dan for x-ray results, Alene decided to find her way to the hospital cafeteria. The emergency room receptionist told them how to get there by going through the hospital building. On the way, they passed a number of rooms in which patients were visible. In one particular ward, one patient could be seen with one arm and one leg raised in traction. Shirley slowed her steps and stared. "Why is he like that?" she asked her mother. "I guess he was in an automobile accident," Alene replied. A couple of hours later, Shirley and Alene were able to take Dan, now with a cast on his broken arm, back to his apartment.

About a week later, Shirley had her first toileting accident at school. "I forgot to go potty," she told one of her teachers. The teacher took her to the bathroom, found some extra pants and underwear for her, and helped her change. Two days later, Shirley had another accident, and thereafter the rate increased so that within a week, she was having two to four accidents a day. The teachers talked with Alene, who indicated that Shirley was waking up wet at night and had begun to have bowel accidents as well. A parent-teacher conference was quickly scheduled to explore possible causes and solutions. At this meeting, Alene and the teachers agreed that Shirley was undoubtedly reacting to the stress of the divorce.

Their agreed-on strategy was to be matter-of-fact about the accidents while the teachers, Alene, and Dan would all try to be reassuring and understanding with Shirley. About a week later, the toileting accidents decreased and then disappeared.

Not long after, Shirley was gone from school for a week while she and her mother visited relatives. When they returned, Alene met with one of Shirley's teachers to relay some news. While they were out of town, Shirley had asked her mother one day, "Mommy, are you going to have an audiovisual accident, too?" Taken aback, Alene asked Shirley what she meant. The story, when it emerged, was that Shirley had been worried that her mother, who worked in the university's audiovisual department, would have an "audiovisual accident" like the man who was "tied up at the hospital" and then not be able to live at home. Daddy had an accident and now was not at home; the man at the hospital had an "audiovisual accident" and could not live at home because he had to be tied up; Mommy worked in audiovisual so she might have an accident too and have to stay at the hospital; then who would take care of Shirley?

"Is that what you've been worried about, Shirley?" asked Alene. Alene explained to Shirley what an "automobile accident" is and they talked about the fact that she would not leave Shirley.

As Alene told the teachers, "It sure is easy to jump to conclusions. We all decided that Shirley was upset about the divorce. Yet, in her complicated mind, she had put together a story that none of us could have guessed at!"

● Bathroom Facilities

It is best for children if toilets and sinks are child-sized and easy to reach. If you have adult facilities, sturdy, wide steps should be placed in front of toilets and sinks. Children should also be able to reach toilet paper, soap, and towels with ease. Having to overreach can cause accidents.

Ideally, bathrooms should be adjacent to the classroom and easy to supervise. Children are more likely to have an accident when they have to ask for permission to go to the bathroom than when they can go on their own when they need to. Some schools have one large bathroom for all—find an arrangement that promotes independence but lets you know where each child is at all times. Taking children to the bathroom in large groups may prolong waiting, and promote pushing, shoving, or even toilet accidents if a child just can't wait.

Some centres and most elementary schools have separate washrooms for girls and boys. However, open toileting has been a tradition in most early childhood programs, not just for convenience, but because it allows children to learn about anatomical and toileting differences in a matter-of-fact way. A parent cooperative preschool, located in an elementary school, used the girls' washroom—which was upstairs, while the preschool was downstairs—at a time prearranged with the school for two reasons: (1) it was more convenient for supervision and (2) the 2- and 3-year-olds did not receive mixed messages about their anatomy.

● Toothbrushing

Especially in child care centres, toothbrushing supplies are often located in the bathroom. Wet toothbrushes should not be stored in a closed cabinet, but in an out-of-the-way place where they can air out after each use. Each child should have an individual, clearly marked brush; disposable paper cups can be used for rinsing. Once they are around age 2, the children can dispense the toothpaste, preferably from a pump, with supervision. It is important to the establishment of good hygiene habits that children be allowed to brush their teeth after meals. As toothbrushing often occurs after toileting, it is important to ensure that the children are supervised to ensure handwashing before toothbrushing.

Sleep and Rest Times

Infants and young toddlers spend a considerable period of time napping. But older children need rest too. When children spend all day at a child care centre, a rest or nap time should be an integral part of the day. Not all children need a nap, especially as they get older, but for children who are on the go all day, a time to slow down is important. According to Dr. Richard Ferber (1985), director of the Centre for Pediatric Sleep Disorders in Boston, *most children—but not all—*sleep 11 to 12 hours at night by age 2, with a 1-to-2-hour nap after lunch. Most children continue to take naps until at least age 3, though some children still nap until they are 5 and others stop at age 2.

● Children Who Don't Need to Sleep

A variety of arrangements can be made for those children who do not take a nap in the middle of the day. In some programs, children are asked to lie on a cot quietly for a period of relaxation; if this is not handled punitively, children can enjoy a short period of rest and quiet. In other centres, children who do not sleep are allowed to engage in a quiet activity, such as book browsing, while they are on their cots. Nonsleepers are usually placed apart from those who are expected to fall asleep, so they are not disturbed. Some children, when they lie down in a relaxed atmosphere, will eventually fall asleep. Those who don't can get up after about a half-hour and move into an activity apart from the sleepers. Another alternative is to have a quiet time, where non-nappers, rather than lying down, participate in a period of individual, restful activity, for instance, book browsing, or playing quietly with manipulatives.

● Nap Guidelines

Sleep, which is a natural part of the body's daily rhythm, requires that the body and mind be relaxed and at ease. If children are anxious or wound up, they will have a difficult time falling asleep. Thus, the way you prepare for nap time and set up the environment will either facilitate or hinder sleep.

Children should not be expected to move directly from a high-energy activity, such as outdoor play, into nap; rather, a transition is needed to let children slow down gradually. A predictable pre-nap routine that is followed every day is as important as the nap itself (Ferber, 1985). One reviewer noted that she takes children for outside play after lunch, and then inside for a "wind-down activity" such as a story or relaxation exercises. She has found this routine really simplifies nap time. Others might suggest a leisurely ten-minute period is set aside for children to go to the bathroom, get a drink of water, take off shoes and tight clothing, get a favourite stuffed animal and blanket, and settle down on cots. The lights are dimmed, and drapes or shades are drawn. Cots are spaced far enough apart, and friends who enjoy talking are separated, to facilitate sleeping. Once all the children are settled down, a teacher may read a story or play a story record, sing softly, or lead the children in relaxation exercises. In fact, Bob Munsch, the renowned and much-loved Canadian children's author, got his start telling stories to the children in the sleep room at the University of Guelph's child care centre.

After these preliminaries, the teachers move from child to child, gently rubbing backs, whispering a soothing word, or stroking children's hair. Children who need a midday nap will fall asleep in a conducive atmosphere in which lighting is dim, the temperature is comfortable, the room is relatively quiet, and the teachers convey a gentle, soft mood.

Because sleeping children would need extra help to move out of the building in case of an emergency, it is especially important that teachers be aware of exits and alternative escape routes.

Children should not sleep for too long; an average of an hour to two suffices for most preschool children, although younger children and infants of course need more. Some children need time to wake up gradually, so an unstructured transition in which children can join the class at their own pace is helpful. An afternoon snack, to which children can move as they are ready, often helps provide that transition.

● Problem Sleepers

Occasionally you will encounter children who consistently resist sleep, even though they need the rest. A few children have genuine sleep problems, stemming from such conditions as chronic middle-ear infection, the use of certain medications, and some cases of brain damage. For other children, falling asleep represents a letting go, where anxieties and fears can surface, and their sleep reluctance comes from a need to avoid such scary thoughts. Most children's difficulty in falling asleep, however, results from poorly established sleep habits and routines (Ferber, 1985).

Three-year-old Becky had a very hard time going to sleep, both at home and at school, and engaged in a variety of disruptive stalling techniques to avoid nap time. Often, by late afternoon she was grumpy and tired, and she invariably fell asleep in the car on the way home or "crashed" in the classroom around 4:00 p.m. Her teachers eventually decided that it was not worth trying to put Becky down for nap with the other children because she prevented everyone from sleeping when she was in the nap room. Instead, once the other children had fallen asleep, one teacher would sit with Becky in the rocking chair and read a quiet story to her. This seemed to work about three days out of the week, when Becky would fall asleep on the teacher's lap and then be put down on her cot.

Factors That Affect Group Behaviour

Each of the previously discussed routine elements of the child's day is important and needs careful consideration as you decide how best to guide the group of children in your care. We will now turn to another aspect of guidance, those times of the day when all the children participate together in a common activity. Although it is important to consider each child as an individual within that group, some factors can facilitate group guidance.

● The Physical Environment

For one thing, it is important to examine the physical environment in relation to group behaviour. Are several children running in the classroom, for instance, although the rule is "Walk inside, run outside"? Perhaps too much open space invites children to run. Critically examine room arrangement in relation to group behaviours. (See Chapter 7 for more detail on this topic.)

● Developmentally Appropriate Expectations

Another important factor in setting expectations for the group is the developmental level of the children. Carefully examine activities, the daily schedule, and materials to be sure they are appropriate to the ages of the children. Keep in mind the attention span, social ability, activity level, muscle control, and cognitive skills of your group and plan accordingly (look back at Chapter 5). Realistic expectations are essential to good group guidance and have to be aligned with the children's developmental level so you do not have either under- or over-expectations. Frequently refer to the literature on developmentally appropriate practice in early childhood programs (e.g., Bredekamp, 1987; Bredekamp & Rosegrant, 1992; Bredekamp & Copple, 1997; Gestwicki, 1999). Children who are expected to behave beyond their capability will become frustrated, and frustration results in misbehaviour. Similarly, if the expectations are too simple for the children's abilities, the children will easily get bored; this can also lead to misbehaviour.

A relevant incident occurred recently in one child care centre's 2-year-old class during large group time. About seven children were grouped on the floor in front of a standing adult, who flashed alphabet cards while reciting the letters "A, B, C ... ," and obviously was not using developmentally appropriate methods.

During this activity, one child was crying, another poked her neighbour, several stared vacantly into space, one untied his shoelaces with the help of a friend, and two were about to get up to look for an alternative activity. There was also a distinctive smell that indicated that at least one child in the group had a physical need more immediate than hearing the alphabet recitation. The well-intentioned teacher was pleased that she was furthering the academic development of the children in her class. A better grasp of child development would have helped her recognize the inappropriateness of the activity and the normalcy of the inattentive children's reactions. Activities have to be age-appropriate, and this is an important responsibility of the teacher.

Another example in which the need for understanding of child development provides the teacher with guidance is in the pacing of activities. Avoid occasions in which a group of children must wait for more than a minute or two. For instance, it is generally unrealistic to make children wait until everyone is seated to start, or until everyone is finished to move on to the next activity. Also, standing in line to wait for a turn to get a drink, go outside, go to the bathroom, go to lunch, or wash hands is difficult for active preschoolers. There are other methods of moving children from one place to another without chaos, which we will discuss later in this chapter.

Also keep in mind that although developmental guidelines help you identify appropriate expectations for the age of the children, each child is an individual and will conform to some but not to other developmental milestones. You may also have children in your class who have special needs and in some ways do not fit the profile for their age group. Be sensitive to their unique needs and characteristics, make alternative arrangements if they cannot be expected to participate in the same way as the other children in some activities, but help them fit into the group as smoothly as possible.

● Conveying Expectations

Young children are exuberant and active, so you may find times when their voices or activity levels get too high. Shouting "Quiet down!" or "Settle down!" will only add to the confusion. A more effective way of controlling children's voice levels is to whisper softly. Move from small group to small group and speak in a soft, slow voice. Children will quiet their pitch so they can hear you. You will find the noise level quickly reduced by your modelling.

You might want to let the children know that it will be "shout time when we go outside." Similarly, an elevated activity level, if it seems unproductive, also can be reduced by a quiet voice, dimmed lights, or soft music that induces relaxation rather than agitation.

As individual children quiet or settle down, let them know with a smile or nod that you appreciate how they are speaking or behaving, rather than calling attention to inappropriate behaviour; appropriate behaviour can be contagious. Teachers will frequently praise the behaviour of one compliant child publicly in the hopes that others will behave similarly because they also want to be acknowledged.

According to Hitz and Driscoll (1988), however, research shows that praise given in this manner can lead to resentment and anger because it is manipulative rather than sincere. "Teachers of preschool-age children … may get away with blatant manipulation and fool themselves into thinking that it works. But eventually most children come to resent this type of control" (p. 10).

● Rules

Another way of encouraging good behaviour from the group is by letting the children know just what is expected. You probably only need one rule: *You may not hurt yourself, others, or the things around you.* Children should know what the limits are and why they are set. Like adults, children are much more likely to follow rules if they understand the reasons behind them. Rules should be discussed with children to emphasize and explain them. Another way of reinforcing rules is by posting them so that children can easily "read" them. One example is a picture poster of dos (smiling face) and don'ts (frowning face) with contrasting photographs or sketches for the two categories (for instance, pounding clay versus hitting another child). Such a poster makes it easy to call children's attention to the rule if there is an infraction and to encourage them to verbalize the expected behaviour.

Group behaviour, as indicated in the previous discussion, can be affected by such factors as room arrangement, developmental level of the children, and clearly-spelled-out expectations. These factors are, in a sense, constants that do not change from day to day, although they do change over longer periods of time as the children change. They provide a framework for the group guidance techniques that relate to specific parts of the daily schedule and that a teacher uses in the minute-by-minute functioning of the class.

Group Guidance and the Program

In Chapter 7, we discussed some guidelines for program planning. Many have a direct effect on group guidance because the schedule is a very important element in successful control of group behaviour and needs to be thought through carefully (Essa & Rogers, 1992). The actual sequence and timing of the daily schedule, and the length of activities, will have a bearing on group guidance.

There must be a logical rhythm and flow to the sequence of daily activities that relates to the developmental level of the children. If children are expected to sit quietly for several activities in a row, they will tend to find unacceptable ways to release some of the energy that is pent up during this overly long period; if too many boisterous activities are scheduled one after another, the children may tire or get too keyed up. All elements of the schedule should be carefully timed to avoid boredom because activities last too long or frustration when activities are not long enough.

Let's look at some specific aspects of the daily routine in relation to group guidance techniques. At certain times in the schedule, careful forethought, and planning can make the difference between a chaotic and a well-ordered classroom.

● Activity Time

A good part of the day will be scheduled for activities that children select from several planned by the teachers or from the classroom learning centres. Children have the opportunity to engage in a decision-making process at these times (e.g., Gestwicki, 1999; Hohmann, Banet, & Weikart, 1979). Some group guidance principles can help keep activity time blocks running smoothly.

One of the main guidance problems during activity time can arise from the grouping and distribution of children among activities. What if ten children want to participate in the water play activity, eight more are in the housekeeping area, and only one chooses to do the art project you planned so carefully? Chances are problems will develop at the water table and in dramatic play. How can you avoid such a situation?

Several methods can help you control the number of children who go to a given classroom area. Some methods strictly control the number of children, while others involve decision making. The former methods are more appropriate for younger preschoolers, whereas the others should be used with children over the age of 3.

One way to establish limits is to post happy faces in a conspicuous place at the entrance to each learning centre. The number of happy faces corresponds with the number of children who can be in a given area at one time. Thus, four happy faces above the water table means that only four children at one time may be in that area. The teacher can help the child count the number of happy faces and match it to the number of children in the area. In this concrete way, a child can be helped to understand why there is no more room. The child can then be redirected to another area with an assurance that she or he will be informed if a child leaves the desired area and there is room for one more.

The number of children can also be limited by the availability of materials and equipment in an area. Thus, five chairs around the art table indicates how many artists can work at one time; six play dough boards tells how many youngsters can engage in that activity; four hard hats set the limits in the block area, and so forth.

With older children, you may want to involve them consciously in decision making through some type of planning board (Baker, 1982). You might adopt medallions or individual symbols. Medallions are simple necklaces (for instance, a string with a symbol) that children put on if they want to play in a given area. The symbol can be colour-coded (for instance, green for the block area, red for science) or have a pictorial representation of that area on it (for instance, a book for the library, a record player for the music area). The number of medallions available limits the number of children in each area. Medallions are kept on a board by each area, and children put one around their necks when they enter that area and take it off again when they leave.

Individual symbols are similar in function, but rather than being coded for an activity, they are coded individually for each child. Laminated poster-board symbols with a different picture for each child, a photograph of the child, the child's name, or any combination of these can be used. Each activity area has a specified number of hooks on which symbols can be hung, and the number of hooks limits the number of children allowed in an area at one time. Hooks can be placed in each area on a board, a nearby wall, or, as in one school, on thick dowels set in large coffee cans filled with plaster of paris.

If you try using medallions or individual symbols, and you find yourself always reminding children how the system works, it is time to reevaluate. Perhaps the children are not ready for such a system. You may want to try it later, or you might want to use the system for only a small part of each day until the children catch on.

● Meals

Breakfast, lunch, dinner, or snack can pose group guidance problems if these times are not carefully planned. What happens before, during, and after a meal will directly affect group control, not to mention digestion.

Before the children sit down to eat, tables should be set and the food ready. Children should be involved in this process. It provides an excellent opportunity for young children to be engaged in a practical activity that builds self-concept, self-confidence, social competence, eye-hand coordination, and cognitive skills. Special helpers can assist in setting the table; putting out a plate, napkin, and silverware for each child; pouring juice or milk; and passing food.

Once the children have washed their hands and are ready to sit down, waiting should be kept to a minimum. Children, especially toddlers and young preschoolers, should not have to wait for everyone to be seated. And infants should never wait. With older preschoolers, in whom patience is beginning to develop, it is possible for them to wait one or two minutes until all the children at their table are seated. If, for some reason, the children are at the table and have to wait for more than a minute, initiate a song or finger play to keep the youngsters occupied until they can eat. Waiting for any prolonged period, especially quietly with hands folded in their laps, only frustrates children and is an invitation to guidance problems.

During the meal, establishing a few simple rules about eating (as discussed earlier in this chapter) and a pleasant, relaxed atmosphere are important. Conversation with peers and adults should be encouraged; silence is not an asset to a pleasant mealtime. The focus should be on appropriate eating and social behaviours. Children will seek your attention by doing what is expected if you praise and attend to those behaviours.

After the meal, children should again follow a few simple rules about clearing their dishes and cleaning their area at the table. Children should not have to wait until everyone is finished eating. They should be able to engage in a self-directed, quiet activity such as book browsing or move individually to the next activity. The staff should be distributed according to where the children are. As more children finish eating and move to another area, so should more of the staff move. One staff member should stay with the eaters until all are finished and then clear away all food and utensils (unless there is a separate kitchen staff that does this).

● Group Times

One of the most rewarding as well as most difficult parts of the preschool day occurs when children participate in teacher-initiated group activities. Good guidance is particularly important at group times because the success of such activities may well depend on your ability to keep the group attentive. This is no simple task, because you are trying to move children gradually from their egocentric focus toward some specific social behaviours, ones that will be particularly important when they start elementary school. The control you maintain over the group will, to a great extent, be a function of the environment and activities you provide for group times.

The physical environment within which group activities are conducted has to be carefully thought out. It should be relatively free from distractions so the children focus on the activity. If, for instance, a shelf of attractive materials competes for the children's attention, a simple covering of butcher paper or fabric can be used during group activities. Also, if children cannot see you or are crowded, they will respond with frustration or lose interest in the activity.

Therefore, arrange the group seating with thought. A carpeted area works best; children should be physically comfortable. Depending on the activity, a circle or semicircle around which children sit works well. If the activity is basically verbal with no visual props, such as group discussion, use a circle. If there is something to look at such as a book or flannel board, a semicircle works better, because in a circle the children next to the teacher will not be able to see the visuals very well. The visual prop should be held at or slightly above the children's eye level; if it is too high, the children will have to tilt their heads back at an uncomfortable angle. Get down on the floor with the children to see what they see or how they see it.

Sometimes, however, as much as you try to delineate an outer edge for the group, the children gradually creep closer and closer until you have a knot of little people sitting in no designated order. This may particularly happen with a group of younger preschoolers. Some things can be done to help children stay on the periphery of the group area. You might simply outline the area with masking tape and mark X's or dots at intervals where children are to sit. Or you may use carpet samples from a local carpet or interior design business; carpet squares can provide a colourful and appealing outline for your group area. You can set out the squares yourself, or you can have the children select a colour and place the square in the circle to sit on.

Another way of keeping the shape of the circle is to set out cues on the floor that the children must then match. You might, for instance, use the youngsters' name tags (whether these are just printed names, photographs, individual symbols, or a combination). You could use some other cue with which the children are not familiar. In this way you can achieve three things: (a) you delineate the outline of the group area, (b) you incorporate an active cognitive task with your group activity, and (c) you can arrange seating and thus control potential problems by separating children who tend to distract each other.

The timing of group activities is also important. Remember the discussion in Chapter 7 about the length of group times. Be aware of the developmental abilities of your group to sit quietly and pay attention. Begin the year with relatively short group times and lengthen these as the children are able to sit for increasingly longer times. You may plan several short group times at the beginning of the year and fewer longer ones later in the year.

A stimulating, longer group activity is sometimes fine, but as a rule don't expect children to sit quietly and attend for extended periods. It may also happen that although the group as a whole can pay attention for a certain period of time, one child lacks the maturity of the rest. In such a case, provide that child with a quiet alternative away from the group, rather than punishment as the child is not developmentally ready.

What happens during group times is very important to group guidance. Your activities must be age-appropriate to hold the children's interest. A wide variety of appropriate activities can be included during group time. Most popular among early childhood teachers are books, stories, and music activities (McAfee, 1985), but there are many other possibilities, as we discussed in Chapter 7.

You should plan a clear beginning—a calm one, a middle part that presents your activity or is action-oriented, and a gradual ending for the circle, but children should be free to leave when they are ready. This means you may not have the entire group with you for some circles. Remember to have visual aids or real objects to keep the children's interest.

It is also important to be prepared for whatever you plan to cover during group time; you should have read the stories, have all props prepared and at hand, and know songs and finger plays by heart. If you try to wing it, you may well lose the all-important sense of pacing. Several group guidance techniques help keep the children's attention while you are reading or telling a story.

If you see a child's attention wavering, you might try saying, "And do you know what happened next, Amy?" to gently bring Amy back to the group. To involve children in the story process, plan enough time to stop every so often to ask the children questions or to have them find something in a picture. Another way to heighten interest in a story is to periodically substitute the names of some of the children in the group for those of the characters in the story.

When you are using finger plays and songs during group activity, keep in mind that some of these excite and others quiet children. Have a repertoire of songs and finger plays on hand to use as a stimulant or a relaxant, as needed. Children should learn an increasingly larger number of songs and finger plays as the year goes on. Remember, young children enjoy and need repetition, so when you introduce a new song, give the children enough time to learn it thoroughly, then continue to use it periodically thereafter.

Songs and finger plays serve an excellent group guidance function at the beginning and end of group time. At the beginning, they provide a good transition from the previous activity; start a familiar song as soon as a couple of children are seated in the group area, or even before children arrive as a signal that the group is starting.

Don't wait for everyone to be seated before you start. You can also end your group with a familiar song or finger play, particularly if you need a good transitional device to move children to the next activity. (This will be discussed in more detail in the discussion on transitions, which follows.)

One more group activity, a favourite of many teachers, is Show and Tell, or "sharing time," which is often used to allow children to share something special and personal with their classmates. Such an activity can be tiresome and difficult, or it can provide a rich learning experience for all of the children (Oken-Wright, 1988).

Show and Tell gives children a chance to be in the limelight and to practice talking before a group. But it has to be planned and carried out carefully. As with other preschool activities, you should keep in mind the attention span of the group. It is not necessary for all of the children to participate on the same day. The ages of the children will determine how many youngsters should share on one day. Show and Tell has to be handled skillfully by the teacher so that children who do not have many possessions are as valued as those that do.

One alternative to Show and Tell, especially for young preschoolers and children from disadvantaged homes, is to select a "special child" for each day. Part of what the special child can do on his or her day is to share something from home. One thing to consider is storage for the children's personal treasures. It is not a good idea to allow the entire group to play with a special item, in case it gets broken or lost. Instead, arrange a place to store these items, whether in the children's own cubbies or in a specially designated place. When a child shares a treasured item, be sure you are very interested in what the child shows and tells about. A half-hearted comment from you could be crushing.

Transitions

A very important, though often unplanned-for or neglected part of the day's schedule, is not the daily activities but what happens in the gaps or transitions between them (Alger, 1984). Transitions really have to be thought of as part of the routine, a part that provides many opportunities for children to learn. Learning certainly takes place as children have to cooperate and be considerate of each other during toileting before lunch. They also learn to classify, seriate, match, and organize during cleanup. When outdoors, they need to bend, lift, stretch, and pull when they put outdoor toys away.

A beautifully planned day can fall apart if no thought is given to transitions between activities. Carefully think through what has to happen at the beginning of an activity, at the end of an activity, and between activities. In fact, to help you plan transitions, role-play with the rest of the staff what occurs during transition times. Fix in your mind the sequence and steps of various transitions so your guidance and expectations of the children are appropriate.

Children should always be aware of upcoming transitions, and you can do this in a variety of ways. For instance, you might use a cue or signal to let children know a change is coming. A song, chant, record, bell, flick of the lights, or specific clapped or drummed beat can be used regularly as transitional signals. For instance, such cues can announce cleanup time, group time, or outside time.

Even before you announce the end of an activity, however, and the transition to the next, give children a warning. Do this to help children finish activities they may still be involved in. For older preschoolers who are more product-oriented with projects or who are concerned with completing a game, a longer warning will be needed. As a rough guide, allow one minute of warning for each year of age (two minutes for 2-year-olds, three minutes for 3's). "In a few minutes, it will be time to put your blocks away so we can get ready for snack." This is the first warning, to be followed within a few minutes by the cue that signals a transition time.

Try to involve children in cleanup; they are *usually* willing helpers. "Jimmy, you get to put the shoes on the shelf and the purses and hats on the hat rack; Lesley, please stack the dishes in the cupboard on the top shelf; Tom, you can put all the long blocks on top of the red rectangle on the block shelf."

Cleanup will, of course, be facilitated by an orderly, well-thought-out environment (also see Chapter 9), where every item has a logical place. Sometimes you may have to devise games to encourage assistance with cleanup, especially for reluctant helpers, until they accept it as part of the routine. Suggestions to "drive your truck into the garage" or "swim like a fish to the sink and get the sponge to wash this table" can help encourage cleanup participation.

Sometimes a transition needs to be used to limit the flow of children to the next activity. For instance, you may have snack following group activity, with handwashing between the two. Sending 20 children at one time to a bathroom with two sinks is asking for problems. Think through ahead of time how many children can be in the bathroom comfortably at one time, and plan accordingly. A familiar song or finger play is a good device for such controlled flow. For instance, sing "Five Little Monkeys" using five children as participants at one time, and send each "monkey" to the bathroom as it "falls off the bed."

The position of teachers, as in the previous example of moving children from group to bathroom to snack, is an important factor in smooth transitions. The teachers should be positioned in key places (in the bathroom, in the group area, at the snack table). As the bulk of the group moves to the next area, so should the adults.

It is important to consider and plan for transitions as part of the program, because children spend a considerable part of their day involved in transitions. In an analysis of time spent in various activity categories in five different early childhood settings, Berk (1976) found that children spent from 20 to 35 percent of their total time in transitions. Because the teachers involved in this study ranked transitions low in relation to other activities, Beck suggests that teachers need to consider transitions a legitimate part of the curriculum.

The Unusual Situation

A regular program and routine are essential to help young children work comfortably in their environment; they need the security and regularity. But sometimes the unusual or unexpected comes along. It is important that children be able to handle deviations from the usual since life is full of the unexpected.

Some guidance techniques will help you give the children in your group the coping skills to deal with unusual situations if and when they come up. It should be noted, by the way, that if children are allowed to make choices frequently, they won't panic when the unexpected happens. Unusual situations can be grouped into two categories—the planned and the unplanned.

● Planned Unusual Situations

These include such changes from the regular routine as special events, special circumstances that you know about ahead of time, and field trips. Children can be prepared for expected changes, although it is advisable not to prepare them too far in advance to avoid undue anxiety or disappointment if they become ill. Also keep in mind that children's time sense is not the same as adults'; a week can seem like an eternity! When you prepare children, tell them exactly what will happen during the special event. If the Santa Claus is coming tomorrow, tell the children that they will sing some songs for Santa and then they will each have a chance to sit on Santa's lap if they would like. A calendar that refers to the special coming event can help older preschoolers "see" the time span in a concrete way.

If you can anticipate a special circumstance that will involve a change—for instance, if you will be away from school for a few days next week and a substitute teacher will be taking your place—prepare the children. Discuss your upcoming absence and reassure the group that you will still be their teacher, even if you are gone for a few days. If possible, have the substitute teacher visit your class so the children have a concrete idea of who Mrs. Carlton is.

Field Trips.   This is probably the most common example of a planned unusual event, and some of the principles we just discussed also apply here. Children should be well prepared ahead of time so they know what to expect. Permission slips should be obtained and typically, informing the parents about the trip encourages discussion at home. Review the schedule for the field trip with the children, any "rules," the return time ("We'll get back just before lunch"), the transportation arrangements, and the transportation rules. It is particularly important to review safety rules with the children. If necessary, role-play or present a flannel board story to cover key points that the children need to know before leaving. Before leaving, also put a name tag on each child's outer garment with the child's name and the school's name and phone number.

If you are going by car, assign children and adults to a specific car in which they must go and return. This avoids a child being left behind accidentally because everyone assumes she is in the other car. In the car, be strict about safety rules and expectations. If the children do not comply with the rules (and in the excitement of the trip this could well happen), pull the car to the nearest curb and tell the children that the trip will continue when everyone obeys the safety rules again. Be familiar with the child safety restraint laws of your province and follow these carefully on car trips. Before and frequently during the trip, count noses. It is also advisable to get extra adult supervision for field trips (parents are often willing to go along and help) because any environment outside the school will be less familiar and less controlled, and therefore less safe. Also be certain that all staff—and all volunteers—are familiar with the policies you follow on trips.

Walks.   Similar to field trips but with some different guidelines are walks. When you take the group on a walk, you again need to inform the children of expectations and safety rules. A buddy system works well. Children are paired off, and each partner is responsible for the other by holding hands. It's a good idea to establish an engine and a caboose if the children have to walk in a line (such as along a sidewalk). An adult at the beginning and end of the line are essential on a walk. Any additional adults can walk in between or act as rovers.

An alternative arrangement is to have each adult in charge of a small group of children, but enough adults must be available for this to work. Especially with a group of young preschoolers, there may be some strayers in the group. If you know who they are, be sure an adult is holding their hands. If there are too many strayers in the group, it is probably better not to leave the building at all. One thing that works with some children who tend to run off is a rope. Take a sturdy, smooth, long rope and have the children hold onto it at intervals; knots tied in the rope can indicate handholds. Often a strayer will hang onto a piece of rope and not a hand. A rope is more important with toddlers, and, if they are quite young, a rope with individual harnesses is necessary.

● Unplanned Unusual Events

There are times when the really unexpected occurs. A fire drill or a real fire, a serious accident to a child, or any other emergency can throw the class into an agitated state or even panic. Although you cannot foretell unplanned unusual events, you can prepare the children for these situations with some discussion and practice. As with planned unusual happenings, you can role-play, present a flannel-board story, use puppets, or otherwise pose hypothetical problem situations so children know what may happen and what they are to do.

Emergency procedures should be thought through so that both teachers and children know what to do. A written policy for handling emergencies should be visibly posted. Such a policy statement can be written in another language if some of the parents or staff are not native English speakers. One example of a carefully planned emergency procedure is fire drills. These should be part of any preschool program. It can also be helpful to have an "emergency pack" available by the exit, which might include a class list, phone numbers, a flashlight, and a couple of favourite children's books in case there is a wait.

Another type of emergency situation that is helped by forethought occurs if a child is seriously injured. One teacher should stay with the child while another moves the rest of the group away. It should be agreed on ahead of time who is responsible for which tasks; a teacher who has had first-aid training should, of course, stay with the hurt child. If necessary, a responsible child can be sent to get additional help—the director, secretary, cook, janitor—so arrangements for needed medical care can be made. Once the emergency is settled, review with the children what happened so they can express their concerns and feelings and be reassured.

It is a good idea to devise a cue for emergencies that tells children that this is a "red flag" situation. A combined visual and auditory signal can let children know that the teacher's attention needs to be focused on one child. This cue tells the children what they are to do—for instance, move to a self-directed, independent activity. This can be especially useful if one teacher is in charge of a group.

The unexpected does not always have to be a dire emergency. Less serious occurrences such as broken glass, spilled paint, or a minor injury can still be disconcerting to children. If children realize that the teacher's attention must be focused temporarily on the calamity, they can take responsibility for being self-directed if they have been prepared to do so.

The teacher should set the stage by verbalizing what is happening: "Usually we get ready for snack at this time. But because this window was broken, we will have to take care of the broken glass first. So instead of snack right now, we get to do something else. Jenny, get the 'Goldilocks' flannel-board pieces and all of you help Jenny tell the story. Bobby, please get the broom and dustpan from the bathroom. Anita and Todd, go to the office and tell Mrs. Arnold we have a broken window." When adults are organized—even in unexpected situations—know what to do, and do not panic, children will respond in a similarly calm manner, particularly if they have been prepared for unexpected events.

● What Is the Difference Between Normal and Problem Behaviour?

If you view guidance as an ongoing process that contributes to the socialization of the child, it is easier to consider a solution to a problem behaviour as a change that has a far-reaching impact, rather than as a stopgap measure to make your class run more smoothly. Although many children go through temporary periods in their early years that can be difficult for the adults around them, children pass through these without too many residual effects. The negative stage of many toddlers, for instance, often dissolves within a few months into a period of cooperation. But some behaviours persist and may become more problematic as children get older.

Problem behaviours are one of the greatest challenges facing teachers of young children. Remember that all children misbehave at some time; it is normal for them to test the limits. Some children, although they misbehave, can easily be rerouted by the adults around them. Other children have diagnosed deficits, and knowing the diagnosis gives you some direction about handling the problem behaviours. For instance, a child with diagnosed *hyperactivity*, known as **attention deficit disorder with hyperactivity (ADHD)**, has particular needs that can be readily identified—but not so readily met, as Don Shattuck notes in A Canadian Professional Speaks Out. And then some children totally frustrate all their teachers' attempts to deal with them. Teachers can go through a series of up-and-down feelings about their own competence as they try to cope with such children in the classroom.

But which behaviours are normal, and which should send up a red flag? Some guidelines follow that can help you make that distinction.

- Know the developmental stages of the children! Many children go through phases that usually pass. For example, the propensity of 4-year-olds to blur the line between truth and fantasy does not predict a life of dishonesty and pathological lying.

- Have realistic expectations for the age group, tempered by a recognition of individual variations among children. If a child appears extremely different from his or her age-peers, be concerned. For example, a 4-year-old who acts more like a 2-to-3-year-old in social behaviour, might or might not be developmentally delayed; if other areas of development also are delayed, there is more reason for concern.

- Look for signs of possible medical causes for problem behaviours. Chronic infections, allergies, nutritional deficiencies, and sensory deficits, for example, can profoundly affect behaviour.

- When the behaviour of a child in your class is out of hand so frequently that you feel there is a preponderance of negative experiences between you and the child, *it is time to bring in professional assistance to help you deal with the situation.* Consulting an outside professional is particularly appropriate if other teachers, who are generally very effective in dealing with children, share your experience and feel as baffled and frustrated by this child as you do. If a child is so frequently disruptive and not able to get along in the early childhood program without continuous help, do not blame yourself: that child needs professional, one-on-one help that cannot be given in a group school setting.

- Teachers generally notice acting-out children because they draw attention because of their behaviour. But also be alert to the extremely withdrawn child who stays away from social interactions, is reluctant to participate in activities, avoids eye contact, or refuses to talk. Many children are shy, but extreme withdrawal might signal a deeper problem.

- A child whose behaviour changes suddenly and drastically may be signalling a problem requiring attention. You should feel concerned about the generally happy, outgoing child who suddenly becomes antisocial, or the active, assertive child who inexplicably becomes withdrawn and passive, particularly if the changed behaviour persists for more than a few days. Your first source of information, of course, is the child's parents. But if they too are baffled, a more thorough search for the cause of the change is in order.

THE NEEDS OF THE ADHD CHILD

Don H. Shattuck, Ph.D., C.Psych., Chief Psychologist, Kawartha Pine Ridge School Board

Attention Deficit-Hyperactivity Disorder (ADHD) is the technical term for what you may know as *hyperactivity*. The hyperactive child—or the child with ADHD—is the one who seems always on the go, always moving or talking, and bouncing from one activity to another. These children are often doing things they should not, seemingly oblivious to rules or the possibility of danger. They butt into other's activities, do not seem to listen to instructions and are constantly getting into trouble for something they have said or done.

Obviously, these children show a wide range of problematic behaviours and are not simply overactive. This is why the condition is not technically known as hyperactivity. There are two other aspects to this syndrome which are frequently even more problematic. First, these children have *trouble paying attention*. They cannot concentrate on their work for long periods and often do not finish their assignments. They have trouble listening to instructions and seem easily bored. Second, they are often *very impulsive* and act without thinking. Running into the street and other risky behaviours are always a concern. Further, saying and doing the wrong things at the wrong times makes it difficult to be liked. If others do not like you, it is hard to like yourself, and not having friends makes it hard to learn social skills. Not surprisingly, then, ADHD children often have low self-esteem, may be easily frustrated and many show signs of depression and anxiety. For some reason, a large percentage also have learning disabilities, in spite of average intelligence. As well, middle ear infections, allergies and asthma seem to appear more frequently than with most children.

Attention Deficit-Hyperactivity Disorder is relatively common. How common is unclear, but probably about 5% of children have the disorder in varying degrees, usually boys, with some being much more affected than others. The cause or causes are unknown. Genetics may play a role; bad parenting does not, although this may make the problems worse. Elevated lead levels in children, and alcohol and nicotine use during pregnancy are correlated with ADHD symptoms, but their importance is not known. Popular opinion to the contrary, sugar or food additives have not been shown to be a problem.

Ritalin, a stimulant medication related to the caffeine in coffee, has been shown over and over to be a relatively safe and effective medication in the treatment of ADHD. Unfortunately, it only partially relieves some of the symptoms. Although most of these children make successful adult adjustments and their symptoms sometimes diminish with age, there is no cure. For the ECE teacher, however, it is important to know that there are a number of behavioural techniques, some of which are discussed in this book, that can be very helpful for an ADHD child. If you become an early childhood educator, you will meet ADHD children. When you do, seek help from professional people and follow their advice. Few of these children meet caring, helpful adults. Try to be one.

- Finally, if you notice unexplainable bruises, abrasions, cuts, or burns on a child, consider the possibility of child abuse. Other forms of abuse—verbal and sexual abuse and/or neglect—do not leave physical scars but are just as damaging. An abused child usually also exhibits behavioural symptoms of the problem. If you have reason to suspect child abuse, speak to your supervisor or director so the concern can be followed up by notifying the appropriate authority in your province.

When a competent teacher finds that a particular child's behaviour is just beyond that teacher's capacity to cope, it is time to look beyond a teacher's own resources. *Getting professional help is not a sign of weakness, but rather of your strength in being able to recognize the limits of your professional expertise.* Just as you would have a physician, not yourself, prescribe medication, there are times when a psychologist, psychiatrist, or other appropriate professional should be asked to help with a challenging behaviour. These community professionals also have a share of responsibility for the care and guidance of young children in your community.

● Factors That Affect Children's Behaviour

In dealing with children's behaviour, it is important to examine all potential factors that might be affecting that behaviour. All kinds of subtle influences can contribute to behaviour, even the weather (Essa, Hilton, & Murray, 1990; Faust, Weidmann, & Wehner, 1974). But most behaviours have identifiable causes, some external, others internal. When you are concerned about a behaviour, give careful thought to what might be triggering it. In this section, we will examine some factors that can affect children's behaviour.

● Clear-Cut Guidelines

Children generally abide by rules that are logical, simple, and few in number. There is no need to overwhelm children with too many rules; as we suggested before, the rule that children should not hurt themselves, others, or things would suffice in most programs.

Sometimes children's behaviour is a function of not understanding what is expected. When a child engages in a behaviour that you see as a problem, do not jump to the conclusion that the child is misbehaving deliberately. The child may simply be acting out of ignorance or may not understand your expectations. For example, by their second week in school, 4-year-old twins Trevor and Teddy seemed constantly to be testing the preschool program limits. One day they climbed over the six-foot chain-link playground fence. Another time they were each swaying in the tops of two trees on the playground; on yet another day, they were found exploring and sampling the contents of the refrigerator in the school's kitchen.

The teachers were disconcerted by what they *perceived* as the boys' constant misbehaviour. It occurred to one teacher that Trevor and Teddy may not have

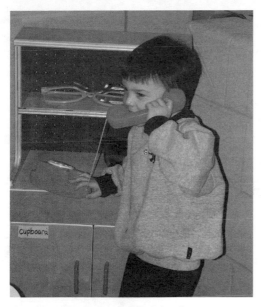

Courtesy of Eglinton Public School.

understood the expectations. Indeed, in talking to their mother, the teacher found that the type of exploration the boys engaged in at school was encouraged at home. The teacher decided to talk to the boys about the school rules, which no one had reviewed with them as relative new-comers to preschool. Once the children discussed these with the teacher, they agreed that the rules made sense. They diverted their abundant energy to other, more acceptable activities with the help of the staff, who made greater efforts to inform the boys of their expectations.

Gartrell (1998) might place Trevor and Teddy's behaviour into the first and second levels in his classification of three levels of mistaken behaviour. The first, the **experimentation level**, is the mildest form of mistaken behaviour; at this level, children try to figure out how things work and what the consequences might be. Gartrell identifies the second as the social habit level, in which the child erroneously thinks the behaviour is appropriate, it has been acceptable in another context, or peers respond positively to it. The **deep emotional needs level** is the third, reflecting a more troubled cause and possibly erupting in extreme behaviours. Gartrell suggests that understanding the child is vital to effective intervention.

● Health and Related Problems

Children often react in unacceptable ways because their bodies are not functioning well or are sending messages of discomfort or pain. When children do not feel well, they cannot be expected to behave normally. Think how most adults become very irritable when ill. Children are no different. In fact, children have fewer resources to control their behaviour when they don't feel well (Essa, 1995), and sometimes problem behaviours emerge when they do not feel well.

Some children are also affected by environmental or food allergies which can affect behaviour in unpredictable ways. Other children might have an undetected **sensory deficit** that affects behaviour. Could the clumsy child who is unwilling to try anything new have a vision deficit? Might the child who is often distractible and seems to ignore what you tell him have trouble hearing? Three-year-old George, for example, was uncooperative and inattentive at school, but his mother reported he would sit for long periods at home while she read to him and where he complied with her requests. At the suggestion of the director, George's mother had his hearing tested. It turned out that he had a severe hearing loss from frequent ear infections, a situation that was remedied when tubes were inserted in his ears. George then became an entirely different child, attending, responding to adults and children, and becoming involved in activities; he could hear and interpret specific sounds in the group setting rather than hearing only undifferentiated noise as he had before the tubes were inserted.

Nutrition, both the quality and the quantity of food, is another factor that can affect children's behaviour (Lozoff, 1989; Ricciuti, 1993; World Health Organization [WHO], 1996). A child who comes to school hungry or malnourished may be irritable or listless, may not work to potential, and/or may misbehave. Studies have linked nutrition to behaviour and learning (e.g., Barrett, 1986; Lozoff, 1989; McDonald, Sigman, Espinosa, & Neumann, 1994; Ricciuti, 1993; WHO, 1996; Van Heerden, 1984). Immigrant children from Third World countries may be at special risk as a World Health Organization study (WHO, 1996) found that at least half of the children in southeast Asia, 30 percent of the children in sub-Saharan Africa, and 10 percent of those in the western hemisphere are malnourished. This deprivation affects cognitive and social as well as physical development (Ricciuti, 1993; WHO, 1996). Of course, it is not only immigrant children who are at risk. Canadian children from all social strata are at risk for malnutrition and undernutrition—some do not get proper nutrients because of costs, others subsist on a diet high in sugar, fats, additives, and empty calories.

● Individual Temperament

To a large degree, children's personalities are molded by their environment, but research has also shown that children are born with a certain **temperament** (Thomas & Chess, 1969), which we discussed in Chapter 5. Thomas, Chess, and Birch (1968), in a classic and enduring work on temperament, found that the children they studied could be classified children into three general categories: easy, slow to warm up, and difficult. They concluded that the largest group in their sample—40 percent—were classified as easy children, whereas 15 percent belonged to the slow-to-warm-up category and 10 percent to the difficult category; 35 percent of the children did not fit neatly into any of these categories.

Easy children, from their earliest days, follow a regular cycle in sleeping, eating, and eliminating; are readily adaptable to change; have a reasonable attention span; display a moderate level of activity; are not overly sensitive to stimuli; and have a generally happy disposition. Difficult children, on the other hand, show opposite traits such as irregularity, intensity in reactions, an inability to adapt, and a high activity level, and they are often out of sorts. Slow-to-warm-up children fall in between these two extremes.

It is not easy to deal with difficult children because they often defy all attempts to pacify or engage them. "When children are difficult, less confident adults will doubt themselves, feel guilty, and be anxious about the child's future and their relationship" (Soderman, 1985, p. 16). Thomas and Chess (1969) encouraged parents to accept a difficult child positively by seeing his or her traits in terms of self-assertion. Soderman advises teachers to deal with difficult children through respect, objectivity, environmental structure, effective limits, positive interaction, patience, and cooperation with colleagues and parents, all characteristics of sensitive, effective teachers. She further warns against inappropriate reactions such as ignoring the difficult behaviours, coercing compliance, shaming, labelling, or punishing.

As you pursue your early childhood teaching career, you will likely be entrusted with one or more temperamentally difficult children. Many beginning (as well as veteran) teachers have found this to be a real test of their self-confidence. Keep in mind that consistent, positive guidance skills and ingenuity can help channel the child's energy, perhaps into a leadership role, rather than into that of an unhappy outcast. Rely on your teaching strengths, examine and acknowledge your own feelings, and then continue to view every child—whether easy or difficult—as an individual worthy of your respect and support.

● The Child's Family

A child's behaviour may be a reaction to stress or change at home. The statistics in Chapter 1 (e.g., Statistics Canada, 1997e, Oct. 14; Statistics Canada, 1998g, May 12) told us that a large number of young children will experience their parents' divorce, enter a single-parent family where there will most likely be financial and emotional stresses, or experience reconstitution of a family as one of their natural parents remarries. Such major changes, even when parents are very sensitive to and mindful of the needs and feelings of their youngsters, are invariably upsetting to children who cannot fully understand what is happening. Other changes, such as a new baby in the family, a visit from grandparents, a parent away on a business trip, the death of a family member or pet, or moving to a new house, can also trigger behavioural responses.

It is important to maintain frequent and open communication with parents to find out what is happening at home. If you know, for example, that Eddie's parents are heading toward a divorce, you can better understand his sudden angry outbursts. You cannot put Eddie's family back together, but you can convey to him that you understand his distress and are there for them. If Eddie hits out at other children, you can let him know that you do not condone his behaviour and will take measures to stop it, but that you do acknowledge his pain.

Behaviour problems have also been linked to parenting style. Patterson, DeBaryshe, and Ramsey (1989) proposed a developmental model of antisocial behaviour. Poor parental discipline and monitoring can lead to **child conduct disorders** in early childhood; in middle childhood, such parenting practices may result in rejection by peers and academic failure; finally, in later childhood and adolescence, poor parenting can lead to affiliation with a deviant peer group and delinquency. Antisocial behaviour is more likely to develop in children of families with a history of antisocial behaviour and stressors such as unemployment, marital conflict, and divorce. The authors, in summarizing the literature on intervention efforts, conclude that intervention at adolescence produces short-lived results. *But intervention at earlier ages has proven to be more effective.*

A Closer Look provides insight into a disturbing family-based problem, drug-exposed babies and children, that poses many challenges for the early childhood profession.

A Closer Look

THE PLIGHT OF DRUG-EXPOSED CHILDREN

Just a few years ago the media began to reflect a concern about "crack babies," children born of mothers who had taken crack cocaine during pregnancy. Now, many of these babies are in their preschool and early elementary school years, and the focus of attention has turned to how these youngsters will function in the school environment. Some early childhood teachers have already experienced drug-exposed children who have been mainstreamed into their classrooms.

Over the years, many children exposed prenatally to drugs have been born. Stories of newborns suffering withdrawal symptoms are not new. Research has documented tremors, irritability, oversensitivity to stimuli, and other problems in infants whose mothers took a variety of illicit drugs. But one problem in studying this population of children is that it is difficult to tell what drugs or combination of drugs their mothers took, when during the pregnancy these children were exposed, how frequently they were exposed, and the quantity to which they were exposed. To complicate matters, many of the mothers had inadequate prenatal nutrition and no prenatal care.

Once born, drug-exposed babies are often taken away from addicted mothers and placed in foster care, subjecting already vulnerable children to a host of potential social risk factors. Thus, many unknown variables make it difficult to generalize about children who were exposed to drugs prenatally. There are no prototypes of drug-exposed children.

In recent years, several early childhood programs have been developed specifically to work with this group of children. Two such programs in California have concluded that the children do best in a high-quality early childhood environment.* The preschool program provides a secure base for children who are attached insecurely, according to one administrator. The focus of these programs is not on the children's history but on their current needs, which, most often, involve social-emotional and language problems.

Although there are no long-term studies to document the success of these children, staff members are very positive about the prognosis for those they have served. Several youngsters have moved into regular kindergarten classrooms, while others have required some limited special education services; none has required full special education placement. The staff feel that the children they have worked with would be best served in mainstreamed early childhood programs. Furthermore, they are very concerned that these youngsters not be stuck with a label that will follow them through their school years.

Other experts are not so optimistic, however. Many are particularly concerned about unexpected emotional swings that some drug-exposed children have demonstrated; such outbursts often result in unpredictable aggression. Although most children who react aggressively do so in response to some external provocation, the aggression of some drug-exposed children tends to come with no warning and often for no apparent reason. Some see this as a symptom of neurological damage. One child development expert feels that it is irresponsible to mainstream children who are so unpredictable. Unless a full-time aide is provided, the teacher should not be expected to add "just one more child" into the class.

The question of how to help children who were exposed to drugs before birth and often end up in unstable care once they are born is a difficult one to answer. As those who work with these youngsters in special programs indicate, the children can be helped, but the social service delivery system too often enmeshes them in a cumbersome and inconsistent bureaucracy. Some of the conflicting opinions and concerns about this group of children may be resolved as more longitudinal research continues to follow their progress.

*From conversations in May 1991 with Mary Ann Nielsen, Assistant Superintendent, Diagnostic Center for Neurologically Handicapped Children, California State Department of Education, and Carol Cole, early childhood special education teacher with the Los Angeles Unified School District.

● Some Guidance Techniques

Keep in mind that your attitude toward your job and toward children, your skill as a teacher, your ability to be consistent and flexible—and a good sense of humour—all contribute to setting the tone for the classroom. A respect for all children and a willingness to get to know each child as an individual are basic ingredients in positive guidance. So is a sense of partnership with the children ("me with the children") rather than a "me against them" attitude. There is no doubt: you, the teacher, are central to establishing a productive, lively, happy environment for children of all ages.

We have discussed guidance from the viewpoint of what kinds of adults we would like children to grow up to be, within the context of some different philosophical approaches, and as it is related to and distinguished from some other terms.

Before we turn to some specific techniques that can help you better deal with children's behaviour, however, remember that behaviour management focuses on observable traits that can be *noted and measured*, such as crying, hitting, or whining, not on unobservable qualities, such as jealousy, insecurity, or separation anxiety. When a behaviour is a problem and needs to be changed, you *carefully measure* it (e.g., the number of aggressive incidents are counted) and quantify it, perhaps using a graph (Essa, 1995). If, for example, Edward has been hitting other children frequently, it is more accurate to know that after two weeks of a behaviour management program he has decreased his rate of hitting from an average of five times to two times a day than to conclude that the program is not working because Edward is still hitting.

● Thorough and Creative Planning

Remember, when children are engrossed in meaningful activities that they find rewarding and interesting, they are much less likely to misbehave. A well-planned, developmentally appropriate curriculum is integrally tied to your guidance approach (e.g., Gartrell, 1998; Gestwicki, 1997, 1999; Gordon & Browne, 1993; Marion, 1999; Miller, 2000; Reynolds, 2001) and will in itself provide a key preventive technique.

● Prevention

It is much easier on you, as the teacher, as well as on children to prevent problems before they occur. Prevention is an excellent guidance technique, because you step in to stop a problem before tempers flare. Keep an eye on as much of the group as possible; both inside and on the playground, position yourself where you can watch the majority of the children, even though generally you are with an individual child or a small group. Prevention is particularly important at the beginning of the school year, when you set expectations for the rest of the year.

Also know what triggers certain children's problem behaviours. If Solomon tends to hit others when he gets frustrated, be available when you see him trying a difficult puzzle; if Rana cries when she does not get to be "Mommy" in housekeeping play, be available to guide children's role selection if needed; if Jarrod hits children when it is crowded, ensure that he has more space; if Shaheen has a difficult time sharing, watch the block area when Andy approaches it.

● Redirection

Another way to prevent problems is by redirection. For instance, distract Sylvia if she is about to kick over the block tower by steering her to the water table, or provide Yusuf with an alternative toy to replace the one he is about to snatch from Richie. Redirection works particularly well with very young preschoolers whose self-control is just emerging and who do not yet have the verbal and social skills required for sharing. Sensitive teachers can help 2-year-olds develop these attributes over time and through many positive interactions.

Distraction through humour also can be effective ("Laughing all the way," 1988). Many potential "me against you" situations can be avoided by using the light touch. Distraction works particularly well with younger children; most toddlers readily change focus when distracted. Telling a child, "Now … let … me … see … you … walk … slow … slow … like … a … turtle" will be more effective than saying, "How many times do I have to tell you not to run in the classroom?"

● Positive Reinforcement

Positive reinforcement is perhaps the most widely used application of behaviour management, but it is one that teachers frequently forget to use in abundance. You use it every time you smile at the children who are playing cooperatively in the dramatic play area, gently touch the head of the child who is engrossed in putting together a puzzle, or say thank you to the children for helping to clean up after snack; such subtle social reinforcers come naturally to most teachers. In behaviour management, reinforcers are often used systematically to encourage specified behaviours. If Julio gets positive attention every time he hangs up his coat, he is more likely to repeat the behaviour.

Behaviourists may resort to more powerful reinforcers such as food, toys, tokens, or privileges to reward a child, but only if that child does not respond to social reinforcement (e.g., Blanco, 1982; Lexmond, 1987; Sheppard, 1973; Zlomke & Piersel, 1987). Reinforcement, because it follows the behaviour ("Everyone who helps in cleanup will get a special sticker") needs to be distinguished from bribes ("If I give you a special sticker, will you help clean up?").

It is important that reinforcement immediately follow the behaviour to be effective, although the frequency of reinforcement will vary. When you first attempt to help a child acquire a new behaviour (for instance, Julio hanging up his coat when he comes inside), the reinforcement must be applied every time the behaviour appears; however, once the child is on the way to remembering to hang up his coat, the reinforcement schedule can be decreased gradually until eventually Julio is reinforced for this behaviour about as frequently as the other children (Patterson & Gullion, 1971).

While positive reinforcement can be a powerful tool, ineffective praise, for example, general or gratuitous statements such as "Good job!" or "Good boy!" can actually be counterproductive (Hitz & Driscoll, 1988).

Rather than fostering positive self-concept and autonomy, ineffective praise can lower self-confidence and lead to dependency, because the teacher has placed herself or himself in the position of telling children what is right or wrong (Kamii, 1984). Ineffective praise can also decrease motivation by making the reward rather than the activity the goal. When praising one child's appropriate behaviour is used to encourage the others to follow suit, children may react with anger and resentment because they feel manipulated.

Instead, it is recommended that you use **effective praise** or encouragement, which focuses on the activity and process, allows children to evaluate their own work, and discourages competition. Following are some examples of encouragement, as proposed by Hitz and Driscoll (1988, p.12):

- Denise has played with Jimmy at the sand table; they experimented with funnels for more than 20 minutes. *Encouraging statement:* "You and Jimmy played together for a long time at the sand table."

- Dhanni seldom talks in the group, but today she told a short story about Halloween. *Encouraging statement:* "That was a very scary story you told. It gave me goose bumps."

- Guzmayadi has just finished a painting. He comes to you, the teacher, and says, "Look at my painting, isn't it beautiful!" *Encouraging statement:* "You look happy about your painting. Look at all the colours you used."

● Attention

Reinforcement is a form of attention, but attention is more than reinforcement. All human beings need acknowledgment of their existence, affirmation of their linkage to others, acceptance of their membership in the human race. Sometimes we communicate through nurturance, caring, gentleness, sensitivity, and tenderness; we do this not because we are reacting to a desired behaviour, as in reinforcement, but simply because we are responding to a human need.

Reinforcement is given conditionally on the basis of the child responding in a specific way, but children also need **unconditional attention**, which makes an enormous difference to a child. Unconditional acceptance and response begin in earliest infancy and lay the foundation for feelings of trust. As a result, many children, receiving such attention in ample supply at home and in infant and toddler care programs, have strong, trusting relationships in their lives. By 3 years old, these children are full of independence and openness to new experiences. Other children, whose foundation for trust is not so firmly established or has been shaken by a disruptive experience such as divorce, may seem unduly demanding; they may constantly seek your attention, possibly through misbehaviour.

Most often, a child who engages in a lot of attention-getting behaviour is expressing a need for attention. It is not wise to provide attention when a child expresses that need through some form of misbehaviour; that only reinforces the child's mistaken notion that the main way to get attention is to do something unacceptable. Such attention is generally negative and will not help the child feel good about herself or himself. Two kinds of attention should be provided instead. One is reinforcement of appropriate behaviours, as we have already discussed. The other is unconditional attention.

Unconditional attention tells the child that you value *her*, as a person in her own right, not just because she behaves as you want her to behave. You can give unconditional attention in a number of ways, such as greeting children at the beginning of the day with *genuine* statements such as, "Good morning, Jenny! I'm so glad to see you!" During the day, teachers also provide such attention when they smile at, hug, cuddle, or soothe a child or when they respond to the child who requests help or attention.

One mechanism for providing unconditional attention to a child who particularly seems to need extra attention is special time (Essa, 1995). The teacher sets aside just a few minutes a day, or even two or three times a week, just for the child. This one-on-one time is not conditional on the child behaving in a particular way (for instance, "If you ——, then we will spend **special time**") but is unconditional, not at all tied to the child's behaviour. The teacher conveys the message, "I want to spend time with just you because you are you." The teacher can ask what the child would like to do for special time and then follow up on that suggestion, whether it is going for a short walk, reading a book, or playing a game; the specific activity is less important than the teacher's undivided attention during this time together.

Such a time investment can have great payoffs. Early childhood educators who have used special time with children who seem to be seeking extra attention have found that these children seem to feel better about themselves and greatly decrease their acting-out behaviour. Some schools also recommend this method to parents (Keele, 1966), with the result that children whose parents regularly spend a few minutes using an individual time formula in one-on-one interaction seem much more self-assured and secure.

Modelling

Modelling, advocated by social learning theorists, is effective because research has told us that children are likely to imitate those they admire and like. Observational learning occurs frequently in the classroom, and we use it when we model politeness, friendliness, or caring, although modelling is not a simple cause-effect phenomenon. Certain conditions, for instance, children seeing a model being reinforced, will be more likely to result in imitation of the behaviour (Bandura, 1977).

Shaping

Shaping is another behavioural technique, perhaps used more frequently with children who have special needs. A behaviour is broken down into smaller steps, and **successive approximations** to the desired behaviour are reinforced, until the final behaviour is achieved (Peters, Neisworth, & Yawkey, 1985; Sheppard, 1973). Thus, each time children come closer to the goal or target behaviour, they are reinforced. For instance, to increase a child's attention to any given activity when that child remains at one task only for an average of three minutes, the time required for reinforcement is increased gradually, moving from three minutes to five minutes to eight minutes to ten minutes to fifteen minutes (Peters et al., 1985).

Cuing

Cuing is a technique used to help children remember what is expected. Thus, teachers may use a specific cue such as a bell to tell children that it is time to come in from outside play, or a specific song to signal a transition time as discussed above. It may suffice for the teacher to catch a child's eye and give a nod of the head to remind the child of what is expected.

Ignoring

Just as positive reinforcement strengthens behaviours, withdrawing it, through **ignoring** or **extinction**, can weaken and eliminate behaviours. We often inadvertently reinforce a negative behaviour by our reactions: frowning when a child shouts in the classroom; repeatedly saying, "Stop shouting, you are disturbing everyone!"; or taking the child aside and sitting with her or him until she or he promises to stop making noise. Each of these reactions tells children that they have successfully attracted our attention. Ignoring can extinguish the behaviour, if it is persistent and complete. But ignoring is not always the best method to use, especially when aggression is involved (Essa, 1995; Morrison, 1988). Aggressive behaviour must be dealt with more firmly and quickly for the safety of all involved.

Ignoring works well for annoying behaviours that are clearly a bid for your attention. Persistent and repeated instances of whining, pouting, baby talk, crying as a means of getting attention, tantrums (for older infants, toddlers, and younger preschoolers), and deliberately creating annoying noises are some examples of behaviours that can be changed through ignoring.

● Time-Out

Although consistent ignoring should gradually eliminate an undesirable behaviour, psychologists (e.g., Blanco, 1982; Lexmond, 1987; Zlomke & Piersel, 1987), on rare occasions, when the behaviour is serious, recommend **time-out** as a method for speeding up the removal of reinforcement that maintains the behaviour. Consistent time-out can be effective in eliminating undesirable behaviours, but it should be used *sparingly*, only for situations in which the removal of the child is the best response, and *only in conjunction with a program of positive reinforcement.*

While time-out can be a powerful technique, it has been subject to overuse and abuse in most of Canada. For this reason, every reviewer for this text, all of them recognized Canadian experts in early childhood education, expressed some concern about the inclusion of this approach in an introductory text. They cited the many abuses of time-out they have seen in the field. If you remember this unanimous concern, and only use the technique after all else has failed, you should avoid the regular pitfalls. As Peters, Neisworth, and Yawkey (1985, p.126) note, "Time-out must not be used to get rid of the child, but to weaken specific behaviour." Moreover, *time-out should be used only when a child engages in a behaviour consistently, not for one-time occurrences. It is also most effective when used very infrequently and for very short durations, two to three minutes at most* (Blanco, 1982; Lexmond, 1987; Zlomke & Piersel, 1987). Time-out also *must be paired with ample attention for appropriate social interactions or it will not work* (Blanco, 1982; Lexmond, 1987; Risley & Baer, 1973; Zlomke & Piersel, 1987).

Blanco (1982) notes that time-out, which entails removal from others, is *totally inappropriate even for school-aged children who are frightened of being alone*. It is a punishment in these circumstances, not a removal from reinforcement. It also should not be used for very young children. Time-out is usually carried out in an identified location, often a chair in the place in the classroom that has the least chance of offering stimulation and opportunities for reinforcement. **Self-selected time-out** (Essa, 1995) is a variant that gives a child the responsibility of removing himself or herself when losing control is a concern. Another variation is **time-away** which allows the child to get away from a particular activity, for a few minutes rather than be removed from the room. If Theomoor hit someone in the block area, you might choose to tell him, "It's time to talk with me now." Then, while he has time-away from the block area, you would ask him or review (at younger ages) why he was removed from the block area, discuss the rule about hurting people, and say he can return when he can play without hitting.

Time-out and time-away, used for no more than two minutes, can allow children to regain their composure when they lose self-control. *It should be reempha-*

sized that time-out should not be overused. It should also never be considered the primary method of disciplining children. Finally, it must always be paired with positive reinforcement for positive behaviours, and empowering guidance techniques. In fact, psychologists typically use time-out as a technique to deal with very serious behaviour problems, as the other behavioural techniques, including positive reinforcement, unconditional attention, prevention, redirection, ignoring, and discussing, are more effective and less intrusive than this procedure. Information about guidance strategies may be found on the Internet.

● Discussion

Talking about behaviour can be effective with some children, especially older preschoolers and school-aged children. Older children often respond well to such discussion, particularly if they have adequate verbal skills, the budding ability to look at themselves, and the motivation to change a behaviour that makes them unhappy. Infants and toddlers, in contrast, are quite unlikely to benefit from discussions. In essence, the teacher and child form a partnership: The child agrees to try to make some behavioural changes while the teacher promises to support the child and be there to help or remind.

All the techniques we discussed in this chapter have merit and have proven their effectiveness. They are effective for dealing with most behaviour situations. Remember, however, that each child is a unique individual and may not fit into a "formula approach."

Key Terms

attachment	morality of autonomy
attention deficit disorder with hyperactivity (ADHD)	morality of obedience
	nutrients
child conduct disorders	positive discipline
consequences	positive reinforcement
cuing	punishment
deep emotional needs level	self-selected time-out
discipline	sensory deficit
eclectic	separation anxiety
effective praise	shaping
experimentation level	special time
extinction	successive approximations
guidance	temperament
ignoring	time-away
inductive reasoning	time-out
modelling	unconditional attention

Key Points

Important Definitions

1. Although the word *discipline* often has negative connotations, the terms *guidance* and *positive discipline* are more concerned with the ongoing process involved in raising children. Punishment as a technique is discouraged because it is ineffective in the long run.

2. Prosocial behaviours have to be nurtured.

3. An eclectic approach to guidance allows you to select approaches that work best for you.

Arrival at School

4. Some young children experience separation anxiety on leaving their parent.

5. A well-thought-out procedure for arrival, particularly when children don't all arrive at the same time, will help get the day off to a good start.

6. It is important to help the new child adjust to the early childhood program.

Meals and Eating Behaviour

7. Nutritious, healthy foods for meals and snacks must be served at school as these are part of the child's daily intake of nutrients. Some specific mealtime guidelines can help encourage children, including finicky and overweight eaters to form good eating habits.

Toileting

8. Occasional toileting accidents should be expected in a group of young children and should never be considered a cause for punishment or shame.

Sleep and Rest Times

9. A nap or rest time is important for children who spend all day in a child care centre. A consistent pre-nap routine and a relaxing atmosphere will facilitate sleep.

Factors That Affect Group Behaviour

10. Group guidance can be facilitated by such factors as a well-set-up environment, schedule, activities, materials, and expectations that are appropriate for the developmental level of the children. When expectations are inappropriate, frustration or boredom are likely to result.

11. Children are most apt to follow rules if there are few of them and if they understand the reasons for these rules.

Group Guidance and the Daily Program

12. A number of strategies are outlined above for preventing problems during various routines. Crowding should be avoided, and remember that effective group activities require careful planning and preparation, and attention to seating arrangements.

Transitions

13. Children best respond to upcoming transitions, such as cleanup time, if they know what to expect; therefore, a warning a few minutes before the change will help them be prepared for it.

The Unusual Situation

14. Careful planning and forethought are important to ensure safety and enjoyment on field trips and walks. Children cannot be prepared for all unexpected or emergency situations, but some specific teacher strategies can help them respond calmly.

What Is the Difference Between Normal and Challenging Behaviour?

15. All children misbehave at times; the early childhood educator must distinguish between normal behaviours and those that merit concern and intervention. An understanding of developmental stages, coupled with a recognition of children's individual differences, helps the teacher distinguish between normal and problem behaviours.

16. Children who are continually disruptive and unmanageable may need professional, one-on-one help. Watch for very withdrawn children, sudden inexplicable behaviour changes, and signs of child abuse.

Factors That Affect Children's Behaviour

17. Many times the causes of misbehaviour are not within the control of the child but come from some source beyond the child's ability to change. For example, family problems, allergies, sensory deficits, and poor nutrition all can affect behaviour, as can temperament and parenting style.

Some Techniques of Guidance

18. A number of guidance techniques were reviewed, including reinforcement, unconditional attention, ignoring, time-out, prevention, distraction, and talking.

Key Questions

1. List the behaviours you think are desirable in young children. Then list the characteristics you like to see in adults. Compare the two lists. Are the qualities on your two lists similar? Do you see a link between your expectations of children's behaviours and the outcomes you find desirable in adults?

2. Observe children arriving at school with their parents. What differences do you note in the ways in which they leave their parents?

3. A 3-year-old in your class consistently refuses to go to sleep during nap, but then almost always falls asleep later in the afternoon. What strategies might you use in such a situation?

4. Ask three teachers what rules they set for the young children in their classes. Are there commonalities among the rules listed by the different teachers? Are there differences? Which rules seem reasonable and understandable to preschoolers? Do any of the rules seem inappropriate?

5. Observe a preschool class during transitions between activities. What strategies does the teacher use? Do these strategies reflect a sense of preparedness and forethought? Did the transitions go smoothly or were there some problems? How could these transitions be improved?

6. You are going to take a group of children on the first field trip of the year. How will you and the other staff members prepare for this trip? How will you prepare the children?

7. Organize a class discussion—or even a debate—on time-out. Try to identify situations where it would be an appropriate technique and situations where it would be inappropriate. Have you seen abuses of the technique in the field or in your community?

8. Observe a group of children and note any aggressive behaviour. What was the nature of the aggression? How did the victim of the aggression react? What did the teacher do? Was the teacher's action or reaction effective? Why or why not?

Part 4

How? Curriculum

In Part 4, we continue to explore the basic hows of early childhood education, examining the following fundamental intricacies of what you now know to be quality programs. Some basic components of the environment and curriculum, such as materials, and planning and implementation guidelines, are addressed.

- In Chapter 9, **Curriculum**, we discuss curriculum in terms of process and content. Then we address the issue of accountability, examining observation, assessment, standards, learning outcomes, and evaluation.

- In Chapter 10, **Development Through the Curriculum**, we focus on creative, physical, cognitive, language, and social development, and talk about how the curriculum can foster development in these spheres.

Courtesy of Eglinton Public School.

Chapter 9

Curriculum

A program is the structure within which certain things occur. Program components, as we have just discussed in Chapters 7 and 8, include such things as schedules, the environment, times for certain types of activities, and personal care, which are devised on the basis of knowledge of child development and imply certain guidelines for incorporating these into the day. Curriculum, essentially, is what happens during these times.

Think about your own school experience now. Your program, and even each particular class, may involve individual and group times, a variety of materials, and a balanced time frame, which are appropriate practices for adult learning. But it is the curriculum that you are learning during these times.

What Is Curriculum?

Unfortunately, quality early childhood education programs do not come in ready-made, hand-delivered packages. They entail a great deal of teacher time—time planning activities and organizing the environment so that child-initiated, play-based, teacher-supported learning will occur. The amount of planning and the terms used vary somewhat with the age of the children in the program.

As Gonzalez-Mena and Eyer (1997) note, most people and texts (e.g., Almy, 1975; Gestwicki, 1999; Maxim, 1989; Shimoni et al., 1992) prefer to avoid the term **curriculum** when describing programs for infants and toddlers.

Traditionally, the word is used to describe the content of a program designed to develop cognitive skills. For infants and toddlers, all experiences are curriculum—and cognition cannot be parcelled out from other areas of development. However, the word *curriculum* comes from the Latin word describing the race course a chariot followed. If you think of curriculum as the *course of the day* for children in a program, then the term is appropriate for all ages. Programs for infants and toddlers are carefully planned, the environment is carefully and safely structured, and teachers in these settings have a knack for using many diverse opportunities for learning. However, the very short attention spans and more demanding care-taking needs of infants and younger toddlers in the sensorimotor stage of development mean that extended periods of self-directed play are out of the question.

The longer attention spans and reduced caretaking needs of preoperational preschoolers and preoperational and concrete-operational school-aged children require different forms of program planning. Consequently, people are more likely to use the term *curriculum* when discussing programs for preschool children. **Lesson plan** almost always creeps into the terminology when school-aged children are being discussed. Notwithstanding the variations in terminology, quality early childhood education settings have developmentally and individually appropriate programs and/or curricula that have been carefully planned and regularly evaluated by their teachers.

In the following sections, we will consider some of the elements of the early childhood program or curriculum. Our goal is not to provide actual step-by-step lesson plans but to introduce you to a framework for planning. Content and applications are far more vital than format. Is your rationale sound? Is the content appropriate? Do you plan effectively? Do you know how to observe and document children as they engage in the activities? Can you assess and evaluate their development? Then, in Chapter 10, we will consider five developmental domains—creative, physical, cognitive, language, and social—and will provide guidelines for supporting them through the curriculum. Some ingredients will be found in all programs, regardless of the children's ages. Caring, warm adults who welcome parent involvement in a developmentally appropriate program are taken as givens. Choice, variety, and challenge in an anti-bias program are also basics. But young children also need the sense of security that a predictable, yet fully flexible program can offer. Finally, young children—especially children in full-day programs—also need time, time to do what comes naturally, time to pause and reflect, time to be alone, and time to be with others. If the program has all of these ingredients, the environment will also have children and adults who are enjoying each day; you will hear sounds of delight, joy, pleasure, and humour from both children and teachers who approach each day with enthusiasm.

Elements of the Curriculum

The early childhood curriculum is the result of both long-range and short-term planning, and the children's developmental levels. Long-term planning is perhaps inappropriate for infants and toddlers because they change so quickly—almost daily. In contrast, in late August, a kindergarten teacher might outline what she or he would like to accomplish over the year, and then revise and refine the outline upon meeting the children in the program in September.

Curriculum has to be integrally related to several important factors—program philosophy, learning outcomes, observation, and evaluation—as we will discuss (Epstein, Schweinhart, & McAdoo, 1996; Gestwicki, 1997, 1999; Howe, Jacobs, & Fiorentino, 2000; Jalongo & Isenberg, 2000; Schweinhart & Epstein, 1996).

These factors form a cyclical pattern: program philosophy guides goals and objectives, which are part of learning outcomes or expectations; these, coupled with observation, lead to development of content and activities; content and activities are evaluated on an ongoing basis; and learning outcomes are reassessed and adjusted as needed, starting the cycle anew (Gestwicki, 1997, 1999; Howe, Jacobs, & Fiorentino, 2000; Jalongo & Isenberg, 2000; Lawton, 1988).

● Program Philosophy and Curriculum

Curriculum takes its direction from the overall philosophy of your program. For instance, underlying beliefs and values about how children learn will have an impact. Another factor shaping the curriculum will be reliance on a particular theorist's works. For instance, programs derived from the theory of Jean Piaget will focus on developmentally appropriate cognitive tasks, whereas programs based on behaviourist theory may rely more on a direct instructional approach. Montessori programs will have equipment and activities, some of which you are unlikely to find in a Piagetian or behavioural program. Likewise, Reggio Emilia takes its approach from Piaget, Vygotsky, and Dewey's perspectives.

Finally, the children in your program and your assumptions about how best to meet their specific requirements will also affect the curriculum. For instance, you might increase the language component of your program if you have children from low-income families. You would also adjust your program if you think that some children in your program have special needs, including a need for positive socialization experiences, an improved self-concept, or cognitive stimulation.

● Standards, Learning Outcomes, and Curriculum

Objectives or **goals** stem from a program's philosophy—they are **standards** you aim to achieve. The objectives or goals are then translated into concrete learning outcomes (e.g., Johnny will be able to tie his shoe and Rana will be able to count to two.) Standards and learning outcomes are expectations about what we want a person (e.g. college student, preschooler, or staff member) to know or be able to do—they refer to knowledge and sets of skills that can cover a wide range of topics and developmental domains. These provide the basis for the curriculum, elevating activities above a utilitarian rationale, such as "We have to keep the kids busy!" Standards are designed both to promote and facilitate growth in developmental areas and to convey specific content related to the curriculum. Outcomes, in turn, give direction to the activities that are planned and the learning to be done.

● Observation and Curriculum

It would be impossible to determine if your outcomes were appropriate or had been achieved without observation. Outcomes must be describable and measurable. We have to see and recognize progress, and we need to be able to make changes where necessary. Observation is one of the most critical tools for curriculum planning and will be looked at more closely later in this chapter.

● Assessment, Evaluation, and Curriculum

A curriculum has to be closely matched to the needs of the children in the program. For this reason, evaluation is an important element in curriculum development. It is essential to evaluate, on an ongoing basis, whether the topics and activities of the curriculum are appropriate and meaningful for the children. This can be done by observing and documenting the children's engagement in activities and by reviewing not only their comprehension of concepts you deem important but the emergence of concepts you were not planning or looking for. If your assessment leads you to question aspects of the program, then modify or change the objectives and the curriculum as needed.

● Children's Development and Curriculum

You know from our earlier discussion in Chapter 7 of developmentally appropriate practices and individually appropriate, anti-bias, multicultural, inclusive programs that what you include in the curriculum must be directly related to the children in your program. A curriculum that does not accommodate and adjust for the comprehension levels, abilities, needs, and interests of the children is meaningless. To plan an appropriate program requires knowledge about the age group of your class, family characteristics and backgrounds, and individual variations among the children in the class.

The NAEYC's books we discussed earlier—*Developmentally Appropriate Practice in Early Childhood Programs Serving Children from Birth Through Age 8* (Bredekamp, 1987) and *Developmentally Appropriate Practice in Early Childhood Programs* (Bredekamp & Copple, 1997)—are invaluable when you are developing curriculum as are Bredekamp's and Rosegrant's 1992 and 1995 texts on curriculum and assessment. In addition, texts such as Fraser's (2000) *Authentic Childhood: Experiencing Reggio Emilia in the Classroom* and Goffin's (1994) *Curriculum Models and Early Childhood Education* provide more detailed analyses of the philosophical rationale underlying curriculum models and specific program information on different curricula.

Curriculum Content

What, then, is appropriate in an early childhood curriculum? What interests the children in your program? What is relevant to them? What is developmentally relevant?

Perhaps the best way to define what is appropriate in a curriculum is to say that it should be derived from the children's life experiences, based on what is concrete, and tied to their emerging skills (Bredekamp, 1987; Bredekamp & Copple, 1997; Bredekamp & Rosegrant, 1992, 1995). Consider that young children have been part of their physical and social world for only a very short time. They have so much to learn about the people, places, objects, and experiences in their environment.

When you give careful consideration to making the elements of the environment meaningful and understandable to children, you need not seek esoteric and unusual topics. Children's lives offer a wide variety of topics on which to build a curriculum, including learning about themselves, their families, and the larger community in which they live (Essa & Rogers, 1992; Gestwicki, 1999; Jalongo & Isenberg, 2000).

● Children as the Focus of the Curriculum

The most crucial attributes with which young children can be armed to face the future are feelings of self-worth and competence. Children are well equipped for success if they are secure about their identities, feel good about themselves, and meet day-to-day tasks and challenges with a conviction that they can tackle almost anything. The curriculum can foster such attributes by contributing to children's self-understanding and providing repeated reinforcement and affirmation of their capabilities, individual uniqueness, and importance.

Self-understanding comes from learning more about oneself—one's identity, uniqueness, body, feelings, physical and emotional needs, likes and dislikes, skills and abilities, and self-care. Children enjoy learning about themselves, so a focus on children as part of the curriculum can and should take up a significant portion of time. It is important, however, to ensure that planned activities are age-appropriate so they contribute to both self-understanding and positive self-esteem. Infants will enjoy playing patty-cake, for example. Two-year-olds are still absorbed in learning to label body parts; thus, activities that contribute to sharpening this language skill are appropriate. Older preschoolers, on the other hand, are more interested in finer details. For example, they enjoy examining hair follicles under a microscope or observing how the joints of a skeleton move in comparison with their own bodies. Still older children are interested in processes such as digestion and respiration, when presented in a concrete way. But all children are interested in exploring through doing and creating, so this should become the cornerstone of practice.

● The Family as the Focus of the Curriculum

The family is vitally relevant to children and provides another rich basis for curriculum topics. We can help children build an understanding and appreciation of the roles of the family, similarities among families, the uniqueness of each family, different family forms, the tasks of families, and relationships between family members. An examination of the children's family homes, means of transportation, food preferences, celebrations, parental occupations, and patterns of communication also provide appropriate curriculum topics. You might invite family members to come into the classroom and share special knowledge and talents. Alternatively, children as well as teachers might bring photographs of their families to share.

A curriculum focus on the family contributes to children's feelings of self-esteem and pride. They can share information about something central to their lives while, at the same time, expanding their understanding of the family life of the other children. While such learning strengthens children's emerging socialization, it also contributes to cognitive development. Teachers help children make comparisons, note similarities and differences, organize information, and classify various aspects of family structure.

● The Community as the Focus of the Curriculum

The open schools have aptly demonstrated that children's awareness of their world can particularly be expanded through the community. Older toddlers and preschoolers have had experience with numerous aspects of their community, especially shopping, medical, and recreational elements. School-aged children know even more about it. The community and those who live and work in it can certainly extend the walls of your program and offer a wealth of learning opportunities and curriculum material.

From the community and the people who work in it, children can learn, through projects and investigations, about local forms of transportation; food growing, processing, and distribution; health services, including the role of doctors, nurses, dentists, dental hygienists, health clinics, and hospitals; safety provisions such as fire and police departments; communications facilities, including radio and television stations, newspapers, telephone services, and libraries; and local recreational facilities, such as parks and museums. Children can visit an endless variety of appropriate places through field trips. In addition, community professionals can be invited to visit your class and share information and tools of their professions with the children.

You can help children begin to build an understanding of the community as a social system by focusing on the interrelatedness of the people who live and work in your area. For instance, people are both providers and consumers of goods and services; the dentist buys bread that the baker produces, and the baker visits the dentist.

In addition, the larger physical environment of the area in which you live provides a setting worth exploring with the children in your class. Your approach will differ depending on whether your community is nestled in the mountains, by the ocean, or in the midst of rolling prairies. Most young children living in Saskatchewan, for instance, will not have experienced the ocean. It is difficult to convey what the ocean is like to someone who has never seen it, and this is particularly true for children who rely on concrete, firsthand experience. Therefore, it makes little sense to plan a unit on the ocean when it is more than a thousand miles away. Instead, focus on what is nearby and real in the environment, on what children are familiar with and can actually experience. You may choose a unit on farming if it is harvest time in Saskatchewan, whereas you may choose shellfish as a topic in Nova Scotia during lobster season. If you are visiting a barn with horses and pigs, you will not select tender fruit farming as a topic.

In Exhibit 9-1 we provide an example of a curriculum that begins with the child and builds outwards. In the past, the arrows often moved inwards, imposing the outside world onto the child. In this sense, developmental objectives for what the child should know dictated learning. In this model, the arrows move outwards. The curriculum evolves as the child learns. In this sense, learning is leading development. This model is child-centred, open-ended, divergent, and flexible.

EXHIBIT 9-1 *The Self-Concept Curriculum Model*

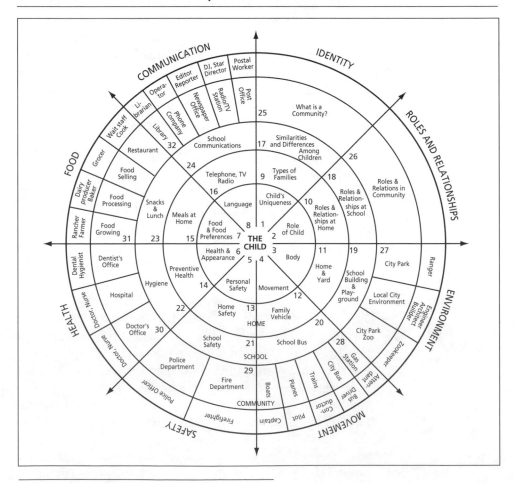

SOURCE: Adapted from Essa & Rogers (1992).

Planning the Curriculum

In some programs, especially those with infants and toddlers, long-term plans and objectives are inappropriate. Short-term objectives, however, are reasonable. With older preschoolers and school-aged children, your plans and objectives may cover a longer time span. Flexible long-term objectives are also appropriate at the primary-school level. Teachers try to plan their programs so that the whole child is challenged every day. Quite frequently, the only effective way of making sure you do this is to develop global plans for each week and more specific ones for each day. This means planning not what is done and said every minute since we wish to be flexible enough to accommodate the unexpected, but rather your approach to the day, some of the things you and the children would like to accomplish, and what you need to accomplish them.

Planning precedes and goes far beyond the actual implementation. Planning means coming up with ideas. Think about the difference between the following two scenarios and how it relates to teaching and learning. An architect shows up and says, "Here is the blueprint I designed. This is the building we will build." In contrast, there is the architectural team who collaborate. The team members, including the client, know they want to build a building, but they first discuss the type of building; investigate possible sites; research; design; and determine needed materials and equipment, staff requirements, length of project, and ways to measure its progress and evaluate their work. Changes are welcome along the way as new information arises and problems are solved. Which scenario would engage you and teach you more?

Daily plans describe each activity planned for that day, objectives for the activities, and the time frame within which they are carried out. In addition, a daily plan can indicate which teacher will be in charge of an activity, in what part of the classroom each activity is to be carried out, and what materials are needed. Plans can take many forms, but they should be complete enough so that any teacher can pick them up and know for any given day what activities are planned and why they are planned.

Each plan may be part of a project or theme and, as such, related to broader goals and objectives. But each plan should also be complete in itself by providing a balanced day for the children. Within each plan, there should be provision for activities that meet needs in all developmental domains. There should be activities that promote creative expression. Communication should be woven throughout activities, so children exercise receptive and expressive language, as well as a variety of nonverbal means of communication. And there should be opportunity for exploring new topics in a variety of ways through multiple activities in a leisurely, unrushed manner.

While beginning teachers find planning time-consuming, they also find that written plans are useful as they help to organize thinking about objectives, materials, and evaluation. Written plans are also helpful when teachers work in teams and when unexpected illness necessitates a supply teacher. Plans for older children who are working on themes keep parents informed about what their child has been experiencing, discussing, and investigating. But for plans, as for schedules, flexibility is critical. You may need to abandon your plan completely, or you may need to revise it as you go along. With older preschoolers and school-aged children, you probably will also want to consider using projects and themes in your program.

● Themes and Projects

Themes and projects, which can be traced back to the open education model and to Dewey in North America, provide a unifying element around which activities are planned (Katz & Chard, 1993; Katz & Chard, 2000). While **theme** and **project** are often used to mean the same thing, themes are generally less specific than projects. You might have a theme titled "Spring," but that does not provide much information on what you will do. A related project would be more specific, for example, "What happens in the garden—or fields or the ranch or fisheries— during spring?" (The term *unit* is often used to mean theme. However, a unit also is used to describe a series of teacher-initiated, prearranged lessons on specific topics. As such, a unit would be more appropriate at the upper limits of the early childhood years, especially if provincial or territorial directives require teachers to cover certain topics.)

Reflective Exercise 9-2

Brainstorm with a group of children for possible topics you could select for a project. Then compare notes as a class. What guidelines will you follow when narrowing down to a single topic?

A project or theme can last any length of time, from a day or two to a month or more. The interest-value and relevance of the topic to the children should dictate how much time is spent on a theme. Furthermore, the length of a project or theme should be flexible enough so you can spend more time if the topic intrigues the children or cut it shorter if the children seem ready to move on.

Planning a project or theme should begin with a careful consideration of your objectives and the children's interests. What is it that you and the children want to learn about the topic? What concepts, skills, and information can this project convey? Most important, are these relevant, age-appropriate, and of interest to the children, and will the children enjoy them? Children have to be the starting point for planning, and they can be involved in the planning. Consult them when you are planning to find out what their ideas are, and incorporate these ideas into your plan. Prior knowledge is critical. Teachers so often create elaborate lessons and teach this new knowledge without first exploring what the children already know. Don't you find it tedious to be taught something you already know? If the group is planning a project called "How to Make Bread," you might hope to cover the following concepts:

- Bread is baked at the bakery.

- The baker is the person who bakes bread.

- Many loaves of bread are baked at the bakery (mass production).

- Bread is made up of many ingredients.

- Bread is taken by trucks to grocery stores, where it is sold to people such as those in the children's families.

- Different bakeries make different types of bread (e.g., Rajeev's baker makes chapatis and puris, Rana's baker makes pita bread, Maria's baker makes tortillas, Albino's baker makes crusty cornbread, and Freddie's mother makes lavash).

A project usually begins with an introduction in which the theme is initially presented or arises out of the children's interests, and often this introduction is a field trip or investigation of prior knowledge and experiences. Early on in a project, you will want to focus on the children's familiarity with the subject or closely related areas, and adjust your plans to fit with their existing knowledge. Thus, if you plan a theme on the topic "bread," you can discuss types of bread with which the children are familiar, the food group to which bread belongs (if you have already spent time discussing nutrition and the four basic food groups), the process of baking (for those children who have helped their parents make bread), and the different ways in which bread is used in meals.

New ideas and activities can be introduced logically and sequentially. New material should always be presented first in a concrete manner. While field trips are frequent starting points, concrete experiences also can be brought into the classroom through objects or guests. In the case of the bread unit, you may want to plan a field trip to the local bakery at the beginning of the unit so the children can see how bread is made. On the other hand, some in-class experiences with bread baking can be a wonderful preparation for a trip to the bakery. Alternatively, Rajeev's and/or Maria's mother and father may agree to help the children make chapatis and tortillas. In either case, *it cannot be emphasized enough that any new concept should begin with the concrete, with firsthand experience.*

Courtesy of Yes I Can! Nursery School.

Once children have had a chance to observe and learn through firsthand experience, they can begin to assimilate this information through subsequent activities. After the field trip, children should have opportunities to represent factually what they observed by talking about and dictating accounts of the visit to the bakery, drawing pictures of what they saw on the field trip, and otherwise recalling and replicating their visit. This factual recounting allows children to fix the experience in their minds.

Children can begin to use new information in creative ways once it has been integrated into their existing memory and experiential store. They can play with the information through such activities as art, dramatic play, puppets, or blocks. This element of the project offers a wide variety of possibilities that children can approach in their unique ways.

Finally, a project is ended through a summarizing component. Younger children may enact baking in the bakery they have made in the home or dramatic play centre. Older children may have individual and group projects they would like to share with others. Visitors also may be invited to see the children's creations—and to taste them. Usually, the teacher also evaluates the children's responses to the project and makes notes about changes for future years. Several Web sites highlight Sylvia Chard's approach to projects, while the High/Scope site discusses curriculum, for those who would like to learn more on this topic.

● Activities

The play in which children are involved is as important as any planning for from this emerges new ideas, new insights, and new questions upon which more planning can be based. Children at play are constructing new knowledge, for which we could not possibly plan, as they bring their unique experiences and dispositions to the situation.

It is important to be aware of the objectives of a given activity as well as to think through how the activity will be carried out so that the children will gain the intended knowledge and skills. However, there is a danger in creating lesson plans that focus on very specific skills: you tend to watch only for those skills to determine whether they were achieved. With this narrow focus, it is easy to overlook other important learning that is occurring.

● Environment

An environment that is designed to promote play and learning opportunities facilitates children's propensity to explore and investigate. This, in turn, piques their curiosity and desire to find out more, which generates questions. It is from these queries that teachers and children discover interests and generate ideas for projects. In A Closer Look, we examine two environments. We enter a playground that, through design, provides opportunities for play, creativity, spontaneity, planned events, and ongoing projects, and acts as a springboard for endless new activities. Some of these activities are child-initiated, some teacher-initiated, but all activities are agreeable to both children and staff on the basis of common interests and mutual respect. Next we observe a classroom on the basis of a curriculum that supports emergent literacy. The environment provides materials that immerse the child in literacy, and the teacher has a set of general goals and objectives for the children. However, rather than present structured lessons, the teacher is guided by principles that she can apply in either an emergent or a planned way.

● Team Planning

Planning for an individual child or class without regard for the system to which they belong is fruitless. The school as a whole must buy into the philosophy, goals, and curriculum. Teachers must work as an interconnected, interrelated system so that continuity is evident through the program. The entire program must reflect the attitude of respect toward all persons and uphold the value and worth of children, families, and teachers.

Working as a group ensures that all members are familiar with, accountable to, and responsible for objectives and activities because they took part in their development. It can also lead to greater commitment to the program because everyone's ideas were incorporated. Personal investment in the curriculum can contribute to the overall cohesiveness of the program. In A Canadian Professional Speaks Out, Carolyn Simpson relates how team planning, program planning, program philosophy, children's development, and accountability (our next topic) merge to create a high-quality inclusive program.

A Closer Look

ENVIRONMENTS THAT SUPPORT CURRICULUM

1. A Playground for Learning

St. Elizabeth's Child Care Centre, in a metropolitan community in Nova Scotia, serves a large population of children from low-income families. Several years ago, one of the staff members was particularly interested in transforming the original blacktop playground—with its traditional swings, slides, and jungle gyms—into a more exciting and flexible outdoor area that would enhance and extend learning. She devised a plan that, through extensive fundraising and the cooperative efforts of staff, parents, and the community, eventually became a reality.

This new outdoor area now includes multiple, well-defined learning centres. Included in this carefully and esthetically landscaped space are an amphitheatre for storytelling and dramatic play; a fenced animal care area for rabbits; a covered art area; a "freeway" network of paths for riding toys; an extensive sand area; a woodworking centre; a "meditation garden" or quiet area surrounding a shady willow tree; a boat-shaped centre with props and equipment for housekeeping dramatic play and a car engine with which children can tinker; a five-opening drainage pipe tunnel; and many places that can be used to climb, swing, and build. Storage spaces are provided wherever materials and props are needed.

Building materials throughout the area were selected and arranged to provide various textures, multiple sizes, and esthetic appeal. Equipment was selected to encourage children to observe and classify, make comparisons, and note similarities and differences. Movable equipment, such as planks and tires, was added to promote problem-solving skills. In addition, this outdoor play area is a delight to the senses, with its dwarf-tree fruit orchard, vegetable garden, strawberry patch, raised herb garden for easy sniffing, and flower beds, all of which children and teachers help tend. This playground has a wide range of activities to engage children, activities that promote all areas of development. Through the imaginative planning of one teacher and the efforts of the many people who helped make it a reality, this playground has enriched the play of many young children (Essa, 1981).

Not all early childhood programs have the luxury of such an exciting playground, because each school is unique in its approach as well as limited by space, weather, funding, and other resources. All playgrounds have the potential to be improved, however, through added movable props, the enhancement of natural features, and the careful arrangement of learning centres.

2. A Classroom for Emergent Literacy

Mary was hired to teach a class of fifteen 5-year-olds at a school in which most of the children came from low-income families. Her first task was to get rid of the desks, both the small ones and the one intended for the teacher, and to set up a developmentally appropriate environment with learning centres. She particularly focused on providing a whole-language environment. She carefully selected materials and arranged the room to reinforce language in as many ways as possible, also using day-to-day spontaneous conversations and planned activities.

As she found on the first day, many of the children came to school having had few or no experiences with art materials. From that very first day, she encouraged each child to draw many pictures on any topic. "I remember one little boy who drew a line and said, 'It's a dog,'" Mary recalled. She wrote the word "dog" next to his line and encouraged him to make other pictures. "His picture was typical of this group's artwork in September," she said. In addition to the daily art, Mary posted labels around the room, talked about the labels, sounded them out, read many stories, had the children discuss and act out the stories, talked and encouraged the children to talk all the time, included letters and letter lotto games to allow the children to manipulate them, and generally enriched their environment with lots of written and oral language.

Mary also enlisted the help and support of the parents, who became very interested in what their children's teacher was doing. She talked with parents every day, showed them what the children were doing, and explained the importance of the children's work. She sent notes home and made phone calls to those parents she did not see. In addition, she put together a "writing suitcase," an old briefcase with a variety of writing and reading materials that the children took turns taking home.

By January, some of the children were drawing very detailed pictures and taking an interest in the letters of their names. One day, Lishana, after spending considerable time working on a complex picture that featured a lot of red, suddenly jumped up screaming, "I did it! I did it!" Mary went to Lishana to see what the excitement was about. She found, to her delight, the phrase "I like red" written at the top of the picture. "Obviously she had been thinking about what letters mean, and from that time on, she put letters into words. It clicked for her," explained Mary.

By the end of the school year, all fifteen children were writing often long and complex stories on their own. They continued to use invented spelling, to read many of the words in their environment and in books, and to use a lot of verbal language. According to Mary, "Given the right environment, these children could do a lot. They just blossomed!"

Accountability

As with anything we do, we need to provide a sound rationale for why we do things, a plan for getting them done, and evidence that we did them. We must also have some way of measuring our success and our satisfaction. In essence, we must be held accountable for our actions. Accountability means setting goals on the basis of observation and information, documenting progress and evidence, and evaluating the results so that improvements and achievements can be addressed.

Working with young children and planning a program for them requires a sense of direction and purpose. In order to plan, we need to assess situations. Assessment involves such components as observation, documentation, and collaboration. These can be expressed as a set of standards and learning outcomes that include broad goals and more specific objectives. Goals and objectives provide the roadmap for the early childhood program journey. But not just any map will provide the specific information needed for your specific program. Goals and objectives should reflect the individual character and uniqueness of your class, school, and program. One way of identifying that individuality is through systematic evaluation.

In order to determine if you accomplished what you set out to do, to learn what new knowledge and skills emerged or how existing knowledge and skills were applied, you must evaluate the process and the outcomes. Evaluation holds you accountable to your plan and actions and helps you to make adjustments. It also helps gather the evidence and support you need to keep your program credible. This process occurs at all levels of the system. We assess and evaluate individual children, our curriculum, our program, our environment, the model of service delivery, and our practices. Staff is evaluated on an ongoing basis as well, and this includes reciprocal and self-evaluation. The information we glean from this process assists us in making decisions, recommendations, and modifications with regard to the children, family programs, the team, and ourselves. In this section, we look at accountability and its constituents, including standards and learning outcomes, observation and documentation, and assessment and the process of evaluation.

● Standards and Learning Outcomes

Standards.   Standards provide a general overview of what you and the team expect the children, yourself, the family, the team, and the centre to gain from the program. They are long-term (i.e., for the year) and are commonly referred to as "aims" or goals. Goals should be based on a sound understanding of process and needs, reflecting appropriate expectations and practices. Goals are often based on facilitating and encouraging healthy development in the social, emotional, cognitive, creative, language, behavioural, and physical domains; the acquisition of skills; and the construction of new knowledge in and about these domains. Hence, as a teacher and, therefore, an employee, you would require a written plan about your career goals. The program must have goals which are conveyed to parents. The families clearly have goals they expect of the centre. Of course, the teachers, centre, and families have goals for the children. The children, too, have goals. The common thread that ties these goals together is communication and collaboration. Goals reflect the theoretical rationale on which the program is based.

Another way of identifying goals, related to a developmental approach, focuses on important processes that we all begin to acquire in the early years. Frazier (1980) suggested that these might include:

- *Communicating*—expressing, taking in, responding

- *Relating* to others

- *Finding out*—inquiring, investigating

- *Discovering*

- *Making*—constructing, creating, inventing

- *Choosing*—seeking, preferring, holding on to

- *Controlling*—directing, leading, managing

- *Persisting*—staying with, enduring

Keep in mind that there is no one way of wording goals and objectives.

Learning Outcomes.   A **learning outcome** is a more specific interpretation of a general goal, and it provides a more practical and direct tool for planning. Goals can be identified at the beginning of the program year to provide direction; learning outcomes are useful for short-term planning (i.e., lesson and daily planning) and should be an integral part of it. Learning outcomes have often been referred to as objectives. However, recent thinking has differentiated objectives and outcomes; objectives tend to refer to what the child should

INCLUSION IN EARLY CHILDHOOD EDUCATION

Carolyn Simpson, Holland College, Prince Edward Island

Making the decision to utilize an early childhood program is often difficult for parents, and especially so for parents with children who have special needs. Matching the service to family needs can prove especially challenging. These parents must also match the quality and philosophy of services with other resources that may be required to meet their children's needs.

In Prince Edward Island, once the parent and ECE supervisor agree that his service will best meet the needs of the family, the supervisor can apply for funding under the Ministry of Health and Community Services (formerly the Department of Health and Social Services) for a Special Needs Grant. Prior to 1988, funding for specialized programming was available to families through either the Child Care Subsidy Program or Family Support Program; eligibility was determined by an income test. With the implementation of the Special Needs Grant in 1988, funding is now granted to licensed centres directly. The grant allows for a higher child-staff ratio and for the purchase of additional resources (i.e., materials, equipment, or environmental modifications) as required, thus enabling the centre to be in a better position to deliver a high-quality inclusive program.

The grant is individualized, and approval is based on an assessment of the child's needs, the appropriateness of proposed program activities and curriculum, the availability of funds, and the agreement of the centre to administer any funds according to the policies of the Special Needs Grant.

Another strength of the program is its accountability. Centres are required to submit quarterly progress reports and salary reports, and to hold annual case conferences, the first being six months into the program, with the transdisciplinary team. As well, should this team decide that a child of school age would benefit from one year longer in the ECE environment, the Department of Education and Health and Social Services [now the Ministry of Health and Community Services] have worked together to provide services for this child.

As a result of the Special Needs Grant, Island children and their families are receiving early education and intervention that may not otherwise have been possible.

do, whereas outcomes reflect what the child should learn. We will use the terms interchangeably while the field sorts out the transition. Objectives will differ depending on whether they are developed for a group as a whole or for an individual. The inherent danger with objectives is that they can be limiting. They are often very teacher-determined and can limit the teacher to observing only that which she or he has deemed important. This is one reason why team input is so vital.

Objectives must include not only what you want to teach the children or what you want to learn about them but the conviction that you want to learn about them. They help you evaluate what you do with the children, what the children know and have learned, and how they approached learning. This evaluation helps you to determine the children's learning styles and problem-solving skills over and above the actual facts they have accumulated. Often what you intend children to get out of a lesson and what they actually get out of it are quite different. You must be able to tie together what you planned, what you did, and what you saw. Objectives encompass several areas to help you plan for, observe, assess, and evaluate an activity, a skill, knowledge, or performance.

Developmental Objectives.   **Developmental objectives** help you focus on the developmental domains by directing your attention to development and the wholeness of your activity. Is it open-ended enough to enlist all the domains in its implementation?

Content Objectives.   Content objectives are also identified for the content or subject matter of the curriculum (Bredekamp & Rosegrant, 1995; Essa & Rogers, 1992; Lawton, 1988; Peters, Neisworth, & Yawkey, 1985). A **content objective** relates to the information that an individual activity conveys. Appropriate topics can be drawn from meaningful aspects of the children's environment to expand their understanding of the world. They also help you focus on the wholeness of your activities. A content objective also gives direction to the teacher carrying out an activity (Essa & Rogers, 1992). Assume the lesson plan indicates that you will help the children make fruit salad. What direction does this activity description give you? What will you discuss with the children? Where is your focus? Do you talk about the colour of the fruit, its texture, and its sweetness? Do you help children label the individual fruits? Do you relate the fruit salad to what might be served in a restaurant? What about at home? Do you discuss the fact that chefs, or mothers and fathers, make fruit salad? Do you focus on safety and health? Or should you incorporate measurement and math concepts? The objectives will determine the focus and purpose of the activity and will help guide your teaching style and handling of the activity.

Behavioural Objectives.   Although developmental and content objectives usually apply to planning for the total group, a **behavioural objective** is generally used in planning for an individual. Behavioural objectives are very specific and are based on observable and measurable actions or skills. Behavioural objectives can help you to document program and teacher effectiveness as well as individual progress. Words such as "label," "name," "identify," "match," "sort," "classify," or "order from largest to smallest" relate to a child's actions which you can observe. On the other hand, words such as "think," "enjoy," "consider," "appreciate," or "be aware of" describe an internalized process. If, for instance, an objective stated that Simon would *understand* the colour red, you would have no way to measure this because you cannot see Simon understanding the concept of redness (Deiner, 1983).

Behavioural objectives can be useful, particularly in planning for an individual child in an area needing attention. Such objectives have also been criticized, however. Because they specify how a child will behave, they eliminate spontaneity, creativity, and playfulness; by spelling out and directing the content of activities, they ignore a child's internal motivation to master a topic or skill; they demand a great deal of work from the teacher because each identified behaviour will require developing a list of objectives; they also encourage teachers to "teach the objective" rather than to observe for it in context; and, because they are broken into such small components, it is sometimes difficult to keep in touch with the larger goals for the child (Lawton, 1988). However, it is possible to write objectives that are open-ended yet measurable.

Personal Objectives.   Personal objectives occur when an individual determines what learning will occur and why. For example, an individual may have a list of skills and knowledge that she or he views as essential for personal growth, progress, success, and satisfaction.

● Observation and Documentation

It would be impossible to set standards and learning outcomes without observation and documentation to provide evidence and rationale for your plans. One of the most effective informal methods of assessment, program planning, and evaluation is focused observation. Early childhood teachers use observation as a primary method of gaining insight into the various facets of children's development at different times and in different contexts (Wortham, 1990). As well, observation is integral to making program and curriculum changes. Environment and approach have strong impacts on behaviour. In Chapter 7, we noted that watching children's play like Rubin and his colleagues have done can be very rewarding. Often, however, we tend to look for something specific. If we get in the habit of watching with an open mind, we will learn a great deal about the children and gain many insights. As well, we remind you to watch children watching and you'll note they are continually processing, deciding, analyzing, and absorbing. Their facial expressions, body language, language, and actions reveal much about their overall development.

Observation is valuable as a team tool in improving team function and sharing teaching strategies. Observation can provide us with detailed information about behaviour, help us understand it, and provide the basis for predicting behaviour (Borich, 1999; Jalongo & Isenberg, 2000; Richarz, 1980). One of the most appealing features of observation is that it is unobtrusive and natural. It does not interfere with the child's ongoing activity and behaviour, in contrast with more formal tests that require the child to perform specified tasks in an isolated setting.

● Confidentiality and Objectivity

Observation, assessment, and evaluation are meant to be a positive, supportive tool to improve the lives of those it measures. Information is shared verbally or written, only with permission of all parties and only as a tool that will positively enhance the lives of the participants. Being objective supports fairness and confidentiality protects the rights and privacy and therefore the integrity and dignity of all.

● Documentation

Obviously observation and assessment imply documentation since you must record what you see and hear. Writing is the most common method of recording. However, videotapes, audiotapes, photographs, interviews, and children's work all lend insight to observations. Formal and informal assessment methods provide concrete information primarily about children's overall development.

● Parental Involvement

Parental consent is mandatory as is their input. Their input must be actively sought and supported from the very beginning. Parents should not be simply the recipients of information after the process is concluded. Their observations, interpretations, experience, and recommendations are integral to the true picture of the child or situation.

● Types of Observations

Anecdotal Record.   Observation can take a variety of forms. One of the most often used is the **anecdotal record**, a brief description or "word picture" of an event or behaviour (Cartwright & Cartwright, 1974). A collection of well-written and accurate anecdotes can provide a very descriptive characterization of a child. Anecdotal records come only from direct observation, are written down promptly and accurately, describe the context of the behaviour, are factual rather than interpretive, and can focus either on a typical or an unusual aspect of the child's behaviour (Wortham, 1990).

Running Record.   A **running record** is a more detailed account of a child's behaviour over a period of time (Wortham, 1990). Whereas the anecdote focuses on a single event, the running record keeps track of everything that happens in a specified time period, whether it is a half-hour or several months. Such a record can be very useful when you are trying to pinpoint the source of a problem. It was most helpful in getting a handle on the disruptions in one class, where 3-year-old Erin seemed to be always at the centre of aggressive outbursts. A careful running record, kept over a period of three days, helped the teachers see that Erin was responding to rather subtle taunts from two other children.

ABC Analysis.   One helpful device in keeping a running record is the **ABC analysis**, in which three columns identify the antecedent (what occurred just prior to the episode), the behaviour, and the consequence of incidents (Bijou,

Peterson, & Ault, 1968). This helps you focus not only on the child's behaviour but also on what precipitates and what follows it.

Time Sampling.   **Time sampling** provides a way of measuring the frequency of a behaviour over a period of time (Wortham, 1990). Time sampling is a quantitative method of observation in that you count how often a behaviour occurs at uniform time intervals (Genishi, 1982). You may, for instance, want to know just how often the adults in the classroom attend to Yanik because you suspect he is often overlooked and neglected. Since you don't have time to observe Yanik all day long, you might determine that every half-hour you will spend five minutes watching Yanik, noting every time a teacher attends to or interacts with him. Over a period of a week, you should have a representative sampling of the attention Yanik receives from adults. You might also decide, for purposes of comparison, to observe Brittany at the same time because Brittany appears to get frequent adult attention.

Event Sampling.   When you want to observe a less frequent behaviour, **event sampling** can be used (Genishi, 1982; Wortham, 1990). In this case, you wait until a given behaviour occurs and then write a descriptive record of the event. Event sampling can be useful if you have noted that Kareem has periodic crying spells, and you have trouble pinpointing the cause. Thus, each time Kareem engages in this behaviour, one of the teachers stands back and records carefully what is happening. The ABC analysis can be very useful in recording such an event because you are trying to get a sense of its causes and consequences (Wortham, 1990).

● Characteristics of Good Observations

One of the requirements of good observation is that it be objective. Your role as observer is to be as impartial as possible, to stand back and record what you see rather than what you think the child is feeling or experiencing. Compare the two records in Exhibit 9-2. What distinguishes the two? The first observation tells you how the observer is interpreting the incident; the second describes what is happening. Can the first observer really know that Letitia does not like Erica? Can she be certain that the teacher is angry and that Letitia made a conscious decision to pick on Erica?

Another characteristic of good observation is that it is *adequately descriptive*. Cohen and Stern (1978) provide some helpful suggestions to beginning observers in the use of descriptive vocabulary. The verb "run," for instance, has many synonyms that can evoke a clearer image of what is being described. Examples include "stampede," "whirl," "dart," "gallop," "speed," "shoot across," "bolt," "fly," "hippity-hop," or "dash." Adding descriptive adverbs, adjectives, and phrases will also enliven an anecdote. Although synonyms can add authenticity and life to your observational anecdote, be sure to use the dictionary to ensure that the word means what you intend. What descriptive words in the second example of Exhibit 9-2 make the incident come alive?

EXHIBIT 9-2 *Observations*

Observation 1

Letitia comes into the classroom and immediately decides to pick on Erica, whom she doesn't like. She approaches Erica and, in her usual, aggressive way, grabs the doll with which Erica is playing. Letitia doesn't really want the doll; she just wants what Erica has. When the teacher sees what has happened, she gets upset with Letitia and makes her give the doll back to Erica. Because of this, Letitia gets really angry and has one of her nasty tantrums, which upsets everyone in the class.

Observation 2

Letitia marches into the classroom. She looks around for a few seconds then ambles to the dramatic play area, where Erica is putting a doll into the cradle. Letitia stops two feet in front of the cradle, standing with her legs apart and hands on hips. She watches Erica put a blanket on the doll then steps right up to it, grabs the doll by an arm, and pulls it roughly out of the cradle. She runs with the doll into the block area and turns around to look back at Erica. As Letitia is running off, Erica yells, "No! I was playing with the doll." Erica looks at Mrs. Wendell, whose eyes move toward the dramatic play area. Erica's shoulders drop and she says in a softer whimper, "Letitia took the doll I was playing with," then starts to cry. As Mrs. Wendell walks toward Letitia, Letitia drops the doll and darts to the art area. Mrs. Wendell catches up with Letitia, and urges her back to the block area by pointing and stating matter-of-factly, "Go back to the block centre." She picks up the doll. "Letitia, we need to give this doll back to Erica. She was playing with it." Letitia, her lips pressed together over clenched jaws, pulls away from Mrs. Wendell and throws herself on the floor, kicking her feet and screaming.

Good observations also describe **nonverbal cues**, some of the nuances of body language as well as voice inflection which can give deeper meaning to an anecdote. Children, like adults, share subtle movements of face and body and shadings of voice that describe common feelings and reactions. Izard (1982), for instance, used common facial nuances in infants and children to measure emotion. Body language is not easy to read, requiring experience and practice to interpret accurately. In Exhibit 9-2 do you see some descriptions of such nonverbal signs?

● Interpreting Observations

As we have indicated, observational information must be gathered objectively, without inserting personal bias. But there comes a point, once you have gathered a collection of anecdotes, when you can look for patterns (Beaty; 1990; Borich, 1999; Cohen & Stern, 1978). Interpretations, however, should always be kept clearly separate from observations (Beaty; 1990; Borich, 1999; Cartwright & Cartwright, 1974). In reviewing observations that span a period of time, you

should be able to find clues to children's unique ways of behaving and responding. When a set of observations shows repeatedly that a child reacts aggressively to conflict or becomes pleasurably involved in messy media or talks to adults far more than to other children, you can see a characteristic pattern for that child.

Interpretation should be undertaken cautiously and consensus reached through team effort. Human behaviour is complex, not easily pigeon-holed, and there is the danger of overzealous interpretation when a pattern is more in the mind of the observer than representative of the child.

● Some Observational Techniques

Finding time to observe can be challenging for the busy teacher. Some authors (e.g., Beaty; 1990; Borich, 1999; Cartwright & Cartwright, 1974; Hymes, 1981) have recommended setting specific time frames and a fixed number of anecdotes per day can be helpful for the observing teacher. Practical strategies like always carrying a pencil and pad in your pocket and setting ten minutes aside at the end of the day for writing your records also help. Keeping anecdotal and event sampling records, as examples, can also pinpoint children who are being overlooked when, over a period of time, you find very few or no records on some youngsters (Hymes, 1981). Beaty (1990) offered a comprehensive approach in her text *Observing the Development of the Young Child.*

Early childhood student-teachers and, in some programs, teachers, may be asked specifically to record observations for a period of time. If you are assigned a role as an outside observer rather than as a teacher, try to be as unobtrusive as possible so that children's behaviour is minimally affected by your presence. If children come to you to ask what you are doing, as they invariably will, give a simple answer that does not invite further conversation (e.g., "I am writing").

Assessment

● Instruments

Checklists for Children. A **checklist** itemizes behaviours, skills, concepts, or attributes and contains a space for noting their presence or absence at a point in time or over a period of time.

Rating Scales for Children. **Rating scales** provide more qualitative information than checklists because they indicate to what extent the child engages in or has mastered a behaviour. For example, as a student, you are judged on a rating scale that usually takes the form of letter grades ranging from A (excellent) to F (unsatisfactory).

The dimensions of ratings applied to children will depend on what you want to measure. You may, for instance, want to determine the frequency of each child's participation in various types of activities. In that case, you might graph the children on a continuum that goes from "daily" to "never" (Beaty; 1990; Borich, 1999; Cartwright & Cartwright, 1974; Wortham, 1990). Rating scales can also be used to show where a child is in the process of mastering certain tasks by using such words as "emerging," "developing," and "developed."

Standardized Tests.   Whereas observations and teacher-devised instruments are informal methods of gathering information about children, **standardized tests** are considered formal assessments. Such instruments are developed by professionals and are distributed commercially. Standardized tests are developed, tested, and refined so that they have **validity** and **reliability**. "Validity" means that tests measure what they purport to measure. "Reliability" means that tests are stable and consistent; you know that when a child's score changes, it is because the child has changed, not the test (NAEYC, 1988). When standardized tests are administered, specific standards for testing conditions are required to ensure uniformity. Over the past few years, the use of standardized tests to evaluate caregiving environments and young children's development has increased. While a comprehensive overview of standardized tests may be offered in advanced courses you will take, we will just briefly examine some general test categories and consider several sample instruments.

Environmental Checklists and Rating Scales.   Several standardized rating scales and checklists have been developed and published that help in the evaluation of early childhood programs. The **Early Childhood Environment Rating Scale** (Harms & Clifford, 1998), initially developed by Harms and Clifford in 1980, is perhaps the best known. The **Family Day Care Home Rating Scale** (Harms, Clifford, & Padan-Belkin, 1983) and the **Infant/Toddler Environment Rating Scale** (Harms, Cryer, & Clifford, 1990) are useful for evaluating family child care and infant programs respectively.

These **environmental checklists** are rating scales that can help you both when you are evaluating a program and when you are comparing several programs. The results can help you pinpoint areas of the program that need improvement. The results also are useful if you are doing research related to early childhood education. Goelman and Pence (1990), for example, used the Early Childhood Environment Rating Scale and the Family Day Care Home Rating Scale in the Victoria and Vancouver studies.

Goelman and Pence also used Caldwell and Bradley's (1979) **Home Observation for Measurement of the Environment (HOME)** in the Vancouver study. HOME is used to assess the quality of stimulation in the home environment, and this makes it useful for home-based child care. A number of studies (e.g.,

Bradley & Caldwell, 1984; Gottfried, 1984) have demonstrated that HOME scores are highly correlated with child development. A parent or caregiver who scores highly on HOME:

1. Is verbally and emotionally responsive.

2. Does not restrict the child's activity and does not punish the child.

3. Provides age-appropriate play materials.

4. Arranges the environment so it is safe and organized.

5. Is involved with the child and usually is within sight.

6. Provides variety in the available stimulation. In addition to reading to the child several times a week, the parent or caregiver takes the child on outings and arranges for the child to eat meals with the family at least once a day.

Of course, these behaviours also can be found in good teachers in centre-based programs.

Screening Tests.   **Screening tests** provide a quick method of identifying children who may be at risk for a specified condition, for instance developmental delay. Screening is not an end in itself but is meant to be followed by more thorough **diagnostic testing** if screening shows a possible problem. Because most screening tests are quick and easy to administer, they can be used by a wide variety of people who may have no specialized training.

A wide variety of tests are available. One that is widely used is the **Denver Developmental Screening Test (DDST)** (Frankenburg, Dodds, Fandal, Kajuk, & Cohr, 1975), which is used with infants and children up to age 6. This test, often used by medical as well as early childhood professionals, examines the child's functioning in self-help, social, language, fine motor, and gross motor areas. The child's test scores are compared with **norm-referenced** scores. By testing a large number of children at each age, the test developers were able to determine what the average child of each age could do—or what the norm was for each age. For each item on the test, you can determine if the child is functioning around the norm or average level, or above or below average. If a child appears to be well below or above average, more testing might be recommended.

Reflective Exercise 9-3

Discuss possible disadvantages of screening tests.

Developmental Tests. Frequently a screening test will indicate the necessity for more complete assessment and is then followed by a more thorough and time-intensive **developmental test**. Such tests usually measure the child's functioning in most or all areas of development. Developmental assessments are usually **criterion-referenced** rather than norm-referenced. Thus, children are measured against the test developer's educated understanding of what children, at various ages, can be expected to achieve.

One older but still widely used developmental test is the **Brigance Diagnostic Inventory of Early Development** (Brigance, 1978). With some training, early childhood teachers can use this test. It contains subtests for fine motor, gross motor, language, cognitive, and self-help areas for children from birth to age 7.

Intelligence or IQ Tests. One of the oldest types of standardized assessments is the intelligence test. Such tests have stirred considerable controversy, much of it loaded with emotion, because they raise the question of whether intelligence is a fixed biological trait or whether it is malleable and can be raised through an enriched environment (Bowd et al., 1998). Some controversial features of standardized tests are definite cultural bias and their tendency to favour white, middle-class children and their experiences (Bowd et al., 1998).

Reflective Exercise 9-4

Discuss your views on whether intelligence is malleable. How does this relate to the views of children we discussed in Chapter 2?

The **Wechsler Preschool and Primary Scale of Intelligence—Revised (WPPSI-R)** (Wechsler, 1989) is a commonly used IQ test for 3-to-7-year-old children. The **Wechsler Intelligence Scale for Children—III (WISC-III)** (Wechsler, 1991) is also available for use with children from 6 to 16 years of age. Both Wechsler tests were revised sometime ago, and one might question the currency of the norms.

Readiness Tests. The specific purpose of readiness tests—to determine whether a child is prepared to enter a program such as kindergarten or first grade—differentiates them from other types of assessments. Such tests should not be used to predict school success, because they merely measure a child's level of achievement of specified academic tasks at the time of testing (Meisels, 1986; Meisels, Liaw, Dorfman, & Nelson, 1995). One study, in fact, found that the **predictive validity** of one widely used readiness test, when compared with first-grade teacher judgment and report cards, was very modest, raising questions about the usefulness of the test and about the potential harm to the many children misidentified as not ready for school (Graue & Shepard, 1989). Increasingly, early childhood educators have questioned why school is not ready for children! The NAEYC has developed a position on this topic as well that you can access through their excellent Web site.

Success on readiness tests, as you might suspect, depends on the child's having been exposed to the concepts, not on innate ability. Unfortunately, readiness tests do not distinguish between the child who has had limited exposure to the concepts and the child who has actual learning difficulties. The use of these tests has driven many prekindergarten programs to incorporate activities designed to prepare children for readiness testing, often at the expense of other appropriate activities, particularly exploratory, hands-on experiences (Schickedanz, Hansen, & Forsyth, 1990). Moreover, virtually all of the available readiness tests have technical problems in the areas of reliability and predictive validity (Salvia & Ysseldyke, 1991). Unless the appropriate research is conducted to determine the ability of these tests to predict school achievement, they should not be used to make major educational decisions.

● Concerns About Using Assessment Instruments

All of these informal and formal evaluation instruments can give us useful insights into the environments we provide and the children in our care. Although using a variety of methods to better understand children has always been an important part of early childhood education, there is a growing concern about potential misuses, particularly of standardized evaluations.

The 1980s brought an increased emphasis on testing, particularly as a way of proving that educational goals are being met (Wortham, 1990). The back-to-basics movement has become a powerful lobby group, and it continues to ask for more frequent standardized testing, especially for school-aged children. In the 1990s, the provincial and territorial ministers of education met on a regular basis to develop a national testing program. Pilot testing of selected grades across the country began in the 1993–94 school year, and before the new millennium, many jurisdictions were administering standardized tests to all school-aged children.

One major concern involves the misuse of readiness tests. With increasing frequency, such tests are being used to decide children's placement. For instance, a test is used to decide which children will be allowed to move on to first grade, which ones will be placed in a transitional class, and which ones will be retained in kindergarten (Wortham, 1990). Thus, children are often labelled as failures when, in fact, they are expected to conform to inappropriate expectations (NAEYC, 1988). How devastating such practices are on children's self-concepts! Read the eloquent discussion of these concerns in NAEYC's "Position statement on standardized testing of young children 3 through 8 years of age," which was released in *Young Children* in 1988.

Tests are being used by prestigious (and expensive) private schools, not just in large cities such as New York but also in smaller cities in Canada, to determine which children will be admitted. A corollary to this testing trend is that many early childhood programs have adopted curricula whose main aim is to prepare children for readiness tests (Bredekamp & Shepard, 1989). Thus, preschool and kindergarten programs promote developmentally inappropriate methods to meet such goals, intensifying the problem of "failures" and children who are "unready" (NAEYC, 1988). In fact, the NAEYC became so concerned about this that it had Constance Kamii, an eminent early childhood educator, edit a book on the topic. *Achievement Testing in the Early Grades: The Games Grown-Ups Play* (Kamii, 1990) is a book you will want to consult if testing becomes a problem in your community.

It has long been acknowledged that standardized tests have a variety of limitations. For instance, a test cannot ask every possible question to evaluate what a child knows on a topic. Another criticism of standardized tests is that they are culture-biased. However, test designers have found it impossible to devise tests that are completely culture-free (Wortham, 1990). In addition, it is very difficult to establish reliable and valid instruments for young children, given the rapid changes that occur in development as well as the normal individual variations among children (NAEYC, 1988). This also calls into question the use of norm groups against which individuals are rated.

In addition to the potential problems with tests, there are difficulties in evaluating young children that can affect the accuracy of test results. These might include the child's attention and interest, the familiarity (or unfamiliarity) with the surroundings, the trust the child has in the adult tester (or whether the child has even seen this person before), the time of day, the fact that the child slept poorly the night before, or the fact that the mother forgot to kiss the child goodbye. In too many instances, tests are given to young children in large groups, a practice that further decreases reliability (NAEYC, 1988).

In a number of Canadian settings, there is also concern that tests are not always administered and interpreted by individuals with the qualifications to do so. Even some major school boards (but by no means all) in some Canadian jurisdictions rely upon unqualified individuals to complete the testing process, much to the chagrin of Canadian psychologists. An unqualified tester is likely to obtain misleading, unreliable results which might still be used in educational decisions regarding a young child. Parents are frequently upset if testing is recommended and tend to be overwhelmed by the testing process. They often do not know—or feel they know—what cautions and questions are appropriate and are reluctant to seek a second opinion, which can be invaluable.

If so many problems are inherent in standardized tests, what is the answer to the dilemma of their increasing use with young children? NAEYC (1988) recommends that the relevance of tests be carefully evaluated by administrators: Will results from the test contribute to improving the program for the children? Will the children benefit from the test? If the benefits are meager in relation to the cost (expense and time), perhaps the test should not be used. Furthermore, it is recommended that:

- Tests be carefully reviewed for reliability and validity

- Tests match the program's philosophy and goals

- Only knowledgeable and qualified persons administer and interpret results

- Testers be sensitive to individual and cultural diversity

- Tests be used only for the purpose for which they were intended

- No major decision related to enrollment, retention, or placement in a remedial program be made on the basis of only one test, but that multiple sources of information be used for this purpose

It is important to keep in mind that any information gathered about children and their families—whether from test results, observations, or something a parent shared—needs to be treated with complete **confidentiality** and respect.

Evaluation

Evaluation is closely tied to goals, objectives, observation, and assessment as a beginning, an ending, and an ongoing process. To set appropriate goals and objectives, we need to know something about the group. **Preassessment** can help us learn about the children in the group. Later, to find out whether the children (or group) have met our goals and objectives, we can conduct a **summative evaluation** at the ends of units, for example. In addition, ongoing **formative evaluation** is characteristic in good early childhood programs as it allows us to determine if our planned activities, methods, and topics are accomplishing what we want them to. Evaluation can be carried out in many ways, by different disciplines of qualified persons, depending on whether they are informal or formal types of assessment.

Evaluation is a two-directional interaction. However, you will find that it is often only used one way. For instance, in your course, your instructor will hand you a course evaluation so you can comment on the strengths and needs of the course's goals and objectives, course content, and teaching methods, as well as how you, as a student, contributed to the class's success. But not very often does the instructor get to evaluate the class. This would allow for a comparison between what both parties felt, observed, and experienced and therefore would be more accurate in identifying the needs that changed and why. Together the two-way evaluation gives a more holistic view by combining and comparing vantage points. Similarly, when you are evaluated on your job, you should complete an evaluation on yourself which can be compared to the one that peers, administrators, and parents complete on the work environment. Once the evaluations are compared, they should be discussed with you, and changes, comments, goals, recommendations, timelines, and responsibilities should be agreed upon, recorded, and signed. This process is repeated for each team member. Families are part of this process since their input on teacher, school, and program is an essential team component.

● Selecting and Using Assessment and Evaluation Methods

We have looked at formal and informal methods of gathering information. Selecting an appropriate method will depend on how the results are to be used. The key is to use a combination of methods that involve the entire team in the process from beginning to end. But how will we use this information? Once information is gathered, we must make sense of it and then apply it. We gain knowledge that we must share (1) about children, (2) for program planning purposes, and (3) for parent feedback. In the Partnerships box we discuss sharing evaluations with parents.

● Information About Children

Effective teaching depends on knowing as much as possible about the children in the class. A variety of data-gathering methods can be used as follows:

1. Ongoing observation and documentation, including a portfolio of their work, can provide valuable insight into all children, their functioning as part of the class, and their growth in all developmental areas.

2. A screening test coupled with parent interviews might help with those children who, on the basis of your observations, seem to have problems.

3. A developmental assessment can be given to children whose performance on the screening test indicated a need for further evaluation. Periodic reassessment may be appropriate.

4. You may decide that a referral to an outside professional (e.g., psychologist, speech pathologist, doctor) is needed.

5. Feedback from each team member can be solicited.

Utilizing a combination of evaluation and assessment methods is the most comprehensive approach to planning.

● Information for Program Planning

One of the main purposes of assessment is to help direct program development. Once you have an idea of strengths and areas that need attention, both for individual children and for the group as a whole, you can plan a prescriptive curriculum (Beaty; 1990; Hendrick, 1986; Wright, 1983). Some useful data-gathering methods include the following:

1. Information from observations and documentation can provide excellent programming direction.

2. Checklists and rating scales allow you to evaluate the functioning of the group of children on a variety of factors that the team identified as being important.

Courtesy of George Brown College.

Evaluation as a team—of the team itself, the children, the team members, and the program—provides a forum for improvement.

● Information for Parent Feedback

All forms of evaluation provide information to share with parents from the beginning to the end of the process. It is important to examine the child's strengths, and it is vital that all information be as accurate, realistic, and unbiased as possible. Data that is carefully collected over a period of time and thoughtfully evaluated provides the basis for good parent feedback conferences. As well, parents shed tremendous light on their children's behaviour.

Partnerships
SHARING EVALUATIONS WITH PARENTS

The results of tests, observations, and other measures provide valuable information that can be shared with parents. As you read this information, you might also briefly review the discussion of parent conferences in Chapter 6 for the methods described are important to sharing evaluation results. We expect that any evaluation that teachers administer to a child is used because the teachers expect it to offer relevant insights. Thus, if this information is important to teachers, it will also be important to parents, who certainly have a right to know how their child is performing (Wortham, 1990).

There are a number of points to keep in mind when sharing evaluation results with parents. In all instances, tests or other evaluation information should never be given in isolation, out of the context of the child's overall nature. As we will continue to stress throughout this book, children cannot be divided into separate developmental compartments. Thus, to tell parents that their 4-year-old daughter is performing below (or, for that matter, above) the norm in fine motor skills is only part of the picture. It is equally important to tell them that their child has excellent social skills, that she shows leadership qualities, that she has a delightful sense of humour, that she particularly seems to enjoy sensory activities, and so forth. Such information does not rely just on the results of a developmental assessment, which yielded the fine motor score, but is reinforced by observations, anecdotes, and the teacher's reflections about this child.

Another point to remember when sharing evaluation results with parents is that you should be able to explain the measures that were applied. Some standardized tests are rather complicated to use, score, and interpret. Be sure that you understand what the test results mean and that you can explain them. It does not help a parent who asks, "What do you mean she scored below the norm?" to be told, "Well, I'm not exactly sure what 'norm' means." If your school uses any kind of standardized test, read its manual carefully, understand how the test was constructed, know how results should be interpreted and used, and be familiar with the terminology.

At the same time, it is also important to keep in mind and convey to parents that tests have their limitations. Consider the preceding discussion about the shortcomings of and concerns about tests, and let parents know that the test results represent only part of the input used in evaluation. Also remind parents, as well as yourself, that young children are amazingly flexible and often will experience a quick change or growth spurt in their development that could suddenly modify the test findings. Do not present any evaluation results as the definitive answer about the child's abilities and functioning.

A similar point is that each child is individual and unique, and test results will show a wide variety of profiles that fall within a normal range. It is reassuring to parents to be reminded that many factors affect a child's performance, particularly when parents compare the child with siblings or other children (Wortham, 1990). Keep in mind, however, that when you share test scores or other evaluation results, you should present only the child's scores, not the child's score in relation to other children's.

Finally, when sharing evaluation results with parents, be prepared to defend the measures you used. A parent may well ask you, "Why did you give this test to my child?" Be able to answer such a question because it is certainly logical and valid. You need to feel that the test provides valuable information, and you should be able to specify how such information will be used. For instance, such measures should help plan relevant and appropriate learning experiences for the child (Wortham, 1990).

Key Terms

ABC analysis
anecdotal record
behavioural objective
Brigance Diagnostic Inventory of Early Development
checklist
confidentiality

content objective
criterion-referenced
curriculum
Denver Developmental Screening Test (DDST)
developmental objectives
developmental test

diagnostic testing
Early Childhood Environment Rating
   Scale
environmental checklists
event sampling
Family Day Care Home Rating Scale
formative evaluation
goals
Home Observation for Measurement of
   the Environment (HOME)
Infant/Toddler Environment Rating Scale
learning outcome
lesson plan
nonverbal cues
norm-referenced
objectives

preassessment
predictive validity
project
rating scales
reliability
running record
screening tests
standardized tests
summative evaluation
theme
time sampling
validity
Wechsler Preschool and Primary Scale of
   Intelligence—Revised (WPPSI-R)
Wechsler Intelligence Scale for Children—
   III (WISC-III)

Key Points

1. Elements of the curriculum include both long- and short-term planning based on ongoing philosophy, knowledge of development, observation, assessment, and evaluation.

2. Curriculum has three focal points—the children themselves, their families, and their community, and it evolves continuously from there.

3. To ensure continuity, the school and team as a whole must buy into the philosophy, goals, and curriculum and agree to be accountable and make necessary adjustments.

4. A project begins with an introduction that arises from the children's interests and experiences, and then new ideas are presented sequentially and completed with a summarizing component.

5. A learning outcome (objective) is a more specific interpretation of a standard general goal, and it provides a practical and direct tool for planning.

6. Although developmental and content objectives usually apply to planning for the total group, behavioural and personal objectives are generally used in planning for an individual.

7. Observation must be unobtrusive and as natural as possible, objective, descriptive, and carefully interpreted.

8. Formal and informal assessment and evaluation instruments give us useful insight into the environments we provide and the children in our care but are subject to misinterpretation and misuse.

9. A combination of assessment and evaluation methods provides a more comprehensive portrait of the child (family, program, etc.).

Key Questions

1. What are your memories of your earliest school experiences? What kinds of activities were involved? Can you glean from your recollections what type of curriculum your preschool or child care or kindergarten teacher might have been following?

2. Review a lesson plan containing specific objectives. Do you see a relationship between the objectives and the planned activities? How do the objectives give direction to the teachers who carry out the activities?

3. With a fellow student, spend about 15 minutes observing the same child. Each of you should write an anecdotal observation involving this child for the exact same period of time. Now compare your two observations. Do they describe the same behaviours, activities, and interactions? Do they convey the same "picture" of this child? If the two observations differ significantly, why? Are there some subjective elements in either observation that might contribute to this difference?

4. Design a checklist of ten items for a group of preschoolers to assess social development. How did you decide which items to include? What resources did you use to put this checklist together? If possible, observe a group of preschoolers and apply this checklist to several of the children.

5. Have you been tested with a standardized instrument? Recall how you felt about the testing situation and the questions asked. What emotional impact did the test have on you? How might young children feel about being tested? What can a tester do to help children perform to the best of their abilities?

6. Given the information from this chapter about the values and potential misuses of evaluation procedures, develop a set of criteria that might guide you, as an early childhood professional, in using assessments in the most effective way. What do you consider to be the three most important benefits of such testing? What should you avoid?

Chapter 10

Development Through the Curriculum

*I*n Chapters 7 and 8, we looked at play and guidance because they occur wherever there are children. Teachers gently and positively guide as children play.

When you enter a child care program, the very first thing you will likely see is children playing. Eventually you will observe the teacher guiding and the result of this interaction. Each interaction impacts upon the child's emotional development and well-being.

In Chapters 7 and 8, we also looked at some of the intricacies of small- and large-group times, routines, equipment and materials, schedules, the physical environment, and appropriate practices for guiding and planning for children. Chapter 9 expanded on how to plan effectively, focusing on curriculum. We examined elements of the curriculum and curriculum content, and looked at accountability for our planning, which encompassed standards and learning outcomes, observation, assessment, and evaluation. We used the analogy of your attending school to clarify appropriate practices and curriculum. There is a general schedule, appropriate content is determined, and different types of activities are planned (i.e., individual or group), all in the context of experience-(play-)based learning

with a teacher who uses positive guidance techniques. How does the teacher support your construction of new knowledge?

This chapter looks at supporting the development of five domains—creative, physical, cognitive, language, and social—in relationship to the curriculum. It is not focused on activities (e.g., art activities), developmental milestones (e.g., children walk at 12 months), or theories (e.g., Piaget's theory of cognitive development). This chapter focuses on defining each domain (i.e., by asking, for example, "What is creativity?"), looking at environments and attitudes that foster this development, and providing guidelines for supporting its development across the curriculum. A good teacher—one armed with knowledge on child development, excellent guidance techniques, and strategies—will have little difficulty in supporting, creating, locating, assessing, planning, implementing, and evaluating activities that are appropriate, enriching, and rewarding for children.

Judy Wainwright's contribution in this chapter in A Canadian Professional Speaks Out, and the description of the Reggio Emilia model in Chapter 3, have already given you some insight into the principles of the emergent curriculum. In it, the traditional word-for-word themed curriculum, planned in advance, is abandoned. Instead, a broad set of goals and guiding principles, based on knowledge of development, is coupled with observation and dialogue to help teachers and children plan and create projects that are meaningful. The image of the child as a competent partner suggests a relationship fostered through dynamic and ongoing communication. Hence, there is not necessarily a standard art centre or home centre or science centre. Projects, by their very nature, and teachers, through their interaction, foster all the domains. As you read, think about how the children's emerging interest in, say, birds could evolve into projects—not preplanned by you but planned in relation to what has happened, is happening, and could happen.

In this sense, curriculum does not guide development. Rather, development guides curriculum. Instead of children adjusting to a preplanned curriculum, the curriculum is adjusted to adapt to the changing interests, strengths, and needs of the children. Planning is definitely required, but rather than a preplanned lesson based on an arbitrary theme, it would entail a well-planned project based on real interests.

Creative Development

The preschool years have been described as a "golden age of creativity, a time when every child sparkles with artistry" (Gardner, 1982, p. 86). One of the most rewarding joys of working with young children is watching them approach experiences with that spark of freshness and exuberance that opens the door to creativity. Each of us possesses some measure of creativity—some more, some less. This is especially true of young children. Unfortunately, there is the danger of their creativity being stifled through increasing pressure to conform to adult expectations (Mayesky, 1990).

A Canadian Professional Speaks Out

TAILORING CURRICULUMS TO ABILITY AND INTEREST

Judy Wainwright, Mount Royal College, Calgary

My desire for Canadian children enrolled in child care centres is that each child will receive quality, individualized care from educated, caring, and committed adults. Nice idea, you say, but hardly practical. I disagree. For many young children this idea is reality, and with some changes it can become a reality for all children. From my perspective, theme planning and "recipe card" manuals should be discarded. Play experiences for children should be planned using playroom staff's educational expertise and information gathered through frequent, firsthand observations of each child's needs, interests, and abilities.

Let's suppose from recent observations and conversations with children, parents, and other playroom staff that Timothy is interested in dinosaurs, Rachel in colours, and Kent in changes. Michael's mother had a new baby and he needs to learn how to understand and express his feelings, positive and negative, about his sibling. Attiya is thrilled about her newly acquired skill of printing the letters in her name. Heather and Pam are frustrated that their block structures continue to tumble. Just as you were leaving the centre yesterday, Sharon's mother called to say that their family dog had been killed by a car. This is the information that forms the backbone of your upcoming daily play programs. For each child you develop a variety of play experiences for active and quiet play throughout the planned environment.

Here are some possible play opportunities that meet the individual needs of the children and more than likely will appeal to several others:

- At the easel, primary colours of paint, large pieces of paper cut in circles, and one-inch, long-handled brushes (Rachel, Attiya, Michael, Kent).

- Beside the sandbox, a box of dinosaurs, a variety of twigs and branches gathered from yesterday's walk in the nearby park, and a container of water (Timothy, Kent).

- On the manipulative table, three different types of paper, preschool pencils, erasers, rulers, crayons, stencils, and scissors. At a nearby table, alphabet blocks with small people and animals (Attiya, Kent, Rachel, Michael, Sharon).

- At the science table, bean and onion seeds, soil, clear plastic cups for planting, watering can, and magnifying glasses with pictures of growing plants on the nearby bulletin board (Kent, Michael).

- In the dramatic-play area, several stuffed [toy] baby zoo animals with appropriate foodstuffs, zookeeper shirts, hats, gloves, and cleaning supplies with a stack of hollow blocks that could be used to construct habitats (Michael, Sharon, Pam, Heather).

(cont'd)

TAILORING CURRICULUMS *cont'd*

- Newborn babies [dolls], bottles, blankets, a carriage, and a cradle are available in the family area (Michael).

- The water table has clear water, and beside it are props for making bubbles (liquid soap, straws, tennis racquets, and plastic tubes with terry towel wrapped around one end) (Kent, Rachel, Michael).

- In the block area, several flat pieces of masonite are on the floor along with three large cardboard boxes (Heather, Pam, Kent).

- Added to the bookshelf are alphabet, dinosaur, plant, and animal books.

- For children who wish to join a group activity, there are scales for weighing and measuring people; conversations about growth of nails, hair, skin, and feet; and clothes of different sizes.

- When children arrive, Sharon's primary caregiver will be there to talk and support her in the playroom and is prepared to talk about her feelings about her dead pet at appropriate opportunities.

- Materials added to the outdoor playground will be sponges, chamois, cloths, brushes, buckets, and water for washing bikes, windows, and equipment, woodworking materials, and some musical instruments.

- Throughout the day adults will interact with children as they self-select play experiences.

Using all knowledge and information available, early childhood professionals must trust their own judgment on what is best for each child and provide daily, numerous, real, firsthand play experiences that allow children to self-select from a wide range of opportunities to foster their own growth and development with supportive guidance from competent, confident adults. Children will feel valued and respected; learning opportunities will be individually and developmentally appropriate; and individual and group needs will be met in a responsive environment that recognizes the uniqueness of each child in the playroom. The result will be quality care for each child.

● What Is Creativity?

Creativity has been defined in a number of ways. Most definitions include such concepts as originality, imagination, divergent thinking (seeing things from different viewpoints), and the ability to create something new or to combine things in novel but meaningful ways. Creativity is more likely to occur when the person possesses traits such as curiosity, flexibility, and interest in investigation and exploration (traits manifested by most children).

J. P. Guilford (1962), dissatisfied with the limited definition of intelligence imposed by tests that measure it by a series of single, "correct" answers, developed a new way of looking at intelligence that includes some of these traits. In Guilford's structure of the intellect, divergent thinking is differentiated from convergent thinking, both of which are involved in the creative process.

- **Divergent thinking,** by one definition, is "the making in the mind of many from one," for instance, by elaborating on a topic as in brainstorming (Hampden-Turner, 1981, p. 104).

- **Convergent thinking** is defined as "the making of one from many" through narrowing down many ideas to a single, focused point (Hampden-Turner, 1981, p. 104).

- **Fluency** is the ability to generate many relevant ideas on a given topic in a limited time. Five-year-old Michelle wonderfully displayed fluency when she was confronted with a sheet of paper containing 20 circles. She drew as many different items from these circles as she could—face, balloon, ball, sun, orange, and flower. She then created an ashtray, glass, light bulb, and pencil eraser as they would be seen from the top. She had used all but one row of the circles when the teacher reminded her that she needed to finish up. Michelle, after a moment's thought, drew two parallel lines under the remaining row of circles, connected them with crosshatches, then put boxes on top of the circles, creating a quick but recognizable train.

- **Flexibility** is the ability to adapt readily to change in a positive, productive manner. Three-year-old Ramon showed flexibility when another child accidentally knocked water on the lines that he had carefully painted in different hues of water colours. After a fleeting look of dismay crossed his face, Ramon surveyed his picture and declared, "Look, the water made new colours!"

- **Sensitivity** is a receptivity to external and internal stimuli. Creative people have a heightened awareness of their world and often experience through their senses what others miss (Lowenfeld, 1962). The creative child will more likely be the one who points out that a cloud looks like a speeding motorboat, appreciatively sniffs the aroma of freshly sawed wood at the woodworking activity, or delights in the softness of the soapy water when blowing bubbles.

● Esthetic Appreciation

Esthetics, an enjoyment and appreciation of beauty, is related to art in all its forms. Evans (1984) considers the inclusion of esthetics in education as contributing to a "quality of life that is uniquely human" by exposing children to "sublime experiences" (p. 74), that sense of wonder and enjoyment when we are touched by beauty. Esthetics includes sensitivity and appreciation for both natural beauty and synthetic creations (Feeney & Moravcik, 1987). A teacher who is sensitive to beauty can help children find it in their surroundings.

The early childhood setting should provide an environment in which these traits are encouraged and valued. Such an environment, however, goes far beyond providing materials for artistic and other expression. The creative environment is made up not just of the physical arrangement, but is permeated by an attitude of openness, acceptance, and encouragement. We will examine both of these aspects—the physical parameters of such an environment and the attitudes that promote creativity. You may wish to check some Web sites for ideas for children.

● Environments That Encourage Creativity

The physical setting can support creativity through provision of and access to a wide range of **open-ended materials**, that is, materials that lend themselves to various uses. Children have to make choices about how to use open-ended materials and employ their imagination in doing so because these materials do not dictate a single outcome. Furthermore, each time they use the materials, they can do so in a unique way. They love to practise familiar songs over and over, to read and act out favourite stories, to participate in both open-ended and themed dramatic-play centre, and to create endlessly with art materials. In art, for example, children do not need a different art activity each day. When a different set of limited materials is provided every day, children never get the chance to explore in depth or experiment with common, basic materials (Clemens, 1991).The easel should be out every single day, and the creative shelf should be stocked with ample materials from which the children can create limitless things.

A well-stocked early childhood program will be full of open-ended materials. Examples include a wide variety of art materials, manipulatives, blocks, sensory materials, puppets, dramatic-play props, musical instruments, and versatile outdoor equipment. (This is not to say that single-purpose materials, e.g., puzzles, are unimportant, but they meet different developmental needs and are not particularly suited to creative development.) One study demonstrated that children who were offered a large selection of art materials from which to choose, rather than provided with materials limited to a single project, produced significantly more creative artwork, as judged by a panel of artists (Amabile & Gitomer, 1984).

The physical arrangement of the room can also facilitate creativity. Clearly organized classroom areas let children know where they can engage in various creative activities, for instance, where they can build or where they might experiment with messy media. Classroom areas should be set up so that traffic flow does not interfere or disrupt ongoing activity.

At the same time, children should be able to move freely from one activity to another. When materials are organized and visible on accessible shelves, the children know what is available for their independent use. These materials should be attractively displayed and uncluttered so that children can see possible new combinations they might try. You may also want to label the materials available. Such orderly display also conveys a respect for the materials. Similarly, a display area for children's work tells the children that their creative endeavours are valued and respected. Even though many children will not be interested in the finished product, it is also important to have an area where you can store the children's work.

Creativity can and should occur in every aspect of the early childhood program. Although art and music foster creativity, they also promote cognition, socialization, language, emotional release, sensory stimulation, and muscle development. Similarly, language, outdoor motor, and manipulative activities can be very creative. As you read on, keep in mind that good early childhood activities serve many purposes, meet many needs, and, above all, contribute to the development of the whole child. Creativity is not limited to art, music, or drama but is the essence of process in everything the child (and teacher) does.

A Canadian Professional Speaks Out

CREATIVITY IN ART: AN EXPRESSION OF THE INNER SELF

Elizabeth Wood, Early Childhood Studies, Nova Scotia Community College

Young children come to our day care centres as avid participants in the discovery of their world. They are curious, excited, and creative when they arrive at our door. It is our responsibility and challenge, as child care professionals, to ensure they maintain these positive qualities.

Our child care facilities should provide programs that meet the social, physical, emotional, and intellectual needs of the young child. Such a program enables each child to develop to his or her fullest potential, feeling confident and willing to take risks. Having opportunities to participate in creative art activities enhances all areas of development in a relaxed, positive atmosphere. Through creative activities, children grow socially as they share materials and ideas. Fine and gross motor skills are developed as they manipulate a variety of art media. Intellectually, children learn about spatial awareness, colours, textures, and problem solving. The children learn to express their emotions in a positive manner and gain confidence in their capabilities.

As adults we must learn to appreciated the uniqueness of each child's artistic presentations. We should share in their joy as they utilize paints, crayons, clay, and other art media to produce original works of art. Frequently, as adults, we are tempted to try to channel the child's art by providing predesigned crafts or gifts, colouring sheets, glue and paste activities, or stencils for them to complete. These types of activities stifle imaginative thought and rob the children of the freedom to express their own ideas. According to Piaget's stages of intellectual development, children do not perceive the world as adults do. Neither are they developmentally capable of representing their world in an artistic form determined by adult standards. Robert Schirrmacher believes that as the creative process blossoms within each child, "the emphasis is on the making and doing rather than on the finished product." The making and doing of creative activities comes naturally from within the child, and adults do not need to impose their ideas on them.

(cont'd)

CREATIVITY IN ART *cont'd*

The child care professional plays an important role in the development of the children's creativity. One of our greatest creative resources is the environment. By providing daily access to an art centre with a variety of art media, children are given the freedom to explore the materials and create as they desire to do so. The materials in the art centre should be changed frequently to maintain interest and stimulate creative thought. In addition to the art centre, the adult needs to plan a variety of sensory experiences for the children. As they participate in the experiences, they will acquire information that will then be expressed through their artistic representations. An effective creative art program encourages children to portray their perceptions of the world in a variety of ways. Only through an open-ended approach will we create an atmosphere where children will become creative, confident people who are willing to risk sharing their ideas and feelings.

Partnerships

PARENTAL INVOLVEMENT IN THE CURRICULUM

As we've indicated many times, the curriculum should reflect the backgrounds, needs, and interests of the children and their families. One excellent resource, as you plan the curriculum for your group of children, is their parents. Frequent parent-teacher communication and an open-door policy that conveys the school's emphasis on the importance of the family can encourage parents to be part of the early childhood program. As parents investigate your school in order to decide whether to enrol their child, your open-door policy regarding family should be explained and discussed. As the central focus toward ensuring quality, parent involvement in the curriculum can take many forms. Helping parents feel welcome and genuinely soliciting their ongoing input benefits both parties. Each feels reciprocally valued and respected as an integral component in the overall well-being of the child.

Most parents are interested in what their children do each day. The overall curriculum, the units, and the daily lesson plans should be available for the parents' review and input. A Parents' Night should be planned early in the year to discuss plans and responsibilities. A school newsletter might be the place to share information about the overall curriculum and philosophy throughout the year. Lesson and unit plans, and progress reports of ongoing projects, can be posted in a prominent place, for instance, just outside the classroom door or on a parent bulletin board, where parents can look at the activities, objectives, and outcomes. The children can be videotaped and the video presented on a Parents' Night, or photos of the children in action can be sent home. Parents appreciate knowing what activities their children engaged in during their day at school, something that is often a topic of conversation between parent and child on the way home from school. Anything that highlights their child and the positive experiences of his or her day helps parents to relax and share in the successes of the program and child.

Parents can also be called on to participate in the curriculum. There are many areas in which their expertise and input can greatly enhance the program. Parents can provide information about special family, cultural, religious, or ethnic customs, celebrations, foods, or dress. They can visit the classroom to share occupational information or special skills. A parent who makes pottery, weaves baskets, plays an instrument, or knows origami will contribute a fascinating element to the classroom. Knowing parents' interests is as important as knowing their children's. Whether parents prefer to work behind the scenes or in the class, asking for, supporting, and honouring parents' suggestions and encouraging their participation will prove a strengthening factor in the overall integrity of the curriculum.

An early childhood program in which adults model, emphasize, and value prosocial behaviours will facilitate development of such traits in children. Alice Honig (1988a), who considers a prosocial curriculum based on caring and kindness as a crucial goal of early childhood programs, has highlighted the importance of such behaviours. Previous sections of this chapter presented activities and strategies that can encourage developmentally appropriate and positive social attitudes and behaviours. In the context of a supportive atmosphere, understanding of child development, concern for children's needs, respect for their opinions, encouragement of their autonomy, support for their individuality, and provision of a stimulating program and environment, such activities will help promote positive socialization.

Parents and teachers must, of course, work together toward creating such an atmosphere and must communicate regularly to build a bridge between home and school. When children see parents working together in a positive, prosocial manner, they trust that their own strengths and needs will be cared for. Partnerships suggests ways parents can foster development by being involved in the curriculum.

● Attitudes That Encourage Creativity

Creativity, as you have seen, is related to flexibility, divergent thinking, and openness to new ideas. Young children's minds strive to make sense of their world by organizing information and input. Once they become familiar with and master new concepts, they are free to use these in various ways. If we use what we learn in only one way, we are limited and rigid in our approach. Flexible or creative thinking is a mindset that can be encouraged in an open classroom atmosphere. A creative environment promotes new perceptions of and responses to the world.

Creativity has to be nurtured; it does not develop on its own. The teacher plays an important role in fostering creativity by providing a variety of materials and encouraging imaginative use of them. When children are allowed creative expression, each child will produce a different outcome. The teacher's acceptance of each child's work and unique responses gives children the opportunity to learn that people feel and think differently, and to value this difference.

Creativity does not always result in a product, although we traditionally tend to think of the song, the picture, the story, or the dance as the creative product. It is the process, not the product, that is important for young children—and the younger they are, the more this applies. All too frequently, you see adults imposing their desire for a finished product on young children. Infants and toddlers are not inclined to take paintings home. And preschoolers may have painted a beautiful picture in red, yellow, and blue that they then cover with black paint. By the time they are school-aged, however, many children will want a completed product to take home. But this product should still be a result of the child's chosen process as opposed to a teacher-imposed craft.

If you watch young children involved in creative activities, you will better understand why the process is so valuable. In the process, the child can:

- Experiment ("What will happen if I put this block across the top of these two?")

- Enjoy the sensory experience ("Squishing the play dough between my fingers feels nice!")

- Communicate ("I'm a bird!")

- Relive experiences ("I'll tell the 'baby' she has to go to bed because that's what big people always tell me")

- Work out fears ("I'll be the doctor, and my dolly will be the baby who gets the shot!")

As children mature, as their motor and perceptual skills improve, and as they plan ahead more, their creative efforts may well result in purposeful products. But young preschoolers are much more involved in the process of creative experiences. For children up to 4 years, any end product is usually secondary to the enjoyment of doing the activity.

By encouraging children to solve problems, the teacher also fosters creativity. By helping children think through different alternatives and find various solutions, the teacher expands their creative capacity. The teacher, however, is a facilitator rather than the one who comes up with answers or solutions. Divergent thinking involves the opportunity to go off in different directions and to explore various strategies. The teacher's acceptance of children's suggestions and willingness to try these tells them that they are capable of worthwhile ideas.

Another way of accepting and encouraging children's creative work is through uncritical acknowledgment. Well-intentioned praise ("I like your picture") can

Courtesy of Play and Learn.

stifle creativity because it imposes a value judgment, or becomes meaningless when it is repeated to every child. Rather than evaluate, compare, or try to read meaning into nonrepresentational art, a teacher can remark on the process ("You glued the squares on first, then you glued circles over them"); recognize the work that has gone into the picture ("You've worked 20 minutes on this sculpture!"); or comment on its design qualities ("You're using lots of big circles!") (Schirrmacher, 1986).

In setting up an appropriate climate for creativity, it is important to provide enough time for children to get involved in and complete their projects. When the time set aside for child-selected activity is short, children tend not to get very involved (Christie, Johnsen, & Peckover, 1988), thus missing opportunities to engage in creative activity. Children may continue to pursue a creative project over a period of time.

● Factors That Decrease Creativity

A discussion about creative development should include a few words about the all-too-present factors in our society that often blunt children's creative impulses. As we have discussed, creativity depends on flexible, open, divergent thinking, which is encouraged in children through a flexible and open environment.

Conversely, creativity can be diminished by socializing factors that narrow, stereotype, or limit ideas. An atmosphere that promotes racial, cultural, or sex stereotypes, for instance, imposes a narrow view of people that restricts potential. An environment in which the adult is always right and children are expected to do what they are told without asking questions is not conducive to creativity. When children are always shown how to do tasks, they will not have the opportunity to engage in problem solving and creative thinking. When adults laugh at, rather than appreciate, a child's unique or unusual response, that child is discouraged from expressing other creative ideas.

Television and Creativity.   One pervasive factor in children's lives that can affect creativity is television and, increasingly, videotapes. On average, children spend more time watching television than they do engaging in any other activity except sleep (Huston, Watkins, & Kunkel, 1989; Levin & Carlsson-Paige, 1994). In 1996, Canadian children watched almost 18 hours of television per week (Statistics Canada, 1999e). What children see—program content—as well as how much time they spend in front of the TV set can decrease creative thinking.

Programs on this medium tend to convey a very stereotyped view of people, one in which recognition and respect are accorded primarily to those who are white, male, young, and beautiful (Liebert & Sprafkin, 1988). Television also generally promotes the view that an effective way of solving problems is through violence, another narrow attitude that often does not model a variety of constructive problem-solving strategies. Even more disturbing are the results from a number of studies showing that frequent and consistent viewing of violent television programming is strongly related to aggressive behaviour (e.g., Huesmann, Lagerspetz, & Eron, 1984; Joy, Kimball, & Zabrack, 1986; McCreary, 1997; Singer, Singer, & Rapaczynski, 1984).

The amount of viewing time can also affect creativity. Creative learning is an active process, dependent on ample time spent exploring, investigating, manipulating, and reflecting. Television viewing is basically a passive occupation; thus, the more a child sits in front of the TV, the less time there is for active, self-directed play. On the other hand, some researchers feel that television is active in that children process what they see in relation to their own background and experience (Anderson & Lorch, 1983).

There are worthwhile children's programs on television that model and teach children positive, **prosocial behaviours** and promote appreciation of nature, esthetics, and culture. Four rules can help ensure that young children benefit from the positive values of television:

1. Parents at home and teachers at school must carefully monitor the content so children watch only age-appropriate programs.

2. Television viewing should be allowed only in small doses.

3. Adults should watch television with children so discussion can take place.

4. Videos may be a better choice if you cannot be with the children throughout the program. You can choose an age-appropriate, commercial-free video with which you are familiar.

Reflective Exercise 10-1

Watch a children's television program, for instance, a cartoon. What messages does this program convey to children? Does it promote stereotypes? If a child frequently watches programs such as this one, how might such viewing affect creativity?

Physical Development

One of the major aspects of the early years is physical growth and development. At no other time in life is there such a rapid rate of change in size, weight, and body proportion, and in increased control and refinement in the use of body parts (Allen & Marotz, 1989). Physical changes, which are readily observable, profoundly affect and are affected by all areas of development.

● What Is Physical Development?

As children start the preschool years, they have rudimentary movement ability and control, but by the time they enter middle childhood, their movements have become much more refined and competent, allowing for a wider repertoire of activities and choices. This is due to an integration of three components:

1. **Gross motor development** is involved in control of the large muscles of the legs, arms, back, and shoulders needed for movements such as running, jumping, and climbing. The preschool development of six important elements of body control—walking, running, jumping, hopping, throwing, and balancing—have been described by Keogh and Sugden (1985). Walking is the basic means of locomotion or self-movement from place to place; running, jumping, hopping, and throwing are fundamental play skills; and balancing provides one way of assessing postural control. All of these important skills become more accurate, controlled, and efficient as children develop coordination during the preschool years.

2. **Fine motor development** is involved in use of the small muscles of the fingers and hands necessary for such tasks as writing, drawing, and buttoning. During the infant and toddler years, children develop basic grasping and manipulation skills, which are refined during the preschool years. The preschooler becomes quite adept in self-help (i.e., feeding, dressing, toileting), construction (i.e., building and manipulating materials), **holding grips** (i.e., for writing, grasping, and drawing) (Keogh & Sugden, 1985), and **bimanual control** tasks—those requiring use of both hands.

   Toys that require some kind of manipulation with fingers and hands can be categorized as **manipulatives**. Manipulative materials enhance fine motor development because they require controlled use of hand and finger muscles. But they contribute much more. Manipulatives are sensory materials, involving visual and tactile discrimination and **eye-hand coordination**; they require skill in coordinating the eyes with what the hands do. Manipulatives can reinforce a variety of concepts such as colour, shape, number, and size, and encourage one-to-one correspondence, matching, patterning, sequencing, and grouping. Some manipulative toys, such as puzzles, are **self-correcting**, fitting together in only one specific way. Such toys allow children to work independently and know when they have achieved success. These toys contribute to children's growing attention span and the satisfaction of staying at a task until it is completed (Table Toys, 1979).

3. **Sensory-perceptual development** involves conveying information that comes through the senses and the meaning that it is given. Closely intertwined with

motor development are sensory and perceptual functioning. Sensory input involves the collection of information through the senses of sight, hearing, taste, smell, and touch. The **kinesthetic sense** provides people with a sense of awareness, a feel, for their body in space so that they can make judgments about movement. Perceptual input involves attention to, recognition of, and interpretation of that information to give it personal meaning. Thus, perception is a cognitive process as it integrates sensory and kinesthetic information into knowledge and behaviour.

Any activity involves a sensory component, because we use sight, hearing, or touch almost all of the time. But some activities are specifically geared to enhance sensory awareness. Most young children seem to enjoy and become thoroughly immersed in activities such as sand and water play. These are completely open-ended, tactile, and soothing.

● Environments That Encourage Physical Development

In addition to internal influences, external factors also influence physical development (Henniger, 1999; Keogh & Sugden, 1985). Early childhood educators should arrange the environment to facilitate children's exploration, creativity, and discovery. Through movement, in interacting with the environment, children engage in problem solving (Curtis, 1987; Henniger, 1999). In other words, the environment provides materials, equipment, and activities that motivate, challenge, and stimulate the child. The child exercises his or her muscles while engaging in thinking, socialization, language, and creative development at the same time.

In a quality setting, teachers ensure that infants and toddlers are given a responsive environment to explore, one that enhances their existing schemes of the world. Teachers who have physically challenged children in their class can ensure that these children also have a responsive environment.

● Attitudes That Encourage Physical Fitness, Health, and Well Being

Physical Fitness. Physical fitness is concerned with overall health—nutrition, alertness and energy level, and integration of the range of skills covered by gross motor, fine motor, and sensory-perceptual skills such as eye-hand coordination, dexterity, heightened senses, quickness, precision, and accuracy. Physical fitness is important to every aspect of daily living and stress reduction. Specifically, it contributes to the development and maintenance of an "adequate level of cardiovascular endurance, muscular strength, muscular endurance, flexibility, and body leanness" (Poest, Williams, Witt, & Atwood, 1990, p. 5), also imperative to health and daily functioning. The sizable and growing number of overweight North American preschool-aged children further attests to a need for physical fitness.

Exercise occurs in many early childhood activities. Vigorous, active play is important not only to muscle development but also to the establishment of life-long health habits (Henniger, 1999; Seefeldt, 1984). Yet a recent large-scale survey found that preschool children are not engaging in enough physical activity (Poest, Williams, Witt, & Atwood, 1989, 1990). Children whose parents engage in exercise are more likely to do so as well.

Javernick (1988) feels that teachers of young children often neglect gross motor development, paying it only lip service, and instead emphasize fine motor, cognitive, and social areas in the curriculum. A number of physical education proponents express the concern that free play alone does not adequately meet the motor development needs of young children (Seefeldt, 1984; Skinner, 1979). They advocate that regular physical fitness activities (not organized sports) be part of the early childhood curriculum. It is important to note, however, that no norms exist for what physical fitness in preschoolers should involve (Poest et al., 1990).

The term "physical fitness" often conjures up our own childhood experiences involving games and sports. Play, games, and sports have characteristics that are tied to developmental readiness and appropriateness (Coleman & Skeen, 1985). Play is free from time, space, and rule constraints, and reward is inherent in the play rather than dependent on winning. Play involves such activities as creeping, running, crawling, climbing, and throwing. Games are more structured than play. Although time limitations and rules can be altered to meet the needs of the players involved, games with more than a few simple rules are beyond the ability of most preschoolers. However, non-rule-based jumping and running games can be played. Children are famous for making up games, which encourages creativity and cognitive, language, and social development. Teacher-imposed competition can have detrimental effects on children, and teachers' interference in children's devised games, which sometimes involve competition, places value judgments on them and minimizes group skills. If the group is cooperating and the basic rule of no hurting is being respected, then the teacher must respect the group's decision to follow through with its devised game.

Young children need to develop physical capabilities through many play experiences in which they can explore their world (Coleman & Skeen, 1985). The challenge to early childhood educators is not just to develop appropriate gross motor and physical fitness activities but to allow time to play, to be active, to observe people in action, to discuss the value of activity, health, and fitness, and to plan as a group for it. Early childhood educators must model fitness and health practices as part of everyday living. Javernick (1988) suggested some guidelines for teachers of young children as shown in Exhibit 10-1.

The research implies that early childhood teachers need to be more concerned with providing physical fitness as part of the daily program. Vigorous daily activities that are fun and enjoyable contribute to establishing a foundation for lifelong health habits and attitudes.

Caring for the Body. The early childhood program should help lay the foundation for good health habits. In addition to establishing routines and activities that emphasize the importance of physical exercise, the preschool or child care centre also can help children of all ages learn about appropriate nutrition, health, and safety concepts.

EXHIBIT 10-1 *Guidelines for Supporting Physical Development*

- Activities should be presented in ways that will interest and intrigue children.

- Physical activities such as calisthenics, "adventurecises," walks, hikes, bike rides, swimming, or obstacle courses should be planned for every day.

- Music and movement activities should also be part of every day. Many excellent children's tapes and CDs are available to enhance exercise and movement activities.

- Children should be provided with opportunities to make choices from a diverse range of materials and should have input into suggesting activities, events, equipment, and projects.

- The teacher must be an active participant in physical activity. Children are much more attracted to activities in which a teacher is enthusiastically involved.

- Outside and inside activities must provide and encourage a mix of game time, active and passive time, individual and group time, teacher- and child-initiated activities, materials that promote doing, and play time within and away from the playground and the classroom.

- Materials need to be open-ended with varying attributes of size, shape, colour, and texture to encourage a variety of physical and creative uses.

- Many open-ended sensory activities such as sand and water provide excellent forums for physical, social, language, and creative skills. These activities are very soothing and relaxing.

Reflective Exercise 10-2

Talk to two or three children who are 4 or 5 years old. Ask them what they like about their classroom and playground. Are the features they mention ones that you consider particularly interesting and noteworthy? What do their answers tell you about these children's interests, attitudes, and needs in relation to the environment?

Nutrition   Because food is a basic human need and so often provides great pleasure, nutrition education experiences should be an integral part of the curriculum. Nutrition concepts can be explored with the children in an understandable, interesting manner, and they can be reinforced by such things as hands-on cooking activities. Nutrition and cooking, while promoting understanding of a basic physical need, equally involve cognitive, language, creative, and social areas of development.

Nutrition education, attitudes toward food, and food behaviours are all of interest to children. When you are planning food-related activities, consider concepts such as the variety and sources of foods, and the many variations in foods such as texture, smell, colour, sound, and shape (Herr & Morse, 1982). The different ways you can prepare and eat foods also are of interest to young children . Of course, the contributions that nutritious foods make to health, growth, and energy levels are worthy topics in the program. *Canada's Food Guide* highlights different types of foods and their nutritional value. Personal preferences for foods can also be a topic for lively discussions.

If you are in a full-day setting, where meals are a standard feature, you will probably discuss many of these topics informally while eating. Exploring children's prior knowledge, interests, and questions will provide an excellent starting point for determining what the group can investigate in more depth. Limitless options for projects will unfold from the children's growing of their own food, planning a banquet, or studying anatomy. Herr and Morse (1982) recommended that nutrition be an integral part of the early childhood program, covered on an ongoing basis. Local and provincial marketing boards (e.g., egg, beef, and milk producers' boards) often have excellent photographs, activities, or speakers available free of charge for teachers. Local markets, restaurants, agricultural associations, public health departments, and provincial bodies are also excellent resources.

Cooking Experiences   Among the most enjoyable activities for young children are those that involve food preparation. Such activities are multisensory; involve children in a process they have observed but in which they may not have participated; teach and reinforce a variety of concepts related to nutrition, mathematics, science, and language; and are very satisfying because they result in a tangible (and delicious) end product (Cosgrove, 1991).

Some cooking activities are more appropriate than others and should be carefully selected to meet specific criteria and objectives. The following are guidelines to keep in mind when planning food activities:

1. The activity should be matched to the children. Older infants might help poke some bread dough, for example, but they would not be able to knead it, whereas older children could. Heat, sharp utensils, and a need for precise fine motor control place age constraints on activities, so for younger children think

of activities that do not require them. Examples include tearing lettuce for a salad, plucking grapes from the stem for fruit salad, mixing yogurt and fruit in individual cups, or spreading tuna salad on crackers with a spoon. Older preschoolers and school-aged children have more refined muscle control and can follow more complex instructions. More involved recipes that might require use of knives, electrical appliances, and multiple ingredients can be planned.

2. Safety is of utmost importance. Many cooking tools are potentially dangerous, and careful adult supervision is required. Some steps in cooking require that only one child at a time be involved with a teacher (e.g., flipping pancakes in an electric skillet or griddle). Other cooking activities may well require that the number of children be limited, for instance, to five or six at a time, so that the adult can supervise and observe all of the children adequately. The process can then be repeated with additional groups of children so that everyone who is interested has the opportunity to participate. However, limitations on the number of children who can be involved at one time have to be thought out before the activity is presented to the children.

3. The recipe should involve enough steps so that all of the children in the group make a significant contribution. Some recipes can be prepared individually by each child in single-serving sizes. Other recipes will require group cooperation. Such an appealing activity as cooking should have enough ingredients and steps (i.e., five or six) so that each child in the group is an active participant. If children are making muffins, for instance, one child can break and stir the eggs while others add and stir in the butter, flour, milk, honey, nuts, raisins, flavourings, and leavening; then they can take turns stirring the dough.

4. Children can be helped to understand the entire process. It is helpful to prepare a pictorial recipe chart (or use one that is commercially made) that shows ingredients and amounts, allowing children to experience measuring as well as mixing. Point out the changes in ingredients as they are mixed with others (e.g., the flour loses its dry "powderiness" as it joins the liquids). Discuss and point out the effect of heat, which changes the semi-liquid dough into firm muffins, for instance.

5. The activity should focus on wholesome, nutritious foods. It is important to set a good example in the planned cooking activities to reinforce nutritional concepts. A wide selection of available cookbooks focus on healthy recipes for preschoolers.

6. The importance of hygiene and cleanliness must be stressed. Require that children as well as adults wash their hands before participating in cooking experiences. Make sure that cooking surfaces and tools are clean. Multisensory learning is enhanced if you allow children to taste at various points during the cooking process; however, instead of letting children use their fingers for tasting, provide individual spoons or popsicle sticks.

Health and Hygiene   Young children get many messages about health needs and practices from what is expected of them, what they are told, and what adults model. School routines (discussed in Chapters 7 and 8) set many expectations and structure the schedule to encourage and facilitate increasing self-care in toileting, cleanliness, and eating. But health information should also be conveyed as part of the curriculum. Discussions and activities can heighten children's awareness of such topics as the relationship between health and growth, the body's need for both activity and rest, temperature regulation through appropriate clothing, hygiene practices as part of disease prevention, the importance of medical and dental care, and health professionals and facilities that care for children in the community. In addition, if a child in the class has a specific allergy or a chronic illness, you can help all of the children to understand this condition better by sensitively including the topic in the curriculum.

It was helpful in one preschool program, for instance, when the teacher discussed why Dorothea could not eat certain foods. The children became more sensitive to Dorothea's allergies and the restrictions it caused, and they saw that her special snacks were not a privilege but a necessity.

Safety   Young children begin to acquire safety information and precautions, although it is important to remember that adults must be responsible for ensuring children's safety by providing a safe environment and preventing accidents. Because toddlers and very young preschoolers may not process safety information accurately, it should be conveyed with a great deal of caution. Some 2-year-olds, or young 3-year-olds, may fail to understand the negative message in "Don't do ———" or may get ideas from well-intentioned cautions (Essa & Rogers, 1992). Through curriculum topics, older preschoolers can gradually acquire information and learn some preventive precautions related to fire, electricity, tools, traffic, potential poisons, and strangers, as well as learn about community safety personnel and resources, and what to do in case of an accident.

Cognitive Development

Young children's thinking ability is quite amazing. Within just a few years of their birth, preschoolers have acquired an immense repertoire of information and cognitive skills. A child, who two or three or four years before was a helpless baby responding to the environment mainly through reflexes, is now a competent, thinking, communicating, reasoning, problem-solving, exploring person. In studying children's cognition, you should be concerned more with the process of knowing than with what children know. In particular, we are interested in how children acquire, organize, and apply knowledge (Copple, DeLisi, & Sigel, 1982).

● What Is Cognition?

Most people think of cognition only as knowledge, and many think of knowledge simply as facts. Cognition goes far beyond this. It involves:

- *Modes* (i.e., some people learn best by seeing, others by touch, others by hearing, and most of us in combinations)

- *Strategies* (i.e., some people write things down, others repeat them over and over)

- *Skills* (e.g., reading, writing)

- *Acquisition* (i.e., resourcefulness)

- *Processing* (which involves memory and the storing and retrieving of information)

- *Comprehension* (i.e., some people know a lot of facts but do not know what they mean; comprehension is understanding meaning)

- *Application* (i.e., some people have the knowledge, for example, that smoking is dangerous, but they do not use it; application is using the knowledge)

Virtually every activity involves cognition. Children actively learn, use problem-solving strategies, construct new knowledge, and use new knowledge in all activities, be they science and math or art, music, movement, manipulatives, storytelling, or dramatic play. Some specific cognitive skills include:

- *Classification*—the ability to sort and group objects, ideas, and information into categories

- *Seriation*—the ability to understand and relate to the order of things, ideas, and events

- *Number concepts*—the understanding of quantity

- *Temporal concepts*—the understanding and awareness of the principles of time

- *Spatial concepts*—the understanding and awareness of the principles of space

These skills are not strictly mathematical concepts but ones that transcend all facets of daily interactions and decisions from passing in traffic to meal planning to deciding what to wear to planning your day. As these skills develop in children, their knowledge and ideas about the world, people, and things grow and develop.

Children develop their own theories of mind—theories about thinking and how the mind works. Children have theories on just about everything though. This is what Piaget found so fascinating about interviewing children: their answers to questions such as "Why is the sky blue?" Children of different ages would, of course, give very different answers, but most children answer confidently and without hesitation, secure in the conviction that the answer is obvious and therefore correct. Intelligence is generally related to facts and how many of these one knows. As we saw in Chapter 2, however, Piaget and Gardner felt there were several types of knowledge.

People gather knowledge, approach a task, use knowledge, and remember and understand things differently. We sometimes call this a person's "learning style." There are learning style inventories on the market which are interesting to do with a team since they build understanding of one another's style and approach to problem solving. Early childhood philosophy caters well to a classroom of diverse learning styles since it is open-ended and therefore accommodating and flexible. Many elementary, secondary, and postsecondary programs, as well as corporations, have recognized this open-ended, accommodating style as an excellent approach to teaching and learning and have begun to adapt it to their environments.

● Environments and Attitudes That Encourage Cognitive Development

While young children learn about the properties of objects, compare objects to discover what makes them similar and different, begin to understand quantity and number concepts, and start to develop a sense of time and space, they also learn a wide variety of facts and information. Some of this information emerges from repeated daily experiences; other items seem to pique children's interest and stick in their memories.

Young children generally do not discriminate or differentiate between facts, but collect and store much information. The early childhood curriculum helps support children as they learn to sort and classify. Attitudes that provide for and encourage opportunities to explore, question, practise, and discuss enable children to construct new knowledge.

As we discussed in Chapter 9, appropriate topics for curriculum development can revolve around children, families, and the community. These familiar subjects, which offer innumerable learning possibilities, hook into a child's prior or current knowledge about a topic and can then be expanded and built on to help children gain additional information that has relevance in the context of their lives and experiences. Teachers must realize that each child brings unique experiences and interests to school.

Acquisition of information, and of the concepts related to classification, seriation, numbers, time, and space, occurs in many ways in the early childhood program. Just about any activity in which young children engage involves one or several of these concepts. Although the acquisition of information and concepts is often associated with specific curriculum areas, especially math and science, it is not so easy to place them in discrete categories. Children's thinking is ongoing and involves a constant taking in, sifting, connecting, and storing of experiences, concepts, and information. Teachers are constantly listening, observing, questioning, and adjusting to these processes as the children engage in learning.

A Word About Math and Science. Remember that math and science are as much a part of other activities (e.g., blocks, cooking, woodworking, manipulatives, dramatic play, art) as they are separate activities. It is easy to see that the acquisition of number concepts is central to math. But math is not central to the acquisition of number concepts. Classification, seriation, and temporal and spatial concepts are equally integral to both math and science. Yet, these concepts supply some of the tools required to carry out many other endeavours, for instance, measuring, grouping, and comparing which are crucial for managing in all aspects of one's day.

Having children take part in artificial activities to learn math, asking them endless "test" questions (e.g., "What is 2 + 2?" "How many fingers?") or cornering them to make every instance a teachable moment is unrealistic and inappropriate. So much of what children know is demonstrated as they play, and we need to watch for this. Though we must always help children find ways to explain and explore phenomena and answer their queries, math, as with anything, is best learned in the context of experience and guided learning. Math can be identified, pointed out, explored, and enhanced in many indirect, as well as direct, ways throughout the curriculum, both by children and teachers, as interests and circumstances warrant. Remember that the goal of teaching is not to show how much you know but to learn about what the children know. The math centre should not contain math worksheets but the tools of math that can be utilized over the entire curriculum throughout the day. Measuring tapes, rulers, scales, counters, calculators, pencils and paper, and software are only a few examples. If children wish to make comparisons, predictions, or plans on the playground, in the block centre, in the art centre, or in home centre or kitchen, they can! If you want to review software, you might check the SuperKids Web page.

Science, as well, needs to be woven throughout the curriculum. A science centre consisting of a pine cone and magnifying glass is insufficient. Caring for plants and animals, using binoculars, keeping records, using observations, and making predictions help children acquire not only the facts but also the tools for getting the facts. Children's scientific needs can be identified, supported, and enhanced through both the context of the day and their interests and experiences. Exhibit 10-2 outlines guidelines for supporting children in their growth.

Language Development

Children's early development is particularly astounding when we consider the acquisition of language. Infants arrive in the world with no language, but within a year they are starting to converse. And they have done this without any direct instruction

EXHIBIT 10-2 *Guidelines for Supporting Cognitive Development*

Recognize interests, respect ideas, and support efforts.

Encourage children to use the same strategies you use to create an atmosphere of exploration, discovery, excitement, warmth, teamwork, respect, and positive relationships:

• Observe	• Evaluate
• Predict	• Plan
• Record	• Listen
• Hypothesize	• Present
• Discuss	• Elaborate
• Experiment	• Expand
• Question	• Explain
• Research	• Attend to
• Brainstorm ideas	• Compare
• Problem-solve	• Support
• Implement	• Encourage
• Assess	

This list is by no means complete. How we implement these guidelines is demonstrated through positive words and actions and voice tone, as well as all the other guidance techniques we discussed in Chapter 7 for building learning, self-esteem, and prosocial behaviours. These strategies, or ways of doing things to acquire and use information, can be applied in any situation with any project, short- or long-term, in any area of the curriculum throughout the day. Help children to understand these words and to use them. As children learn about learning, they gain lifelong strategies for learning and interacting in a positive and productive way.

in one of the most complex cognitive tasks, one that is unique to humans. The toddler makes rapid gains in language and by the preschool years has acquired an enormous vocabulary, a fundamental grasp of the rules of grammar, and an understanding of the subtleties of the social aspects of communication. In addition, young children begin to develop the skills needed for the complex process of reading and writing, which they begin to tackle soon after they enter school.

These are truly amazing accomplishments. We know much about this language acquisition process, although language researchers certainly are far from understanding completely how children learn to communicate with such speed and accuracy (Gineshi, 1987). Don Rutledge, the former Associate Director of the Toronto Board of Education and the Chair of Ontario's Inquiry into Deaf Education, comments on the process of language acquisition in the next A Canadian Professional Speaks Out box.

EARLY LANGUAGE ACQUISITION

Donald G. Rutledge, Chair, Ontario's Inquiry into Deaf Education

About fifty years ago Noam Chomsky put forth the idea that human language ability is biologically determined, specific to our species, and genetically transmitted. Skeptics abounded. Maybe the skepticism was caused by the name attached to the notion—Language Acquisition Device. It seemed to suggest a single black box in the head. But now the idea that human beings are predisposed from birth to discover specific patterns in language and so "soft-wire" their brains as they grow is commonly accepted. The linguistic evidence as we watch children develop is simply overwhelming, and it is confirmed as neurologists begin to identify specific sites in the brain which deal with various aspects of language. They even begin to discern an intricate pattern of interrelated neurons that can represent objects, metaphors, analogies and other subtle operations peculiar to the human brain ... a constellation of Language Acquisition Devices. We know now that any normal human being can learn any of the more than five hundred human languages—not to mention dialects, pidgins, and creoles. We also know that infants and children can learn languages much more easily than adults—a strong sign of innate endowment.

The question of *how* this is done is now under intense scrutiny. Perhaps the most puzzling thing of all is **syntax**—the art of creating sentences. Implicitly "known" rules seem to govern this. Children try out rules as they learn language, and they all try out the same rules in the same order. Negation is a good example. The child first puts a negative word at the front of the sentence—*No I want sleep*. This later becomes *I no want sleep*, and even later the auxiliaries appear: *I don't want to sleep.* The same regularity of progression is seen in shaping questions and in all other features of language acquisition. We can't escape the conclusion that somehow children "know" the rules in advance, and are just working out how they apply. It is obvious that this innate capacity must develop in response to a linguistic environment, and it is now also obvious that the early years are critical. That's when the neurological architecture of the brain is chiefly decided.

Linguists see a powerful pattern in the language progress we are all familiar with, a pattern which may be important to human success as a species. Infants discover *phonemes*, begin categorizing them, and discover about nine new *words* a day. From 18 to 36 months of age they gradually discover *syntax*—patterns of words called *phrases and clauses*—and they begin to master plurals and past tenses. After *syntax*, or even simultaneously, they develop a sense that *narratives* have a beginning, middle, and end.

This powerful and relatively swift organization of experience, pyramidical yet having separate rules at each level, is accompanied by attendant developments in the neurological structure of the brain. Because each development bootstraps further developments, early success is crucial to optimum brain development in any individual. When a child is eight years old, much of the prime time for language and brain development is past.

The implications are obvious, and should lead to increased emphasis on a rich early environment for the child. But it is also clear that reasonably healthy development will occur in almost any normal social environment, that cultural environments and emphases are diverse throughout the world, and that developed intelligence can occur in all them. The enrichment of the early environment in a literate society takes its own peculiar form. The great Russian psychologist Vygotsky pointed out that learning to read "alters the tools of thinking available to the child." He summed up the power of language acquisition admirably:

> *As the child discovers speech and, literally begins to talk to himself, he inherits far more than words and grammar. He is inducted into ways of being and thinking. Intelligence is a cultural product in which the organic potential of the child interacts with ways of living, thinking and talking to shape the structure of knowing and being.*

● What Is Language?

Language is a complex system involving a variety of components. Included are:

- Vocabulary—learning words

- **Semantics**—understanding word meaning

- **Morphology**—knowing the rules for creating and using words accurately

- **Grammar and syntax**—learning the rules for putting words together meaningfully

- **Pragmatics**—obtaining a growing grasp of the appropriateness of what is being communicated

Any theory of language development indicates that children's early years are particularly crucial in the evolution of language skills.

● What Is Communication?

Language is only part of the communication process. Children can communicate well even when they are unable to talk. Gestures; body language; eye contact; use of picture symbols; assistive devices that replace or augment talking such as picture boards, voice synthesizers, or sign language; facial expressions; sounds;

written symbols; and creative media such as art, dance, music, audio and visual effects, pictures, and drama all communicate ideas and messages.

Language is simply one tool of many that we use to interact with others to share and exchange information and ideas. A conversation is a good example of a communicative interaction. But a dance between two people, exchanging letters, or a chat room on the Internet are also examples, each of which have their own unique characteristics. The interaction can be positive or negative. Certain factors can extend the communication, that is, keep it going. Other factors can stop or prevent the communication.

To keep the communication going, especially in a conversation, we generally do things such as nod, ask questions for clarification or more information, confirm what we heard, pay attention, make eye contact, listen, give positive reinforcement, use body language that says we are interested (e.g., leaning forward), and use an expressive tone and face. Things that typically end communication quickly are a lack of acknowledgment, interruptions, negative comments, inattentiveness, misunderstandings, and a lack of response.

In early childhood education, our aim is to keep the communication and the interactions going, whether they are verbal, written, or expressed through actions or activity. We strive to communicate many positive messages to parents, children, and others through what we do and say and how we present the environment. Messages such as "Welcome," "It is safe here," "I will help you," "You can trust me," "I respect you," and "You can do it" are all evident in the many ways in which we present information and interact.

● What Is Multilingualism?

Canadian early childhood educators in some areas of the country have been familiar with the issue of **bilingualism** for a long time. However, with our changing immigration patterns, **multilingualism** in the program is now an issue, especially in some of our larger urban centres. Early childhood programs increasingly include children from varied linguistic and cultural backgrounds, children who may speak only a language other than English, children who are in the process of acquiring English as a second language, and children who have grown up acquiring more than one language simultaneously.

In some programs, English-speaking children are also exposed to a second language, particularly if that language and culture are important parts of the community. Bilingualism and multilingualism, although often considered a matter of language learning, are intricately tied to cultural and social dimensions (Hakuta & Garcia, 1989). Awareness of and sensitivity to family values is particularly important in working with children learning English as a second language (Sholtys, 1989). In general, young children have little difficulty acquiring more than one language and eventually speaking each language with no interference from the other (Obler, 1985).

Second-Language Teaching Strategies. Although there are no definitive guidelines for helping children learn a second language, the following strategies, which are important for all young children, can also be helpful to those learning a new language (Saville-Troike, 1982; Sholtys, 1989).

1. A new experience such as preschool can be bewildering to any young child, particularly if the child cannot understand the language. A friendly, consistent, supportive atmosphere can help make the child feel welcome and comfortable, which, in turn, will facilitate learning English.

2. If someone who speaks the child's first language is available, enlist that person to help the child learn the routines and expectations, as well as the new language. If another child in the class speaks the language, interaction between the two should be encouraged, although certainly not forced.

3. Encourage all of the children to talk to and include the child in activities.

4. Use the child's name frequently, being sure to pronounce it properly when talking to the child.

5. A non-English-speaking child should not be forced to speak because the natural process of learning a second language usually entails a time of silent assimilation.

6. Involve the child in the classroom through non-language activities (e.g., helping to set the table for snack) to help the child become part of the group.

7. Language should be presented in a natural, meaningful way in the context of the child's experiences and interests.

8. Concrete objects or demonstration of actions should be paired with new words. For example, say the word "milk" when helping the child pour it at snack.

9. Repetition of new language learning is important, provided it is done naturally. Meaningless drill does not help. Consistently using the same wording each day, for instance, to signal classroom transitions, will help the child connect words and meaning more easily.

10. When a child shares feelings or an idea verbally, such communication should be encouraged through uncritical acceptance. Correcting grammar or pronunciation tends to inhibit rather than foster language.

● Environments and Attitudes That Encourage Language Development

The following sections will examine several important aspects of language. First, we will discuss the spontaneous, informal, ongoing use of language that should be a natural accompaniment to whatever children are doing. We next look at the story as a means to enhance language development. Finally, we will examine children's emerging literacy, their awareness that language extends to reading and writing, and how this is supported through integrated language experiences.

Spontaneous Language.   Because language is used in almost everything children do, it must be central to the early childhood program. Children are constantly involved in communication—in listening, hearing, talking, interpreting, representing, writing, and reading. All forms of language surround them as they interact with one another, with adults, with media, with activities, and with varied materials. Language activities do not need to be structured to teach language, because preschool-aged children have already acquired an elaborate and complex language system. Rather, early childhood language experiences should emerge from natural and meaningful conversations, interactions, and experiences between adults and children and among children. Such talk is used to inform, tell stories, pretend, plan, argue, discuss, express humour, and so on (Gineshi, 1987). Classrooms for young children, therefore, are not quiet. They are abuzz with language almost all of the time.

Almost every aspect of the early childhood environment and program facilitates language. For instance, the knowledgeable teacher, who values what children have to say and listens to them carefully, promotes language development. Similarly, a daily program that provides large blocks of time in which children can become immersed in activities and interactions fosters language usage. In addition, language growth is encouraged by a curriculum that introduces interesting and stimulating objects, experiences, and concepts, just as a classroom environment that is set up to invite small groups of children to work together promotes language.

Conversations   A natural way of using language is through conversation. In good early childhood programs, there is an almost constant, ongoing buzz of conversations between children and teachers and among children. For children, conversation is an art that takes time to develop since it involves learning a number of elements, such as how to initiate and end conversations, maintain coherent dialogue, take turns, and "repair" a conversation that breaks down (McTear, 1985). It is important, therefore, that there be many opportunities for children to practise their emerging conversational skills.

Teachers' ability to engage in effective conversations with children is also an art. Dialogue between adults and small groups or individual children is essential in teaching preschoolers (Lay-Dopyera & Dopyera, 1987a). Unfortunately, research has found that there is generally little extended conversation between teachers and young children.

An in-depth study of one skilled teacher's conversational strategies revealed some significant findings (Rogers, Perrin, & Waller, 1987). "Cathy" (the teacher) maintained an equal relationship in her conversation; the number of words and length of sentences were relatively equal to those used by the child. Particularly important was Cathy's genuine interest in what the child was telling her. Cathy's interactions were based on the child's actions and interests and, more often than not, were in response to the child's initiation.

The most significant observation of this study was Cathy's avoidance of "know-answer questions," questions to which the teacher already knows the answer (e.g., "What colour did you paint the sky?" or "How many cookies are on your plate?").

Such questions are answered by a simple response from the child and may be evaluated by the teacher. Children may fear giving a wrong answer and therefore avoid conversation with the teacher. Thus, teacher–child conversations should arise from natural situations and be based on genuine interest in what the child is doing.

Playing with Language   Another facet of language that teachers can use to enrich its use in the early childhood setting is children's language play. Once children have a good grasp of the principles of language and the correctness of a concept, they delight in confirming this by expressing the opposite, usually accompanied by much laughter and giggling (Geller, 1985). Expressions of humour through silliness, nonsense words, or rhymes particularly enthrall preschoolers. Children enjoy humour, and teachers can use it to capture and maintain children's attention, both in the stories they read or tell and in their conversations with children.

Stories.

In a language-rich early childhood program, you will find that language permeates every activity. You will hear it in the washroom, at the meal table,

in the block centre, and on the playground. You will hear children talking to themselves, with their teachers, and with their peers. A quiet program is cause for concern. In addition to the ongoing use of language in the early childhood program, specific activities based on language use and elaboration are also incorporated. Such activities are often presented at large- or small-group times, enhancing not just language but listening skills, group social skills, creative thinking, concept formation, and other areas of development. The story is at the core of many of those experiences.

Stories, in their various forms, are the most popular vehicle for language activities. Stories can be told or read by teachers, children, or both together; they can be enacted by children or with flannel-board pieces, puppets, or play dough; or they can come from the rich store of children's literature or from the children's own experiences. Stories can exist in a variety of forms such as poems, rhymes, songs, actions, pictures, videos, dramas, writing, or drawing. In this section, we discuss the significance for development of preschool experiences with stories.

The Story Schema   As adults, you know that most simple stories have a regular, predictable structure—a beginning, a middle, and an end. Preschoolers, in communicating, tell us their stories constantly in relaying events about their day, families, projects, experiences, play, ideas, and other matters. Everything in life has this basic structure of a beginning, a middle, and an end. In essence, you have a story. The beginning of the "story," or "once upon a time" section, introduces the setting, the time, and the characters. In the middle, there is a complication—something unusual or unexpected happens. Then, in the end, or the "lived happily ever after" section, the complication is resolved or settled and the characters reach a more stable state. This simple structure is known as the **story schema**. Children need to gain a sense of this sequence in order to communicate effectively and to understand the world around them. It has been the subject of fairly extensive research since the 1980s.

Both children and adults use the story schema to help them understand, remember, and retell stories. As long as stories follow that structure or schema, they are easy to understand and to remember. Experience with stories in the preschool years is critical for the development of the story schema (Young, 1987, 1993a).

By reading lots of stories in your program, you are helping children to learn about the story schema and to develop cognitive skills they will need throughout their lives. And you are contributing to significant cognitive growth through a developmentally appropriate activity.

Emergent Literacy. As we have seen, children learn to understand and express language in a natural way through a process that begins very early in life. They also learn about the story schema without direct instruction. Similarly, preschool children begin to form an understanding of reading and writing, something that has only come to interest researchers and educators relatively recently. The term "emergent literacy" acknowledges that learning to read and write (in other words, to become literate) is a dynamic, ongoing, emerging process. In fact, all aspects of language—listening, speaking, writing, and reading—are intertwined and develop concurrently, not sequentially (Teale & Sulzby, 1986).

Children develop an understanding of reading and writing through a supportive, literate environment, starting at home and continuing in the early childhood program. And this is done without formal instruction. If a young child is in a story- and print-rich environment, the child will develop the foundations of literacy that are required for reading and writing.

Catherine Snow concluded that when parents read to and with their young children, the children's language is more complex than it is during other times of play. Furthermore, in the process of early reading, teachers and parents help their children acquire some of the basic rules of literacy—learning that books are for reading rather than manipulating or that books represent a separate, fictional world (Snow & Ninio, 1986). Both home and school experiences with books provide children with further insights, for example, that print should make sense, that

---

Reflective Exercise 10-3

Read a book written for preschool-aged children. Does this book appeal to you? Do you think it will appeal to children? Is the story schematic? Evaluate this book according to the criteria outlined in the text.

print and speech are related, that book language is different from speech, and that books are enjoyable (Schickedanz, 1986). Out of many experiences with the printed form of the language come the foundations for writing and reading.

Learning to Write   The beginnings of writing emerge early in life through a number of steps. Vygotsky (1978a) traced the roots of writing to earliest infant gestures, described as "writing in the air." In late infancy, infants will try to copy a parent's list writing, and a toddler engages in more complex writing behaviours. During the preschool years, children become aware of the differences between drawing and writing, a distinction that is evident in their own efforts. By age 3, many children begin to use **mock writing**, a series of wavy, circular, or vertical lines that deliberately imitate adult writing and are distinctly different from drawing. Within the next couple of years, mock writing increasingly becomes a mixture of real letters and innovative symbols.

By late kindergarten or Grade 1, most children who have grown up in a pleasurable, literate environment and who recognize most or all of the letters of the alphabet begin to use **invented spelling** by finding the speech sound that most closely fits what they want to write (Atkins, 1984). Five-year-old Abby wrote, "I M GNG TO DRV MI KAR AT HOM" (I am going to drive my car at home) in one of her stories, which was accompanied by a picture of Abby atop a blue vehicle. Analysis of the errors seen in invented spelling indicates that children are trying to work out a system of rules, just as they did as toddlers when they were acquiring oral language. Because reading and writing are intertwined processes, such early attempts at spelling are soon replaced with more conventional forms as children repeatedly come across the same words in their reading (Atkins, 1984).

Learning to Read   When children read and write, they are "making sense out of or through print," although this sense does not require an understanding of a conventional alphabetic code (Goodman, 1986, p. 5). Eventually, children do acquire this understanding as they learn the consistent relationship between the letters of the alphabet and their use in the written form. Early literacy, however, is based on the growing awareness that print means something, for instance, that a stop sign indicates that a driver should step on the brake.

Some 2-year-olds already display such awareness, for example, pointing to a word in a book and saying, "That's my name" (Walton, 1989). By age 3, children clearly have substantial understanding of why and how print is used. Many 4-year-olds have developed the ability to recognize a variety of words when these are presented in their appropriate context, for instance, common labels and signs. Experiences in recognizing words in their environmental context help children learn about the process of reading and lead to eventual recognition of these words out of their context (Kontos, 1986).

Children actively seek to make sense of print in their environment by using a variety of strategies that they themselves invent (Willert & Kamii, 1985). Younger preschoolers' strategies focus on such clues as the first letter of a word ("That's my name," says Paul, "because it's got a 'P'"); looking at the shape of the word, such as its length or spacing if there is more than one word in a configuration; and using pictures as clues to help decipher accompanying words. As children get older and more experienced in acquiring reading skills, they use some additional strategies. Included are looking for familiar letters or combinations of letters in words; spontaneously and repeatedly practising the spelling and copying of words; and inventing a phonological system, similar to that used in invented spelling, to sound out words.

Implications   As the preceding discussions suggest, young children have a natural interest in the print environment around them, an interest most of them express through their own inventive attempts at writing and reading. This developmentally appropriate view of how children learn to read and write is far removed from some of the stereotyped notions of reading and writing as formal subjects best begun in first grade. Thinking of literacy merely as recognizing words or the sounds of letters "is as dangerous as it is erroneous" (Gibson, 1989, p. 30).

Yet, all too often, young children are placed into high-powered, rigid, formalized programs that focus on isolated skills involved in the reading process rather than on the integration of all aspects of language. In fact, a statement expressing concern over this developmentally inappropriate practice was jointly prepared by a group of relevant organizations (International Reading Association, 1986).

Reading and writing emerge from many successful and enjoyable experiences with language, both oral and written. According to research, literacy best develops through meaningful context in an informal, supportive environment (Kontos, 1986). As Judith Schickedanz (1982), one of the leading authorities in children's emergent literacy, wrote:

> *We need to abandon ideas and practices that assume early literacy development to be simply a matter of teaching children a few basic skills such as alphabet recognition or letter-sound associations. Much more is involved. Limiting children's reading experiences to contacts with bits and pieces of print isolated from meaningful contexts may actually prevent them from developing broader and more complex insights that are key to understanding what written language is all about. (P. 259)*

Promoting Literacy Development   Literacy, like oral language, emerges in a natural way that does not require formal teaching to prompt interest. What it does need is a language-rich environment to encourage its development. Literacy is best promoted in the context of a **whole language approach**, one in which high-quality oral and print language surrounds children, children can observe others using literacy skills, and children are encouraged to experiment with all forms of language. Such an approach integrates all forms of communication, including speaking, listening, writing, reading, art, music, and math (International Reading Association, 1986). Exhibit 10-3 provides excellent ideas for promoting literacy and language development.

EXHIBIT 10-3 *Guidelines for Supporting Language and Literacy Development*

The following suggestions for supporting literacy development come from a variety of sources. The term "story" can be interchanged with "project" or another medium where appropriate.

- The aim of supporting literacy development in young children should be to enhance their desire to read and write by building on their intrinsic motivation to learn these skills (Willert & Kamii, 1985).

- A language-rich environment must contain many materials, opportunities, and experiences for planned and spontaneous interaction with language, both oral and written. This means providing appropriate materials and scheduled time blocks for children to pursue language activities (Machado, 1985; Teale & Martinez, 1988).

- A carefully selected library of high-quality children's books must be available for children to browse through or to ask a teacher to read.

- Stories should not just be read but also discussed when the children want to do so. Children understand stories better when they have opportunities to ask and answer questions about the plot and characters of a story and to relate the story to their own lives (Teale & Martinez, 1988; Walton, 1989). But stories need not be stopped and interrupted with a barrage of questions. A few key questions can be used to assess prior knowledge and experience, to check for key concepts, and to check for understanding occasionally to ensure the children are following the story line.

- Children need many story-reading experiences to acquire the story schema. Knowing, for instance, how a story begins and ends and the story's sequence of events is important to literacy development (Jensen, M. A., 1985; Young, 1987, 1993a).

- Books should be read more than once. Children are more likely to reenact a book on their own if they have heard it at least three times (Teale & Martinez, 1988).

- Children should be encouraged to "read" to one another, whether or not they actually know how to read. Such activities promote emergent literacy (Teale & Martinez, 1988).

- If some children in the class seem to have had few one-on-one reading experiences at home, time should be set aside when a teacher can spend time reading to just one or two children (Jensen, 1985b).

- Print awareness can be supported through books and other forms of print in the school environment. Charts, lists, labels, and bulletin boards that surround children in the environment contribute to print awareness, as does a teacher who interprets, calls attention to, and gets the children's input when creating print (Goodman, Smith, Meredith, & Goodman, 1987; Schickedanz, 1986).

(cont'd)

EXHIBIT 10-3 *cont'd*

- Children gradually learn that there is a relationship between written and spoken words. When children read certain books frequently, they often become so familiar with the stories that they know which words correspond with which pages. Such experiences contribute to making the connection between speech and print (Schickedanz, 1986).

- Children should be provided with a variety of reading and writing materials to incorporate into their play. For example, paper, pencils, markers, and other implements in the art, language arts, dramatic play, science, and math centres should be included to suggest a link between the activities that go on in those areas and reading/writing.

- Given a supportive atmosphere, older children will engage in story writing. Although children may not be using conventional letters and words, their stories as well as the writing process are still full of meaning. The sensitive teacher must carefully attend to what children are conveying to understand that meaning (Harste, Short, & Burke, 1988).

- One way of promoting storytelling and writing is to include a "publishers' workshop" as an ongoing activity centre in the classroom (Bakst & Essa, 1990). The teacher writes down children's dictated stories but also encourages the children to write their stories. Books are designed, made, and presented and stories are displayed and recorded.

- Stories should be shared, something that can be done informally as other children come to the publishing area or more formally during a large-group activity. When their stories are shared, children develop audience awareness, an appreciation that their stories are a form of communication that should make sense to others (Bakst & Essa, 1990).

- Some children show little interest in reading and writing, perhaps because they have had little access to materials that promote these activities. One successful strategy to stimulate this interest is to provide a "writing suitcase" that the children can take home overnight or over a weekend. This suitcase can include such materials as various sizes and shapes of paper and notebooks; chalk and chalkboard, pencils, crayons, and markers; magnet, cardboard, or plastic letters and stencils; favourite picture books; scissors; and tape, glue, stapler, hole punch, and ruler (Rich, 1985).

- Stories can be input on the computer.

- Stories can be represented through creative media.

- Post children's work everywhere.

- Share books and stories between home and school.

- Make comparisons between salient features of books, such as authors' backgrounds, illustrators' methods, themes, size, shape, colour, and texture of the book.

- Stories should be read often for the sheer pleasure they give with no strings attached!

Social Development

One major function of the early childhood program is to support the process of socialization, the means through which children become a functioning part of society and learn society's rules and values. Although socialization is a lifelong process, it is particularly crucial early in life, when the foundation for later attitudes, values, and behaviours is laid. Unquestionably, socialization begins with the parent-child and caretaker-infant relationships in infancy, where patterns of response, need fulfillment, and give-and-take have their roots. Children who do not come to an early childhood program until they are older already have had numerous socializing experiences. They may have learned to trust or be wary of others, to meet new experiences enthusiastically or with caution, to care about others' feelings because their needs have always been considered, or to think of others as competitors for affection or resources. The term "curriculum" includes all the elements in the environment that lead to conversations and activities that promote socialization.

● What Is Social Development?

As increasing numbers of infants, toddlers, and preschoolers enter group care, these children experience increasingly intimate peer contact (Howes, 1987). By age 3 or 4, most children are part of a social world that is truly egalitarian, a world of peers who are equals (Moore, 1982). In this world, as young children go through this process of becoming socialized to the peer society, they are expected to:

• Share and cooperate

• Learn the rules and expectations

• Gain skill and competence in peer interaction

• Enter into friendships

• Develop gender identity

• Adopt racial and cultural attitudes

• Form a sense of morals and values

• Acquire a host of prosocial behaviours

The opportunity to develop multicultural, multiracial, and multieconomic acceptance will, to a large extent, depend on the integrative nature of the early childhood program. Environment, attitude, and actions combine to guide social development.

● Environments and Attitudes That Encourage Social Development

Peer Interaction.   Peer interaction is an essential ingredient in the process of childhood socialization, in fact, in the total development of the child (Hartup,

1983a). As with any skill, it is through practice in real situations that children develop competence in peer interaction. The many naturally occurring opportunities of day-to-day life allow children to be sympathetic and helpful to peers (Honig, 1982). These social skills include the many strategies children learn to help them initiate and continue social interactions, negotiate, and settle conflicts (C. A. Smith, 1982).

For young children who are just entering peer relationships, adult guidance—not interference—is important; as children get older and less egocentric, the presence of an adult becomes less necessary (Howes, 1987; Oden, 1982). The teacher, in facilitating social development, must first of all provide children with ample time and space, and appropriate materials, to facilitate social interaction. A child who has difficulty engaging in social play can be helped through sensitive teacher guidance, for instance, directing that child to a group with similar play interests or pairing the child with a more socially competent peer (Rogers & Ross, 1986).

Older children also provide excellent models for younger ones. In one study, the pretend play of 2-year-olds was characterized as much more cooperative and complex when they were paired with 5-year-olds than with fellow toddlers (Howes & Farver, 1987). This research supports the idea of providing children in early childhood programs with some opportunities for mixed-age interaction.

Friendship. One special type of peer relationship is friendship, that close link between people typified by mutual concern, sharing, and companionship. Recent research points to the importance of early friendship to later emotional well-being (Flaste, 1991). Young children's concept of friendship primarily revolves around the immediate situation. As children grow older, their friendships typically become more stable (Damon, 1983).

Preschoolers view friends in terms of their accessibility, physical attributes, and actions (Rubin, 1980). In other words, a friend is "someone you play with a lot," "someone who wears a Batman T-shirt," "someone who invites you to her birthday party," or "someone who isn't mean." Another insight into early friendship can be found in the often-heard question, "Are you my friend?" which can be translated to mean, "Will you play with me?" (Edwards, 1986).

Preschoolers expect friendships to maximize enjoyment, entertainment, and satisfaction in play (Parker & Gottman, 1989). Typically young children are focused on themselves—their own feelings and needs (Rubin, 1980). Yet, as many observers have noted, young children are surprisingly capable of caring about and giving emotional support to one another (Levinger & Levinger, 1986); for instance, observe the concern of onlookers when a child cries because he or she is hurt or distressed.

Trust is the basic foundation on which friendship is built. Children who are trustworthy, who share and cooperate, are more likely to be considered as friends by their peers. Trust in the peer relationship, however, does not simply emerge but is built on the sense of trust that children established early in life (as described by Erikson), when nurturing adults met their needs consistently. Teachers can help children develop a sense of trust, which can enhance friendships, through their support and guidance. More specifically, they can help children recognize their own needs and goals and those of others, develop more effective social skills, recognize how their behaviour affects others, and become aware of their own social successes so they can be repeated (Buzzelli & File, 1989).

It is wise to remember that friendships cannot be imposed or forced. To tell children, "We are all friends at school" or "Go find another friend to play with" sends a mixed message about the meaning of friendship. Young children will develop friendships on the basis of trust and criteria meaningful to them. Teachers should respect their right to choose friends.

● Inclusion and Diversity

The theme of inclusion and diversity—respecting, valuing, and including all people by affording them the same access to rights, choices, and opportunities and acknowledging their commonalities while respecting their individuality and unique strengths and needs—is a thread we have attempted to weave throughout this text. Here we look at three areas, gender, race and culture, and special needs, in order to provide helpful strategies that incorporate awareness, advocacy, sensitivity, and empathy in the curriculum so that inclusion becomes a way of life for the children as they grow.

Gender Role Development.   Research has shown that one of the most powerful determinants of peer interaction and friendship is the children's sex. If you work with young children, you will have observed that the majority of their playmate choices are of the same sex. This holds true in all cultural settings, not just in North America (Maccoby, 1990). Cross-sex friends are not uncommon; however, as they get older, girls increasingly choose to play with other girls, and boys seek out other boys as play partners.

Children choose same-sex friends spontaneously, and attempts to change or influence their choices to encourage more cross-sex interaction have generally not been very successful (Howes, 1988; Katz, 1986; Maccoby, 1990). Children value the concrete symbols of their gender that confirm their maleness or femaleness, and they construct and adopt a rigid set of rules and stereotypes about what is gender-appropriate. This rigidity is consistent with a similar approach to other cognitive concepts. In acquiring same-sex values, children also form an identity with same-sex people.

This rigidity, children's gravitation toward same-sex peers, and their engagement in gender-stereotyped activities are often troublesome to adults who want children to be broadminded and tolerant of others. Despite many parents' and teachers' efforts to present non-sexist models to the children in their lives, these same children will often display highly sex-stereotyped behaviours and attitudes. Some guidelines can help the early childhood teacher lay the foundation for non-biased attitudes toward the sexes based on respect for each person as an individual, which includes their unique gender. These are found in Exhibit 10-4.

EXHIBIT 10-4 *Guidelines for Supporting Social Development I*

Non-Sexist Teaching

- *Value each child as an individual.* Focus on the strengths and abilities of each child as a person, and help children recognize and value these characteristics.

- *Help children learn that gender identity is biologically determined.* Before they develop gender constancy, children may feel that it is their preference for boy or girl activities that makes them boys or girls. Reassure them that their bodies, not their activities, determine their sex (Derman-Sparks, 1989).

- *Be aware of possible gender biases in your own behaviour.* Studies have shown, for instance, that adults tend to protect girls more, react to boys' misbehaviours more, encourage independence more in boys, and expect girls to be more fearful (Honig, 1983).

- *Listen carefully to all children.* Adults tend to interrupt or speak simultaneously more with girls than with boys, suggesting that what girls have to say is less important (Honig, 1983).

- *Help children find the words to get their nurturance needs met.* Little boys are not as likely to ask for a hug or a lap to sit on as girls. Teachers can help all children find the right words to communicate their needs for affection (Honig, 1983).

- *Use language carefully, avoiding bias toward male identity.* The English language tends to assume male identity when sex is not clear. We generally say "he" when we don't know whether an animal, person, or storybook character is male or female, and this tricks children into thinking that "he's" are more important than "she's" (Sheldon, 1990).

- *Provide materials that show males and females in a variety of roles.* Puzzles, lotto games, posters, and photographs can portray males and females in non-traditional roles. Dramatic-play props can draw children into a variety of roles sometimes stereotyped as male or female.

- *Select children's books that portray non-sexist models.* Children's literature includes a range of characters from the very sex-stereotyped to the very non-sexist. A study of widely read children's books, including award-winning ones, showed that male and female roles are often distorted and stereotyped. Males appear far more often; females, when they are portrayed, tend to be shown as passive and dependent (Flerx, Fidler, & Rogers, 1976).

- *Plan a wide range of activities, and encourage all children to participate.* Children will participate in and enjoy a variety of activities—cooking, woodworking, blocks, housekeeping, book browsing, sewing, sand and water, art—if they are well planned and the teacher's words or attitudes do not promote sex stereotyping.

- *Discuss obvious sex stereotyping with children.* Older preschoolers and school-aged children, especially if they have been around adults who are sensitive to using non-biased concepts and vocabulary, can engage in discussions about sex stereotypes in books, favourite television programs, or movies.

Racial and Cultural Awareness and Attitudes.   Similarly to their early recognition of gender differences, children also develop an awareness of racial variations at an early age. Preschoolers use the most readily visible physical differences as cues; skin colour in particular, and hair and eye colour, provide a basis for comparison and classification.

A rather subtle variation in learning about different people arises when children begin to discover cultural differences. Family, neighbourhood, school, church, books, and mass media can introduce children to the fact that people meet their daily needs in different ways. All people need to communicate, but they may do so in different languages; all people need to eat, but they don't all eat the same types of foods; all people require clothing, shelter, and transportation, but they meet these needs in different ways.

Although children's cognitive development steers them toward noting differences and classifying accordingly, society applies the comparative values that lead to stereotypes and prejudice. Children are bombarded with subtle and not-so-subtle messages about the worth of people. Parents, as the primary socializers of their children, seem the obvious transmitters of racial and cultural attitudes; yet, research has shown little relationship between children and their parents in this respect (Katz, 1982). A more plausible source of racial and cultural information may be television, movies, and books that, by their portrayals or omissions, imply superiority of some and inferiority of other groups.

In forming their own attitudes, young children continually strive to fit together the multiple and often contradictory sources of information about other people. The early childhood program is an ideal place to help children learn about themselves and others, learn to value and have pride in themselves, and learn to respect others. This involves conveying accurate knowledge about and pride in children's own racial and cultural groups, accurate knowledge about and appreciation of other racial and cultural groups, and an understanding of racism and how to counter it (Derman-Sparks, Higa, & Sparks, 1980). One excellent resource for helping teachers of young children in this task is Louise Derman-Sparks' *Anti-Bias Curriculum: Tools for Empowering Young Children* (1989). This book sensitively and succinctly discusses and suggests strategies for helping children learn about and respect racial, gender, cultural, and physical differences and promotes anti-discrimination and activism. Derman-Sparks and Ramsey's 1993 article "Early childhood multicultural, anti-bias education in the 1990s: Toward the 21st century" would also be a useful resource. Exhibit 10-5 outlines guidelines, gleaned from various sources, that can help you provide children with a developmentally appropriate understanding of other races and cultures.

Sensitivity Toward People with Diverse Abilities.   Children learn attitudes of understanding, acceptance, and sensitivity toward those who have special needs. More and more children with disabilities are included in early childhood programs. In Prince Edward Island, for example, direct funding to licensed centres for children with disabilities has been available since 1988. Consequently, the number of children with disabilities included in the province's child care centres has risen quickly. The following factors are important considerations in helping children develop sensitivity.

Spending Time Together Children with special needs can benefit from a quality inclusive program by experiencing success in a variety of developmentally appropriate activities through relationships with age-mates, where both assume roles of model and friend, and through exposure to the many opportunities for informal, incidental learning that take place in all early childhood programs (Deiner, 1983; Spodek, Saracho, & Lee, 1984). At the same time, all children benefit by learning that children who are in some way different from them have, nonetheless, far more commonalities than differences (Karnes & Lee, 1979). Inclusion provides children with the opportunity for positive experiences that build a good foundation for lifelong learning about and from others. Its intent is to decrease isolation from others and increase knowledge about others. This, in turn, decreases prejudice toward and stereotypes of those initially perceived as different (Deiner, 1983, p. 14).

Planning As we discussed in Chapter 5, simply including children with and without disabilities does not ensure interaction and acceptance. The benefits do not happen automatically. Inclusion does not mean simply enrolling children with special needs in a preschool or child care program. Current information and ongoing planning, preparation, modification, evaluation, and support inclusive of the team are necessary for success. Early childhood educators, because they know a great deal about children and how best to work with them, have many skills needed for working with all children, including those with special needs. The Web site of Assistive Technology might be of interest if you have children with special needs in your program.

Team Effort Teachers need to recognize their skills and the influence they have. Just as we attempt to empower children by involving them in the decision-making process and creating ownership—a vested personal interest—so the entire school needs to be involved in the process of inclusion. Making decisions together holds each team member responsible and accountable for the success of the process.

In working with children and their families, you will find that the greatest emotion is the fear of the unknown. Parents of typical children will worry about the effect inclusion will have on their child. Parents of the child with special needs will worry about their child being able to manage. Children will have questions. The new child will have all the anxieties of any new child plus the additional fears of being taken care of adequately. Teachers will worry whether they are prepared to handle the situation.

To reduce these fears, schools often arrange for the child to spend some time in the program before they are to start. The teacher can spend time in the child's current program as well. Each gets an opportunity to know and understand the

EXHIBIT 10-5   *Guidelines for Supporting Social Development II*

Racial and Cultural Awareness and Attitudes

- *When children bring up racial/cultural differences*, discuss them honestly. Help children recognize that there are differences between people but that these differences do not make them superior or inferior to others.

- *Help children develop pride through positive racial/cultural identity.* Children's self-concepts are tied to feeling good about all aspects of their beings. Acknowledgment and positive comments about the beauty of different skin, hair, and eye colours is important to developing feelings about self-worth.

- *Help children develop positive attitudes about other races.* Children need accurate information about other races. Modelling acceptance and appreciation of all races is an important factor.

- *Help children see skin colour variations as a continuum rather than as extremes.* Colour charts to which children can match their own skin colour can help them recognize that everyone is a shade of brown.

- *Help children learn that darker colours are not dirty.* A common misconception among children is that a child of a darker colour is dirty or unwashed. Be careful in your choice of words (e.g., do not say, "Wash that black dirt off your hands"). Doll-washing activities, for instance, bathing an obviously dirty white doll and a clean black doll, can help begin to dispel this notion.

- *Post photographs of children and their families.* This can help children begin to acquire the concept of racial constancy as teachers point out similarities (and differences) between family members. Help dispel misconceptions about racial constancy as these come up spontaneously. Be prepared for questions if a child in your class was adopted by parents of a different race.

- *Ensure that the environment contains materials representing many races and cultures.* Books, dolls, pictures, posters, dramatic-play props, manipulatives, puzzles, and other materials should portray people of all colours and cultures in very positive ways. This is particularly important if your class is racially/culturally mixed. It is also important, however, to expose children in homogeneous classes to different racial and cultural groups through the environment.

- *Discuss incidents of racism and racial stereotypes with the children.* Model anti-racist behaviours by challenging incidents of racism or racial stereotyping. Help children find alternative words if they use racial slurs in arguments with one another.

- *Focus curriculum material about cultures on similarities between people rather than on differences.* Children can identify with shared experiences engaged in by people of other cultures. All people eat, wear clothes, need shelter, share special occasions, and value family activities. Focusing on "exotic" aspects of a culture only points out how different these are and robs them of the shared human factor.

(cont'd)

EXHIBIT 10-5 *cont'd*

- *Avoid a "tourist" approach to teaching about cultures.* Do not teach children about other cultures out of context. For instance, avoid using only the holidays celebrated by other cultures or a one-shot "cultures week" to focus on this topic (e.g., Monday—Mexico, Tuesday—Japan, Wednesday—Africa, Thursday—Germany, and Friday—France). Also avoid using an ethnic cooking activity and a display of ceremonial clothing as the main components of these occasions. Such an approach is disconnected from everyday life, trivializes cultural diversity, and merely represents multiculturalism as a token gesture rather than as a genuine reflection of life around the world.

- *Make cultural diversity part of daily classroom activity.* Integrate aspects of the children's cultures into the everyday life of your class. Consider that the typical housekeeping centre in many early childhood classrooms conveys a single culture: a white, middle-class model. Many ways of life should be reflected throughout the classroom. For instance, you can include dolls of different races, post pictures showing different ethnic groups, introduce in the housekeeping cupboard food packages that reflect cultural preferences, or include home or cooking implements used by families of children from different cultures.

- *Convey the diversity of cultures through their common themes.* Read about different cultures to find out how various cultural groups meet their physical needs, engage in celebrations, and adapt to their environment. For instance, although Canadians and Americans carve pumpkins into jack-o'-lanterns at Halloween, other cultures also commonly carve fruits and vegetables on certain occasions.

- *Consider the complexity involved in celebrating holidays when their observance might be counter, even offensive, to some families' beliefs or cultures.* The celebration of Christmas could offend the non-Christian families with children in your program. Thanksgiving as a holiday might be an occasion of loss rather than celebration for Canadian Aboriginal families. The celebration of holidays should not be avoided but should be considered carefully, taking into account the attitudes, needs, and feelings of the children, families, and staff. Holiday celebrations should focus on respect and understanding of cultural observances.

- *Do not single out a child in a way that would make that child feel different.* Learning about a child's culture should be done in the context of learning about all of the children's cultures. Help such a child and the others in the class recognize that a particular culture is shared by many other people in the world.

- *Involve children's families.* Families are a prime source of information about cultural diversity. Invite parents to participate in the class and share ideas about how all of the children can learn more about their unique backgrounds. Particularly in child care centres, parents may not have the time to join the class, but they should always feel welcome.

SOURCES: Derman-Sparks (1989); Derman-Sparks & Ramsey (1993); Dimidjian (1989); Edwards (1986); Phenice & Hildebrand (1988); Ramsey (1982, 1987); "Suggestions for developing positive racial attitudes" (1980).

other. Then a planning session with all parties helps address needs, answer questions, and delegate responsibilities and develops a network of support for parents. Following this, parents and teachers often state that their fears were unfounded or addressed and that they felt confident, prepared, and excited about having the child in the class.

Continuity and Communication　Continuity between teachers and programs can be a serious barrier to inclusion. Teams need to include the transitional partner from the very beginning in a gradual process of transfer in which trust, goals, needs, and information are clearly defined and considered in the context of the family. Ongoing communication and interaction is essential before, during, and after the process has been initiated. This is done with the family as the central focus. No decisions or discussions should occur without the parents present and actively involved. As well, too much or too little information can be damaging by creating either unnecessary bias or work. Parental consent, presence, and review of information to be exchanged is critical before exchanging information.

Honesty　Children need accurate information, presented in a sensitive manner, about why a peer (or a teacher) looks, moves, sounds, or behaves differently from themselves. Children need the chance to express fears or misgivings and to ask questions. It is not unusual for children to be apprehensive about things that are unfamiliar and different or to worry that the disability could happen to them as well. Children's questions are honest and without value judgments. Offering a simple, honest explanation will answer the child's concern and respect the person's disability (Derman-Sparks, 1989).

When a child with cerebral palsy was enrolled at one school, one student called her a "baby." Initially, the teacher thought of an explanation: "Roberta cannot walk because there is something wrong with the muscles in her legs. She can get around on this scooter board by using her arm muscles. Would you like to ask Roberta if you can try her scooter board so you can see what it feels like?" However, the teacher concluded there were three difficulties with this answer:

1. The teacher felt she needed to explore with the child why she thought Roberta was a baby. Sometimes children's questions have nothing to do with the disability, yet we assume they do. Perhaps Roberta was acting like a baby as many children do when they play. Or perhaps it was because Roberta was so small. Asking for reasons for, and clarification of, a child's comments or queries helps us provide the child with the appropriate response. This is a springboard for discussion to clarify the child's misconceptions or fears.

2. The teacher realized she needed to word statements objectively and without value. "Something wrong" would devalue Roberta as a person. Children can identify and accept matter-of-fact statements, so "Roberta was born with cerebral palsy" would prove a better choice. It is simply a statement and does not imply good or bad or right or wrong.

3. The teacher realized Roberta's scooter board was very personal, and she did not want to put Roberta in the awkward position of choosing between a yes and a no answer. She decided to provide some additional scooter boards in the class so that children could use them as they wished. This would create natural instances for discussion as the children compared their self-directed activities and experiences.

Sincerity, Credibility, and Trust   Think how often we say we are going to "help" children accept and include peers with disabilities. Relationships are two-way and both parties must do the accepting. People can't accept others simply because they are told to or because they live next door. Acceptance is based on credibility and trust, so children need opportunities to establish this. Having a disability is not a basis for friendship or permission to behave in a hurtful way. Children need the skills to go beyond the disability to determine the personality of the person who has it and pursue genuine friendships.

● Moral Development

One primary aim of socialization is for children to learn and internalize standards of what is right and wrong, in other words, to develop a conscience. **Moral development** is a long-term process to which many factors contribute. Children are surrounded by a social climate in which the actions of others convey degrees of fairness, consistency, respect, and concern for others. Children's observations of how others behave, how they are treated, and their own cognitive maturation contribute to their emerging sense of morality.

Children adopt a more mature set of standards if they are raised in an atmosphere of clearly set and enforced standards, support and nurturance, open communication in which their viewpoint is valued, and other-oriented reasons for expected behaviour (Maccoby & Martin, 1983). There is also evidence that the onset of the distinction between right and wrong may be an inborn trait, emerging by children's second birthday (Kagan, 1987).

Another factor with which children have to contend, especially in a diverse society such as ours, is that moral standards vary across cultures. Some universal **interpersonal moral rules**—ones prohibiting harm to others, murder, incest, and theft—are found in different cultures. Other **conventional moral rules** are arrived at by general consensus and are more culture-specific, such as wearing clothes in public or chewing with your mouth closed. In addition, every society specifies some regulations that ensure orderly and safe functioning, for instance, stopping at red traffic lights. Implied in this differentiation is that some rules are more important than others. This is usually reflected in the classroom, where some transgressions, such as harm to others, are considered more serious than others (Edwards, 1986).

Much of today's theoretical writing about moral development derived from Piaget's work on children's developing understanding of rules (1932). From his observations of children at play, Piaget formulated a stage theory of moral development that moves from an early childhood view, in which rules are unchange-able and derived from a higher authority (e.g., God or parents), to the more mature perspective that rules are made by and can be changed through mutual consent of the players.

Lawrence Kohlberg (1969) took Piaget's stage theory and developed a more elaborate framework for considering moral development based on why people make certain choices rather than on what those choices are (Edwards, 1986).William Damon (1977, 1983) further delineated children's thought processes as they move from the very concrete to the wider range of self in rela-tion to others. It is important for caregivers to help children attend to inner cues to label and interpret emotions as they begin to make decisions based as much on their "rightness" and internal reward as on their external rewards. Exhibit 10-6 outlines some helpful strategies for promoting moral development.

EXHIBIT 10-6   *Guidelines for Supporting Social Development III*

Promoting Moral Development

It is important to recognize children's abilities and limits in terms of moral reasoning and to guide them on the road to moral understanding. The fol-lowing guidelines will help in this task.

- *Use other-oriented reasoning with children*. For example, rather than stating, "Our rule is that we don't run inside," say, "We don't run inside because we could hurt other children by bumping into them."

- *Use stories to promote thinking and discussion about moral issues.* Favourite children's stories often pose interesting moral dilemmas that, with teacher guidance, encourage discussion. Krogh and Lamme (1985) recommended such books as *The Little Red Hen* by Paul Galdone (1973), *Angus and the Cat* by Marjorie Flack (1931), and *Peter's Chair* by Ezra Jack Keats (1967) for this purpose.

- *Provide ample time for child-selected play and materials that promote cooperation.* Dramatic play, for example, allows children to take the viewpoints of others; equipment that requires more than one child to operate it encourages cooperation.

- *Provide activities that help children become more aware of how the face conveys emotions.* Collages, masks, photos, acting out feelings, and "emotion puzzles" can strengthen this awareness.

- *Initiate thinking games that encourage children to seek multiple alterna-tives for social problems.* Puppets can enact a common social dilemma, for instance, one dealing with a refusal to share, and children can gen-erate alternative solutions to the situation.

(cont'd)

EXHIBIT 10-6 *cont'd*

- *Plan thinking games that deal with moral intentionality.* Children over the age of 4 can begin to differentiate between intended naughtiness and an accident that happened while a child was trying to help. Discuss the context of consequences in each instance.

- *Use any teachable moments that arise to encourage moral development.* For example, if you accidentally spill a large jug of juice, discuss the concept of intent regarding accidentally or purposely spilling a small glass of juice.

- *Realize that not all cultures share the same values.* Communication with parents can help teachers find which values are important to families and reinforce these as appropriate with the children (Edwards, 1986; Krogh & Lamme, 1985).

● Development of Prosocial Behaviours

Peer interactions, friendship, gender role acquisition, racial and cultural awareness, and moral development are all part of an intertwined process that involves the emergence of a number of other related traits. Researchers have looked at how such social characteristics as nurturance, empathy, altruism, generosity, sharing, and tolerance evolve in young children. Children's social cognition will affect how they respond to others. With age comes greater comprehension, although a higher level of understanding will not ensure that children's responses will necessarily be appropriate. Other factors contributing to the emergence of prosocial behaviours include the modelling by the significant people in children's lives as well as the kinds of other-oriented values that have been stressed (Schickedanz, Hansen, & Forsyth, 1990).

Key Terms

bilingualism
bimanual control
conventional moral rules
convergent thinking
divergent thinking
esthetics
eye-hand coordination
fine motor development
flexibility
fluency
grammar and syntax

gross motor development
holding grips
interpersonal moral rules
invented spelling
kinesthetic sense
manipulatives
mock writing
moral development
morphology
multilingualism
open-ended materials

pragmatics
prosocial behaviours
self-correcting
semantics
sensitivity

sensory-perceptual development
story schema
syntax
whole language approach

Key Points

1. Creativity includes originality, imagination, divergent thinking, and the ability to create something novel in meaningful ways when combined with flexibility, investigation, and exploration.

2. Creativity can be diminished by socializing factors and thoughtless actions by adults.

3. Television and prerecorded videotapes can enhance creativity when used properly.

4. Vigorous daily activities that are fun and enjoyable help establish a foundation for life-long health habits and attitudes.

5. Children's thinking is ongoing and involves a constant taking in, sifting, connecting, and storing of experiences, concepts, and information.

6. Language involves vocabulary, semantics, morphology, grammar and syntax, and pragmatics, whereas communication involves body language, sounds, and creative media such as art and dance.

7. Conversation with and reading to children aid them in acquiring the basic rules of literacy in the context of the whole language approach.

8. Socialization is a crucial process early in life, created by peer interaction, friendships, and racial and cultural attitudes, for developing the beginnings of a conscience in children.

9. Inclusion of children with special needs in early childhood programs makes it essential that teachers help children develop sensitivity to and acceptance of others unlike themselves.

Key Questions

1. If you have access to a computer and early childhood software, try out one early childhood activity on the computer. After you have mastered the activity, evaluate the software according to the criteria presented in this chapter. What do you think young children will learn from the activity? What feature(s) do you think might be appealing, unappealing, or frustrating to preschoolers?

2. Which of your friends or acquaintances do you consider to be creative? What creative characteristics do they possess? Do they fit the definition of creativity presented in this

chapter? How do they use creativity in ways other than the conventional sense (for instance, art or music expression)?

3. Observe a group of children. What expressions of creativity do you see? What factors in the environment or in the teachers' behaviour encourage or discourage creativity? Does any child in this group stand out as particularly creative? What characteristics does this child possess? Is your criterion for identifying a creative child different from one used to identify a creative adult?

4. Observe preschoolers of various ages at play. What differences in physical development do you see as a function of age? What do these abilities tell you about appropriate activities and expectations?

5. Observe a young child for about 20 minutes. How does this child use cognitive skills? Note the many ways in which the child uses her or his thinking abilities, including evidence of problem solving, symbolic representation, memory, classification, seriation, time and space concepts, and number concepts.

6. Listen to a young child's spontaneous language usage. What components of language do you note? Consider both the child's understanding of the meaning of language and the child's grasp of language rules.

7. Some teachers appear to be biased in favour of one gender over the other, and this can create many difficulties for the less favoured gender. Examine your views on this, and discuss ways teachers can avoid gender bias.

Part 5

Why?

In Chapter 11, **Quality in Early Childhood Programs**, we discuss current research on the quality of early childhood education programs across the country. The different variables that contribute to high-quality programs are discussed with special reference to recent Canadian studies.

In Chapter 12 of this final section, **The Future of Early Childhood Education**, we consider where the profession will go at the dawn of the 21st century. What issues and challenges do we face and what new ones will arise? What problems must the profession confront? What does the future hold for early childhood education in Canada? How can we ensure the availability of affordable, high-quality child care for very young Canadians?

Chapter 11

Quality in Early Childhood Programs

*N*ow that you are quite familiar with program terminology and models, developmentally appropriate practices, and curriculum, we will return to the all-important issue of quality. We will continue our exploration of the factors that affect the quality of a program and the effects of program quality on the well-being of children. We will also look at what kinds of programs are best for teachers and their satisfaction levels.

Program Quality

The quality of a program should be examined from several different perspectives—the children's, the parents', and the teachers':

1. What is the program's impact on the child? Does it support the child's well-being and meet the child's needs?

2. What is the program's impact on the parents? Does it support the parents' well-being and meet their needs?

3. What is the program's impact on the teachers? Does it support the teacher's well-being and meet their needs?

In Chapter 1, we considered some of the research on program quality, and then at more of the quality-related research in Chapter 3 when we discussed specific models. In Chapter 4, we had a look at Canadian practices in child care and how this country was measuring up in terms of quality. Now we will turn to additional studies that tell us even more about what makes a program good for children, parents, and teachers. Being very familiar with what that research tells us about quality will help you in your quest to be an exemplary teacher.

Recent studies have tried to identify the factors that make a program a "good program" in the same way you might try to figure out what ingredients were used in those great cookies Aunt Martha used to make. Quality early childhood pro-

grams, just like cookies, have certain ingredients, and the more research can tell us about those ingredients, the more likely we are to see exemplary programs for young children. We have gone far beyond the old question "Is child care necessary?" With so many Canadian children in some form of care (see Exhibit 4-9) and knowing how critical the early years are, today's researchers try to find out how to make child care better for young children. The emerging picture is complex: quality in child care is not dependent on just one or two things, but rather it is dependent on the complex interplay of multiple factors, some more important than others. Early in 1995, a Canadian educator, Gillian Doherty-Derkowski, summarized the extensive and widely-scattered research on quality in child care available at that time in her text *Quality Matters*. Doherty-Derkowski noted that high-quality programs can have positive effects on children, parents, and teachers, but conversely, poor or low-quality programs also can have severe, possibly irreversible effects on children and perhaps their parents and teachers. Since 1995, there have been a number of additional studies that have furthered our knowledge about the ingredients of high-quality programs.

As a student who has spent most of the past year studying this field, you will be pleased to know that courses directly related to early childhood education continue to be a strong predictor of quality, as you will see below. The relevance of your studies to a career in early childhood education is clearly something you can control. However, as a beginning teacher, there may be things about an early childhood program you do not like or agree with—but those things are beyond your control. Recall that in Chapter 1, we briefly examined some elements that contribute to the quality of early childhood programs (and you might want to review that brief section). Exhibit 11-1 lists those variables and categorizes them in terms of your ability as a beginning teacher to influence them. Some of the variables, such as education, professional development, and the developmental appropriateness of the program, are within your control. Other variables, such as salary and teacher-child ratios, are not. Your first few years of teaching will be challenging and exhausting enough; therefore it makes little sense to expend effort on

---

Reflective Exercise 11-1

In recent months, have there been any stories in the local or national news about low-quality child care? Discuss any such news reports. Has poor-quality animal care been in the news lately? Elaborate upon and discuss these findings.

changing things beyond your control. Take salaries for example: you and your colleagues could ask for pay increase, but if the answer is no, you have only a few choices available:

1. Try to find a position with a higher salary.

2. Stay, but keep asking.

3. Advocate for higher salaries from your professional association.

You can always advocate for changes with your association, and, as the histories of ECE in the provinces and territories showed, the associations usually are behind any government changes in the legislation covering early childhood education.

Some situations are more complex, such as group size. Say, for example, that the management of your program would like to have smaller group sizes, but the facility is housed in a 60-year-old building with two large rooms. As budgets are tight, they cannot afford to do major alterations. However, you and your colleagues propose to your director that you ask for parent volunteers to help you to build portable room dividers or partitions so that you can move off with smaller groups of children. That proposed compromise might well be accepted; parents can be very resourceful when they realize that their volunteer work will enhance their children's programs.

Some situations are even more complex such as the ones with "BUT" beside them. Let's consider the quality of adult-child interactions. You, as the teacher, definitely have an influence over that, but if you have an unsupportive management team, poor facilities, and a rock-bottom salary, that BUT is a large factor—it is unlikely that you will be able to maintain positive interactions if you are working in an unpleasant setting with minimal support and sparse materials. It is unfortunate that possibilities like this need to be discussed, but the available research makes it clear that there is tremendous variability in the quality of early childhood programs in Canada, and there is a real possibility that someone in your class might find a position in a low-quality setting. Knowledge about the variables found in high-quality programs will put you in the proverbial "driver's seat": You will know what to look for and what to ask when it comes time to search for that first teaching position. For that reason, we will examine the most recent research and see if there are any additional variables that should be added to the list.

Several large-scale studies that have been published since Doherty-Derkowski's text was prepared, and they deserve attention. The studies are listed below by date:

1. *Cost, Quality, and Child Outcomes in Child Care Centers* (Helburn et al., 1995; Peisner-Feinberg & Burchinal, 1997; Peisner-Feinberg, Burchinal, Clifford, Culkin, Howes, & Kagan, 1999)

2. *Child Care and Child Development: The NICHD Study of Early Child Care* (National Institute of Child Health and Human Development, 1994)

EXHIBIT 11-1 *Variables an Early Childhood Educator Can Influence*

Variables Known to Affect Quality	Variables You Can Influence with or Without Management's Support	Variables You and Management Both Influence	Variables Determined by Management and Legislation
Teacher qualifications	√	√	√
Developmental appropriateness of the program	√	√	√
Group size*	☹	√	√
Teacher-child ratio	☹	☹	√
Quality of child-adult interaction**	√ BUT	√	√
Quality of the physical environment**	√ BUT	√	√
Ongoing professional development	√	√	√
Staff consistency**	☹ BUT	√	√
Family involvement	√ BUT	√	√
Mixed-age grouping*	√	√	√
Salary	☹	√ BUT	√

QUALITY IS A COMBINATION OF FACTORS

*May be constrained by the physical layout of the facility.
**Depends on the goodwill of the management.

3. The You Bet I Care! series of studies:

   i. *You Bet I Care! A Canada-wide Study On: Wages, Working Conditions, and Practices in Child Care Centres* (Doherty, Lero, Goelman, La Grange, & Tougas, 2000)

ii. *Caring and Learning Environments: Quality in Child Care Centres Across Canada* (Goelman, Doherty, Lero, La Grange, & Tougas, 2000)

iii. *Caring and Learning Environments: Quality in Regulated Family Child Care Across Canada* (Doherty, Lero, Goelman, Tougas, & La Grange, 2000)

iv. *Policies and Practices in Canadian Family Child Care Agencies* (Doherty, Lero, Tougas, La Grange, & Goelman, 2001)

Initially, we will look at each study individually, and for obvious reasons we will look at the Canadian studies in greater detail than the American ones. Then, we will consider them collectively along with the studies we already have looked at in Chapters 1 and 3 from the three perspectives mentioned above—the children's, the parents', and the teachers'. Prior to discussing the studies, however, it is worth reviewing the features of two assessment tools first mentioned in Chapter 9, as they were used in virtually all of the studies that examined program quality:

1. The **ECERS** or Early Childhood Environment Rating Scale (Harms & Clifford, 1998), a preschool classroom evaluation tool

2. The **ITERS** or Infant/Toddler Environment Rating Scale (Harms, Cryer, & Clifford, 1990), an evaluative tool for infant and toddler classrooms

The ECERS is perhaps the best-known standardized rating scale that can be used to evaluate early childhood programs, and it is one of the few supported by appropriate validity and reliability studies. Both teachers and observers report that the scales help them to think systematically about the environment in early childhood programs for children between 2 and 6 years of age. Harms and Clifford (1980, p. iv) described the original scale in the following terms:

> *The scale has proven to be a good beginning place for looking at the various rooms and groupings within a … school. It offers a relatively short and efficient means of looking seriously at the quality of the environment currently being provided and for planning improvements.*

A number of studies we reviewed in Chapter 1 (e.g., Howes, Phillips, & Whitebook, 1992; Kontos & Fiene, 1987; Phillips, Scarr, & McCartney, 1987; Phillips, Howes, & Whitebook, 1991) have found that scores on the ECERS are good predictors of program quality. For example, developmentally appropriate activities are more likely to be found in programs that have favourable group sizes and a supportive environment for the adult staff, both of which were measured by the ECERS. Similarly, programs with higher scores on the ECERS have the lowest rates of teacher turnover.

During the 17 years that the original ECERS was in use, inclusive environments for children with disabilities had become more prevalent and the program variables that reflected sensitivity to cultural diversity had become better understood (Harms, Clifford, & Cryer, 1998). For those reasons, the scale needed updating—the revised scale "is indeed a revision of the ECERS; it is not a new scale" (Harms et al., 1998, p. 1).

Both the ECERS and the ITERS have seven subscales focused on the following areas:

1. Space and furnishings
2. Personal care routines
3. Language-reasoning
4. Activities
5. Interaction
6. Program structure
7. Parents and staff

Within each of these seven areas, there are series of questions with descriptors that use a seven-point scale. Although handwashing is not a separate item, it is a consideration in the Personal Care Routines section of the scale and would work well as an example. Handwashing as you observed it in a centre would be rated on a seven-point scale with a rating of 1 being inadequate and a rating of 7 being excellent. An example of the descriptors and the format of the items is given in Exhibit 11-2.

Both the ECERS and the ITERS have established two important attributes of rating scales: validity and reliability; essentially, this means that the scale measures quality as it is meant to and that there is consistency in measurements over time. The content of many of the individual items on both scales will become evident below as we discuss the results from the research studies that have used them. You might

EXHIBIT 11-2 *Example of the Rating System and Items Used in ECERS and ITERS*

Inadequate 1	Minimal 3	Good 5	Excellent 7
Handwashing never observed during entire observation and no reminders given. Children holding guinea pig came straight to lunch with no wash-up.	Children and staff were observed washing hands a few times. Reminder was heard once.	Teachers usually reminded children to wash hands after using the wash-room and before meals and snacks.	Teachers always reminded children to wash hands after using the wash-room and checked to see they did. Supervised wash-up time before meals and snacks.

also ask your instructor to bring in copies of the scales for you to review. Certainly, once you are working in the field, it is desirable to use the instruments with your colleagues to assess and continually improve upon practice in your own program.

Cost, Quality, and Child Outcomes Study

Overview.   This large-scale study was based on children in 228 infant/toddler classrooms and 521 preschool classrooms across four different states, California, Colorado, Connecticut, and North Carolina (Helburn et al., 1995; Peisner-Feinberg & Burchinal, 1997). The CQCO (Cost, Quality, and Child Outcomes) study painted a poor picture of child care in the United States that made national news in January 1995. Headlines reflected the major finding that the quality of most centres is poor to mediocre and quality is even lower in infant/toddler centres. Very few centres were considered to be excellent.

The Cost, Quality, and Child Outcomes Study Team (Helburn et al., 1995), the authors of the first report, used the ECERS and ITERS as assessment tools to assess the centres. Although there was great variation between programs, the average ECERS' scores across all preschool centres on the 7-point scale we just discussed was 4.0, a score that reflects mediocre care. Almost three-quarters or 75 percent of the centres rated provided mediocre care, while 12 percent of the centres provided totally inadequate care, leaving only 14 percent of the centres that provided good-quality care. Less than 1 percent of the CQCO centres were rated as having excellent (7 on the ECERS and ITERS) care. The situation for infants was even worse, with only 8 percent of the centres providing high-quality care, 52 percent providing mediocre care, and 40 percent offering totally inadequate care. The authors clearly describe the sorry state of affairs:

> *Babies in poor-quality rooms are vulnerable to more illness because basic sanitary conditions are not met for diapering and feeding; are endangered because of safety problems that exist in the room; miss warm supportive relationships with adults; and lose out on learning because they lack the books and toys required. ... (Helburn et al., 1995, p. 2)*

The CQCO study team also found that the children's cognitive and social development were correlated with the child care centre's quality of program. Contrary to previous expectations, this correlation between program quality and development was just as strong for children with mothers with high educational levels (usually predictive of social class) as it was for children with mothers with very little education. The association between quality and development also did not vary with the child's ethnicity or gender. Not surprisingly, the children in the higher-quality centres, when compared to age-peers in the lower-quality centres, had better-developed language skills, and higher scores on measures of school readiness and social skills (Helburn et al., 1995; Peisner-Feinberg & Burchinal, 1997). Moreover, the children in the better programs were less likely to be seen as having behaviour problems. Even in Grade 2, the differences between children who had been in poor-quality centres and those who had been in good centres were still marked in language and mathematics, even when they took into account

the types of programs the children had attended post–child care.

The authors of the study found these results disturbing enough to conclude that quality in most American child care centres is sufficiently poor to affect young children's emotional and cognitive development. Regardless of their family backgrounds, children in lower-quality child care were found to be less competent developmentally than those in higher-quality programs. The difference was even more marked for at-risk children.

After our review of the Canadian Acts and Regulations governing child care in Chapter 4, it should not surprise you to learn that the CQCO authors also found that the states with higher regulatory standards for child care also had higher-quality infant and preschool child care programs. This finding is significant for those who advocate positive changes to legislation that further regulate quality—clearly regulation works to enhance the quality of care. The CQCO report identifies better teacher-child ratios and supervisors and directors with prior experience as the variables having the strongest association with high-quality programming. Minimal wages, little specialized training, and little unrelated education were the features that had the strongest relationship with low-quality care.

A provocative finding of the CQCO study was that while such a high percentage of programs was rated by professionals as being mediocre or poor, 90 percent of parents considered their children's centres to be very good. We know, for example, that only 34 percent of the parents had infants and toddlers in programs the research labelled as low-quality, yet 30 percent of those parents considered their infants' and toddlers' programs to be high-quality and only 4 percent thought the programs were mediocre. Of course, one suspects it would be very difficult for a parent who *had* to work to think that the quality of care was poor. Still, it appears as if many parents need education about the variables that define high-quality programs. Even though the overall level of quality of the CQCO programs is quite poor, most parents think they are acceptable. The more parents understand about the variables that define quality (cf. Exhibit 11-1), the more likely they are to insist on programs that have those defining features.

Clearly, parents tend to overestimate quality. Why would there be this discrepancy? The researchers speculate that parents have relatively little opportunity to observe in the facility, and some parents may never have seen high-quality child care; therefore, they have no basis for comparison. Parents may also feel they have no choice; therefore, it is easier for them to consider that their children are cared for appropriately. Since this study found little difference in the cost between high- and low-quality child care, the researchers conclude that parents simply are not demanding quality, although they state that quality in their children's care is important to them. In the A Canadian Professional Speaks Out, Mary Louise Vanderlee describes Havenwood Place, a high-quality program designed to foster school readiness.

HAVENWOOD PLACE: AN INTEGRATED SERVICES APPROACH TO SCHOOL READINESS

Mary-Louise Vanderlee, Co-chair, Havenwood Place Steering Committee

Background

The Havenwood community is located in the Dixie/Bloor area within the Peel Region in Mississauga, Ontario. *Portraits of Peel* (Balkwill, McGrath, & Rice, 1996) presented the educational risk factors related to the success of children in school and found that the Havenwood community had the second-highest percentage of the factors that indicate the need for support programs for children and their families. The risk index included factors such as parental education, socioeconomic status, housing, and the impact of immigration on families. There was a strong sense from the area service providers and educators that the many programs offered in the Peel region were not being used to their fullest potential or by those most in need. Thus, Havenwood Place was established in an effort to moderate the risk factors and improve young children's opportunities to experience success in school by six.

Havenwood Place, which opened its doors in September 1997, is a school-based family resource centre that provides an integrated system of services to support and enhance the experiences of the families living in the Havenwood community. The primary goal is to advance parents' and caregivers' ability to promote the healthy, holistic (i.e., emotional, social, physical, and cognitive) development of young children and family functioning. To this end, staff and volunteers provide information, support, and enriching programs for infants, toddlers, and preschoolers as well as for their families and caregivers.

● Child Care and Child Development: The NICHD Study of Early Child Care

Overview.   The National Institute of Child Health and Human Development's (NICHD) (1994) study *Child Care and Child Development: The NICHD Study of Early Child Care* (Clarke-Stewart, 1999; NICHD Early Child Care Research Network, 1994, 1996, 1999; Vandell, 1999) is a longitudinal one of 1300 children from diverse backgrounds who were born in 1991. Some of the 1300 participants have not been in child care, while others have spent time in non-parental care including family-based and centre-based child care. The sample used is diverse geographically, ethnically, and socially, as the study has been carried out in different locations in the United States. As the study is longitudinal in nature, the results continue to accumulate.

Reflective Exercise 11-2

Listen to a young child's spontaneous language usage. What components of language do you note?

Observe a teacher of young children engage in spontaneous conversation with children. What techniques does she or he use? How are the children encouraged to interact with each other as well as with the teacher? Did you hear examples of language play or humour?

Clarke-Stewart (1999) and Vandell (1999) have reported on NICHD data related to quality in recent years, and their participants were both in centre-based and family child care settings. As in the CQCO study, it appears that higher-quality care is associated with developmental gains in the areas of language and social development (Clarke-Stewart, 1999; Vandell, 1999). The NICHD study has also shown definitively that the quality of attachment in child care attendees did not differ from that of matched children who did not attend child care, and this was true even if the quality of care was poor. If the quality of care was poor, however, *and* the mother was relatively insensitive and unresponsive, insecure attachment is more likely. Seefeldt and Galper (1998) suggest that this is because the infant is placed in a dual-risk situation. Children who had been in more than one child care setting before 15 months of age also had an increased risk of insecure attachments.

You Bet I Care! Series of Studies

This Canadian series, by the Child Care Visions Project funded by Human Resources Development, Canada, a branch of the federal government, consists of three main studies:

1. *A Canada-wide Study On: Wages, Working Conditions, and Practices in Child Care Centres* (Doherty, Lero, Goelman, La Grange, & Tougas, 2000)

2. *Caring and Learning Environments: Quality in Child Care Centres Across Canada* (Goelman, Doherty, Lero, La Grange, & Tougas, 2000)

3. *Caring and Learning Environments: Quality in Regulated Family Child Care Across Canada* (Doherty, Lero, Goelman, Tougas, & La Grange, 2000)

A fourth study is, in some senses, just another part of the third study, a study of the agencies that run regulated family homes:

4. *Policies and Practices in Canadian Family Child Care Agencies* (Doherty, Lero, Tougas, La Grange, & Goelman, 2001)

● A Canada-wide Study on: Wages, Working Conditions, and Practices in Child Care Centres

Overview.   In Chapter 5, when we discussed the status of the profession, we touched upon several findings from the *You Bet I Care!* study. We noted that, in 2000, 8.5 out of 10 early childhood educators had postsecondary degrees or diplomas, and we complained that despite this level of education, the average wage nationally was comparable to that of parking lot attendants. The *You Bet I Care!* study was a country-wide survey; questionnaires about the work and working conditions of early childhood professionals, about centres, and about directors were mailed out to selected centres across the country in 1998. Finances would not allow the authors to mail the survey to every licensed centre in the country, but they tried to obtain a representative sample. The difficulty with surveys, however, is you are never certain if the sample is representative—you always learn more about those who return the survey than those who do not! Nevertheless, the authors did receive responses from 4154 teachers, and 848 directors. The 848 directors also returned the same number of questionnaires about their centres—with about 63 percent of them being nonprofit. The authors assume there are close to 40,000 professionals in the field, so this study sampled about an eighth of them. Directors especially might find the Web site of the Center for Early Childhood Leadership worthwhile.

The Study Sample.   The 4154 teachers and 848 directors were from across Canada; responses were received from every province and territory (although Nunavut was not yet separate in 1998 when the survey was mailed out). About 73 percent of the respondents were teachers, while 12 percent were directors and 15 percent were assistant teachers. About 90 percent of the respondents worked full-time, and had been in the field for more than a year. The vast majority were between 25 and 45 years of age—but there were regional differences. In Alberta, New Brunswick, and Newfoundland/Labrador, there were high proportions of under-25s with no previous experience in the field. In contrast, in Manitoba, Ontario, and Quebec, there were few teachers under 25, and few new to the field. In part, differences in legislation about teacher education requirements would explain these demographic differences (cf. Chapter 4). Almost 55 percent of those who returned the questionnaire were the primary wage earner in the home, contributing between 50 and 100 percent to household expenses. About three-quarters of the teachers had lived in their communities for more than five years.

By and large, the teachers were quite an experienced group: nearly a third had been in the field for over ten years, almost another third for over five years, and only 5 percent for less than a year. Again, there were regional variations with Newfoundland, Price Edward Island, New Brunswick, and Alberta having close to 12 percent of their teaching staff in the field for less than a year. Assistant teachers were more likely to be new to the field which you would expect, and directors were more likely to have been in the field for over ten years. Around two-thirds of the experienced teachers had worked in only one centre for their entire career, but just over a half of the directors and assistants had stayed at the same centre. The percentage of "teachers" coming to child care from an unrelated field—and probably no related education—was highest for assistants, with about 17 percent being new to the field. Only 7 percent of directors and 10 percent of teachers had worked in an unrelated field prior to coming to the child care centre. Percentages of new staff from an unrelated field were highest in Alberta, New Brunswick, and Saskatchewan. Just over 20 percent of the teachers had at least one promotion in their current placement, and, not surprisingly, the figure was higher for directors, falling at 67 percent.

Results from the *You Bet I Care!* Study

Teachers   Over 80 percent of the teachers surveyed felt their work was stimulating, used their skills, and left them with a sense of accomplishment. Close to 95 percent of the individuals surveyed said they felt they made a positive difference in the lives of the children in their care. However, around half of the teachers thought there was not enough time in the day to do all that should be done and left feeling exhausted at the end of each day. Only 12 percent of the respondents felt frustrated in their work, and almost 80 percent did not expect to change careers in the following year. Assistant teachers were most likely to think they would change careers within the year. Those thinking of leaving mentioned wages as one reason and wanting a career change as another; what is not clear is if moving into a different careers was perceived as a necessary—but perhaps not preferred—step to obtain higher wages.

The teachers were well educated, as we have already noted. Assistant teachers were more likely to have lower levels of education, but only 3 percent of the sample had less than a high school diploma. In for-profit centres, 20 percent of the staff had a high school education or less, while only 12 percent of the nonprofit centres had comparable qualifications. Exhibit 11-3 shows the percentages of staff in the child care centres by level of education. Overall, educational levels are very high, and only 11 percent of all teaching staff have no training at all. Because the rate of no training is much higher in New Brunswick, Saskatchewan, and Manitoba, they are added for comparison purposes beside the bars showing how many Canadian teachers have high school or less. The Early Childhood Education Web Guide provides teachers with updated Internet resources.

Relative to the *Caring for a Living* study, educational levels have increased, and the numbers of untrained staff have decreased from 42 percent to 11.4 percent. Much of that latter change is due to the introduction of legislated requirements for teacher training in Alberta; in the 1992 study, 72 percent of the respondents reported they had no training, but the figure plummeted to 9.2 percent in the 2000 results.

It appeared that staff training was lower in commercial centres, but the data is confounded as more for-profit centres exist in provinces with minimal or no requirements for teacher training. Suffice it to say that New Brunswick,

EXHIBIT 11-3 *Educational Levels in the* You Bet I Care! *Study*

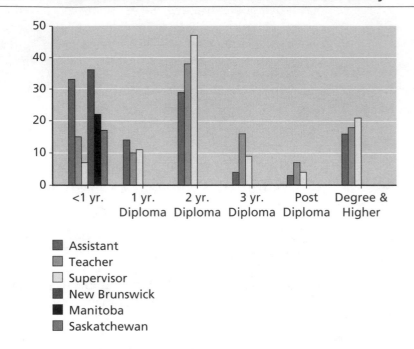

- ■ Assistant
- ■ Teacher
- □ Supervisor
- ■ New Brunswick
- ■ Manitoba
- ■ Saskatchewan

Newfoundland, Prince Edward Island, and Labrador all have minimal or no regulations about training and also a much higher percentage of commercial centres than the other provinces and territories.

About three-quarters of the teachers had participated in professional development activities in the previous year. Almost half of the teachers said they would have attended more, but costs were prohibitive. Not being given release time, not having information about events, and not being close to their communities were also factors preventing teachers from participating. In British Columbia and Prince Edward Island, ongoing professional development is regulated and teaching licences are renewed *only if* you attend such activities. Needless to say, the rates for involvement in professional development activities are much higher in those two locations—close to 90 percent and far higher than all other jurisdictions. Again, this points up the benefits of legislation on issues that contribute to quality programs—if it is in the law, people tend to comply. An encouraging finding was that centres paid for professional development activities for over half of the teachers who had attended them, and almost 40 percent were given paid release time to attend. Teachers in for-profit centres were far less likely to receive financial compensation for expenses than those in nonprofit centres—46 percent versus 66 percent—and fewer participated in these activities (about 58 percent in for-profit centres versus 82 percent in nonprofit centres).

A number of the teachers in the study had additional teaching and/or supervisory responsibilities. Almost half the teachers sampled supervised college students studying early childhood when they were on their field placements. Over 70 per-

Courtesy of Play and Learn.

cent of the centres had children with special needs, and 12 percent had more than five such children. Finally, over 40 percent of the centres had infants and toddlers in their programs, and 41 percent of the teachers worked with the very young. These additional responsibilities are quite compatible with the educational background of most of the teachers—but would not be appropriate for those without early childhood training.

Working Conditions   Most teachers worked almost a 40-hour week in their positions, but they typically spent about five-and-a-half hours in unpaid preparation time. Some spent over a day per week preparing for the centre, doing unpaid work. The directors also spend a number of unpaid hours working. In some jurisdictions, Alberta, for example, a significant percentage of teachers are hired on a part-time basis without benefits and sent home if numbers are down. Temporary layoffs are close to 20 percent in Prince Edward Island, New Brunswick, the Northwest Territories, and Newfoundland/Labrador. One might speculate that the seasonal nature of some employment in those locations leads to great fluctuations in the need for child care. However, very few teachers (4.2 percent) have this occur once they have been in a centre for a year. It happens most frequently (15 percent) with assistant teachers. While it is quite likely that some of these layoffs are for financial reasons, and probably more frequent in for-profit centres, it also may be that a director's concern about quality of care enters into this. Although the questionnaire in the study does not allow us to interpret these results, the Canadian author speculates that some directors intentionally start untrained assistants on a part-time basis to ensure that their caregiving skills are appropriate. With Canadian employment laws, it is much easier to bid farewell to a part-time employee whose style does not fit your centre, than it is to dismiss a full-time employee.

Wages remain a critical concern as we know from Chapter 5, but there are many regional differences and no data are available for either the Northwest Territories or Nunavut. In this study, wages are lowest in New Brunswick and Newfoundland where the cost of living is low, and highest in British Columbia and Ontario where the cost of living is high. In addition, there are government grants to enhance the salaries in Ontario, British Columbia and Saskatchewan. Salaries are lowest in Alberta, Newfoundland, New Brunswick, and Prince Edward Island, all provinces that have suspended or frozen operating grants. Unions are most common in British Columbia, Ontario, Quebec, Saskatchewan, and Manitoba, where between 8 and 19 percent of the teachers are unionized. Nationally, unionized teachers make over $3 more per hour than non-unionized teachers.

The authors draw comparisons between different occupations and child care teachers. Though most teachers have a year more of college than practical nurses, they earn about $7000 less a year nationally. Their salaries are comparable nationally to those of kindergarten assistants—and, as you already know, of parking lot attendants! Of course, average salaries nationally hide many of the facts—many salaries are higher than the average and some are less. Nonprofit child care centres, for example, tend to pay salaries well above the national average. Graduates from early childhood education programs who are knowledgable, motivated, and caring tend to enter higher-level positions. Sometimes finding a higher-paying position means relocating, but it may be worth it.

Satisfaction levels are not as high as they were in the 1992 study, but given that just two paragraphs ago you were reading about government freezes and cutbacks in the 1990s this should not come as a surprise.

Directors   The *You Bet I Care!* study has a brief chapter discussing directors of the different centres (Doherty, Lero, Goelman, La Grange, & Tougas, 2000). As you know from the large-scale CQCO study, the director's background education was one of the best predictors of quality. How do our Canadian directors look? Almost all are female and over 70 percent of them are over 35 years old. Over 60 percent have been in the field for over 11 years, and only 6 percent had been in the field for less than 4 years. Directors who only did administrative tasks and head supervisors of centres that were part of an organization with several centres generally had a two-year early childhood credential or higher degree or credential. Teacher-directors who still had responsibility for teaching usually had a two-year credential. What is troubling, however, is that a quarter of the administrative directors had absolutely no educational background in early childhood education. Another warning bell is sounded by the fact that under 3.5 percent of the directors had only a high school diploma—but not surprisingly, 13.9 percent of this group were from New Brunswick where they still have not legislated teacher training requirements. Fortunately, close to 90 percent of the directors had been involved in professional development activities in the previous year, and many were furthering their studies at the same time. Directors tended to stay at the same centre, but there were some regional variations. Mobility between centres was highest in Prince Edward Island and lowest in Manitoba, Newfoundland, Nova Scotia, and Quebec.

What Do These Results Mean?   The *You Bet I Care!* study reinforces the need for concern about the quality of child care in Canada. Clearly, there are many well-educated, dedicated, and satisfied professionals in the field. Yet is also is evident that there are people in the field who have no formal training in early childhood and little formal education. There are also great fluctuations in terms of salaries, benefits, working conditions, and turnover. While variability between provinces in training for professions like nursing, medicine, teaching, and law does occur, it never reaches the extremes seen in child care. The fact that some provinces refuse to legislate requirements for all ultimately demeans the profession. The importance of ongoing advocacy for standards in every province and territory that contribute to quality programs for all children cannot be overemphasized. Additional requirements for directors also seem necessary especially in view of the CQCO findings about directors. An administrative director with no early childhood background might well recommend larger classrooms and group sizes, for example, as they would make sense in the business end of child care but, as you know, there is a point in group size beyond which quality suffers.

● Caring and Learning Environments: Quality in Child Care Centres Across Canada

Overview.   In many ways, the *Caring and Learning Environments: Quality in Child Care Centres Across Canada* (QCCCC) study is similar to the CQCO study though it does not have the long-term, post-program follow-up component. Goelman et al. completed the QCCCC study in 122 infant/toddler rooms and 227 preschool rooms in a total of six provinces and one territory: Yukon, British Columbia, Alberta, Saskatchewan, Ontario, Quebec, and New Brunswick. In addition to using the ECERS and ITERS, the authors used the 23-item Caregiver Interaction Scale (CIS) (Arnett, 1987) which had been used by the CQCO study team and by Whitebook et al. (1989) in the *National Child Care Staffing Study*, the large-scale U.S. study we discussed in Chapter 1. The CIS has four items related to detachment (i.e., how involved is the teacher?), nine items related to harshness (i.e., is the teacher harsh in setting limits, irritable, and/or negative in tone and behaviour?), and ten items related to sensitivity (i.e., how warm, encouraging, and child-oriented is the teacher?). In addition, participants answered a lengthy questionnaire with questions about their program, their experiences, their education and specialized training, and themselves. There were also questions related to the child care field and professional development.

The original intent for the QCCCC study was to have 40 preschool rooms and 20 infant/toddler rooms participate in it. Whenever possible, half of the rooms in each province or territory were to be in profit-making centres and half were to be nonprofit (although Saskatchewan had only nonprofit centres in the list of possible centres). The authors elected to use centres in major cities because of cost and convenience. About half of the centres that had been chosen for possible participation refused to become involved, so additional centres had to be contacted. This certainly compromised the representative nature of the centres that the authors had aimed for, and a number of additional methodological modifications had to be made. As the authors suggest, it is quite likely that those who agreed to participate might differ in a systematic way from those who refused—and in a study of quality, one might expect that individuals who knew the quality of their program was questionable might well refuse to participate. The CQCO and National Child Care Staffing Study in the United States encountered similar difficulties.

The Study Sample.   There were 234 infant and child care centres in the study, and 68 percent of them were nonprofit. In the nonprofit centres, 62 percent of the teachers had a two-year diploma in early childhood education, while only 50 percent of the teachers in for-profit centres did. Salary levels were higher in nonprofit centres and these centres spent more of their annual budget on wages than the for-profit centres. Additionally, more teachers in nonprofit centres than for-profit centres returned the questionnaires for the study. A total of 1352 teachers returned the questionnaire, and information about their education is shown in Exhibit 11-4. Only 24 percent or 326 of those teachers agreed to participate in the observational component of the study where the CIS, ECERS, and ITERS were used. The educational characteristics of those teachers who agreed to be observed are

EXHIBIT 11-4   *Characteristics of Canadian Teachers Responding to QCCCC Study Questionnaire*

High school or less	17.9 %	No ECE	12.1%
Community college	67.7%	College ECE	80.6%
B.A. or higher	13.4%	University ECE	7.3%

shown in Exhibit 11-5. The teachers who were observed had more education on average than those who did not wish to be observed, and it is reasonable to assume this self-selected group of teachers were better than those who did not agree to the observational component.

EXHIBIT 11-5   *Characteristics of Canadian Teachers Observed in QCCCC Study*

High school or less	12%	No ECE	9.3%
Community college	75.7%	College ECE	85.5%
B.A. or higher	12.3%	University ECE	5.2%

Around 80 percent of the directors returned the questionnaires about their centres and themselves, although for some unknown reason, only 34 percent of directors in Quebec returned the questionnaire about themselves. The directors had an average of 8.6 years in their current centres, 6.3 of them in the current position. Exhibit 11-6 summarizes the educational characteristics of the directors.

EXHIBIT 11-6   *Characteristics of Centre Directors Responding to QCCCC Study Questionnaire*

High school or less	7.1 %	Some postsecondary ECE	18.3%
Community college	59.6%	College ECE	61.6%
B.A. or higher	33.3%	University ECE	24.7%

Results of the QCCCC Study

CIS Scores   The CIS scores for sensitivity range from 1 to 4, with 4 being the best for sensitivity. Overall, the teacher ratings on the CIS were quite positive: 3.25 for sensitivity. The harshness and detachment scales work the opposite way: 1 is not at all harsh or detached, and therefore the most positive, whereas a rating of 4 would indicate a high level of harshness and/or detachment. The teachers did receive low scores on the latter items: 1.28 for harshness, and 1.38 for detachment. Teacher sensitivity scores tended to be slightly higher in the three western provinces for reasons unknown.

ITERS and ECERS Scores   You will recall from the foregoing discussion that a score below 3 on the ECERS and ITERS means that even basic health and safety needs are not being met. Scores between 3 and 4.9 indicate that health and safety concerns are met, but the program does not offer a stimulating program. When scores are above 5, the program would have positive interactions, quality programming, diverse materials, and excellent personal care.

The average ITERS score across all locations was 4.4, and there was variation across locations: teachers in British Columbia, Alberta, and the Yukon had overall average scores above 5; Saskatchewan and Ontario teachers had scores just above 4; and the average score across teachers in both Quebec and New Brunswick were high 3's. When summed across locations, the highest rating of 5.5 was in the area of adult-child interactions, a critically important area. Interestingly, the lowest score, 3.8, was for learning activities. The scores for the other scales were all in the 4-range. The average score for commercial centres was 4.0 and it was 4.5 for nonprofit centres.

The average ECERS score for the total sample was 4.7, and Alberta and British Columbia had averages above 5. The Yukon and Ontario teachers had average scores of 4.9, and the remaining locations all had scores above 4. The two highest scores were for adult-child interactions (5.4) and program structure (5.2). The lowest score, 4.0, was for learning activities, the low being comparable to the ITERS results. The average score for all commercial centres was 4.4, while it was 4.8 for the nonprofit centres.

The relationship between scores on the two observation scales also were correlated with scores on the CIS. As you would expect, teachers with more positive scores on the CIS also had higher scores on the ECERS and ITERS when their classes were observed.

What Do These Results Mean?   The results on the ECERS and ITERS raise a series of concerns, especially as it is likely that weaker teachers were the ones who refused to participate in the observational component of the study. Exhibit 11-7 summarizes the scores, using the 1-point increases that characterize the scales. Over half of the Canadian preschool programs observed received scores below 5 on both scales, suggesting that health and safety concerns are met, but there is not a stimulating, developmentally appropriate program. Of even greater concern is the fact that nearly three-quarters of the infant/toddler programs fall in

EXHIBIT 11-7   *ECERS and ITERS Scores for Centres in QCCCC Study*

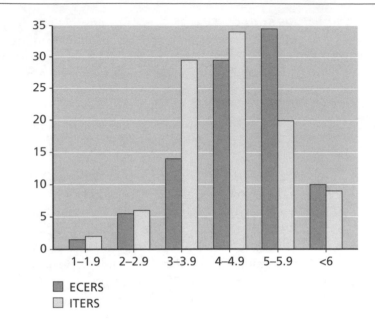

- ■ ECERS
- □ ITERS

this range. Of course, the greatest concern lies with the smaller percentage of programs have scores below 3 on the ECERS and ITERS—meaning that basic health and safety needs are not met in these centres. Only 10 percent of the preschool programs have scores above 6, while 8.7 percent of the infant/toddler centres do; given that the sample is likely biased toward better teachers and better centres, this means there are astonishingly few outstanding programs.

Another finding of concern was the low scores in both infant/toddler and preschool rooms on personal care routines. This seems to be attributable primarily to the handwashing item. Handwashing should be a major concern, especially as young children who are just moving into a group setting—whether it be at 3 months or 3 years of age—are particularly susceptible to gastrointestinal disorders and hepatitis. There is an extensive literature on the topic, with available research generally conducted in child care centres (e.g., Black et al., 1981; Gelbach et al., 1973; Hayes et al., 1990; Silva, 1980). Some years ago, Klein from Boston University School of Medicine (1986) stated the findings succinctly:

Hand washing is the single most important technique for prevention of gastrointestinal and many respiratory infections. Compulsory hand washing after ... blowing noses ... and using toilet facilities should be expected. (P. 12)

Courtesy of George Brown College.

Black et al. (1981) found that rigorous enforcement of child and teacher hand washing led to a 50 percent decrease in diarrhea in four child care centres. Clearly, the importance of this practice is not being stressed in training programs to the extent it should be. When you begin teaching, it is worth remembering the importance of this practice, and you will have to stress that with volunteers and student teachers.

The promotion of diversity and attention to different cultures and ethnic groups also was a weak point on both the ECERS and ITERS. Pretend play, art, and active physical play were neglected (and received scores below 4) in the infant/toddler rooms. In the preschool classes, the provision of science materials and activities, the use of television and computers, and music and movement all had scores below 4. Teachers in both infant/toddler and preschool classes did not have enough opportunities for professional growth. The facilities for the preschool staff also were sparse.

Questionnaire Results and Quality.   In infant/toddler rooms, teacher-child ratio and group size were not related to total ITERS scores. However, teacher education was: the percentage of teachers with early childhood training predicted quality—higher-quality programs had more trained staff. Child care fees, the receipt of government and non-government assistance (e.g., subsidized rents and utilities), being used for student placements, and expenditures on benefits for staff all were positively correlated with quality on the ITERS. Similar findings were reported for the ECERS. There were no significant correlations with the many items related to directors.

Wages, teacher satisfaction levels, educational levels, specific knowledge about early childhood, promotion of diversity, group size, and the number of adults in the infant/toddler rooms all predicted quality. Teachers who had another adult present had higher scores than those in very small programs where they were alone with the infants. Support from another adult seems important in this setting, a finding that would not surprise most parents. In the preschool rooms, wages, teacher satisfaction levels, specific knowledge about early childhood, promotion of diversity, participation in professional development activities and anti-bias courses, clearly identified goals, and number of hours worked all correlated positively with the ECERS scores. Interestingly, teachers who worked fewer hours had higher ECERS scores—but how few is not clear.

The authors of the QCCCC study note that the difference between the ITERS and ECERS scores mirror the results that Scarr, Eisenberg, and Deater-Deckard reported in their 1994 study. Infant/toddler programs appear to receive lower overall ratings. The authors also compare their results with similar studies done using the ECERS in British Columbia (Hunter, 1995), New Brunswick (Lyon & Canning, 1995), and Ontario (Doherty, 1995) in the mid-1990s.

While the studies differ in some ways, it is interesting to note that the ECERS scores increased over time in British Columbia, while they decreased in Ontario and New Brunswick. What is fascinating is that wage enhancement grants came into being in British Columbia during that time period, while cutbacks came into place in Ontario and New Brunswick! Although the authors do not draw any causal links, the suggestion of one is not surprising. Job satisfaction at all levels is related to feeling that you are being paid what you deserve! The child care field is not unusual in this dimension—what is unusual is that the salaries have been so low for so long for highly trained professionals.

● Caring and Learning Environments: Quality in Regulated Family Child Care Across Canada

Overview.   Now that you know the details of the QCCCC study, you will find that the *Caring and Learning Environments: Quality in Regulated Family Child Care Across Canada* (QFCCC) research asked similar questions using similar methods, except that it looked at family-based as opposed to centre-based care. The QFCCC study was conducted in the same six provinces and territory as the QCCCC study. In British Columbia, Saskatchewan, and New Brunswick, providers receive licences on an individual basis. In the Yukon, Ontario, Quebec, and Alberta, licences come through agencies that monitor the quality of care and compliance with licensing regulations for the provinces.

Rather than the ECERS or ITERS, the authors used the Family Day Care Rating Scale (FDCRS), a scale that is similar in organization to the ECERS and ITERS, but addresses items suited to a family-based environment. The FDCRS (Harms & Clifford, 1989) follows the same 7-point scoring system as the ITERS and ECERS. The authors also used the same Caregiver Interaction Scale (CIS) (Arnett, 1987) in this study. In addition, providers had a brief interview and also answered several questionnaires with questions about their program, their experiences, their education and specialized training, and themselves. There were also questions about professional development, fees and wages, available supports, and home visitors.

The Study Sample.   A total of 231 providers of regulated family-based child care providers participated in the study. Most of the providers selected tended to be in or close to several major cities, except in New Brunswick where all 22 licensed providers were invited to participate, and in the Yukon where only places by Whitehorse were selected. The authors aimed to find 40 providers from each province and territory included, but there were only 17 and 22 licensed providers in the Yukon and New Brunswick respectively. Again, as in the QCCCC study, there were recruitment problems that may be a source of bias in the study. A total of 136 individual providers and 3 agencies, one in Alberta and two in Quebec, refused to participate. The agencies made the initial contacts with individual providers so that their response rate is not known. Most of the agencies/providers who were willing to be contacted for the study participated. Again, this difference in refusal rates may well mean that the sample obtained is "better than average."

All of the providers who participated were women; most were married; and nearly half had at least one child of their own under 12 years at home. There were only 15 percent of providers over 50, and most were between 30 and 49 years of

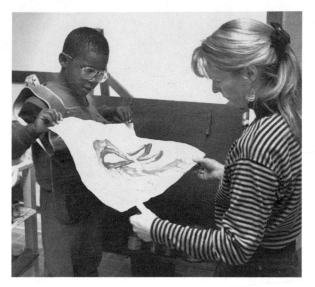

age. Relative to the "average" provider, there is some suggestion that the study participants are a little older, better educated, and more experienced. In addition, as someone who has been observed when on your practicums, you will undoubtedly agree that the providers' willingness to agree to a three-hour observation period says something about their confidence levels—or need for adult company! One-third of the 24 agencies were for-profit, two in Ontario and six in Alberta.

Results of the QFCCC Study. Information about the education of the providers is summarized in Exhibit 11-7. Just over 40 percent of the providers had taken courses related to family child care. This was more common in British Columbia, Alberta, and Quebec, where such courses are widely available. Over a third of the participants had degrees or diplomas in or related to the early childhood field. Almost two-thirds of the sample had taken either a family-child care course or a postsecondary diploma or degree related to the field. Perhaps this is why their participation in ongoing professional development activities was quite high: almost 90 percent of the providers had been in such activities in the previous three years.

The providers generally entered the family child care field because they liked children, wanted to work with them, and wanted to earn money while home with their own children. There were some curious regional differences: providers in British Columbia were more likely to emphasize liking children, while Ontario providers were more likely to mention earning money while being home with their own children. Ontario providers also mentioned finding companions for their own children more frequently than providers in the other locations.

Fluctuations in income and the lack of benefits in the position were stressors for a number of the providers, and to a lesser extent, problems with parents (e.g., late pickups, late payments) and having a child leave were concerns. Only about 15 percent of the providers expected to leave the field within three years.

FDCRS Scores On average, the CIS scores for the providers indicated that they were warm, sensitive caregivers who were neither harsh nor detached. The average FDCRS score across all items was 4.5 (out of a possible 7), indicating an acceptable, but not good level of care. Exhibit 11-8 shows the range of overall FDCRS scores.

Adult needs received the highest score (5.5), while basic care received the lowest (4.0), again because of handwashing and food-related hygiene practices. A lack of attention to issues around diversity and gender led to a low social development score (3.0).

Like their colleagues in group-based care in the QCCCC study, diversity was not given sufficient attention and cultural awareness had an average score below

3. Average scores below 3 were also found on items related to safety, child-related displays, and the provision of sand and water activities.

As in the study of group care, FDCRS scores were positively correlated with CIS scores. Providers with high-quality programs were more sensitive and involved, and not harsh. Interestingly, individually licensed providers had higher scores overall than those with agencies.

What Do These Results Mean?   While some of the results are heartening, others raise concerns. As there was some sampling bias that probably favoured more positive outcomes, the low scores for about a third of the centres shown in Exhibit 11-8 are alarming. If this many centres are at best custodial in nature, what is the situation in the unregulated world of family child care? Of greater concern is the fact that only a third of the programs are in the good range or above with a self-selected sample.

Perhaps the only heartening comparison is with the results of Kontos et al.'s (1995) comparable study of 112 providers in the United States. The FDCRS scores they reported were lower than those in the QFCCC study, and their CIS harshness and detachment scores were higher.

Questionnaire Results and Quality.   The questionnaire data provided additional information, though we will only touch on a few salient results. The providers cared on average for six children coming from five families for a median fee of just over $20 per child per day. Most had at least one child under 3 in care, and all had at least one child under 6 years. Only half the sample looked after school-aged children. Their days almost always are long—from 7:00 until 7:00,

EXHIBIT 11-8 *Range of FDCRS Scores for QFCCC Study*

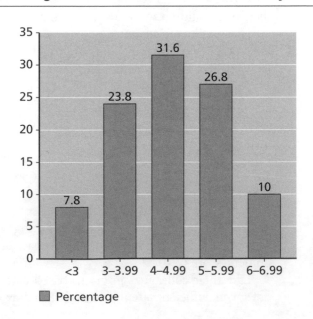

and almost all providers have at least one child in care for over 50 hours a week. Annual gross incomes ranged from $15,000 to $25,000, and expenses were considerable. About 60 percent of the providers spent between a third and a half of their income on expenditures related to care, and only a few (13.5 percent) covered at least 80 percent of their household expenses with their earnings. Contact with other providers, and community resources such as toy libraries, book and video libraries, and stores with bulk buying privileges were important to the providers.

A small number of providers had a second provider in the home, and this was associated with higher-quality care. Educational level made a difference in quality, with higher levels in any field being associated with higher FDCRS scores and more positive CIS scores. Years of experience as a provider did not contribute to quality, but prior experience in a child care setting did correlate positively with total FDCRS scores as well as scores on furnishings, language, and reasoning and learning activities. Specific training in early childhood education and in family child care predicted quality quite well; providers without specific training had lower overall scores. Some items related to working conditions such as gross income, number of vacation days taken, payment during absences, and actual fees were positively correlated with quality on both the FDCRS and the CIS. In addition, the number of extra unpaid hours spent on their work was also positively associated with the overall FDCRS score. Networking with other providers, associations, resource teams, and provincial associations also contributed to the quality of care. Finally, both independently licensed and agency providers seemed to find the visits of the inspectors and home visitors valuable.

● Policies and Practices in Canadian Family Child Care Agencies

The briefest study in the You Bet I Care! series is *Policies and Practices in Canadian Family Child Care Agencies* (CFCCA), and though published under separate cover it is related to the family child care study we just discussed. The agencies that were responsible for family child care programs described in the preceding section on the QFCCC study were also asked to complete a questionnaire, and this study summarizes those results. For reasons of brevity, we will only highlight the major findings of interest in the present context.

Eight agencies from Alberta, eight from Ontario, and another eight in Quebec were in the study which is based on the questionnaires the 24 agency directors completed. The directors identified certain difficulties with family child care as they experience it (which may differ in many ways from how independently licensed providers and directors experience it). Certain themes and findings overlap with those from the group care studies so they deserve to be highlighted.

The agency directors report that funds are inadequate and recruitment of providers is difficult. In addition, they report high turnover rates that just compound the recruitment problems. In fact, at least 30 percent of the providers reported they either were not sure where they would be in three years or they definitely would not be, though there is a suggestion that 50 percent of the Alberta providers expected to be elsewhere in three years. Some leave for work outside the home, but some may leave just so they can earn more in family child care as private cases pay higher rates than agency-sponsored cases. In family-based care, as in group-based care, high turnover rates seem to be strongly associated with low salaries.

On average, providers had 14 days of vacation a year, little opportunity for advancement within child care, and an annual *gross* salary between $10,000 and $24,999. Few have disability insurance and benefits, but two-thirds have liability insurance for their homes.

● What Have We Learned About the Quality of Child Care?

These studies underscore a number of important issues. High-quality child care is an elusive and rare phenomenon in both Canada and the United States—even good-quality child care is not readily available to most families. The available research tells us that the majority of children in Canada and the United States are receiving mediocre care at best. The CQCO study has shown us that adverse outcomes are associated with this poor-quality care, no matter how resourceful the child's family. In addition, the developmental consequences of low- and mediocre-quality care as a preschooler was still evident in Grade 2. Allowing mediocre care to be acceptable puts the future of our children, indeed the future of countries in general, in jeopardy. Governments must make a strong commitment so that all children and their families have access to quality child care. This commitment involves educating parents to help them both understand and demand appropriate quality for their children. Your role as an early childhood educator is important in this endeavour, because you can be a force in ensuring that the children you work with experience a quality program and you can help to educate parents about what quality means.

At the start of this chapter, we said that the quality of a program should be examined from several different perspectives—the children's, the parents', and the teachers':

1. What is the program's impact on the child? Does it support the child's well-being and meet the child's needs?

2. What is the program's impact on the parents? Does it support the parents' well-being and meet their needs?

3. What is the program's impact on the teachers? Does it support the teacher's well-being and meet their needs?

The series of studies we have just reviewed provide a reasonable amount of information on the first and third questions, while answering the second one requires some speculation. High-quality infant and preschool programs have a positive impact on children's development, and the gains stay with them into elementary school. Low-

quality programs have negative impacts on development. High-quality programs meet children's needs and foster well-being—but they are rare.

As long as parents are warm, approachable, and caring, even poor-quality child care does not have a negative impact on attachment—but it does have a negative impact on development. In this way, we know that mediocre and poor programs will ultimately have an impact on parents. The CQCO study, for example, found fewer reports of behaviour problems in children who had been in good-quality programs. The children who had been in high-quality programs also had better readiness skills, social skills, and language skills than those in poor-quality programs. In Grade 2, the quality of care—despite subsequent educational experiences—still manifests itself: language, math skills, and behaviour were still better if your child was in high-quality care. Parents who switch their infants under 15 months from one program to another also are at increased risk of having a child with attachment problems. Yet we also learned that parents have great difficulty judging quality.

There are multiple responses to the third question. When salaries are low, working conditions are poor, and professional development is limited, even teachers who have the potential to offer good programs do not meet the standard. Teachers need to be supported in the program if they are to offer a high-quality program. When they have a director with education and experience in the field who supports their efforts, then they feel supported and their programs reflect that. We also know that many programs in this country and the United States do not meet the teachers' needs and do not foster well-being. Teachers in poor-quality centres often look for a new career. If you want to network with other teachers and discuss these issues, visit the Web site of the Teacher Information Network.

The most striking finding across all the studies is perhaps the way government can help to ensure high-quality programs. In places that have stricter legislated requirements, quality is higher—when legislated standards are low, quality suffers and so do children, parents, and teachers. Advocating for legislative changes takes time and patience, but the efforts of many of our predecessors have paid off. In

Reflective Exercise 11-3

Perhaps as a class assignment, you could develop an information workshop for parents in your community to discuss "How do you find a high-quality child care program for your child?

this new millennium, perhaps you can help with your colleagues and professional associations to ensure that high-quality care becomes more available and accessible across the whole country.

In 2000, 95 percent of the educators surveyed reported they made a difference in children's lives, and about 85 percent found the work made good use of their skills and was stimulating and challenging. Despite that level of satisfaction and challenge, approximately 75 percent of the teachers and supervisors reported that poor pay and lack of opportunity for promotion were the most negative aspects of the job. As in the 1992 study, the educators thought the public undervalued the profession—although some noted that other professionals respected their work. Changes in salary levels and the public perception of the profession are definitely needed in this country. As a student entering the profession, you and your classmates are most likely to effect these long-overdue changes!

Key Terms

ECERS   ITERS

Key Points

1. For an early childhood education program to meet the criteria for high quality, it must respect the emerging abilities of young children without imposing inappropriate expectations and be staffed by specifically trained individuals. Low teacher turnover and positive child interaction are essential.

2. Studies show that smaller groups receive more stimulation than large ones; however, the parameters of the physical environment also need to be considered.

3. Mixed-age groups benefit both younger and older children.

4. A child-oriented environment, open communication, and family involvement benefit the child.

5. Staff must be respected, receive appropriate benefits, and work in a satisfying environment. Qualified staff is an important factor in any quality program.

6. Quality is not defined by a single factor but rather depends on the complex interaction of a variety of elements in which the professional plays a key role.

7. There is no federal legislation for child ratios and group size or centre size. Every province regulates this separately.

Key Questions

1. Observe preschoolers of various ages at play. What differences in physical development do you see as a function of age? Discuss these differences with the staff and ask them what that should tell you about appropriate activities and expectations.

2. Observe a group of young children during a time when they can self-select activities. How and when do their teachers intervene?

3. Have each student in your class visit an early childhood setting, and then return to class to compare notes. Look around the early childhood classroom to assess how it promotes positive (or negative) attitudes toward other people in relation to sex, race, culture, or disabling condition. What recommendations can you make for setting up a nonbiased classroom?

4. Select two different manipulative materials. What do you think children can potentially learn from each of them? Now spend ten minutes using each manipulative. Would you add any additional items to your lists?

Chapter 12

The Future of Early Childhood Education

*T*eachers and children are the critical ingredients in early childhood education. By this stage in the text and your academic year, you know that you can make the difference between a quality program and a mediocre one. You also understand that as a teacher in ECE, you will face a number of issues and dilemmas that are of concern to all in the profession. Your commitment to bettering the profession and your involvement in advocacy for the field will benefit generations to follow.

In this chapter, we will look at the field of early childhood education and its future from the teacher's perspective. We will examine the following topics:

1. Although early childhood education presents teachers with exciting challenges, it also presents some issues and dilemmas that we will consider.

   - Some problems faced by early childhood educators are rooted in the historic antecedents of the field.

   - Early childhood education educators have faced some serious concerns, including teacher shortages, turnover, low pay, burnout, and scarcity of males in the field.

   - Through advocacy and empowerment of early childhood professionals, these issues are beginning to be addressed.

2. We will end the chapter by examining trends and drawing some conclusions about what the future holds for the field of early childhood education.

Some Current Issues and Dilemmas

Early childhood education is, in many ways, a field of contradictions and extremes. Those who try to define it often find themselves in a dilemma, not clear on what to include and what to exclude. Where does a program fit that barely meets minimum standards, and what about the program that genuinely strives for excellence in meeting the needs of its children and families? Are the kindergarten teacher, the child care provider, the preschool demonstration teacher, and the family-based child care provider all included? Are the preschool teacher who holds a master's degree in early childhood education and the high school graduate who works in a child care centre equals in the same field? Can the child care provider who earns minimum wage and no benefits for the eight hours a day spent caring for children 50 weeks of the year be lumped with the kindergarten teacher who earns a public school salary, often greater then $60,000, for ten months of teaching?

How can the teacher job description that calls for someone who "likes children" be compared with the one that requires "a degree in early childhood education or child development"? How can the lack of licensing requirements for teachers of young children in some Canadian jurisdictions be reconciled with educators' insistence that those who work with young children need specific training? In fact, is there a good reason to justify why some of you are enrolled in an academic program while others with no academic training may equally qualify for a position?

These questions and others are at the heart of the dilemma facing the early childhood profession. We will review some specific issues and look at some possible ways of addressing these. Although we will divide some of these issues into categories such as teacher shortage and low pay, these issues are intertwined in the same way the variables defining quality are linked.

The purpose of presenting these issues in this chapter is aimed not at discouraging you, but at enlightening and motivating you. If you enter the field knowing the risks, issues, and challenges that face you, then you also enter the profession prepared to face and meet these problems head on.

We end this section by discussing the positive impact of empowerment and activism and by outlining five key recommendations for resolving these issues. You should also note that these issues can also be found in other fields and professions and are not necessarily exclusive to early childhood education.

Some Web sites may be of interest. The site The Future of Children discusses the future of children while the site of the World Bank Group discusses Third World ECE programs and has a number of links to related sites.

● A Historical Perspective

It might be helpful to look at the road travelled by the field of early childhood education to gain a perspective on its current status. Early childhood education today is inextricably linked to the role and status of women in North America.

Between the mid-18th and mid-19th centuries, "womanhood was redefined, its image re-created and reimagined, its social function reviewed, its links to child rearing and socialization forged, and its authority over the moral and cultural development of the nation rationalized" (Finkelstein, 1988, p. 12). When, in the latter half of the 19th century, the kindergarten became firmly established as a

Canadian institution, women had found their niche in an environment that was not quite domestic, yet not quite public either.

The early 20th-century pioneers of the early childhood movement, while building a scientific basis for child study, continued to see women as the guardians of the young with a specialized role in upholding moral and cultural standards, a noble role above concerns for economic and material comforts. Unfortunately, this legacy of "unselfishness" has followed early childhood educators to the beginning of the new millennium, endowing them with a realization of the importance of their work, yet placing them in a low-paying profession that has low status in our social structure (Varga, 1997). Varga warns about a return to the philanthropy of the 19th century—providing child care for good will and low pay results in children and caregivers becoming exploited and devalued under legislation that reduces standards of care (Varga, 1997).

● Teacher Shortage/Turnover

Over the past several years, increasing attention has been focused on the shortage of qualified early childhood educators. This shortage is partly caused by the high demand for child care as increasing numbers of mothers with children enter the workforce. The Statistics Canada figures we discussed in Chapter 1 suggest that there will be growing demand for child care facilities and teachers. Yet, particularly in areas where there is low unemployment and a high cost of living, early childhood educators are scarce.

Teacher shortage can be tied to the high rate of turnover among early childhood educators. *Caring for a Living* (Canadian Child Day Care Federation & Canadian Day Care Advisory Association, 1992), one Canadian survey of early childhood teachers, found the national teacher turnover rate to be 26 percent. In the 1992 report, it ranged from a low of 16 percent in Prince Edward Island to a high of 84 percent in the Yukon. The *You Bet I Care!* study (Doherty et al., 2000) we discussed in the previous chapter found that turnover rates had dropped to 21.7 percent when they collected their data in 1998. Again, there were very significant regional variations: Alberta had a high of 44.8 percent and Prince Edward Island and Ontario had lows of 15 and 16 percent respectively. The turnover rate was higher in for-profit centres, at 32 percent, almost double the 17 percent turnover rate in nonprofit centres. A similar pattern was seen in the National Child Care Staffing Study in the United States (Whitebook, Howes, & Phillips, 1989): the 1988 U.S. turnover rate was 41 percent ranging from a *74 percent* annual staff change in chain, for-profit centres to a 30 percent rate in nonprofit programs.

High turnover rates are a problem for many—for children and directors to name a few. The literature does tell us that frequent turnover has a negative impact on child development. For a director of a licensed centre, the sudden of departure of a teacher means finding a supply teacher and then filling the position as quickly as possible; otherwise, it would mean reducing numbers of children in order to meet licensing requirements. Reducing numbers suddenly would leave many parents in a quandary. Teacher turnover rates and teacher shortages are not issues that can be viewed separately—there is little doubt that they must be viewed along with information on teacher salaries.

● Teacher Turnover and Low Pay

You have already entered this field knowing that salaries are lower than they should be in your chosen profession and for females in general. Our goal here is to inform you early on why this is so. You can then begin making career-path choices within the field of early childhood education: investigating programs, sending away for information, asking questions, focusing some of your assignments on these issues, lobbying for change, and ultimately having an impact on your field from day one. Students can be a very powerful and visible force to the public and the politicians.

Beach and her colleagues noted in their study of the Canadian child care workforce that turnover will always be a problem if wages stay low (Beach, Bertrand, & Cleveland, 1998). Certainly high turnover rates are not characteristic of kindergarten and primary-level programs where the rate of pay is much higher (Cleveland & Krashinsky, 2001)—in fact, some Canadian teachers' federations are offering incentives for early retirement in an attempt to persuade aging teachers to leave the lucrative profession and create positions for young graduates in the teaching profession.

The staffing shortage in non-school-based early childhood programs would undoubtedly be much less of a problem if early childhood teachers were paid adequate salaries and if they received appropriate recognition and status. For most teachers of young children, however, monetary rewards are not equal to their professional training and value. Although there is wide variation in pay, early childhood teachers are generally paid poorly as we know from the previous chapter. Yet, as we noted, there is considerable variation in salaries across the provinces and territories. Unionized teachers have higher salaries, and some public sector positions pay very well.

Courtesy of George Brown College.

The low wages of Canadian early childhood educators still remain somewhat discouraging given that 8.5 of every 10 teachers in the *You Bet I Care!* survey had postsecondary-level diplomas or degrees. Historically, the profession has been dominated by females, and historically, predominantly female occupations are associated with low pay and low status. Thus, this problem of low pay does not belong exclusively to our profession or our field. Moreover, over the years, females also have been less likely to protest their wages. However, this is definitely changing. In April 1993, for example, the Confédération des syndicats nationaux (CSN) organized a walkout of all unionized child care teachers in Quebec to support demands for a wage increase of $3.50 per hour (Child Care Resource and Research Unit, 1994).

Benefits are another issue of concern. Generally, teachers of early childhood programs sponsored by larger institutions, such as municipalities, hospitals, school boards, or universities, benefit from the policies of their sponsoring agencies. In a similar way, teachers of employer-sponsored child care programs also often receive their company's benefits package. However, benefits are rare in smaller centres, especially profit-making ones (Beach et al., 1998). Teacher turnover in Canadian child care is lower in those centres with benefit plans and pension plans (Beach et al., 1998). Certainly, Canadian teachers' responses to the *You Bet I Care!* and *Caring for a Living* surveys suggest that the high turnover rate in non-school-based early childhood programs is related to low wages. In the United States, Whitebook et al. (1989) found an inverse relationship between rate of pay and percentage of turnover. Those at the lower end of the pay scale changed jobs at twice the rate of those at the higher end. At the same time, however, they found that there was less turnover among teachers with early childhood training.

High staff turnover takes its toll in several ways. The National Child Care Staffing Study (Whitebook et al., 1989) found that in centres with a high turnover rate, children spent less time in social activities with peers and tended more to wander aimlessly. Very young children such as toddlers have been found to be very susceptible to turnover, exhibiting withdrawal and aggressiveness two years later (Howes & Hamilton, 1993). In addition, separation from parents becomes more critical when caregivers change frequently (Galinsky, 1989). Teachers also suffer when their co-workers change frequently, because they have to assume the additional burden of orienting and training new staff (Whitebook, 1986). In a follow-up study, Whitebook and her colleagues (Whitebook, Phillips, & Howes, 1993) made similar observations four years later. They confirmed that the rate of teacher turnover is affected by quality, salaries, and type of program (i.e., for-profit or non-profit).

Low pay fuels a vicious cycle. Poor pay causes qualified teachers to seek work elsewhere; as a result, jobs are often filled by unqualified staff. They, in turn, reinforce the low status in which early childhood education is held and negate the need for higher pay (Katz, 1984a). In a call for an "all-out effort to improve compensation and status," Marcy Whitebook (1986), director of the U.S. Child Care Employee Project under which the National Child Care Staffing Study was carried out, warned that child care:

> could become a less and less attractive career choice despite the many inherently gratifying aspects of working with young children. The most likely and scariest prospect is that the pressure will build at a faster pace to lower standards for child care personnel—some of which are already frighteningly inadequate—in order to fill teaching vacancies. (P. 11)

Kyle (1992a) expressed similar concerns about teacher shortages in Ontario:

> There is also some concern that the [Ministry's] development of an options paper "to provide alternatives for determining equivalency" may result in the

watering down of present training requirements in order to allow more semi-trained or untrained staff to work in child care centres. (P. 444)

Semi-trained and untrained teachers might well solve the teacher shortage problem, and possibly reduce child care fees, but at what cost? While professionals with training command higher salaries, they also bring considerably more to their programs and enhance the quality of care young children receive.

● Low Wages and Affordable Child Care

The low wages of early childhood educators are inextricably related to the issue of affordable child care. Teachers' wages and benefits (if they receive them) constitute the largest expenditure in early childhood programs—just over 75 percent for salaries and almost 9 percent for benefits according to the *You Bet I Care!* survey. However, that allocation varies considerably from one jurisdiction to another. In Newfoundland and New Brunswick, for example, only 66 percent of a centre's budget is used for salaries, while that figure jumps to 80 and 82 percent for Saskatchewan and Manitoba respectively. The proportion of money going to benefits is 8.9 percent nationally, but again there is regional variation. In Alberta, Newfoundland, and New Brunswick, only 4.2 , 3.5, and 2.5 percent of income goes to benefits, while Saskatchewan, Ontario, and Quebec centres spend between 10 and 11 percent of their budgets on benefits. Salaries may improve in Newfoundland, however, now that teacher certification has been embedded in the regulations. In the A Canadian Professional Speaks Out box, Joanne Morris, a faculty member at the College of the North Atlantic in St. John's, discusses the certification requirements that Newfoundland introduced in 1999.

Of course, the fee parents pay for a program is directly affected by how much is allocated to salaries. The higher the teachers' cheques are, the greater the cost of the program. Teacher-child ratios and group-size regulations have a similar impact on budgets and fees. The more children per adult, the lower the cost because fewer adults have to be hired. On the other hand, high child-adult ratios are associated with higher levels of teacher stress and decreased responsiveness to children (Phillips & Howes, 1987; Whitebook, Howes, Darrah, & Friedman, 1982).

Yet the answer is not simply a matter of raising the cost of child care charged to parents. Although some families can afford to pay higher rates to ensure high-quality care offered by well-trained and well-paid professionals, many others cannot. Experts contend that the cost parents pay for child care includes a hidden subsidy—the low wages teachers receive (Willer, 1990). Many professionals advocate aggressive lobbying for public support of child care. Some advocates maintain that only when teachers collectively insist on higher wages and benefits will there be sufficient economic impetus to force a solution to the problem.

Since any additional costs would have to be borne by parents, parents will become more interested in the problem, unless they find public funds. If they cannot afford child care, parents will become involved in the political process of vying for funds. According to Morin (1989):

A Canadian Professional Speaks Out

CERTIFICATION WITHIN REGULATION

Joanne Morris, Education and Training Representative, Child Care Human Resources Round Table, College of the North Atlantic, St. John's, Newfoundland

The province of Newfoundland and Labrador has embedded certification of all individuals who work within the regulated child care sector into the Child Care Services Regulations, 1999. The Regulations stipulate that specific levels of certification must be held by individuals who fulfill specific positions such as operator (program director) and the lead staff within each group of children as defined for centre-based care, and for family child care providers and home visitors. In addition, all individuals who have contact with the children must minimally hold an entry level of certification which is usually achieved through the completion of a provincial orientation course. The Association of Early Childhood Educators of Newfoundland and Labrador is working in partnership with the provincial government through the position of a Registrar for Certification who assesses levels of certification and delivers the orientation course.

The underlying goal of this initiative is to improve the quality of early childhood care and education that children are receiving through the enforcement of qualified educators and care providers. To do so means building on the system that is in place. The model and strategy that derived from a research and development project has three components: certification; education through distance methodologies; and prior learning assessment and recognition (PLAR). Many individuals within the child care system of this province were impacted by new regulations requiring them to upgrade their education in order to maintain their positions. In order to support them in doing so, the Department of Health and Community Services provided the public college with funding to partially offset tuition fees, and the costs associated with completion of practicum requirements.

The College of the North Atlantic, the provincial public college, offers a diploma in Early Childhood Education in two locations within the province for full-time studies. In addition, in St. John's, the diploma is offered by distance education to students in locations throughout the province. Limited access to educational opportunities led to this program design in order to address the vast geographic distances that exist between communities. Faculty have assured quality through the development of the curriculum using various technologies including print and media resources, computer access, teleconferencing, and individual availability to students for instruction. Students complete practicum requirements by participation in summer institutes held at the College's Children's Centre as well as in their own places of employment through faculty observation and evaluation of their practice. Students can continue their employment and upgrade toward certification levels.

Prior learning assessment and recognition, the third component of the model to support implementation of certification and education, is a process of assessing the knowledge, skills and attitudes which derive from work and life experience. Students develop a comprehensive portfolio through a course, documenting their learning, which is further verified through evaluation of their practice. This challenge for credit may result in credits or exemptions within the diploma program. The value of this process for those who are becoming certified is that they begin their studies in areas they need to work on and avoid having to repeat learning in areas in which they can already demonstrate equivalency to course outcomes. Some individuals may achieve their required levels through PLAR alone.

This new legislated approach to certification has long been awaited by the profession and the provincial government. As further recognition, annual educational supplements are being given to individuals who are working in lead staff and supervisory positions once they have met their certification levels. This enhancement of wages is a step in the direction of supporting the funding of a major cost within a quality child care system. It is anticipated that these new directions will lead to a greater sense of professionalism within the field and greater public awareness of the importance of quality child care. Future possibilities may include an early childhood educators act, portability of certification across the country, and eventually a national certification system.

Our advocacy efforts have been directed primarily toward increasing the supply of affordable care for parents, not to increasing compensation for employees. Common practice is to shield parents from the true cost of child care by having employees work at compensation levels that subsidize the cost to parents. (P. 19)

● Burnout Syndrome

Teacher burnout is another issue in the field, and it too is linked with teacher shortages, high turnover rates, low salaries, and the stress that arises as a consequence. Burnout is complex, resulting from multiple causes. It is characterized by job dissatisfaction, stress, loss of energy, irritability, and a feeling of being exploited. The **burnout syndrome** has been described as a feeling of exhaustion that results from too many demands on one's energy and resources (Mattingly, 1977; Schneider & Boyd, 1996; White & Mill, 2000). And burnout typically occurs in professions that require extensive contact with people.

Many factors contribute to burnout. Some of the factors cited in the research (White & Mill, 2000; Schneider & Boyd, 1996; Whitebook et al., 1982) are long working hours, unpaid overtime (e.g., time planning, parent functions), maintenance

> ## *Reflective Exercise 12-1*
>
> What impact did the events of September 11, 2001, have on teacher and parent stress levels? Which young children in local centres were troubled by the events? Which ones seemed not to notice?

duties, and few or no breaks. In addition, the intensity of working closely with children, lack of power in the decision-making process, and poor adult-child ratios all can contribute to burnout.

Although burnout is a final outcome for some of those who work in early childhood programs, most find great job satisfaction, which balances some of the negative aspects. Both the *You Bet I Care!* (Doherty et al., 2000) study and the *Caring for a Living* (Canadian Child Day Care & Canadian Day Care Advisory Association, 1992) study found Canadian teachers find their involvement with and their positive influence on young children very satisfying. They also enjoy the collegiality that accompanies their positions. The opportunity for reflection and self-development, satisfying staff relations, job flexibility, autonomy, and staff interdependence have also been reported as positives in U.S. studies (Whitebook et al., 1982, 1989).

● Men in Early Childhood Education

A somewhat different issue concerns the role of men in early childhood education. Both the *Caring for a Living* and the *You Bet I Care!* study have reported that 98 percent of Canadian early childhood teachers were females. The figure is in the same range in the United States—Seifert (1988) and Whitebook et al. (1989) both reported that in the United States 95 to 97 percent of practitioners are females.

There have been and continue to be male teachers who have a high commitment to the education and well-being of young children. For some children who grow up in single-parent homes without a father figure, a male teacher can fill a particularly special role. Yet men leave the field of early childhood education at an even greater rate than women do. Some male teachers who changed careers reported that they were subject to subtle prejudicial attitudes from parents, female co-workers, and administrators. They were considered inferior to women because they had never been mothers. Suspicion that was initially based on vague sex stereotypes was intensified during the 1980s by several highly publicized cases of sexual abuse involving male teachers in child care settings (Robinson, 1988). Similarly, the 1993 abuse trial of four male police officers, one unrelated woman, and a family (father, mother, and son) who operated an unlicensed child care facility in Martensville, Saskatchewan again raised public suspicions about men in child care (and about child care in general). While these are exceptional cases, they nonetheless have a deterrent effect on some men considering the child care field.

There has been considerable speculation that economic reasons prevent more men from entering the field of early childhood education or cause them to leave the field more readily if they do spend some time as preschool teachers. Robinson (1988) found that 85 percent of his sample of male early childhood teachers were married with at least one child and were the major wage earners in their families. Low pay compelled them to look elsewhere for work. In part, men leave the field or do not enter it because they have more and better-paying career choices than women, not because of the nature of the job (Seifert, 1988).

The absence of a substantial number of men in the field is undoubtedly another contributing factor to low salaries, though it has been argued that "recruiting more men would enhance the professional self-image of early childhood education" (Seifert, 1988, p. 114). La Grange (2001), however, in a recent article on Canadian child care workers discusses the fact that few men joined the Early Childhood Services (ECS) project between 1973 and 1989 when it existed in Alberta. ECS provided programs for children from birth to 8 years, and teachers received their credentials through the Department of Education. The salaries of the ECS teachers. Teachers working in ECS were affiliated with the Alberta Teachers' association, and their salaries were on a par with elementary school teachers. Even then, when salaries were high, few men chose to work there; La Grange "suspect[s] that this has something to do with issues of 'women's work' and the way we treat and view workers who care for young children" (p. 393).

Recruiting men in the absence of increasing salaries is ineffective—but it also may be ineffective with higher wages. Nonetheless, low wages are a pivotal factor affecting professionalism.

● Changes in Professional Education for an Early Childhood Workforce

At a 1998 symposium on child care, summarized in *Our Children's Future: Child Care Policy in Canada* (Cleveland & Krashinsky, 2001), there was considerable discussion about the need for an advanced credential for teachers in early childhood education (e.g., Bertrand, 2001; Doherty, 2001; Goelman, 2001; Juorio, 2001; La Grange, 2001; Pollard, Bernhard, & Corson, 2001). La Grange maintained that the early childhood field is lagging behind other professions—nurses and teachers have raised educational requirements in recent years, and the increase in educational levels has been met with an increase in salary levels, won partly through unionization. Groups such as the British Columbia Nurses Association and the Ontario Teachers Federation have helped set standards for the profession, and advocated for the profession at the same time. The early childhood field should be turning to these exemplars—professions in which the majority of the members are again female.

There were diverse views about what the advanced credential should be. Some proposed a four-year degree (Goelman, 2001), some a three-year degree (Bertrand, 2001; La Grange, 2001); and others wanted to broaden the discussion to include family-based care (e.g., Doherty, 2001; Pollard et al., 2001). Notwithstanding this debate, there is a suggestion that directors and senior teachers should have a post-diploma credential. A model suggested by Doherty (2001) is based on the model used in France where one teacher with a master's degree has responsibility for as many as twenty-eight 3-to-6-year-old children in a program. Only the teacher is specified in the ratio requirements. However, that teacher has an assistant who helps with feeding, naps, and other routines. In addition, there is a cook and a maintenance worker so the overall ratio is far better. A similar situation occurs in the infant/toddler rooms where the official ratio is 1:5, but there is a floating staff person plus the cook and maintenance person. Doherty suggests that a similar model would allow for more task differentiation, and, at the same time, open up possibilities for advancement and different salary levels. The head teacher would concentrate on programming, while the assistants would help with routines, with program, and so on.

A related issue that emerged in the discussion was the problem of transferability of an early childhood diploma to the university setting. In Quebec, the transition from the CEGEP programs in early childhood to university programs is straightforward, but it can be difficult in some locales. Several universities—Manitoba, Victoria, Brock, and Ryerson, for example—have transfer credits in place, but most do not.

● Empowerment and Activism

We have raised several issues that face the early childhood profession. It is heartening that increasingly more effort is being devoted to solving these issues. Articulate public statements, relevant publications, thoughtful research, and energetic political advocacy and lobbying are making an impact. There is no question but that the needs of young children and families, the importance of high quality in child care, and the needs of early childhood teachers are becoming highly visible public matters.

Changes in the current realities of early childhood education can be brought about through joint political action and the empowerment of teachers (Dresden & Myers, 1989). Training for advocacy is being incorporated into some higher-education programs, so students learn how policies are made, how the political system operates, and how they can affect it (Lombardi, 1986). You may well be taking a course that covers advocacy as part of your program of study, something that probably would not have been part of the curriculum 15 or 20 years ago.

Reflective Exercise 12-2

What do you think about the idea of an advanced credential? Would it interest you? Do the institutions near you allow transfer of credit?

Courtesy of Play and Learn.

What is clear is the resolve of professionals and organizations to push for change. Interest in and support for quality child care comes from many sectors both within and outside of the field of early childhood education, including parents, teachers, administrators, resource and referral agencies, related service providers, professional organizations, teacher trainers and educators, researchers, civic and religious groups, business and labour organizations, volunteer service organizations, philanthropic organizations and foundations, and civic leaders. A coalition including members of such constituency groups can be a powerful force in beginning to address issues (Lombardi, 1990). However, the ultimate responsibility for enhancing the prestige—and the salaries—of early childhood educators lies with the members of the profession. As one of the reviewers of this text noted, some early childhood professionals "are quite apathetic and want other groups to plead their cause." In order to effect real change, professionals must be willing to commit their own time to lobbying efforts, and then other groups—parents, for example—may join them.

The United States National Child Care Staffing Study (Whitebook et al., 1989) ended with five major recommendations for change and suggestions for achieving these. These continue to be as relevant to the Canadian context as they are to that of the United States.

1. *Increase salaries.* To reach this goal, some of the recommendations are to establish salary levels that are competitive with jobs requiring comparable training and education, earmark government funds for salary enhancement, raise the minimum wage, and invest more public and private funds in child care to help low- and middle-income families.

2. *Promote education and training.* This goal can be reached by establishing a career ladder, as well as stipend programs to cover early childhood training costs.

3. *Adopt standards that will lead to higher-quality programs.* Such standards should establish national criteria for child-adult ratios, staff training, education, and compensation, and they should be required of recipients of any public funds.

4. *Develop industry-wide standards.* To increase the quality of early childhood programs, recommendations include a minimum allocation of a centre's budget for teaching staff expenditures, a benefits package for all teaching staff, inclusion of time for curriculum preparation and staff meetings, and encouragement of staff to join a professional organization.

5. *Promote public education.* To educate the public about the importance of well-trained and adequately paid teachers, it is recommended that administrators, educators, professional organizations, and referral agencies participate in a concerted effort to promote this issue and its importance.

There are a number of resources for professionals in the field on the Internet that may be of interest.

The Future of Early Childhood Education

Up to this point, we have examined issues that Canadian early childhood teachers face as a profession. At the dawn of the 21st century, we can look back and unravel some of the factors that have shaped the field as it exists today. But what lies ahead? Are there more changes in store? Will unresolved social issues be addressed? Will early childhood education become an important force in considering these issues? Lacking the aid of a crystal ball, we might, nonetheless, try to predict what lies ahead by extrapolating from current trends.

- From all economic and social indications, it is reasonable to expect that a high percentage of families will continue to have two parents in the workforce. Thus, while they are at work, dual-income families, along with working single parents, will continue to need care for their young children.

- At the same time, the actual number of children potentially requiring child care will continue to grow.

Courtesy of Play and Learn.

- Employment opportunities in early childhood education will continue to increase.

- The number of young children who live in poverty will continue to increase. However, recent economic and political realities in Canada have not made people optimistic about federal increases in funding for child care.

- Employer involvement in child care sponsorship has been one of the fastest-growing trends during the past 15 years. This interest is likely to increase as employers recognize the need to provide child care benefits for parent-employees to help maintain a productive workforce. A shift in type of program sponsorship, along with new job opportunities, is likely to accompany such a trend.

- All indications are that the number of positions for early childhood professionals will

continue to rise because of the ongoing need of families for child care, projected expansion in publicly funded programs for children at risk, and increasing numbers of employer-sponsored programs. Yet there are and will continue to be grave concerns about the stability of the early childhood workforce. In no other industry is there such a high turnover of employees as in child care. Unless wages are attractive, this turnover is likely to continue.

- Professionals working with young children are realizing that teacher training programs for those specializing in early childhood are fragmented in most Canadian jurisdictions. Programs for elementary school teachers often do not put enough stress on the early years, while programs for child care teachers do not put enough stress on school-related issues. More formal liaison mechanisms between programs and joint offerings are likely to increase.

- As more children are in school-aged care, new issues emerge. The need for improved communication between child care facilities and elementary schools is becoming more urgent. Similarly, there will be a greater need for teacher training programs to broaden their focus to include non-school-based care in the curriculum.

- As we have discussed, stability of staff is an important element in the quality of early childhood programs, because children's trust and attachment to the adults in their lives depends on that stability. As a result, there has been increasing concern about the interplay between the needs of children for quality care, the needs of parents for affordable child care, and the needs of early childhood professionals for appropriate compensation and status. This concern, expressed both from within and from outside the early childhood profession, will continue to be articulated. We can expect greater focus on and increasing public awareness of this issue in the future.

- As issues related to early care and education continue to occupy public attention, it becomes more and more apparent that our country lacks a cohesive and consolidated social policy within which to consider child and family matters. For instance, a wide variety of agencies initiate, license, administer, and evaluate varying programs for children and families, often relying on disparate philosophies, approaches, and regulations. Even within provinces, there are different regulations governing variables such as teacher-child ratios, for example, depending on which ministry is involved. But, at the same time, because of increased public attention, there also seems to be greater willingness to address such issues with more depth, integration, and forethought. It can be expected, therefore, that efforts to coordinate early childhood policies and approaches will continue in the future, and perhaps a national policy will eventually be a reality.

- Many programs for young children, compensatory education and kindergarten programs, for example, often are operated only part-day. Such scheduling is

Courtesy of George Brown College.

problematic for working parents who need full-day care for their children. This conflict may prevent youngsters, who would potentially benefit, from participating in such programs. Because limited funding is the major stumbling block to extending these programs to meet working parents' needs, this issue will continue to be raised.

- Within the early childhood profession, there is a continued focus on the pluralistic nature of our society and the shrinking world in which children are growing up. Many early childhood programs can be expected to focus more than ever on an unbiased curriculum that includes children and families from all cultural, ethnic, linguistic, and economic backgrounds, as well as children with disabilities. Special programs that preserve the culture of Aboriginal groups are also likely to become more numerous.

- Finally, there will be continued efforts to integrate children with disabilities into programs with other children. The parent groups representing children with disabilities are a powerful lobby, and they are likely to pressure provinces without legislation about integration to enact legislation.

As you complete your studies and enter the field, remember that you can make a difference in the field of early childhood education and enhance its status in Canada. Just as you can be a powerful influence on the development of the young children in your program, you can have a major impact on the development of the field in the 21st century. Finally, you also will have a major impact on the lives of the young children you teach and care for in your program, and on their families.

A Closer Look
_____

ST. PETER'S AND JACK SPRAT

A look at two early childhood centres in one community points up some of the reasons why there is great satisfaction and stability in one while there is a high rate of teacher burnout resulting in frequent staff turnover in the other. St. Peter's Child Care Centre is a church-sponsored facility begun by a group of interested parents in the 1970s. It has an active and supportive board made up of church, parent, and community professional representatives. Most of the staff have worked at St. Peter's for ten years or more, and the rare job openings tend to elicit many applicants. Salaries are a little above the average for the community, but not as high as at some other centres.

The staff report high job satisfaction; they enjoy their work with the children, appreciate each other, and value their input into the decision-making process. The director meets weekly with the staff, discussing concerns and promoting group problem-solving strategies. She spends a good part of each day in the classrooms, with the staff and children. A child-adult ratio of 7 to 1, team teaching, flexible scheduling to accommodate the staff's personal needs, and response to staff requests for material and equipment also contribute to their level of satisfaction. One staff member summed up the feelings of her colleagues by saying, "I love this job and wouldn't trade it for the world. I work with a very special group of people whom I highly respect as well as really like. It's a pleasure to come to work. Each day is a challenge, and it's exhilarating. I suppose I could make more money at another job, but where else could I find this special combination of great people, little and big, and the chance to grow and develop personally as I have done in the 12 years I have been here!"

Jack Sprat, a privately owned child care program in the same community, suffers from constant staff turnover. Seven months is the longest any staff member has been at Jack Sprat. Most of the children have had as many teachers as the number of months they have been in the program. A director spends part of her time at this facility and part of her time at another one that belongs to the same owner. Each teacher has charge of a group of 13 to 17 children in isolated rooms, and there is little interaction among staff.

The owner subscribes to a monthly curriculum service and teachers are expected to follow this program, which involves letter and number recognition activities, dittoed exercises, and group discussions that focus on specific letters, numbers, names of the months, animals, and occupations. Each child is expected to complete a specific number of dittos each day. Teachers complain about feeling isolated, having no say over what they do with the children, being forced to carry out activities neither they nor the children enjoy, a lack of resources, an inability to request additional supplies, and a lack of support in dealing with the children.

The contrast between St. Peter's and Jack Sprat is underlined by the frequent teacher turnover in the latter and the almost total absence of staff changes in the former. St. Peter's gives priority to meeting the needs of children and staff, allows staff to participate in decision making, promotes communication and camaraderie among staff, and exudes an atmosphere of mutual respect among teachers, administration, and children.

Key Term

burnout syndrome

Key Points

Current Issues and Dilemmas

1. The history of women over the past two centuries is closely linked with the development of the field of early childhood education.

2. Low pay and poor benefits for early childhood teachers are directly tied to the cost of child care for parents.

3. Some early childhood teachers experience burnout.

4. More than 98 percent of early childhood teachers are women, and male teachers leave the field at an even greater rate than female teachers do.

5. The issues and dilemmas facing early childhood education and its teachers are being addressed through vigorous advocacy and lobbying to help bring about change through political action and empowerment of teachers.

The Future of Early Childhood Education

6. Economic and social factors point up a continued growing need for early childhood education. These include an expected increase in the number of women in the workforce, an increase in the number of children in poverty, and greater employer sponsorship of child care.

7. The need for qualified early childhood educators will increase, and provinces with minimal requirements for teachers in early childhood settings will be pressured to raise their standards.

8. The early childhood profession will continue to address issues related to quality care and the needs of staff.

Key Questions

1. Discuss teacher salaries, burnout, and teacher turnover as a class. Try to determine the best way of resolving these issues.

2. What would you do to encourage more men to enter early childhood education? In what ways would more male teachers be beneficial for young children in child care settings?

3. We have speculated about the future of early childhood education on the basis of current trends. What issues do you think the field will face in the future? What will the field look like in ten years?

4. Discuss teacher turnover and issues related to a child's attachment to a caregiver. What impact might this have on the public's perceptions of the profession?

Glossary of Key Terms

ABC analysis—An observational technique in which the observer records observations in three columns, identifying antecedent, behaviour, and consequence.

absorbent mind—Maria Montessori's term to describe the capacity of young children to learn a great deal during the early years.

abstract thinking—According to Jean Piaget, the ability to solve a variety of problems abstractly, without a need to manipulate concrete objects.

academic materials—See *conceptual materials*.

accommodation—According to Jean Piaget, one form of adaptation, which takes place when an existing concept is modified or a new concept is formed to incorporate new information or a new experience.

active learning—A teaching style in which children are active seekers of knowledge, not passive recipients of it.

active listening—Thomas Gordon's term for the technique of reflecting back to children what they have said as a way to help them find their own solutions to problems.

activities—Well-planned, self-selected learning opportunities, usually placed in activity centres, for children in an active learning program.

activity centres (also called **learning** or **interest areas**)—Well-planned, self-selected learning opportunities, usually placed in special locations, for children in an active learning program; the locations themselves, where materials and equipment are combined around common activities, such as art, science, or language arts.

activity time—Largest block(s) of time in the early childhood program day during which children can self-select from a variety of activities.

adaptation—Jean Piaget's term for the process that occurs whenever new information or a new experience occurs.

adoptive parents—A person (or persons) who become parents through a legal process.

adult-child ratio—The number of children for whom an adult is responsible, calculated by dividing the total number of adults into the total number of children. A high ratio means there are fewer children per teacher; a low ratio means there are more children.

aesthetics—The enjoyment and appreciation of beauty, particularly related to all forms of art.

aggression—Behaviour deliberately intended to hurt others.

aide—See *assistant teacher*.

allergies—Physiological reactions to environmental of food substances that can affect or alter behaviour.

anal stage—The second stage of development described by Sigmund Freud, occurring during the second two years of life, in which pleasure and conflict derive from bowel control and elimination.

anecdotal record—A method of observation involving a written "word picture" of an event or behaviour.

assimilation—According to Jean Piaget, one form of adaptation, which takes place when the person tries to make new information or a new experience fit into an existing concept.

assistant teacher (also called **aide**, **helper**, **auxiliary teacher**, **associate teacher**, or **small-group leader**)—Works under the guidance of the head teacher in providing a high-quality program for the children and families in the class.

associate teacher—See *assistant teacher*.

associative play—A category of play in which children interact to some extent and may share materials, but are not really engaged in a common activity.

atelier—A workshop that provides learning through visual arts and an esthetically pleasing environment.

atelierista—A teacher who provided the framework for learning through visual arts and an esthetically pleasing environment.

attachment—The child's bond with the mother, established during the first year of life.

attention deficit disorder with hyperactivity (ADHD)—A psychological disorder manifested by short attention span, restlessness, poor impulse control, distractibility, and inability to concentrate.

authority stage—A stage of parenting defined by Ellen Galinsky typifying parents of young preschoolers who are defining rules as well as their own parenting role.

auto-education—See *self-education*.

autonomy—See *Autonomy vs. Shame and Doubt*.

Autonomy vs. Shame and Doubt—The second stage of development described by Erik Erikson, occurring during the second two years of life, in which toddlers assert their growing motor, language, and cognitive abilities by trying to become more independent.

auxiliary teacher—See *assistant teacher*.

back-to-basics movement—A movement that advocates a return to teacher-centred, subject-centred education that stresses the basic subject areas.

Bank Street model—An early childhood education program model, developed at the Bank Street College of Education in New York, that draws upon progressive education and the open education model seen in the British infant schools.

behaviour modification—The systematic application of principles of *reinforcement* to modify behaviour.

behaviour setting—According to Kounin and Sherman, different environments elicit behaviours that are fitted to the setting; thus children act "schoolish" at school.

behavioural objective—Aim or goal, usually set for an individual child, that describes in very specific and observable terms what the child is expected to master.

behaviourism—The theoretical viewpoint, espoused by theorists such as B. F. Skinner, that behaviour is shaped by environmental forces, specifically in response to reward and punishment.

bibliotherapy—The use of books that deal with emotionally sensitive topics in a developmentally appropriate way to help children gain accurate information and learn coping strategies.

bilingualism—The ability to use two languages.

bimanual control—The ability to use both hands in tasks for which each hand assumes a different function.

biological parents—The natural mother and father of a child.

blended family—The merging of two or more families.

board of directors—Policymaking or governing board that holds ultimate responsibility, particularly for not-for-profit programs.

Brigance Diagnostic Inventory of Early Development—A developmental assessment tool for children from birth to age 7.

British Infant school—Schools for 5-to-8-year-olds where the open model was developed.

burnout syndrome—A condition experienced by professionals as a result of undue job stress, characterized by loss of energy, irritability, and a feeling of being exploited.

Canada Assistance Plan (CAP)—Canadian federal legislation which requires the federal government to share child-care funding, only for those in need, with the provinces on a 50-50 basis.

Canadian National Child Care Study (CNCCS)—A federally funded study of child care in Canada.

caregiver—Term traditionally used to describe a person who works in a child care setting.

casa dei bambini **("children's house")**—Montessori's first school in Rome, founded in 1907.

centre size—Refers to the total number of children in a child care facility.

checklist—A method of evaluating children that consists of a list of behaviours, skills, concepts, or attributes that the observer checks off as a child is observed to have mastered the item.

child care centres—School programs for young children that usually include larger groups of children than are found in home-based programs.

child care worker—A term traditionally used to describe a person who works in a child care setting.

child conduct disorders—Label for serious psychological problems.

child study movement—Occurred earlier in the 20th century in the United States when many university preschools were established to develop scientific methods for studying children.

child-centred—An approach to childhood education that allows children to self-select activities.

classical conditioning—A learning technique in which a stimulus that usually evokes a reflex is paired with one that does not usually evoke the reflex, until the latter eventually evokes the reflex by itself.

classification—The ability to sort and group objects by some common attribute or property, for instance, colour or size.

code of ethics—Agreed-upon professional standards that guide behaviour and facilitate decision making in work situations.

cognitive development theory—A theory formulated by Jean Piaget that focuses on how children's intelligence and thinking abilities emerge through distinct stages.

Colour Tablets—Two sets of wooden tablets of many colours that children match and sort by shades in Montessori programs.

common law—A partnership that is not sanctioned by a marriage ceremony, but by the law.

communication book—A book that teachers and parents use for communication purposes.

community professionals—Professionals in the community, such as physicians, psychologists, and social workers.

competency-based program—Programs that give paraprofessionals credit for the knowledge they acquire through experience, and thus, facilitate in-service training of early childhood professionals.

computer literacy—Familiarity with and knowledge about computers.

conceptual materials—Montessori academic materials related to math, reading, and writing.

concrete operations period—According to Jean Piaget, the period of development spanning approximately ages 7 to 11, when children do not depend solely on visual cues but can apply logic to explain physical tasks or operations.

confidentiality—Requirement that results of evaluations and assessments be shared with only the parents and appropriate school personnel.

conservation—Ability to recognize that objects remain the same in amount despite perceptual changes, usually acquired during the period of concrete operations.

content objective—Purpose or rationale for an activity that specifies that the activity is intended to promote specific subject matter.

conventional moral rules—Standards, which are generally culture-specific, arrived at through general consensus.

convergent thinking—The act of narrowing many ideas into a single, focused point.

core knowledge base—The framework within which to work and improve.

creative development— Most accepted definitions of creativity include a requirement that the product is novel. Creative development is the growth of the ability to put things together in novel or original ways.

criterion-referenced—A characteristic of tests in which children are measured against a predetermined level of mastery rather than against an average score of children of the same age.

cuing—A technique used to help children remember what is expected by giving them a specific signal.

curriculum—Overall master plan of the early childhood program, reflecting its philosophy, into which specific activities are fit.

daily living—A Montessori classroom area that focuses on practical tasks involved in self-care and environment care.

deep emotional needs level—Misbehaviour that stems from a child's serious emotional needs.

Denver Developmental Screening Test (DDST)—A quick test for possible developmental delays in children from infancy to age 6.

development of concepts—Growth or positive change in concepts.

developmental objective—Purpose or rationale for an activity that specifies that the activity is intended to promote an aspect of physical, social, emotional, or cognitive development.

developmental test—Measures the child's functioning in most or all areas of development, although some such tests are specific to one or two areas.

developmentally appropriate practices—A term coined by the NAEYC to describe programs that match children's developmental and personal histories.

diagnostic testing—Another term for *screening tests*, which might indicate that more thorough testing should be carried out.

director—Often a label for the teacher in Montessori programs.

discipline—Generally considered a response to children's misbehaviour.

discovery learning—See *active learning*.

disequilibrium—According to Jean Piaget, the lack of balance one feels when existing mental structures and new experience do not fit exactly.

DISTAR—An ECE program developed by Bereiter and Engelmann that draws on behaviour theory.

divergent thinking—The act of expanding or elaborating on an idea, such as in brainstorming.

early childhood—Term used for the period between birth and 8 years of age.

early childhood education—Term encompassing developmentally appropriate programs that serve children from birth through age 8; a field of study that trains students to work effectively with young children.

early childhood education models—Approaches to early childhood education, based on specific theoretical foundations, for instance, the behavioural, Piagetian, or Montessori view.

early childhood educator—A specifically trained professional who works with children from infancy to age 8.

Early Childhood Environment Rating Scale—A rating scale to help in the evaluation of early childhood programs.

early childhood teacher—A specifically trained professional who works with children from infancy to age 8.

ECERS—See *Early Childhood Environment Rating Scale*.

eclectic approach—An approach in which various desirable features from different theories or methods are selected; drawing elements from different sources.

ecological model—A framework for viewing development that takes into account the various interconnected contexts within which individuals exist, for instance, the family, neighbourhood, or community.

effective praise—A form of encouragement that focuses on children's activities rather than on teacher evaluation of their work; praise that is meaningful to children rather than general or gratuitous.

ego—According to Sigmund Freud, the rational facet of personality that helps find appropriate ways of achieving the pleasure goals of the *id* and mediating between the id's demands and the *superego*'s restrictions.

emergent curriculum—Education through continuous dialogue and documentation.

empowerment—Helping parents gain a sense of control over events in their lives.

entrepreneur—One who creates and implements new ideas.

environmental checklists—Standardized checklists that help you assess the early childhood program and environment.

equilibrium—According to Jean Piaget, the state of balance each person seeks between existing mental structures and new experiences.

equipment—Large items such as furniture that represent a more expensive, long-term investment in an early childhood facility.

event sampling—A method of observation in which the observer records a specific behaviour only when it occurs.

exosystem—According to ecological theory, that part of the environment that includes the broader components of the community that affect the functioning of the family, such as governmental agencies or mass media.

experience—Guiding children through various adult roles through dramatic play.

experimentation level—Misbehaviour that results from the child "experimenting" with the limits.

exploration—To search for knowledge through various activities.

extended family—Family members beyond the immediate nuclear family, for instance, aunts and uncles, grandparents, or cousins.

extinction—In behavioural theory, a method of eliminating a previously reinforced behaviour by taking away all reinforcement, for instance, by totally ignoring the behaviour.

eye–hand coordination—Integrative ability to use the hands as guided by information from the eyes.

family day care—Child care offered in a family setting.

Family Day Care Home Rating Scale—A rating scale to help in the evaluation of home-based early childhood programs.

family involvement—The commitment of parents to the early childhood program through a wide variety of options.

family systems theory—A view of the family as an ever-developing and -changing social unit in which members constantly accommodate and adapt to each other's demands and outside demands.

family-centred model—Encompasses all aspects of involvement and acknowledges the family as the focal point of care.

feral children—Children who, lost or abandoned by their parents, are said to have been reared by animals in the wild.

fine motor development—Development of skills involving the small muscles of the fingers and hands, necessary for such tasks as writing, drawing, or buttoning.

flexibility—A measure of creativity involving the capability to adapt readily to change in a positive, productive manner.

fluency—A measure of creativity involving the ability to generate, in a limited time, many relevant ideas on a given topic.

formal operations period—According to Jean Piaget, the last period of development spanning approximately ages 11 to 15, characterized by sophisticated, abstract thinking and logical reasoning abilities.

formative evaluation—Ongoing assessment to ensure that planned activities and methods accomplish what the teacher intended.

foster parents—People assigned to the care of minors by a legal agency.

games with rules—Type of play, usually engaged in by older children, in which there are accepted, prearranged rules.

generativity—According to Erik Erikson, the stage of human development in which the mature adult focuses on the care and nurture of the young.

genital stage—The last stage of development described by Sigmund Freud, beginning with the onset of puberty, during which adolescents become increasingly aware of sexuality.

goal—An overall, general overview of what children are expected to gain from an educational program.

Golden Beads—Montessori manipulative materials that represent the decimal system in a concrete way. A single bead is one unit, and large units include 10s, 100s, and 1000s.

good teacher-child ratio—A good or high ratio means there are fewer children per teacher. For calculation, see *adult-child ratio*.

grammar and syntax—The rules for putting words together meaningfully.

gross motor development—Development of skills involving the large muscles of the legs, arms, back, and shoulders, necessary for such tasks as running, jumping, and climbing.

group size—Term used to describe the number of children together in a room in an early childhood setting, which usually differs from the teacher-child ratio.

guidance—An ongoing process of directing children's behaviour based on the types of adults children are expected to become.

Head Start—A comprehensive, federally funded early childhood program in the United States for children from poverty backgrounds.

helper—See *assistant teacher*.

holding grip—Placement of the hands in using a tool for drawing or writing.

Home Observation for Measurement of the Environment (HOME)—An evaluation tool used to assess the quality of stimulation in the home environment. Useful for home-based child care.

Home Rating Scale—A scale used to rate family settings for the young child.

home visit—A one-on-one interaction between the teacher and the parent(s) of the child that takes place in the child's home.

hothousing or **hurrying**—Term taken from horticulture in which plant growth is speeded up by forced fertilization, heat, and light; refers to accelerated learning programs for young children.

human development theory—A way to describe what happens as individuals move from infancy through adulthood, identifying significant events that are commonly experienced by all people, and explaining why changes occur as they do.

human resources—Any structure defined by individuals who are connected with it or have a stake or interest in the system.

id—According to Sigmund Freud, a largely unconscious facet of personality that seeks immediate pleasure and gratification.

ignoring—A principle of behaviour management that involves removing all reinforcement for a given behaviour to eliminate that behaviour.

image of the child—A view of the child and childhood that varies according to culture, history, and theory.

inclusive education—The integration of children with special needs into regular programs by recognizing their rights as children first and affording them the same choices and opportunities granted to any child.

increasing competence—The process by which children gain skills.

inductive reasoning—A guidance approach in which the adult helps the child see the consequences of a behaviour on other people through logic and reasoning.

Industry vs. Inferiority—The fourth stage of development described by Erik Erikson, starting at the end of the preschool years and lasting until puberty, in which the child focuses on development of competence.

infant—In eight of the thirteen provinces and territories, infants are defined as children who are between 0 and 18 months of age.

infant stimulation programs—Compensatory programs for infants at risk for developmental delays.

Infant/Toddler Environment Rating Scale—Rating scale for assessing quality of infant and toddler programs.

Initiative vs. Guilt—The third stage of development described by Erik Erikson, occurring during the preschool years, in which the child's curiosity and enthusiasm lead to a need to explore and learn about the world, and in which rules and expectations begin to be established.

integrated day—A day in which there are no lessons at prescribed times, as subjects are integrated into activities offered throughout the day.

interaction—Working together for the good of everyone.

interest areas—See *activity centres*.

interpersonal moral rules—Rules considered as universal, including prohibitions against harm to others, murder, incest, and theft.

interpretive stage—A stage of parenting defined by Ellen Galinsky typifying the parent of an older preschooler who faces the task of explaining and clarifying the world to the child.

invented spelling—Used by young children in their early attempts to write by finding the speech sound that most closely fits what they want to convey.

invitational education—A perceptually based self-concept approach to teaching, learning, and caring in which: (1) people should be treated as able, valuable, and responsible; (2) education should be cooperative; (3) process is the product in the making; (4) people possess untapped positive potential in all areas of endeavour; (5) potential can best be realized by places, policies, processes, and programs designed to invite development, and by people who are inviting with themselves and others.

isolation of a single quality—A Montessori term denoting how materials are designed to emphasize only one attribute—such as size as opposed to colour and texture for the Pink Tower.

ITERS—See *Infant/Toddler Environment Rating Scale*.

key experiences—In the cognitively oriented curriculum, the eight cognitive concepts on which activities are built.

kindergarten—German word, literally meaning "garden for children," coined by Friedrich Froebel for his program for young children.

kinesthetic sense—Information from the body's system that provides knowledge about the body, its parts, and its movement; involves the "feel" of movement without reference to visual or verbal cues.

large-group times—Time blocks during the day when all of the children and teachers join in a common activity.

latency stage—The fourth stage of development described by Sigmund Freud, occurring during middle childhood, during which sexuality is repressed until adolescence.

lattice—Structure like a net.

lead teacher—See *senior teacher*.

learning areas—See *activity centres*.

learning centres—See *activity centres*.

learning outcome—A specific interpretation of a general goal that provides a more practical and direct tool for planning and evaluation.

learning style—Each child is a unique person with an individual learning style; for example, some are strong verbal learners while others favour visual learning.

legal guardians—Persons with legal authority to care for and/or make decisions for a child.

legislation—Laws governing or concerning an issue.

lesson plan—A working document from which the daily program is run, specifying directions for activities.

logical consequences—Rudolf Dreikurs' technique of allowing children to experience the natural outcome of their actions.

logical thinking—According to Jean Piaget, the ability that begins to emerge at around age seven in which children use mental processes to solve problems rather than relying solely on perceived information.

macrosystem—According to ecological theory, the broadest part of the environment, which includes the cultural, political, and economic forces that affect families.

Malting House School—The name of Susan Isaacs' famous nursery school in Cambridge where open education was refined and exemplified.

manipulatives—Toys and materials that require the use of the fingers and hands, for instance, puzzles, beads, and pegboards.

marriage—A legal ceremony uniting a man and a woman in matrimony.

maturation—The unfolding of inherited potential; the nature side of the nature-nurture controversy emphasizes this.

mental representation—Piagetian term that describes the ability to picture something in the mind.

mesosystem—According to ecological theory, the linkages between the family and the immediate neighbourhood and community.

microsystem—According to ecological theory, that part of the environment which most immediately affects a person, such as the family, school, or workplace.

mixed-age grouping—Programs in which children of different ages, for instance, 3-to-6-year-olds, are together in one class.

mock writing—Young children's imitation of writing through wavy, circular, or vertical lines, which can be seen as distinct from drawing or scribbling.

modelling—In social learning theory, the process of imitating a model.

moral development—The long-term process of learning and internalizing the rules and standards of right and wrong.

morality of autonomy—A sense of morality based on self-integrity.

morality of obedience—A sense of morality based on doing what one is told to do.

morphology—The study of word rules, for instance, tense, plurals, and possessives.

Movable Alphabet—Montessori-designed individual wooden letters that can be combined to form words.

multilingualism—Ability to use multiple (more than two) languages.

nanny—A caregiver who comes to the child's home and often lives there.

National Day Care Study (NDCS)—A study of child care availability in Canada summarized in *The Status of Day Care in Canada 1990* (National Child Care Information Centre, 1991, Child Care Programs Division).

nature—Theorists in the nature camp believe that children's development follows an inborn plan, that is, it is largely determined by heredity.

negative punishment—The removal of a pleasant stimulus.

negative reinforcement—The removal of an unpleasant stimulus.

nonverbal cues—Some of the subtle cues of body language or voice inflection that can give an observer deeper meaning in a record of behaviour.

norm-referenced—A test in which scores are determined by using a large group of same-age children as the basis for comparison, rather than using a predetermined criterion or standard of performance.

norms—That which is usual, average, or customary in development, behaviour, or expectations.

nuclear family—The smallest family unit, made up of a couple or one or two parents with children.

number concepts—One of the cognitive concepts young children begin to acquire, involving an understanding of quantity.

nursery schools—Half-day programs for preschoolers that have an educational emphasis.

nurture—A theory that children's development is affected primarily by external, environmental factors, not heredity.

nurturing stage—A period of development that parents of an infant are expected to experience.

nutrients—Nutritional components required for health and well-being, including proteins, fats, vitamins, and minerals.

objectives—Aims; specific interpretations of general goals, providing a practical and directive tool for day-to-day program planning.

object permanence—Part of Jean Piaget's theory, the recognition that objects exist even when they are out of view; a concept that children begin to develop toward the end of their first year of life.

observable behaviour—Actions that can be seen rather than those that are inferred.

observing—Watching.

open education—A program that operates on the assumption that children, if provided a well-conceived environment, are capable of selecting and learning from appropriate activities.

open-ended materials—Early childhood materials that are flexible rather than structured and can be used in a variety of ways rather than in only a single manner.

Open Model—early childhood model developed in Britain.

operant conditioning—The principle of behavioural theory whereby a person deliberately attempts to increase or decrease behaviour by controlling consequences.

oral stage—The first stage of development described by Sigmund Freud, during infancy, in which pleasure is derived from the mouth.

organization—According to Jean Piaget, the mental process by which a person organizes experiences and information in relation to each other.

parent education—Programs aimed at enhancing parent-child relations and improving parenting.

parent cooperative—A (usually) part-day preschool program staffed by one paid professional head teacher and a rotating staff of parents. As part of enrolling their children in the program, parents are required to assist a specified number of days in the classroom.

parent–teacher conference—A one-on-one interaction between the teacher and the child's parent(s).

partnership—A relationship with mutual respect and an equal balance of power regarding decision making.

pay equity—Equal pay for equal work, regardless of gender.

perceived competence—Children's belief in their ability to succeed in a given task.

personal control—The feeling that a person has the power to make things happen.

phallic stage—The third stage of development described by Sigmund Freud, occurring during the preschool years, in which pleasure is derived from the genitals.

Pink Tower—A set of ten pink wooden cubes, developed by Montessori, that vary from one to ten cubic centimetres in size and are used to build a tower.

plan-do-review cycle—The heart of the cognitively oriented curriculum, through which children are encouraged to make deliberate, systematic choices with the help of teachers by planning, carrying out, then recalling each day's activities.

planning time—In the cognitively oriented curriculum, the time set aside during which children decide what activities they would like to participate in during the ensuing work time.

play—An activity of children that is intrinsically motivated; focused on means, not ends; occurs with familiar objects; involves pretending and has non-literal qualities; has no externally imposed rules such as appear in games; requires active involvement; is not predetermined or scripted.

pleasure principle—According to Sigmund Freud, the principle of maximizing what is pleasant and avoiding anything unpleasant, which motivates all behaviour.

poor teacher-child ratio—A poor or low ratio means there are more children for whom an adult is responsible. For calculation, see *adult-child ratio*.

positive discipline—Synonymous with guidance, an approach that allows the child to develop self-discipline gradually.

positive punishment—The addition of an unpleasant stimulus.

positive reinforcement—The addition of a pleasant stimulus.

practice play—A term used by Piaget to describe repeated actions, such as banging or playing patty-cake, that infants make.

pragmatics—Rules that govern language use in social contexts.

preassessment—A form of evaluation given before teaching a specific concept or topic to assess how much children know about it and to compare later how much they have learned.

predictive validity—An attribute possessed by any test that is a valid predictor of future events, such as school achievement.

preoperational period—In Jean Piaget's theory, the second stage of cognitive development, approximately covering the preschool years, in which children are able to use various forms of mental representation but do not yet think logically.

prepared environment—Maria Montessori's term to describe the careful match between appropriate materials and what the child is most ready to learn at any given time.

preschool—Term to describe a setting for children who are not of elementary school age.

pretend play—Children's dramatic or symbolic play that involves more than one child in social interaction.

problem solving—Using physical and social skills to encourage and guide children in creating and/or finding solutions.

professional development—Growth in a manner congruent with a particular code of ethics.

progressive education—The type of education advocated by John Dewey, who maintained that teachers be guided by the child's interests and that education should emphasize active learning through real experiences.

projects—Like *themes*, projects are a unifying element around which activities are planned; projects, however, are more specific. You might have a theme titled "Spring," while a related project would be more specific, for example "What happens in the fishery during spring?"

prosocial behaviour—Positive, commonly valued social behaviour such as sharing, empathy, or understanding.

psychoanalytic theory—The branch of psychology founded by Sigmund Freud; it focuses on unconscious drives and the importance of the early years to later personality development.

psychosocial theory—The branch of psychology founded by Erik Erikson, in which development is described in terms of eight stages that span childhood and adulthood, each offering opportunities for personality growth and development.

punishment—An aversive consequence that follows a behaviour for the purpose of decreasing or eliminating the behaviour; not recommended as an effective means of changing behaviour.

rating scales—Assessments of specific skills or concepts that are rated on some qualitative dimension of excellence or accomplishment.

reality principle—According to Sigmund Freud, the reality-based principle by which the *ego* functions to counter the pleasure-seeking goals of the *id*.

recall time—In the cognitively oriented curriculum, the time when children review their work time activities.

Reggio Emilia—An approach to teaching and learning that originated in Italy under the supervision of Loris Malaguzzi (1920–1994); the approach believes in the emergent curriculum, projects, and collaboration. It has received worldwide attention and its popularity grew in the 1990s.

reinforcement—In behavioural theory, any response that follows a behaviour and that encourages repetition of it.

reliability—A measure of a test indicating that it is stable and consistent, to ensure that changes in score are due to the child, not the test.

representation—According to Jean Piaget, the ability to depict an object, person, action, or experience mentally, even if it is not present in the immediate environment.

respect for children—A characteristic feature of Montessori's original program.

restraining order—A court order that prevents someone from seeing someone else.

routines—Regular, predictable behaviours that are repeated every day—or almost every day—in early childhood programs.

running record—A type of observation that provides an account of all of the child's behaviour over a period of time.

scaffolding—Assistance to the child, adjusted as he or she masters the task at hand.

schemata (*pl.*; **schema** *sing.*)—According to Jean Piaget, cognitive structures into which cognitive concepts or mental representations are organized.

school readiness—The age and stage at which a child is prepared to enter school.

screening tests—A quick method of identifying children who might exhibit developmental delay; only an indicator, which must be followed up by more thorough and comprehensive testing.

self-concept—Perceptions and feelings children have about themselves, gathered largely from how the important people in their world respond to them.

self-correcting materials—Learning materials such as puzzles that give the child immediate feedback on success when the task is completed.

self-education—A term used by Montessori to describe how child educates herself or himself by activity in the prepared environment.

self-esteem—Children's evaluation of their worth in positive or negative terms.

self-selected time-out—A technique in which children are given the responsibility for removing themselves from the classroom if they feel they are about to lose control.

semantics—Related to the understanding and study of word meaning.

senior teacher—The person in charge of a class who is ultimately responsible for all aspects of class functioning.

sensitive periods—Maria Montessori's term describing the times when children are most receptive to absorbing specific learning.

sensitivity—Related to creativity, this term refers to a receptivity to external and internal stimuli.

sensorial—A Montessori classroom area in which materials help children develop, organize, broaden, and refine sensory perceptions of sight, sound, touch, smell, and taste.

sensorial materials—Learning materials in Montessori classroom area that help children develop, organize, broaden, and refine sensory perceptions of sight, sound, touch, smell, and taste.

sensorimotor period—In Jean Piaget's theory, the first stage of cognitive development, covering approximately the first two years of life, in which the child learns primarily through movement and the senses.

sensory deficit—A problem, particularly of sight or hearing.

sensory education—A term used to describe the emphasis Montessori placed on education through the senses.

sensory-perceptual development—Giving meaning to information that comes through the senses.

separation anxiety—Emotional difficulty experienced by some young children when leaving their mothers.

seriation—A relationship among objects in which they are placed in a logical order, such as from longest to shortest.

shaping—In behavioural theory, a method used to teach a child a new behaviour by breaking it down into small steps and reinforcing the attainment of each step systematically.

small-group activity time—Time set aside for children to work with a teacher in a smaller group than usual.

small-group leader—See *assistant teacher*.

social mediation—Intervening to help a social situation.

social reinforcers—In behavioural theory, rewards that convey approval through such responses as a smile, a hug, or attention.

social skills—Actions that encourage sharing, cooperating, and planning, in a context in which several children can interact.

software—The "instructions" that direct a computer to perform an activity; usually stored on a disk or directly in the computer. Much software is written for young children.

Sound Boxes—Montessori equipment that includes two sets of cylinders, both of which are filled with various materials (e.g., rice, beans, and salt), and then matched by the sounds they make.

spatial relationships—The relative positions to each other of objects and people in space.

special time—A method for spending a few minutes a day with just one child as a way of providing unconditional attention.

Sputnik—The name of the first space missile, launched by the Russians in 1957.

stage theorist—Any theory that delineates specific stages in which development is marked by qualitatively different characteristics and accomplishments and where each stage builds on the previous one.

standardized tests—Tests that have been developed and used with a large population of children. The standardized scores for these tests are based on comparisons with the scores of children tested during test development (e.g., How does this 5-year-old child do compared to the 200 5-year-old children tested during test development?).

stepparent—The spouse of a child's biological parent.

story schema—A term used to describe the regular, predictable structure of simple stories.

successive approximations—Breaking down a complex behaviour into smaller steps and reinforcing the child for each step as she or he comes closer to attaining the final behaviour.

summative evaluation—An assessment that follows a specific lesson or unit to evaluate whether the children have met the objectives.

superego—According to Sigmund Freud, the facet of personality called the conscience, which is based on the moral norms of society as passed on by parents and other adults.

supervisor—The lead person in a child care facility.

support staff—In early childhood programs, these might include people involved in food preparation, maintenance, and office management.

symbolic play—A term used by Piaget to describe play by children who can mentally represent objects and therefore can pretend.

syntax—Involves the grammatical rules that govern the structure of sentences.

systems approach—A way of thinking of something that recognizes the many parts that work both dependently and independently to keep a system working.

teacher-child ratio—See *adult-child ratio*.

team teaching—An approach that involves co-teaching in which status and responsibility are equal rather than having a pyramid structure of authority, with one person in charge and others subordinate.

teenage parents—13-to-19-year-old person(s) who conceive a child.

temperament—Inborn characteristics such as regularity, adaptability, and disposition that affect behaviour.

themes—Topics—for instance, "Spring" or "Community Helpers"—that provide a unifying element around which activities are planned. See also *projects*.

time sampling—A quantitative measure or count of how often a specific behaviour occurs within a given amount of time.

time-away—A technique in which the child removes himself or herself from the *reinforcement* and stimulation of the classroom in order for the teacher to stay in control.

time-out—A technique in which the child is removed from the *reinforcement* and stimulation of the classroom in order for the teacher to stay in control.

toddler—In the majority of Canadian jurisdictions, children between 19 and 35 months of age.

Tonal Bells—Two sets of bells, one brown, one white, that children in Montessori programs match by the sound they make.

Trust vs. Mistrust—The first stage of development described by Erik Erikson, occurring during infancy, in which the child's needs should be met consistently and predictably.

unconditional attention—Attention that is given, not in response to a specific behaviour, but as a way of conveying acceptance to children by letting them know they are valued and liked no matter what they do.

validity—A characteristic of a test that indicates it actually measures what it purports to.

volunteers—People who volunteer to work in the class.

Wechsler Intelligence Scale for Children—III (WISC-III)—An intelligence test for 6-to-16-year-olds that gives a verbal IQ score, a performance IQ score, and an overall IQ score. A score of 100 is average for the WISC-III.

Wechsler Preschool and Primary Scale of Intelligence—Revised (WPPSIR)—An intelligence test, like the WISC-III, but for 3-to-7-year-old children.

whole language approach—Strategy for promoting literacy by surrounding children with high-quality oral and print language.

work time—In the cognitively oriented curriculum, the large block of time during which children engage in self-selected activities.

zone of proximal development (ZPD)—The area in which a child finds a task too difficult to complete alone but can with assistance.

References

Adler, S. (1993). Teacher education research as reflective practice. *Teacher and Education, 9,* 159–167.

Alberta. Family and Social Services. (1990). *Alberta day care reforms*. Edmonton, AB: Government of Alberta.

Alexander, N. P. (1986). School-age child care: Concerns and challenges. *Young Children, 42*(1), 3–10.

Alford, B. B., & Bogle, M. L. (1982). *Nutrition during the life cycle*. Englewood Cliffs, NJ: Prentice-Hall, Inc.

Alger, H. A. (1984). Transitions: Alternatives to manipulative management techniques. *Young Children, 39*(6), 16–25.

Allen, J. (1988). Children's cognition of stressful events. *Day Care and Early Education, 16*(3), 21–25.

Allen, J., & Pettit, R. B. (1987). Mighty Mouse and MX missiles: Children in a violent society. *Day Care and Early Education, 15*(1), 6–9.

Allen, K. E., & Marotz, L. (1989). *Developmental profiles: Birth to six*. Albany, NY: Delmar Publishers Inc.

Almy, M. (1975). *The early childhood educator at work*. New York: McGraw-Hill Book Co.

Almy, M., Monighan, P., Scales, B., & Van Hoorn, J. (1984). Recent research on play: The teacher's perspective. In L. G. Katz (Ed.), *Current topics in early childhood education* (Vol. 5, pp. 1–26).

Alper, C. D. (1987). Early childhood music education. In C. Seefeldt (Ed.), *The early childhood curriculum: A review of current research* (pp. 211–236). New York: Teachers College Press, Columbia University.

Amabile, T. M., & Gitomer, J. (1984). Children's artistic creativity: Effects of choice in task materials. *Personality and Social Psychology Bulletin, 10,* 209–215.

American Academy of Pediatrics. (1985). *Pediatric Nutrition Handbook* (2nd ed.). Elk Grove Village, IL: American Academy of Pediatrics.

Ames, L. B., Gillespie, C., Haines, J., & Ilg, F. L. (1980). *The child from one to six: Evaluating the behaviour of the preschool child*. London: Hamish Hamilton.

Anastasiow, N. (1988). Should parenting education be mandatory? *Topics in Early Childhood Special Education, 8*(1), 60–72.

Anderson, D. R., & Lorch, E. P. (1983). Looking at television: Action or reaction. In J. Bryant & D. R. Anderson (Eds.), *Understanding TV: Research in children's attention and comprehension* (pp. 1–33). New York: Academic Press.

Andrews, J. H. (1988). Poetry: Tool of the classroom magician. *Young Children, 43*(4), 17–25.

Anthony, S. (1972). *The discovery of death in childhood and after*. New York: Basic Books.

Arent, R. P. (1984). *Stress and your child: A parents' guide to symptoms, strategies and benefits*. Englewood Cliffs, NJ: Prentice-Hall.

Aries, P. (1962). *Centuries of childhood: A social history of family life* (R. Baldick, Trans.). New York: Alfred A. Knopf.

Arnett, J. (1987). *Caregivers in day care centers: Does training matter?* Paper presented at the biennial meeting of the Society for Research in Child Development, Baltimore, MD.

Arnett, J. (1989). Caregivers in day care centers: Does training matter? *Developmental Psychology, 10,* 541–552.

Atkins, C. (1984). Writing: Doing something constructive. *Young Children, 40*(1), 3–7.

Ayers, W. (1989). *The good preschool teacher: Six teachers reflect on their lives.* New York: Teachers College Press, Columbia University.

Baker, B. B. (1982). *The planning board: Ideas for construction and use with young children.* ERIC microfiche, #ED 233801.

Baker, R. & Wakefield, P. (1985). *Early childhood education for a multicultural society: A handbook for educators.* Vancouver: Pacific Educational Press.

Bakst, K., & Essa, E. L. (1990). The writing table: Emergent writers and editors. *Childhood Education, 66,* 145–150.

Balaban, N. (1992). The role of child care professionals in caring for infants, toddlers and their families. *Young Children, 47*(5), 66–71.

Bandura, A. (1977). *Social learning theory.* Englewood Cliffs, NJ: Prentice-Hall.

Banta, T. (1969). Research on Montessori and the disadvantaged. In R. Orem (Ed.), *Montessori and the special child.* New York: Putnam.

Baratta-Lorton, M. (1979). *Workjobs: Activity-centred learning for early childhood education.* Menlo Park, CA: Addison-Wesley Publishing Co.

Barnes, B. J., & Hill, S. (1983). Should young children use micro-computers: LOGO before LEGO? *The Computing Teacher, 10*(9), 11–14.

Barrett, D. E. (1986). Behaviour as an outcome in nutrition research. *Nutrition Reviews, 44,* 224–236.

Baumrind, D. (1967). Child care practices anteceding three patterns of preschool behaviour. *Genetic Psychological Monographs, 75,* 43–88.

Baumrind, D., & Black, A. E. (1967). Socialization practices associated with dimensions of competence in preschool boys and girls. *Child Development, 38,* 291–327.

Bayless, K. M., & Ramsey, M. E. (1982). *Music: A way of life for the young child.* St. Louis, MO: The C. V. Mosby Co.

Baynham, P., Russell, L., & Ross, L. (1988). Wages and work experience survey of child care staff in an Ontario community. *The Canadian Journal of Research in Early Childhood Education, 2*(2), 159–164.

Beach, J., Bertrand, J., & Cleveland, G. (1998). *Our child care workforce: From recognition to remuneration—More than a labour of love.* Ottawa: Child Care Human Resources Steering Committee.

Beaty, J. (1990). *Observing the development of the young child.* Columbus, OH: Merrill.

Becher, R. M. (1986). Parent involvement: A review of research and principles of successful practice. In L. G. Katz (Ed.), *Current topics in early childhood education* (Vol. 6, pp. 85–122). Norwood, NJ: Ablex Publishing Corp.

Bereiter, C. (1986). Does direct instruction cause delinquency? *Early Childhood Research Quarterly, 1,* 289–292.

Bereiter, C. (1999). How sound is High/Scope research? *Educational Leadership, 56*(6), 83–84.

Bereiter, C., & Engelmann, S. (1966). *Teaching disadvantaged children in the preschool.* Englewood Cliffs, NJ: Prentice-Hall, Inc.

Bereiter, C., (1967). *Acceleration of intellectual development in early childhood.* Washington, DC: Department of Health, Education, & Welfare, U.S. Office of Education, Bureau of Research.

Berk, L. E. (1976). How well do classroom practices reflect teacher goals? *Young Children, 32*(1), 64–81.

Berlyne, D. (1969). Laughter, humor, and play. In G. Lindzey & E. Aronson (Eds.), *The handbook of social psychology* (Vol. 3). Reading, MA: Addison-Wesley.

Berns, R. M. (1989). *Child, family, community: Socialization and support* (2nd ed.). New York: Holt, Rinehart and Winston, Inc.

Berrueta-Clement, J. R., Schweinhart, L. J., Barnett, W. S., Epstein, A. S., & Weikart, D. P. (1984). Changed lives: The effects of the Perry Preschool program on youths through age 19. *Monographs of the High/Scope Educational Research Foundation, #8.* Ypsilanti, MI: High/Scope Press.

Bertrand, J. (2001). Working with young children. In G. Cleveland & M. Krashinsky, *Our children's future: Child care policy in Canada* (pp. 372–389). Toronto: University of Toronto Press.

Bessell, H., & Palomares, U. (1973). *Methods in human development: Theory manual.* El Cajon, CA: Human Development Training Institute.

Biber, B. (1984). *Early education and psychological development.* New Haven, CT: Yale University Press.

Bijou, S. W., Peterson, R. F., & Ault, M. H. (1968). A method to integrate descriptive and experimental field studies at the level of data and empirical concepts. *Journal of Applied Behaviour Analysis, 1,* 175–191.

Birch, L. L. (1980a). Effects of peer models' food choices and eating behaviours on preschoolers' food preferences. *Child Development, 51,* 489–496.

Birch, L. L. (1980b). Experiential determinants of children's food preferences. In L. G. Katz (Ed.), *Current topics in early childhood education* (Vol. 3, pp. 29–46). Norwood, NJ: Ablex Publishing Corp.

Birch, L. L., Marlin, D. W., & Rotter, J. (1984). Eating as the "means" activity in a contingency: Effects on young children's food preferences. *Child Development, 55,* 431–439.

Bjorklund, G., & Burger, C. (1987). Making conferences work for parents, teachers, and children. *Young Children, 42*(3), 26–31.

Black, R. E., Dykes, A. C., Anderson, K. E., Wells, J. G., Sinclair, S. P., Gary, G. W., Hatch, M. H., & Gangarosa, E. J. (1981). Handwashing to prevent diarrhea in day care centers. *American Journal of Epidemiology, 113*(4), 445–451.

Blanco, R. (1982). *Prescriptions for children with learning and adjustment problems* (2nd ed.). Springfield, IL: Charles C Thomas.

Blocks: A creative curriculum for early childhood. (1979). Washington, DC: Creative Associates, Inc.

Blom, G. E., Cheney, B. D., & Snoddy, J. E. (1986). *Stress in childhood: An intervention model for teachers and other professionals.* New York: Teachers College Press, Columbia University.

Bloom, B. (1964). *Stability and change in human characteristics.* New York: Wiley.

Bohannon, J. N., & Warren-Leubecker, A. (1985). Theoretical approaches to language acquisition. In J. B. Gleason (Ed.), *The development of language* (pp. 173–226). Columbus, OH: Charles E. Merrill Publishing Co.

Borich, Gary (1999). *Observation skills for effective teaching.* Upper Saddle River, NJ: Prentice Hall.

Borstellman, L. J. (1983). Children before psychology: Ideas about children from antiquity to the late 1800s. In P. H. Mussen (Ed.), *Handbook of child psychology* (4th ed.): *Vol. 1. History, theory, and methods* (pp. 1–40). New York: John Wiley and Sons.

Bowd, A., McDougall, D., & Yewchuk, C. (1998). *Educational psychology for Canadian teachers* (2nd ed.). Toronto: Harcourt Brace & Company.

Bowlby, J. (1951). *Maternal care and mental health.* Geneva: World Health Organization.

Boxhill, N. A. (1989, December). Quoted in S. Landers, Homeless children lose childhood. *The APA Monitor,* pp. 1, 33.

Bradley, R., & Caldwell, B. M. (1984). The relation of infants' home environments to achievement test performance in first grade: A follow-up study. *Child Development, 55,* 803–809.

Braun, S. J., & Edwards, E. P. (1972). *History and theory of early childhood education.* Worthington, OH: Charles A. Jones Publishing Co.

Brazelton, T. B. (1992). *On becoming a family: The growth of attachment.* New York: Delacorte Press.

Bredekamp, S. (1997). NAEYC issues revised position statement on developmentally appropriate practice in early childhood programs. *Young Children, 52*(2), 34–40.

Bredekamp, S. (Ed.). (1987). *Developmentally appropriate practice in early childhood programs serving children from birth through age 8.* Washington, DC: National Association for the Education of Young Children.

Bredekamp, S. (Ed.). (1997). *Developmentally appropriate practice in early childhood programs serving children from birth through age 8* (2nd ed.). Washington, DC: National Association for the Education of Young Children.

Bredekamp, S. Quoted in E. R. Shell (1989, December). Now, which kind of preschool? *Psychology Today*, pp. 52–57.

Bredekamp, S., & Copple, C. (Eds.). (1997). *Developmentally appropriate practice in early childhood programs* (Rev. ed.). Washington, DC: National Association for the Education of Young Children.

Bredekamp, S., & Rosegrant, T. (Eds.). (1992). *Reaching potentials: Appropriate curriculum and assessment for young children* (Vol. 1). Washington, DC: National Association for the Education of Young Children.

Bredekamp, S., & Rosegrant, T. (Eds.). (1992). *Reaching potentials: Appropriate curriculum and assessment for young children* (Vol. 1). Washington, DC: National Association for the Education of Young Children.

Bredekamp, S., & Rosegrant, T. (Eds.). (1995). *Transforming early childhood curriculum and assessment* (Vol. 2). Washington, DC: National Association for the Education of Young Children.

Bredekamp, S., & Shepard, L. (1989). How best to protect children from inappropriate school expectations, practices, and policies. *Young Children, 44*(3), 14–24.

Bredekamp, S., & Willer, B. (1992). Of ladders and lattices, cores and cones: Conceptualizing an early childhood professional development system. *Young Children, 47*(3), 47–50.

Bredekamp, S., & Willer, B. (1993). Professionalizing the field of early childhood education: Pros and cons. *Young Children, 48*(2), 82–84.

Brenner, A. (1984). *Helping children cope with stress.* Lexington, MA: Lexington Books.

Brigance, A. H. (1978). *Brigance Diagnostic Inventory of Early Development.* Woburn, MA: Curriculum Associates.

Briggs, B. A., & Walters, C. M. (1985). Single-father families. *Young Children, 40*(3), 23–27.

Briggs, D. (1975). *Your child's self-esteem.* New York: Doubleday.

Bronfenbrenner, U. (1971). Who cares for America's children? *Young Children, 26*(3), 157–163.

Bronfenbrenner, U. (1979). *The ecology of human development.* Cambridge, MA: Harvard University Press.

Bronfenbrenner, U. (1986). Ecology of the family as a context for human development: Research perspectives. *Developmental Psychology, 22,* 723–742.

Bronfenbrenner, U., & Crouter, A. C. (1983). Ecology of the family as a context for human development research perspectives. In P. H. Mussen (Ed.), *Handbook of child psychology* (4th ed.): *Vol. 1: History, theory and methods* (pp. 357–414). New York: John Wiley and Sons.

Brooks, R. L., & Obrzut, J. E. (1981). Brain lateralization: Implications for infant stimulation and development. *Young Children, 36*(3), 9–16.

Brown, R. (1973). *A first language.* Cambridge, MA: Harvard University Press.

Bruner, J. (1980). *Under five in Britain.* Ypsilanti, MI: High/Scope Press.

Bruner, J., Jolly, A., & Sylva, K. (1976). *Play: Its role in development and evolution.* Markham, ON: Penguin Books.

Bullock, J. (1986). Teacher-parent conferences: Learning from each other. *Day Care and Early Education, 14*(2), 17–19.

Bundy, B. F. (1989). Effective record keeping. *Day Care and Early Education, 17*(1), 7–9.

Bundy, B. F. (1991). Fostering communication between parents and preschools. *Young Children, 46*(2), 12–17.

Burts, D. C., Hart, C. H., Charlesworth, R., & Kirk, L. (1990). A comparison of frequencies of stress behaviours observed in kindergarten children in classrooms with developmentally appropriate versus developmentally inappropriate instructional practices. *Early Childhood Research Quarterly, 5,* 407–423.

Bushell, D. (1982). The behavior analysis model for early education. In B. Spodek (Ed.), *Handbook of research in early childhood education* (pp. 156–184). New York: The Free Press.

Buzzelli, C. A., & File, N. (1989). Building trust in friends. *Young Children, 44*(3), 70–75.

Cairns, R. B. (1983). The emergence of developmental psychology. In P. H. Mussen (Ed.), *Handbook of child psychology* (4th ed.): *Vol. 1. History, theory, and methods* (pp. 41–102). New York: John Wiley and Sons.

Cairns, R. B. (1983). The emergence of developmental psychology. In P. H. Mussen (Ed.), *Handbook of child psychology* (4th ed.): *Vol. 1. History, theory, and methods* (pp. 41–102). New York: John Wiley.

Cairns, R., Moore, C., Redshaw, D., & Wilson, T. (1992a). Addendum: Child care in the Northwest Territories, 1988–1990. In A. Pence (Ed.). (1992). *Canadian child care in context: Perspectives from the provinces and territories*. Ottawa: Statistics Canada & Health and Welfare Canada.

Cairns, R., Moore, C., Redshaw, D., & Wilson, T. (1992b). An historical overview of child care in the Northwest Territories. In A. Pence (Ed.), *Canadian child care in context: Perspectives from the provinces and territories*. Ottawa: Statistics Canada & Health and Welfare Canada.

Cairns, R., Moore, C., Redshaw, D., & Wilson, T. (1992c). An overview of child care legislation in the Northwest Territories. In A. Pence (Ed.), *Canadian child care in context: Perspectives from the provinces and territories*. Ottawa: Statistics Canada & Health and Welfare Canada.

Cairns, R., Moore, C., Redshaw, D., & Wilson, T. (1992d). A socio-geographic overview of the Northwest Territories. In A. Pence (Ed.), *Canadian child care in context: Perspectives from the provinces and territories*. Ottawa: Statistics Canada & Health and Welfare Canada.

Caldwell, B. M. (1968). The fourth dimension in early childhood education. In R. D. Hess & R. M. Bear (Eds.), *Early Education*. Chicago: Aldine Press.

Caldwell, B. M. (1971). Impact of interest in early cognitive stimulation. In H. Rie (Ed.), *Perspectives in child psychopathology*. New York: Aldine Atherton.

Caldwell, B. M. (1973a). What does research teach us about day care? *Young Children, 29,* 197–208.

Caldwell, B. M. (1973b). Infant day care: The outcast gains respectability. In P. Roby (Ed.), *Child Care: Who Cares?* New York: Basic Books.

Caldwell, B. M. (1977). Aggression and hostility in young children. *Young Children, 32*(2), 4–13.

Caldwell, B. M. (1977). Aggression and hostility in young children. *Young Children, 32*(2), 4–13.

Caldwell, B., & Bradley, R. (1979). *Home observation of the environment*. Little Rock: University of Arkansas Press.

Camp, B. W., & Bash, M. A. (1981). *Think aloud: Increasing social and cognitive skills—A problem solving program for children*. Champaign, IL: Research Press.

Campaign 2000. (1998). *Child poverty in Canada: Report card 1998*. [Brochure]. Toronto: Family Service Association.

Canadian Child Care Federation. (1996). Canadian Child Care Federation proposal. In *Visions: Special research and development competition on child care* (pp. 6–7). Ottawa: Canadian Child Care Federation.

Canadian Child Care Federation. Inside the federation: Partnerships and projects. *Interaction* (Fall), 2. Ottawa: Canadian Child Care Federation.

Canadian Child Day Care Federation & Canadian Day Care Advocacy Association (1992). *Caring for a living: Executive summary*. Ottawa: Authors.

Canadian Child Day Care Federation (1991). *National statement on quality child care*. Ottawa: Canadian Child Day Care Federation.

Canning, P., & Irwin, S. (1992). A socio-geographic overview of Nova Scotia. In A. Pence (Ed.), *Canadian child care in context: Perspectives from the provinces and territories*. Ottawa: Statistics Canada & Health and Welfare Canada.

Canning, P., Irwin, S., & Lewis, L. (1992). An overview of child care legislation in Nova Scotia. In A. Pence (Ed.), *Canadian child care in context: Perspectives from the provinces and territories.* Ottawa: Statistics Canada & Health and Welfare Canada.

Caplan, F., & Caplan, T. (1974). *The power of play.* New York: Anchor Press.

Carlsson-Paige, N., & Levin, D. E. (1985). *Helping young children understand peace, war, and the nuclear threat.* Washington, DC: National Association for the Education of Young Children.

Carlsson-Paige, N., & Levin, D. E. (1990). *Who's calling the shots? How to respond effectively to children's fascination with war play and war toys.* Philadelphia, PA: New Society Publishers.

Carrière, Y. (1992). A socio-geographic overview of Quebec. In A. Pence (Ed.), *Canadian child care in context: Perspectives from the provinces and territories.* Ottawa: Statistics Canada & Health and Welfare Canada.

Carter, D. B. (1987). Early childhood education: A historical perspective. In J. L. Roopnarine & J. E. Johnson (Eds.), *Approaches to early childhood education* (pp. 1–14). Columbus, OH: Merrill Publishing Co.

Cartwright, C. A., & Cartwright, G. P. (1974). *Developing observation skills.* New York: McGraw-Hill Book Co.

Cartwright, S. (1990). Learning with large blocks. *Young Children, 45*(3), 38–41.

Casler, L. (1961). Maternal deprivation: A critical review of the literature. *Monographs of the Society for Research in Child Development, 26*(2, Serial No. 80).

Cass, J. E. (1973). *Helping children grow through play.* New York: Schocken Books.

Cataldo, C. Z. (1987). *Parent education for early childhood: Child-rearing concepts and program content for the student and practicing professional.* New York: Teacher's College Press, Columbia University.

Chafel, J. A. (1990). Children in poverty: Policy perspectives on a national crisis. *Young Children, 45*(5), 31–37.

Charles, C. M. (1974). *Teachers.* Belmont, CA: Petit Piaget Pitman Learning.

Charlesworth, R. (1987). *Understanding child development.* Albany, NY: Delmar Publishers.

Charlesworth, R., & Lind, K. K. (1990). *Math and science for young children.* Albany, NY: Delmar Publishers Inc.

Chattin-McNichols, J. (1992). *The Montessori controversy.* Albany, NY: Delmar Publishers Inc.

Chattin-McNichols, J. P. (1981). The effects of Montessori school experience. *Young Children, 36*(5), 49–66.

Chess, S., & Thomas, A. (1987). *Know your child: An authoritarian guide for today's parents.* New York: Basic Books.

Child Care Resource and Research Unit (1990). *Child care information sheets.* Toronto, ON: Centre for Urban and Community studies, University of Toronto.

Child Care Resource and Research Unit (1993, May). *What's happening in child care policy: A cross Canada overview.* Paper presented at the Canadian Child Care Federations third National Child Care Conference.

Child Care Resource and Research Unit. (1994). *Child care in Canada: Practices and territories 1993.* Toronto: CRRU.

Child Care Resource and Research Unit. (1997). *Child care in Canada: Provinces and territories 1995.* Toronto: Centre for Urban and Community Studies, University of Toronto.

Child Care Resource and Research Unit. (2000). *Early childhood care and education in Canada: Provinces and territories 1998.* Toronto: Centre for Urban and Community Studies, University of Toronto.

Child Care Visions Call for Proposals. (1997). Hull, PQ: Employability and Social Partnerships Division, Human Resources Development Canada.

Chisholm, P. (1997, February 24). Growing up poor. *Maclean's,* 42–45.

Chomsky, N. (1972). *Language and mind.* New York: Harcourt Brace Jovanovich, Inc.

Christie, J. F. (1982). Sociodramatic play training. *Young Children, 37*(4), 25–32.

Christie, J. F., Johnsen, E. P., & Peckover, R. B. (1988). The effects of play period duration on children's play patterns. *Journal of Research in Early Childhood, 3,* 123–131.

Ciaranello, R. D. (1983). Neurochemical aspects of stress. In N. Garmezy & M. Rutter (Eds.), *Stress, coping and development in children* (pp. 85–105). New York: McGraw-Hill Book Co.

Cicerelli, V. (1969). *The impact of Head Start: An evaluation of the effects of Head Start on children's cognitive and affective development.* Athens, OH: Westinghouse Learning.

Clark, E. V. (1978a). Non-linguistic strategies and the acquisition of word meaning. In L. Bloom (Ed.), *Readings in language development* (pp. 433–451). New York: John Wiley & Sons.

Clark, E. V. (1978b). Strategies for communicating. *Child Development, 49,* 953–959.

Clarke-Stewart, A. (1988a). "The 'effects' of infant day care reconsidered" reconsidered. *Early Childhood Research Quarterly, 3,* 293–318.

Clarke-Stewart, A. (1999). *How child care relates to children's cognitive and language development: NICHD Study.* Paper presented at the American Association for the Advancement of Science meetings, Anaheim, CA, January 21–26.

Clarke-Stewart, K. (1988b). Evolving issues in early childhood education: A personal perspective. *Early Childhood Research Quarterly, 3,* 13–149.

Clarke-Stewart, K. (1989). Infant day care: Maligned or malignant? *American Psychologist, 44,* 266–273.

Clarke-Stewart, K. A. (1983). Exploring the assumptions of parent education. In R. Haskins & D. Adams (Eds.), *Parent education and public policy* (pp. 257–276). Norwood, NJ: Ablex Publishing Corp.

Clarke-Stewart, K. A. (1984). Day care: A new context for research and development. In M. Perlmutter (Ed.), *Parent-child interaction and parent-child relations in child development: The Minnesota symposia on child psychology* (Vol. 17, pp. 61–100). Hillsdale, NJ: Lawrence Erlbaum Associates.

Clarke-Stewart, K. A. (1987a). In search of consistencies in child care research. In D. A. Phillips (Ed.), *Quality in child care: What does research tell us?* (pp. 105–120). Washington, DC: National Association for the Education of Young Children.

Clarke-Stewart, K. A. (1987b). Predicting child development from child care forms and features: The Chicago Study. In D. A. Phillips (Ed.), *Quality in child care: What does research tell us?* (pp. 21–41). Washington, DC: National Association for the Education of Young Children.

Clarke-Stewart, K., & Fein, G. (1983). Early childhood programs. In P. H. Mussen (Ed.), *Handbook of child psychology* (4th ed.): *Vol. 2. Infancy and developmental psychobiology* (pp. 917–1000). New York: John Wiley and Sons.

Clarke-Stewart, K., & Gruber, C. (1984). Daycare forms and features. In R. C. Ainslie (Ed.), *Quality variations in daycare* (pp. 35–62). New York: Praeger.

Clemens, S. G. (1991). Art in the classroom: Making every day special. *Young Children, 46*(2), 4–11.

Clements, D. H. (1987). Computers and young children: A review of research. *Young Children, 43*(1), 34–44.

Cleveland, G. & Krashinsky, M. (2001). *Our children's future: Child care policy in Canada.* Toronto: University of Toronto Press.

Cleveland, G., & Krashinsky, M. (1998). *The benefit and cost of good child care: The economic rationale for public investment in young children.* Toronto: Childcare Research and Resource Unit, Centre for Urban and Community Studies, University of Toronto.

Cleveland, G., & Krashinsky, M. (2001). What special arrangements are necessary for lone-parent families in a universal child care program? In G. Cleveland & M. Krashinsky, *Our children's future: Child care policy in Canada* (pp. 315–333). Toronto: University of Toronto Press.

Clewett, A. S. (1988). Guidance and discipline: Teaching young children appropriate behaviour. *Young Children, 43*(4), 26–31.

Click, P. M., & Click, D. W. (1990). *Administration of schools for young children* (3rd ed.). Albany, NY: Delmar Publishers Inc.

Clifford, Howard (1992). Foreword. In A. Pence (Ed.), *Canadian child care in context: Perspectives from the provinces and territories* (pp. xiii–xvii). Ottawa: Statistics Canada & Health and Welfare Canada.

Cochran, M. (1988). Between cause and effect: The ecology of program impacts. In A. R. Pence (Ed.), *Ecological research with children and families: From concepts to methodology* (pp. 143–169). New York: Teachers College Press, Columbia University.

Cohen, D. H., & Stern, V. (1978). *Observing and recording the behavior of young children* (2nd ed.). New York: Teachers College Press, Columbia University.

Cole, E., & Schaefer, C. (1990). Can young children be art critics? *Young Children, 45*(2), 33–38.

Coleman, J. S., et al. (1966). *Equality of Educational opportunity*. Washington, DC: United States Government Printing Office.

Coleman, M., & Skeen, P. (1985). Play, games, and sport: Their use and misuse. *Childhood Education, 61,* 192–198.

Comenius, J. (1967). *The great didactic* (M. W. Keating, Ed. & Trans.). New York: Russell & Russell. (Original work published 1896, 1910).

Consortium for Longitudinal Studies. (1978). *Lasting effects after preschool*. (DHEW Publication No. OHDS 79-30178). Washington, DC: US Government Printing Office.

Consortium for Longitudinal Studies. (1983). *As the twig is bent: Lasting effects of preschool programs*. Hillsdale, NJ: Erlbaum.

Cook, R. E., Tessier, A., & Armbruster, V. B. (1987). *Adapting early childhood curricula for children with special needs*. Columbus, OH: Merrill Publishing Co.

Copple, C. E., DeLisi, R., & Sigel, E. (1982). Cognitive development. In B. Spodek (Ed.), *Handbook of research in early childhood education* (pp. 3–26). New York: The Free Press.

Corbett, B. (1994). Froebel Education in Canada. In E. Essa & R. Young (Eds.), *Introduction to early childhood education* (p. 38). Toronto: Nelson Canada.

Cosgrove, M. S. (1991). Cooking in the classroom: The doorway to nutrition. *Young Children, 46*(3), 43–45.

Cox, M. V. (1986). *The child's point of view: The development of cognition and language*. New York: St. Martin's Press.

Cratty, B. J. (1982). Motor development in early childhood: Critical issues for researchers in the 1980s. In B. Spodek (Ed.), *Handbook of research in early childhood education* (pp. 27–46). New York: The Free Press.

Critics challenge proposed program for pre-schoolers. (1993, February 24). *The St. Catharines Standard*, p. 8.

Cuddigan, M., & Hanson, M. B. (1988). *Growing pains: Helping children deal with everyday problems through reading*. Chicago: American Library Association.

Culture and children. (1985). Austin, TX: Texas Department of Human Resources.

Curtis, S. R. (1987). New views on movement development and the implications for curriculum in early childhood. In C. Seefeldt (Ed.), *The early childhood curriculum: A review of current research* (pp. 257–270). New York: Teachers College Press, Columbia University.

Daehler, M. W., & Bukatko, D. (1985). *Cognitive development*. New York: Alfred A. Knopf, Inc.

Dale, P. *Language development* (2nd ed.). New York: Holt, Rinehart and Winston.

Damon, W. (1977). *The social world of the child*. San Francisco: Jossey-Bass.

Damon, W. (1983). The nature of social-cognitive change in the developing child. In W. F. Overton (Ed.), *The relationship between social and cognitive development* (pp. 103–141). Hillsdale, NJ: Lawrence Erlbaum Associates, Publishers.

Davidson, J. (1982). Wasted time: The ignored dilemma. In J. F. Brown (Ed.), *Curriculum planning for young children* (pp. 196–204). Washington, DC: National Association for the Education of Young Children.

Davidson, J. I. (1989). *Children and computers together in the early childhood classroom*. Albany, NY: Delmar Publishers Inc.

Day care, families, and stress: A day care provider's guide. (1985). Austin, TX: Child Development Program Division, Texas Department of Human Resources.

Debelack, M., Herr, J., & Jacobson, M. (1981). *Creating innovative classroom materials for teaching young children.* New York: Harcourt Brace Jovanovich Inc.

Deiner, P. L. (1983). *Resources for teaching young children with special needs.* New York: Harcourt Brace Jovanovich.

Deiner, P. L. (1993). Family day care and children with disabilities. In D. L. Peters & A. R. Pence (Eds.), *Family day care: Current research for informed public policy* (pp. 129–145). Toronto: Canadian Scholars' Press.

Delacato, C. H. (1964). *The diagnosis and treatment of speech and reading problems.* Springfield, IL: Thomas Publishers.

Delacato, C. H. (1966). *Neurological organization and reading.* Springfield, IL: Thomas Publishers.

deMause, L. (Ed.). (1974). *The history of childhood.* New York: Harper & Row.

Derman-Sparks, L. (1989). *Anti-bias curriculum: Tools for empowering young children.* Washington, DC:

Derman-Sparks, L., & Ramsey, P. (1993). Early childhood multicultural, anti-bias education in the 1990s: Toward the 21st century. In J. L. Derman-Sparks, L., Higa, C. T., & Sparks, B. (1980). Children, race and racism: How race awareness develops. *Interracial books for children bulletin, 11*(3–4), 3–9.

Desjardins, G. (1992). An historical overview of child care in Quebec. In A. Pence (Ed.), *Canadian child care in context: Perspectives from the provinces and territories.* Ottawa: Statistics Canada & Health and Welfare Canada.

deVilliers, J. G., & deVilliers, P. A. (1973). A cross-sectional study of the acquisition of grammatical morphemes in child speech. *Journal of Psycholinguistic Research, 2,* 267–278.

deVilliers, P. A., & deVilliers, J. G. (1979). *Early language.* Cambridge, MA: Harvard University Press.

Dewey, J. (1897). *My pedagogic creed.* Washington, DC: The Progressive Education Association.

Dewey, J. (1900). *The school and society.* New York: McLure, Phillips & Company.

Dewey, J. (1902). *The child and the curriculum.* Chicago, IL: University of Chicago Press.

Dewey, J. (1916). *Democracy and education: An introduction to the philosophy of education.* New York: Macmillan.

Dill, N. (1992). Addendum: Child care in Saskatchewan, 1988–1990. In A. Pence (Ed.), *Canadian child care in context: Perspectives from the provinces and territories.* Ottawa: Statistics Canada & Health and Welfare Canada.

Dimidjian, V. J. (1989). Holidays, holy days, and wholly dazed: Approaches to special days. *Young Children, 44*(6), 70–74.

Dinkmeyer, D., & McKay, G. D. (1976). *Systematic training for effective parenting: Parent's handbook.* Circle Pines, MN: American Guidance Services.

Division for Early Childhood, Council for Exceptional Children. (1993). *DEC recommended practices: Indicators of quality in programs for infants and young children with special needs and their families.* Reston, VA: Author.

Dixon, G. (1994). The first years of kindergarten in Canada. *Canadian Children, 19*(2), 6–9.

Doherty, G. (1995). *Quality measures in child care projects. Final report.* Unpublished manuscript. Toronto: Child Care Branch, Ontario Ministry of Community and Social Services.

Doherty, G. (1996). School for three- and four-year olds. What does the research tell us? *Canadian Journal of Research in Early Childhood Education, 5,* 135–142.

Doherty, G., Goelman, H., La Grange, A., Lero, D. S., Tougas, J. (1999). *You bet I care!* Retrieved March 8, 2002 from action.web.ca/home/cfwwb/readingroom.shtml.

Doherty, G., Lero, D., Goelman, H., La Grange, A., & Tougas, J. (2000). *You bet I care! A Canada-wide study on: Wages, working conditions, and practices in child care centres.* Guelph, ON: Centre for Families, Work and Well-Being, Department of Family Relations and Applied Nutrition, University of Guelph.

Doherty, G., Lero, D., Goelman, H., Tougas, J., & La Grange, A. (1999). Wages and long-term income security in child care centers. *Interactions, 13*(3), 32–35.

Doherty, G., Lero, D., Goelman, H., Tougas, J., & La Grange, A. (2000). *Caring and learning environments: Quality in regulated family child care across Canada.* Guelph, ON: Centre for Families, Work and Well-Being, Department of Family Relations and Applied Nutrition, University of Guelph.

Doherty, G., Lero, D., Tougas, J., La Grange, A., & Goelman, H. (2001). *Policies and practices in Canadian family child care agencies.* Guelph, ON: Centre for Families, Work and Well-Being, Department of Family Relations and Applied Nutrition, University of Guelph.

Doherty-Derkowski, G. (1995). *Quality matters: Excellence in early childhood programs.* Don Mills, ON: Addison-Wesley Publishers.

Doman, R. J., Spitz, E. B., Zucman, E., & Delacato, C. H. (1960). Children with severe brain injuries: Neurological organization in terms of mobility. *Journal of the American Medical Association, 174,* 257–262.

Douvan, E. (1990). Psychoanalytic theory of human development. In R. M. Thomas (Ed.), *The encyclopedia of human development and education: Theory, research, and studies* (pp. 83–88). New York: Pergamon Press.

Doxey, I. (1990). The Canadian child. In I. Doxey (Ed.), *Child care and education: Canadian dimensions* (pp. 3–12). Toronto: Nelson Canada.

Doyle, A. B., & Connolly, J. (1989). Negotiation and enactment in social pretend play: Relations to social acceptance and social cognition. *Early Childhood Research Quarterly, 4,* 289–302.

Doyle, A. B., Gold, D., & Moskowitz, D. S. (Eds.). (1984). *Children and families under stress.* San Francisco, CA: Jossey-Bass Inc., Publishers.

Drabman, R. S., Cordua, G. D., Hammer, D., Jarvie, G. J., & Horton, W. (1979). Developmental trends in eating rates of normal and overweight preschool children. *Child Development, 50,* 211–216.

Dresden, J., & Myers, B. K. (1989). Early childhood professionals: Toward self-definition. *Young Children, 44*(2), 62–66.

Dumas, J. (1997). Marriage and divorce in Canada: What the statistics can and cannot tell us. *Transition, 27*(4), 9–11.

Dunst, C. J., & Trivette, C. M. (1988). Toward experimental evaluation of the family, infant, and preschool program. In H. B. Weiss & F. H. Jacobs (Eds.), *Evaluating family programs* (pp. 315–346). New York: Aldine de Gruyter.

Early Childhood Educators of British Columbia. (1997). *Code of ethics.* Vancouver: ECEBC.

Edwards, C. P. (1986). *Promoting social and moral development in young children.* New York: Teachers College Press, Columbia University.

Elkind, D. (1981). *The hurried child: Growing up too fast too soon.* Reading, MA: Addison Wesley.

Elkind, D. (1983). Montessori education: Abiding contributions and contemporary challenges. *Young Children, 38*(2), 3–10.

Elkind, D. (1986). Formal education and early childhood education: An essential difference. *Phi Delta Kappan, 67,* 631–636.

Elkind, D. (1987a). The child yesterday, today, and tomorrow. *Young Children, 42*(4), 6–11.

Elkind, D. (1987b). *Miseducation: Preschoolers at risk.* New York: Alfred A. Knopf, Inc.

Elkind, D. (1988a). *The hurried child: Growing up too fast too soon.* Reading, MA: Addison-Wesley.

Elkind, D. (1988b). The resistance to developmentally appropriate educational practice with young children: The real issue. In C. Warger (Ed.), *A resource guide to public school early childhood programs* (pp. 53–62). Alexandria, VA: Association for Supervision and Curriculum Development.

Elkind, D. (1990). Academic pressures—Too much, too soon: The demise of play. In E. Klugman &

S. Smilansky (Eds.), *Children's play and learning* (pp. 3–17). New York: Teachers College Press.

Employment and Immigration Canada (1992). *Labour market information.* St. Catharines, ON: Employment and Immigration Canada.

Endres, J. B., & Rockwell, R. E. (1980). *Food, nutrition, and the young child.* St. Louis, MO: C. V. Mosby Co.

Epstein, A. S., Schweinhart, L. J., & McAdoo, L. (1996). *Models of early childhood education.* Ypsilanti, MI: High/Scope Press.

Eriksen, A. (1985). *Playground design: Outdoor environments for learning and development.* New York: Van Nostrand Reinhold Co.

Erikson, E. H. (1963). *Childhood and society* (2nd ed.). New York: Norton.

Esbensen, S. (1990). Designing the early childhood setting. In I. Doxey (Ed.), *Child care and education: Canadian dimensions* (pp. 178–192). Toronto, ON: Nelson Canada.

Essa, E. L. (1981). An outdoor play area designed for learning. *Day Care and Early Education, 9*(2), 37–42.

Essa, E. L. (1987). The effect of a computer on preschool children's activities. *Early Childhood Research Quarterly, 2,* 377–382.

Essa, E. L. (1990). *Practical guide to solving preschool behavior problems* (2nd ed.). Albany, NY: Delmar.

Essa, E. L. (1995). *Practical guide to solving preschool behaviour problems* (3rd ed.). Albany, NY: Delmar Publishers Inc.

Essa, E. L. (1999). *Practical guide to solving preschool behaviour problems* (4th ed.). Albany, NY: Delmar Publishers Inc.

Essa, E. L., & Rogers, P. R. (1992). *An early childhood curriculum: From developmental model to application.* Albany, NY: Delmar Publishers Inc.

Essa, E. L., Hilton, J. M., & Murray, C. I. (1990). The relationship of weather and preschool children's behaviour. *Children's Environments Quarterly, 7*(3), 32–36.

Essa, E., & Young, R. (1994). Introduction to early childhood education (1st Canadian ed.). Toronto: ITP Nelson Canada.

Ethics Commission. (1987). Ethics case studies: The working mother. *Young Children, 43*(1), 16–19.

Evans, E. (1975). *Contemporary influences in early childhood education* (2nd ed.). New York: Holt, Rinehart, & Winston.

Evans, E. D. (1982). Curriculum models and early childhood education. In B. Spodek (Ed.), *Handbook of research in early childhood education* (pp. 107–134). New York: The Free Press.

Evans, E. D. (1984). Children's aesthetics. In L. G. Katz (Ed.), *Current topics in early childhood education* (Vol. 5, pp. 73–104). Norwood, NJ: Ablex Publishing Corp.

Faggella, K., & Horowitz, J. (1990). Different child, different style. *Instructor, 100*(2), 52.

Fassler, J. (1978). *Helping children cope.* New York: Free Press.

Faust, V., Weidmann, M., & Wehner, W. (1974). The influence of meteorological factors on children and youths. *Acta Paedopsychiatrica, 40,* 150–156.

Feeney, S. (1988a). Ethics case studies: The aggressive child. *Young Children, 43*(2), 48–51.

Feeney, S. (1988b). Ethics case studies: The divorced parents. *Young Children, 43*(3), 48–49.

Feeney, S., & Chun, R. (1985). Effective teachers of young children. *Young Children, 41*(1), 47–52.

Feeney, S., & Freeman, N. K. (1999). *Ethics and the early childhood educator: Using the NAEYC code.* Washington, DC: National Association for the Education of Young Children.

Feeney, S., & Kipnis, K. (1985). Professional ethics in early childhood education. *Young Children, 40*(3), 54–56.

Feeney, S., & Moravcik, E. (1987). A thing of beauty: Aesthetic development in young children. *Young Children, 42*(6), 7–15.

Feeney, S., Christensen, D., & Moravcik, E. (1991). *Who am I in the lives of young children?* New York: Merrill.

Fein, G. G. (1979). Play and the acquisition of symbols. In L. G. Katz (Ed.), *Current topics in early childhood education* (Vol. 2, pp. 195–225). Norwood, NJ: Ablex Publishing Corp.

Fein, G. G. (1982). Pretend play: New perspectives. In J. F. Brown (Ed.), *Curriculum planning for young children* (pp. 22–27). Washington, DC: National Association for the Education of Young Children.

Fein, G., & Clarke-Stewart, A. (1973). *Day care in context*. New York: John Wiley & Sons.

Fein, G., & Fox, N. (1988). Infant day care: A special issue. *Early Childhood Research Quarterly, 3,* 227–234.

Fein, G., & Schwartz, P. M. (1982). Developmental theories in early education. In B. Spodek (Ed.), *Handbook of research in early childhood education* (pp. 82–104). New York: The Free Press.

Ferber, R. (1985). *Solve your child's sleep problems*. New York: Simon & Schuster.

Fernandez, J. P. (1986). *Child care and corporate productivity*. Lexington, MA: Lexington Books.

Finkelstein, B. (1988). The revolt against selfishness: Women and the dilemmas of professionalism in early childhood education. In B. Spodek, O. N. Saracho, & D. L. Peters (Ed.), *Professionalism and the early childhood practitioner* (pp. 10–28). New York: Teachers College Press, Columbia University.

Flack, M. (1931). *Angus and the cat*. New York: Doubleday.

Flanagan-Rochon, K. F. (1992a). Addendum: Child care in Prince Edward Island, 1988–1990. In A. Pence (Ed.), *Canadian child care in context: Perspectives from the provinces and territories*. Ottawa: Statistics Canada & Health and Welfare Canada.

Flanagan-Rochon, K. F. (1992b). An overview of child care legislation on Prince Edward Island. In A. Pence (Ed.), *Canadian child care in context: Perspectives from the provinces and territories*. Ottawa: Statistics Canada & Health and Welfare Canada.

Flanagan-Rochon, K. F., & Rice, C. (1992). An historical overview of child care on Prince Edward Island. In A. Pence (Ed.), *Canadian child care in context: Perspectives from the provinces and territories*. Ottawa: Statistics Canada & Health and Welfare Canada.

Flaste, R. (1991, April 28). Sidelined by loneliness. *New York Times Magazine*, pp. 14–15, 23–24.

Flavell, J. (1963). *The developmental psychology of Jean Piaget*. Princeton, NJ: Van Nostrand.

Fleming, W. G. (1971). *Ontario's educative society: Vol. 5. Supporting institutions and services*. Toronto: University of Toronto Press.

Flerx, V. C., Fidler, D. S., & Rogers, R. W. (1976). Sex role stereotypes: Developmental aspects and early intervention. *Child Development, 67,* 998–1007.

Fogel, A. (1991). *Infancy: Infant, family, and society* (2nd ed.). St. Paul., MN: West Publishing.

Forman, G. E., & Kuschner, D. S. (1977). *The child's construction of knowledge: Piaget for teaching children*. Monterey, CA: Brooks/Cole Publishing Co.

Forman, G., & Kaden, M. (1987). Research on science education for young children. In C. Seefeldt (Ed.), *The early childhood curriculum: A review of current research* (pp. 141–164). New York: Teachers College Press, Columbia University.

Fowler, W. (1971). *Demonstration program in infant care and education: Final report*. Toronto, ON: Ontario Institute for Studies in Education, University of Toronto.

Fowler, W. (1972). A developmental learning approach to infant care in a group setting. *Merrill-Palmer Quarterly, 18,* 145–175.

Fowler, W. (1973). *The development of a prototype infant, preschool and child daycare centre in Metropolitan Toronto: Year II Progress Report*. Toronto, ON: Ontario Institute for Studies in Education, University of Toronto, 1973.

Fowler, W. (1974, June). *From intuitive to rational humanism: The comparative effects of group and home care on infant development*. Paper presented at the annual meeting of the Canadian Psychological Association, Windsor.

Fowler, W. (1978). *Day care and its effects on early development: A study of group and home care in multi-ethnic, working-class families* (Research in Education Series, No. 8). Toronto, ON: Ontario Institute for Studies in Education, University of Toronto.

Fowler, W., & Khan, N. (1974, April). *A follow-up investigation of the late development of infants in enriched group care*. Paper presented at the annual meeting of the American Education Research Association, Chicago.

Frankenburg, W. K., Dodds, J. B., Fandal, A. W., Kajuk, F., & Cohr, M. (1975). *Denver Developmental Screening Test: Revised reference manual*. Denver: Ladoca Publishing Foundation.

Fraser, S. (2000). *Authentic childhood: Experiencing Reggio Emilia in the classroom*. Toronto: ITP Nelson.

Frazier, A. (1980). Making a curriculum for children. *Childhood Education, 56*, 258–263.

Friedman, D. (1989, August). A more sophisticated employer response to child care. *Child Care Information Exchange*, pp. 29–31.

Friendly, M. (1994). *Child care policy in Canada: Putting the pieces together*. Don Mills, ON: Addison-Wesley Publishers.

Friendly, M. (1997). What is the public interest in child care? *Policy Options, 18*(1), (pp. 3–6).

Friendly, M. (1998). Canadian child care: Can we make order out of chaos? *Perception, 22*(2), 6–7.

Friendly, M. (2000). Child care as a social policy issue. In L. Prochner & N. Howe (Eds.), *Early childhood care and education in Canada* (pp. 252–272). Vancouver: UBC Press.

Friendly, M., & Oloman, M. (2000). Early childhood education on the Canadian policy landscape. In J. Hayden (Ed.), *Landscapes in early childhood education: Cross-national perspectives on empowerment—A guide for the new millennium* (pp. 69–81). New York: Peter Lang.

Friesen, J. (1992). An overview of child care legislation in Manitoba. In A. Pence (Ed.), *Canadian child care in context: Perspectives from the provinces and territories*. Ottawa: Statistics Canada & Health and Welfare Canada.

Friesen, J., Humphrey, M., & Brockman, L. M. (1992a). Addendum: Child care in Manitoba, 1988–1990. In A. Pence (Ed.), *Canadian child care in context: Perspectives from the provinces and territories*. Ottawa: Statistics Canada & Health and Welfare Canada.

Friesen, J., Humphrey, M., & Brockman, L. M. (1992b). An historical overview of child care in Manitoba. In A. Pence (Ed.), *Canadian child care in context: Perspectives from the provinces and territories*. Ottawa: Statistics Canada & Health and Welfare Canada.

Froschl, M., Colon, L., Rubin, E., & Sprung, B. (1984). *Including all of us: An early childhood curriculum about disability*. New York: Educational Equity Concepts, Inc.

Frost, J. L., & Henniger, M. L. (1982). Making playgrounds safe for children and children safe for playgrounds. In J. F. Brown (Ed.), *Curriculum planning for young children* (pp. 48–55). Washington, DC: National Association for the Education of Young Children.

Frost, J. L., & Klein, B. L. (1979). *Children's play and playgrounds*. Boston: Allyn and Bacon, Inc.

Frost, J. L., & Wortham, S. C. (1988). The evolution of American playgrounds. *Young Children, 43*(5), 19–28.

Fullum, H. (1992a). Addendum: Child care in Quebec, 1988–1990. In A. Pence (Ed.), *Canadian child care in context: Perspectives from the provinces and territories*. Ottawa: Statistics Canada & Health and Welfare Canada.

Fullum, H. (1992b). An overview of child day care legislation in Quebec. In A. Pence (Ed.), *Canadian child care in context: Perspectives from the provinces and territories*. Ottawa: Statistics Canada & Health and Welfare Canada.

Furman, E. (1982). Helping children cope with death. In J. F. Brown (Ed.), *Curriculum planning for young children* (pp. 238–245). Washington, DC: National Association for the Education of Young Children.

Furman, E. (1987). More protection, fewer directions. *Young Children, 42*(5), 5–7.

Furth, H. G. (1969). *Piaget and knowledge: Theoretical foundations*. Englewood Cliffs, NJ: Prentice-Hall.

Galdone, P. (1973). *The little red hen*. New York: Seabury.

Galinsky, E. (1981). *Between generations: The six stages of parenthood*. New York: Times Books.

Galinsky, E. (1988). Parents and teacher-caregivers: Sources of tension, sources of support. *Young Children, 43*(3), 4–12.

Galinsky, E. (1989). Update on employer-supported child care. *Young Children, 44*(6), 2, 75–77.

Galinsky, E. (1990). Why are some parent/teacher partnerships clouded with difficulties? *Young Children, 45*(5), 2–3, 38–40.

Gallagher, J. M., & Coche, J. (1987). Hothousing: The clinical and educational concerns over pressuring young children. *Early Childhood Research Quarterly, 2*, 203–210.

Gallimore, R., & Tharpe, R. (1990). Teaching mind in society: Teaching, schooling and literate discourse. In L. C. Moll (Ed.), *Vygotsky in education* (pp. 175–205). New York: Cambridge University Press.

Gamble, J. (1992a). An historical overview of child care in New Brunswick. In A. Pence (Ed.), *Canadian child care in context: Perspectives from the provinces and territories*. Ottawa: Statistics Canada & Health and Welfare Canada.

Gamble, J. (1992b). A socio-geographic overview of New Brunswick. In A. Pence (Ed.), *Canadian child care in context: Perspectives from the provinces and territories*. Ottawa: Statistics Canada & Health and Welfare Canada.

Gandini, L. (1997a). Foundations of the Reggio Emilia approach. In J. Hendrick (Ed.), *First steps toward teaching the Reggio way* (pp. 14–25).

Gandini, L. (1997b). The Reggio Emilia story: History and organization. In J. Hendrick (Ed.), *First steps*

toward teaching the Reggio way* (pp. 1–13). Upper Saddle River, NJ: Merrill/Prentice Hall.

Garbarino, J. (1990, June). Child abuse: Why? *The World and I*, pp. 543–553.

Garcia Coll, C., Kagan, J., & Reznick, J. S. (1984). Behavioural inhibition in young children. *Child Development, 55*, 1005–1019.

Garcia, E. E. (1982). Bilingualism in early childhood. In J. F. Brown (Ed.), *Curriculum planning for young children* (pp. 82–101). Washington, DC: National Association for the Education of Young Children.

Gardner, D. (1949). *Education under eight*. London: Methuen & Co.

Gardner, H. (1982). *Art, mind, and brain: A cognitive approach to creativity*. New York: Basic Books, Inc.

Gardner, H. (1983). *Frames of mind*. New York: Basic Books.

Gardner, H. (1989). Learning, Chinese-style. *Psychology Today, 23*(12), 54–56.

Garmezy, N. (1984). Stressors of childhood. In N. Garmezy & M. Rutter (Eds.), *Stress, coping and development in children* (pp. 43–84). New York: McGraw-Hill Book Co.

Garn, S. M., & Clark, D. C. (1976). Trends in fatness and the origins of obesity. *Pediatrics, 57*, 443–456.

Gartrell, D. (1987). Punishment or guidance? *Young Children, 42*(3), 55–61.

Gartrell, D. (1995). Misbehaviour or mistaken behaviour? Young Children (July), 27–34.

Gartrell, D. (1998). *A guidance approach for the classroom* (2nd ed.). New York: Delmar Publishers.

Gehlbach, S. H., MacCormack, J. N., Drake, B. M., & Thompson, W. V. (1973). Spread of disease by fecal-oral route in day nurseries. *Health Service Reports, 88*, 320–322.

Geller, L. G. (1985). *Word play and language learning for children*. Urbana, IL: National Council of Teachers of English.

Gelman, R., & Gallistel, C. R. (1978). *The child's understanding of number*. Cambridge, MA: Harvard University Press.

Genishi, C. (1982). Observational research methods for early childhood education. In B. Spodek (Ed.), *Handbook of research in early childhood education* (pp. 564–591). New York: The Free Press.

Gersten, R. (1986). Response to "Consequences of three preschool curriculum models through age 15." *Early Childhood Research Quarterly, 1,* 293–302.

Gessell, A. (1923). *The preschool child: From the standpoint of public hygiene and education.* Houghton Mifflin.

Gessell, A. (1928). *Infancy and human growth.* New York: Macmillan.

Gestwicki, C. (1987). *Home, school, and community relations: A guide to working with parents.* Albany, NY: Delmar Publishers Inc.

Gestwicki, C. (1997). *The essentials of early education.* New York: Delmar Publishers.

Gestwicki, C. (1999). *Developmentally appropriate practice* (2nd ed.). New York: Delmar Publishers.

Gestwicki, C. (2000). *Home, school, and community relations: A guide to working with parents* (4th ed.). Albany, NY: Delmar Publishers Inc.

Gettman, D. (1987). *Basic Montessori: Learning activities for under-fives.* New York: St. Martin's Press.

Gibson, L. (1989). *Through children's eyes: Literacy learning in the early years.* New York: Teachers College Press, Columbia University.

Gilkeson, E., & Bowman, G. (1976). *The focus is on children: The Bank Street approach to childhood education as enacted in Follow Through.* New York: Bank Street College of Education.

Gilmore, B. (1971). Play: A special behavior. In R. Haber (Ed.), *Current research in motivation* (pp. 343–355). New York: Harper.

Gineshi, C. (1987). Acquiring oral language and communicative competence. In C. Seefeldt (Ed.), *The early childhood curriculum: A review of current research* (pp. 75–106). New York: Teachers College Press, Columbia University.

Ginsburg, H., & Opper, S. (1969). *Piaget's theory of intellectual development: An introduction.* Englewood Cliffs, NJ: Prentice-Hall, Inc.

Glassman, M. (1992a). An historical overview of child care in Newfoundland. In A. Pence (Ed.), *Canadian child care in context: Perspectives from the provinces and territories.* Ottawa: Statistics Canada & Health and Welfare Canada.

Glassman, M. (1992b). A socio-geographic overview of Newfoundland. In A. Pence (Ed.), *Canadian child care in context: Perspectives from the provinces and territories.* Ottawa: Statistics Canada & Health and Welfare Canada.

Glazer, J. I. (1986). *Literature for young children* (2nd ed.). Columbus, OH: Charles E. Merrill Publishing Co.

Gleason, J. B. (1985). Studying language development. In J. B. Gleason (Ed.), *The development of language* (pp. 1–35). Columbus, OH: Charles E. Merrill Publishing Co.

Goelman, H. (1988). The relationship between structure and process variables in home and day care settings on children's language development. In A. R. Pence (Ed.), *Ecological research with children and families: From concepts to methodology* (pp. 16–34). New York: Teachers College Press, Columbia University.

Goelman, H. (2001). Training, quality, and the lived experience of child care. In G. Cleveland & M. Krashinsky, *Our children's future: Child care policy in Canada,* (pp. 142–168). Toronto: University of Toronto Press.

Goelman, H., & Pence, A. (1990). The Victoria and Vancouver research projects. In Doxey, I. (Ed.), *Child care and education: Canadian dimensions* (pp. 269–277). Toronto: Nelson Canada.

Goelman, H., Doherty, G., Lero, D., La Grange, A. & Tougas, J. (2000) *Caring and learning environments: Quality in child care centres across Canada.* Guelph, ON: Centre for Families, Work and Well-Being, Department of Family Relations and Applied Nutrition, University of Guelph.

Goffin, S. G. (1987). Cooperative behaviours: They need our support. *Young Children, 42(2),* 75–81.

Goffin, S. G. (1994). *Curriculum models and early childhood education: Appraising the relationships.* New York: Merrill.

Goldfarb, W. (1943). The effects of early institutional care on adolescent personality. *Journal of Experimental Education, 12,* 106–129.

Gonzalez-Mena, J. (1993). *Multicultural issues in child care.* Mountain View, CA: Mayfield Publishing Company.

Gonzalez-Mena, J., & Eyer, D. W. (1997). *Infants, toddlers, and caregivers* (4th ed.). Toronto: Mayfield Publishing Company.

Good discipline is, in large part, the result of a fantastic curriculum! (1987). *Young Children, 42*(3), 49.

Goodman, K. S., Smith, E. B., Meredith, R., & Goodman, Y. M. (1987). *Language and thinking in school: A whole-language curriculum* (3rd ed.). New York: Richard C. Owen Publishers, Inc.

Goodman, Y. M. (1986). Children coming to know literacy. In W. H. Teale & E. Sulzby (Eds.), *Emergent literacy: Writing and reading* (pp. 1–14). Norwood, NJ: Ablex Publishing Corp.

Goodwin, W. L., & Goodwin, L. D. (1982). Measuring young children. In B. Spodek (Ed.), *Handbook of research in early childhood education* (pp. 523–563). New York: The Free Press.

Goodz, N. S. (1982). Is before really easier to understand than after? *Child Development, 53,* 822–825.

Gordon, A. M., & Browne, K. W. (1989). *Beginnings and beyond: Foundations in early childhood education* (2nd ed.). Albany, NY: Delmar Publishers Inc.

Gordon, A. M., & Browne, K. W. (1993). *Beginnings and beyond: Foundations in early childhood education* (3rd ed.). Albany, NY: Delmar Publishers Inc.

Gordon, I. (1967, June). *The young child: A new look.* Paper presented at the conference on The Young Child: Florida's Future, University of Florida.

Gordon, T. (1974). T.E.T.: Teacher effectiveness training. New York: Peter H. Wyden Publisher.

Gordon, T. (1976). *P.E.T. in action.* New York: Peter H. Wyden Publisher.

Gottfried, A. (1984). Home environment and early cognitive development: Integration, meta-analyses, and conclusions. In A. Gottfried (Ed.), *Home environment and early cognitive development.* San Francisco: Academic Press.

Gould, R. L. (1978). *Transformations: Growth and change in adult life.* New York: Simon and Schuster.

Graue, M. E., & Shepard, L. A. (1989). Predictive validity of the Gessell School Readiness Test. *Early Childhood Research Quarterly, 4,* 303–315.

Greenberg, P. (1987). Lucy Sprague Mitchell: A major missing link between early childhood education in the 1980s and progressive education in the 1890s–1930s. *Young Children, 42*(5), 70–84.

Greenberg, P. (1988). Ideas that work with young children: Avoiding me against you discipline. *Young Children 44*(1), 24–29.

Greenleaf, P. (1978). *Children throughout the ages: A history of childhood.* New York: Barnes & Noble.

Greenspan, S., & Greenspan, N. T. (1986). *First feelings: Milestones in the emotional development of your baby and child.* New York: Penguin Books.

Greenwood-Church, M., & Crozier-Smith, D., (1992). A socio-geographic overview of Alberta. In A. Pence (Ed.), *Canadian child care in context: Perspectives from the provinces and territories.* Ottawa: Statistics Canada & Health and Welfare Canada.

Griffin, E. F. (1982). *Island of childhood: Education in the special world of nursery school.* New York: Teachers College Press, Columbia University.

Griffin, S. (1992). Addendum: Child care in British Columbia, 1988–1990. In A. Pence (Ed.), *Canadian child care in context: Perspectives from the provinces and territories (pp. 87–99).* Ottawa: Statistics Canada & Health and Welfare Canada.

Grimsley, R. (1976). Jean-Jacques Rousseau. In P. Edwards (Ed.), *The encyclopedia of philosophy* (Vols. 7–8, pp. 218–225). New York: Macmillan Publishing Co., Inc. & The Free Press.

Guilford, J. P. (1962). Creativity: Its measurement and development. In S. Parnes & H. Harding (Eds.), *A sourcebook for creative thinking* (pp. 151–168). New York: Charles Scribner's Sons.

Gunnar, M., Senior, K., & Hartup, W. (1984). Peer presence and the exploratory behavior of eighteen- and thirty-month-old children. *Child Development, 55,* 1103–1109.

Gunsberg, A. (1989). Empowering young abused and neglected children through contingent play. *Childhood Education, 66,* 8–10.

Hakuta, K. (1988). Why bilinguals? In F. S. Kessel (Ed.), *The development of language and language researchers* (pp. 299–318). Hillsdale, NJ: Lawrence Erlbaum Associates, Publishers.

Hakuta, K., & Garcia, E. E. (1989). Bilingualism and education. *American Psychologist, 44,* 374–379.

Halpern, R. (1987). Major social and demographic trends affecting young families: Implications for early childhood care and education. *Young Children, 42*(6), 34–40.

Hampden-Turner, C. (1981). *Maps of the mind: Charts and concepts of the mind and its labyrinths.* New York: Collier Books.

Harms, T., & Clifford, R. (1980). *Early childhood environment rating scale.* New York: Teachers College Press.

Harms, T., & Clifford, R. M. (1989). *Family Day Care Rating Scale (FDCRS).* New York: Teachers College Press.

Harms, T., & Clifford, R. M. (1998). *Early Childhood Environment Rating Scale—Revised (ECERS).* New York: Teachers College Press.

Harms, T., Clifford, R., & Padan-Belkin, E. (1983). *The day care home environment rating scale.* Chapel Hill, NC: Homebased Day Care Training Project.

Harms, T., Cryer, D., & Clifford, R. (1990). *Infant/toddler environment rating scale.* New York: Teachers College Press.

Harris, J. D., & Larsen, J. M. (1989). Parent education as a mandatory component of preschool: Effects on middle-class, educationally advantaged parents and children. *Early Childhood Research Quarterly, 4,* 275–287.

Harsh, A. (1987). Teach mathematics with children's literature. *Young Children, 42*(6), 24–27.

Harste, J. C., Short, K. G., & Burke, C. (1988). *Creating classrooms for authors: The reading-writing connection.* Portsmouth, NH: Heinemann Educational Books, Inc.

Hartup, W. (1983b). Peer relations. In P. H. Mussen (Ed.), *Handbook of child psychology* (4th ed.): *Vol. 4. Socialization, personality, and social development* (pp. 103–196). New York: John Wiley and Sons.

Hartup, W. W. (1983a). Peer interaction and the behavioural development of the individual child. In W. Damon (Ed.), *Social and personality development: Essays on the growth of the child* (pp. 220–233). New York: W. W. Norton & Co.

Haskins, R. (1985). Public school aggression among children with varying day care experience. *Child Development, 56,* 698–703.

Haugland, S. W., & Shade, D. D. (1990). *Developmental evaluations of software for young children.* Albany, NY: Delmar Publishers Inc.

Hautman, L., Read, M., & Greenwood-Church, M. (1992). An overview of child care legislation in Alberta. In A. Pence (Ed.), *Canadian child care in context: Perspectives from the provinces and territories.* Ottawa: Statistics Canada & Health and Welfare Canada.

Hayes, C. D., Palmer, J. L., & Zaslow, M. J. (1990). *Who cares for America's children: Child care policy for the 1990's.* Washington, DC: National Research Council, Panel on Child Care Policy, National Academy Press.

Hayward, D., Rothenburg, M., & Beasley, R. (1974). Children's play and urban playground environments: A comparison of traditional, contemporary, and adventure playground types. *Environment and Behaviour, 6*(2), 131–168.

Health Canada (2001). *Canada's food guide to healthy eating.* Ottawa: Author.

Healy, J. M. (1991). Ten reasons why "Sesame Street" is bad news for reading. *The Education Digest,* February, 63–66.

Helburn, S., Culkin, M. L., Howes, C., Bryant, D., Clifford, R., Cryer, D., Peisner-Feinberg, E., & Kagan, S. L. (1995). *Cost, quality, and child care outcomes in child care centers.* Denver: University of Colorado at Denver.

Helfer, R. E. (1987). The developmental basis of child abuse and neglect: An epidemiological approach. In R. E. Helfer & R. S. Kempe (Eds.), *The battered child* (4th ed., pp. 60–80). Chicago, IL: The University of Chicago Press.

Hendrick, J. (1986). *Total learning: Curriculum for the young child* (2nd ed.). Columbus, OH: Merrill Publishing Co.

Hendrick, J. (1997). Reggio Emilia and American schools: Telling them apart and putting them together—Can we do it? In J. Hendrick (Ed.), *First steps toward teaching the Reggio way* (pp. 41–53). Upper Saddle River, NJ: Merrill/Prentice Hall.

Hendrick, J. (Ed.). (1997). *First steps toward teaching the Reggio way.* Upper Saddle River, NJ: Merrill-Prentice Hall.

Henkens-Matzke, A., & Abbott, D. A. (1990). Game playing: A method for reducing young children's fear of medical procedures. *Early Childhood Research Quarterly, 5,* 19–26.

Herr, J., & Morse, W. (1982). Food for thought: Nutrition education for young children. In J. F. Brown (Ed.), *Curriculum planning for young children* (pp. 151–159). Washington, DC: National Association for the Education of Young Children.

Herrera, J. F., & Wooden, S. L. (1988). Some thoughts about effective parent-school communication. *Young Children, 43*(6), 78–80.

Hess, R. D., & Shipman, V. (1965a). Early blocks to children's learning. *Children, 12,* 189–194.

Hess, R. D., & Shipman, V. (1965b). Early experience and socialization of cognitive modes in children. *Child Development, 36,* 869–886.

Hess, R. D., & Shipman, V. (1968). Maternal influences upon early learning: The cognitive environments of urban pre-school children. In R. D. Hess & R. M. Bear (Eds.), *Early education.* Chicago: Aldine-Atherton.

Hetherington, E. M., Stanley-Hagan, M., & Anderson, E. R. (1989). Marital transitions: A child's perspective. *American Psychologist, 44,* 303–312.

Hildebrand, V., & Hearron, P. F. (1999). *Guiding young children* (6th ed.). Upper Saddle River, NJ: Prentice Hall.

Hills, T. W. (1987). Children in the fast lane: Implications for early childhood policy and practice. *Early Childhood Research Quarterly, 2,* 265–273.

Hilton, J. M., Essa, E. L., & Murray, C. I. (1991). Are families meeting the nonphysical needs of their children? A comparison of single parent, one-earner and two-earner households. *Family Perspectives, 25*(2), 41–56.

Hinde, R. A. (1983). Ethology and child development. In P. H. Mussen, (Ed.), *Handbook of child psychology* (4th ed.): *Vol. 4. Infancy and developmental psychobiology* (pp. 27–93). New York: John Wiley & Sons.

Hitchcock, N. E., Gracey, M., Gilmour, A. I., & Owles, E. N. (1986). *Nutrition and growth in infancy and early childhood: A longitudinal study from birth to 5 years.* New York: Karger.

Hitz, R., & Driscoll, A. (1988). Praise or encouragement? New insights into praise: Implications for early childhood teachers. *Young Children, 44*(5), 6–13.

Hofferth, S. L., & Phillips, D. A. (1987). Child care in the United States, 1970 to 1995. *Journal of Marriage and the Family, 49,* 559–571.

Hoffman, W. (1989). Effects of maternal employment in the two-parent family. *American Psychologist, 44,* 283–292.

Hohmann, M., & Weikart, D. P. (1995). *Educating young children: Active learning practices for preschool and child care programs.* Ypsilanti, MI: High/Scope Press.

Hohmann, M., Banet, B., & Weikart, D. P. (1979). *Young children in action: A manual for preschool educators.* Ypsilanti, MI: High/Scope Press.

Honig, A. (1993). The Eriksonian approach. In J. L. Roopnarine & J. E. Johnson (Eds.), *Approaches to early childhood education* (2nd ed.) (pp. 47–70). New York: Merrill.

Honig, A. S. (1979). *Parent involvement in early child-hood education*. Washington, DC: National Association for the Education of Young Children.

Honig, A. S. (1982). Prosocial development in young children. *Young Children, 37*(5), 51–62.

Honig, A. S. (1983). Sex role socialization in early childhood. *Young Children, 38*(6), 57–70.

Honig, A. S. (1985a). Research in review. Compliance, control, and discipline. (Part 1). *Young Children, 40*(2), 50–58.

Honig, A. S. (1985b). Research in review. Compliance, control, and discipline. (Part 2). *Young Children, 40*(3), 47–52.

Honig, A. S. (1986a). Stress and coping in children. (Part 1). *Young Children, 41*(4), 50–63.

Honig, A. S. (1986b). Stress and coping in children. (Part 2). Interpersonal family relationships. *Young Children, 41*(5), 47–59.

Honig, A. S. (1987). The shy child. *Young Children, 42*(4), 54–64.

Honig, A. S. (1988a). Caring and kindness: Curricular goals for early childhood educators. In G. F. Robertson & M. A. Johnson (Eds.), *Leaders in education: Their views on controversial issues* (pp. 58–70). New York: University Press of America.

Honig, A. S. (1988b). Humor development in children. *Young Children, 43*(4), 60–73.

Honig, A. S. (1990). Parent involvement in early childhood education. Washington, DC: National Association for the Education of Young Children.

Honig, A. S., & Oski, F. A. (1984). Solemnity: A clinical risk index for iron deficient infants. In A. S. Honig (Ed.), *Risk factors in infancy* (Special issue). *Early child development and care, 16*(1–2), 69–83.

Honig, A. S., Wittmer, D. S., & Gibralter, J. (1986). *Discipline, cooperation, and compliance: An annotated bibliography*. Urbana, IL: ERIC Clearinghouse on Elementary and Early Childhood Education.

Hough, R. A., Nurss, J. R., & Wood, D. (1987). Tell me a story: Making opportunities for elaborated language in early childhood classrooms. *Young Children, 43*(1), 6–12.

Howe, N., Jacobs, E., & Fiorentino, L. M. (2000). The curriculum. In L. Prochner & N. Howe (Eds.), *Early childhood care and education in Canada* (pp. 208–235). Vancouver: UBC Press.

Howes, C. (1983). Caregiver behavior in center and family day care. *Journal of Applied Developmental Psychology, 4,* 99–107.

Howes, C. (1987). Social competency with peers: Contributions from child care. *Early Childhood Research Quarterly, 2,* 155–167.

Howes, C. (1988). Same- and cross-sex friends: Implications for interaction and social skills. *Early Childhood Research Quarterly, 3,* 21–37.

Howes, C., & Farver, J. A. (1987). Social pretend play in 2-year-olds: Effects of age of partner. *Early Childhood Research Quarterly, 2,* 305–314.

Howes, C., & Hamilton, C. E. (1993). The changing experiences of child care: Changes in teachers and teacher-child relationships and children's social competence with peers. *Early Childhood Research Quarterly, 8,* 15–32.

Howes, C., & Olenick, M. (1986). Family and child care influences on toddlers' compliance. *Child Development, 57,* 202–216.

Howes, C., Philips, D.A., & Whitebook, M. (1992). Thresholds of quality: Implications for social development of children in center-based care. *Child Development, 63*(4), 449–460.

Huesmann, L. R. (1986). Psychological processes promoting the relation between exposure to media violence and aggressive behaviour by the viewer. *Journal of Social Issues, 42,* 125–139.

Huesmann, L. R., Lagerspetz, K., & Eron, L. D. (1984). Intervening variables in the TV violence-aggression relation: Evidence from two countries. *Developmental Psychology, 20,* 746–775.

Humphrey, J. H., & Humphrey, J. N. (1985). *Controlling stress in children*. Springfield, IL: Charles C Thomas Publisher.

Hunt, J. McV. (1961). *Intelligence and experience*. New York: Ronald Press.

Hunt, J. McV. (1968). Revisiting Montessori. In J. L. Frost (Ed.), *Early childhood education rediscovered* (pp. 102–127). New York: Holt, Rinehart & Winston.

Hunter, T. (1995). *Quality assessment of early childhood programs demonstration project. Final Report.* Victoria, BC: Unit for Child Care Research, School of Youth and Child Care, University of Victoria.

Huston, A. C., Watkins, B. A., & Kunkel, D. (1989). Public policy and children's television. *American Psychologist, 44,* 424–433.

Hymes, J. L. (1981). *Teaching the child under six* (3rd ed.). Columbus, OH: Merrill Publishing Co.

Hyson, M. C. (1986). Lobster on the sidewalk: Understanding and helping children with fears. In J. B. McCracken (Ed.), *Reducing stress in young children's lives* (pp. 2–5). Washington, DC: National Association for the Education of Young Children.

International Reading Association (1986). Literacy development and pre–first grade: A joint statement of concerns about present practices in pre–first grade reading instruction and recommendations for improvement. *Young Children, 41*(4), 10–13.

Irwin, S., & Canning, P. (1992a). Addendum: Child care in Nova Scotia, 1988–1990. In A. Pence (Ed.), *Canadian child care in context: Perspectives from the provinces and territories.* Ottawa: Statistics Canada & Health and Welfare Canada.

Irwin, S., & Canning, P. (1992b). An historical overview of child care in Nova Scotia. In A. Pence (Ed.), *Canadian child care in context: Perspectives from the provinces and territories.* Ottawa: Statistics Canada & Health and Welfare Canada.

Isaacs, Susan (1933). *Intellectual growth in young children.* New York: Schocken.

Ishee, N., & Goldhaber, J. (1990). Story re-enactment: Let the play begin. *Young Children, 45*(3), 70–75.

Izard, C. (1982). *Measuring emotions in infants and children.* New York: Cambridge University Press.

Jalongo, M. R. (1983). Using crisis-oriented books with young children. *Young Children, 38*(5), 29–36.

Jalongo, M. R. (1986). Using crisis-oriented books with young children. In J. B. McCracken (Ed.), *Reducing stress in young children's lives* (pp. 41–46). Washington, DC: National Association for the Education of Young Children.

Jalongo, M. R., & Collins, M. (1985). Singing with young children! Folk singing for nonmusicians. *Young Children, 40*(2), 17–22.

Jalongo, M. R., & Isenberg, J.P. (2000). *Exploring your role.* Upper Saddle River, NJ: Prentice-Hall.

Javernick, E. (1988). Johnny's not jumping: Can we help obese children? *Young Children, 43*(2), 18–23.

Jenkins, S. (1987). Ethnicity and family support. In S. L. Kagan, D. R. Powell, B. Weissbourd, & E. F. Zigler (Eds.), *America's family support programs: Perspectives and prospects* (pp. 282–294). New Haven, CT: Yale University Press.

Jensen, A. R. (1985a). *Compensatory education and the theory of intelligence.* Phi Delta Kappan, *66,* 554–558.

Jensen, M. A. (1985b). Story awareness: A critical skill for early reading. *Young Children, 41*(1), 20–24.

Johnson, J. (1993). Evaluation in early childhood education. In J. L. Roopnarine & J. E. Johnson (Eds.), *Approaches to early childhood education* (2nd ed.) (pp. 317–336). New York: Merrill.

Johnson, L., & Joe, M. J. (1992). An historical overview of child care in Yukon. In A. Pence (Ed.), *Canadian child care in context: Perspectives from the provinces and territories.* Ottawa: Statistics Canada & Health and Welfare Canada.

Johnston, J. R., & Slobin, D. I. (1979). The development of locative expressions in English, Italian, Serbo-Croatian, and Turkish. *Journal of Child Language, 6,* 529–545.

Jones, C., Marsden, L., & Tepperman, L. (1990). *Lives of their own: The individualization of women's lives.* Toronto, ON: Oxford University Press.

Jones, E., & Prescott, E. (1978). *Dimensions of teaching—Learning environments, II: Focus on day care.* Pasadena, CA: Pacific Oaks College.

Jones, J. M. Cheek, & S. R. Briggs (Eds.), *Shyness: Perspectives on research and treatment* (pp. 81–90). New York: Plenum Press.

Jordan, N. H. (1993). Sexual abuse prevention in early childhood education: A caveat. *Young Children, 48*(6), 76–69.

Jorde-Bloom, P. (1988a). *A great place to work: Improving conditions for staff in young children's programs.* Washington, DC: National Association for the Education of Young Children.

Jorde-Bloom, P. (1988b). Teachers need "TLC" too. *Young Children, 43*(6), 4–8.

Joy, L. A., Kimball, M. M., & Zabrack, M. L. (1986). Television and children's aggressive behaviour. In T. M. Williams (Ed.), *The impact of television: A natural experiment in three communities* (pp. 303–360). Orlando, FL: Academic Press, Inc.

Juorio, M. (2001). The need for a well-trained child care workforce. In G. Cleveland & M. Krashinsky, *Our children's future: Child care policy in Canada* (pp. 397–402). Toronto: University of Toronto Press.

Kagan, J. (1987). Introduction. In J. Kagan & S. Lamb (Eds.), *The emergence of morality in young children* (pp. ix–xx). Chicago: The University of Chicago

Kagan, S. L., & Newton, J. W. (1989). For-profit and non-profit child care: Similarities and differences. *Young Children, 44*(6), 4–10.

Kamii, C. (1982). *Number in preschool and kindergarten.* Washington, DC: National Association for the Education of Young Children.

Kamii, C. (1984). Obedience is not enough. *Young Children, 39*(4), 11–14.

Kamii, C. (Ed.). (1990). *Achievement testing in the early grades: The games grown-ups play.* Washington, DC: National Association for the Education of Young Children.

Kamii, C. K., & DeClark, G. (1985). *Young children reinvent arithmetic: Implications of Piaget's theory.* New York: Teachers College Press, Columbia

Kamii, C., & DeVries, R. (1980). *Group games in early childhood.* Washington, DC: National Association for the Education of Young Children.

Kamii, C., & Lee-Katz, L. (1982). Physics in preschool education: A Piagetian approach. In J. F. Brown (Ed.), *Curriculum planning for young children* (pp. 171–176). Washington, DC: National Association for the Education of Young Children.

Kaplan, P. (1991). *A child's odyssey* (2nd ed.). St. Paul, MN: West Publishing.

Karnes, M. (1969). *Research and development project on preschool disadvantaged children.* Washington, DC: U.S. Office of Education.

Karnes, M., & Lee, R. C. (1979). Mainstreaming in the preschool. In L. G.

Karnes, M., Shwedel, A., & Williams, M. (1983). A comparison of five approaches for educating young children from low-income homes. In The Consortium for Longitudinal Studies, *As the twig is bent … Lasting effects of preschool programs.* Hillsdale, NJ: Lawrence Erlbaum Associates.

Katz, L. G. (1972). *Teacher-child relationships in day care centres.* ERIC document #046 494.

Katz, L. G. (1977). *Talks with teachers: Reflections on early childhood education.* Washington, DC: National Association for the Education of Young Children.

Katz, L. G. (1980). Mothering and teaching: Some significant distinctions. In L. G. Katz (Ed.), *Current topics in early childhood education* (Vol. 3, pp. 47–63). Norwood, NJ: Ablex Publishing.

Katz, L. G. (1984a). The education of preprimary teachers. In L. G. Katz (Ed.), *Current topics in early childhood education* (Vol. 5, pp. 209–227). Norwood, NJ: Ablex Publishing Corp.

Katz, L. G. (1984b). The professional early childhood teacher. *Young Children, 39*(5), 3–10.

Katz, L. G. (1988). Where is early childhood education? In B. Spodek, O. N. Saracho, & D. L. Peters (Eds.), *Professionalism and the early childhood practitioner* (pp. 75–83). New York: Teachers College Press, Columbia University.

Katz, L. G. (1989). *Engaging children's minds: The project approach*. Norwood, NJ: Ablex Publishing Corp.

Katz, L. G. (1998). What can we learn from Reggio Emilia? In C. Edwards, L. Gandini, & G. Forman (Eds.), *The hundred languages of children: The Reggio Emilia approach—Advanced reflections* (2nd ed., pp. 27–45). Greenwich, CT: Ablex Publishing.

Katz, L. G. (Ed.). (1981). *Current topics in early childhood education* (Vol. 2, pp. 13–42). Norwood, NJ: Ablex Publishing.

Katz, L. G., & Chard, S. (1993). The project approach. In J. L. Roopnarine & J. E. Johnson (Eds.), *Approaches to early childhood education* (2nd ed.) (pp. 209–222). Columbus, OH: Merrill Publishing Co.

Katz, L. G., & Chard, S. C. (2000). *Engaging children's minds: The project approach* (2nd ed.). Stamford, CT: Ablex Publishing.

Katz, L. G., Evangelou, D., & Hartman, J. A. (1990). *The case for mixed-age grouping in early education*. Washington, DC: National Association for the Education of Young Children.

Katz, P. A. (1982). Children's racial awareness and intergroup attitudes. In L. G. Katz (Ed.), *Current topics in early childhood education* (Vol. 4, pp. 17–54). Norwood, NJ: Ablex Publishing Corp.

Katz, P. A. (1983). Developmental foundations of gender and racial attitudes. In R. L. Leahy (Ed.), *The child's construction of social inequality* (pp. 41–78). New York: Academic Press.

Katz, P. A. (1986). Modification of children's gender-stereotyped behaviour: General issues and research considerations. *Sex Roles, 14*, 591–602.

Keats, E. J. (1967). *Peter's chair*. New York: Harper and Row.

Keele, V. S. (1966). Individual-time formula: The golden formula for raising happy secure children. Unpublished paper.

Kellogg, R. (1969). *Analyzing children's art*. Palo Alto, CA: Mayfield Publishing Co.

Kelly, F. J. (1981). Guiding groups of parents of young children. *Young Children, 37*(1), 28–32.

Kelly, J. (1989). *Early, middle, or late immersion?* Unpublished master's thesis, Brock University, St. Catharines, ON.

Kempe, R. S., & Kempe, C. H. (1978). *Child abuse*. Cambridge, MA: Harvard University Press.

Keogh, J., & Sugden, D. (1985). *Movement skill development*. New York: Macmillan Publishing Co.

Kersey, K. (1985). *Helping your child handle stress: The parents' guide to recognizing and solving childhood problems*. New York: Acropolis.

Kessen, W. (1965). *The child*. New York: Wiley.

Ketchel, J. A. (1986). Helping the young child cope with death. *Day Care and Early Childhood, 14*(2), 24–27.

Kids freed from carpet factories join protest against child labor. (1993, February 16). *St. Catharines Standard*, p. C10.

Kilpatrick, W. H. (1914). *The Montessori system examined*. Boston: Houghton Mifflin.

Kinsman, C. A., & Berk, L. E. (1982). Joining the block and housekeeping areas. In J. F. Brown (Ed.), *Curriculum planning for young children* (pp. 28–37). Washington, DC: National Association for the Education of Young Children.

Kleckner, K. A., & Engel, R. E. (1988). A child begins school: Relieving anxiety with books. *Young Children, 43*(5), 14–18.

Klein, J. O. (1986). Infectious disease and day care. In M. T. Osterhold, J. O. Klein, S. S. Aronson, & L. K. Pickering (Eds.), *Infectious diseases in child day care: Management and prevention*. Chicago, IL: University of Chicago Press, 9–13.

Kohlberg, L. (1966). A cognitive-developmental analysis of children's sex-role concepts and attitudes. In E. E. Maccoby (Ed.), *The development of sex differences* (pp. 82–173). Stanford, CA: Stanford University Press.

Kohlberg, L. (1969). Stages and sequence: The cognitive development approach to socialization. In D. A. Goslin (Ed.), *Handbook of socialization theory and research* (pp. 347–480). Chicago: Rand McNally.

Kontos, S. (1986). What preschool children know about reading and how they learn it. *Young Children, 42*(1), 58–66.

Kontos, S., & Fiene, R. (1986). *Predictors of quality and children's development in day care.* Unpublished manuscript. Harrisburg, PA: Pennsylvania State University.

Kontos, S., & Fiene, R. (1987). Child care quality: Compliance with regulations and children's development: The Pennsylvania Study. In D. Philips (Ed.), *Quality in child care: What does the research tell us?* (pp. 57–79). Washington, DC: National Association for the Education of Young Children.

Kontos, S., Howes, C., & Galinsky, E. (1996). Does training make a difference to quality in family child care? *Early childhood Research Quarterly, 11,* 427–445.

Kontos, S., Howes, C., Shinn, M., & Galinsky, E. (1995). *Quality in family child care and relative care.* New York: Teachers College Press.

Kopp, C. B. (1982). Antecedents of self-regulation: A developmental perspective. *Developmental Psychology, 18,* 199–214.

Kostelnik, M. J., Whiren, A. P., & Stein, L. C. (1986). Living with He-man. *Young Children, 42,* 3–9.

Kounin, J. S., & Sherman, L. W. (1979). School environments as behaviour settings. *Theory into Practice, 18*(3), 145–151.

Kritchevsky, S., Prescott, E., & Walling, L. (1977). *Planning environments for young children: Physical space.* Washington, DC: National Association for the Education of Young Children.

Krogh, S. L., & Lamme, L. L. (1985). "But what about sharing?" Children's literature and moral development. *Young Children, 40*(4), 48–51.

Kubler-Ross, E. (1969). *On death and dying.* New York: Macmillan.

Kushner, D. (1989). "Put your name on your painting, but … the blocks go back on the shelves." *Young Children, 45*(1), 49–56.

Kyle, I. (1992a). Addendum: Child care in Ontario, 1988–1990. In A. Pence (Ed.), *Canadian child care in context: Perspectives from the provinces and terri-* tories. Ottawa: Statistics Canada & Health and Welfare Canada.

Kyle, I. (1992b). An historical overview of child care in Ontario. In A. Pence (Ed.), *Canadian child care in context: Perspectives from the provinces and territories.* Ottawa: Statistics Canada & Health and Welfare Canada.

Kyle, I. (1992c). An overview of child care legislation, programs and funding in Ontario. In A. Pence (Ed.), *Canadian child care in context: Perspectives from the provinces and territories.* Ottawa: Statistics Canada & Health and Welfare Canada.

Kyle, I. (1992d). A socio-geographic overview of Ontario. In A. Pence (Ed.), *Canadian child care in context: Perspectives from the provinces and territories.* Ottawa: Statistics Canada & Health and Welfare Canada.

Labi, N. (1998). Burning out at 9? *Time, 44,* 152.

Labov, W. (1970). *The study of nonstandard English.* Urbana, IL: National Council of Teachers of English.

Lally, J. R., Mangione, P. L., & Honig, A. S. (1988). The Syracuse University Family Development Research Program: Long-range impact on an early intervention with low-income children and their families. In D. R. Powell (Ed.), *Emerging directions in parent-child intervention* (pp. 79–104). Norwood, NJ: Ablex Publishing Corp.

Lamb, M. E., & Bornstein, M. H. (1987). *Development in infancy: An introduction.* New York: Random House.

Lambert, W. (1977). The effects of bilingualism on the individual: Cognitive and sociocultural consequences. In P. Hornby (Ed.), *Bilingualism: Psychological, social and educational implications.* New York: Academic Press.

Lambert-Lagace, L. (1983). *Feeding your child: From infancy to six years.* New York: Beaufort Books, Inc.

Landsberg, Michelle. (2001, May 19). *The Toronto Star.*

Langenbach, M., & Neskora, T. W. (1977). *Day care curriculum considerations.* Columbus, OH: Charles E. Merrill Publishing Co.

Larsen, J. M., & Robinson, C. C. (1989). Later effects of preschool on low-risk children. *Early Childhood Research Quarterly, 4,* 133–144.

Laughing all the way. (1988). *Young Children, 43*(2), 39–41.

Lavatelli, C. S. (1970). *Piaget's theory applied to an early childhood curriculum.* Boston, MA: American Science and Engineering, Inc.

Lawton, J. T. (1988). *Introduction to child care and early childhood education.* Glenview, IL: Scott, Foresman & Co.

Lay-Dopyera, M., & Dopyera, J. (1987b). *Becoming a teacher of young children* (3rd ed.). New York: Random House.

Lay-Dopyera, M., & Dopyera, J. E. (1987a). Strategies for teaching. In C. Seefeldt (Ed.), *The early childhood curriculum: A review of current research* (pp. 13–33). New York: Teachers College Press, Columbia University.

Lazar, I., & Darlington, R. (1982). Lasting effects of early education: A report from the Consortium for Longitudinal Studies. *Monographs of the Society for research in Child Development, 47*(2–3, Serial No. 195).

Lee, V. E., Brooks-Gunn, J., Schnur, E., & Liaw, F. R. (1990). Are Head Start effects sustained? A longitudinal followup comparison of disadvantaged children attending Head Start, no preschool and other preschool programs. *Child Development, 61,* 495–507.

Lennenberg, E. H. (1967). *Biological foundations of language.* New York: John Wiley & Sons, Inc.

Lepper, M. R., Greene, D., & Nisbett, R. E. (1973). Undermining children's intrinsic interest with extrinsic reward: A test of the "overjustification" hypothesis. *Journal of Personality and Social Psychology, 28,* 129–137.

Lero, D. S. (1994). In transition: Changing patterns of work, family life, child care ideas. *The Journal of Emotional Well Being in Child Care, 1*(3), 11–14.

LeShan, E. J. (1968). *The conspiracy against children.* New York: Athenaeum.

Levinger, G., & Levinger, A. C. (1986). The temporal course of close relationships: Some thoughts about the development of children's ties. In W. W. Hartup & Z. Rubin (Eds.), *Relationships and development* (pp. 111–133). Hillsdale, NJ: Lawrence Erlbaum Associates, Publishers.

Levinson, D. J. (1978). *The seasons of a man's life.* New York: Alfred Knopf.

Lexmond, T. (1987). Temper tantrums. In A. Thomas & J. Grimes (Eds.), *Children's needs: Psychological perspectives* (pp. 627–633). Washington, DC: National Association of School Psychologists.

Lieberman, A. F. (1994). *The emotional life of the toddler.* New York: The Free Press.

Liebert, R. M., & Sprafkin, J. N. (1988). *The early window: Effects of television on children and youth* (3rd ed.). New York: Pergamon Press.

Lillard, P. P. (1973). *Montessori: A modern approach.* New York: Schocken Books.

Lindauer, S.L.K. (1987). Montessori education for young children. In J. L. Roopnarine & J. E. Johnson (Eds.), *Approaches to early childhood education* (pp. 109–126). Columbus, OH: Merrill Publishing Co.

Lindauer, S.L.K. (1993). Montessori education for young children. In J. L. Roopnarine & J. E. Johnson (Eds.), *Approaches to early childhood education* (2nd ed.) (pp. 243–260). Columbus, OH: Merrill Publishing Co.

Linderman, C. E. (1979). *Teachables from trashables: Homemade toys that teach.* St. Paul, MN: Toys 'n Things Training and Resource Centre, Inc.

Lindfors, J. W. (1987). *Children's language and learning* (2nd ed.). Englewood Cliffs, NJ: Prentice-Hall, Inc.

Lombardi, J. (1986). Training for public policy and advocacy: An emerging topic in teacher education. *Young Children, 41*(4), 65–69.

Lombardi, J. (1990). Developing a coalition to reach the full cost of quality. In B. Willer (Ed.), *Reaching the full cost of quality in early childhood programs* (pp. 87–96). Washington, DC: National Association for the Education of Young Children.

Long, S. M. (1985). Mobile lifestyles: Creating change and adaptation for children and adults. *Dimensions, 13*(2), 7–11.

Lovell, P., & Harms, T. (1985). How can playgrounds be improved? A rating scale. *Young Children, 35*(2), 3–8.

Lowenfeld, V. (1962). Creativity: Education's stepchild. In S. Parnes & H. Harding (Eds.), *A sourcebook for creative thinking* (pp. 9–17). New York: Charles Scribner's Sons.

Lozoff, B. (1989). Nutrition and behaviour. *American Psychologist, 44,* 231–236.

Lutes, D. (1992). An overview of child care legislation in New Brunswick. In A. Pence (Ed.), *Canadian child care in context: Perspectives from the provinces and territories.* Ottawa: Statistics Canada & Health and Welfare Canada.

Lutes, D., & Gamble, J. (1992). Addendum: Child care in New Brunswick, 1988–1990. In A. Pence (Ed.), *Canadian child care in context: Perspectives from the provinces and territories.* Ottawa: Statistics Canada & Health and Welfare Canada.

Lyon, M., & Canning, P. (1995). *The Atlantic day care study.* St. John's, NF: Memorial University of Newfoundland.

Maccoby, E. E. (1990). Gender and relationships. *American Psychologist, 45,* 513–520.

Maccoby, E. E., & Jacklin, C. N. (1987). Gender segregation in childhood. In H. W. Reese (Ed.), *Advances in child development and behaviour* (Vol. 20, pp. 239–288). New York: Academic Press.

Maccoby, E. E., & Martin, J. A. (1983). Socialization in the context of the family: Parent-child interaction. In E. M. Hetherington (Ed.), *Handbook of child psychology* (4th ed.): *Vol. 4. Socialization, personality, and social development* (pp. 1–101). New York: John Wiley & Sons.

Maccoby, E., & Jacklin, C. (1974). *The psychology of sex differences.* Stanford, CA: Stanford University Press.

Mace, F. C., Page, T. J., Ivancic, M. T., & O'Brien, S. (1986). Effectiveness of brief time-out with and without contingent delay: A comparative analysis. *Journal of Applied Behaviour Analysis, 19,* 79–86.

Machado, J. M. (1985). *Early childhood experiences in language arts* (3rd ed.). Albany, NY: Delmar Publishers Inc.

Maier, H. W. (1965). *Three theories of child development.* New York: Harper and Row.

Maier, H. W. (1990). Erikson's developmental theory. In R. M. Thomas (Ed.), *The encyclopedia of human development and education: Theory, research, and studies* (pp. 88–93). New York: Pergamon Press.

Malaguzzi, L. (1993). A bill of three rights in innovations in early education. *The International Reggio Exchange, 2*(1), 9.

Malaguzzi, L. (1998). History, ideas, and basic philosophy: An interview with Lella Gandini (L. Gandini, Trans.). In C. Edwards, L. Gandini, & G. Forman (Eds.), *The hundred languages of children: The Reggio Emilia approach—Advanced reflections* (2nd ed., pp. 49–96). Greenwich, CT: Ablex Publishing.

Marcotte, R., & Young, R. (1992). *The effects of changing themes on children's play in the drama centre.* Unpublished manuscript. Brock University, St. Catharines, ON.

Mardell-Czudnowski, C. D., & Goldenberg, D. S. (1983). *Developmental Indicators for the Assessment of Learning—Revised (DIAL-R).* Edison, NJ: Childcraft Education Corp.

Marion, M. (1999). *Guidance of young children* (5th ed.). Upper Saddle River, NJ: Prentice Hall.

Marotz, L. R., Rush, J. M., & Cross, M. Z. (1989). *Health, safety, and nutrition for the young child.* Albany, NY: Delmar Publishers Inc.

Marshall, H. H. (1989). The development of self-concept. *Young Children, 44*(5), 44–51.

Maslow, A. (1970). *Motivation and personality.* New York: Harper & Row.

Mattingly, M. (1977). Introduction to symposium: Stress and burnout in child care. *Child Care Quarterly, 6,* 127–137.

Mauch, D. (1992a). Addendum: Child care in Yukon, 1988–1990. In A. Pence (Ed.), *Canadian child care in context: Perspectives from the provinces and territories.* Ottawa: Statistics Canada & Health and Welfare Canada.

Mauch, D. (1992b). An overview of child care legislation in Yukon. In A. Pence (Ed.), *Canadian child care in context: Perspectives from the provinces and territories*. Ottawa: Statistics Canada & Health and Welfare Canada.

Mauch, D. (1992c). A socio-geographic overview of Yukon. In A. Pence (Ed.), *Canadian child care in context: Perspectives from the provinces and territories*. Ottawa: Statistics Canada & Health and Welfare Canada.

Mavrogenes, N. A. (1990). Helping parents help their children become literate. *Young Children, 45*(4), 4–9.

Maxim, George (1989). *The very young* (3rd ed.). Columbus, OH: Merrill Publishing Co.

May, K. A., & Perrin, S. P. (1985). Prelude: Pregnancy and birth. In S.M.H. Hanson & F. W. Bozett (Eds.), *Dimensions of fatherhood*. Beverly Hills, CA: Sage.

Mayesky, M. (1990). *Creative activities for young children* (4th ed.). Albany, NY: Delmar Publishers Inc.

Mayfield, M. (1990). *Work-related child care in Canada*. Ottawa: Labour Canada.

McAfee, O. D. (1985). Circle time: Getting past "two little pumpkins." *Young Children, 40*(6), 24–29.

McCain, M. N., & Mustard, J. F. (1999). *Early Years Study: Reversing the real brain drain*. Toronto: Publications Ontario.

McCarthy, D. (1972). *Manual for the McCarthy Scales of children's abilities*. New York: Psychological Corp.

McCaughey, W. G. (1997). *Multiple intelligences: An introduction to the work of Howard Gardner. A workshop for adult learners*. Brock University, St. Catharines, ON.

McCracken, J. B. (Ed.). (1986). *Reducing stress in young children's Lives*. Washington, DC: National Association for the Education of Young Children.

McCreary, D. R. (1997). Media influences. In S. W. Sadava & D. R. McCreary (Eds.), *Applied social psychology*. Upper Saddle River, NJ: Prentice Hall.

McDonald, D. T., & Ramsey, J. H. (1982). Awakening the artist: Music for young children. In J. F. Brown (Ed.), *Curriculum planning for young children* (pp. 187–193). Washington, DC: National Association for the Education of Young Children.

McDonell, L. (1992). An historical overview of child care in British Columbia. In A. Pence (Ed.), *Canadian child care in context: Perspectives from the provinces and territories*. Ottawa: Statistics Canada & Health and Welfare Canada.

McDonell, L., & Griffin, S. (1992). An overview of child care legislation in British Columbia. In A. Pence (Ed.), *Canadian child care in context: Perspectives from the provinces and territories*. Ottawa: Statistics Canada & Health and Welfare Canada.

McIntosh, A., & Rauhala, A. (February 3, 4, 6–8, 1989). Who's minding the children? *The Globe and Mail*. Toronto, ON.

McIntyre, M. (1984). *Early childhood and science*. Washington, DC: National Science Teachers Association.

McLaughlin, B. (1984). *Second-language acquisition in childhood: Preschool children* (Vol. 1, 2nd ed.).

McMillan, M. (1919). *The nursery school*. London: J. M. Dent & Sons.

McMillan, M. (1930). *The nursery school* (rev. ed.). London: J. M. Dent & Sons.

McTear, M. (1985). *Children's conversations*. Oxford England: Basil Blackwell.

McWilliams, M. (1986). *Nutrition for the growing years*. New York: John Wiley & Sons.

Mead, M., & Metraux, R. (1993). A new understanding of childhood. In R. H. Wozniak (Ed.), *Worlds of childhood*. New York: Harper Collins College Press.

Meddin, B. J., & Rosen, A. L. (1986). Child abuse and neglect: Prevention and reporting. *Young Children, 41*(4), 26–30.

Medeiros, D. C., Porter, B. J., & Welch, I. D. (1983). *Children under stress*. Englewood Cliffs, NJ: Prentice-Hall, Inc.

Meisels, S. J. (1986). Testing four- and five-year-olds: Response to Salzer and to Shepard and Smith. *Educational Leadership, 44*(3), 90–92.

Meisels, S. J., Liaw, F., Dorfman, A., & Nelson, R. F. (1995). The work sampling system: Reliability and validity of a performance assessment for young children. *Early Childhood Research Quarterly, 10,* 277–296.

Miesels, S., & Sternberg, S. (1989, June). Quality sacrificed in proprietary child care. *Education Week,* p. 36.

Miezitis, S. (1972). The Montessori method: Some recent research. *American Montessori Society Bulletin, 10*(2).

Milkovich, G., & Gomez, L. (1976). Day care and selected employee work behaviours. *Academy of Management Journal, 19,* 111–115.

Miller, C. S. (1984). Building self-control: Discipline for young children. *Young Children, 40*(1), 15–19.

Miller, G. A., & Gildea, P. M. (1987, September). How children learn words. *Scientific American,* pp. 94–99.

Miller, L. B., & Bizzell, R. P. (1983). Long-term effects of four preschool programs: Sixth, seventh, and eighth grade. *Child Development, 54,* 727–741.

Miller, L. B., & Dyer, J. L. (1975). Four preschool programs: Their dimensions and effects. *Monographs of the Society for Research on Child Development* (5–6, Serial No. 162).

Minuchin, P. (1987). Schools, families, and the development of young children. *Early Childhood Research Quarterly, 2,* 245–254.

Mitchell, A., & Modigliani, K. (1989). Young children in public schools? The only ifs reconsidered. *Young Children, 44*(6), 56–61.

Monighan-Nourot, P. (1990). The legacy of play in American early childhood education. In E. Klugman & S. Smilansky (Eds.), *Children's play and learning* (pp. 59–85). New York: Teachers College Press.

Montessori, M. (1965). *The Montessori method* (A. E. George, Trans.). Cambridge, MA: Robert Bentley (Original work published 1912).

Montessori, M. (1967). *The absorbent mind* (A. Claremont, Trans.). New York: Holt, Rinehart & Winston.

Moore, R. C., Goltsman, S. M., & Iacofano, D. S. (1987). *Play for all guidelines: Planning, design and management of outdoor play settings for all children.* Berkeley, CA: MIG Communications.

Moore, S. G. (1982). Prosocial behaviour in the early years: Parent and peer influences. In B. Spodek (Ed.), *Handbook of research in early childhood education.* New York: Free Press.

Morado, C. (1986). Prekindergarten programs for 4-year-olds. *Young Children, 41*(5), 61–63.

Morgan, E. L. (1989). Talking with parents when concerns come up. *Young Children, 44*(2), 52–56.

Morin, J. (1989). We can force a solution to the staffing crisis. *Young Children, 44*(6), 18–19.

Morrison, G. (1984). *Early childhood education today* (3rd ed.). New York: Merrill.

Morrison, G. (1991). *Early childhood education today* (5th ed.). New York: Merrill.

Morrison, G. (2001). *Early childhood education today* (8th ed.). New York: Merrill.

Morrison, G. S. (1988). *Education and development of infants, toddlers, and preschoolers.* Glenview, IL: Scott, Foresman/Little, Brown College Division.

Morrow, R. D. (1989). What's in a name? In particular, a Southeast Asian name? *Young Children, 44*(6), 20–23.

Moskowitz, B. A. (1982). The acquisition of language. In *Human communication: Language and its psychobiological bases: Readings from Scientific American* (pp. 121–132). San Francisco, CA: W. H. Freeman & Co.

Mullen, S. (1992). A socio-geographic overview of Prince Edward Island. In A. Pence (Ed.), *Canadian child care in context: Perspectives from the provinces and territories.* Ottawa: Statistics Canada & Health and Welfare Canada.

Munro, J. G. (1986). Movement education: Balance. *Day Care and Early Education, 14*(2), 28–31.

Mussen, P. H., Conger, J. J., Kagan, J., & Huston, A. C. (1990). *Child development and personality* (7th ed.). New York: Harper & Row, Publishers.

Mussen, P., & Eisenberg-Berg, N. (1977). *Roots of caring, sharing, and helping: The development of pro-social behaviour in children*. San Francisco: W. H. Freeman and Co.

Musson, S. (1994). *School-age care*. Don Mills, ON: Addison-Wesley.

Myers, B. K., & Maurer, K. (1987). Teaching with less talking: Learning centres in the kindergarten. *Young Children, 42*(5), 20–27.

Myers-Walls, J. A., & Fry-Miller, K. M. (1984). Nuclear war: Helping children overcome fears. *Young Children, 39*(4), 27–32.

NAEYC (National Association for the Education of Young Children). (1988). Position statement on standardized testing of young children 3 through 8 years of age. *Young Children, 43*(3), 42–47.

NAEYC Information Service. (1990). *Employer-assisted child care: An NAEYC resource guide*. Washington, DC: National Association for the Education of Young Children.

NAEYC. (1989a). *Developmentally Appropriate Practice in Early Childhood Programs Serving Infants*. Washington, DC: National Association for the Education of Young Children.

NAEYC. (1989b). *Developmentally Appropriate Practice in Early Childhood Programs Serving Toddlers*. Washington, DC: National Association for the Education of Young Children.

NAEYC. (1993). Position statement on violence in the lives of children. *Young Children 49*(3), 68–77.

NAEYC. (1996). NAEYC position statement: Responding to linguistic and cultural diversity—Recommendations for effective early childhood education. *Young Children, 51*(2), 4–12.

NAEYC. (1996b). NAEYC position statement: Responding to linguistic and cultural diversity—recommendations for effective early childhood education. *Young Children, 51*(2), 4–12.

NAEYC. (1996c). NAEYC position statement: Technology and young children—ages three through eight. *Young Children, 51*(6), 11–16.

Napier-Anderson, L. (1981). *Change: One step at a time*. Toronto, ON: Faculty of Education, University of Toronto.

National Child Care Information Centre, Child Care Programs Division (1991). *The status of day care in Canada 1990*. Ottawa: Minister of Health and Welfare.

National Child Care Staffing Study (1989). *Who cares? Child care teachers and the quality of child care in America*. Child Care Employee Project. Oakland, CA: National Child Care Staffing Study.

National Council of Welfare (1988). *Childcare: A better alternative*. Ottawa: Supply and Services.

National Council of Welfare (1990). *Women and poverty revisited*. Ottawa: Supply and Services.

National Dairy Council (1980). *Food … Early choices: A nutrition learning system for early childhood*. Rosemont, IL: National Dairy Council.

National Guide. (1996). *College and University Programs, 1996*. Ottawa: Public Works and Government Services Canada.

National Institutes of Health. (1999, November 7). *Only small link found between hours in child care and mother-child interaction*. Retrieved March 8, 2002 from www.nichd.nih.gov/new/releases/timein-childcare.htm.

National Longitudinal Survey of Children and Youth. (1996). *Growing up in Canada* (Catalogue No. 89-550-MPE, No. 1). Ottawa: Statistics Canada.

Nauta, M. J., & Hewett, K. (1988). Studying complexity: The case of the child and family resource program. In H. B. Weiss & F. H. Jacobs (Eds.), *Evaluating family programs* (pp. 389–405). New York: Aldine de Gruyter.

Neisworth, J., & Buggey, T. (1993). Behavior analysis in early childhood education. In J. L. Roopnarine & J. E. Johnson (Eds.), *Approaches to early childhood education* (2nd ed.) (pp. 113–136). New York: Merrill.

Neugebauer, R. (1988, January). How's business? Status report #4 on for profit child care. *Child Care Information Exchange*, pp. 29–34.

Neugebauer, R. (1991, January/February). How's business? Status report #7 on for profit child care. *Child Care Information Exchange*, pp. 46–50.

Niagara Early Childhood Mentoring Program. (1997). Information package. St. Catharines, ON: Early Childhood Community Development Centre.

NICHD (National Institute of Child Health and Human Development) Early Child Care Research Network. (1994). Child care and child development: The NICHD study of early child care. In S. L. Friedman and H. C. Haywood (Eds.), *Development follow-up: Concepts, domains, and methods* (pp. 377–396). San Diego, CA: Academic Press.

NICHD Early Child Care Research Network. (1996). Characteristics of infant child care: Factors contributing to positive caregiving. *Early Childhood Research Quarterly, 11,* 269–306.

Norris, D., & Boucher, J. (1980). *Observing children.* Toronto: Board of Education for the City of Toronto.

Northway, M. (1973). Child study in Canada: A casual history. In L. Brockman, J. Whiteley, & J. Zubek (Eds.), *Child development.* Toronto: McClelland & Stewart.

Nova Scotia government promises more money for day cares, child development. (2001, March 5) *Halifax Chronicle Herald.*

Noyes, D. (1987). Indoor pollutants: Environmental hazards to young children. *Young Children, 42*(6), 57–65.

Nurss, J. R., & McGauvran, M. E. (1986). *Metropolitan readiness assessment program* (5th ed.). Orlando, FL: Harcourt Brace Jovanovich.

Nykyforuk, J. (1992a). An historical overview of child care in Saskatchewan. In A. Pence (Ed.), *Canadian child care in context: Perspectives from the provinces and territories.* Ottawa: Statistics Canada & Health and Welfare Canada.

Nykyforuk, J. (1992b). A socio-geographic overview of Saskatchewan. In A. Pence (Ed.), *Canadian child care in context: Perspectives from the provinces and territories.* Ottawa: Statistics Canada & Health and Welfare Canada.

Obler, L. K. (1985). Language through the life-span. In J. B. Gleason (Ed.), *The development of language* (pp. 277–305). Columbus, OH: Charles E. Merrill Publishing Co.

Oden, S. (1982). Peer relationship development in childhood. In L. G. Katz (Ed.), *Current topics in early childhood education* (Vol. 4, pp. 87–118). Norwood, NJ: Ablex Publishing Corp.

Oken-Wright, P. (1988). Show-and-tell grows up. *Young Children, 43*(2), 52–58.

Ontario (1965, June 2). *Proceedings of the legislature* (pp. 3582–3583).

Ontario. (1987). *Throne speech.* Toronto: Queen's Printer.

Ontario. (1988). *Day nurseries act.* Revised statutes of Ontario, 1980, Chapter 111 and Ontario regulation 760/83 as amended to Ontario Regulation 143/88. Toronto: Queen's Printer.

Orlick, T. (1978a). *The cooperative sports and games book: Challenge without competition.* New York: Pantheon Books.

Orlick, T. (1978b). *Winning through cooperation.* Washington, DC: Acropolis Books, Ltd.

Orlick, T. (1982). *The second cooperative sports game books.* New York: Pantheon Books.

Owens, R. E. (1984). *Language development: An introduction.* Columbus, OH: Charles E. Merrill Publishing Co.

Paley, V. G. (1995). *Kwanzaa and me: A teacher's story.* Cambridge, MA: Harvard University Press.

Paley, V. G. (1999). *The kindness of children.* Cambridge, MA: Harvard University Press.

Papalia, D. E., Olds, S. W., & Feldman, R. D. (1999). *A child's world: Infancy through adolescence* (8th ed.). Toronto: McGraw-Hill.

Parke, R. D., & Slaby, R. G. (1983). The development of aggression. In P. H. Mussen (Ed.), *Handbook of child psychology* (4th ed.): *Vol. 4. Socialization, personality, and social development* (pp. 547–641). New York: John Wiley & Sons.

Parker, J. G., & Gottman, J. M. (1989). Social and emotional development in a relational context. In T. J. Berndt & G. W. Ladd (Eds.), *Peer relationships in child development* (pp. 95–131). New York: John Wiley & Sons.

Parten, M. B. (1932). Social participation among preschool children. *Journal of Abnormal and Social Psychology, 27,* 243–269.

Patterson, G. R. (1982). *Coercive family practices.* Eugene, OR: Castalia Press.

Patterson, G. R. (1982). *Coercive family practices.* Eugene, OR: Castalia Press.

Patterson, G. R., & Gullion, M. E. (1971). *Living with children: New methods for parents and teachers.* Champaign, IL: Research Press.

Patterson, G. R., DeBaryshe, B. D., & Ramsey, E. (1989). A developmental perspective on antisocial behaviour. *American Psychologist, 44,* 329–335.

Pease, D., & Gleason, J. B. (1985). Gaining meaning: Semantic development. In J. B. Gleason (Ed.), *The development of language* (pp. 103–138). Columbus, OH: Charles E. Merrill Publishing Co.

Peisner-Feinberg, E. S., & Burchinal, M. R. (1997). Relations between preschool children's child-care experiences and concurrent development: The cost, quality, outcomes study. *Merrill-Palmer Quarterly, 43,* 451–447.

Peisner-Feinberg, E. S., Burchinal, M. R., Clifford, R. M., Culkin, M. L., Howes, C., & Kagan, S. L. (1999). *The children of the cost, quality and outcomes student go to school.* Executive summary. Chapel Hill, NC: Frank Porter Graham Child Development Center, University of North Carolina at Chapel Hill.

Pence, A. (1990). The child care profession in Canada. In Doxey, I. (Ed.), *Child care and education: Canadian dimensions* (pp. 87–97). Toronto: Nelson Canada.

Pence, A. (1992a). *Canadian child care in context: Perspectives from the provinces and territories* (pp.

xiii–xvii). Ottawa: Statistics Canada & Health and Welfare Canada.

Pence, A. (Ed.). (1992b). *Canadian child care in context: Perspectives from the provinces and territories.* Ottawa: Statistics Canada & Health and Welfare Canada.

Pence, A., & Moss, P. (1994). Towards an inclusionary approach in defining quality in valuing quality. In P. Moss & A. Pence (Eds.), *Early childhood services* (pp. 1–9). New York: Teachers College Press, Columbia University.

Pence, A., Read, M., Lero, D., Goelman, H., & Brockman, L. (1992). An overview of the NCCS data for British Columbia. In A. Pence (Ed.), *Canadian child care in context: Perspectives from the provinces and territories* (pp. 65–86). Ottawa: Statistics Canada & Health and Welfare Canada.

Peters, D. L. (1988). The Child Development Associate credential and the educationally disenfranchised. In B. Spodek, O. N. Saracho, & D. L. Peters (Eds.), *Professionalism and the early childhood practitioner* (pp. 93–104). New York: Teachers College Press, Columbia University.

Peters, D. L., Neisworth, J. T., & Yawkey, T. D. (1985). *Early childhood education: From theory to practice.* Monterey, CA: Brooks/Cole Publishing Co.

Phenice, L., & Hildebrand, L. (1988). Multicultural education: A pathway to global harmony. *Day Care and Early Education, 16*(2), 15–17.

Philips, D., Howes, C., & Whitebook, M. (1991). Child care as an adult work environment. *Journal of Social Issues, 47,* 49–70.

Phillips, D. A. (1987). *Quality in child care: What does research tell us?* Washington, DC: National Association for the Education of Young Children.

Phillips, D. A., & Howes, C. (1987). Indicators of quality child care: Review of research. In D. A. Phillips (Ed.), *Quality in child care: What does research tell us?* (pp. 1–20). Washington, DC: National Association for the Education of Young Children.

Phillips, D. A., Scarr, S., & McCartney, K. (1987). Dimensions and effects of child care quality: The

Bermuda Study. In D. A. Phillips (Ed.), *Quality in child care: What does research tell us?* (pp. 43–56). Washington, DC: National Association for the Education of Young Children.

Phillips, D., & Whitebook, M. (1986). Who are child care workers? The search for answers. *Young Children, 41*(4), 14–20.

Phyfe-Perkins, E. (1980). Children's behaviour in preschool settings: A review of research concerning the influence of the physical environment. In L. G. Katz (Ed.), *Current topics in early childhood education* (Vol. 3, pp. 91–125). Norwood, NJ: Ablex Publishing Corp.

Piaget, J. (1926). *The language and thought of the child.* London: Routledge & Kegan Paul.

Piaget, J. (1932). *The moral judgment of the child.* New York: Harcourt, Brace & World.

Piaget, J. (1951). *Play, dreams, and imitation in childhood.* New York: Norton.

Piaget, J. (1983). Piaget's theory. In P. H. Mussen (Ed.), *Handbook of child psychology* (4th ed.): *Vol. 1. History, theory, and methods* (pp. 103–128). New York: John Wiley and Sons.

Pipes, P. L. (1989a). Between infancy and adolescence. In P. L. Pipes (Ed.), *Nutrition in infancy and childhood* (4th ed., pp. 120–142). St. Louis, MO: C. V. Mosby Co.

Pipes, P. L. (1989b). Special concerns of dietary intake during infancy and childhood. In P. L. Pipes (Ed.), *Nutrition in infancy and childhood* (4th ed., pp. 268–300). St. Louis, MO: C. V. Mosby.

Plomin, R., & Daniels, D. (1986). Genetics and shyness. In W. H. Jones, J. M. Cheek, & S. R. Briggs (Eds.), *Shyness: Perspectives on research and treatment* (pp. 63–80). New York: Plenum Press.

Poest, C. A., Williams, J. R., Witt, D. D., & Atwood, M. E. (1989). Physical activity patterns of preschool children. *Early Childhood Research Quarterly, 65,* 367–376.

Poest, C. A., Williams, J. R., Witt, D. D., & Atwood, M. E. (1990). Challenge me to move: Large muscle development in young children. *Young Children, 45*(5), 4–10.

Pollard, J., Bernhard, J., & Corson, P. (2001). The professionalization process in child care. In G. Cleveland & M. Krashinsky, *Our children's future: Child care policy in Canada* (pp. 175–176). Toronto: University of Toronto Press.

Powell, D. R. (1986). Parent education and support programs. *Young Children, 41*(3), 47–53.

Powell, D. R. (1987a). After-school child care. *Young Children, 42*(3), 62–66.

Powell, D. R. (1987b). Day care as a family support system. In S. L. Kagan, D. R. Powell, B. Weissbourd, & E. F. Zigler (Eds.), *America's family support programs: Perspectives and prospects* (pp. 115–132). New Haven, CT: Yale University Press.

Powell, D. R. (1989). *Families and early childhood programs.* Washington, DC: National Association of the Education of Young Children.

Powell, D. R. (1989). *Families and early childhood programs.* Washington, DC: National Association of the Education of Young Children.

Prentice, S. (2000). The business of child care: The issue of auspice. In L. Prochner & N. Howe (Eds.), *Early childhood care and education in Canada* (pp. 273–289). Vancouver: UBC Press.

Prescott, E. (1987). The environment as organizer of intent in child-care settings. In C. S. Weinstein & T. G. David (Eds.), *Spaces for children: The built environment and child development* (pp. 73–88). New York: Plenum Press.

Price, G. G. (1989). Mathematics in early childhood. *Young Children, 44*(4), 53–58.

Prochner, L. (2000). A history of early education and child care in Canada, 1820–1966. In L. Prochner & N. Howe (Eds.), *Early childhood care and education in Canada* (pp. 11–65). Vancouver: UBC Press.

Project Head Start Fact Sheet. (1994, January). Washington, DC: Administration on Children, Youth and Families.

Proshansky, H. M., & Fabian, A. K. (1987). The development of place identity in the child. In C. S. Weinstein & T. G. David (Eds.), *Spaces for children: The built environment and child development* (pp. 21–40). New York: Plenum Press.

Provincial and Territorial Child Care Organizations. (1997). Ottawa: Canadian Child Care Federation.

Purkey, W. W., & Novak, J. M. (1996). *Inviting school success: A self-concept approach to teaching, learning, and democratic practice* (3rd ed.). Toronto: Wadsworth Publishing Company.

Radomski, M. A. (1986). Professionalization of early childhood educators: How far have we progressed? *Young Children, 41*(4), 20–23.

Ram, B. (1990). *Current demographic analysis: New trends in the family* (Catalogue No. 91-535E). Ottawa: Supply and Services, Canada.

Ramey, D., Dorvall, B., & Baker-Ward, L. (1983). Group day care and socially disadvantaged families: Effects on the child and the family. In S. Kilmer (Ed.), *Advances in early education and day care* (Vol. 3, pp. 69–132). Greenwich, CT: JAI Press.

Ramsey, P. G. (1982). Multicultural education in early childhood. In J. F. Brown (Ed.), *Curriculum planning for young children* (pp. 131–142). Washington, DC: National Association for the Education of Young Children.

Ramsey, P. G. (1987). *Teaching and learning in a diverse world: Multicultural education for young children.* New York: Teachers College Press, Columbia University.Randell, V. (1992a). Addendum: Child care in Newfoundland, 1988–1990. In A. Pence (Ed.), *Canadian child care in context: Perspectives from the provinces and territories.* Ottawa: Statistics Canada & Health and Welfare Canada.

Randell, V. (1992b). An overview of child care legislation in Newfoundland. In A. Pence (Ed.), *Canadian child care in context: Perspectives from the provinces and territories.* Ottawa: Statistics Canada & Health and Welfare Canada.

Rarick, G. L. (1982). Descriptive research and process-oriented explanations of the motor development of children. In J.A.S. Kelso & J. E. Clark (Eds.), *The development of movement control and coordination* (pp. 275–291). New York: John Wiley & Sons.

Read, M. (1992). Addendum: Child care in Alberta, 1988–1990. In A. Pence (Ed.), *Canadian child care in context: Perspectives from the provinces and territories.* Ottawa: Statistics Canada & Health and Welfare Canada.

Read, M., Greenwood-Church, M., Hautman, L., Roche, E., & Bagley, C. (1992). An historical overview of child care in Alberta. In A. Pence (Ed.), *Canadian child care in context: Perspectives from the provinces and territories.* Ottawa: Statistics Canada & Health and Welfare Canada.

Reiber, J. L., & Embry, L. H. (1983). Working and communicating with parents. In E. M. Goetz & K. E. Allen (Eds.), *Early childhood education: Special environmental, policy, and legal considerations* (pp. 152–183). Rockville, MD: Aspen Systems Corp.

Reifel, S. (1984). Block construction: Children's developmental landmarks in representation of space. *Young Children, 40*(1), 61–67.

Reppucci, N. D., & Haugaard, J. J. (1989). Prevention of child sexual abuse: Myth or reality. *American Psychologist, 44,* 1266–1275.

Resnick, L. B. (1989). Developing mathematical knowledge. *American Psychologist, 44,* 162–169.

Reynolds, E. (2001). *Guiding young children: A problem-solving approach* (3rd ed.). Toronto: Mayfield Publishing Company.

Ricciuti, H. L. (1993). Nutrition and mental development. *Current Directions in Psychological Science, 2*(2), 43–46.

Rich, S. J. (1985). The writing suitcase. *Young Children, 40*(5), 42–44.

Richarz, A. S. (1980). *Understanding children through observation.* St. Paul, MN: West Publishing Co.

Riessman, F. (1962). *The culturally deprived child.* New York: Harper and Row.

Risley, T. R., & Baer, D. M. (1973). Operant behaviour modification: The deliberate development of behaviour. In B. M. Caldwell & H. M. Ricciuti (Eds.), *Review of child development research* (Vol. 3, pp. 283–329). Chicago: University of Chicago Press.

Ritch, A., & Griffin, S. (1992). A socio-geographic overview of British Columbia. In A. Pence (Ed.), *Canadian child care in context: Perspectives from the provinces and territories.* Ottawa: Statistics Canada & Health and Welfare Canada.

Robinson, B. E. (1988). Vanishing breed: Men in child care programs. *Young Children, 43*(6), 54–57.

Rogers, C. S., & Morris, S. S. (1986). Reducing sugar in children's diets: Why? How? *Young Children, 41*(5), 11–16.

Rogers, D. L., & Ross, D. D. (1986). Encouraging positive social interaction among young children. *Young Children, 41*(3), 12–17.

Rogers, D. L., Perrin, M. S., & Waller, C. B. (1987). Enhancing the development of language and thought through conversations with young children. *Early Childhood Research Quarterly, 2,* 17–29.

Rogers, F., & Sharapan, H. B. (1991). Helping parents, teachers, and caregivers deal with children's concerns about war. *Young Children, 46*(3), 12–13.

Roopnarine, J., & Honig, A. S. (1985). The unpopular child. *Young Children, 40*(6), 59–64.

Roopnarine, J., & Johnson, J. (Eds.). (1993). *Approaches to early childhood education* (2nd ed.). New York: Merrill.

Ross, D. P., Scott, K., & Kelly, M. A. (1996). Overview: Children in Canada in the 1990s. In National Longitudinal Survey of Children and Youth, *Growing up in Canada* (pp. 15–45) (Catalogue No. 89-550-MPE, No. 1). Ottawa: Statistics Canada and Human Resources Development Canada.

Rothlein, L. (1989). Nutrition tips revisited: On a daily basis, do we implement what we know? *Young Children, 44*(6), 30–36.

Rothman Beach Associates (1985). A study of work-related day care in Canada. In *Childcare: The employer's role* (pp. 58–138). Ottawa: Status of Women.

Rowland, T., & McGuire, C. (1968). The developmental theory of Jean Piaget. In J. L. Frost (Ed.), *Early childhood education rediscovered* (pp. 145–152). New York: Holt, Rinehart & Winston.

Royce, J. M., Darlington, R. B., & Murray, H. W. (1983). Pooled analyses: Findings across studies.

In The Consortium for Longitudinal Studies, *As the twig is bent ... Lasting effects of preschool programs* (pp. 411–459). Hillsdale, NJ: Lawrence Erlbaum Associates.

Rubin, K. (1977). Play behaviors of young children. *Young Children, 32*(6), 16–24.

Rubin, K. (1982). Early play theories revisited: Contributions to contemporary research and theory. In D. Pepler & K. Rubin (Eds.), *The play of children: Current theory and research.* Basel, Switz.: Karger AG.

Rubin, K., Fein, G., & Vandenberg, B. (1983). Play. In P. H. Mussen (Ed.), *Handbook of child psychology* (4th ed.): *Vol. 4. Socialization, personality, and social development* (pp. 693–774). New York: John Wiley and Sons.

Rubin, Z. (1980). *Children's friendships.* Cambridge, MA: Harvard University Press.

Rudick, E., & Nyisztor, D. (1977). *The emerging educator.* Toronto: Nelson Canada.

Ruopp, R., Travers, J., Glantz, F., & Coelen, C. (1979). *Children at the center: Final report of the National Day Care Study.* Cambridge, MA: Abt Associates.

Rutter, M. (1983). Stress, coping, and development: Some issues and some questions. In N. Garmezy & M. Rutter (Eds.), *Stress, coping, and development in children* (pp. 1–41). New York: McGraw-Hill Book Co.

Saida, Y., & Miyashita, M. (1979). Development of fine motor skill in children: Manipulation of a pencil in young children aged two to six years old. *Journal of Human Movement Studies, 5,* 104–113.

Saltz, E., Dixon, D., & Johnson, J. (1977). Training disadvantaged preschoolers on various fantasy activities: Effects on cognitive functioning and impulse control. *Child Development, 48,* 367–380.

Saltz, R., & Saltz, E. (1986). Pretend play training and its outcomes. In G. Fein & M. Rivkin (Eds.), *The young child at play* (pp. 155–173). Washington, DC: National Association for the Education of Young Children.

Salvia, J., & Ysseldyke, J. (1991). *Assessment* (5th ed.). Boston: Houghton Mifflin Co.

Sameroff, A. J. (1983). Developmental systems: Contexts and evolution. In P. H. Mussen (Ed.), *Handbook of child psychology* (4th ed.): *Vol. 1. History, theory, and methods* (pp. 237–294). New York: John Wiley and Sons.

Samuels, S. C. (1977). *Enhancing self-concept in early childhood*. New York: Human Sciences Press.

Saracho, O. N., & Spodek, B. (1995). Children's play and early childhood education: Insights from history and theory. *Journal of Education, 177*(3), 129–148.

Sarafino, E. P. (1986). *The fears of childhood: A guide to recognizing and reducing fearful states in children.* NY: Human Sciences Press, Inc.

Saunders, R., & Bingham-Newman, A. M. (1984). *Piagetian perspectives for preschools: A thinking book for teachers*. Englewood Cliffs, NJ: Prentice-Hall, Inc.

Saville-Troike, M. (1982). The development of bilingual and bicultural competence in young children. In L. G. Katz (Ed.), *Current topics in early childhood education* (Vol. 4, pp. 1–16). Norwood, NJ: Ablex Publishing Corp.

Scales, B., Almy, M., Nicolopoulou, A., & Ervin-Tripp, S. (1992a). Defending play in the lives of children. In B. Scales, M. Almy, A. Nicolopoulou, & S. Ervin-Tripp (Eds.), *Play and the social context of development in early care and education* (pp. 15–31). New York: Teachers College Press.

Scales, B., Almy, M., Nicolopoulou, A., & Ervin-Tripp, S. (Eds.). (1992b). *Play and the social context of development in early care and education.* New York: Teachers College Press.

Scarr, S., Eisenberg, M., & Deater-Deckard, K. (1994). Measurement of quality in child care centers. *Early Childhood Research Quarterly, 9,* 131–151.

Scarr, S., Phillips, D., & McCartney, K. (1990). Facts, fantasies and the future of child care in the United States. *Psychological Science, 1*(1), 26–35.

Schickedanz, J. A. (1982). The acquisition of written language in young children. In B. Spodek (Ed.), *Handbook of research in early childhood education* (pp. 242–263). New York: Free Press.

Schickedanz, J. A. (1986). *More than ABCs: The early stages of reading and writing*. Washington, DC: NAEYC.

Schickedanz, J. A., Hansen, K., & Forsyth, P. D. (1990). *Understanding children*. Mountain View, CA: Mayfield Publishing Co.

Schilder, P., & Wechsler, D. (1934). The attitudes of children toward death. *Journal of Genetic Psychology, 45,* 406–451.

Schirrmacher, R. (1986). Talking with young children about their art. *Young Children, 41*(5), 3–10.

Schirrmacher, R. (1990). *Art and creative development for young children*. Albany, NY: Delmar Publishers Inc.

Schneider, N. I., & B. J. Boyd. (1996). Burnout in Canadian child care providers. *Canadian Journal of Research in Early Childhood Education, 5,* 3–11.

Schwarz, S., & Robison, H. (1982). *Designing curriculum for early childhood*. Boston, MA: Allyn & Bacon.

Schweinhart, L. J., & Epstein, A. S., (1996). Adopting a curriculum model: Is it really worth the effort? *High/Scope Resource, 15*(1), 4–7.

Schweinhart, L. J., & Weikart, D. P. (1985). Evidence that good early childhood programs work. *Phi Delta Kappan, 66,* 545–551.

Schweinhart, L. J., & Weikart, D. P. (1993). Changed lives, significant benefits. *High/Scope Resource, 12*(3), pp. 1, 10–14.

Schweinhart, L. J., Weikart, D. P., & Larner, M. B. (1986a). Consequences of three preschool models through age 15. *Early Childhood Research Quarterly, 1,* 15–45.

Schweinhart, L. J., Weikart, D. P., & Larner, M. B. (1986b). Child-initiated activities in early childhood programs may help prevent delinquency. *Early Childhood Research Quarterly, 1,* 303–312.

Sciarra, D. J., & Dorsey, A. G. (1990). *Developing and administering a child care centre* (2nd ed.). Albany, NY: Delmar Publishers Inc.

Seaver, J. W., & Cartwright, C. A. (1986). *Child care administration*. Belmont, CA: Wadworth Publishing Co.

Seefeldt, C. (1987). The visual arts. In C. Seefeldt (Ed.), *The early childhood curriculum: A review of current research* (pp. 183–211). New York: Teachers College Press.

Seefeldt, C. (Ed.). (1987). *The early childhood curriculum*. New York: Teachers College press, Columbia University.

Seefeldt, C., & Galper, A. (1998). *Continuing issues in early childhood education* (2nd ed.). Upper Saddle River, NJ: Prentice-Hall.

Seefeldt, V. (1984). Physical fitness in preschool and elementary school-aged children. *Journal of Physical Education, Recreation, and Dance, 55*(9), 33–40.

Seefeldt, V., & Haubenstricker, J. (1982). Patterns, phases, or stages: An analytical model for the study of developmental movement. In J.A.S. Kelso & J. E. Clark (Eds.), *The development of movement control and co-ordination* (pp. 309–318). New York: John Wiley & Sons.

Seifert, K. (1988). Men in early childhood education. In B. Spodek, O. N. Saracho, & D. L. Peters (Ed.), *Professionalism and the early childhood practitioner* (pp. 105–116). New York: Teachers College Press, Columbia University.

Seifert, K. (1993). Cognitive development in early childhood education. In B. Spodek (Ed.), *Handbook on research on the education of young children* (pp. 9–23). New York: Macmillan.

Seitz, V., Rosenbaum, L. K., & Apfel, N. H. (1985). Effects of family support intervention: A ten-year follow-up. *Child Development, 56,* 376–391.

Selye, H. (Ed.). (1980). *Guide to stress research* (Vol. 1). New York: Van Nostrand Reinhold.

Shapiro, E., & Biber, B. (1972). The education of young children: A developmental-interaction approach. *Teachers College Record, 74,* 55–79.

Shatz, M., & Gelman, R. (1973). The development of communication skills: Modifications in the speech of young children as a function of listener.

Monographs of the Society for Research in Child Development, 38(5, Serial No. 152).

Sheehy, G. (1976). *Passages: Predictable crises of adult life*. New York: Dutton.

Shefatya, L. (1990). Socioeconomic status and ethnic differences in sociodramatic play: Theoretical and practical implications. In E. Klugman & S. Smilansky (Eds.), *Children's play and learning* (pp. 137–155). New York: Teachers College Press.

Sheldon, A. (1990). "Kings are royaler than queens": Language and socialization. *Young Children, 45*(2), 4–9.

Sheldon, J. B. (1983). Protecting the preschooler and the practitioner: Legal issues in early childhood programs. In E. M. Goetz & K. E. Allen (Eds.), *Early childhood education: Special environmental, policy, and legal considerations* (pp. 307–341). Rockville, MD: Aspen Systems Corp.

Sheppard, W. C. (1973). *Teaching social behaviour to young children*. Champaign, IL: Research Press.

Shimoni, R., & Baxter, J. (1996). *Working with families: Perspectives for early childhood professionals*. Don Mills, ON: Addison-Wesley Publishers.

Shimoni, R., Baxter, J., & Kugelmass, J. (1992). *Every child is special*. Don Mills, ON: Addison-Wesley Publishers Ltd.

Sholtys, K. C. (1989). A new language, a new life. *Young Children, 44*(3), 76–77.

Shore, R. (1997). *Rethinking the brain: New insights into early development*. New York: Families and Work Institute.

Shure, M. B., & Spivak, G. (1978). *Problem solving techniques in childrearing*. San Francisco, CA: Jossey-Bass.

Shweder, R. A., Mahapatra, M., & Miller, J. G. (1987). Culture and moral development. In J. Kagan and S. Lamb (Eds.), *The emergence of morality in young children* (pp. 1–83). Chicago: The University of Chicago Press.

Siegel, A. W., & White, S. H. (1982). The child study movement: Early growth and development of the symbolized child. *Advanced in Child Development and Behavior, 17,* 233–285.

Siegler, R. S. (1983). Information processing approaches to development. In P. H. Mussen (Ed.), *Handbook of child psychology* (4th ed.): *Vol. 1. History, theory, and methods* (pp. 103–128). New York: John Wiley & Sons.

Siegler, R. S. (1986). *Children's thinking*. Englewood Cliffs, NJ: Prentice-Hall, Inc.

Sigel, I. E. (1987). Does hothousing rob children of their childhood? *Early Childhood Research Quarterly, 2*, 211–225.

Silberman, C. (1970). *Crisis in the classroom*. New York: Random House.

Silberman, C. (1990). *Crisis in the classroom*. New York: Random House.

Silberman, C. *Crisis in the classroom*. New York: Random House.

Silin, J. G. (1985). Authority as knowledge: A problem of professionalization. *Young Children, 40*(3), 41–46.

Silva, R. J. (1980). Hepatitis and the need for adequate standards in federally supported day care. *Child Welfare, 59*(7), 387–400.

Silver, R. A. (1982). Developing cognitive skills through art. In L. G. Katz (Ed.), *Current topics in early childhood education* (Vol. 4, pp. 143–171). Norwood, NJ: Ablex Publishing Corp.

Simons, J. A., & Simons, F. A. (1986). Montessori and regular preschools: A comparison. In L. G. Katz (Ed.), *Current topics in early childhood education* (Vol. 6, pp. 195–223). Norwood, NJ: Ablex Publishing Corp.

Singer, J. L., Singer, D. G., & Rapaczynski, W. (1984, Spring). Family patterns and television viewing as predictors of children's beliefs and aggression. *Journal of Communication*, 73–89.

Skeels, H. (1966). Adult status of children with contrasting early life experiences. *Monographs of the Society for Research in Child Development, 31*(3, Serial No. 105).

Skinner, B. F. (1957). *Verbal behaviour*. New York: Appleton-Century-Crofts.

Skinner, B. F. (1969). *Contingencies of reinforcement: A theoretical analysis*. New York: Appleton-Century-Crofts.

Skinner, B. F. (1974). *About behaviorism*. New York: Alfred A. Knopf.

Skinner, L. (1979). *Motor development in the preschool years*. Springfield, IL: Thomas Publishers.

Smilansky, S. (1968). *The effects of sociodramatic play on disadvantaged preschool children*. New York: John Wiley & Sons.

Smilansky, S. (1987). *On death: Helping children understand and cope*. New York: Peter Lang.

Smilansky, S. (1990). Sociodramatic play: Its relevance to behavior and achievement in school. In E. Klugman & S. Smilansky (Eds.), *Children's play and learning* (pp. 18–42). New York: Teachers College Press.

Smith, C. A. (1982). *Promoting the social development of young children*. Palo Alto, CA: Mayfield Publishing Co.

Smith, C. A. (1989). *From wonder to wisdom: Using stories to help children grow*. New York: New American Library.

Smith, D. (1991). Here they come: Ready or not! In B. Scales, M. Almy, A. Nicolopoulou, & S. Ervin-Tripp (Eds.), *Play and the social context of development in early care and education* (pp. 51–61). New York: Teachers College Press.

Smith, M. M. (1990). NAEYC annual report. *Young Children, 46*(1), 41–48.

Smith, P. K., & Connolly, K. J. (1980). *The ecology of preschool behaviour*. Cambridge, England: Cambridge University Press.

Smith, P. K., & Connolly, K. J. (1981). *The behavioural ecology of the preschool*. Cambridge, England: Cambridge University Press.

Smith, R. F. (1982). Early childhood science education: A Piagetian perspective. In J. F. Brown (Ed.), *Curriculum planning for young children* (pp. 143–150). Washington, DC: National Association for the Education of Young Children.

Snow, C. E., & Ninio, A. (1986). The contracts of literacy: What children learn from learning to read books. In W. H. Teale & E. Sulzby (Eds.), *Emergent literacy: Writing and reading* (pp. 116–138). Norwood, NJ: Ablex Publishing Corp.

Sobel, J. (1983). *Everybody wins: Non-competitive games for young children.* New York: Walker & Co.

Soderman, A. K. (1985). Dealing with difficult young children. *Young Children, 40*(5), 15–20.

Spitz, H. (1986). *The raising of intelligence: A selected history of attempts to raise retarded intelligence.* Hillsdale, NJ: Lawrence Erlbaum.

Spitz, R. (1945). Hospitalism.: An inquiry into the genesis of psychiatric conditions in early childhood. Part I. *Psychoanalytic Studies of the Child, 1,* 53–74.

Spodek, B. (1985). *Teaching in the early years* (3rd ed.), Englewood Cliffs, NJ: Prentice-Hall, Inc.

Spodek, B., & Saracho, O. N. (1982). The preparation and certification of early childhood personnel. In B. Spodek (Ed.), *Handbook of research in early childhood education.* New York: The Free Press.

Spodek, B., & Saracho, O. N. (1988). Professionalism in early childhood education. In B. Spodek, O. N. Saracho, & D. L. Peters (Ed.), *Professionalism and the early childhood practitioner* (pp. 59–74). New York: Teachers College Press, Columbia University.

Spodek, B., & Saracho, O. N. (1994). *Dealing with individual differences in the early childhood classroom.* New York: Longman.

Spodek, B., Saracho, O., & Lee, R. C. (1984). *Mainstreaming young children.* Belmont, CA: Wadsworth Publishing Co.

Sponseller, D. (1982). Play and early education. In B. Spodek (ed.), *Handbook of research in early childhood education* (pp. 215–241). New York: The Free Press.

Stapleford, E. M. (1976). *History of the Day Nurseries Branch: A personal record.* Toronto, ON: Ontario Ministry of Community and Social Services.

Statistics Canada (1985). *Women in Canada.* Ottawa: Statistics Canada.

Statistics Canada. (1991). Families: Number, type and structure. Catalogue No. 93-312. Ottawa: Supply and Services Canada.

Statistics Canada. (1993a). Basic facts on families in Canada, Past and present. Catalogue No. 89-516. Ottawa: Supply and Services Canada.

Statistics Canada. (1993b). *Labour force activity of women by presence of children.* Ottawa: Statistics Canada.

Statistics Canada. (1997a). *Census families by presence of children,* 1996 Census. Retrieved January 28, 2002 from www.statcan.ca/english/Pgdb/People/Families/famil54c.htm.

Statistics Canada. (1997b). *A national overview—Population and dwelling counts (data products: 1996 Census of Population)* (Catalogue No. 93-357-XPB). Ottawa: Statistics Canada. Retrieved January 28, 2002 from www.statcan.ca/english/census96/table15.htm.

Statistics Canada. (1997c, July 29). Age and sex, 1996 Census. *The Daily.* Retrieved January 28, 2002 from www.statcan.ca/Daily/English/970729/d97079.htm.

Statistics Canada. (1997d, August 26). Earning characteristics of two-partner families, 1995. *The Daily.* Retrieved January 28, 2002 from www.statcan.ca/Daily/English/970826/d970826.htm.

Statistics Canada. (1997e, October 14). 1996 Census: Marital status, common-law unions and families: Marriage a fragile bond for more people. *The Daily.* Retrieved January 28, 2002 from www.statcan.ca/Daily/English/971014/d971014.htm.

Statistics Canada. (1997f, November 4). 1996 Census: Immigration and citizenship. *The Daily.* Retrieved January 28, 2002 from www.statcan.ca/Daily/English/971104/d971104/d971104.htm.

Statistics Canada. (1998a). *Census families, number and average size* (Catalogue No. 91-213-XPB). Retrieved January 28, 2002 from www.statcan.ca/english/Pgdb/People/Families/famil40.htm.

Statistics Canada. (1998b). *Census families in private households by number of persons, 1971–1996 Censuses, Canada*. Retrieved January 28, 2002 from www.statcan.ca/english/Pgdb/People/Families/famil50a.

Statistics Canada. (1998c). *Census families in private households by number of persons, 1996 Census*. Retrieved January 28, 2002 from www.statcan.ca/english/Pgdb/People/Families/famil50d.htm.

Statistics Canada. (1998d). *Population estimates for 1996 and projections for the years 2001, 2006, 2011, 2016, 2021 and 2026, July 1*. Retrieved January 28, 2002 from www.statcan.ca/english/Pgdb/People/Population/demo23a.htm.

Statistics Canada. (1998e, January 13). 1996 Census: Aboriginal data. *The Daily*. Retrieved January 28, 2002 from www.statcan.ca/Daily/English/980113/d980113.htm.

Statistics Canada. (1998f, March 17). 1996 Census: Labour force activity, occupation and industry, place of work, mode of transportation to work, unpaid work. *The Daily*. Retrieved January 28, 2002 from www.statcan.ca/Daily/English/980317/d980317.htm.

Statistics Canada. (1998g, May 12). 1996 Census: Sources of income, earnings and total income, and family income. *The Daily*. Retrieved January 28, 2002 from www.statcan.ca/Daily/English/980512/d980512.htm.

Statistics Canada. (1998h, June 9). 1996 Census: Private households, housing costs and social and economic characteristics of families. *The Daily*. Retrieved January 28, 2002 from www.statcan.ca/Daily/English/980609/d980609.htm.

Statistics Canada. (1998i, June 24). Demographic situation in Canada: Substantial decline in natural growth since 1991. *The Daily*. Retrieved January 28, 2002 from www.statcan.ca/Daily/English/980624/d980624.htm.

Statistics Canada. (1999a, May 18). Divorces. *The Daily*. Retrieved January 28, 2002 from www.statcan.ca/Daily/English/990518/d990518b.htm.

Statistics Canada. (1999b, September 1). Employment after childbirth. *The Daily*. Retrieved January 28, 2002 from www.statcan.ca/Daily/English/990901/d990901a.htm.

Statistics Canada. (1999c, October 14). National Longitudinal Survey of Children and Youth: School component. *The Daily*. Retrieved January 28, 2002 from www.statcan.ca/Daily/English/991014/d991014a.htm.

Statistics Canada. (1999d, October 28). Marriages. *The Daily*. Retrieved January 28, 2002 from www.statcan.ca/Daily/English/991018/d991028c.htm.

Statistics Canada. (1999e). *Canada Yearbook 1999*. Ottawa: Statistics Canada.

Stevens, H. (1992). A socio-geographic overview of Manitoba. In A. Pence (Ed.), *Canadian child care in context: Perspectives from the provinces and territories*. Ottawa: Statistics Canada & Health and Welfare Canada.

Stevenson, J. (1990). The cooperative preschool model in Canada. In I. Doxey (Ed.), *Child care and education: Canadian dimensions* (pp. 221–239). Toronto: Nelson Canada.

Stevenson, R. L. (1985). *A child's garden of verse* (M. Forman, Illustrator). New York: Delacorte Press.

Stone, J. (1993). Caregiver and teacher language: Responsive or restrictive? *Young Children, 48*, 12–18.

Suggestions for developing positive racial attitudes (1980). *Interracial books for children bulletin, 11*(3–4), 10–15.

Sunal, C. S., & Hatcher, B. (1985). A changing world: Books can help children adapt. *Day Care and Early Education, 13*(2), 16–19.

Sutherland, Z., & Arbuthnot, M. H. (1986). *Children and books* (7th ed.). Glenview, IL: Scott, Foresman and Co.

Swick, K. J. (1994). Family involvement: An empowerment perspective. *Dimensions of Early Childhood, 22*(2), 10–13.

Swigger, K. M., & Swigger, B. K. (1984). Social patterns and computer use among preschool children. *AEDS Journal, 17*(3), 35–41.

Sword, J. (1987). Help! I'm selecting children's books. *Day Care and Early Education, 15*(2), 26–28.

Table toys: A creative curriculum for early childhood. (1979). Washington, DC: Creative Associates, Inc.

Teale, W. H., & Martinez, M. G. (1988). Getting on the right road to reading: Bringing books and young children together in the classroom. *Young Children, 44*(1), 10–15.

Teale, W. H., & Sulzby, E. (1986). Emergent literacy as a perspective for examining how young children become writers and readers. In W. H. Teale & E. Sulzby (Eds.), *Emergent literacy: Writing and reading* (pp. vii–xxv). Norwood, NJ: Ablex Publishing Corp.

Teale, W. H., & Sulzby, E. (Eds.). (1986). *Emergent literacy: Writing and reading* (pp. vii–xxv). Norwood, NJ: Ablex Publishing Corp.

The Bookfinder: A guide to children's literature about the needs and problems of youth aged 2–15 (Vol. 1). (1977). Circle Pines, NM: American Guidance Service.

Thomas, A., & Chess, S. (1969). *Temperament and development.* New York: New York University Press.

Thomas, A., Chess, S., & Birch, H. G. (1968). *Temperament and behavior disorders in children.* New York: New York University Press.

Thomas, R. M. (1990a). The encyclopedia of human development and education: *Theory, research, and studies.* New York: Pergamon Press.

Thomas, R. M. (1990b). Basic concepts and applications of Piagetian cognitive development theory. In R. M. Thomas (Ed.), *The encyclopedia of human development and education: Theory, research, and studies* (pp. 53–56). New York: Pergamon Press.

Thomson, C. L., & Ashton-Lilo, J. (1983). A developmental environment for child care programs. In E. M. Goetz & K. E. Allen (Eds.), *Early childhood education: Special environmental, policy, and legal considerations* (pp. 93–125). Rockville, MD: Aspen Systems Corp.

Thorndike, R., Hagen, E., & Sattler, J. (1985). *Stanford-Binet Intelligence Scale* (4th ed.). Chicago, IL: The Riverside Publishing Company.

Thornton, J. R. (1990). Team teaching: A relationship based on trust and communication. *Young Children, 45*(5), 40–43.

Tietze, W. (1987). A structural model for the evaluation of preschool effects. *Early Childhood Research Quarterly, 2,* 133–153.

Tire hazards, woodworking, and crib safety. (1986). *Young Children, 41*(5), 17–18.

Tizard, B., Mortimer, J., & Burchell, B. (1981). *Involving parents in nursery and infant schools.* Ypsilanti, MI: The High/Scope Press.

Torrance, E. P. (1963). *Adventuring in creativity. Childhood Education 40,* 79–87.

Townson, M. (1985). Financing child care through the Canada Assistance Plan. In Status of Women, Canada (Ed.), *Financing child care: Current arrangements. A report prepared for the Task Force on Child Care, Series 1.* Ottawa: Status of Women, Canada.

Trahms, C. M. (1989). Factors that shape food patterns in young children. In P. L. Pipes (Ed.), *Nutrition in infancy and childhood* (4th ed., pp. 160–170). St. Louis, MO: C. V. Mosby Co.

Tribe, C. (1982). *Profile of three theories: Erikson, Maslow, Piaget.* Dubuque, IA: Kendall/Hunt Publishing Co.

Truemner, T. (1992). An overview of child care legislation in Saskatchewan. In A. Pence (Ed.), *Canadian child care in context: Perspectives from the provinces and territories.* Ottawa: Statistics Canada & Health and Welfare Canada.

U.S. firms join forces to build daycare centres (1992, July 10). *The Toronto Star*, p. D1.

Ulich, R. (1947). *Three thousand years of educational wisdom.* Cambridge, MA: Harvard University Press.

Ulich, R. (1967). Johann Heinrich Pestalozzi. In P. Edwards (Ed.), *The encyclopedia of philosophy* (Vols. 5–6, pp. 121–122). New York: Macmillan Publishing Co., Inc. & The Free Press.

Van Heerden, J. R. (1984). Early under-nutrition and mental performance. *International Journal of Early Childhood, 16*(1), 10–16.

Vandell, D. L. (1999). *Cognitive, linguistic, and social consequences of early experience: Child care and social competence*: NICHD Study. Paper presented at the American Association for the Advancement of Science meetings, Anaheim, CA, January 21–26.

Vandell, D. L., & Corasaniti, M. A. (1990). Variations in early child care: Do they predict subsequent social, emotional, and cognitive differences? *Early Childhood Research Quarterly, 5,* 555–572.

Vandell, D. L., & Su, H. (1999). Child-care and school-aged children. *Young Children, 54*(6), 62–71.

Vander Ven, K. (1986). "And you have a ways to go": The current status and emerging issues in training for child care practice. In K. Vander Ven & E. Tittnich (Ed.), *Competent caregivers—Competent children: Training and education for child care practice*. New York: Hawthorne Press.

Varga, D. (1997). *Constructing the child: A history of Canadian day care*. Toronto: James Lorimer Publishers.

Varga, D. (2000). A history of early-childhood-teacher education. In L. Prochner & N. Howe (Eds.), *Early childhood care and education in Canada* (pp. 66–95). Vancouver: UBC Press.

Vygotsgy, L. S. (1962). *Thought and language* (E. Haufmann & G. Vakar, Eds., Trans.). Cambridge, MA: MIT Press.

Vygotsky, L. (1976). Play and its role in the mental development of the child. In J. Bruner, A. Jolly, & K. Sylva (Eds.), *Play—Its role in development and evolution* (pp. 537–554). Harmondsworth, Eng.: Penguin Books.

Vygotsky, L. S. (1978a). The prehistory of written language. In M. Cole, V. John-Steiner, S. Scribner, & E. Souberman (Eds.), *Mind and society: The development of higher psychological processes* (pp. 105–119). Cambridge, MA: Harvard University Press.

Vygotsky, L. S. (1978b). *Mind in society*. Cambridge, MA: Harvard University Press.

Wade, M. G., & Davis, W. E. (1982). Motor skill development in young children: Current views on assessment and programming. In L. G. Katz (Ed.), *Current topics in early childhood education* (Vol. 4, pp. 55–70). Norwood, NY: Ablex Publishing Corp.

Wadsworth, B. J. (1984). *Piaget's theory of cognitive and affective development* (3rd ed.). New York: Longman.

Walker, D. K., & Crocker, R. W. (1988). Measuring family systems outcomes. In H. B. Weiss & F. H. Jacobs (Eds.), *Evaluating family programs* (pp. 153–176). New York: Aldine de Gruyter.

Wallerstein, J. S. (1983). Children of divorce: Stress and developmental tasks. In N. Garmezy & M. Rutter (Eds.), *Stress, coping, and development in children* (pp. 265–302). New York: McGraw-Hill Book Co.

Wallerstein, J., Corbin, S. B., & Lewis, J. M. (1988). Children of divorce: A ten-year study. In E. M. Hetherington & J. Arasteh (Eds.), *Impact of divorce, single-parenting and stepparenting on children* (pp. 198–214). Hillsdale, NY: Paul Erlbaum, Associates.

Walton, S. (1989). Katy learns to read and write. *Young Children, 44*(5), 52–57.

Wash, D. P., & Brand, L. E. (1990). Child day care services: An industry at a crossroads. *Monthly Labor Review, 113*(12), 17–24.

Washington, V., & Oyemade, U. J. (1985). Changing family trends: Head Start must respond. *Young Children, 40*(6), 12–18.

Wass, H. (1984). *Concepts of death: A developmental perspective*. In H. Wass & C. A. Corr (Eds.), *Childhood and death*. New York: Hemisphere Publishing Corp.

Watson, J. B. (1925a). *Behaviorism*. New York: Norton.

Watson, J. B. (1925b). What the nursery has to say about instincts. In C. Murchison (Ed.), *Psychologies of 1925*. Worcester, MA: Clark University Press.

Watson, J. B. (1928). *Psychological care of infant and child.* New York: W. W. Norton.

Watson, J. B., & Rayner, R. (1920). Conditioned emotional reactions. *Journal of Experimental Psychology, 3,* 1–4.

Weber, E. (1971). *The English infant school and informal education.* Englewood Cliffs, NJ: Prentice-Hall.

Weber, E. (1984). *Ideas influencing early childhood education.* New York: Teachers College Press, Columbia University.

Wechsler, D. (1989). *Wechsler Preschool and Primary Scale of Intelligence—Revised.* San Antonio, TX: The Psychological Corporation.

Wechsler, D. (1991). *Wechsler Intelligence Scale for Children* (3rd ed.). San Antonio, TX: The Psychological Corporation.

Weikart, D. P., & Schweinhart, L. J. (1987). The High/Scope cognitively oriented curriculum of early education. In J. L. Roopnarine & J. E. Johnson (Eds.), *Approaches to early childhood education* (pp. 253–267). Columbus, OH: Merrill Publishing Co.

Weinstein, C. S. (1987). Designing preschool classrooms to support development. In C. S. Weinstein & T. G. David (Eds.), *Spaces for children: The built environment and child development* (pp. 159–185). New York: Plenum Press.

Weiss, H. (1987). Family support and education in early childhood programs. In S. L. Kagan, D. R. Powell, B. Weissbourd, & E. F. Zigler (Eds.), *America's family support programs: Perspectives and prospects* (pp. 133–160). New Haven, CT: Yale University Press.

Werner, E. E. (1984). Resilient children. *Young Children, 40*(1), 68–72.

Werner, E. E. (1986). Resilient children. In H. E. Fitzgerald, & M. G. Walraven (Eds.), *Annual editions: Human development.* Sluice Dock, CT: Dushkin.

Werner, P. (1974). Education of selected movement patterns of preschool children. *Perceptual and Motor Skills, 39,* 795–798.

Wertsch, J. V. (1985). *Vygotsky and the social formation of mind.* Cambridge, MA: Harvard University Press.

West, S. (1988). *A study of compliance with the Day Nurseries Act at full-day child care centres in Metropolitan Toronto.* Toronto, ON: Ministry of Community and Social Services.

White, B. (1968). Informal education during the first months of life. In R. D. Hess & R. M. Bear (Eds.), *Early Education.* New York: Aldine-Atherton.

White, B. (1975). *The first three years of life.* Toronto: Prentice-Hall.

White, D., & Mill, D. (2000). The child care provider. In L. Prochner & N. Howe, *Early childhood care and education in Canada* (pp. 236–251). Vancouver, BC: UBC Press.

Whitebook, M. (1986). The teacher shortage: A professional precipice. *Young Children, 41*(3), 10–11.

Whitebook, M., Howes, C., & Phillips, D. (1989). *Who cares? Child care teachers and the quality of care in America: Executive summary, National Child Care Study.* Oakland, CA: Child Care Employee Project.

Whitebook, M., Howes, C., Darrah, R., & Friedman, J. (1982). Caring for the caregiver: Staff burnout in child care. In L. G. Katz (Ed.), *Current topics in early childhood education* (Vol. 4, pp. 211–235). Norwood, NJ: Ablex Publishing Corp.

Whitebook, M., Phillips, D., & Howes, M. (1993). *National Child Care Staffing Study revisited: Four years in the life of centre-based child care.* Oakland, CA: Child Care Employee Project.

Wilderstrom, A. H. (1986). Educating young handicapped children: What can early childhood education contribute? *Childhood Education 63*(2), 78–83.

Willer, B. (1987). Quality or affordability: Trade-offs for early childhood programs? *Young Children, 42*(6), 41–43.

Willer, B. (1990). Estimating the full cost of quality. In B. Willer (Ed.), *Reaching the full cost of quality in early childhood programs* (pp. 55–86). Washington, DC: National Association for the Education of Young Children.

Willer, B., & Bredekamp, S. (1993). A new paradigm of early childhood professional development. *Young Children, 48*(4), 64.

Willert, M. K., & Kamii, C. (1985). Reading in kindergarten: Direct vs. indirect teaching. *Young Children, 40*(4), 3–9.

Williams, L. R. (1992). Determining the curriculum. In C. Seefeldt (Ed.), *The early childhood curriculum: A review of current research* (2nd ed.) (pp. 1–15). New York: Teachers College Press, Columbia University.

Williams, T. M. (Ed.). (1986). *The impact of television.* Orlando, FL: Academic Press.

Winner, E. (1986). Where pelicans kiss seals. *Psychology Today, 20,* 24–35.

Wolery, M., Holcombe, A., Venn, M. L., Brookfield, J., Huffman, K., Schroeder, C., Martin, C. G., & Fleming, L. A. (1993). Mainstreaming in early childhood programs: Current status and relevant issues. *Young Children 49*(1), 18–88.

Wolf, A. D. (1990). Art postcards: Another aspect of your aesthetics program? *Young Children, 45*(2), 39–43.

Wolff, S. (1969). *Children under stress.* Baltimore, MD: Penguin.

Women's Bureau (1970a). *Women in the labour force: 1970 facts and figures.* Ottawa: Information Canada.

Women's Bureau (1970b). *Working mothers and their child care arrangements* (Catalogue No. L38-2970). Ottawa: Queen's Printer.

Women's Bureau (1990). *Women in the labour force* (1990–1991 edition). Ottawa: Supply and Services.

Woodrich, D. L. (1984). *Children's psychological testing: A guide for nonpsychologists.* Baltimore, MD: Paul H. Brookes Publishing Co.

Wortham, S. C. (1990). *Tests and measurement in early childhood education.* Columbus, OH: Merrill Publishing Co.

Wright, M. (1983). Compensatory education in the preschool: A Canadian approach. *The University of Western Ontario preschool project.* Ypsilanti, MI: High/Scope Press.

Yarrow, L. J. (1961). Maternal deprivation: Toward an empirical and conceptual re-evaluation. *Psychological Bulletin, 58,* 459–490.

Yarrow, M. R., Scott, P. M., & Waxler, C. Z. (1973). Learning concern for others. *Developmental Psychology, 8,* 240–260.

Young, B. (1994). Custody disputes and pick up authorization. In E. Essa & R. Young (Eds.), *Introduction to early childhood education* (pp. 134). Toronto: Nelson Canada.

Young, R. (1981). *Association for Early Childhood Education, Ontario (AECEO) submission to the Minister of Education.* Toronto: AECEO.

Young, R. (1987). *Bringing the "bedtime story" into inner city classrooms.* Toronto, ON: Queen's Park, Ontario Ministry of Education.

Young, R. (1993a). *The acquisition and use of knowledge about the story schema.* Unpublished manuscript, Brock University, St. Catharines, ON.

Young, R. (1993b). *Child care in Canada: History, regulation, teacher training, scope, and parental needs.* Unpublished manuscript. Brock University, St. Catharines, ON.

Young, R. (2001). *Child care in Canada: History, regulation, and teacher training.* Unpublished manuscript. St. Catharines, ON: Brock University.

Young, R., & Shattuck, D. (2000). *The communicative competence of inner-city children.* Paper presented at the Annual Meeting of the American Educational Research Association, New Orleans, LA.

Ziajka, A. (1983). Microcomputers in early childhood education. *Young Children, 38*(5), 61–67.

Ziemer, M. (1987). Science and the early childhood curriculum: One thing leads to another. *Young Children, 42*(6), 44–51.

Zigler, E. F., & Freedman, J. (1987). Head Start: A pioneer of family support. In S. L. Kagan, D. R. Powell, B. F. Weissbourd, & E. F. Zigler (Eds.), *Approaches to early childhood education* (2nd ed., pp. 261–273). Columbus, OH: Merrill.

Zigler, E., & Berman, W. (1973). Discerning the future of early childhood intervention. *American Psychologist, 38,* 894–906.

Zimiles, H. (1981). The Bank Street approach. In J. L. Roopnarine & J. E. Johnson (Eds.), *Approaches to early childhood education* (pp. 163–178). Columbus, OH: Merrill Publishing Co.

Zimiles, H. (1982). Psychodynamic theory of development. In B. Spodek (Ed.), *Handbook of research in early childhood education* (pp. 135–155). New York: The Free Press.

Zion, G. (1965). *Harry by the sea.* New York: Harper & Row.

Zlomke, L., & Piersel, W. (1987). Aggression. In A. Thomas & J. Grimes (Eds.), *Children's needs: Psychological perspectives* (pp. 19–26). Washington, DC: National Association of School Psychologists.

Name Index

Adler, S., 194
Alexander, N. P., 20
Alford, B. B., 266, 283, 284
Alger, H. A., 297
Allen, J., 178
Allen, K. E., 152, 154–57, 365
Almy, M., 160, 192, 239, 320
Amabilie, T. M., 358
Ames, L. B., 154–57
Anastasiow, N., 186
Anderson, D. R., 364
Anderson, K. E., 420, 421
Apfel, N. H., 171, 173
Arnett, J., 26, 417, 422
Ashton-Lilo, J., 245, 249, 250
Atkins, C., 383
Atwood, M. E., 366, 367
Ault, M. H., 338
Ayers, W., 194

Baer, D. M., 314
Baker, B. B., 293
Baker-Ward, L., 173
Bakst, K., 386
Balaban, N., 193
Bandura, Albert, 313
Banet, B., 80, 82, 84, 261, 263, 293
Banta, T., 96
Baratta-Lorton, M., 255
Barnes, B. J., 251
Barnett, W. S., 8, 99
Barrett, D. E., 306
Baumrind, D., 278
Baxter, J., 170, 320
Baynham, P., 21
Beach, J., 433, 434
Beaty, J., 340–42, 348
Becher, R. M., 183
Bereiter, C., 95, 96
Berk, L. E., 298
Berlyne, Daniel, 223
Bernhard, J., 439, 440
Berns, R. M., 186
Berreuta-Clement, J. J., 8, 99
Bertrand, J., 433, 434, 439
Bijou, S. W., 338

Bingham-Newman, A. M., 56
Birch, H. G., 153, 162, 306
Bizzell, R. P., 96
Black, A. E., 278, 420, 421
Blanco, R., 311, 314
Bogle, M.L., 266, 283, 284
Borich, G., 337, 340, 342
Borstellman, L. J., 39, 48
Bowd, A., 344
Bowman, G., 80
Boyd, B. J., 437
Bradley, R., 342, 343
Brand, L. E., 8, 21
Braun, S. J., 39, 41, 44, 45, 46, 50, 60
Brazelton, T.B., 240
Bredekamp, S., 20, 29, 31, 154–56, 194, 196, 205, 239, 240, 290, 323, 346
Brigance, A. H., 344
Brockman, L. M., 113–15
Brockman, L., 5, 6, 8, 12, 13, 15, 19, 20, 45, 46, 146, 170, 214
Bronfenbrenner, U., 28, 165, 166
Brookfield, J., 163
Browne, K. W., 276, 277, 310
Bruner, J., 26, 223
Bryant, D., 404, 408
Buggey, T., 60
Bundy, B. F., 175, 181
Burchell, B., 175
Burchinal, M. R., 404, 408
Burke, C., 386
Bushell, D., 60
Buzelli, C. A., 289

Cairns, R., 47, 60, 135, 136
Caldwell, B. M., 63, 342, 343
Canning, P., 78, 126–28, 421
Caplan, F., 38
Caplan, T., 38
Carlsson-Paige, N., 236
Carriere, Y., 120
Carter, D. B., 4, 41, 44, 46, 50
Cartwright, C. A., 338, 340, 341, 342

Cartwright, G. P., 338, 340, 341, 342
Casler, L., 63
Cass, J. E., 160
Chafel, J. A., 171
Chard, S. C., 157, 328
Charlesworth, R., 227
Chattin-McNichols, J. P., 50, 70–73, 96, 97
Chess, S., 153, 162, 306
Chisholm, P., 9
Christie, J. F., 261, 363
Chun, R., 192
Cicerelli, V., 98
Clarke-Stewart, A., 48
Clarke-Stewart, K. A., 11, 25, 26, 27, 31, 33, 93, 102, 186, 410, 411
Clemens, S. G., 358
Clements, D. H., 251
Cleveland, G., 433, 434
Click, D. W., 207
Click, P. M., 207
Clifford, R. M., 23
Clifford, R., 248, 250, 342, 404, 406, 408, 422
Coche, J., 11, 30
Cochran, M., 173
Coelen, C., 25, 27
Cohen, D. H., 339, 340
Cohr, M., 343
Coleman, J. S., 63
Coleman, M., 367
Comenius, J. A., 44
Connolly, K. J., 27
Consortium for Longitudinal Studies, 171
Copple, C. E., 371
Copple, C., 29, 31, 290, 323
Corasaniti, M. A., 102
Corson, P., 439, 440
Cosgrove, M. S., 369
Crocker, R. W., 165
Crouter, A. C., 166
Crozier-Smith, D., 109
Cryer, D., 404, 406, 408
Culkin, M. L., 404, 408
Curtis, S. R., 97, 366

Damon, W., 388, 397
Darlington, R., 96, 98
Davidson, J. I., 251, 270
Davis, W. E., 315, 325, 351
Deater-Deckard, K., 8
DeBaryshe, B. D., 307
Debelack, M., 255
Deiner, P. L., 163, 392
DeLisi, R., 371
Derman-Sparks, L., 241, 244, 390, 391, 395,
Desjardins, G., 121
Dewey, J., 48
Dill, N., 112, 113
Dinkmeyer, D., 187
Dixon, D., 235
Dodds, J. B., 343
Doherty-Derkowski, G., 20, 21, 25, 171, 195, 213, 405, 406, 411, 416, 421, 432, 438, 439
Dopyera, J. E., 74
Dorfman, A., 344
Dorsey, A. G., 207, 211
Dorvall, B., 173
Douvan, E., 54
Doxey, I., 4, 9
Doyle, A. B., 230
Drake, B. M., 420
Dresden, J., 195, 205, 440
Driscoll, A., 311
Dumas, J., 7
Dunst, C. J., 185
Dyer, J. L., 96, 100
Dykes, A. C., 420, 421

Edwards, C. P., 388, 396, 397, 398
Edwards, E. P., 39, 41, 44, 45, 46, 50, 60
Eisenberg, M., 8
Eisenburg-Berg, N., 277
Elkind, D., 11, 25, 50, 74, 97, 223, 240
Embry, L. H., 175
Endres, J. B., 283
Engelmann, S., 96
Epstein, A. S., 8, 99, 321
Erikson, E. H., 61, 172
Eron, L. D., 364
Ervin-Tripp, S., 239
Essa, E. L., 159, 168, 251, 256, 262, 284, 292, 304, 305, 309, 312, 313, 314, 324, 326, 336, 386, 391
Evangelou, D., 28, 29
Evans, E. D., 69, 97, 357
Eyer, D. W., 320

Fandal, A. W., 343
Farver, J. A., 29, 388
Faust, V., 304
Feeney, S., 48, 192, 201, 357
Fein, G. G., 153, 230, 233, 280
Fein, G., 93, 160, 223, 225, 226, 229, 234
Feldman, R. D., 280
Ferber, R., 288, 289
Fernandez, J. P., 23
Fidler, D. S., 390
Fiene, R., 406
File, N., 289
Finkelstein, B., 431
Fiorentino, M., 321, 322
Flack, M., 397
Flanagan-Rochon, K. F., 125, 126
Flaste, R., 388
Fleming, L. A., 163
Fleming, W. G., 116–18
Flerx, V. C., 390
Forman, G., 90, 91
Forsyth, P. D., 345, 398
Fowler, W., 102
Fox, N., 153
Frankenburg, W. K., 343
Fraser, A. S., 87, 91, 92, 323
Frazier, A., 334
Freedman, J., 171
Friedman, D., 24
Friendly, M., 20, 21
Friesen, J., 113–15
Fullum, H., 122

Galdone, P., 397
Galinsky, E., 172, 179, 434
Gallagher, J. M., 11, 30
Gallimore, R., 62
Galper, A., 411
Gamble, J., 124
Gamble, L., 87, 91–93
Gangarosa, E. J., 420, 421
Garcia., E. E., 378
Gardner, H., 354
Gartrell, D., 276, 277, 305, 310
Gary, G.W., 420, 421
Gelbach, S. H., 420
Geller, L. G., 381
Genishi, C., 339, 375, 380
Gersten, R., 96
Gestwicki, C., 21, 29, 175, 176, 178, 182, 183, 185, 290, 293, 310, 320–22, 324
Gettman, D., 50, 97
Gibson, L., 384
Gilkeson, E., 80

Gillespie, C., 154–57
Ginsburg, H., 56
Gitomer, J., 358
Glantz, F., 25, 27
Glassman, M., 79, 128, 129
Goelman, H., 5, 6, 8, 12, 13, 15, 19, 20, 21, 45, 46, 101, 146, 166, 170, 195, 213, 214, 342, 405, 406, 411, 416, 432, 438, 439
Goffin, S. G., 74, 236, 323
Goldfarb, W., 63
Gomez, L., 23
Gonzalez-Mena, J., 170, 179, 320
Goodman, K. S., 385
Goodman, Y. M., 383, 385
Gordon, A. M., 276, 277, 310
Gordon, T., 65, 187
Gottfried, A., 343
Gottman, J. M., 388
Gould, R. L., 172
Graue, M. E., 344
Greenberg, P., 41
Greenleaf, P., 39
Greenspan, N. T., 159, 222
Greenspan, S., 159, 222
Greenwood-Church, M., 109
Griffin, E. F., 108, 109
Griffin, S., 107, 109
Grimsley, R., 44
Gruber, C., 26
Guilford, J. P., 356
Gullion, M. E., 311
Gunner, M., 282

Haines, J., 154–57
Hakuta, K., 378
Halpern, R., 15
Hamilton, C. E., 434
Hampden-Turner, C., 357
Hansen, K., 345, 398
Harms, T., 248, 250, 264, 342, 406, 422
Harris, J. D., 186
Harste, J. C., 386
Hartman, J. A., 28, 29
Hartup, W. W., 230, 387
Hartup, W., 282
Haskins, R., 102
Hatch, M. H., 420, 421
Haugland, S. W., 251
Hayes, C. D., 420
Hearron, P. F., 277
Helbern, S., 404, 408
Hendrick, J., 348
Henninger, M. L., 366, 367
Herr, J., 255, 369

Herrera, J. F., 280
Hess, R. D., 65
Hewitt, K., 401
Hildebrand, L., 277
Hill, S., 251
Hills, T. W., 11
Hilton, J. M., 304
Hinde, R. A., 280
Hitz, R., 292, 311
Hofferth, S.L., 15
Hohman, M., 80, 82, 84, 261, 263, 293
Holcombe, A., 163
Honig, A. 102, 183, 185, 277, 388, 390, 361
Honig, A. S., 102
Howes, C., 26, 27, 29, 33, 102, 201, 321, 322, 387, 388, 389, 404, 406, 408, 417, 432, 434, 435, 438, 441
Huesman, L. R., 364
Huffman, K., 163
Humphrey, M., 113–15
Hunter, T., 421
Huston, A. C., 363

Ilg, F. L., 154–57
Irwin, S., 78, 126–28
Isenburg, J. P., 322, 324, 337

Jacklin, C. N., 268
Jacobs, E., 321, 322
Jacobson, M., 255
Jalongo, M. R., 322, 324, 337
Javernick, E., 367
Jenkins, S., 168
Jensen, M. A., 385
Joe, M. J., 79, 131
Johnsen, E. P., 261, 363
Johnson, J., 93, 235
Johnson, L., 79, 131
Jolly, A., 223
Jones, E., 249
Jorde-Bloom, P., 33, 250
Joy, L. A., 364
Juorio, M., 439

Kagan, S. L., 21, 22, 404, 408
Kajuk, F., 343
Kamii, C., 277, 278, 346
Kaplan, P., 58
Karnes, M. B., 96
Karnes, M., 96, 163, 392
Katz, L. G., 28, 29, 87, 157, 192, 194, 200, 202, 328, 389, 391, 434
Keats, E. J., 397
Keele, V. S., 312

Kelly, F. J., 182
Keogh, J., 365, 366
Kessen, W., 57
Khan, N., 102
Kilpatrick, W. H., 63
Kimball, M. M., 364
Kipnis, K., 201
Klein, B. L., 420
Kohlberg, L., 397
Kontos, S., 383, 384, 406, 424
Kopp, C. B., 277
Kostelnik, M. J., 235
Krogh, S. L., 397, 398
Kunkel, D., 363
Kyle, I., 115, 116, 120, 434

Labi, N., 11
Lagerspetz, K., 364
La Grange, A., 20, 21, 195, 213, 405, 406, 411, 416, 432, 438
Lally, J.R., 102
Lambert-Lagace, L., 283
Lamme, L. L., 397, 398
Larsen, J. M., 102, 186
Lavatelli, C. S., 56
Lawton, J. T., 74, 322, 336, 337
Lay-Dopyera, M., 74
Lazar, I., 96, 98
Lee, R. C., 163, 392
Lero, D., 5, 6, 8, 12, 13, 15, 19, 20, 45, 46, 146, 170, 214
Lero, G., 20, 21, 195, 213, 405, 406, 411, 416, 432, 438
Levin, D. E., 236
Levinger, A. C., 388
Levinger, G., 388
Levinson, D. J., 172
Lexmond, T., 311, 314
Liaw, F., 344
Lieberman, A.F., 221
Liebert, R. M., 364
Lillard, P. P., 97
Lindauer, S. L. K., 96, 97
Linderman, C. E., 255
Lombardi, J., 440, 441
Lorch, E. P., 364
Lovell, P., 264
Lowenfeld, V., 357
Lozof, B., 306
Lutes, D., 124
Lyon, M., 421

Maccoby, E. E., 268, 276, 389, 396
MacCormick, J. N., 420
Machado, J. M., 385
Maier, H. W., 61

Malaguzzi, L. 51
Mangoine, P. L., 102
Maravick, E., 357
Marion, M., 276, 277, 278, 310
Marotz, L., 152, 154–57, 365
Marshall, H. H., 159
Martin, C. G., 163
Martin, J. A., 276, 396
Martinez, M. G., 385
Maslow, A. 222
Mattingly, M., 437
Mauch, D., 131, 132
Maxim, G., 320
Mayesky, M., 354
Mayfield, M., 23
McAdoo, L., 321
McAfee, O. D. 262
McCartney, K., 33, 406
McCreary, D. R., 364
McDonell, L., 109
McDougall, D., 344
McGuire, C., 64
McIntosh, A., 21, 119
McKay, G. D., 187
McMillan, M., 49
McTear, M., 380
McWilliams, M., 283
Meisels, S. J., 344
Meredith, R., 385
Miesels, S., 21
Miezitis, S., 97
Milkovich, G., 23
Mill, D., 437
Miller, C. S., 268, 269, 276, 277, 310
Miller, L. B., 96, 100
Mitchell, A., 25
Modigliani, K., 25
Monighan, P., 160, 192
Monighan-Nourot, P., 223
Montessori, M., 70
Moore, R. C., 387
Morado, C., 25
Morgan, E. L., 179, 280
Morin, J., 435
Morrison, G. S., 41, 62, 11, 276, 313
Morrow, R. D., 243
Morse, W., 369
Mortimer, J., 175
Moss, P., 197
Mullen, S., 124
Murray, C. I., 304
Mussen, P. H., 20
Mussen, P., 277
Myers, B., 195, 205, 440

Nauta, M. J., 401
Neisworth, J. T., 60, 313, 314, 336
Nelson, R. F., 344
Neugebauer, R., 21
Newton, J. W., 21, 22
Nicolopoulou, A., 239
Ninio, A., 382
Northway, M., 60, 117
Novak, J. M., 180
Nykyforuk, J., 111, 112

Obler, L. K., 378
Oden, S., 388
Oken-Wright, P., 297
Olds, S. W., 280
Olenick, M., 102
Ontario, province of, 78, 118
Opper, S., 56
Orlick, T., 236, 460

Padan-Belkin, E., 342
Palmer, J. L., 420
Papalio, D. E., 280
Parker, J. G., 388
Parten, M. B., 230
Patterson, G. R., 277, 307, 311
Peckover, R. B., 261, 363
Peisner-Feinburg, E. S., 404, 408
Pence, A., 5, 6, 8, 12, 13, 15, 19, 20,
    45, 46, 101, 146, 170, 197, 214,
    342
Perrin, M. S., 380
Peters, D. L., 60, 80, 313, 314, 336
Peterson, R. F., 338
Phillips, D. A., 15, 25, 27, 33, 34,
    192, 406, 27, 33, 435
Phillips, D., 26, 201, 417, 432, 434,
    435, 438, 441
Phyfe-Perkins, E., 246, 249
Piaget, J., 56, 225, 397
Piersel, W., 311, 314
Pipes, P. L., 285
Poest, C. A., 366, 367
Pollard, J., 439, 440
Powell, D. R., 20, 150, 163, 173, 183,
    186
Prentice, S., 20, 21
Prescott, E., 249
Purkey, W. W., 180

Radomski, M. A., 195
Ram, B., 7
Ramey, D., 173
Ramsey, E., 307
Ramsey, P., 241
Randall, V., 140

Rapaczynski, W., 364
Rauhala, A., 21, 119
Rayner, R., 58
Read, M., 5, 6, 8, 12, 13, 15, 19, 20,
    45, 46, 146, 170, 214
Redshaw, D., 136
Reiber, J. L., 175
Reynolds, N. L., 276, 277, 310
Ricciuiti, H. L., 306
Rice, C., 125, 126
Rich, S. J., 386
Richarz, A. S., 337
Riessman, F., 63
Risley, T. R., 314
Ritch, A., 107
Robinson, B. E., 438
Robinson, C. C., 102
Robison, H., 74
Rockwell, R. E., 283
Rogers, D. L., 380, 388
Rogers, P. R., 159, 256, 262, 292,
    324, 326, 336, 391
Rogers, R. W., 390
Rosegrant, T., 29, 290, 323
Rosenbaum, L. K., 171, 173
Ross, D. D., 388
Ross, L., 21
Rothlein, L., 282
Rothman Beach Associates, 23
Rowland, T., 64
Rubin, K. H., 160, 223, 225, 226,
    229, 234
Rubin, K., 223, 230, 388
Ruopp, R., 25, 27
Russell, L., 21

Saltz, E., 235
Saltz, R., 235
Salvia, J., 345
Sameroff, A. J., 60
Samuels, S. C., 159
Saracho, O. N., 162, 192, 392
Saunders, R., 56
Saville-Troike, M., 379
Scales, B., 160, 192, 239
Scarr, S., 8, 33, 406
Schickedanz, J. A., 345, 398
Schickedanz, J., 383, 384, 385, 386
Schirrmacher, R., 363
Schneider, N. I., 437
Schroeder, C., 163
Schwartz, P. M., 280
Schwartz, S., 74
Schweinhart, L. J., 8, 80, 82, 84, 95,
    99, 100, 321
Sciarra, D. J., 207, 211

Seefeldt, C., 367, 411
Seifert, K., 62, 439
Seitz, V., 171, 173
Senior, K., 282
Shade, D. D., 251
Sheehy, G., 172
Shefatya, L., 234
Sheldon, A., 167
Sheldon, J. B., 390
Shepard, L. A., 344
Shepard, L., 346
Sheppard, W. C., 277, 311, 313
Shimoni, R., 170, 320
Shipman, V., 65
Sholtys, K. C., 378, 379
Short, K. G., 386
Shwedel, A., 96
Siegel, A. W., 41
Sigel, E., 371
Sigel, I. E., 11, 30
Silberman, C., 97
Silin, J. G., 195
Silva, R. J., 420
Simons, F. A., 50, 97
Simons, J. A., 50, 97
Sinclair, S. P., 420, 421
Singer, D. G., 364
Singer, J. L., 364
Skeels, H., 63, 240
Skeen, P., 367
Skinner, B. F., 60
Skinner, L., 367
Smilansky, S., 230, 234, 235
Smith, C. A., 388
Smith, D., 239
Smith, E. B., 385
Smith, P. K., 27
Snow, C. E., 382
Soderman, A. K., 306
Spitz, H., 63, 70
Spodek, B., 162, 192, 392
Sprafkin, J. N., 364
Stapleford, E. M., 41, 116, 117,
    118
Stein, L. C., 235
Steinburg, S., 21
Stern, V., 339, 340
Stevenson, J., 14, 113
Su, H., 21
Sugden, D., 365, 366
Sulzby, E., 382
Swick, K.J., 173
Sylva, K., 223

Teale, W. H., 382, 385
Tharpe, R., 62

Thomas, A., 52, 56, 153, 162, 306
Thompson, W. V., 420
Thomson, C. L., 245, 249, 250
Thornton, J. R., 206
Tietze, W., 102
Tizard, B., 175
Torrance, E. P., 228
Tougas, J., 20, 21, 195, 213, 405, 406, 411, 416, 432, 438
Townson, M., 23
Trahms, C. M., 284
Travers, J., 25, 27
Tribe, C., 56, 61
Trivette, C. M., 185

Ulich, R., 45, 46
Van Hoorn, J., 160, 192
Vandell, D. L., 21, 102
Vandenberg, B., 160, 223, 225, 226, 229, 234
Vander Ven, K., 194
Varga, D., 248, 271, 432
Venn, M. L., 163
Vygotsky, L., 226, 383

Wadsworth, B. J., 56
Walker, D. K., 165
Waller, C. B., 380
Walton, S., 383, 385
Wash, D. P., 8, 21
Watkins, B. A., 363
Watson, J. B., 57, 58
Weber, E., 41, 44, 45, 46, 48, 49, 54, 60, 61, 74
Wechsler, D., 344
Weikart, D. P., 8, 80, 82, 84, 95, 99, 100, 261, 263, 293
Weinstein, C. S., 249
Wells, J. G., 420, 421
West, S., 21
Whiren, A. P., 235
White, B., 65, 240
White, D., 437
White, S. H., 41
Whitebook, M., 26, 27, 192, 201, 406, 417, 432, 434, 435, 438, 441
Wilderstrom, A. H., 163
Willer, B., 192, 194, 196, 205, 435
Williams, J. R., 366, 367

Williams, M., 96
Wilson, T., 136
Witt, D. D., 366, 367
Wolery, M., 163
Woodan, S. L., 280
Wortham, S. C., 337, 338, 339, 342, 345, 346, 349, 350
Wright, M., 8, 12, 80, 101, 209, 235, 263, 348

Yarrow, M. R., 63
Yawkley, T. D., 60, 313, 314, 336
Yewchuk, C., 344
Young, B., 40, 63, 107, 116, 119, 140, 141, 142, 143, 144, 146, 235, 382
Young, R., 168
Ysseldyke, J., 345

Zabrack, M. L., 364
Zaslow, M. J., 420
Zigler, E. F., 171
Zlomke, L., 311, 314

Subject Index

ABC analysis, 338, 350
Absorbent mind, 49, 65, 70, 103
Abstract thinking, 56, 65, 193
Accommodation, 55, 65
Accountability, 333–41
Accreditation, program, 214
Active learning, 43, 48, 83, 103
Activities, balancing, 268
Activities, large-group or circle, 262–63
Activities, outdoor, 263–65
Activities, small-group, 263
Activity time, 261–62, 293–94
Adaptation, 54–55, 65, 243
Advocacy, 3, 8–9, 35, 195, 389, 430, 437, 440, 446
   child, 8–9
   in Newfoundland and Labrador, 130
   in Nova Scotia, 127
   in Saskatchewan, 111–12
   parental empowerment and, 172–73
   professional organizations, 215
Aggression, 236, 273, 276, 308, 313, 318
Alberta, 109–11
Allergies, 266, 302, 303, 305, 317, 371
Anecdotal record, 338, 350
Animals, 39, 45, 55, 57, 64, 70, 83, 265, 374, 445
   materials in child care centres, 253, 254, 355, 356
Anti-bias curriculum, 244, 391
Anxiety, 168, 225, 299, 303, 309, 316
   arrival at school, 280–82
   at beginning of teaching experience, 202, 204
Arrival at school, 280–82. See also Children, arrival of
Art, 248, 265, 272, 354, 363, 372, 374, 378, 399, 400
   as communication, 378
   developmentally appropriate material, 252, 253

display of, in classroom, 246, 247
esthetics and creativity, encouraging, 357–60
learning centres, 256–57
Assessment, 114, 164, 235, 323, 341–47, 351, 352, 353, 406, 408
   accountability, as part of, 333
   concerns about assessment instruments, 345–47
   for Special Needs Grant, 335
   methods of, for information about children, 348
   methods of, for parent feedback, 349–50
   methods of, for program planning, 348–49
   observation and, 337–38
Assessment instruments, 341–45
   checklists, 341
   concerns about using, 345–47
   developmental tests, 344
   environmental checklists and rating scales, 342–43
   IQ tests, 344
   rating scales, 341–42
   readiness tests, 344–45
   screening tests, 343
   standardized tests, 342
Assimilation, 55, 65, 90, 225, 379
Assistant teacher, 201, 209, 217, 412, 413
At-risk children, 409
Attachment, 172, 222, 280, 315, 411, 442, 446
   effect of staff turnover on, 32–33
Attention, 27, 97, 154, 252, 258, 271, 291, 306, 315, 336, 339, 346, 366, 378, 381, 385
   and problem eating behaviours, 284
   deflecting, after toilet accidents, 285
   ignoring, 313–14
   of teacher during activities, 262, 263–64
   problem behaviour, 301–2

unconditional, 311–12
   use of, for controlling behaviour, 59, 60, 294
Attention deficit disorder, 302, 303, 315
Attention span of children, 269, 295–97, 303, 365
Autonomy vs. shame and doubt, 53, 66

Bank Street program, 74, 103
Bathroom facilities, 287
Behaviour
   difference between normal and problem, 301–4
   factors that affect children's, 304–15
   guidance techniques, 309
   guidelines for, 304–5
   managing, through positive reinforcement, 310–11
   modification, 58, 66
   problems, prevention of, 310
   redirection as prevention, 310
   setting, 245, 272
Behaviourism, 56–58, 64, 66
Bereiter-Engelmann model (DISTAR), 84–87, 95–96, 100
Bilingualism, 378, 398
Bimanual control, 365, 398
Blocks, 73–74, 77, 82–83, 86, 245–55, 355–56, 358, 374, 381, 385, 390
Board of directors, 205, 211, 218
Body, 52, 84, 155, 288, 324, 337, 340, 377–79
   body language, 340
   caring for, 367–68, 369–71
   cooking experiences, 369–70
   (see also Meals)
   health and hygiene, 371
   nutrition, 369
   physical development, 364–71
   safety, 371
Books, 83, 356, 391, 393, 408
   about open education, 74

for parents, 30
for promoting moral development, 397
group times, 296
NAEYC publications, 216, 323
on curriculum assessment, 323
one-year-old children and, 154
psychological studies, 64–65
See also Literacy, emergent
Brain, 120, 223, 289
Brigance Diagnostic Inventory of Early Development, 344, 350
British Columbia, 107–9
Bulletin boards, 181–82
Burnout syndrome, 437–38

Canadian Child Care Advocacy Association, 215
Canadian National Child Care Study, 8, 12, 34, 107, 123
Caregiver, 2, 3, 15, 21, 27, 33, 53, 101, 133, 134, 153, 191, 192, 217, 221, 229, 271, 343, 356, 397, 417, 432, 434
Centre-based programs, 10, 12–15, 16, 27, 343
Centre size, in Canada, 137–42
Cerebral palsy, 395–96
Checklist, 341, 348, 350, 352
Canadian, 106–47
centre-based, 12–14
chain-owned, 21
child care, 4–25
employer-supported, 23–24
environmental, 342–43
home-based, 15–16
non-profit, 22
profit-making, 20–22
quality of, 25–34, 95–103, 136–47, 402–28, 430–42
typical features of children, 152
Child care worker, 2, 133, 192, 195, 208, 439. *See also* Early childhood educator
Child development, 221, 222, 241, 354, 361
and developmentally appropriate expectations, 290–91
and developmentally appropriate practice, 29
application of theories of, 69–93
books about, 51
communication with parents about, 180, 181
Friedrich Froebel, 46

HOME scores, correlation with, 343
influential theorists of, 51–62
Manitoba, training in, 114
New Brunswick, childcare legislation, 123
Newfoundland and Labrador, training in, 129
NICHD study, 410–11
Nova Scotia, training in, 127
nursery schools as labs for research, 13
Ontario, training in, 117
parental misconceptions, clarifying, 280
parent education, 187
Saskatchewan, training in, 112
staff turnover, effect of, 432
teacher training, 142–45
teacher training in, 26–27, 431
Child Development Associate (CDA), 80
Child study movement, 40, 66, 114, 143
Childhood education, 1, 2
benefits of, 8
child advocacy, 8–9
defining quality in, 25–34
future of, 430–46
history of, 38–67
in Canada, 106–148
inclusion, 335
program models, 68–105
what is included, 9–25
See also Curriculum; Early childhood educator; *individual provinces and territories*
Children, activity level of, 268–69
Children, age-related similarities among, 152–58
characteristics of, 150–64, 282–90
differences, respecting, 161–62
five-year-old children, 156–57
four-year-old children, 156
infants (birth to 12 months), 153
interactions with, 31–32
new at school, 281–82
one-year-old children (1 to 2 years), 153–54
primary or school-aged children, 157–58
three-year-old children, 155–56
two-year-old children, 154–55
See also Inclusion

Children, ages of, 16–17, 19–20
before- and after-school care, 20
infants and toddlers, 16–17
kindergarten and primary children, 19–20
preschoolers, 19
Children, arrival of, 270
Children, developmental level of, 269
Children, recognizing similarities in, 151–52
Classification, 10, 16, 57, 83, 103, 230, 234, 305, 372–74, 391, 400
Clay, 48, 57, 77, 93, 253, 257, 292, 359
Cleanup, 265
Cognitive development, 371–74, 375
Cognitive developmental theory, 54, 67
Cognitively Oriented Curriculum (COC), 80–84, 95–96, 99
Collage, 253, 397
Colour, 50, 181, 355
and creative development, 359
classroom, 245, 246, 250
colour tablets, 73, 74
in books, 386
in DISTAR curriculum, 87
of food, 283, 369
of materials, 255
physical development, 365, 368
racial bias, 391, 393
software, 252
Comenius, John Amos, 43–44
Communication methods, 175, 180–82. *See also* Family, communication with
Community, as curriculum topic, 325–26
Compensatory programs, 12, 17, 40, 114. *See also* Early intervention
Computer literacy, 250, 272
Computers, 250–52
Concrete operations period, 56, 57, 66
Confidentiality, 177, 199, 337, 338, 347, 350
Constructive play, 232, 261
Content objectives, 336, 351
Convergent thinking, 357, 398
Conversations. *See* Language, spontaneous
Cooking, 16, 82, 210, 229, 248, 256, 257, 262, 369–70, 374, 390, 394
Cooperative games, 236, 273
Cost, Quality, and Child Outcomes Study, 408–9

Counting, 87, 211
Creative development, 354–64
Creative playgrounds, 234
Creativity
  attitudes that encourage, 361–63
  environments that encourage,
    358–60, 361
  factors that decrease, 363–64
  television and, 363–64
Cuing, 313, 315
Cultural awareness, 391, 393, 398,
  423
Curriculum
  and program philosophy, 322
  assessment, evaluation, and, 323
  children as focus of, 324
  children's development and, 323
  community as focus of, 325–26
  content, 323–26
  elements of, 321–23
  family as focus of, 324–25
  observation and, 322
  planning, 327–33

Death, 307
Deficit, 315, 317
  ADHD, 301–3
  sensory, 305
Denver Developmental Screening Test
  (DDST), 343, 350
Development, emotional, 221–23
Developmental delay, 17, 79, 161,
  240, 248, 343
Developmental objectives, 264, 324,
  336
Developmental tests, 334
Developmentally appropriate practice,
  19, 27, 29–30, 31, 164, 210, 216,
  290, 323, 402
  and play, 220–73
Dewey, John, 47–48
Diagnostic testing, 343
Dialect, 150
Differences, respecting, 161–62
Director, 72, 201, 202, 205, 207,
  209, 210, 211, 243, 299, 304, 305,
  404, 408, 412, 413, 418, 421, 425,
  432, 434, 436, 440, 445
Discipline, 39, 40, 44, 103, 187,
  275–77, 279, 307, 347
Discrimination, 49, 73, 242, 365, 391
Disequilibrium, 55
DISTAR, 84–87, 95–96, 100
Divergent thinking, 356–57, 361–63
Divorce, 5, 7, 167, 168, 234, 286,
  287, 307, 312

Dramatic play, 73, 75, 77, 232–35,
  236, 247, 252–56, 265, 293, 310,
  330, 331, 340, 355, 358, 390, 393
Drawing, 32, 48, 83, 90, 97, 156, 157,
  181, 257, 329, 332, 365, 381, 383
Drug-exposed children, 308

Early childhood education
  appropriate practices in, 237–44
  benefits of, 8
  careers in, 202
  current issues and dilemmas,
    430–42
  current practices and future
    directions in, 136–47
  future of, 442–44
  growth of, 4–9
  history of, 38–67
  in Canada, 106–48
  roots of, and regulation of, in
    Canada, 107–36 (*see also indi-*
    vidual provinces and territories)
Early childhood education program
  models, 68–105
Early childhood education, training
  and regulation in, 201. *See also*
  Teacher training
Early childhood educator, 191–218
  qualities of, 192–94
  responsibilities of, 199–200
  rights of, 198–99
  roles of, 199
  terminology, 192
Early childhood programs, defining
  quality in, 25–34
  family involvement, 34
  group size, 25–26 (*see also*
    Group size)
  mixed-age grouping, 28–29
  physical environment, 33–34
  program, developmental appro-
    priateness of the, 29–30
  teacher consistency, 32–33
  teacher qualifications, 26–27
    (*see also* Teacher training)
  teacher-child interaction, 31
  teacher-child ratio, 27–28
  teachers, respect and concern for,
    33
Early childhood special education, 214
Early childhood years, rediscovery of,
  64–65
Early intervention, 8, 17, 102, 124,
  202, 208, 285
Eclectic approach, 69, 70, 93,
  100,102, 220, 279

Ecological model, 165
Education, adult, and lifelong
  learning, 185–87
Ego strength, 277
Emergencies, 300, 301
Emergent literacy, 330, 332, 382–86
Emotional development, 221–23
Employer-supported child care,
  23–24, 165
Empowerment and activism, 440–42
Environment
  arranging indoor, 141–42,
    250–63
  arranging outdoor, 48–49,
    141–42, 263–65
  developmentally appropriate,
    245–50
  impact of, on children, 248–49
  impact of, on teachers, 249–50
  physical, 180
Equilibrium, 55
Equipment, developmentally appro-
  priate, 250–52
Equipment, selection criteria, 250
  computers, 250–52
Erikson, Erik, 53, 61
Ethics, 194, 196, 200, 201
Evaluation, 347–50
  for teachers, 213, 214, 242, 244,
    327, 333, 336, 337, 347–50,
    406
  of children, 158, 177, 262, 347,
    348
  of programs/curriculums, 78, 93,
    97–100, 186, 206, 207, 210,
    212, 236, 239, 323, 342, 345,
    347, 348
Event sampling, 339
Exosystem, 166
Expectations, conveying, 291–92
Expectations, developmentally appro-
  priate, 290–91
Extended family, 4, 7, 8, 16, 123,
  131, 133, 134, 165, 166
Extinction, 313
Eye-hand coordination, 294

Families, needs of, 171
Family, as curriculum topic, 324
Family, as decision makers, 185
Family, as resource, 184
Family, communication with, 174–75
  formal contact, 176–78
  informal contact, 175–76
  problems in, 179–80
Family, in the classroom, 184–85

Family, involvement of, 183–84
Family child care home, 10, 11, 15, 16, 19, 24, 113, 122, 135, 171
Family forms, 166–68
Family life, changes in, 4
    family mobility, increasing, 7–8
    single-parent families, 5, 7
    two-income families, 4–5
Family systems theory, 151, 165
Family variations, 168, 170
Fears, 236, 282, 289, 362, 394–95
Field trips, 299–300
Fine motor development, 177, 365
Flannel board stories, 254
Flexibility, 156, 194, 206, 210, 238, 257, 259, 327, 356, 357, 361, 366, 438
Fluency, 357
For-profit programs, 20
Formal operations period, 57
Freud, Sigmund, 52–54, 225
Friendship, 101, 155, 157, 158, 164, 247, 387, 388, 389, 396, 398
Froebel, Friedrich, 46–47
Functional play, 232

Games, 30, 82, 85, 86, 160, 184, 226, 228, 229, 232, 236, 339, 252, 253, 255, 262, 264, 273, 332, 367, 390, 397–98
Gender role development, 389–90. *See also* Social development
Gessell, Arnold, 60–61
Goals, 10, 11, 17, 18, 68, 69, 79, 84, 86, 87, 90, 171, 191, 197, 210, 216, 236, 241, 242, 243, 250, 260, 322, 327, 330, 331, 333, 334, 337, 345, 346, 347, 350, 389, 395, 421
Gross motor development, 249, 365, 367
Group activities, guidance, 295–97
Group communication methods, 180
Group guidance and the program, 292–97
Group size, 137–42, 269
Guidance and discipline, 276–77
Guidance techniques, factors in selecting, 278–79

Head Start, 77–80, 96, 98–99
    Head Start, Canadians and, 78–79
Head teacher, 22, 440
Health check, 281
Health problems, 284
Hearing impairments, 17–19

High/Scope Foundation, 80
Holding grip, 365
Home visits, 178
Hothousing, 11, 12, 30, 43, 84, 223
Human development theory, 52
Humour, 155, 156, 158, 173, 193, 309, 310, 321, 349, 380, 381
Hyperactivity, 302, 303

Ignoring, 306, 313, 314, 315
Illness, 15, 171, 327, 371, 408
Inclusion, 161–62, 162–64. *See also* Social development
Inclusive programs, individually appropriate, 241–44
Inductive reasoning, 277
Industry vs. Inferiority, 53
Infants, 5–6, 9–10, 12–17, 25–34, 136–39, 153, 160–61, 229–30, 364–96, 402–28
Initiative vs. Guilt, 53
Instruments, 341, 342, 345, 346
Integrated curriculum, 19

Kindergarten, 19–20, 24, 46–47, 75–80, 107–35, 141, 230

Language development, 374–86
    early language acquisition, 376–77
    environments and attitudes that encourage, 379–86
    multilingualism, 378–79
    second-language teaching strategies, 378–79
Language, playing with. *See* Language, spontaneous
Language, spontaneous, 380–81
Large-group or circle activities, 262–63
Latch-key children, 145
Learning centres, 20, 33, 230, 247, 248, 256, 257, 293, 331, 332
Learning disabilities, 85, 303
Learning outcomes, 334–36
Lesson plans, 321, 330, 336, 360
Licensing, 15, 21, 108, 109, 110, 112, 114, 117, 126, 129, 130, 135, 136, 145, 147, 207, 422, 431, 432
Literacy, emergent, 382–86
    implications of, 384
    reading, learning, 383–84
    writing, learning, 383
Literacy development, promoting, 384
Locke, John, 44
Locomotion, 252, 365

Logical thinking, 56, 158
Low wages and affordable child care, 435, 437
Luther, Martin, 43

Macrosystem, 166
Mainstreaming, 162
Malaguzzi, Loris, 50–51
Manipulatives, 252, 256, 288, 331, 358, 365, 372, 374, 398
Manitoba, 113–15
Matching, 49, 83, 154, 365
Materials
    developmentally appropriate, 252–57
    for preschool classroom, basic, 253–54
    selection criteria, 252, 255
    teacher-made, 255–56
Math, 20, 50, 59, 153, 158
Maturational theory, 64
McMillan, Margaret, 48–49
Meals, 266–67
    eating behaviour, 282–85
    eating habits, encouraging healthy, 284
    group guidance, 294–95
    nutritious, providing, 282–83
    problem eating behaviours, 284–85
Meetings and other group functions, 182–83
Memory, 97, 153, 330, 372
Men in early childhood education, 438–39
Mesosystem, 165
Microsystem, 165
Mixed-age grouping, 3, 28, 29, 34, 405
Modelling, 62, 291, 313, 393, 398
Montessori, Maria, 49–50
Montessori programs, 70–74, 96, 97
Moral development, 396–98
Morphology, 377, 398, 399
Movement, 29, 254, 262, 267, 271, 340, 365, 366, 368, 372, 432
Music, 12, 81, 82, 85, 86, 248, 254, 256, 257, 265, 269, 272, 280, 291, 293, 296, 359, 368, 372, 378, 384, 421

Naps, 267. *See also* Sleep and rest times
National Association for the Education of Young Children (NAEYC), 215–16

National Child Care Staffing Study,
21, 417, 432, 434, 441
Needs and programs, coordinating,
173–74
New Brunswick, 123–24
New child at school, 281–82
Newfoundland and Labrador,
128–30
NICHD Study of Early Child Care,
410–11
Northwest Territories, 134–36
Not-for-profit programs, 22, 114,
136, 434
Nova Scotia, 126–28
Nuclear family, 7, 166
Number concepts, 83, 372–74
Nunavut, 136
Nutrition education, 369

Object permanence, 57
Observation
  and documentation, 337, 338
  characteristics of good, 339–40
  confidentiality and objectivity,
  337–38
  interpretation of, 340–41
  parental involvement, 338
  techniques, 341
  types of, 338–39
Observational learning, 313
Ontario, 115–20
Open education, 74–77, 96–97
Open-ended materials, 160, 237, 358
Operant conditioning, 59
Organizations, professional, 214–17
  Canada, 214–15
    student memberships, benefits
    of, 216–17
  United States, 215–16
Outdoor play, benefits of, 264–65
Overweight child, 284, 285
Owen, Robert, 45–46

Painting, 30, 77, 83, 97, 104, 154,
311, 362
Parallel play, 231
Parent cooperatives, 14
Parent education, 22, 48, 92
Parent Effectiveness Training (PET),
187
Parent feedback, information for,
349–50
Parent-teacher conferences, 176–78
Parenthood, 172, 188
Parents and teachers, problems
  between, 179

Peer interaction, 155, 234, 248, 251,
387, 388, 389, 397, 399
Perceived competence, 159
Perceptual development, 365
Personal control, 159, 188
Pestalozzi, Johann, 45
Phobia, 241
Physical development, 364–71
  attitudes that encourage, 366–71
  environments that encourage, 366
Physical environment, effect on group
  behaviour, 290
Piaget, Jean, 54–56, 57, 225–26
Plan-do-review cycle, 82
Plants, 46, 47, 56, 71, 73, 246, 254,
265, 355, 374
Play, 223–27
  as creativity, 228
  definitions of, 228
  games, cooperative, 236–37
  guidance of, 237
  need for, 160
  overview of, 229–37
  pretend play, 230, 233–34
  research and value of, 234–35
  superheroes, 235–36
  theories of, 223, 225–27
Play dough, 154, 157, 160, 176, 285,
293
Playgrounds, 283, 304, 310
Positive reinforcement, 59, 310, 311,
313, 314, 315
Poverty, families in, 170–71
Pragmatics, 377, 399
Praise, 59, 72, 84, 100, 155, 291,
292, 294, 311, 362,
Preoperational period, 56, 57, 83
Prepared environment, 49, 70, 71, 84
Prince Edward Island, 124–26
Professional organizations, 201, 202,
204, 214, 218
Professionalism, 194–201
  core knowledge base, 196–98
  ethics, 200–201
  philosophy, developing your,
  197–98
Program models, comparisons of,
95–97
Program models, evaluations of,
97–100
Program models, research and evalua-
tion of, 93–100
Program planning, guidelines for,
267–72
Program planning, information for,
348–49

Program quality, 402–11
Program settings, 12–16
  centre-based programs, 12–15
  home-based settings, 15–16
Programs, age-appropriate, 240
Programs, developmentally appropriate, 239–40
  components of, 260–67
Programs, inclusive, 241–44
Programs, purpose of, 10–12
  children, care of, 11
  compensation, 12
  cultural preservation, 12
  enrichment, 11
  hurrying or hothousing, 11–12
Programs, sources of support, 20–25
  employer-supported programs,
  23–24
  for-profit programs, 20–22
  nonprofit programs, 22
  public school involvement,
  24–25
  publicly supported programs,
  22–23
  university- and college-affiliated
  programs, 24
Programs, staffing, 205–13
  assistant teacher, 209
  board of directors, 211
  community professionals,
  211–12
  director and/or supervisor, 207
  home visitors, 208
  resource teacher, 207–8
  senior teacher, 208–9
  support staff, 210–11
  teaching staff, 208
  team teaching, 209–10
  volunteers, 210
Prosocial behaviours, development of,
398
Psychoanalytic theory, 52, 67
Punishment, 45, 47, 48, 59, 276,
277, 296, 314, 316
Puppets, 300, 237, 254, 330, 358,
381, 398,
Puzzles, 77, 83, 155, 192, 239, 253,
252, 358, 365, 390, 393, 397

Quebec, 120–23

Racial and cultural awareness and attitudes, 391. *See also* Social development
Rating scales, 341, 342, 348, 407
Readiness tests, 344, 345, 346

Reading, 43, 85, 87, 94, 97, 104, 131, 154, 157, 158, 168, 180, 201, 262, 296, 312, 332, 343
Redirection, 310, 315
Reggio Emilia model, 87–93, 100
Reinforcement, 59, 87, 310, 311, 312, 313, 314, 315, 324
Reliability, 193, 342, 345, 346, 347, 351, 406, 407
Rest, 267. *See also* Sleep and rest times
Rousseau, Jean-Jacques, 44
Routines, 265
Rules, and group behaviour, 292

Safety, 12, 20, 21, 114, 120, 122, 123, 125, 135, 222, 248, 249, 262, 264, 265, 268, 299, 300, 313, 317, 325, 336, 408, 419, 420, 424
Sand, 77, 81, 82, 88, 154, 160, 237, 253, 254, 262, 311, 331, 336, 368, 390, 424
Saskatchewan, 111–13
Schedule, 72, 77, 80, 82, 86, 92–93, 257–72
    components of, 260–67
    group guidance and, 292–301
    guidelines for, 260–72, 280–301
Schedules, developmentally appropriate, 257–60
Schemata, 56, 57
Science, 54, 64, 75, 212, 254, 256, 293, 354, 355, 369, 372, 373, 374, 386, 396, 399, 421
Screening tests, 343, 344, 348
Scribbling, 154, 181
Self-concept, 158, 157, 159, 162, 164, 188, 203, 222, 246, 247, 294, 311, 322, 326, 345, 393
Self-correcting materials, 50
Self-esteem, need for, 158–59
Self-selected time-out, 314
Semantics, 377, 399
Senses, 43, 56, 57, 248, 323, 357, 365, 366, 425
Sensitive periods, 49
Sensitivity, 39, 158, 193, 271, 312, 357, 378, 389, 391, 392, 399, 406, 417, 419
Sensory activities, 262, 349, 368

Sensory discrimination, 49
Sensory-perceptual development, 365
Separation anxiety, 280, 309, 316
Seriation, 57, 83, 372, 373, 374, 400
Shaping, 39, 275, 313
Singing, 45, 271, 273
Skinner, B. F., 58–60
Sleep and rest times, 288–90. *See also* Nap
Social cognition, 397
Social development, 387–98
    environments and attitudes that encourage, 387–89
Social play, 160, 230, 246, 338
Solitary play, 230, 232, 261
Spatial concepts, 372, 374,
Special needs, 17, 162, 163, 164, 178, 202, 207, 208, 313, 322, 335, 391, 392
Sputnik, and educational upheaval, 63
Staffing, 21, 22, 136, 185, 205, 208, 218, 241, 273, 432, 433, 434, 441
Staff qualifications, 3, 114, 122, 124, 126, 127, 142, 143, 201, 208, 413, 443
Standardized tests, 18, 342, 345, 346, 350
Stories, 381–82
Story schema, 381–82
Support staff, 133, 136, 210, 211, 218
Symbolic representation, 400
Syntax, 376, 377, 399
Systematic Training for Effective Parenting (STEP), 187

Teacher
    evaluation of, 213–14
    nurturer, role as, 221
    shortage/turnover, 432–33
    turnover and low pay, 433–35
Teacher-child ratios in Canada, 137–42
Teacher-initiated activities, 246, 258, 268, 270
Teacher training
    academic programs, 201
    changes in professional education, 439–40

qualifications, 26–27
    regulation of, and program availability, 142–45
    teachers' developmental stages, 202, 204
Team teaching, 205, 208, 209, 445
Temperament, 93, 150, 153, 161, 162, 188, 220, 238, 306, 317
Temporal concepts, 372
Themes and projects, 328–30. *See also* Curriculum, planning
Theories, application of, in ECE, 69–93. *See also* Cognitively Oriented Curriculum; DISTAR; Head Start; Montessori programs; Open education; Reggio Emilia model
Time-out, 314–15
Time sampling, 339
Toileting, 285–88
Toothbrushing, 287–88
Transitions, 267, 297–98
Trust vs. Mistrust, 53

Unconditional attention, 312, 315
Units, 245, 347, 360
Unoccupied behaviour, 261
Unplanned events, 300–301

Validity, 342, 347, 406, 407
Vocabulary, 87, 155, 157, 158, 252, 339, 375, 377, 390, 399
Volunteers, 76, 79, 91, 113, 183, 187, 205, 207, 210, 217, 218, 300, 404, 421
Vygotsky, Lev, 61–62, 226–27

Walks, 300
"Wasted time," 270–71
Watson, J. B., 56–58
Whole language, 240, 384, 399
Woodworking, 254, 261, 331, 357
Writing, 38, 39, 44, 46, 50, 58, 73, 97, 104, 157, 158, 179, 181, 207, 213, 254, 257, 332, 333, 338, 341, 365, 375, 379, 382–84, 386, 397

You Bet I Care! studies, 411–28
Yukon Territory, 131–32